"I welcome Gregg Allison and Andreas Köstenberger's new book on the Holy Spirit with great interest and excitement. It is grounded deeply in the burgeoning scholarly literature on the Spirit but written in a very accessible way for Bible teachers and preachers. And because it is comprehensive, it will provide a wonderful, often-used reference source for teaching this central truth of the faith. This book belongs on your shelf containing the study tools that you reach for regularly."

—**Leonard Allen**, dean, College of Bible & Ministry, Lipscomb University

"This is a remarkable study, providing both a synoptic overview of biblical and theological approaches to the Holy Spirit, and a much-needed, fresh integration of the two. This should be a go-to book for anyone working on pneumatological issues or wanting to explore how the theology of the Holy Spirit is woven together with a range of key themes both in Scripture and in the life of the Church. I heartily recommend it."

—**Gary D. Badcock**, Peache Professor of
Divinity, Huron at Western University

"*The Holy Spirit* by Gregg Allison and Andreas Köstenberger is a vital new resource for a biblical and theological approach to the third person of the Godhead. Careful biblical analysis grounds systematic synthesis in a robust treatment of the Spirit that combines scholarly vigor with conceptual and expressive clarity. This volume will richly benefit any student or scholar of the person and work of the Holy Spirit. Highly recommended!"

—**Constantine R. Campbell**, senior vice president of Global
Content and Bible Teaching, Our Daily Bread Ministries, and former
professor of New Testament, Trinity Evangelical Divinity School

"This is a significant book. Köstenberger and Allison combine to present the reader with both a biblical and theological treatment of the doctrine of the Holy Spirit. They do so with great aplomb: well-crafted, biblically grounded, theologically perceptive, and relevantly applied. No issues are ducked. These are such capable scholars and theologians and this work shows it to great effect. But most importantly, this is a book that serves the church."

—**Graham A. Cole**, dean and senior vice president
of education, and professor of biblical and systematic
theology, Trinity Evangelical Divinity School

"Biblical and theological studies have been estranged from one another for far too long—rarely cooperating, treating one another as strangers, and conversing only on occasion. The church should be grateful for professors Allison and Köstenberger, for they fuse their disciplines in a delightful project on the Spirit. The authors characterize their work with fully orbed biblical theology, from Genesis to Revelation, and a sensitivity to historical and systematic theology, all supported by careful interaction with secondary sources and helpful charts. What God has joined together, let no one separate."

—**Benjamin L. Gladd**, associate professor of New Testament, Reformed Theological Seminary

"Köstenberger and Allison have written a very fine book. Brimming with biblical insight and alert to the riches of catholic trinitarianism, they offer a deeply edifying account of the Spirit's person and work, both in God and among us. Anyone interested in the pastoral importance of robust pneumatological teaching, its scriptural basis, and the teaching of the doctors of the universal church should read this erudite and comprehensive study."

—**Christopher R. J. Holmes**, associate professor in systematic theology, and head of the Theology Programme, University of Otago, New Zealand

"Commendably well researched and balanced, *The Holy Spirit* deserves wide appreciation even beyond its primary audience. Most treatments of pneumatology address particular issues, but Allison and Köstenberger engage a far more complete range of material."

—**Craig S. Keener**, F. M. and Ada Thompson Professor of Biblical Studies, Asbury Theological Seminary

"This book is rich indeed! The biblical-theological section by Köstenberger is a wonderfully thoroughgoing treatment and will serve as a touchstone for future scholars. And the systematic-historical-theological section by Allison is a solidly evangelical treatment that ranges widely and integrates classical patristic, medieval, and Reformational doctrinal insights with contemporary viewpoints and controversies. The result is a work that should be on the shelf of every student of the Holy Spirit."

—**Matthew Levering**, James N. and Mary D. Perry Jr. Chair of Theology, Mundelein Seminary

"This pneumatology will take the advanced and the novice alike on a delightful journey through the rich diversity of ideas to be found in the Scriptures and the tradition concerning the Holy Spirit. Yet, all along the way, the over-arching themes of a coherent vision are built and become increasingly clear. I have just found my dream textbook on pneumatology."

—**Frank D. Macchia**, professor of Christian theology, Vanguard University of Southern California, and associate director, the Centre for Pentecostal and Charismatic Studies, Bangor University, Wales, UK

"In this volume, a seasoned biblical theologian and a historically-informed systematic theologian team up to provide a resource that will be valuable for both students and scholars. The result of their collaboration is a book that canvasses the breadth of biblical teaching while also drilling down deeply on several issues of historic and contemporary importance. I learned from it and will surely return to it in the future. This book is a substantive contribution to contemporary evangelical pneumatology."

—**Thomas H. McCall**, professor of biblical and systematic theology, and director, Carl F. H. Henry Center for Theological Understanding, Trinity Evangelical Divinity School

"This compendium on the third person of the Trinity will be especially useful for evangelical students as both a textbook and reference work. I am especially impressed with the way biblical and systematic investigations are combined here. An auspicious first volume for an ambitious new series in theology."

—**Fred Sanders**, professor, Torrey Honors Institute, Biola University

"Designating a book as unprecedented and the first of its kind can often be misleading and the fruit of what C. S. Lewis called 'chronological snobbery.' But that is not the case when it comes to this remarkable new volume on the Holy Spirit by Allison and Köstenberger. Having taught graduate courses on the Holy Spirit on multiple occasions, I was repeatedly frustrated by the lack of a biblically solid, evangelical treatment of the third person of the Godhead and his ministry among God's people. But no more. I'm hesitant to speak of any book as exhaustive or comprehensive, but this one comes close! From the Old Testament through the New, into church history and up to the present day, the authors have provided us with the most substan-tive, biblically rooted, and persuasive treatment of the Spirit to date. I cannot recommend it too highly."

—**Sam Storms**, lead pastor of preaching and vision, Bridgeway Church, Oklahoma City, OK

"Could one volume possibly contain everything necessary for a doctrine of the Holy Spirit? Now, we can answer that question with a hearty 'Yes, and Amen!' Andreas Köstenberger and Gregg Allison have collaborated to offer contemporary Christians a summative and substantive treatment of the biblical basis for pneumatology along with an historically adept and culturally relevant systematic treatment of the Spirit's person and work. This is currently and may long remain the premiere introductory volume. Authors, thank you! Readers, take up and read!"

—**Malcolm B. Yarnell III**, research professor of systematic theology, Southwestern Baptist Theological Seminary, and teaching pastor, Lakeside Baptist Church

THE
HOLY
SPIRIT

Gregg R. Allison & Andreas J. Köstenberger

EDITORS

David S. Dockery | *Nathan A. Finn* | *Christopher W. Morgan*

ACADEMIC
NASHVILLE, TENNESSEE

To the administration and faculty, past and present,
at Trinity Evangelical Divinity School
Thank you for launching us on a path of faithful, creative,
and relevant scholarship for the church

ACKNOWLEDGMENTS

Andreas Köstenberger wrote Part 1 in its entirety and Gregg Allison is responsible for all of Part 2. Gregg also wrote the Introduction (except for the first paragraph) and the Conclusion. While we read each other's contributions and gave input, each author takes responsibility for the material he wrote. In a volume of this scope, it is inevitable that two authors differ on certain issues (e.g., Gregg with Andreas on the interpretation of John 16:8–11, Andreas with Gregg on his advocacy of continuationism). We usually do not identify such disagreements explicitly but focus instead on a clear presentation of the topic from our respective areas of expertise and distinctive vantage points.

Gregg would like to thank his faculty colleagues and the Ph.D. students in the department of systematic theology for their interaction with and feedback on his part of the book. Andreas would like to thank Mark Baker, David Phillips, and Jimmy Roh for their help in taking notes on individual books on the Holy Spirit. Both of us would like to acknowledge Lindsay Simpson's capable assistance in compiling the indices. We are also grateful to the three series editors and the B&H in-house editors for their input and assistance in preparing the manuscript for publication.

CONTENTS

Part I: Biblical Theology

Part II: Systematic Theology

DETAILED OUTLINE
OF CONTENTS

Part II: Systematic Theology

SERIES INTRODUCTION

In Ephesians 4:11-16, the Apostle Paul identifies the goals of the teaching ministry of the church: to build up the church, to lead it to maturity in faith, and to lead it to unity. The goals continue to be the focus of ecclesial theologians, those Christian thinkers who understand their calling and work is to be carried out in service to the church, the people of God. Among other things, ecclesial theology must be grounded in the Scriptures; it must be Trinitarian, Christ-centered, Spirit-enabled, and doxological; it must be informed by the thinking of God's people throughout church history; and it must be ministry- and mission-focused.

Theology at its best understands the importance of influencing and speaking to the mind, the heart, as well as the hands. Ecclesial theologians in the twenty-first century must help people develop: a theologically informed way of seeing the world (the mind); a Christian response to life (the heart); and Christian motivations for ministry (the hands). We believe that this full-orbed understanding can only be addressed when we understand that theology finds its focus in the church. This is not to say that there is no place for academic theology that seeks to address the academy or for a public theology that attempts to engage culture and society. It is to say that the purpose of this series has a particular emphasis, which is grounded in a calling to serve the church. For this reason, we have titled the series Theology for the People of God.

Like other similar series, Theology for the People of God is a multi-volume effort that addresses the classical *loci* of systematic theology. What sets this series apart is its perspective, its emphasis, and its scope. In terms of its perspective, each volume in the series is co-authored by two scholars who are deeply committed to a theological outlook that is convictionally Baptist and warmly evangelical. Careful theology is an integrative task, and to that end the volumes in Theology for the People of God emphasize integration of biblical and systematic theology in dialog with historical theology and with application to church and life. Finally, the scope of this series extends beyond the classical *loci* to include other topics that are relevant to the church: spirituality, pastoral ministry, cultural engagement, and global mission.

Our audience is not first and foremost other "professional" theologians, but rather university students, seminarians, pastors, and other church and ministry leaders. However, we also believe that any thoughtful Christian will benefit from the volumes in this series. At its root, all faithful theology is simply thinking rightly about God and his world for the sake of living rightly before God in his world. To that end, all theology is for the people of God, and every believer is called to be a theologian.

It is our prayer that this series may somehow in God's good providence serve as a source of renewal for the people of God in the days to come. We hope that this will take place as people better understand what they believe and why they believe it, for it is the responsibility of theology to expound the whole counsel of God (Acts 20:7). While no single author or volume will be able to do so, together, we trust that the series in a symphonic manner will serve the church in this way. We believe that the sound, reliable theology found in this series will serve as a source of strength and hope for God's people for decades to come.

This series has been many years in the making. We pray that each volume will serve as an instrument of grace for readers and those who will be influenced by the faithful efforts of the authors who have collaborated with us in this project. We are grateful for each author and the skills and gifts that each person brings to this work. We are grateful for our friends at B&H Academic and LifeWay who have supported the idea for this series. We ultimately thank our great God for the privilege to work together with these many colleagues and co-workers.

Finally, we truly believe that healthy theology that matures the head, heart, and hands will not only enable believers to move toward maturity but will result in the praise and exaltation of God, for it is our understanding that all good and edifying theology leads to doxology. With the Apostle Paul, we, too wish to exclaim, "Oh, the depth of the riches of the wisdom and knowledge of God! How unsearchable his judgments and his paths beyond tracing out! . . . For from him and through him and to him are all things. To him be glory forever! Amen" (Rom 11:33, 36).

Soli Deo Gloria
David S. Dockery, Nathan A. Finn, and Christopher W. Morgan, editors

FIGURES

The Holy Spirit,
through whom the prophets prophesied,
and the fathers learned the things of God,
and the righteous were led forth into the way of righteousness;
and who in the end of the times was poured out in a new way
upon mankind in all the earth,
renewing man unto God.

(Irenaeus, *Epideixis*, 6)

ABBREVIATIONS

AB	Anchor Bible
ABD	*Anchor Bible Dictionary*
Adv. Haer.	*Against Heresies* (Irenaeus)
ANF	*Ante-Nicene Fathers*
ANTC	Abingdon New Testament Commentaries
art.	article
BECNT	Baker Exegetical Commentary on the New Testament
BBR	*Bulletin for Biblical Research*
Bib	*Biblica*
bk.	book
BSac	*Bibliotheca Sacra*
BTCP	Biblical Theology for Christian Proclamation
BTNT	Biblical Theology of the New Testament
BZNW	Beihefte zur Zeitschrift für die neutestamentliche Wissenschaft
chap.	chapter
CBQ	*Catholic Biblical Quarterly*
DBSJ	*Detroit Baptist Seminary Journal*
DSS	Dead Sea Scrolls
ed.	edition; editor; edited by
enl.	enlarged
EGGNT	Exegetical Guide to the Greek New Testament
ESV	English Standard Version
EvQ	*Evangelical Quarterly*
1 Clem	*1 Clement*

FRLANT	Forschungen zur Religion und Literatur des Alten und Neuen Testaments
HALOT	*Hebrew and Aramaic Lexicon of the Old Testament*
Heb.	Hebrew
JBL	*Journal of Biblical Literature*
JETS	*Journal of the Evangelical Theological Society*
JPT	*Journal of Pentecostal Theology*
JSNT	*Journal for the Study of the New Testament*
JSNTSup	*Journal for the Study of the New Testament Supplement*
JSOT	*Journal for the Study of the Old Testament*
JSOTSup	*Journal for the Study of the Old Testament Supplement*
KJV	King James Version
LCC	Library of Christian Classics
LHBOTS	Library of Hebrew Bible/Old Testament Studies
LNTS	Library of New Testament Studies
LXX	Septuagint
MT	Masoretic Text
NASB	New American Standard Version
Neot	*Neotestamentica*
NICNT	New International Commentary on the New Testament
NIDNTTE	*New International Dictionary of New Testament Theology and Exegesis*
NIGTC	New International Greek Testament Commentary
NIV	New International Version
NKJV	New King James Version
NPNF[1]	*Nicene and Post-Nicene Fathers*, series 1
NPNF[2]	*Nicene and Post-Nicene Fathers*, series 2
NRSV	New Revised Standard Version
NSBT	New Studies in Biblical Theology
NT	New Testament
NTS	*New Testament Studies*
1QS	Community Rule (Qumran)
Op.	Philo, *De Opificio Mundi*
OT	Old Testament
PNTC	Pillar New Testament Commentary
pt.	part

q.	question
ResQ	*Restoration Quarterly*
rev.	revision
rev. ed.	revised edition
RTR	*Reformed Theological Review*
Sir	Sirach
SNTSMS	Society for New Testament Studies Monograph Series
T. Jud.	*Testament of Judah*
T. Levi	*Testament of Levi*
TrinJ	*Trinity Journal*
TynBul	*Tyndale Bulletin*
VT	*Vetus Testamentum*
WBC	Word Biblical Commentary
Wis	Wisdom of Solomon
WTJ	*Westminster Theological Journal*
WUNT	Wissenschaftliche Untersuchungen zum Neuen Testament
ZNW	*Zeitschrift für die neutestamentliche Wissenschaft*

INTRODUCTION

I (Andreas) still vividly remember the time when, as a new convert, I decided I should get baptized. I went to see my pastor, who said he wanted to talk to me just to make sure I was ready to take this important step of Christian obedience. Things seemed to be going well until, at one point in the conversation, the pastor posed the following question to me: "So, what do you think about the Holy Spirit? Is he a person or a force?" I paused and pondered the question for a moment and then, somewhat hesitantly, responded, "A force." I immediately realized I had given the wrong answer, as the pastor visibly squirmed in his seat and emitted an audible sigh. Not that my "wrong answer" had disqualified me from baptism, but it had become clear that my understanding of the Spirit's person and work displayed some serious deficiencies, which, I am grateful to report, were remedied in the weeks and months that followed by some patient, biblical instruction.

Broadly speaking, two basic yet important questions Christians ask about the Holy Spirit are these: Who is the Holy Spirit? And what does the Spirit do? Church members reciting a creedal or catechetical portion about the Trinity—"God eternally exists as Father, Son, and Holy Spirit"—may wonder about the identity and activity of the last-named person on the list. A new convert, being baptized "in the name of the Father, and of the Son, and of the Holy Spirit," may be led to ponder the character and work of the Third Person of the Godhead. Through sermons and teachings, believers know something of the importance of the Holy Spirit for their Christian growth. Still, they may be perplexed and their faith rendered anemic by their lack of experience of his presence and power. Having heard people claim guidance and even prophetic words from the Holy Spirit, wary and worried pastors may question what is real with respect to his person and work in the lives of certain church members. Others may simply suspect there is more of the Spirit's presence and power than what they currently experience and desire to grow in their understanding of his person and work.

Until about a century ago, biblical scholars and theologians rarely discussed the often-neglected and self-effacing Third Person of the Holy Trinity. Thankfully, we live in an age in which interest in and a craving for a fuller experience of the Holy Spirit are pushing these two questions to the forefront. The Holy Spirit, who inspired the biblical writers, progressively revealed himself and his activity in such a way that we can rightly wonder: *Who is the Holy Spirit? And what does the Holy Spirit do?* In an attempt to address this set of vital questions, the first half of this book on pneumatology—the doctrine of the Holy Spirit—develops a biblical theology of the Holy Spirit. It considers all that Scripture in the Old Testament and New Testament discloses about his person and work. We are convinced that a thorough study of the biblical teaching on the Holy Spirit will not merely be informative but also prove transformative in your lives as it has proven to be illumining and life-changing in our lives.

Moreover, throughout its existence, the church has wrestled to some degree with these two questions. In fact, it continues to do so today with almost unabated enthusiasm and occasional controversy. Accordingly, the second half of this book offers a systematic theology (with some attention to a historical theology) of the Holy Spirit. It considers topics such as the Spirit's relations with the Father and the Son, the Spirit's role—along with the Father and the Son—in creating and sustaining heaven and earth, his mission of anointing and empowering the incarnate Son's life and ministry, the many facets of his work from beginning to end in applying the benefits of Christ to fallen human beings, and his future activity in actualizing the new heavens and the new earth.

Who is the Holy Spirit? And what does the Holy Spirit do? This book invites you to consider these two questions and subsequently act upon the answers provided in this volume as it travels from Genesis to Revelation and from original to new creation.

Veni, Spiritus Sanctus! Come, Holy Spirit!

PART I
BIBLICAL THEOLOGY

Introduction to Biblical Theology of the Holy Spirit

The study of references to the Holy Spirit in Scripture is a fascinating enterprise. This is true especially if such study is approached via a biblical-theological method, tracking the references to God's Spirit book by book in both the OT and the NT, with a view toward connecting the dots between these references. In this way, each biblical author's contribution to a biblical theology of the Holy Spirit is considered and respected while at the same time attention is paid to the gradual unfolding of scriptural revelation regarding the Holy Spirit across the canon of Scripture.

While numerous studies are available on the Holy Spirit in both testaments and in individual biblical authors, and several biblical-theological treatments exist (although most are multi-author collections), it is not often that one finds studies that investigate with a consistent and coherent biblical-theological methodology all biblical references to the Holy Spirit. A case in point is the helpful volume *A Biblical Theology of the Holy Spirit*, in which contributors use different methodologies and, in some cases, adopt a topical approach.[1]

---

[1] Trevor J. Burke and Keith Warrington, eds., *A Biblical Theology of the Holy Spirit* (Eugene: Cascade, 2014). See also M. Turner, "Holy Spirit," in *New Dictionary of Biblical Theology*, ed. T. Desmond Alexander and Brian S. Rosner (Leicester, UK: Inter-Varsity, 2000), 551–58. For broader studies, see G. K. Beale, *A New Testament Biblical Theology: The Unfolding of the Old Testament in the New* (Grand Rapids:

By contrast, in the first half of this volume, we take essentially a narrative-oriented tack; that is, we read a given book (such as Acts) in consecutive order as it was written. In so doing, we focus particularly on references to the person and work of the Holy Spirit, both within that book and within the framework of prior canonical references.[2] In this way, an organic treatment emerges that can (hopefully) serve as a faithful representation of the Bible's own teaching on the Holy Spirit (though there are, of course, passages in which judgment calls have to be made as to whether the referent is the Holy Spirit).

In what follows, then, we will first look at references to God's Spirit in the OT: the Pentateuch, the Historical Books, the Wisdom Books, and key prophetic books, such as Isaiah, Jeremiah, Ezekiel, and certain books from the Twelve (the Minor Prophets), particularly Joel and Zechariah. While it may be interesting to treat OT references in (presumed) chronological order of writing, this would raise many complex questions as to the dating of various books, which is beyond the scope of this study; in any case, the composite picture is not materially affected.

After this, we will turn our attention to the NT, treating, in canonical order, the four Gospels and the book of Acts.[3] Paul's epistles will be discussed in chronological order of writing,[4] as there is a general timeline agreed upon by many scholars, and such an approach will nicely surface developments and respective emphases in Pauline pneumatology. The study will conclude with

---

Baker, 2011), 559–650; E. Kamlah, J. D. G. Dunn, and C. Brown, "Spirit," in *New International Dictionary of New Testament Theology*, ed. C. Brown (Grand Rapids: Zondervan, 1978); 3:689–709, and Charles H. H. Scobie, *The Ways of Our God: An Approach to Biblical Theology* (Grand Rapids: Eerdmans, 2003), 269–97.

[2] The question of various orders in the OT canon cannot be addressed here. We will discuss references to the Spirit within the framework of the order used in most English Bibles. On this question, see esp. Greg Goswell, "The Order of the Books in the Hebrew Bible," *JETS* 51 (2008): 673–88; Goswell, "The Order of the Books in the Greek Old Testament," *JETS* 52 (2009): 449–66. See further my comments in the next paragraph.

[3] Again, we will not be unduly deterred by technical questions regarding the NT canon that exceed the scope of this investigation. See Greg Goswell, "The Order of the Books of the New Testament," *JETS* 53 (2010): 225–41.

[4] Colossians, Philippians, and Philemon do not warrant full, separate treatment due to the paucity of references to the Spirit in these books. The letters to Timothy and Titus will be treated as part of the Pauline corpus.

discussions of references to the Spirit in Hebrews, Peter's and John's letters, Jude and Revelation.[5]

The Holy Spirit is often neglected in the church or, alternately, given disproportionate attention in certain circles. Our purpose here is to provide a nuanced and theologically sensitive and balanced presentation of the biblical teaching on the Holy Spirit that can serve as a reliable foundation for the historical-theological and systematic-theological treatment that makes up the second part of this volume. In this collaborative effort involving biblical, historical, and systematic theology, we hope to make a helpful methodological contribution as well.

---

[5] No separate treatment is required for the book of James.

2

The Holy Spirit in the Old Testament and in the Pentateuch

Old Testament

While the term *Holy Spirit* is exceedingly rare in the OT,[1] there are approximately 100 references to the Spirit of God in the OT, out of close to 400 instances of the Hebrew term *ruach*, which in addition to "S/spirit" can also mean "wind" or "breath."[2] It is challenging at times to distinguish between

---

[1] As noted by, e.g., Walter C. Kaiser Jr., "The Pentateuch," in Trevor J. Burke and Keith Warrington, eds., *Biblical Theology of the Holy Spirit*, 1, the expression "Holy Spirit" is found in the OT in only two passages: Ps 51:11 (where David, after committing adultery with Bathsheba, pleads with God not to take away his Holy Spirit from him) and Isa 63:10–11 (where the Holy Spirit is said to have been active through Moses during the exodus; cf. v. 14: "the Spirit of the LORD"). Contrary to most English versions, the reference in Ps 51:11 may actually be to the human rather than the divine spirit; see Daniel J. Estes, "Spirit and the Psalmist in Psalm 51," in *Presence, Power and Promise: The Role of the Spirit of God in the Old Testament*, ed. David G. Firth and Paul D. Wegner (Nottingham, UK: Apollos, 2011), 122–34, who glosses the phrase "a desire for your [God's] holiness"; and John R. Levison, *Filled with the Spirit* (Grand Rapids: Eerdmans, 2009), 30–31. Victor H. Matthews, "Holy Spirit," *Anchor Bible Dictionary* 3:261, questionably places both passages in the postexilic period.

[2] See Richard E. Averbeck, "The Holy Spirit in the Hebrew Bible and Its Contribution to the New Testament," in Daniel B. Wallace and M. James Sawyer, eds., *Who's Afraid of the Holy Spirit?* (Dallas: Biblical Studies Press, 2005), 16–18; Wilf Hildebrandt, *An Old Testament Theology of the Spirit of God* (Peabody: Hendrickson, 1995), chap. 1; and Robert Koch, *Der Geist Gottes im Alten Testament*

(God's) "Spirit" and (human) "spirit" in some texts, especially since there is often a connection between God as Creator and the human spirit. This connection notwithstanding, passages in which the referent is the human spirit rather than God's Spirit will not be discussed in the text that follows. Also, as noted in the following discussion, OT references to God's *Ruach* are usually better rendered "God's Spirit" rather than "Spirit of God" in order to convey the unity between Yahweh and his *Ruach*. In addition, interpreters discuss a variety of theological questions related to the Spirit's presence and work in the lives of OT believers.[3]

Pentateuch

Overview

The first reference in Scripture to the Spirit is found in Gen 1:2, where the Spirit is shown to be active in creation. At Gen 6:3, God announces before the flood in the days of Noah that the Spirit will not remain or contend with depraved humanity forever. At Gen 41:38, then, surprisingly, it is none other

---

(Frankfurt am Main: Peter Lang, 1991), 13–34. For studies of the Holy Spirit in the OT, see Firth and Wegner, eds., *Presence, Power and Promise*; Hildebrandt, *Old Testament Theology of the Spirit of God*; Koch, *Der Geist*, 9–12; Lloyd R. Neve, *The Spirit of God in the Old Testament* (Cleveland: CPT, 2011); Leon J. Wood, *The Holy Spirit in the Old Testament* (Grand Rapids: Zondervan, 1976); and Christopher J. H. Wright, *Knowing the Holy Spirit Through the Old Testament* (Downers Grove: InterVarsity, 2006), who discusses the creating, empowering, prophetic, anointing, and coming Spirit.

   [3] James M. Hamilton Jr, *God's Indwelling Presence: The Holy Spirit in the Old and New Testaments*, NAC Studies in Bible & Theology (Nashville: B&H, 2006), argues that the Holy Spirit regenerated OT believers but did not indwell them (cf., e.g., 126, 141, 160). Similarly, Larry D. Pettegrew, *The New Covenant Ministry of the Holy Spirit*, 2nd ed. (Woodlands: Kress Biblical Resources, 2013), 24–28. Contra Walter C. Kaiser Jr., "The Indwelling Presence of the Holy Spirit in the Old Testament," *EvQ* 82 (2010): 308–15. The biblical material does not address the issue directly, so the answer can at best be inferred through inductive reasoning. On the limits of biblical theology, see Mark L. Strauss, "Jesus and the Spirit in Biblical and Theological Perspective: Messianic Empowering, Saving Wisdom, and the Limits of Biblical Theology," in *Spirit and Christ in the New Testament and Christian Theology: Essays in Honor of Max Turner*, ed. I. Howard Marshall, Volker Rabens, and Cornelis Bennema (Grand Rapids: Eerdmans, 2012), 266–84, esp. 283–84.

than the Egyptian pharaoh who recognizes that the S/spirit of God dwells in Joseph.

The book of Exodus narrates how those building the tabernacle are endowed with skill and the Spirit of God. In the book of Numbers, God is said to take the S/spirit that is in Moses and put it on the seventy elders (Num 11:17), and when the S/spirit has come to rest on them, they prophesy (Num 11:25). Later in the book, the Spirit of God is said to come on Balaam the prophet (Num 24:2) as well as on Joshua, Moses's successor (Num 27:18; cf. Deut 34:9).

Discussion

At the outset of creation, the book of Genesis describes the universe as "formless and empty" (*tohu wa vohu*; Gen 1:2; cf. Jer 4:23). There is darkness, and the Spirit of God (*ruach elohim*) is hovering over the waters.[4] While the meaning of *ruach* in Gen 1:2 is debated, the term is used in conjunction with *Elohim*, who is featured as the personal God throughout the creation narrative.[5] Thus *ruach* is shown to subsist in close relation to this personal

---

[4] See Craig G. Bartholomew, "The Wisdom Literature," in Burke and Warrington, *Biblical Theology of the Holy Spirit*, 25, citing Basil and Luther, who understands מְרַחֶפֶת ("was hovering") as conveying a sense of "a vibrant presence awaiting the fitting time to actively begin the creation process." The closest OT parallel is Deut 32:11, referring to an eagle hovering over her young to train them how to fly (Kaiser, "Pentateuch," 4). See also Isa 31:5: "Like *hovering* birds, so the LORD of Armies will protect Jerusalem—by protecting it, he will rescue it, by sparing it, he will deliver it." Averbeck, "Holy Spirit in the Hebrew Bible," 22–25, prefers to translate "a mighty wind from the Lord" rather than "the Spirit hovered." See also the discussion in Hildebrandt, *Old Testament Theology of the Spirit of God*, 36–37, "Hovering or Blowing?"

[5] Cf. Paul K. Jewett, "God Is Personal Being," in *Church, Word, and Spirit: Historical and Theological Essays in Honor of Geoffrey W. Bromiley*, ed. J. E. Bradley and R. A. Muller (Grand Rapids: Eerdmans, 1987), 274: "In the context of the Old Testament as a whole it is evident that this animating Power, this creative Breath, is not understood as an impersonal force but rather as a living Subject." For a helpful discussion of Gen 1:2 and the Spirit's role in creation, see Robert L. Hubbard Jr., "The Spirit and Creation," in Firth and Wegner, eds., *Presence, Power and Promise*, 71–91 (see also the chart listing the uses of "Spirit of God/the LORD," 80–81).

God and Creator and serve as his agent in creation (cf. Ps 33:6; Isa 40:13).[6] Into this formlessness and emptiness, God, through the Spirit, brings "order, design and functionality."[7]

Toward the climax of creation, God is shown to infuse the first human, Adam, with the breath of life (Gen 2:7; cf. Job 34:14; 26:4; Isa 2:22), though this is most likely to be distinguished from an impartation of the Holy Spirit. This infusion of the breath of life constitutes the impartation of the energizing principle, or spark of life, that actualizes the material reality of Adam (of the dust of the ground) so that he becomes a living being. Later, every living creature is said to be similarly infused with the breath of life (Gen 6:17; 7:15, 22), though only humanity is created in God's image (Gen 1:26–28; cf. Job 26:4; 27:3; Isa 42:5). Thus God's breathing of life into humanity most likely refers to the impartation not only of physical life but of spiritual life as well. When humans die, therefore, their bodies return to dust, but their spirits return to God (Eccl 12:7).

Next, at the outset of God's universal judgment on sinful, fallen humanity through the flood, the Genesis narrative asserts that God's Spirit will not always remain, or contend, with humanity (Gen 6:3). The word *din* ("contend") casts the Spirit in the role of judge or one who brings a case against someone. In this judicial role, the Spirit apparently had been contending with humanity before the flood to encourage them to repent, but to no avail. While the Spirit's original role, therefore, was to give life, the corollary of his life-giving function is one as an agent of divine judgment.

After a considerable hiatus in the book of Genesis, the first human after the flood to be mentioned in conjunction with the work of the Spirit is Joseph the patriarch. In the wake of Joseph's interpretation of Pharaoh's dreams, which Joseph attributes to divine revelation, the Egyptian king attests that Joseph is a man of unmatched wisdom and discernment, a man "who has

---

[6] Cf. Hildebrandt, *Old Testament Theology of the Spirit of God*, 39–42, who proceeds to discuss other passages in the book of Proverbs, Job, et al.

[7] Kaiser, "Pentateuch," 5. Similarly, Bartholomew, "Wisdom Literature," 25, writes that "the emphasis on the emerging *order of creation* produced by the Spirit and the word resonates with the OT wisdom tradition," providing the foundational premise for the OT wisdom literature that "the creation is ordered and that, to an extent, this order can and should be known."

God's spirit in him" (Gen 41:38). While one may legitimately debate the extent to which Pharaoh understands the full meaning of his words (cf., e.g., similar statements made about Daniel by pagan rulers in Dan 4:8, 9, 18; 5:11, 14), he recognizes that God's Spirit is ultimately what sets Joseph apart from other men in his kingdom.[8]

In the book of Exodus, in conjunction with the construction of the tabernacle, God tells Moses regarding Bezalel, "I have filled him with God's Spirit, with wisdom, understanding, and ability in every craft" (Exod 31:3; cf. 35:31).[9] Similarly, God fills Oholiab with various skills as a craftsman (Exod 35:34–35).[10] The description of these craftsmen's works echoes the creation narrative (cf., e.g., Gen 2:2–3) and is paralleled by creation language used in the book of Proverbs (esp. Prov 3:19–20).[11]

At a later stage in Israel's history, during the exodus from Egypt, people rebel against the daily diet of manna in the wilderness, leading Moses to express to God his displeasure over the heavy burden of responsibility laid upon him. In response, God takes some of the Spirit who has empowered Moses to lead the people and puts him on the seventy elders, who promptly prophesy for a time (Num 11:17, 25).[12] This impartation of the Spirit is

---

[8] See the discussion in Hildebrandt, *Old Testament Theology of the Spirit of God*, 105–6.

[9] Contra Levison, who thinks that the "spirit" that fills Bezalel is not the divine Spirit but rather an increase of the wisdom and skill Bezalel already possesses as an artisan (*Filled with the Spirit*, 62).

[10] See the discussion of the references to the Spirit in conjunction with Bezalel and Oholiab in Hildebrandt, *Old Testament Theology of the Spirit of God*, 106–7. See also Richard S. Hess, "Bezalel and Oholiab: Spirit and Creativity," in Firth and Wegner, eds., *Presence, Power and Promise*, 161–72.

[11] Note the references to "wisdom" and "understanding" in both Exod 31:2–5 (also, "ability") and Prov 3:19–20 (also, "knowledge"). See further the discussion that follows.

[12] See also Isa 63:7–14, esp. vv. 11–12, indicating that God led OT Israel through Moses by the Holy Spirit; and see the reference in Ps 78:40 to Israel grieving the Holy Spirit (though the Spirit himself is not named in this verse) by rebelling against God in the wilderness (Hildebrandt, *Old Testament Theology of the Spirit of God*, 107–8). Regarding "empowering" nomenclature, see Anthony C. Thiselton, *The Holy Spirit in Biblical Teaching, through the Centuries, and Today* (Grand Rapids: Eerdmans, 2013), who prefers to describe the work of the Spirit of God in terms of "enabling" rather than "empowering" because he fears "power" is frequently misconstrued "as

emblematic of the shared leadership and delegation that enable Moses to deal with the mounting pressure of leading a rebellious people. As well, the Spirit's presence with Moses, and subsequently with the seventy elders, highlights God's special empowerment of the leadership of his people by his Spirit, a theme that will continue in both Old and New Testaments. Remarkably, when Joshua tells Moses to stop two men, Eldad and Medad, from prophesying, Moses expresses his desire that all people would be prophets and have God's Spirit in them (Num 11:26, 29).[13]

Later during the exodus, the Israelites are encamped close to Balak, king of Moab, who hires Balaam, a Gentile prophet, to curse the Israelites.[14] However, "when Balaam looked up and saw Israel encamped tribe by tribe, the Spirit of God came on him and he proclaimed his poem" (Num 24:2–3). In a subsequent series of poetic oracles, Balaam proceeds to reveal God's plans for Israel's future. What is more, it is through Balaam, an unlikely source, that the messianic prophecy is uttered that "a star will come from Jacob" and "a scepter will arise from Israel" (Num 24:17). Finally, Joshua, Moses's successor, is said to be "a man who has the Spirit [*ruach*] in him" (Num 27:18) and is identified as one who was "filled with the spirit [or Spirit; *ruach*] of wisdom" (Deut 34:9).

---

an analogy from the industrial age" (11). Thiselton cites Karl Barth and others who "rightly see this enabling in terms of *effectiveness* or *efficaciousness*" (11).

[13] Cf. Thiselton, *Holy Spirit*, who refers to the "striking characteristic of the work of the Spirit of God," namely, "the *Spirit's capacity for being 'shared out' from one figure to others*. The classic example is that of Moses and the seventy elders (Num. 11:25; Deut. 34:9; 2 Kings 2:15; cf. 2:9, 13–14). . . . This principle will have considerable consequences in the New Testament for the sharing of the Messianic Spirit by all Christians" (5). See also Hildebrandt, *Old Testament Theology of the Spirit of God*, 109–11, under the heading "Leadership by the Spirit Democratized" (cf. Hildebrandt, 157–59).

[14] On the controversial figure of Balaam, see Walter C. Kaiser Jr., "Balaam Son of Beor in Light of Deir 'Allā and Scripture: Saint or Soothsayer?" in *"Go to the Land I Will Show You"* (FS Dwight Young), ed. J. Coleson and V. Matthews (Winona Lake: Eisenbrauns, 1996), 95–106; John N. Oswalt, "Is Balaam's Donkey the Real Prophet (Numbers 24:1–4)?" in Firth and Wegner, eds., *Presence, Power and Promise*, 208–19; and Hildebrandt, *Old Testament Theology of the Spirit of God*, 162–66.

Figure 1: References to God's Spirit in the Pentateuch

Scripture Passage	Content
Gen 1:2	The Spirit hovers over the waters at creation
Gen 2:7	God breathes life into Adam
Gen 6:3	God's Spirit will not remain with humanity forever
Gen 41:38	Pharaoh recognizes the presence of God's Spirit on Joseph
Exod 31:3	Bezalel is filled with God's Spirit
Exod 35:31	Bezalel is filled with God's Spirit (cf. Oholiab: Exod 35:34–35)
Num 11:17	God puts the Spirit in Moses into the seventy elders
Num 11:25, 26, 29	The Spirit rests on the seventy elders, and they prophesy, as do Eldad and Medad
Num 24:2	The Spirit of God comes upon Balaam the prophet
Num 27:18	The successor of Moses, Joshua, is a man who has the Spirit in him
Deut 34:9	Joshua is full of the spirit (or Spirit) of wisdom

Summary

The Pentateuch shows the Spirit in three primary roles: (1) as agent in *creation*, preparing the as-yet empty and unformed material world for its future construction, infusing God's human creatures with life-giving breath; (2) as agent in *judgment*, specifically God's universal judgment of depraved humanity in and through the flood; and (3) as agent of *revelation* for (a) Israel's *leaders*, such as Joseph the patriarch, Moses the lawgiver, the seventy elders and tribal leaders, and even (b) Gentile *prophets*, such as Balaam. Thus we see that the Spirit of God is spoken of in connection with Adam and humanity at large, as well as with the heads of the nation of Israel. The Spirit is shown to act in various capacities: infusing with life, judging, and guiding.

3

The Holy Spirit in the Historical and Wisdom Books

Historical Books

For our present purposes, we will define the "Historical Books" as including Joshua, Judges, Samuel, Kings, Chronicles, and Ezra-Nehemiah.[1] Interestingly, the NT writers cite none of the references to the Spirit in the Historical Books.[2] It should be kept in mind that, methodologically, references to the Spirit in the OT (including the Historical Books) must be understood initially on their own terms, and anachronism—reading later (NT) information back into OT texts—should be avoided.[3] What is more, many instances of *ruach* in the OT pertain to the human spirit or to wind or breath.[4] A possible starting point is places in which *ruach* is used in conjunction with *YHWH* or *'elohim*. Also of interest are instances in which

---

[1] The books of Ruth and Esther would be included as well, but neither refers to the Spirit of God.

[2] David Firth, "The Historical Books," in Trevor J. Burke and Keith Warrington, *A Biblical Theology of the Holy Spirit* (Eugene: Cascade, 2014), 12.

[3] See the helpful methodological considerations and appropriate cautions registered in Firth, 12–13.

[4] See Richard E. Averbeck, "Breath, Wind, Spirit and the Holy Spirit in the Old Testament," in *Presence, Power and Promise: The Role of the Spirit of God in the Old Testament*, ed. David G. Firth and Paul D. Wegner (Nottingham, UK: Apollos, 2011), 25–37.

a pronoun is attached that links the Spirit to God,[5] though doubtless the process of determining references to the Spirit in the OT is more complex than this, and the larger narrative context must be taken into account in making a final determination as to whether the referent of a given instance of *ruach* is the Spirit of God. Discounting ambiguous examples, we can identify twenty-four references to the Spirit in the OT Historical Books.[6] As Firth notes, on the whole the Historical Books display "a developing understanding of the work of the Spirit which pivots around David's experience of the Spirit."[7]

Joshua and Judges

As mentioned above, the Pentateuch includes two references to Joshua as "a man who has the Spirit [*ruach*] in him" (Num 27:18) and who is "filled with the spirit [or Spirit; *ruach*] of wisdom" (Deut 34:9). In the conquest of the Promised Land, Joshua is thus assured of God's presence, just as Yahweh had been with Moses during the exodus (Josh 1:5; 3:7). Like Moses, Joshua divides the waters (Josh 3:17; cf. Exod 14:21–23, 29; 15:8), encounters Yahweh on sacred ground (Josh 5:15; cf. Exod 3:5), and intercedes for the Israelites (Josh 7:7; Deut 9:25–29).[8]

The book of Judges contains over one-third of the references to the Spirit in the OT Historical Books.[9] Throughout Judges, the Spirit conveys God's power to deliver his people Israel from other nations. The cycle is repeated over and over again: Israel sins; she is oppressed by a foreign power; she cries out to God for deliverance; and God sends his Spirit to empower a

---

[5] See Leon J. Wood, *The Holy Spirit in the Old Testament* (Grand Rapids: Zondervan, 1976), 18; Wilf Hildebrandt, *An Old Testament Theology of the Spirit of God* (Peabody, MA: Hendrickson, 1995), 18; and implicitly Christopher J. H. Wright, *Knowing the Holy Spirit Through the Old Testament* (Downers Grove: InterVarsity, 2006), passim.

[6] Judg 3:10; 6:34; 11:29; 13:25; 14:6, 19; 15:14; 1 Sam 10:6, 10; 11:6; 16:13; 16:14; 19:20, 23; 2 Sam 23:2; 1 Kgs 18:12; 22:24; 2 Kgs 2:16; 1 Chr 12:18; 2 Chr 15:1; 20:14; 24:20; Neh 9:20, 30. See Firth, "Historical Books," 14.

[7] Firth, 14.

[8] Cf. Hildebrandt, *Old Testament Theology of the Spirit of God*, 108–9.

[9] See the discussion in Hildebrandt, 112–18.

deliverer.[10] Typically, military action is involved, and the Spirit's power coming on a given deliverer conveys Yahweh's presence with him.[11]

The general pattern is established in the narrative regarding *Othniel*:

> The Israelites did what was evil in the LORD's sight; they forgot the LORD their God and worshiped the Baals and the Asherahs. The LORD's anger burned against Israel, and he sold them to King Cushan-rishathaim of Aram-naharaim, and the Israelites served him eight years.
>
> The Israelites cried out to the LORD. So the LORD raised up Othniel son of Kenaz, Caleb's youngest brother, as a deliverer to save the Israelites. The Spirit of the LORD came on him, and he judged Israel. Othniel went out to battle, and the LORD handed over King Cushan-rishathaim of Aram to him, so that Othniel overpowered him. Then the land had peace for forty years, and Othniel son of Kenaz died.[12] (Judg 3:7–11)

Generally, the Spirit empowers a given judge, but not in such a way as to compel him to obey.[13] Also, while Othniel provides the typical pattern, subsequent judges do not necessarily conform completely to this pattern.

The next judge mentioned in conjunction with the Spirit is *Gideon*.[14] A sort of "anti-hero," Gideon is portrayed as timid, if not fearful, even when the Spirit "envelop[s]" him (Judg 6:34; cf. 6:23, 27; 7:3, 10).[15] This shows

---

[10] See Lee Roy Martin, "Power to Save!? The Role of the Spirit of the Lord in the Book of Judges," *JPT* 16 (2008): 21–50.

[11] David G. Firth, "The Spirit and Leadership," in Firth and Wegner, *Presence, Power and Promise*, 259–80, esp. 277. There is a possible connection between the Spirit's "contending" with man in Gen 6:3 (see discussion in chap. 2) and his empowerment of judges. Yet, despite the title "judge," the judges in Judges seem to be less "judicial" (though see Judg 4:5, and the fact that the key verb often used to describe their entire career is "judge" [שׁפט, Judg 3:10; 4:4; 10:2, 3; 12:7, 8, 9, 11, 13, 14; 15:20; 16:31]) and more military (Judg 2:16–18).

[12] Cf. 1:12–15.

[13] Firth, "Historical Books," 16.

[14] See Hildebrandt, *Old Testament Theology of the Spirit of God*, 114–15. Neither Ehud nor Deborah is said to experience the power of the Spirit.

[15] Andreas Scherer, "Gideon—ein Anti-Held? Ein Beitrag zur Auseinandersetzung mit dem sog. 'Flawed-Hero Approach' am Beispiel von Jdc. Vi 36–40," *VT* 55 (2005): 269–73.

that the power to deliver Israel from her enemies comes not from Gideon but from God, a fact underscored further when God significantly reduces Gideon's army in size (Judg 7:2). Later, the Spirit's presence with Gideon does not keep him from sinning, as when he makes an ephod that leads to Israel's downfall (Judg 8:22–27). Thus the Spirit serves as a resource to be drawn upon by a given God-empowered deliverer without necessarily transforming that individual from within.

Like Gideon, *Jephthah* is not a typical hero.[16] While not plagued by fear, he is rejected by his tribe and linked with a gang of "worthless men" (Judg 11:1–3). Like Othniel, he is empowered by the Spirit (Judg 11:29), though hopes that he will be a mighty deliverer like Othniel are immediately dashed by the narration of his rash vow regarding his daughter.[17] While God uses Jephthah to deliver Israel, his career ends in strife, conflict, and major loss of life (Judg 12:1–7).

Matters do not improve with *Samson*.[18] Remarkably, the book of Judges includes a birth narrative signaling Samson's special calling and culminating with a reference to the Spirit's activity in his early life: "The boy grew, and the LORD blessed him. Then the Spirit of the LORD began to stir him" (Judg 13:24–25). Also remarkably, Samson "has more experiences of the Spirit recorded than any other figure in the OT" (Judg 14:6, 19; 15:14).[19] Nevertheless, Samson only *begins* to deliver Israel from the Philistines (Judg 13:5), and the Spirit does not seem to effect any lasting inner transformation of Samson's character until the final moments of his life.[20]

---

[16] See Hildebrandt, *Old Testament Theology of the Spirit of God*, 115–16.

[17] For a summary of the discussion, see Trent C. Butler, *Judges*, WBC 8 (Nashville: Thomas Nelson, 2009), 287–88. See also Tamie S. Davis, "The Condemnation of Jephthah," *TynBul* 64 (2013): 1–16; and Mikael Sjöberg, *Wrestling with Textual Violence: The Jephthah Narrative in Antiquity and Modernity* (Sheffield, UK: Sheffield Phoenix, 2006).

[18] See Hildebrandt, *Old Testament Theology of the Spirit of God*, 116–17; Eugene H. Merrill, "The Samson Saga and Spiritual Leadership," in Firth and Wegner, *Presence, Power and Promise*, 281–93.

[19] Firth, "Historical Books," 17.

[20] One aspect of the Spirit's work through Samson is the way in which he uses him to execute God's righteous judgment upon his enemies (see, e.g., Judg 15:15; cf. 16:23–31). The Spirit does God's work, and part of God's work—reflecting God's holy character—is the punishment of the wicked.

Samuel

Similar to his role in the book of Judges, the Spirit is shown in the books of Samuel to designate a God-chosen leader and to empower that leader to deliver his people. Unlike in Judges, however, this is not necessarily the Spirit's primary role in the books of Samuel. Rather, God's choice and installation of a person as leader and the Spirit's connection with prophecy, in continuation with Num 11:17, 25, emerge as predominant themes.[21]

The Spirit's coming on *Saul* in 1 Sam 10:10 is not linked with a reference to Israel's disobedience, as had typically been the case in the book of Judges. Rather, as the climactic sign in a series of signs (vv. 2–6), it provides validation that the Lord has chosen Saul to lead God's people and deliver them from their enemies (v. 1).[22] As affirmation of God's choice of Saul as king, the Spirit "came powerfully on" Saul (v. 10) and conveyed the power to prophesy, as Saul was "transformed" (vv. 6). The Spirit's coming on Saul and Saul's prophesying constitute signs that God is with Saul (vv. 1, 7) and are accompanied by a change of heart (v. 9). Later, the scriptural narrative records how the Spirit of God comes upon Saul again and how Saul exacts powerful revenge on Israel's enemy, Jabesh-Gilead (1 Sam 11:6). As in Judges, possession of the Spirit does not override a person's choices, including those to sin, as is clear in the case of Saul, who forfeits both his own kingship and his future dynasty (1 Samuel 13–15).[23]

God's rejection of Saul leads to his choice of *David* as king (1 Sam 16:1–13), and from the day of David's anointing by Samuel, "the Spirit of the Lord came powerfully on David" (v. 13). Unlike in previous instances, however, the Spirit's presence with David is not immediately followed by military victory or prophetic activity. Rather, the narrative shifts back to Saul, and the Spirit's coming upon David serves the primary purpose of

---

[21] See the earlier discussion. See also the discussion of "the Spirit and the leadership of kings" in Hildebrandt, *Old Testament Theology of the Spirit of God*, 118–26.

[22] Note here that there is a textual issue in v. 1, which is significantly longer (ESV) in some versions than others (NIV), but the additional text does not seem to add anything that is not at least implicit in the passage.

[23] See the discussion in Hildebrandt, 169–72; see also David G. Firth, "Is Saul Also Among the Prophets? Saul's Prophecy in 1 Samuel 19:23," in Firth and Wegner, *Presence, Power and Promise*, 294–305.

confirming God's selection of David as Israel's king-in-waiting, as it did with Saul; strengthening this assertion is the fact that immediately after the Spirit is said to have come upon David from the day of his anointing forward, the narrator asserts that "the Spirit of the LORD . . . left Saul" (1 Sam 16:14). This shift of the Spirit from Saul to David is of signal importance, reflecting the role of the Spirit in mediating God's presence and empowering the ruler of God's people.

Subsequently, when Saul's men, and then Saul, come to arrest David, the Spirit overrides their intentions and causes them to prophesy instead, apparently in some form of ecstatic experience (1 Sam 19:20, 23–24). Remarkably, this is the first instance in Scripture in which the Spirit acts independently of a given individual.[24]

Finally, in a passage marking an *inclusio* with the reference to the Spirit at the onset of David's activity, David is shown to utter a prophetic word in the Spirit at the end of his life (2 Sam 23:2; cf. 1 Sam 16:13).[25] This incident indicates that David's entire life—from God's selection of him as king onward—is characterized by the Spirit's presence with him. As in the case of individuals featured in the book of Judges, however, this does not preclude David's engaging in sin, most egregiously in his adultery with Bathsheba (2 Samuel 11), at which time he implores the Lord not to take his Holy Spirit away from him (Ps 51:11).[26] On the whole, David serves as a pivotal figure in the depiction of the work of the Spirit in the OT in that he marks a transition in the Spirit's major recorded activity—from empowering leaders to inspiring prophecy.

---

[24] Firth, "Historical Books," 20. It may be that the Spirit overrode Saul's independent action when Saul earlier prophesied in 1 Sam 10:10–13, but that passage is merely suggestive of this possibility, while 1 Sam 19:19–24 is explicit. On the Spirit and ecstasy in the OT, see Charles H. H. Scobie, *The Ways of Our God: An Approach to Biblical Theology* (Grand Rapids: Eerdmans, 2003), 272–73.

[25] See Hildebrandt, *Old Testament Theology of the Spirit of God*, 173–74.

[26] Or, alternatively, remove his desire for God's holiness (see discussion and reference to the works of Estes and Levison in chap. 2, n. 1).

Kings, Chronicles, and Nehemiah

The references to the Spirit in Kings, Chronicles, and Nehemiah all involve his activity in conveying Yahweh's words to his people.[27] The story of the prophets Elijah and Elisha is told in 1 Kings 17–2 Kings 9.[28] The prophet Obadiah predicts that the "Spirit of the LORD" will carry Elijah as he goes on his mission to confront Ahab (1 Kgs 18:12). When the mantle of leadership is passed from Elijah to Elisha, the latter requests "two shares" of Elijah's spirit (2 Kgs 2:9–10). The parting of the Jordan confirms that Elijah's spirit now rests on Elisha (2 Kgs 2:15). When Elijah has vanished, Elisha is told, "Maybe the Spirit of the LORD has carried him away" (2 Kgs 2:16).[29] The passing of Elijah's spirit on to Elisha is reminiscent of the Spirit's passing from Moses to Joshua and the seventy elders and anticipates the anointed Jesus's bestowal of his Spirit upon his followers following his ascension.[30]

Interestingly, none of the references to the Spirit in Samuel finds a parallel in Chronicles, perhaps because the Chronicler takes his point of departure from the characterization of the Spirit as enabler of prophecy at the end of Samuel. In 1 Chr 12:18, the Spirit is said to *envelop* (Heb. *labash*) Amasai, "chief of the Thirty," so he can prophesy regarding David. The same Hebrew verb is used in the final reference to the Spirit in Chronicles, 2 Chr 24:20, where the Spirit is said to empower Zechariah to prophesy and pronounce an indictment of the people for breaking God's commandments.[31] Remarkably,

---

[27] We will not further discuss the passing reference to the Spirit in 1 Kgs 22:24. There, amid a conflict between King Ahab and the prophet Micaiah, Zedekiah the son of Chenaanah strikes Micaiah on the cheek and challenges him, "Did the Spirit of the LORD leave me to speak to you?" Ahab is killed in the ensuing battle, and Micaiah is vindicated. The Spirit here designates Micaiah's authority to prophesy. See further the discussion in Hildebrandt, *Old Testament Theology of the Spirit of God*, 179–82.

[28] See Hildebrandt, 174–79.

[29] See Robert B. Chisholm Jr., "The 'Spirit of the LORD' in 2 Kings 2:16," in Firth and Wegner, *Presence, Power and Promise*, 306–17.

[30] Hildebrandt, *Old Testament Theology of the Spirit of God*, 179. However, it is less clear that "spirit" here refers to the Spirit of God, so we have chosen not to include 2 Kgs 2:9–10, 15 in the summary chart or the appendix.

[31] The only other OT use of לבש is found in Judg 6:34, pertaining to Gideon. See Firth, "Historical Books," 21–22, who argues that both passages in Chronicles evoke this background.

at King Joash's command the people stone Zechariah in the temple court on account of his prophecy (v. 21). These two passages in turn envelop references to the Spirit as coming upon Azariah and Jahaziel, respectively, in 2 Chr 15:1 and 20:14.[32] Azariah prophesies to King Asa, and Jahaziel to King Jehoshaphat, both of whom heed their respective prophecies.

Intriguingly, as indicated by repeated echoes of terminology used in Judges, the characterization of the Spirit's work in Chronicles takes its point of departure from his empowerment of deliverance through military action in Judges while taking it an important step further in focusing on the Spirit's work in empowering prophetic utterances.

The two references to the Spirit's activity in the book of Nehemiah reflect a similar pattern as that in Chronicles. In Nehemiah's prayer in chapter 9, reference is made to the exodus, during which God gave his "good Spirit" to instruct the Israelites (v. 20), perhaps with regard to Moses's role as prophet.[33] Later, reference is made to God's subsequent warning of Israel by his Spirit through his prophets (v. 30). Thus, as in the books of Samuel and especially Chronicles, the emphasis continues to be on the Spirit's work in empowering prophecy.

Figure 2: References to God's Spirit in the OT Historical Books

Scripture Passage	OT Character	Function of God's Spirit	Observations
Judg 3:10	Othniel	Empower deliverer	General pattern
Judg 6:34	Gideon	Empower deliverer	Anti-hero
Judg 11:29	Jephthah	Empower deliverer	Rash vow
Judg 13:25	Samson	Empower deliverer	Birth narrative
Judg 14:6	Samson	Empower deliverer	Tears a lion into pieces

---

[32] Again, there are verbal parallels with the book of Judges, in this case with Othniel and Jephthah (Judg 3:10; 11:29).

[33] See Deut 18:15; cf. Acts 3:22–26 where the term *prophet* is applied to Jesus as the Prophet par excellence. The phrase "your gracious Spirit" is used in Ps 143:10 (cf. "your good spirit" in Neh 9:20).

Judg 14:19	Samson	Empower deliverer	Kills 30 men in anger
Judg 15:14	Samson	Empower deliverer	Kills 1,000 men
1 Sam 10:6	Saul	Enable to prophesy	"Come[s] powerfully on," a "transformed" man
1 Sam 10:10	Saul	Enable to prophesy	"Came powerfully on," among prophets
1 Sam 11:6	Saul	Empower king	"Came powerfully on" Saul
1 Sam 16:13	David	Designate as king	Samuel anoints, Spirit "[comes] powerfully on"
1 Sam 16:14	Saul	Designate as king	Departs from Saul
1 Sam 19:20	Saul	Enable to prophesy	Attempts to arrest David
1 Sam 19:23	Saul	Enable to prophesy	Ecstatic experience
2 Sam 23:2	David	Enable to prophesy	Last words of David
1 Kgs 18:12	Elijah	Deliver from enemy	Will "carry" Elijah
1 Kgs 22:24	Micaiah	Speak to prophet	Zedekiah to Micaiah
2 Kgs 2:16	Elisha	Deliver from enemy	"Carried . . . away" prophet
1 Chr 12:18	Amasai	Enable to prophesy	"Enveloped" leader of 30
2 Chr 15:1	Azariah	Enable to prophesy	Comes upon
2 Chr 20:14	Jahaziel	Enable to prophesy	Comes upon
2 Chr 24:20	Zechariah	Enable to prophesy	"Enveloped" prophet
Neh 9:20	Moses?	Enable to instruct	Instruction at exodus
Neh 9:30	Prophets	Enable to prophesy	Subsequent instruction

Summary

The OT Historical Books exhibit an interesting progression in the characterization of the Spirit of God and his work in the history of his people and their leaders, with primary emphasis on the latter.[34] Judges connects the Spirit primarily with God's power in delivering the people of Israel from their oppressors. The books of Samuel link the Spirit with God's choice of Israel's king, first Saul and later David. In David's case, the Spirit's continued presence with him (and the Spirit's corresponding withdrawal from Saul) confirms God's selection of him as king in the earlier stages of the narrative, while later the Spirit is shown to be active in God's prophetic disclosures in and through David. The emphasis on the Spirit's role in enabling prophetic utterances of the word of Yahweh continues in Chronicles and Nehemiah.

Wisdom Books

The OT Wisdom literature contains few overt verbal references to God's Spirit.[35] Most instances of *ruach* refer to the human spirit.[36] On a conceptual level, however, there is more fertile ground for a theology of the Spirit. In particular, wisdom theology is grounded in creation theology, which, as we saw earlier, features references to the Spirit in the early chapters of the Genesis creation narrative.[37] In this way, God's powerful, effective word is

---

[34] Scobie, *Ways of Our God*, 272, notes that, while at times the Spirit's activity among God's chosen people as a whole is noted, "the predominant emphasis in the OT . . . is on the Spirit as the means by which God confers special powers and gifts on the *leaders* of his people" (emphasis original).

[35] For a helpful discussion, see Tremper Longman III, "The Spirit and Wisdom," in Firth and Wegner, *Presence, Power and Promise*, 95–110, who discusses Prov 1:23; Job 4:7–17; 20:2–3; 26:2–4; 27:1–6; 32:6–10; and Eccl 12:7 (some of these are at best only indirect references to the Spirit of God; cf., e.g., Lindsay Wilson, "Spirit of Wisdom or Spirit of God in Proverbs 1:23?" in Firth and Wegner, 147–58, who concludes that the reference in Prov 1:23 is to the spirit of wisdom rather than to the Spirit of God). The Second Temple literature features more explicit connections between wisdom and the Spirit (e.g., Wis 1:7; 11:24–12:1; Jdt 16:14).

[36] There are twelve such instances in Proverbs; matters are similar in Ecclesiastes, as well as in Job ("spirit of God" in 27:3 [ESV] is no real exception, as the referent there, too, is a human individual).

[37] E.g., Gen 1:2; 2:7; 6:3. See our discussion on these verses in chapter 2.

shown to be the grounds of everything that exists and thus takes on foundational importance for how God's creation functions and is to be inhabited, utilized, and enjoyed.

Discussion

OT Wisdom literature affirms the creation of the universe, including humans, by the "breath" or "Spirit" of God: "The heavens were made by the word of the LORD, and all the stars, by the breath of his mouth" (Ps 33:6; cf. 104:30); "The Spirit of God has made me, and the breath of the Almighty gives me life" (Job 33:4; cf. 27:3).[38] There is thus a close relationship between God's Spirit and the spirit that indwells human beings.[39] This organic link illustrates the intricate intimacy between creature and Creator, between the human spirit and God's Spirit, at least in the original creation. As Bartholomew notes, the portrayal of humans as "spirit" or "breath" in OT Wisdom literature conveys "our creatureliness and contingency, totally dependent upon God."[40] It is thus when we, in our spirits, the essence of our earthly existence, direct ourselves in humble submission toward God that we live most fully in keeping with our God-intended purpose.

As Bartholomew contends, the foundational premise of OT Wisdom literature is the Spirit-engendered order of creation. Within this creational framework, "OT wisdom is a quest for aligning oneself with God and his order for creation in all areas of life."[41] In this vein, the book of Proverbs explores numerous facets of wisdom in keeping with God's purposes in

---

[38] See Rosalind Clarke, "Job 27:3: The Spirit of God in My Nostrils," in Firth and Wegner, *Presence, Power and Promise*, 111–21. G. K. Beale is probably right when he says that Job 33:4 "does not indicate creation from nothing but rather speaks of the initial creation of Job's life in the womb" (except that Elihu is speaking, not Job); cf. Ps 139:13–16; in *A New Testament Biblical Theology: The Unfolding of the Old Testament in the New* (Grand Rapids: Baker, 2001), 560.

[39] See, e.g., Prov 15:4, 13; 16:18, 19; 17:22; 18:14; 29:23; cf. 25:13 (NIV); 20:27 (NIV); Eccl 3:21; 7:9; 12:7; Job 6:4; 7:11; 10:12 (ESV); 17:1; cf. 4:15 (ESV).

[40] Bartholomew, "Wisdom Literature," in Burke and Warrington, *Biblical Theology of the Holy Spirit*, 30, citing Job 34:14–15: "If . . . he withdrew his spirit and breath, all humanity would perish together and mankind would return to the dust" (NIV).

[41] Bartholomew, 25.

creation. Similarly, Ecclesiastes explores the meaning of life "under the sun" (1:3, 9, et al.) contrasting wisdom with the world's ways of trying to find meaning apart from God. In view of the certainty of death, all such worldly pursuits (e.g., accumulating earthly possessions) are thus exposed as ultimately futile. In this way, the Spirit-engendered order of creation under God provides both the foundation and the framework for all of the OT Wisdom literature, including Proverbs and Ecclesiastes.

Because creation theology provides the substructure of wisdom theology, it follows that the scope and sphere of the Spirit's operation in and through both creation and wisdom is all-encompassing and comprehensive, spanning all of creation and all of human life. While the creating God, as *YHWH*, who entered into covenant with Israel, is uniquely Israel's God, he is also the Creator of all things, and thus life in keeping with God's creative purposes is likewise predicated upon reverence for this Creator God.[42]

Bartholomew notes another connection between the OT Wisdom literature and earlier OT historical narrative: the construction of the tabernacle by craftsmen such as Bezalel and Oholiab, who are "filled . . . with God's Spirit" (*ruach 'elohim*; cf. Gen 1:2) and furnished "wisdom, understanding, and ability in every kind of craft" (Exod 31:3; 35:31; cf. 35:35).[43] Here we encounter essentially the same wisdom vocabulary as that found in OT wisdom books such as Proverbs.[44] Similar to his agency in creation, the Spirit thus fulfills a vital role in the construction of the tabernacle, which, for its part, constitutes a "microcosm of the Creation."[45]

---

[42] See, e.g., Prov 1:9. Cf. Bartholomew (26–27), who cites Hendrikus Berkhof as speaking of the Spirit's "universal creativity." Berkhof, *Christian Faith: An Introduction to the Study of the Faith*, 2nd ed. (Grand Rapids: Eerdmans, 1986), 165. Bartholomew himself contends that the "Spirit's work is Creation-wide and he is deeply involved in sustaining and directing the entire Creation dynamically towards its *telos*" (Bartholomew, "Wisdom Literature," 26).

[43] Bartholomew (28) observes that "filling" language here is applied to qualified craftsmen while in the NT all believers are called to be "filled by the Spirit" (Eph 5:18). On the biblical language of being "filled with the Spirit," see Andreas J. Köstenberger, "What Does It Mean to Be Filled with the Spirit?" *JETS* 40 (1997): 229–40; see further the discussion of Eph 5:18 in chap. 21.

[44] See esp. Prov 3:19–20. Cf. Michael V. Fox, *Proverbs 1–9*, AB 18A (New York: Doubleday, 2000), 28–38.

[45] Bartholomew, "Wisdom Literature," 27.

In addition, from the wisdom theology there are entailments of the Spirit on spiritual formation.[46] As Proverbs asserts, a person's steps are directed by the Lord (20:24 NIV), and his "lamp" (the Spirit?) searches his spirit and inmost being (20:27). Elihu, one of Job's counselors, rightly maintains that it is "the breath from the Almighty" that gives a person understanding (Job 32:8).[47] Thus wisdom is a function not merely of a person's age or life experience but of the Spirit of God dwelling within him. The Spirit of God, infused into the human spirit, thus bridges the span between God's mysterious and awe-inspiring transcendence and his caring and life-giving immanence.[48] Wisdom is therefore grounded in reverence for God and the realization that he is God and we are not.

There are also several references to God's Spirit in the book of Psalms. As noted earlier, God's creation through the Spirit is affirmed in both Pss 33:6 and 104:30. In 139:7, the psalmist cries out, "Where can I go from your Spirit?" (NIV), implying the Spirit's omnipresence in God's creation.[49] Psalms 143:10 affirms the Spirit's role in teaching, that is, instructing people in wise living:

> Teach me to do your will,
>> for you are my God;
> may your good Spirit
>> lead me on level ground. (NIV)

Finally, the best understanding of Ps 51:11 points to God's presence with the chosen ruler of his people. There, David pleads for God not to remove his Holy Spirit from him,[50] a prayer that likely has biblical-theological antecedent in the leadership transition from Saul to David. Saul is said three times to have been rejected as king due to his disobedience (1 Sam 15:23, 26; 16:1),

---

[46] See Bartholomew, 30–32.

[47] Conversely, the "breath of God" is active in judgment: Job 4:9 ESV; 15:30. For a discussion of the Spirit in Job, see Longman, "Spirit and Wisdom," 98–104.

[48] Cf. Bartholomew, "Wisdom Literature," 31, who also notes entailments for a theology of suffering (citing Job 6:4; 7:11; 17:1; 27:3; 32:8).

[49] See Jamie A. Grant, "Spirit and Presence in Psalm 139," in Firth and Wegner, *Presence, Power and Promise*, 135–46.

[50] Less likely, it may be that David is pleading that God not to remove David's desire for God's holiness (see discussion and reference to the works of Estes and Levison in chap. 2, n. 1).

and this is immediately followed in the narrative by the anointing of David as king. Once David is anointed, "the Spirit of the LORD came powerfully on David from that day forward" (1 Sam 16:13), and in the same breath, the biblical author informs the reader that "the Spirit of the Lord had left Saul" (v. 14). It is not a large step to see David in Ps 51:11 as fearing that the same withdrawal of the Spirit might follow on the heels of his own disobedience.

Figure 3: References to God's Spirit in the OT Wisdom Literature

Scripture Passage	Major Content	Function of God's Spirit
Job 4:9	"By the breath of God they perish" (ESV)	Agent of God in judgment
Job 15:30	"By the breath of God's mouth, he will depart"	Agent of God in judgment
Job 27:3	"The breath from God . . . in my nostrils"	Agent of God in creation (humanity)
Job 32:8	"The breath from the Almighty"	Gives wisdom and understanding
Job 33:4	"The Spirit of God has made me"	Agent of God in creation (humanity)
Ps 33:6	"The breath of his mouth"	Agent of God in creation (heavens)
Ps 51:11	"Do not. . . take your Holy Spirit from me"	Designates David as king
Ps 104:30	"When you send your breath"	Agent of God in creation (works)
Ps 139:7	"Where can I go to escape your Spirit?"	Omnipresence in creation (David)
Ps 143:10	"May your gracious Spirit lead me"	Teaches God's will (David)
Prov 20:27	God's "lamp" searches the spirit	Examine a person's inner being

Summary

While, as mentioned, explicit references to the Spirit of God in the OT Wisdom literature are relatively uncommon, several important biblical-theological connections ground this body of writings in antecedent OT theology. Most important is the Spirit's work in creation, which imposes an order onto the universe that humans must learn to inhabit and cultivate in wisdom and understanding. Creation by God's "breath" also creates an intimate link between the divine Spirit and the human spirit, which calls God's creatures to relate to their Creator in reverence and humble submission. In another creation-based connection, David's rhetorical question in Ps 139:7 points to the omnipresence of God's Spirit—implying that there is no place anywhere in the created universe where he could escape the Spirit's presence.

Another relevant antecedent OT motif is the work of Spirit-filled craftsmen in building the tabernacle, which connects their work with creation and provides a framework for the depiction of wise living in OT Wisdom literature. In these ways, OT wisdom writings establish a connection between the original creation and wise living that ultimately has a universal scope, reaching beyond the confines of Israel to all those who are created in God's image and desire to be reconciled to their Creator and reconnected to his original design. Psalms 143:10, for instance, explicitly draws the connection between the Spirit and wise living, as David asks that God's Spirit instruct him in this regard.

Finally, David's striking prayer that the Holy Spirit in Ps 51:11 not be taken from him, if a reference to the Holy Spirit, highlights God's empowering presence with the ruler of his people and the possibility of the withdrawal of that special presence due to egregious sin.

4

The Holy Spirit in the Prophetic Books

T he Spirit is mentioned frequently in the Prophetic Books, particularly Isaiah, Ezekiel, and Zechariah.[1] In the Major Prophets, Isaiah shows the Spirit's activity related to the messianic Branch from Jesse, the Davidic Messiah (11:2), as well as through the Servant of Yahweh (42:1; 48:16; 61:1). The Spirit is also mentioned in conjunction with the end-time restoration of God's created order following a new exodus (32:15; 34:16; 40:13).

While Jeremiah features few (if any) references to God's Spirit, Ezekiel contains several significant passages on the Spirit. Most notable is the reference to God's future giving of a new heart and new S/spirit to his people (36:25–27). Also, the Spirit is shown to be at work at Israel's restoration from exile (37:12–14). A third important reference speaks of God's people enjoying the future gift of the Spirit (39:29).

---

[1] For a helpful survey, see W. Hildebrandt, "Spirit of Yahweh," in *Dictionary of the Old Testament Prophets*, ed. Mark J. Boda and J. Gordon McConville (Downers Grove: InterVarsity, 2012), 747–57. Daniel I. Block, "The View from the Top: The Holy Spirit in the Prophets," in *Presence, Power and Promise: The Role of the Spirit of God in the Old Testament*, ed. David G. Firth and Paul D. Wegner (Nottingham, UK: Apollos, 2011), 175–207, provides an integrated treatment of the Spirit in the Prophets along the following topical lines: the Spirit as (divine) breath, mind/disposition, or *alter ego*; the Spirit as (divine) agent of conveyance, inspiration, empowerment, judgment, or animation; and the Spirit as the (divine) mark of ownership. Block also notes the presence of the Aramaic phrase the "spirit of the holy gods" in the book of Daniel (4:8, 9, 18; 5:11, 14).

In the Minor Prophets, the S/spirit is mentioned with regard to God's activity at creation (Zech 12:1; Mal 2:15), as an emblem of divine judgment (translated "wind" in Hos 4:19; 8:7; 12:1; 13:15–16; Jon 1:4; 4:8; Hab 1:11; Zech 2:6; "Spirit" in Zech 6:8), as involved in restoring Yahweh's covenant relationship with Israel (Mic 3:8; Zech 7:12), with regard to God's outpouring of the Spirit on the Day of the Lord (Joel 2:28–39; Zech 12:10), and as empowering prophecy (Hos 9:7 ESV; Mic 3:8; Zech 7:12).

Major Prophets

Isaiah

Together with Ezekiel, Isaiah is the crown jewel of prophetic books featuring God's Spirit. Several references relate the Spirit to the ministry of a coming messianic figure. In Isa 11:1–5 the prophet speaks of a "shoot . . . from the stump of Jesse" and a "branch from his roots" that shall bear fruit. Regarding this messianic figure, the prophet asserts:

> The Spirit of the LORD will rest on him—
> a Spirit of wisdom and understanding,
> a Spirit of counsel and strength,
> a Spirit of knowledge and of the fear of the LORD (v. 2)

This figure's reign will be characterized by righteousness and faithfulness. He will judge the poor equitably and have regard for the meek of the earth, but the wicked he will kill with the breath of his lips (vv. 3–5).[2]

The prophet thus predicts the coming of an individual in the line of David who, like David, will be designated as king by the Spirit. The abiding presence of the Spirit will endow this messianic figure with wisdom to exercise God's rule righteously.

---

[2] See Hilary Marlowe, "The Spirit of Yahweh in Isaiah 11:1–9," in Firth and Wegner, *Presence, Power and Promise*, 220–32. For a discussion of the Spirit of the Lord and the Messiah in Isaiah see Robert Koch, *Der Geist Gottes im Alten Testament* (Frankfurt am Main: Peter Lang, 1991), 82–123 (but note that Koch distinguishes between Proto-Isaiah's depiction of the Messiah as a charismatic king and Deutero- and Trito-Isaiah's portrait of the Messiah as a Spirit-endowed prophet).

In Isa 30:1–2, most likely with reference to the struggle against the Assyrians in the eighth century BC, Isaiah declares the word of the Lord, excoriating Israel as "rebellious children" who "carry out a plan, but not mine; they make an alliance, but against my will," with Egypt. The failure to confer with the prophetic voice in the nation and to seek God's guidance results in political failure and national bondage (cf. 1 Kgs 22:24).

Later, the prophet envisions a future king who will reign in righteousness, and a time when "the Spirit from on high is poured out on us" (Isa 32:15). Justice and righteousness will prevail, resulting in human flourishing and prosperity, peace, quietness, and trust (vv. 15–17). The Spirit is here shown to restore God's order to its original pristine state in the end times.[3] Ma speaks of the "idea of a holistic and transformative effective of the Spirit . . . , affecting material, land and people with moral, social and communal dimensions, until *shalom* is reached, the central characteristic of God's rule."[4] He elaborates, "God's Spirit is re-creating a paradise that was once lost."[5]

In Isa 40:12–15 the prophet extols the unparalleled wisdom of Yahweh in creation and asks, "Who has directed the Spirit of the LORD, or who gave him counsel?" (v. 13).[6] The Spirit's agency in creation grounds the expectation of a new exodus (vv. 1–11), and the nations are said to be no match for Yahweh's—and the Spirit's—matchless power and understanding.[7] As in the creation narrative, we see here the seeds of the divine personhood of both Yahweh and the Spirit, who, while working in tandem, are nonetheless distinct in some way.

Then, in Isa 42:1, the first of the four Servant Songs picks up on the earlier depiction of the Davidic "Branch" in chapter 11:

---

[3] Wonsuk Ma, "Isaiah," in Burke and Warrington, *Biblical Theology of the Holy Spirit*, 41–43, discusses this passage under the rubric of the "creation Spirit tradition." Ma has also written *Until the Spirit Comes: The Spirit of God in the Book of Isaiah*, JSOTSup 271 (Sheffield: Sheffield Academic Press, 1999). However, Ma's distinction between different traditions (charismatic and non-charismatic) in Isaiah's theology of the Spirit is problematic.

[4] Ma, "Isaiah," 42.

[5] Ma, 42.

[6] Ma, 43–44, discusses this passage under the rubric of "wisdom Spirit traditions."

[7] See, e.g., Isa 40:15–17, 21–23.

This is my servant; I strengthen him,
this is my chosen one; I delight in him.
I have put my Spirit on him;
he will bring justice to the nations.

As in the earlier passage, the Spirit-endowed figure's work extends beyond the confines of Israel to the nations and involves the execution of justice. He will be meek and faithful and will persist until his mission of bringing justice to the nations has been accomplished (vv. 2–4).

While the depiction of God's Spirit-enabled Servant in these two Isaianic passages builds on earlier characterizations of the Spirit's empowering God's chosen leaders to deliver his people in the book of Judges and of the Spirit's designating Saul and David as kings in the books of Samuel, the scope of the Servant's activity is broader and the vision of his activity more sweeping and all-encompassing.

The dimensions of bringing justice to the poor and of promoting meekness on the earth are also more pronounced than in the earlier references to the Spirit in the OT Historical Books. Most striking—especially when compared to fallible figures such as Gideon, Samson, Saul, or even David—is the moral excellence of the Servant and the thoroughgoing spiritual nature of his mission.[8]

In chapter 44 Isaiah resumes a theme struck earlier in chapter 32 when declaring Yahweh's words to his servant Israel:

I will pour water on the thirsty land,
and streams on the dry ground;
I will pour out my Spirit on your descendants,
and my blessing on your offspring. (v. 3)

Remarkably, God's blessing upon Israel, mediated by the Spirit, will result in witness and mission (v. 5).

Subsequently, the Servant Song of Isaiah 61 continues the depiction of Yahweh's Servant in chapter 42:

---

[8] See the discussion in Ma, "Isaiah," 35–38. Ma subsumes these two Isaianic passages under "leadership Spirit traditions."

The Spirit of the Lord God is on me,
because the Lord has anointed me
to bring good news to the poor.
He has sent me to heal the brokenhearted,
to proclaim liberty to the captives
and freedom to the prisoners;
to proclaim the year of the Lord's favor,
and the day of our God's vengeance;
to comfort all who mourn. (Isa 61:1–2)

Remarkably, while in chapter 11 the prophet introduces this Spirit-endowed figure, and in chapter 42 it is God who announces the coming of his Servant, in present passage the Servant himself elaborates on the nature of his mission. This makes this passage uniquely suited for Jesus to use in his inaugural homily in his hometown synagogue of Nazareth.[9]

"Anointing" language points to Jesus's messianic consciousness, and, similar to previous characterizations, it is the poor, the brokenhearted, captives, and those who mourn who are the primary intended recipients of this messianic figure's message of good news of justice, liberation, and comfort.[10]

The work of the Spirit is to undergird and empower the mission of the coming messianic Davidic king. While combining political and prophetic dimensions, the Servant's role transcends a one-dimensional characterization and links the Servant directly with God, who commissions him, and with the Spirit, who designates him as the Lord's Servant and empowers him for his mission.[11]

Finally, Isaiah includes several remarkable references to the activity of the Holy Spirit in manifesting God's presence among the Israelites and guiding them during the exodus, even after they had rebelled and grieved the Spirit (Isa 63:10–11, 14). Isa 63:10–11 refers to the Spirit as "the Holy Spirit," a rarity in the OT.[12] The reference to "grieving" the Holy Spirit in v. 10 implies

---

[9] See Luke 4:18–19, on which see further in chapter 6. Cf. also Isa 48:16: "And now the Sovereign Lord has sent me, endowed with his Spirit" (NIV).

[10] Cf. Isa 42:7.

[11] Cf. Isa 59:21.

[12] The only other possible OT reference to "the Holy Spirit" is found in Ps 51:11 (but see discussion in chap. 2, n. 1).

his distinct personality.[13] The reference to the Holy Spirit's presence among the Israelites during the exodus similarly indicates the Spirit's distinct operation in conjunction with Yahweh at this critical juncture of Israel's history.[14] The Holy Spirit is said to have guided Moses's right hand when he parted the waters so that the Israelites could pass through the Red Sea and to have given the Israelites rest from their enemies. By leading his people in such a powerful, miraculous way, God brought glory to himself (v. 14).

Figure 4: References to God's Spirit in Isaiah[15]

Scripture Passage	Major Content	Function of God's Spirit
Isa 11:2	Shoot/Branch from Jesse	Rests on Branch, gives understanding
Isa 30:1	Alliance with Egypt v. Assyrians	Provides guidance in war (resisted)
Isa 32:15	Spirit "poured out on us"	End-time restoration of God's order
Isa 34:16	His Spirit will gather together	End-time restoration of God's order
Isa 40:13	New exodus/creation	Agency and wisdom in creation
Isa 42:1	Servant Song (God speaking)	Put on Servant, justice to nations
Isa 44:3	Witness and mission	Poured out on Israel's offspring
Isa 48:16	Endowed with his Spirit	Sovereign Lord sends the Servant

---

[13] Isaiah's reference to "griev[ing] the Holy Spirit" is echoed by Paul in Eph 4:30, on which see the discussion in chap. 21. See also the brief discussion on Isa 63:10–11 in the introduction.

[14] The reference to those who "shared in the Holy Spirit" in Heb 6:4 may likewise suggest the Spirit's presence in the midst of the Israelites during the exodus.

[15] The phrase "the breath of the Lord" in Isa 40:7 and 59:19 (NIV) likely refers to the wind, not the Spirit of God.

Isa 59:21	My Spirit on you will not depart	Yahweh's covenant, Redeemer in Zion
Isa 61:1	Servant Song (Servant speaking)	Anoints the Servant, good news
Isa 63:10–11, 14	The Holy Spirit during the exodus	Manifests God's presence, guides

The major highlight of the Spirit's work according to Isaiah is doubtless his activity in and through the Messiah, God's end-time Servant.[16] This Servant (or Branch) is identified as Davidic in origin in the first part of the book (11:1–5). In the second part, he is the focal point of the Servant Songs, which describe the Spirit's work of designating this messianic figure as God's Servant and of anointing him to bring good news to the poor and oppressed and to bring justice to the nations. All of this is canvassed against the backdrop of a new creation and a new exodus to be accomplished by Yahweh's sending his Servant on whom the Spirit rests. It is not hard to see in this arrangement the seeds of the economic Trinity, though it is of course left to the NT writers and later theologians to develop this doctrine more explicitly.

Jeremiah

As Andrew Davies notes, "There is not a single specific and unambiguous reference to the Spirit of God in Jeremiah."[17] Of the eighteen times *ruach* is used in Jeremiah, not one of them refers to the Spirit of God; invariably, other meanings of "spirit" related to the natural world are in view.[18] That said,

---

[16] See the discussion in Wilf Hildebrandt, *An Old Testament Theology of the Spirit of God* (Peabody: Hendrickson, 1995), 127–37.

[17] Andrew Davies, "Jeremiah," in Burke and Warrington, *Biblical Theology of the Holy Spirit*, 46, who notes the differences between the MT and LXX versions of Jeremiah, provides further bibliographic references (46, n. 1), and observes that pneumatology is clearly not among Jeremiah's primary theological interests (47). Elsewhere, however, Davies speaks repeatedly of Jeremiah's distinctive "pneumatology" (53).

[18] Possible meanings include "wind," "breath," "air," "(the human) spirit," and others (*HALOT*, 1197); see Jer 2:24; 4:11–12; 5:13; 10:13–14; 13:24; 14:6; 18:17; 22:22; 49:32, 36 (× 2); 51:1, 11, 16–17 (= 10:13–14).

it is not hard to see a connection between the natural and the spiritual world with regard to some of the instances of *ruach* in Jeremiah. Characteristically, wind (*ruach*) scatters and disperses (Jer 13:24; 18:17; 49:32, 35–36), which associates *ruach* with divine judgment.[19]

A key text illustrating the association between Yahweh and *ruach* in conjunction with divine judgment is Jer 4:11–12: "At that time it will be said to this people and to Jerusalem, 'A searing wind blows from the barren heights in the wilderness on the way to my dear people. It comes not to winnow or to sift; a wind too strong for this comes at my call. Now I will also pronounce judgments against them.'" In Jer 22:22, reference is made to "the wind," or spirit (*ruach*), who will "take charge of all your shepherds" (i.e., the rulers of Israel), again with *ruach* possibly exercising the divine function of holding the shepherds of the people accountable.[20]

The difference between Jeremiah and the two other major prophetic books that precede and follow it in the OT canon is palpable. While Isaiah and Ezekiel both style their books in terms of their visionary experience (Isa 1:1; Ezek 1:1), Jeremiah focuses more squarely on the words of Yahweh he is transmitting to the people while looking forward to the day when God's law will be inscribed on people's hearts, removing any further need for intermediaries (Jer 31:31–34).[21] In this way, Jeremiah is distinct from Isaiah, who envisions, as we have just seen, a Spirit-anointed Davidic messianic figure bringing about both a new exodus and a new creation.[22]

---

[19] Note the association between the Holy Spirit and judgment in NT passages such as John 16:8–11, on which see further the discussion in chap. 19.

[20] See the discussion of Jer 4:11–12 and 22:22 in Davies, "Jeremiah," 48–49 and 50, respectively. Davies also proposes that Jer 10:12–16 may contain two related word plays between the רוּחַ of Yahweh and that of idols and between two different kinds of breath, רוּחַ and הֶבֶל. (51–52). While Yahweh commands entire storehouses full of רוּחַ (v. 13), the idols lack רוּחַ (v. 14); they are a mere הֶבֶל (v. 15).

[21] See Sigmund Mowinckel, "'The Spirit' and the 'Word' in the Pre-Exilic Reforming Prophets," *JBL* 53 (1934): 199–227; Mark J. Boda, "Word and Spirit, Scribe and Prophet in Old Testament Hermeneutics," in Kevin L. Spawn and Archie T. Wright, eds., *Spirit and Scripture: Exploring a Pneumatic Hermeneutic* (London: T&T Clark, 2012), 25–45.

[22] See the discussion of Isaiah above. Regarding the comparison between Isaiah, Ezekiel, and Jeremiah, see also Davies, "Jeremiah," 46–47.

Why is Jeremiah so exceedingly subtle in his references to the divine *ruach*? Andrew Davies cites Lloyd Neve, who, building on the work of Sigmund Mowinckel, has suggested that references to the Spirit of God recede after the days of Joel, Isaiah, and Micah: "After 700 BCE until the first exile . . . no prophet speaks of the spirit [*sic*] of God, neither Jeremiah, Zephaniah, Habakkuk, nor Nahum."[23] In addition, Neve observes that the preexilic writing prophets are reluctant to claim inspiration and resistant toward ecstatic prophetic experiences.

Neve attributes these phenomena to the transition from prophetic to dynastic leadership in Israel, which commences with the establishment of the monarchy and of the Davidic line but is not fully completed until the northern kingdom's fall and Assyrian exile in 722 BC. Consequently, one looks in vain in Jeremiah for references to the Gifts of the Holy Spirit: Prophecy or empowering him to declare Yahweh's words.[24] Instead, Jeremiah speaks of receiving and declaring the "word of the Lord" as his faithful herald, messenger, and steward, in contrast to the false prophets, who will "become . . . wind" because the "word is not in them."[25]

In summary, references to the Spirit of God in Jeremiah are few and far between. The term *ruach* routinely refers to "spirit" as part of the natural order. It is therefore open to debate as to whether Jeremiah has a pneumatology at all. If he makes any contribution to a biblical theology of the Spirit, it is (1) with reference to *ruach*—that is, wind as emblematic of God's Spirit—as an agent of divine judgment; and (2) with regard to the fact that not all self-proclaimed prophets speak of God's Spirit but rather are but wind,

---

[23] Lloyd R. Neve, *The Spirit of God in the Old Testament* (Cleveland: CPT, 2011), 33.

[24] Though Jeremiah does speak of being touched by God's hand (Jer 1:9; 15:17). Cf. Matthijs J. De Jong, "Why Jeremiah Is Not among the Prophets: An Analysis of the Terms נָבִיא and נְבִיאִים in the Book of Jeremiah," *JSOT* 35 (2001): 483–510, who challenges the classification of Jeremiah as a prophet in the conventional sense because he is never called a נָבִיא.

[25] Jer 5:13. See the discussion of this passage in Davies, "Jeremiah," 54–55, who notes the apparent word play in the Hebrew between Spirit-inspired prophets and prophets who are nothing but wind. Similarly, Jude speaks in the NT of false teachers "not having the Spirit" (Jude v. 19). References to receiving or speaking the word of the Lord in Jeremiah include 1:2, 4, 11, 13; 2:1, 4, 31; et al. For a full list of references, see Davies, "Jeremiah," 54n26.

devoid of genuine divine revelation.[26] It is certainly understandable that in a period as ominous as the impending exile, references to God's Spirit would recede into the background and references to God's judgment predominate.

Ezekiel

As in the case of Jeremiah, Ezekiel's prophetic activity takes place during the Babylonian exile.[27] This is a time of intense spiritual crisis, as the Davidic dynasty seems to have failed (2 Samuel 7; cf. Psalm 89), the temple has been desecrated (Lam 1:10), and God's people have been forcibly removed from the Promised Land. Instead, they weep as they sit by the rivers of Babylon and remember Jerusalem (Ps 137:1).

Unlike Jeremiah, however,[28] Ezekiel's prophetic message entails a pronounced and pervasive focus on *ruach*, God's Spirit.[29] In fact, one commentator has called Ezekiel "the prophet of the Spirit," which, as we will see in the paragraphs ahead, is hardly an exaggeration, especially compared with the paucity of references to the Spirit in Jeremiah.[30]

Investigating the instances of *ruach* in Ezekiel, Robson observes that the term's "fluidity enabled a deliberate exploitation of its polyvalency for rhetorical purposes."[31] At the same time, Robson, following Johnson, opines that in the OT, the *ruach* of Yahweh is better understood as an extension

---

[26] See Davies, 56, who refers to this feature as the "slightly darker side to Jeremiah's pneumatology."

[27] See the discussions in Koch, *Geist Gottes*, 124–25, 130–33; Hildebrandt, *Old Testament Theology of the Spirit of God*, 187–90; and Block, "View from the Top," 175–207, citing John Woodhouse, "The 'Spirit' in the Book of Ezekiel," in B. G. Webb, ed., *Spirit of the Living God Part One*, Explorations 5 (Sydney: Lancer, 1991), 1–22.

[28] See the discussion in the previous section.

[29] James E. Robson, "Ezekiel," in Burke and Warrington, *Biblical Theology of the Holy Spirit*, 57–70; see also Robson, *Word and Spirit in Ezekiel*, LHBOTS 447 (New York: T&T Clark, 2006).

[30] Daniel I. Block, "The Prophet of the Spirit: The Use of *Rwḥ* in the Book of Ezekiel," *JETS* 32 (1989): 27–49. Robson ("Ezekiel," 58) counts as many as fifty-one instances of רוּחַ in Ezekiel, many of them in relation to Yahweh.

[31] Robson, 59 (see discussion on 58–59).

of his personality than as an independent agent.[32] Thus, as mentioned, it is better to translate "God's Spirit"—conveying the unity between Yahweh and his *ruach*—rather than "Spirit of God," which would imply a distinction in personhood.[33]

One possible approach to analyzing the instances of *ruach* in Ezekiel is to canvass a semantic domain and to assign each instance an appropriate place within this semantic range that encompasses "wind," the human spirit, and the divine spirit. Another approach is to consider "wind" the foundational category that is developed in the book in two ways, direction and agency.[34] However, care must be taken not to lose sight of the fluidity among the various instances of *ruach* in the book.

While *ruach* may refer to the wind, be used in conjunction with the chariot, or denote Ezekiel's own spirit, our discussion here will focus on passages in which explicit reference is made to *ruach* in relation to Yahweh, that is, when Yahweh promises to put his Spirit ("my Spirit") on a restored, rescued remnant subsequent to its return from exile.[35] The first of these is found in Ezek 36:25–27, where the prophet delivers the following message, which Yahweh tells him to convey to his people:

> I will also sprinkle clean water on you, and you will be clean. I will cleanse you from all your impurities and all your idols. *I will give you a new heart and put a new spirit within you*; I will remove your heart of stone and give you a heart of flesh. *I will place my Spirit within you* and cause you to follow my statutes and carefully observe my ordinances.

It is instructive to compare Ezekiel's prophecy with that of Jeremiah, who declares a similar (and yet differently worded) message to God's people at the same juncture:

---

[32] Robson, 59, citing Aubrey R. Johnson, *The One and the Many in the Israelite Conception of God* (Cardiff, UK: University of Wales Press, 1961), 15.

[33] Firth and Wegner, "Introduction," in *Presence, Power and Promise*, 20.

[34] For a discussion of these various options with additional bibliographic references, see Robson, "Ezekiel," 59–60.

[35] For a discussion of the first three categories of usage, see Robson, 60–66.

"Look, the days are coming"—this is the Lord's declaration—
"when I will make a new covenant with the house of Israel and with
the house of Judah. . . . *I will put my teaching within them and write
it on their hearts.* I will be their God, and they will be my people."
(Jer 31:31–34)

While there is obvious congruity between both prophecies in that both
prophets speak of a future time when God will change people's hearts so
that they will obey him, only Ezekiel articulates this heart change in terms
of *ruach*: "I will give you . . . a new spirit. . . . And I will put my Spirit within
you . . ." This comes on the heels of similar passages in Ezek 11:19 and 18:31,
though now, in escalating fashion, Yahweh makes references to "my" *ruach*.
These two references to *ruach*—both human and divine—in Ezek 36:27 are
framed by references to a new creation, even resurrection (Ezek 37:1–10; cf.
Gen 2:7), a new exodus (Ezek 36:24; 37:12), and a restored covenant (Ezek
36:28; 37:12–13; cf. Jer 31:31).

The second reference to God's Spirit is found in Ezek 37:14 at the culmination of the remarkable vision of the valley of dry bones.[36] There the
prophet is told to convey the following oracle to exiled Israel:

Therefore, prophesy and say to them: "This is what the Lord God
says: I am going to open your graves and bring you up from them,
my people, and lead you into the land of Israel. You will know that I
am the Lord, my people, when I open your graves and bring you up
from them. I will put my Spirit in you, and you will live, and I will
settle you in your own land." (Ezek 37:12–14)

In response to the question in Ezek 33:10, "How then can we live?" (ESV),
Yahweh's message to the exiles is that "the word spoken by Ezekiel the
prophet and made effective by *rûaḥ* is the route to life for the 'dead' exiles."[37]
In this regard, the prophet represents humanity as "son of man [*ādām*],"

---

[36] Note that the term רוּחַ dominates the vision, occurring as many as ten times,
designating the Spirit of Yahweh (v. 1), the breath of life entering the dry bones (vv.
5–6, 8, 10), and the wind or four winds (v. 9).

[37] Robson, "Ezekiel," 68.

envisaging a new creation.[38] As recipient of God's Spirit (Ezek 2:2; cf. 37:1–2, 10), he is the first among God's people to experience the restoration of the exiles as promised.

The third reference to God's Spirit is found at the end of Ezekiel's oracle against Gog. According to the prophet, God will restore the fortunes of Israel and return them to the land:

> "They will know that I am the LORD their God when I regather
> them to their own land after having exiled them among the nations.
> I will leave none of them behind. I will no longer hide my face from
> them, for I will pour out my Spirit on the house of Israel." This is
> the declaration of the Lord GOD. (Ezek 39:28–29)

While the point of reference is the same as in the previous two passages, 36:27 and 37:14, the language used builds on these references by speaking of Yahweh as no longer hiding his face but instead pouring out his Spirit. All three prophecies promise restoration from exile and a return to the land, resulting in obedience (Ezek 36:27), life (Ezek 37:14), and enjoyment of God's gracious, even generous, gift of the Spirit (Ezek 39:29).

Figure 5: References to God's Spirit in Ezekiel

Scripture Passage	Major Content	Function of God's Spirit
Ezek 36:27	God will give exiles a new spirit	Restoration and renewal
Ezek 37:14	God will raise and restore exiles	Resurrection and new life
Ezek 39:29	God will pour out his Spirit	Restoration and renewal

What is at best implicit in Jeremiah bursts forth into broad daylight in Ezekiel. In the dark days of the exile, God's promises of future restoration and renewal shine the brightest. The answer to the exiles' question,

---

[38] Robson, 69, calls Ezekiel "an Adamic figure" and adduces several parallels with the Genesis creation account.

"How then can we live?" (33:10 ESV) is abundantly supplied by the prophet Ezekiel, the prototypical new Adam and "son of man," who three times speaks of Yahweh's giving or even pouring out his Spirit upon his people, restoring their fortunes after the traumatic event of the exile. In this way, the Spirit of Yahweh becomes the embodiment of the hope of a new creation, a new exodus, and a renewed covenant between God and his people.

Minor Prophets

While not every instance of *ruach* in the twelve so-called Minor Prophets (also called "the Twelve") is directly theological or pneumatological in nature, there is often an implicit connection, which is why it will be helpful to provide a brief survey of several types of usage in this corpus.[39] First, several passages refer to God as the Giver of the life-giving spirit to humanity, harking back to Gen 2:7.[40] Conversely, idols are said to have no life (lit., "breath") in them (Hab 2:19). These passages underscore that God alone has the power to give life.

Second, similar to what we have seen in Jeremiah, *ruach* may refer to wind as an emblem of divine judgment.[41] Thus the use of *ruach* may convey "divine agency in punishing disobedience and realigning human actions and expectations with those of Yahweh."[42]

Third, *ruach* is active in restoring Israel's relationship with Yahweh, whether by enabling prophets to prosecute covenant infringements (Mic 3:8; Zech 7:12; cf. Jeremiah 7) or by enabling the rebuilding of the Jerusalem

---

[39] On "the Twelve," see Richard Alan Fuhr Jr. and Gary Yates, *The Message of the Twelve: Hearing the Voice of the Minor Prophets* (Nashville: B&H Academic, 2006). See also Paul House, *The Unity of the Twelve* (Sheffield, UK: Sheffield Academic Press, 1990); and James D. Nogalski and Marvin Sweeney, *Reading and Hearing the Book of the Twelve* (Atlanta: SBL, 2000).

[40] See discussion of Gen 2:7 under "Pentateuch" above. Potentially relevant passages in the Twelve include Amos 4:13; Zech 12:1; and Mal 2:15.

[41] See, e.g., Hos 4:19; 8:7; 12:1; 13:15–16; Jon 1:4; 4:8; Hab 1:11; Zech 2:6. See also the reference to the "Spirit of the Lord" being angry in Mic 2:7, and see Hildebrandt, *Old Testament Theology of the Spirit of God*, 190–92.

[42] Martin Clay, "The Book of the Twelve," in Burke and Warrington, *Biblical Theology of the Holy Spirit*, 75.

temple following the exile (Zech 4:6–7; Hag 1:14; 2:3–5).[43] This strikes the theme of the Spirit's empowerment of prophets and other leaders (Micah, Zechariah, and Haggai) in calling God's people back to the law and the covenant and overcoming both internal and external obstacles in this regard. In all these ways, then, the Spirit is shown to promote unity and a restored relationship between Yahweh and Israel.

Fourth, two passages in the Twelve Prophets speak of the outpouring of the Spirit (Joel 2:28–29; Zech 12:10; cf. Isa 32:15; 44:3; Ezek 39:29). Both Joel 2:28–29 and Zech 12:10 place the Spirit's outpouring in the context of the "day of the LORD."

The first of these, Joel's well-known prophecy, will be central later on in Peter's Pentecost sermon in Acts 2:17–21:

> After this
> I will pour out my Spirit on all humanity;
> then your sons and your daughters will prophesy,
> your old men will have dreams,
> and your young men will see visions.
> I will even pour out my Spirit
> on the male and female slaves in those days. (Joel 2:28–29)

Accompanied by signs and wonders, and preceding the day of the Lord, this universal outpouring of the Spirit will enable all those who call on the Lord to be saved:[44]

> I will display wonders in the heavens and on the earth: blood, fire, and columns of smoke. The sun will be turned to darkness and the moon to blood before the great and terrible day of the LORD comes. Then everyone who calls on the name of the LORD will be saved. (Joel 2:30–32)

This series of events, in turn, is placed within the context of Israel's restoration and the judgment of the nations "in the Valley of Jehoshaphat" (Joel 3:1–2). Note that the outpouring of the Spirit is not only universal on

---

[43] See the detailed exegetical discussion of key passages in Clay, 75–78.

[44] For a discussion of whether the phrase "all flesh" refers to all humanity or only to Israel, see Clay, 81–83. After lengthy discussion, Clay himself opts for the former.

all humanity (contingent on their "call[ing] on the name of the LORD") but also indiscriminate of gender (sons and daughters), age (old and young), or social status (even male and female servants), a fact Paul will seize upon in the NT.[45]

The second passage, Zech 12:10, is likewise well known and significantly cited in the NT: "I will pour out a spirit of grace and prayer on the house of David and the residents of Jerusalem, and they will look at me whom they pierced. They will mourn for him as one mourns for an only child and weep bitterly for him."[46] "Grace," or favor, may refer to Yahweh's own grace toward his people, while "pleas for mercy," or "supplication," may refer to prayer for Yahweh to show grace or mercy toward those who have pierced him.[47] Again, the context is Yahweh's judgment of the nations ("that day," vv. 8–9, 11; 13:1–2) and Israel's subsequent restoration to her covenant relationship in conjunction with a national day of mourning (vv. 10–14) and the removal of idolatry, immorality, and false prophets (Zech 13:1–9).

In addition, several passages in the Minor Prophets feature the Spirit as empowering prophecy (Hos 9:7 ESV; Mic 3:8; Zech 7:12).

Figure 6: References to God's Spirit in the Twelve Minor Prophets

Scripture Passage	Major Content	Function of God's Spirit
Hos 9:7	Prophet is "the man of the Spirit" (ESV)	Empowers prophecy
Joel 2:28–29	Spirit to be poured out on "all humanity"	End-time salvation and judgment
Mic 2:7	"Is the Spirit of the LORD impatient?"	(Presumed question by the people)

---

[45] See Gal 3:28. On the passage in Joel, see the treatment by Erika Moore, "Joel's Promise of the Spirit," in Firth and Wegner, *Presence, Power and Promise*, 245–56.

[46] Cf. John 19:37; Rev 1:7.

[47] The NT writers apply this reference to Jesus's crucifixion (e.g., John 19:37; Rev 1:7).

Mic 3:8	"Filled with power, . . . Spirit of the LORD"	Filling with power for prophecy
Hag 2:5	"My Spirit is present among you"	Manifests God's presence
Zech 4:6	Not by human power but by Spirit	Deliverance
Zech 6:8	"Pacified my Spirit"	Vision of four chariots
Zech 7:12	The words God sent by his Spirit	Empowers prophecy
Zech 12:10	God will pour out a spirit of grace	End-time salvation and judgment

The most significant references to the activity of God's Spirit in the Twelve Prophets—Joel 2:28–29 and Zech 12:10—both relate to the provision of end-time salvation and divine judgment. The reference in Joel speaks of a universal outpouring of God's Spirit on "all humanity," regardless of ethnicity, gender, or social status; Peter interprets this passage as fulfilled at Pentecost. The reference in Zechariah speaks of God's pouring out a spirit of grace when people look upon the one they have pierced, a passage NT writers interpret as a messianic reference to Jesus's crucifixion.

5

The Old Testament's Contribution to a Biblical Theology of the Holy Spirit

The OT contributes various tributaries flowing into the stream of biblical revelation regarding the Holy Spirit. To begin with, the Spirit is shown to be active in creation, serving as God's powerful agent acting through his creative word, a theme highlighted several times throughout the OT (Genesis, Job, Psalms, Isaiah). The Spirit is also associated with God's prophetic revelation as early as the time of Moses and with God's judgment of humanity in the flood.

In the Historical Books, the Spirit is shown to empower national deliverers without altering their personalities or overriding their individual choices, although elsewhere it is demonstrated that he may override human intention as necessity demands (1 Sam 19:19–24). With the judges, the Spirit typically comes upon them at the occasion of military deliverance (e.g., at least three distinct times in the case of Samson), and elsewhere the Spirit comes upon others at the occasion of their prophesying (e.g., at least two distinct times in the case of Saul). We also find, however, that the Spirit can remain upon God's chosen leaders in a somewhat different manner, as seen in the withdrawal of the Spirit's presence from Saul and his continuing presence with David (1 Sam 16:13–14). The Historical Books also show the continued and consistent association of the Spirit with prophetic activity.

While God's Spirit is mentioned in the Wisdom literature only infrequently, we do find connections between the Spirit and God's creative work and between the Spirit and wise living. As well, David prays that the Spirit not be taken from him (Ps 51:11), which highlights the presence of the Spirit with the rulers of God's people. The important pneumatological reference in Ps 139:7 speaks of the pervasive presence of God's Spirit, providing an important antecedent for later NT revelation.

God's putting his Spirit on his (messianic) Servant is a major theme in Isaiah (see esp. 42:1–4 and 61:1–2) in further development of God's promise of a messianic deliverer in the Davidic line (e.g., 11:1–3). Isaiah's distinction between God, his Spirit, and his Servant provides a significant backdrop for subsequent NT teaching. Jeremiah gestures toward the corollary of the Spirit's activity in the form of divine judgment in times of national crisis, while Ezekiel envisages the Spirit's postexilic activity in the form of restoration, even resurrection, as part of a new creation and new exodus, themes also struck in the second half of the book of Isaiah (e.g., chs. 40, 65–66).

Finally, the Twelve Prophets, especially Joel and Zechariah, envision an outpouring of God's Spirit in the last days, when people look on God's pierced Messiah in grief and mourning, an outpouring not limited to judges, kings, or prophets but universal among God's people. This fascinating panorama of OT passages pertaining to God's Spirit provides a fruitful field from which the NT writers, in light of the Messiah's coming, reap a rich pneumatological harvest, as we will see in our survey of the NT's teaching on the Spirit in chapters 6–10.[1]

---

[1] For a brief history of the major developments in a modern theology of the Holy Spirit, see John R. Levison, *Filled with the Spirit* (Grand Rapids: Eerdmans, 2009), xiv–xxv.

6

The Holy Spirit in the New Testament and in the Gospels

The New Testament

As the NT opens, we see the Spirit actively at work in strategic salvation-historical individuals such as John the Baptist, Mary, Elizabeth, Zechariah, and Simeon (Luke 1–2) in anticipation of the coming Messiah, Jesus, through whom God will be present with his people in an unprecedented manner. During this earthly ministry, Jesus is shown to possess the Spirit to an unlimited degree (John 3:34), and the Spirit is depicted at Jesus's baptism as descending onto Jesus and resting on him (Matt 3:16/Mark 1:10/Luke 3:22/John 1:32–33).

The future holds the promise of even more significant pneumatological developments for God's people. John the Baptist, and later Jesus himself, indicates that the Messiah will baptize not merely with water but with the Holy Spirit (Matt 3:11/Mark 1:8/Luke 3:16/John 1:33; Acts 1:5). At this future giving of the Spirit (John 7:38), both Jesus and his Father will make their home with believers by the Spirit, who will be with them forever (John 14:16–17, 21; cf. John 20:22; Luke 24:49).

Jesus's promise is realized following his ascension, when believers are filled with the Holy Spirit at Pentecost (Acts 2:4) in fulfillment of the promise of Joel 2:28 that in the last days God would pour out his Spirit "on all humanity" (see also Acts 2:16–21). Now it is not only the leaders of God's people but everyone who calls on the name of the Lord who experiences the presence of the Spirit. Soon it is clear that the same presence of the Spirit is available to Gentile believers in Jesus as well (Acts 10:44–47), in keeping with John the Baptist's prophecy (Acts 11:15–17).

The NT epistles reinforce the notion that every believer now enjoys the Spirit's indwelling presence. Believers have "received" the Spirit given to them (Rom 8:15; cf. 5:5). The Spirit is "in" believers (1 Cor 6:19) and "lives" in them (Rom 8:9, 11; 1 Cor 3:16). They possess the Spirit as "firstfruits" (Rom 8:23) and a "down payment" (2 Cor 1:22; 5:5). In terms of his activity, as will be further developed in the biblical-theological summary below, the Spirit is shown to mediate God's presence, to impart life, to reveal truth, to foster holiness, to supply power, and to effect unity.

The Gospels

The Gospel accounts make no attempt to explain the presence of the Spirit. The Holy Spirit was not unknown to the evangelists, for they knew the OT and Second Temple literature.[1] Jesus is shown to accomplish his ministry by

---

[1] Gerald F. Hawthorne, *The Presence and the Power: The Significance of the Holy Spirit in the Life and Ministry of Jesus* (Dallas: Word, 1991), 2. On the Spirit in Second Temple literature, see esp. Andrew W. Pitts and Seth Pollinger, "The Spirit in Second Temple Jewish Monotheism and the Origins of Early Christology," in *Christian Origins and Hellenistic Judaism: Social and Literary Contexts for the New Testament*, ed. Stanley E. Porter and Andrew W. Pitts (Leiden, NL: Brill, 2013), 135–76, esp. 153–64. See also Victor H. Matthews, "Holy Spirit," *ABD* 3:263–65; Cornelis Bennema, *The Power of Saving Wisdom: An Investigation of the Spirit and Wisdom in Relation to the Soteriology of the Fourth Gospel* (Tübingen, DEU: Mohr Siebeck, 2002); Mehrdad Fatehi, *The Spirit's Relation to the Risen Lord in Paul: An Examination of Its Christological Implications* (Tübingen, DEU: Mohr Siebeck, 2000); Desta Heliso, "Divine Spirit and Human Spirit in Paul in the Light of Stoic and Biblical-Jewish Perspectives," in *Spirit and Christ in the New Testament: Essays in Honor of Max Turner*, ed. I. Howard Marshall, Volker Rabens, and Cornelis Bennema (Grand Rapids: Eerdmans, 2012), 162–67; Levison, *Filled with the Spirit*, 118–21; Levison, "Spirit, Holy," in *The Eerdmans Dictionary of Early Judaism*, ed. John J. Collins and Daniel C. Harlow (Grand Rapids: Eerdmans, 2010), 1252–55; Levison, *The Spirit in First Century Judaism* (Leiden, NL: Brill, 1997); Rodrigo J. Morales, WUNT 2/282, *The Spirit and the Restoration of Israel: New Exodus and New Creation Motifs in Galatians* (Tübingen, DEU: Mohr Siebeck, 2010), 13–77; Max Turner, *Power from on High: The Spirit in Israel's Restoration and Witness in Luke-Acts* (Sheffield, UK: Sheffield Academic

the power of the Holy Spirit, but his possession of the Spirit is a function of his divinity rather than the latter being merely the result of the former.

The Gospels' teaching on the Spirit's role in Jesus's ministry should thus be viewed within the context of a divine Christology and monotheism, designating Jesus as the Spirit-anointed Messiah and Son of God.[2]

What is more, by beginning the account of Jesus's life with the agency of the Holy Spirit at Jesus's birth, the Gospels connect the work of the Spirit in the OT and NT. The NT is not just the story of Jesus but also the story of the work of the Spirit, first in the life of Jesus, then in the lives of his followers.[3]

Synoptic Gospels

Matthew writes his Gospel to furnish proof that Jesus is the long-awaited Jewish Messiah and to chronicle scriptural fulfillment in the various events and activities constituting Jesus's public ministry. Mark, who according to patristic tradition based his work on Peter's testimony, most likely writes for a Roman audience, highlighting Jesus's messianic authority over the elements of nature and the supernatural realm as well. Luke, himself not an eyewitness, bases his account on the (oral and written) eyewitness accounts of others, stressing (as Matthew does) scriptural fulfillment in Jesus's messianic mission, but showing more keenly its applicability not only to Jews but to Gentiles as well.[4]

Press, 1996), 86–104; and M. Wenk, "Holy Spirit," in *Dictionary of Jesus and the Gospels*, 2nd ed. (Downers Grove: InterVarsity, 2013), 388–89. Also, see various essays in *The Holy Spirit, Inspiration, and the Cultures of Antiquity: Multidisciplinary Perspectives*, ed. Jörg Frey and John R. Levison (Berlin: de Gruyter, 2014).

[2] John R. Coulson, "Jesus and the Spirit in Paul's Theology: The Earthly Jesus," *CBQ* 79 (2017): 93–96; contra James D. G. Dunn, *Jesus and the Spirit: A Study of the Religious and Charismatic Experience of Jesus and the First Christians as Reflected in the New Testament* (London: SCM, 1975).

[3] Hawthorne, *Presence and the Power*, 2. John D. Harvey, *Anointed with the Spirit and Power: The Holy Spirit's Empowering Presence* (Phillipsburg: P&R, 2008), 69, holds that during his earthly ministry, Jesus acted primarily out of the empowerment of the Holy Spirit.

[4] For introductory matters regarding the Synoptic Gospels, see Andreas J. Köstenberger, L. Scott Kellum, and Charles L. Quarles, *The Cradle, the Cross, and the*

While there is considerable overlap in these accounts with regard to their presentation not only of Jesus but also of the Holy Spirit, each evangelist tells the story of Jesus in his own way. This means selecting material that suits the evangelist's overriding purposes and stressing distinctive aspects of Jesus's messianic nature and mission important to the evangelists and judged significant for their respective audiences.[5] In this way, the Gospels are best understood as direct or indirect eyewitness testimony continuing the narration of God's mighty acts of deliverance in OT times.[6] This means that their story is in many ways building on the story of Israel,[7] and this includes their portrayal of the Spirit, as we will see in the remainder of this chapter.[8]

Figure 7: Frequency of References to the Spirit in the Gospels and Acts

Gospel/Acts	Number of References	Word Total	Percentage
Matthew	12	18,346	0.07
Mark	7	11,304	0.06
Luke	17	19,482	0.09
John	16	15,635	0.10
Acts	49	18,450	0.27

Crown: An Introduction to the New Testament, 2nd ed. (Nashville: B&H Academic, 2016), chs. 4–6.

[5] This is insufficiently recognized by Keith Warrington, "The Synoptic Gospels," in *Biblical Theology of the Holy Spirit*, who provides a topical treatment but does not trace references to the Spirit in each Synoptic Gospel in narrative fashion.

[6] See Richard Bauckham, *Jesus and the Eyewitnesses: The Gospels as Eyewitness Testimony* (Grand Rapids: Eerdmans, 2006; 2nd ed., 2017).

[7] See N. T. Wright, *The New Testament and the People of God*, Christian Origins and the Question of God 1 (Minneapolis: Fortress, 1992).

[8] For frequencies of mentions of the Spirit in the Gospels and Acts, see figure 7. Note that frequencies in Luke's Gospel are in keeping with the other Gospels, while a notable spike occurs in the book of Acts.

Matthew

Prolegomena to Jesus's Ministry. There are at least four important clusters of references to the Spirit in Matthew's prolegomena to Jesus's ministry (1:18–4:11). First, the "Holy Spirit" is twice identified as the agent of the virginal conception of Jesus in his mother Mary's womb (1:18, 20).[9] Second, John the Baptist predicts that Jesus will baptize with the Holy Spirit and with fire (3:11)—a reference to the judgment that Jesus's proclamation of God's kingdom will bring to those who reject his message. Third, in the account of Jesus's baptism by John, reference is made to the "Spirit of God," who descends on Jesus like a dove and rests on him (3:16).[10] Fourth, immediately following Jesus's baptism, the "Spirit" is shown to lead Jesus into the wilderness to be tempted by the devil (4:1).[11] The cumulative picture that emerges from Matthew's prolegomena to Jesus's ministry is that the Spirit is strategically involved in key events, such as the virgin birth and Jesus's baptism, acting with divine power and taking decisive initiative, as well as serving as an agent of divine judgment. There is some diversity of nomenclature, as the terms "Holy Spirit," "Spirit of God," and "Spirit" are used interchangeably, with no discernible difference in meaning or referent.

Commissioning of the Twelve. The commissioning of the twelve apostles is set within the scope of the spiritual warfare Jesus wages with Satan and his demons, a warfare into which Jesus's followers are drawn by following Jesus and being sent out by him. They will do battle with the unclean spirits (10:1, 8) just as Jesus does (cf. 8:28–34: the Gadarene demoniac). Also, they will face persecution similar to Jesus's (10:16–23), but the "Spirit of your Father" will speak through them (v. 20). The phrase "Spirit of your Father" is remarkable

---

[9] G. K. Beale finds parallels between the Spirit's work in creation in Genesis 1 and the Spirit's association with Jesus's birth as "the very beginning of the new age, the new creation" (*New Testament Biblical Theology*, 566.

[10] Craig S. Keener, *The Spirit in the Gospels and Acts: Divine Purity and Power* (Grand Rapids: Baker Academic, 1997), 60, suggests that the form of the dove stems from the flood narrative (see Gen 8:8–12), with the dove symbolizing new creation. This marks Jesus, who is bringing the Spirit, as the one ushering in a new world in the kingdom.

[11] Matthew contrasts the role of the Spirit (ὑπὸ τοῦ πνεύματος) and the role of the devil (ὑπὸ τοῦ διαβόλου), highlighting the Spirit's role in Jesus's overcoming of Satan (Hawthorne, *Presence and the Power*, 140).

and unique in Matthew's Gospel, intimating a close, even familial, relationship between the disciples and both God the Father and the Spirit of God.
The Spirit will thus empower the mission of Jesus's followers and give them
boldness in times of persecution sure to come.

The Ministry of God's Servant and Blasphemy of the Holy Spirit. The last
two major clusters of references to the Holy Spirit in Matthew's Gospel
before the final reference to him in the penultimate verse of the Gospel are
found in chapter 12.[12] The first of these is part of a citation of one of Isaiah's
Servant Songs. There Yahweh declares that he will put his Spirit on his chosen Beloved. In the Matthean context, this citation indicates fulfillment of
Isaiah's vision of the messianic ministry of healing that God's Servant will
perform with gentleness and that will extend not only to Jews but even to
Gentiles (12:18–21; cf. Isa 42:1–4). [13]

Second, in the context of a demon exorcism performed by Jesus, the
Pharisees attribute Jesus's power over the evil spirits to Beelzebul, the prince
of demons (i.e., Satan; 12:24; cf. the foreshadowing of this controversy in
9:3). Jesus's shot across the bow is pointed: while people who blaspheme
him—the Son of Man—will be forgiven, no one who blasphemes the Spirit
will be forgiven (vv. 31–32).[14] Several pertinent observations may be noted:
(1) the fact that the Spirit can be the object of blasphemy clearly implies
his divinity; (2) the activity of God's Spirit in and through Jesus's ministry
heralds the coming of the kingdom of God (v. 28);[15] (3) the Spirit's power

---

[12] Matthew refers to the Spirit only once in passing in chapters 13–27 (this
is similar to Luke; see the section titled "Luke" later in this chapter). In 22:43 he
indicates that David was "speaking by the Spirit" when he wrote Psalm 110 (NIV).
Jesus's statement here recorded by Matthew helpfully contributes to a biblical understanding of the inspiration of Scripture.

[13] See discussion of this point in Beale, *New Testament Biblical Theology*, 568–69.

[14] For a helpful discussion of this difficult passage, see Duane Litfin, "Revisiting
the Unpardonable Sin: Insight from an Unexpected Source," *JETS* 60 (2017):
713–32.

[15] Cf. Dunn, *Jesus and the Spirit*, 47, who says, "The outpouring of the prophetic Spirit in plentiful supply upon Israel was commonly regarded as one of the
chief blessings and hallmarks of the new age." Again he writes, "Jesus saw his exorcisms not merely as the healing of demented people, not merely as the casting out of
demons, not merely as a victory over Satan, but as that binding of the powers of evil
which was looked for at the end of the age" (48).

exceeds that of Satan and his demons (v. 29; Satan is the "strong man" whose house is invaded and who is bound and rendered powerless).[16]

The Great Commission. After a lengthy hiatus, Matthew's final reference to the Spirit is found at the end of his Gospel as part of the baptismal formula in the so-called Great Commission: "Go, therefore, and make disciples of all nations, baptizing them in the name of the Father and of the Son and of the Holy Spirit, teaching them to observe everything I have commanded you. And remember, I am with you always, to the end of the age" (Matt 28:19–20).

The risen Jesus here commands the Eleven (the Twelve minus Judas) to engage in mission following his ascension, charging them to make disciples of all nations—not only Jews but also Gentiles—and as part of this discipleship mandate to baptize converts "in the name of the Father and of the Son and of the Holy Spirit" and to teach them to observe everything he has commanded them.

The closing reference to the Holy Spirit in Matthew's Gospel is remarkable in several ways:

(1) "The name" is singular, joining Father, Son, and Spirit in missional unity.

(2) The phrase "Holy Spirit" closes a book that begins with references to the Holy Spirit's agency in Jesus's virgin conception (1:18, 20).

(3) Matthew presents on Jesus's lips a full-fledged trinitarian formula, "in the name of the Father and of the Son and of the Holy Spirit," which at a very early stage of doctrinal formulation (in fact, shortly after the resurrection) juxtaposes the three divine persons into what will later come to be called "the Holy Trinity." This has led some critical scholars to suggest that the formula reflects Matthean parlance rather than Jesus's *ipsissima verba*.[17] However, there is no reason why Jesus himself could not have instituted baptism in the name of the Father, the Son, and the Holy Spirit and done so following his resurrection.

---

[16] Note that the reference to the "Spirit of God" at the occasion of Jesus's baptism at the inception of his ministry in 3:16 and the present reference in 12:28 are the only two uses of "Spirit of God" in Matthew's Gospel.

[17] Some, such as F. C. Conybeare, "The Eusebian Form of the Text of Mt. 28:19," *ZNW* 2 (1901): 275–88, have argued that the trinitarian formula is not in the Matthean original.

(4) The Spirit's continual presence with the church as she engages in mission seems implied also in the closing reference: "And remember, I am with you always, to the end of the age" (v. 20). In this way Jesus ("I") identifies himself closely with the Spirit—presenting him, as it were, as his Spirit continually conveying his own presence. This concluding reference also forms an *inclusio* with the statement at the beginning of the Gospel that Jesus is Immanuel, "God with us" (1:23).[18]

Both the close identification of Jesus and the Spirit and the close intertwining of the presence of God the Father, Jesus the Son, and the Holy Spirit are brought out more explicitly in John's Gospel, as we will see in the section titled "The Gospel of John" later in this chapter.

Figure 8: References to the Spirit in Matthew's Gospel

Scripture Passage	Content
Matt 1:18, 20	Holy Spirit to conceive Jesus in womb of mother Mary
Matt 3:11	Jesus will baptize with the Holy Spirit and fire
Matt 3:16	Spirit of God descends and rests on Jesus at baptism
Matt 4:1	Spirit leads Jesus into wilderness to be tempted by the devil
Matt 10:20	Spirit of the Father will speak for persecuted believers
Matt 12:18; cf. Isa 42:1	Spirit-anointed Servant of the Lord is gentle; healing ministry
Matt 12:28–32	Warning against blasphemy of the Holy Spirit
Matt 22:43	David, in the Spirit, calls him "Lord"
Matt 28:19–20	Great Commission to baptize in name of Father, Son, and Holy Spirit

---

[18] Wenk, "Holy Spirit," 391, suggests that the references to the Spirit in Matt 1:18 and 28:19 serve as an *inclusio* for the book as well.

Mark

Moving from Matthew to Mark, we find no new references to the Spirit to consider; all references to the Spirit in Mark are found also in Matthew. Mark, too, includes John the Baptist's prediction that Jesus will baptize with the Holy Spirit (1:8), the Spirit's descent on Jesus as a dove at his baptism (1:10), and the Spirit's driving Jesus into the wilderness, where he is tempted by Satan (1:12)—and all within the scope of five short verses.[19] Mark likewise includes the pericope concerning the blasphemy of the Holy Spirit (3:29). Mark also includes Jesus's assurance that his followers will receive help from the Holy Spirit in times of persecution, albeit not in the context of the commissioning of the Twelve but as part of Jesus's Olivet discourse (13:11; cf. 6:7–13).[20]

In contrast to Matthew, Mark's Gospel includes a reference neither to the Spirit's agency in the virginal conception nor to the trinitarian formula in the Great Commission.[21] Finally, Mark does not include Matthew's central affirmation of the Spirit's empowerment in Jesus's messianic healing ministry taken from Isaiah (Matt 12:18; cf. Isa 42:1). Thus we see that, on the assumption of Markan priority, Matthew has strengthened Mark's pneumatological web of references quite considerably while incorporating Mark's essential framework.[22] On the assumption of Matthean priority, Mark omits Jesus's birth narrative as well as Jesus's healing ministry as Isaiah's Servant of

---

[19] Note that the Spirit is introduced as "the Holy Spirit" in 1:8 and subsequently referred to as "the Spirit" in 1:10 and 12. This is in keeping with customary discourse flow in the narrative genre. Hawthorne argues that the use of εἰς in Mark 1:10 is significant, indicating that the Spirit descends *into* Jesus, coming on him in a new and different way than he has known the Spirit before (*Presence and the Power*, 127).

[20] But note that Matthew's terminology here is "the Spirit of your Father" (Matt 10:20).

[21] This is true whether or not one accepts the longer ending of Mark as original, as it does not contain a reference to the Holy Spirit.

[22] But cf. Morna D. Hooker, "John's Baptism: A Prophetic Sign," in *The Holy Spirit and Christian Origins: Essays in Honor of James D. G. Dunn*, ed. Graham N. Stanton, Bruce W. Longenecker, and Stephen C. Barton (Grand Rapids: Eerdmans, 2004), 27. Cf. Keener, *Spirit in the Gospels and Acts*, 50, 61, 68–71.

the Lord and does not refer to the Holy Spirit in the commissioning at the end of his Gospel.[23]

Figure 9: References to the Spirit in Mark's Gospel

Scripture Passage	Content
Mark 1:8	Jesus will baptize with the Holy Spirit
Mark 1:10	Holy Spirit descends on Jesus at his baptism
Mark 1:12	The Spirit drives Jesus into the wilderness to be tempted by the devil
Mark 3:29	Warning against blasphemy of the Holy Spirit
Mark 12:36	David spoke in the Holy Spirit (cf. Matt 22:43)
Mark 13:11	The Holy Spirit will help believers in times of persecution

Luke

Prolegomena to Jesus's Ministry. Luke places greater emphasis on the Holy Spirit than does either Matthew or Mark.[24] References to the Holy Spirit in Luke's Gospel number seventeen in all,[25] compared to twelve in Matthew and six in Mark.[26] Narrating the prolegomena to Jesus's ministry (1:1–4:15), Luke first indicates that John the Baptist will be filled with the Holy Spirit from his mother's womb (1:15). Both of John's parents, Elizabeth and Zechariah, are likewise said to be filled with the Holy Spirit (1:41, 67). Like Matthew, Luke refers to Jesus's conception in Mary's womb by the Holy

---

[23] On the relationships between the Gospels, see Köstenberger, Kellum, and Quarles, *Cradle, the Cross, and the Crown*, 175–91. For a study of Markan pneumatology, see Emerson B. Powery, "The Spirit, the Scripture(s), and the Gospel of Mark: Pneumatology and Hermeneutics in Narrative Perspective," *Journal of Pentecostal Theology* 11 (2003): 184–98.

[24] For a succinct summary see Köstenberger, Kellum, and Quarles, *The Cradle, the Cross, and the Crown*, 340.

[25] Luke 1:15, 35, 41, 67; 2:25, 26, 27; 3:16, 22; 4:1 (2x), 14, 18; 10:21; 11:13; 12:10, 12; 24:49 (implied).

[26] See Darrell L. Bock, *A Theology of Luke and Acts: God's Promised Program, Realized for All Nations*, BTNT (Grand Rapids: Zondervan, 2011), 211.

Spirit ("The Holy Spirit will come upon you, and the power of the Most High will overshadow you"; 1:35).[27]

The Holy Spirit is said also to be upon Simeon, who had received revelation from the Holy Spirit and entered the temple area in the Spirit (2:25–27)—a remarkable concatenation of three references to the Holy Spirit in as many verses.[28] Similar to Elizabeth and Zechariah before him, Simeon then bears witness to the remarkable salvation-historical events about to unfold through John the Baptist, the forerunner, and Jesus, the long-awaited Messiah.[29] In keeping with Luke's special focus on the lowly and outcast in

---

[27] The discussion of the Holy Spirit's overshadowing Mary calls to mind the OT narratives of God's glory filling the tabernacle (Exod 40:35) as well as God's protective presence for people who trust him (Ps 91:4 [90:4 LXX]). The conception of Jesus in Mary's womb by the Holy Spirit suggests that he is filled with the Spirit from birth. While Luke does not explicitly say this regarding Jesus, he does say it regarding John, and if John is full of the Spirit at birth, it is likely that Jesus is as well. The likelihood is increased further by Luke's consistent emphasis on Jesus's superiority over John in the birth narratives. See Hawthorne, *Presence and the Power*, 71–90. The results of Jesus's being filled with the Spirit are that he (1) is called the Son of God; (2) will be called "holy"; and (3) will be the start of a new humanity (his conception by the Spirit marking a new creation, 1:35).

[28] For a thorough study of this passage, see John R. Levison, "The Spirit, Simeon, and the Songs of the Servant," in Marshall, Rabens, and Bennema, *Spirit and Christ in the New Testament*, 18–34.

[29] Cf. Mark L. Strauss, "Jesus and the Spirit in Biblical and Theological Perspective: Messianic Empowering, Saving Wisdom, and the Limits of Biblical Theology," in *Spirit and Christ in the New Testament and Christian Theology: Essays in Honor of Max Turner*, ed. I. Howard Marshall, Volker Rabens, and Cornelis Bennema (Grand Rapids: Eerdmans, 2012), 266–70, who provides a helpful discussion of scholarship on the Spirit in Luke-Acts starting with James D. G. Dunn's *Baptism in the Holy Spirit* (Philadelphia: Westminster, 1970; 2nd ed. London: SCM, 2010), who stresses the Spirit's role in designating Jesus as the Son of God serving as a model for all believers; and Robert P. Menzies, *The Development of Early Christian Pneumatology with Special Reference to Luke-Acts* (Sheffield, UK: JSOT, 1991), who limits the Spirit's role to prophecy and empowerment for witness. Strauss himself follows the mediating position advocated by Turner, *Power from on High*, who notes the Spirit's salvation-historical embeddedness in the Isaianic new exodus motif and his role as empowering the messianic community's eschatological salvation and/or restoration (see esp. 110). Dunn reiterates the main contours of his position and responds to Menzies's critique in "'The Lord, the Giver of Life': The Gift of the Spirit as Both Life-giving and Empowering," in Marshall, Rabens, and Bennema, 1–17.

society, Simeon stresses the implications of Jesus's coming not only for the people of Israel but also for the Gentiles (2:32).

The characterization of Jesus as filled with wisdom and understanding may further underscore his possession of the Spirit (2:40, 47).[30] Thus Luke features more references to the Holy Spirit in his first two chapters than Mark does in his entire Gospel. Like Matthew and Mark, Luke then narrates the Holy Spirit's dove-like descent on Jesus at his baptism, accompanied by the heavenly voice testifying to Jesus's divine sonship (3:22).

Beginning of Jesus's Ministry: Temptation and Inaugural Address. Luke's temptation narrative includes two references to the Holy Spirit, rather than one, as in Matthew and Mark (Luke 4:1).[31] Not only does the Spirit lead Jesus into the wilderness, where he is tempted by the devil, but Jesus himself is said to be "full of the Holy Spirit" at the very outset of the temptation narrative. This entails a remarkable distinction between the Spirit's own independent personality, which allows him to take initiative and lead Jesus into the wilderness, and Jesus, whom the Spirit continually fills with his presence. At the other end of the temptation narrative, Luke refers to Jesus's return to Galilee "in the power of the Spirit" (4:14).[32] Thus references to the Spirit

---

[30] Cf. Isa 11:2: "The Spirit of the LORD will rest on him, a Spirit of wisdom and understanding." See Hawthorne, *Presence and the Power*, 106–7; see also 97–102 for a discussion of Luke 2:40 and 102–9 for a treatment of Luke 2:41–52. Harvey, *Anointed with the Spirit and Power*, detects a parallel between Luke 2:40 indicating that Jesus was "filled" (πληρούμενον) with wisdom, and John, Elizabeth, and Zachariah, who are similarly "filled" with the Spirit (1:15, 41, 67). OT evidence likewise suggests that "*wisdom* characterizes the individual on whom the Spirit rests" (70).

[31] Luke uses the imperfect in 4:1 to speak of the Holy Spirit's leading, clarifying his ongoing role during the wilderness temptation (Hawthorne, *Presence and the Power*, 139). Turner detects continuity between Second Temple Jewish expectation of the deliverance of Israel by the Spirit-anointed Messiah and Luke's description here; Max Turner, *The Holy Spirit and Spiritual Gifts in the New Testament Church and Today*, rev. ed. (Grand Rapids: Baker, 2012), 36; cf. 3–20. For this same argument in more detail, see M. M. B. Turner, "The Spirit of Prophecy and the Power of Authoritative Preaching in Luke-Acts: A Question of Origins," *NTS* 38 (1992): 66–88.

[32] Like Gordon D. Fee, *God's Empowering Presence: The Holy Spirit in the Letters of Paul* (Peabody: Hendrickson, 1994), passim, Hawthorne notes that "power" and "Spirit" are virtually synonymous (*Presence and the Power*, 154–55).

in 4:1, 14 frame the entire pericope, with the added reference to the Spirit's power in v. 14 indicating Jesus's victory over Satan.

Almost seamlessly, Luke follows the temptation narrative with Jesus's inaugural appearance in his hometown synagogue of Nazareth, where he is revealed as Isaiah's Servant of the Lord in the words of Isa 61:1–2:

> The Spirit of the Lord is on me,
> because he has anointed me
> to preach good news to the poor.
> He has sent me
> to proclaim release to the captives
> and recovery of sight to the blind,
> to set free the oppressed,
> to proclaim the year of the Lord's favor. (Luke 4:18–19)

While Matthew draws on Isaiah 42 in conjunction with Jesus's messianic healing ministry at the center of his Gospel, Luke daringly presents Jesus as the Spirit-anointed Servant of the Lord at the very outset of his ministry in the words of Isaiah 61. This reference, together with the Spirit's descent on Jesus at his baptism, puts the Spirit's work in and through Jesus front and center in Luke's Gospel. Several important observations may be made: (1) the "anointing" language indicates God's choice of Jesus as his royal Messiah; (2) Jesus's proclamation of good news to the poor is at the heart of Luke's emphasis on Jesus's concern for the lowly and outcast in society and the reversal that his coming will entail;[33] (3) Luke also stresses that Jesus's Spirit-anointed ministry will bring liberation (*aphesis*, mentioned twice in v. 18) and healing and will convey God's favor. It is hard to imagine a

---

[33] Longenecker, "Rome's Victory and God's Honour," in Stanton, Longenecker, and Barton, *Holy Spirit and Christian Origins*, 101, notes the importance of the Spirit's empowerment in Luke-Acts regarding the lowly and outcast: "The initial enactment of this reconciliation of the needy, the marginalised, the despised, and the forlorn within the empire of God is narrated within Luke's two volumes, an enactment orchestrated by the Spirit that empowered both Jesus and those who followed in his name. . . . This Spirit-driven process, Luke is convinced, cannot be stopped." Cf. Dunn, *Jesus and the Spirit*, 61, who stresses that the Spirit of God is at work not only in Jesus's healings and exorcisms but also in his proclamation of the good news to the poor.

more dramatic portrayal of Jesus's messianic claim than his assertion, "Today as you listen, this Scripture [Isa 61:1–2] has been fulfilled" (v. 21).

Remainder of Jesus's Ministry (Including the Lukan Travel Narrative). The remainder of Jesus's ministry in Luke—including the Lukan "travel narrative" in 9:51–19:27—features several references to the Holy Spirit. At the return of the seventy-two, Jesus is filled with joy in the Holy Spirit and gives thanks to the Father for hiding himself from the wise and learned but revealing himself to little children (10:21). In a passage similar to that found in Matthew's Sermon on the Mount, Luke speaks of the giving of the Holy Spirit to those who ask the Father, an example of the good gifts God gives to the children he loves (11:13; cf. Matt 7:7–11 with reference to bread and fish). In short order, Luke then groups together two references to the Holy Spirit found also in both Matthew and Mark: Jesus's warning against blaspheming the Holy Spirit (12:10; though note that Matthew and Mark include considerably more detail) and the Holy Spirit's giving Jesus's followers the words to say when they are persecuted (12:11–12).[34] After a very lengthy hiatus spanning almost half the Gospel, oblique reference is made to the impending outpouring of the Spirit when Jesus tells his disciples that he will send "the promise of my Father" upon his followers but that they should remain in Jerusalem until they are "empowered from on high" (24:49; cf. Acts 2:14–36).[35]

---

[34] In Luke 11:20, Jesus speaks of casting out demons "by the finger of God." In the Matthean parallel (Matt 12:28) we read that Jesus casts out demons "by the Spirit of God" (see discussion in this chapter's section titled "Matthew" above). While Luke does not explicitly mention the "Spirit," the effect is the same: Jesus is exorcising demons by God's power and agency. For a discussion of the differences between Luke and Matthew, as well as the exodus imagery (Exod 8:19) that stands behind the reference to "the finger of God," see Darrell L. Bock, Luke 9:51–24:53, BECNT (Grand Rapids: Baker, 1996), 1079; Dunn, *Jesus and the Spirit*, 46–47; I. Howard Marshall, *The Gospel of Luke*, NIGTC (Grand Rapids: Eerdmans, 1978), 475–76. On Luke 12:12, see Steve Walton, "Whose Spirit? The Promise and the Promiser in Luke 12:12," in Marshall, Rabens, and Bennema, *Spirit and Christ in the New Testament*, 35–51, who stresses the unity between Jesus and Yahweh in Jesus's saving and aiding activity, noting that in his exalted state Jesus "can be present as widely as YHWH can" (49).

[35] The "promise of the Father" may encompass the "broader eschatological hope associated with the Spirit" in first-century Judaism (Matthias Wenk, "Acts," in

Figure 10: References to the Spirit in Luke's Gospel

Scripture Passage	Content
Luke 1:15	John the Baptist to be filled with the Holy Spirit from mother's womb
Luke 1:35	Holy Spirit will come upon Mary, and his power will overshadow her
Luke 1:41	Elizabeth, mother of John the Baptist, is filled with the Holy Spirit
Luke 1:67	Zechariah, father of John the Baptist, is filled with the Holy Spirit
Luke 2:25–27	Holy Spirit is upon Simeon, who comes to the temple in the Spirit
Luke 3:16	John the Baptist says Jesus will baptize with the Holy Spirit
Luke 3:22	Holy Spirit descends and rests upon Jesus at his baptism
Luke 4:1	Spirit leads Jesus into wilderness, Jesus is full of the Spirit
Luke 4:14	Jesus returns to Galilee in the power of the Spirit
Luke 4:18–19; cf. Isa 61:1–2	The Spirit of the Lord is upon Jesus, the Servant of the Lord
Luke 10:21	Jesus is filled with joy in the Holy Spirit, praising the Father
Luke 11:13	The Holy Spirit is the supreme good gift God the Father gives

---

Burke and Warrington, *Biblical Theology of the Holy Spirit*, 118). Turner, "The Spirit and Salvation in Luke-Acts," in Stanton, Longenecker, and Barton, *Holy Spirit and Christian Origins*, 110, suggests there is an allusion here and in Acts 1:8 to Isa 32:15 that looks to the restoration of Israel from exile when God pours out his Spirit. Luke is indicating that it will be by the power of the same Spirit that the Christian community experiences and enjoys restoration and salvation.

Luke 12:10	Warning against blasphemy of the Holy Spirit
Luke 12:11–12	Holy Spirit will give Jesus's followers words to say during persecution
Luke 24:49	Promise of the Father will "empower" believers with power from on high

Summary

The NT opens with Matthew's identification of the Holy Spirit as the agent in Jesus's virginal conception and birth. John the Baptist predicts that Jesus will baptize with the Holy Spirit. The Spirit is shown to descend on Jesus and rest on him at his baptism and subsequently to lead Jesus into the wilderness to be tempted by the devil. Thus Matthew makes clear that the Spirit is strategically involved in key events of Jesus's ministry, acting with divine power, taking decisive initiative, and serving as an agent of judgment. Later in Matthew's narrative, believers are assured that the Spirit will speak for them in times of persecution, and Jesus is identified as the Spirit-anointed Servant of the Lord in his gentle healing ministry. Jesus warns against blaspheming the Holy Spirit, a clear acknowledgment of the Spirit's deity. The Gospel closes with a trinitarian reference in the Great Commission.

Mark includes some of the same material as does Matthew (but no reference to the Spirit's involvement in the virgin birth, since he does not feature a birth narrative).

Most of the references to the Spirit in Luke's Gospel are found in the opening chapters of his narrative, including in the birth narratives of John the Baptist and Jesus and the account of the eight-day-old Jesus being circumcised at the temple. A programmatic reference to Jesus's anointing with the Spirit is found at Jesus's inaugural synagogue sermon at 4:18–19, with reference to Isa 61:1–2. The reference to the imminent coming of "what my Father promised" at 24:49 prepares the way for the account of the pouring out of the Spirit in Acts 2.

The Gospel of John

Anyone seeking to explore the role of the Spirit in John's Gospel is initially struck by the way the Son-Father relationship between the Word-made-flesh and God the Father completely dominates the first half of John's Gospel.[36] This is not to say that the Spirit is completely absent; yet it is not until the second half of the Gospel, with the Son's departure to the Father being imminent, that the Spirit moves into the foreground.

There is no reference to the Spirit in John's introduction, and act 1 of the Johannine drama features a mere handful of passages in which reference to the Spirit is made, all of which relate to his role in Jesus's ministry. The Spirit rests on Jesus (1:32–33), is involved in regeneration (3:5) and worship (4:23–24), and rests on Jesus to an unlimited degree (3:34). It is the Spirit who gives life (6:63), and the Spirit will be given only after Jesus's glorification (7:39).

References to the Spirit in the second half of the Gospel increase dramatically in both number and prominence, in keeping with the Spirit's pivotal role in the disciples' mission subsequent to Jesus's departure and return to the Father. The three names for the Spirit used by John in the second half of his Gospel are "Spirit of truth" (14:17; 15:26; 16:13), "Holy Spirit" (14:26; 20:22; cf. 1:33), and *paraklētos*, or "helping presence," translated "Helper" in the ESV (14:16, 26; 15:26; 16:7).

Book of Signs

John's and Jesus's Early Ministries. The initial references to the Spirit are in conjunction with Jesus's baptism by John (1:32–33). The Baptist testifies that he saw the Spirit descend from heaven as a dove and remain on Jesus. He had been told by God that the person so designated would be the one who would baptize—not with water, as John does, but with the Holy Spirit (1:33).[37] Thus the Spirit's first appearance in the Gospel serves both to highlight his ongoing presence with Jesus and to confirm Jesus as the God-sent future dispenser of the Spirit.

---

[36] This section adapts material from Andreas J. Köstenberger, *A Theology of John's Gospel and Letters: The Word, the Christ, the Son of God*, BTNT (Grand Rapids: Zondervan, 2009), 393–402. See there for further bibliography, along with the recent Michael Becker, "Spirit in Relationship: Pneumatology in the Gospel of John," in Frey and Levison, eds., *Holy Spirit, Inspiration, and the Cultures of Antiquity*, 331–41.

[37] Cf. Matt 3:11; Mark 1:8; Luke 3:16; Acts 1:5; see also John 14:26; 20:22.

Cana Cycle. The next possible cluster of references is found in Jesus's interchange with Nicodemus. Jesus's reference to being "born again" (3:3) is explicated as being "born of water and spirit" (3:5; i.e., being reborn spiritually as opposed to physically).[38] In addition, it is possible that the agent of the new birth is here identified, at least on a secondary level (for John's readers) as the person of the Spirit (cf. Ezek 36:26). In either event, the reference conveys the notion of spiritual birth effecting cleansing and renewal. Most likely, the primary emphasis in Jesus's statement seems to lie on the spiritual nature of the birth required for entering God's kingdom, as is apparent from the analogy between wind and spirit in v. 8.[39]

The next unambiguous mention of the Spirit is found in 3:34. In a section explicating the significance of the Baptist's testimony for John's readers, the evangelist comments that "he" (most likely God; made explicit in the NIV) gives the Spirit without measure (i.e., to an unlimited extent; cf. 1:33). That is, Jesus is no mere prophet; he is the Messiah on whom the Spirit has come to rest in all his fullness.

The reference to worship "in Spirit and in truth" in 4:23–24 sustains a close connection with the reference to being born "of water and the Spirit" in 3:5. While possibly containing a secondary reference to the Spirit, Jesus's statement here focuses primarily on the kind of worship those who would please God should render, namely, worship that is spiritual rather than focused on physical location.[40] Nevertheless, while *pneuma* may not refer directly to the Spirit here, one may reasonably infer that a person is qualified to worship "in Spirit and in truth"—existing in the realm of spirit (as God

---

[38] My translation (cf. ESV: "born of water and the Spirit"). See further the discussion of 4:23–24 later in this section, where a similar dynamic and contrast between physical and spiritual realities is at work.

[39] See also 3:6: "That which is born of flesh is flesh, and that which is born of spirit is spirit" (my translation; alternatively, "That which is born of the flesh is flesh, and that which is born of the Spirit is spirit." ESV). Turner, *Holy Spirit*, 67–69, sees this passage as a reference to the Holy Spirit, contending that Ezek 36:26 constitutes a prophecy regarding the Holy Spirit. Cf. Linda Belleville, "'Born of Water and Spirit': John 3:5," *TrinJ* 1, no. 2 (Fall 1980): 125–41.

[40] That is, whether in the Jerusalem temple (the Jewish people) or in the sanctuary on Mount Gerizim (the Samaritans). A direct reference to the Spirit would hardly have been intelligible to the Samaritan woman, though it may have been intelligible to John's first readers.

himself is in that realm)—by the new birth God grants (cf. 3:6: "that which is born of spirit [or: the Spirit] is spirit").

Festival Cycle. The first of several instances in which Jesus refers to the Spirit in this Gospel is found in the context of Jesus's instruction to the Twelve subsequent to a mass defection by Jesus's other followers (6:63). Jesus affirms that the Spirit gives life and that Jesus's words are spirit and life. The latter reference should probably be taken to mean that Jesus's words are life-giving because they are infused with the Spirit who rests on Jesus (1:33) to an unlimited degree (3:34).

The next reference to the Spirit is part of an aside by the evangelist, who explains a given utterance of Jesus with reference to the Spirit (7:39). The context is Jesus's invitation for people to come to him and drink, uttered on the final day of the Feast of Tabernacles (7:37).[41] The festival was celebrated in hopes of Israel's joyful restoration and the ingathering of the nations. Jesus here presents himself as God's agent in bringing about these end-time events.

The Scripture adduced in Jesus's saying, "The one who believes in me, as the Scripture has said, will have streams of living water flow from deep within him" (7:38), is likely common prophetic teaching.[42] "From deep within him" probably refers to believers in Jesus rather than to Jesus himself, with the first clause, "The one who believes in me," serving as a pendent subject.[43] The evangelist adds that Jesus's reference is to the future giving of the Spirit to those who believe in him (7:39; cf. 1:33; 4:13–14).[44]

---

[41] The present passage harks back to Jesus's interchange with the Samaritan woman in 4:7–15.

[42] Suggestions of specific passages include Ps 77:16, 20 LXX (with the epithet "living" coming from Zech 14:8) or Isa 58:11 (cf. Prov 4:23; 5:15). See D. A. Carson, *The Gospel according to John*, PNTC (Grand Rapids: Eerdmans, 1991), 325–28.

[43] So a majority of commentators, including Herman N. Ridderbos, *The Gospel of John*, trans. John Vriend (Grand Rapids: Eerdmans, 1997), 273; and Carson, *Gospel according to John*, 323–25. Less likely, Jesus is presented as the source of "streams of living water." Other examples of pendent subjects in this Gospel include 1:12; 6:39; 15:2; and 17:2.

[44] This reflects hindsight and represents an effort by the evangelist to preserve the historical perspective before Jesus's "glorification," a Johannine euphemism for the cluster of events centering in the crucifixion. See D. A. Carson, "Understanding Misunderstandings in the Fourth Gospel," *TynBul* 33 (1982): 59–91; and Eugene E. Lemcio, *The Past of Jesus in the Gospels*, SNTSMS 68 (Cambridge: Cambridge

Book of Exaltation

In the first half of the Gospel, the fourth evangelist's treatment of the Spirit largely resembles that of the Synoptics. Yet the adoption of a post-exaltation vantage point leads to a vastly enhanced portrait of the Spirit in the Farewell Discourse.[45]

Farewell Discourse. The historical setting of the Farewell Discourse is the preparation of Jesus's followers for the time following his departure. References to the Spirit in chapters 14–16 are numerous, with Jesus envisioning the giving of the Spirit following his exaltation.[46] Contrary to the disciples' sentiments at the time, Jesus's departure will benefit them in several ways. Most important, Jesus will petition the Father to send the *paraklētos*, "another helping presence" like Jesus.

The term *paraklētos*[47] does not occur in the LXX[48] and is found elsewhere in the NT only at 1 John 2:1, which describes Jesus as believers' "advocate"

University Press, 2005). Since the reference in 11:33 is to *Jesus's* spirit (as also in 13:21 and 19:30), not the Holy Spirit, this concludes the fairly sparse list of references to the Spirit in the first half of the Gospel.

[45] For a treatment of the Spirit-Paraclete in the context of the references to the Spirit in the entire Gospel narrative, see Margaret Davies, *Rhetoric and Reference in the Fourth Gospel*, JSNTSup 69 (Sheffield, UK: JSOT, 1992), 139–53. For a comparison of the treatments of the Spirit in John and the Synoptics, see Andreas J. Köstenberger, *Encountering John: The Gospel in Historical, Literary, and Theological Perspective*, 2nd ed. (Grand Rapids: Baker, 2013), 145–46.

[46] This section adapts material from Andreas J. Köstenberger and Scott R. Swain, *Father, Son and Spirit: The Trinity and John's Gospel*, NSBT 24 (Downers Grove: InterVarsity, 2004), 96–103.

[47] Unsatisfactory approaches to resolving the meaning of παράκλητος in John's Gospel are legion. For a brief yet informative history of interpretive options such as "advocate," "comforter," "exhorter," "helper," and "counselor," see Turner, *Holy Spirit*, 77–79. Antony Billington, "The Paraclete and Mission in the Fourth Gospel," in *Mission and Meaning: Essays Presented to Peter Cotterell*, ed. Antony Billington, Tony Lane, and Max Turner (Carlisle, UK: Paternoster, 1995), 90–115, rightly stresses the Paraclete's role in mission. For a discussion of the παράκλητος as part of the Gospel's lawsuit motif, esp. in 15:26–16:15, see Andrew T. Lincoln, *Truth on Trial: The Lawsuit Motif in the Fourth Gospel* (Grand Rapids: Baker, 2000), 110–23, esp. 113–14.

[48] Though see Aquila's and Theodotion's use of a related noun form in Job 16:2.

with God the Father.[49] Jesus's reference to the Spirit as "another *paraklētos*" in 14:16 indicates that the Spirit's presence with the disciples will replace Jesus's encouraging and strengthening presence with them while on earth (cf. 14:17). When the Spirit comes to indwell believers, it will be as if Jesus himself is taking up residence in them.[50] Thus Jesus can refer to the Spirit's coming by saying, "*I* am coming to you" (14:18).[51]

This relieves a primary concern for Jesus's first followers in the original setting of the Farewell Discourse: Jesus's departure will not leave them as orphans (cf. 14:18); just as God has been present with them through Jesus, he will continue to be with them through his Spirit.[52] The Spirit thus ensures continuity between Jesus's pre- and post-glorification ministry. What is more, the Spirit's coming will constitute an advance in God's work with and through the disciples (16:7; cf. 14:12). The changing relationship between believers and the Spirit pre-Pentecost and post-Pentecost is nothing less than programmatic, highlighting a fundamentally changed relationship of the Spirit with the people of God.

The initial reference to the Spirit as *paraklētos* in 14:17 is the first of five Paraclete sayings in the Farewell Discourse (14:26; 15:26; 16:7–11, 12–15),

---

[49] For a survey of all known examples from the fourth century BC to the third century AD, see Kenneth Grayston, "The Meaning of Παράκλητος," *JSNT* 13 (1981): 67–82, who concludes that παράκλητος was a more general term often used in legal contexts, meaning "supporter" or "sponsor." The closest contemporaneous usage is found in Philo conveying the notion of rendering general help, whether by giving advice or support. In later rabbinic usage, the term regularly denotes an advocate (συνήγορος). For a study of the Paraclete in the patristic period, see Anthony Casurella, *The Johannine Paraclete in the Church Fathers: A Study in the History of Exegesis* (Tübingen, DEU: Mohr Siebeck, 1983).

[50] Leon Morris, *Jesus Is the Christ: Studies in the Theology of John* (Grand Rapids: Eerdmans, 1989), 159: "The Spirit is the divine presence when Jesus's physical presence is taken away from his followers."

[51] Alternatively, the statement may refer to Jesus's post-resurrection appearances to his followers (so, e.g., Ridderbos, *Gospel of John*, 505).

[52] As Raymond E. Brown, *Gospel According to John XIII–XXI*, AB 29B (Garden City: Doubleday, 1970), 642, notes, the promise of the divine presence with Jesus's followers in 14:15–24 includes the Spirit (14:15–17), Jesus (14:18–21), and the Father (14:22–24), involving all three persons of the Godhead.

in each case referring to the Holy Spirit.[53] As Jesus's emissary, the Spirit will have a variety of functions in the lives of Jesus's followers:

(1) He will bring to remembrance all that Jesus taught them (14:26).

(2) He, together with Jesus's followers, will testify regarding Jesus (15:26).

(3) He will, presumably through Jesus's followers, convict the world of sin, (lack of) righteousness, and judgment (16:8–11).

(4) He will guide Jesus's followers in all truth and disclose what is to come (16:13).

Clearly, these statements pertain initially to Jesus's historical followers. In their case, the Spirit, as "another *paraklētos*," will pick up seamlessly where Jesus left off during his early ministry with them: he will remind them of Jesus's teaching and help them understand it; he will empower their post-Pentecost witness and the early Christian mission; he will vindicate Jesus historically by showing that the decision, arrived at by an unholy alliance between the Roman governor and the Jewish authorities, to crucify Jesus was unjust and that Jesus was innocent. He will disclose to Jesus's followers what is to come, engendering the formation of the NT canon as apostolic testimony to Jesus.[54]

Beyond this, while the Spirit's activity as set forth in the Farewell Discourse is initially focused on the Eleven, in a secondary, derivative sense he fulfills similar roles in believers today as he illumines the spiritual meaning of Jesus's words and works both *for* believers and *through* believers to the unbelieving world. He also guides believers in truth and aids and empowers

---

[53] See Stephen S. Smalley, "'The Paraclete': Pneumatology in the Johannine Gospel and Apocalypse," in *Exploring the Gospel of John: In Honor of D. Moody Smith*, ed. R. Alan Culpepper and C. Clifton Black (Louisville: Westminster John Knox, 1996), 289–300. In 14:26, the Spirit is also referred to appositionally as the "Holy Spirit." It appears that παράκλητος and "Spirit of truth" are the more common designations for the Spirit in the Farewell Discourse. On the "Holy Spirit," see further the discussion of the commissioning scene in this chapter below.

[54] Cf. Peter Stuhlmacher, "Spiritual Remembering: John 14.26," in Stanton, Longenecker, and Barton, *Holy Spirit and Christian Origins*, 63, who draws a connection between the Spirit's role in bringing Jesus's teachings to remembrance and the repeated statements in John that Jesus's followers did not understand the meaning of a certain saying or event at the time but did so only after the resurrection (cf. 2:22; 12:14–16; 20:9).

their witness. In all these functions, the ministry of the Spirit remains closely linked to Jesus. Just as Jesus is the Sent One who is fully dependent on and obedient to the Father, so is the Spirit said to be "sent" by both the Father and Jesus (14:26; 15:26) and to illumine the spiritual significance of God's work in Jesus (14:26; 15:26; 16:9).

The Spirit is also called "Spirit of truth" (14:17; cf. 15:26; 16:13).[55] Jesus has just characterized himself as "the truth" (14:6) in keeping with statements already made in the prologue (1:14, 17). The concept of truth in John's Gospel encompasses several aspects,[56] and the Spirit is involved in each. He accurately represents the truth regarding Jesus (as one of the witnesses featured in John's Gospel, the Spirit testifies to Jesus; 15:26); he is the eschatological gift of God (whose coming/sending is placed in the future from the historical vantage point of Jesus's original followers; 7:37–39; 20:22); he imparts true knowledge of God (indwelling the disciples, he will help them understand Jesus's union with the Father; 14:16–20); he is operative in both worship and sanctification (true worship must take place in the realm of the spirit, which may hint at the Spirit's involvement; 4:23–24; 6:63; cf. 17:17); and he points people to the person of Jesus (he will make known what he receives from Jesus and guide his followers in[to] all truth; 16:12–15).

This Spirit of truth, then, is the "other helping presence" who takes the place of Jesus following his exaltation. While the world cannot accept him because it neither sees nor knows him, Jesus's followers do accept him because "he resides with you and will be in you" (14:17 NET; cf. 1 John 3:24; 4:13).[57] The Spirit, in turn, is part of a cosmic drama in which Jesus and

---

[55] The expression "spirit of truth" was current in Judaism (e.g., T. Jud. 20:1–5). The Qumran literature affirms that God placed within man "two spirits so that he would walk with them until the moment of his visitation; they are the spirits of truth and of deceit" (1QS 3:18; cf. 4:23–26). Yet these parallels are primarily those of language, not thought; see Elizabeth W. Mburu, *Qumran and the Origins of Johannine Language and Symbolism*, Jewish and Christian Texts (London/New York: T&T Clark, 2010).

[56] For detail on this point, see Scott R. Swain, "Truth in the Gospel of John" (ThM thesis; Wake Forest, NC: Southeastern Baptist Theological Seminary, 1998).

[57] D. Moody Smith, *John*, ANTC (Nashville: Abingdon, 1999), 274–75, notes that "you" here is plural, which leads him to infer that the statement does not

his followers are opposed by the devil.[58] Contra the theology of Qumran, however, the struggle is not between two equally matched dualities of good and evil.[59]

Commissioning Scene. The final reference to the Spirit is found in the context of Jesus's commissioning statement, "As the Father has sent me, I am sending you" (20:21 NIV),[60] which climaxes the characterization of Jesus as the sent Son.[61] The disciples are drawn into the unity and mission of Father and Son.[62] Succession is important both in the OT and in Second Temple literature, as well as in the early church.[63] In the present Gospel, Jesus succeeds the Baptist and is followed by the Spirit and the Twelve (sans Judas), who serve as representatives of the new messianic community.

---

necessarily refer to personal indwelling. Yet the statement certainly does not rule out the indwelling of individual believers (cf., e.g., the singular pronoun κἀκεῖνος in 14:12).

[58] Variously called "the devil" (13:2), "Satan" (13:27), the "prince of this world" (12:31 NIV), or the "evil one" (17:15). This pattern continues in 1 John; see esp. 3:7–15, and here esp. vv. 8–10. See Köstenberger, *John*, chap. 11; Köstenberger, "The Cosmic Trial Motif in John's Letters," in *Communities in Dispute: Current Scholarship on the Johannine Epistles*, Early Christianity and Its Literature 13, ed. R. Alan Culpepper and Paul N. Anderson (Atlanta: SBL, 2014), 157–78.

[59] Cf. Richard Bauckham, "The Qumran Community and the Gospel of John," in Lawrence H. Schiffman, Emanuel Tov, and James C. Vanderkam, eds., *The Dead Sea Scrolls Fifty Years After Their Discovery: Proceedings of the Jerusalem Congress, July 20–25, 1997* (Jerusalem: Israel Exploration Society, 2000), 105–15.

[60] The statement harks back to 17:18, albeit without reference to the sphere of the disciples' commission (i.e., the world), indicating the emphasis in the present passage is on the disciples' authorization rather on the realm of their activity (Ridderbos, *Gospel of John*, 643). Compare the general statement in 13:20, which suggests that the present passage extends beyond the original disciples to later generations of believers. Cf. Leon Morris, *The Gospel according to John*, rev. ed., NIGTC (Grand Rapids: Eerdmans, 1995), 746n55.

[61] Andreas J. Köstenberger, *The Missions of Jesus and the Disciples according to the Fourth Gospel* (Grand Rapids: Eerdmans, 1998), esp. 96–121, 180–98.

[62] Cf. 17:21–26; Ridderbos, *Gospel of John*, 642.

[63] OT narratives involving succession feature Joshua (following Moses) and Elisha (succeeding Elijah). Second Temple literature includes several exemplars of the testamentary genre, such as *The Testaments of the Twelve Patriarchs*. In Acts and Paul, see the Pauline circle, including Timothy, Titus, Luke, Barnabas, Mark, Silas, Priscilla and Aquila, and others.

The reference to Jesus's breathing on his disciples while saying, "Receive [the] Holy Spirit"[64] probably represents a symbolic promise of the soon-to-be-given gift of the Spirit, not its actual impartation, which occurs soon thereafter at Pentecost.[65] The present pericope most likely does not constitute a "Johannine Pentecost" but rather represents an anticipatory sign pointing forward to this event.[66] Canonically speaking, therefore, John 20:22 prepares the reader for the account of the pouring out of the Spirit in Acts 2.[67]

Otherwise, John and Acts would be found to stand in conflict. Moreover, John would be conflicted within himself, contradicting his earlier assertions that the Spirit would be given only following Jesus's glorification, which entails his return to the Father.[68] The disciples' behavior following the present incident would also be rather puzzling had they already received the

---

[64] The absence of the article in the expression "Holy Spirit" may indicate a focus on "the quality of the gift of the Holy Spirit rather than on the individuality of the Spirit" (Morris, *Gospel according to John*, 747n59).

[65] See Acts 2; Carson, *Gospel according to John*, 649–55; cf. Ben Witherington III, *John's Wisdom* (Louisville: Westminster John Knox, 1995), 340–41. Contra Turner, *Holy Spirit*, 98, who holds that Jesus imparts the Holy Spirit to the disciples here (see 89–100 for the full argument, including a survey of the major interpretive options). Turner holds to a "qualified" two-stage reception of the Spirit by the apostles, an exception not repeated for believers after Pentecost (98–100). Thomas R. Hatina, "John 20, 22 in Its Eschatological Context: Promise or Fulfillment?," *Bib* 74 (1993): 196–219, implausibly contends the reference is to the indwelling Paraclete.

[66] Cf. Brown, *Gospel According to John XIII–XXI*, 1038; C. K. Barrett, *Gospel According to St. John*, 2nd ed. (Philadelphia: Westminster, 1978), 570, who claims the present passage cannot be harmonized with Acts 2; and Rudolf Bultmann, *The Gospel of John: A Commentary*, trans. George R. Beasley-Murray et al. (Philadelphia: Westminster, 1971), 691. For an argument that "the giving of the Spirit is a process that runs parallel to, and in step with, the process of Jesus's glorification" in John, starting with the cross (John 19:30), fulfilled for the disciples after the resurrection (John 20:22), and for the church at Pentecost (Acts 2), see Cornelis Bennema, "The Giving of the Spirit in John 19–20: Another Round," in Marshall, Rabens, and Bennema, *Spirit and Christ in the New Testament*, 86–104 (quote from 102). However, the Johannine evidence in the remainder of the Gospel seems to speak against an actual bestowal of the Spirit on the disciples in 20:22. It is more likely that they, together with other believers, receive the Spirit at Pentecost and that 20:22 is to be taken symbolically.

[67] See further the discussion of Acts 2 in chap. 7.

[68] E.g., 7:39; 14:12, 16–18, 25–26; 16:12–15; cf. 20:17.

Spirit.[69] Rather, the present gesture, as well as the pronouncement regarding
the authority to forgive or retain sins, is made to the group in its entirety
rather than to separate individuals.[70]

The theological antecedent of the event is plainly Gen 2:7, where the
same verb form is used.[71] There, God imparts physical and spiritual life to
humanity. Here, we are likely to see an escalation of the initial bestowal of
the "breath of life" in man's creation: when commissioning his disciples, Jesus
constitutes them as the new messianic community, in anticipation of the
outpouring of the life-giving Spirit following his ascension.[72] Thus the narrative has come full circle, having progressed from original creation in 1:1–5
to new creation in 20:22.

Figure 11: References to the Spirit in John's Gospel

Scripture Passage	Content
John 1:32–33	The Spirit descends on Jesus; Jesus will baptize with the Spirit
John 3:5–8	Birth of water and spirit/the Spirit necessary to enter God's kingdom
John 3:34	God gives the Spirit to Jesus without measure
John 4:23–24	True worshipers worship God in spirit (realm of the Spirit) and truth
John 6:63	The Spirit gives life
John 7:39	The Spirit will be given subsequent to Jesus's glorification

---

[69] In 20:26, the doors are locked (cf. v. 19), presumably still "for fear of the Jewish
leaders" (v. 19); in 21:3, Peter decides to go fishing and is joined by six others, but
they catch nothing.

[70] Morris, *Gospel according to John*, 747, 749.

[71] The Greek verb ἐνεφύσησεν means "breathed *on*" rather than "breathed *into*."
See also 1 Kgs 17:21; Ezek 37:9; Wis 15:11; cf. Philo, *Op.* 135.

[72] The "new creation" theme is noted by several scholars, including Morris,
Gospel according to John, 747n58 (who also cites Ezek 37:9).

John 14:16	The "other helping Presence" (*paraklētos*) will be with Jesus's followers forever and will teach them all things and remind them of Jesus's words; whom Jesus will send from the Father will bear witness
John 14:17	The "Spirit of truth" will dwell with Jesus's followers and will be in them
John 14:26	The "helping Presence," the "Holy Spirit" whom the Father will send in Jesus's name, will teach Jesus's followers all things and remind them of Jesus's words
John 15:26	The "Spirit of truth" proceeds from the Father and will bear witness to Jesus.
John 16:7	Once Jesus goes to the Father, he will send the "helping Presence" to his followers
John 16:13	The "Spirit of truth" will guide Jesus's followers in(to) all truth and declare what is to come
John 20:22	Jesus provides an anticipatory sign pointing forward to the pouring out of the Spirit in Acts 2

Summary

In the few references to the Spirit in the first half of John's Gospel, Jesus is associated with the Spirit in his present ministry and as the future dispenser of the Spirit subsequent to his exaltation to the Father. References to the Spirit increase dramatically in the second half of the Gospel, which is taken up with the anticipation of the disciples' mission subsequent to Jesus's crucifixion, resurrection, and ascension (his "glorification").

It is this Spirit, the "Spirit of truth," the "Holy Spirit" or "helping presence" sent by Jesus from the Father, who will continue Jesus's ministry and empower the disciples' mission in the unbelieving world. As in the case of the Father-Son relationship, the references to the Spirit in John's Gospel culminate in the commissioning passage in 20:21–22, an anticipatory reference to the disciples' reception of the Spirit for the purpose of their mission of extending forgiveness of sins upon people's belief in Jesus.

7

The Holy Spirit in Acts

The book of Acts presents itself as the "second book" of a two-volume work, ostensibly written to Theophilus, most likely a Roman official. The book provides an account of what Jesus continued to do and teach in and through the person and mission of the Holy Spirit (Acts 1:1). In the first volume, his Gospel, Luke chronicled the Holy Spirit's agency in the virgin birth (Luke 1:35); indicated that Jesus would baptize with the Holy Spirit and with fire (3:16); narrated the Spirit's descent and resting upon Jesus at his baptism (3:22; cf. 4:1,14); presented Jesus as the Spirit-anointed Servant of the Lord who would proclaim good news to the poor (4:18; cf. Isa 61:1); described the Spirit as the Father's good gift to believers par excellence (Luke 11:13); conveyed Jesus's promise that the Spirit would give his followers the words to say in times of persecution (12:11–12); and at the very end of his Gospel reported Jesus's prediction that the "promise of my Father"—i.e., the Spirit—would soon empower his followers "from on high" (24:49).

Luke's Gospel thus provides the perfect prequel to what is an incredibly exciting and unique account of the first days of the early church and the missionary exploits of its major leaders, Peter and Paul, as well as the bold witness of ordinary believers, men and women, old and young alike,[1] for "in

---

[1] As Max Turner notes in "The Work of the Holy Spirit in Luke-Acts," *Word and World* 23, no. 2 (2003): 146, "The Spirit is a major uniting theme within [Luke's] double-volumed work, indeed nothing less than the driving force of the 'salvation history' and mission that Luke describes."

Acts we move into the age of the Spirit."[2] Commentators variously describe the depiction of the Holy Spirit in the book of Acts. Levison contends that "inspired interpreters employ Israel's literature to defend the authenticity of the death, resurrection, exaltation, and spirit-giving reality of Jesus the Lord and Messiah"; Wenk, following Kuecker, argues that in the book of Acts "the underlying motif for Luke's pneumatology is his eschatological vision of the renewed people of God, including those who were traditionally marginalized or had no power in society and comprising both Jews and Gentiles."[3] In what follows we will embark on a biblical-theological survey of the most salient material on the Holy Spirit in the book of Acts, following Luke's narrative.[4]

In both volumes of his work, Luke uses a major discourse toward the beginning of his book containing a significant OT citation to introduce the main characteristics of the key figure of his account, Jesus and the Holy Spirit, respectively (or, alternately, the earthly and the exalted Jesus). In Luke's Gospel, as discussed in chapter 6, Jesus is presented as the Spirit-anointed Servant of the Lord who proclaims good news to the poor (Luke 4:18–19; cf. Isa 61:1–2); in the book of Acts, Peter in his Pentecost sermon characterizes the Holy Spirit as the agent of the exalted Jesus who will empower the witness of the early Christians and bring about a new messianic eschatological community made up of men and women, young and old, Jews and Gentiles, slaves and free (Acts 2; cf. Joel 3:1–5).[5]

---

[2] Donald Guthrie, *New Testament Theology* (Leicester, UK: InterVarsity, 1981), 535.

[3] Levison, *Filled with the Spirit*, 364; Wenk, "Acts," in Burke and Warrington, *Biblical Theology of the Holy Spirit*, 116, citing Aaron J. Kuecker, *The Spirit and the "Other": Social Identity, Ethnicity and Intergroup Reconciliation in Luke-Acts* (London: T&T Clark, 2011), 18; see also Matthias Wenk, *Community-Forming Power: The Socio-Ethical Role of the Spirit in Luke-Acts* (London: T&T Clark, 2004).

[4] On a hermeneutical note, it will be important to remember that Acts is written primarily from a salvation-historical perspective, marking significant turning points and advances in redemptive history. Thus, care must be taken not to read individual pericopes as providing paradigms for individual conversion or reception of the Spirit in the church age. See the appropriate caution in Wenk, "Acts," 122–23.

[5] See Wenk, "Acts," 117–18.

The Risen and Exalted Jesus and the Spirit's Arrival at Pentecost

The Holy Spirit takes center stage almost immediately in the book of Acts.[6] In 1:2, Luke refers to Jesus's ascension "after he had given instructions through the Holy Spirit to the apostles whom he had chosen." Then, in v. 4, he links back to the reference to the "Father's promise" in Luke 24:49 by speaking of Jesus's command to his followers "not to leave Jerusalem, but to wait for the Father's promise." Luke goes on to report Jesus's statement that while John baptized with water, his followers would soon be baptized with the Holy Spirit (v. 5; cited by Peter in Acts 11:16; cf. Luke 3:16).

The disciples take this as their cue to inquire about the restoration of the politically, nationally, and ethnically constrained kingdom to Israel (v. 6).[7] Jesus responds, however, by speaking cryptically of unknown "times or periods that the Father has set by his own authority," indicating at the very least a delay in such restoration. He goes on to state that his followers "will receive power when the Holy Spirit has come on" them so that they will be able to be his "witnesses in Jerusalem, in all Judea and Samaria, and to the end of the earth" (v. 8).[8] In this way, Jesus indicates that his followers will be sent on a Spirit-empowered mission, bearing witness to the risen and exalted Messiah, that will transcend the boundaries of Israel and extend to

---

[6] See the study of James M. Hamilton Jr., "Rushing Wind and Organ Music: Toward Luke's Theology of the Spirit in Acts," *RTR* 65 (2006): 15–33, who sees three distinct manifestations of the Spirit in Acts: "the Spirit as the eschatological gift; the Christian life as characterised by the Spirit; and particular fillings with the Spirit for inspired proclamation" (33).

[7] As Keener, *Spirit in the Gospels and Acts*, 191, notes, the question is understandable: "Because the biblical prophets had associated the coming of the Spirit with the restoration of Israel (e.g., Isa 44:3–4; 59:20–21; Ezek 36:27–28; 37:14; 39:28–29; Joel 2:28–3:1) and subsequent Jewish interpreters had associated this event with the time of the kingdom, the disciples' question . . . represents a natural one."

[8] See Max Turner, *Power from on High: The Spirit in Israel's Restoration and Witness in Luke-Acts* (Sheffield, UK: Sheffield Academic Press, 1996), 300–2, who argues that Acts 1:8 alludes to three passages in Isaiah (32:15; 43:10–12; 49:6–7), with their prophecies of the restoration of Israel.

the farthest corner of the earth—truly a breathtaking vision of missionary expansion and spiritual conquest.[9]

The remainder of the book of Acts then records Jesus's vision becoming a reality within one generation through the Spirit's activity in and through his followers. The day of Pentecost finds Jesus's followers expectantly gathered in one place when "a sound like that of a violent rushing wind" fills the house and "tongues like flames of fire" appear and rest on them.[10] They are filled with the Holy Spirit and miraculously speak in foreign languages, a reversal of the Tower of Babel incident, in which God confuses people's languages so that they can no longer communicate and the people are scattered across the face of the earth (Acts 2:1–13; cf. Gen 11:9).[11]

---

[9] Cf. Keener, *Spirit in the Gospels and Acts*, 191–92.

[10] Pentecost is in Jewish tradition associated with the giving of God's law to Moses at Sinai. It is possible, therefore, that Luke here draws a parallel: just "as Moses went up Sinai to receive the law and then brought it to the people, so Jesus ascended to the Father from whom he received the Spirit, which he in turn gave to his people" (Wenk, "Acts," 119). See also Turner, *Power from on High*, 285–89; Wenk, *Community-Forming Power*, 246–57; Dunn, *Jesus and the Spirit*, 140. While Robert P. Menzies, *The Development of Early Christian Pneumatology with Special Reference to Luke-Acts* (Sheffield, UK: JSOT, 1990), 235–41, denies the connection between Pentecost and the Sinai theophany, Turner rightly shows that Menzies misses several key points of connection between the two accounts (The Holy Spirit and Spiritual Gifts in the New Testament Church and Today, rev. ed. [Grand Rapids: Baker, 2012], 53 n. 52).

[11] See Michaela Greb, *Die Sprachenverwirrung und das Problem des Mythos: Vom Turmbau zu Babel zum Pfingstwunder* (Frankfurt: Peter Lang, 2007), who argues that more than reversal is in view: while Genesis 11 is about people's great works in an attempt to attain to the divine, Acts 2 is about the proclamation of God's great works opening up heaven and pouring out his Spirit on his people. See also Kuecker, *Spirit and the "Other,"* 117–18, who points out that the Spirit in Acts 2 "not only creates common identity, but . . . also powerfully affirms the validity of ethno-linguistic particularity." Keener, *Spirit in the Gospels and Acts*, 194, further develops the connection with the Tower of Babel. Not only do the nations listed relate to the Table of Nations listed in Genesis 10, but the preaching of the gospel to these individuals represents a foreshadowing of the gospel being taken to all the nations (cf. Matt 24:14; Acts 1:6–8). Thiselton, *Holy Spirit*, 54–55, favors the possibility of *glossolalia* and the Pentecost event as a "miracle of hearing." However, Carson's argument is more compelling: "In Luke's description of the utterances on the day of Pentecost we are dealing with *xenoglossia*—real, human languages never learned by the speakers. . . . It goes beyond the text to argue that this was a miracle of hearing rather than

Figure 12: Biblical–Theological Interconnections between Acts 2 and the OT

Tower of Babel	Moses receives Law at Sinai	Joel's Prophecy	Pentecost
(Genesis 11)	(Exodus 20)	(Joel 2)	(Acts 2)

This passage, along with Acts 8:9–17; 9:17; 10:34–48; and 19:1–7, raises important questions concerning the relationship between salvation, baptism in the Spirit, and speaking in tongues. A full discussion of this issue is better reserved for the theological section of this book. However, at least two comments can be made briefly. First, any suggestion that salvation is always accompanied by the gift of speaking in tongues encounters three significant challenges: (1) this is never explicitly taught in the NT; (2) this is not sustainable based on the description of salvation experiences in the book of Acts, where speaking in tongues is recorded in only three instances (Acts 2:1–13; 10:34–48; 19:1–7); and (3) this is explicitly contradicted by passages such as 1 Cor 12:29–30.[12] Second, the idea that there is a second baptism of the Spirit available to all Christians, whether or not accompanied by speaking in tongues, is likewise nowhere explicitly taught in the NT.[13] What is more, the descriptive evidence in the book of Acts of such a secondary experience is questionable. The most important verses used to support this position

---

speech"; D. A. Carson, *Showing the Spirit: A Theological Exposition of 1 Corinthians 12–14* (Grand Rapids: Baker, 1987), 138.

[12] The questions in 1 Cor 12:29–30 are all preceded by the particle μή, indicating that the expected response is negative. Thus the answer to Paul's question "Do all speak in other tongues?" (which he has earlier indicated is a gift distributed by the Holy Spirit, 1 Cor 12:7–11) is meant to be no. See Andreas J. Köstenberger, Benjamin L. Merkle, and Robert L. Plummer, *Going Deeper with New Testament Greek: An Intermediate Study of the Grammar and Syntax of the New Testament,* 2nd edition (Nashville: B&H Academic, 2020), 203.

[13] This viewpoint can be found in, for example, Guy P. Duffield and Nathaniel M. Van Cleave, *Foundations of Pentecostal Theology* (Los Angeles: L.I.F.E. Bible College, 1983), 304–25. James D. G. Dunn, *Baptism in the Holy Spirit* (Philadelphia: Westminster, 1970), 4, argues that it is essential to emphasize the experiential aspect of receiving the Holy Spirit but also that this gift is intimately connected and inseparable from the act/process of becoming a Christian.

are Acts 8:9–17; 9:17; and 19:1–7, on which we see in chapter 21, under "Pentecostal and Charismatic Understanding of Baptism with the Spirit."

Peter promptly invokes Joel's prophecy that "in the last days" God would pour out his Spirit on all people, both men and women, young and old—even male and female servants—with the remarkable result that "everyone who calls on the name of the Lord will be saved" (Acts 2:14–21; cf. Joel 2:28–32).[14] At this, Peter proclaims, "This Jesus of Nazareth was a man attested to you by God with miracles, wonders, and signs that God did among you through him, just as you yourselves know. Though he was delivered up according to God's determined plan and foreknowledge, you used lawless people to nail him to a cross and kill him." God raised him up in keeping with scriptural prophecy (Acts 2:22–28; cf. Ps 15:8–11). "God," Peter testifies, "has raised this Jesus; we are all witnesses of this" (Acts 2:32). According to Peter's logic, the pouring out of the Spirit at Pentecost proves that Jesus is exalted with God the Father, for it is only after such time that the Spirit will be poured out: "Therefore, since he has been exalted to the right hand of God and has received from the Father the promised Holy Spirit, he has poured out what you both see and hear" (Acts 2:33). In keeping with this premise, the primary purpose of the Spirit's coming is to testify to the risen and exalted Jesus.[15]

Peter's Pentecost message culminates in a gospel invitation: "Repent and be baptized, each of you, in the name of Jesus Christ for the forgiveness of your sins, and you will receive the gift of the Holy Spirit. For the promise is for you and for your children, and for all who are far off, as many as the Lord our God will call" (Acts 2:38–39). With regard to the Spirit's characterization in Acts 2 we observe, then, that (1) the Spirit testifies to the risen Jesus, Israel's Messiah and Lord and Savior of all; (2) the Spirit transcends all boundaries of gender, age, race, or socioeconomic background; (3) the

---

[14] For an excellent discussion of the reference to Joel 2:28–32 in Acts 2, see Wenk, "Acts," 118–20. Wenk points out that the call on Israel to repent and turn to God is more prominent in Joel 3 than in other OT passages on the eschatological outpouring of the Spirit (e.g., Isa 32:1–20; 44:1–5; 61:1–2; Ezekiel 36–37).

[15] Keener, *Spirit in the Gospels and Acts*, 198, 217–18, following Kenneth E. Bailey, *Poet and Peasant* (Grand Rapids: Eerdmans, 1976), 65–67, suggests that Peter's sermon is structured as a chiasm. In the structure, the theme of prophecy is linked with the theme of witness, yet another indication of the connection between the gift of the Spirit and the taking of the gospel to the nations.

Spirit is given freely to all on the basis of repentance from sin and trust in the crucified sin bearer, the Lord Jesus Christ; (4) the Spirit is a Spirit of mission, persistently seeking to bring about repentance and faith, drawing more and more people to God, as his people, represented by leaders such as Peter and the other apostles, testify boldly to God's work in and through the Lord Jesus Christ.[16]

While Pentecost is just the beginning, the event includes in seed form what will work itself out in the years to come and in the chapters to come in Acts. The book covers more than two decades and chronicles the expansion of Christianity from a small band of apostles and a group of women to a world-wide community of followers of "the Way" (e.g., Acts 9:2; 22:4)—believers in the risen and exalted Jesus. On this first day, 3,000 people are added to the church (Acts 2:41), and many more follow—not only in Jerusalem and Judea but also in Samaria and increasingly in Gentile territories as well, until by the end of the book the gospel message has reached the ends of the earth—the capital of the world's greatest empire at the time, the city of Rome.

From Jerusalem to Antioch: Boldness, Martyrdom, Witness, and the Missionary Spirit

As the early Christians embark on their mission, they overcome all internal and external obstacles. Peter, "filled with the Holy Spirit," boldly defends his healing of a lame man before the same Sanhedrin that crucified Jesus only weeks earlier (Acts 4:8). The Holy Spirit is also said to have prophesied

---

[16] Keener, *Spirit in the Gospels and Acts*, 194–95, aptly sums up the relationship of the Spirit and mission at Pentecost:

> Luke develops contemporary Jewish expectations. In the end time, representatives from all peoples would gather before the Lord (Isa 60:3–16; Zech 14:16–19; cf. Rev 7:9); in Acts 2, the Spirit had come in advance of that time to initiate the church into the eschatological unity of an ethnically reconciled, cross-cultural people of God in the midst of the present age. The church in Acts, initially divided between Jewish and Gentile believers, had some problems with this reality; but those truly obedient to the Spirit were ultimately forced to cross ethnic boundaries (8:29; 10:19–20; 11:12–18). Thus Luke intimately connects the Spirit with his theme of the Gentile mission. . . . Thus, Luke implies, those who are truly led by God's Spirit will labor on behalf of the Gentile mission.

through David regarding the unholy alliance between the rulers of the earth against the Lord's Messiah (Acts 4:25–26; cf. Psalm 2).[17] When the supreme Jewish council forbids Jesus's followers to spread the good news about Jesus and his resurrection, the believers offer up fervent prayers. "When they had prayed, the place where they were assembled was shaken, and they were all filled with the Holy Spirit and began to speak the word of God boldly" (Acts 4:31). What in the OT are occasional references to the Holy Spirit—and in the Gospels become more frequent references to the Holy Spirit's work in and through Jesus in the present and his followers in the future—have now in the book of Acts burst into full daylight and turned into a mighty crescendo of references to the Holy Spirit and his powerful work among the Jewish people and among the nations.

The personality of the Holy Spirit is accentuated when a man named Ananias and his wife, Sapphira, are struck dead for lying to the Holy Spirit, instilling "great fear" in the hearts of the entire church and all people (Acts 5:1–11).[18] To lie to the Spirit is to lie to God—in saying this, Peter attests to the Spirit's deity—and to be subject to the severest punishment (vv. 3, 9). Again, when Peter and the apostles are told not to testify to Jesus, they boldly retort, "We must obey God rather than people. The God of our ancestors raised up Jesus, whom you had murdered by hanging him on a tree. God exalted this man to his right hand as ruler and Savior, to give repentance to Israel and forgiveness of sins. We are witnesses of these things, and so is the Holy Spirit whom God has given to those who obey him" (Acts 5:29–32).

Soon thereafter, seven men "full of the Spirit" are chosen as precursors of the office of deacon (Acts 6:3), and one of them, Stephen, "a man full of faith and the Holy Spirit" (Acts 6:5; cf. v. 10; 7:55), becomes the first Christian martyr, yet not before excoriating those who stone him as "stiff-necked people, with uncircumcised hearts and ears," who "are always resisting the Holy

---

[17] Note the similar reference earlier in 1:16, where Peter says the Spirit "through the mouth of David foretold" about Judas, then cites Pss 69:25 and 109:8.

[18] Wenk, "Acts," 123–26, provides a helpful discussion of the "proleptic realization of the eschatological restoration through the Spirit" in "renewed community life" and "reconciliation and the Spirit." Wenk shows that this is a common thread connecting Acts 5 (Ananias and Sapphira) with Acts 8–11 (Samaritans, Paul's conversion, Cornelius) and 20:22–21:16 (Paul's arrest in Jerusalem).

Spirit," as did their fathers (Acts 7:51). In this way, Stephen links the ministry of the Spirit to the ministry of the OT prophets: "Which of the prophets did your ancestors not persecute? They even killed those who foretold the coming of the Righteous One, whose betrayers and murderers you have now become" (Acts 7:52). Not only Peter but now Stephen is characterized by amazing boldness, calling to account those who crucified Jesus and are about to martyr him.

Figure 13: Characterization of Stephen and Barnabas as Paradigmatic Believers in Acts

Stephen	*Barnabas*
"Full of faith and the Holy Spirit" (6:5; cf. v. 3)	Joseph, Levite, native of Cyprus (4:36)
"Full of grace and power" (6:8)	Called "Son of Encouragement" by apostles (4:36)
Does "great wonders and signs" (6:8)	Sells field and gives proceeds to apostles (4:37)
Scolds Israelites for resisting Holy Spirit (7:51)	Takes Saul to apostles after conversion (9:27)
Looks to heaven "full of the Holy Spirit" (7:55)	Mediates between Jerusalem and Antioch (11:22, 30)
First Christian martyr, Christlike (7:58–60)	**"Full of the Holy Spirit and of faith"** (11:24)
	Sent out by church in Antioch with Paul (13:2)
	Wants to give Mark a second chance (15:36–39)
Strategic significance:	
One of first deacons, first martyr	First Christian missionary, recruited Paul for mission

Enter Saul, the zealous Pharisee, who ravages the church and drags off men and women alike and has them thrown into prison on account of their faith in Jesus the Messiah (Acts 8:1, 3). In these early days Peter, who had been given the "keys of the kingdom of heaven" by Jesus (Matt 16:19), is charged with authorizing and authenticating the coming of the Spirit on individuals and groups of people. Thus the Samaritans receive the Holy Spirit when Peter and John lay hands on them (Acts 8:15, 17).[19] As Luke's explanation in v. 16—"(They had only been baptized in the name of the Lord Jesus)"—makes clear, the Samaritan experience of the delay of the Holy Spirit is an unusual, rather than typical, experience, as only an unusual experience calls for an explanatory comment.[20] Later, when Simon the Magician offers Peter money so that he too can dispense the Holy Spirit, Peter issues a sharp rebuke (Acts 8:19). Further on in the narrative, the Spirit sends Philip (one of the Seven) on a mission to evangelize an Ethiopian eunuch and subsequently carries Philip away (Acts 8:29, 30).

At a pivotal juncture in the book of Acts and in the early Christian mission, the risen Jesus himself appears to Saul on the road to Damascus, confronting Saul for persecuting him (i.e., the church, with whom Jesus closely identifies; Acts 9:4). Miraculously, Saul, the hardened persecutor, repents at once and receives the Holy Spirit. "At once something like scales fell from his eyes, and he regained his sight. Then he got up and was baptized" (Acts

---

[19] Thiselton, *Holy Spirit*, 65: "The visit of Peter and John and their laying on of hands in practice constituted a visible and tangible act displaying the *unity* of the one Church, and the *solidarity* of the Jerusalem apostles with Samaria. . . . This act of Peter and John safeguarded the oneness, catholicity, and (many would argue) the visibly apostolic nature of the Church. . . . This was the first step of advance beyond Judaism to the world."

[20] The fact that the Samaritan believers receive the Spirit after they put their faith in Jesus is sometimes used as an argument that Christians can and should expect to receive the Spirit in a unique experience that follows salvation. However, it is better to see here, as well as in Acts 10:34–48, that God is working uniquely in situations in which the gospel is taking root among new people groups. Thus in Acts 11:15–18 the giving of the Spirit to the Gentiles is evidence that they have been accepted by God. See A. J. Thompson, *The Acts of the Risen Lord Jesus: Luke's Account of God's Unfolding Plan*, NSBT 27 (Downers Grove: InterVarsity, 2011), 139; A. C. Clark, "The Role of the Apostles," in I. H. Marshall and D. Peterson, eds., *Witness to the Gospel: The Theology of Acts* (Grand Rapids: Eerdmans, 1998), 176. Contra Dunn, *Baptism in the Holy Spirit*, 63–68, who argues that the Samaritans are in fact not Christians after their initial acceptance of the Word and baptism (8:4–8); and Menzies, *Development of Early Christian Pneumatology*, 258–60, who argues that the Samaritans receive the Spirit in order to be incorporated into the church's mission. In Menzies's view, Luke-Acts presents a consistent pneumatology in which the giving of the Spirit is tied to mission but not directly to salvation (278–89).

9:17–18).[21] Shortly thereafter we read in a Lukan summary statement that
the church in Judea, Galilee, and Samaria grew, "living in the fear of the Lord
and encouraged [*paraklēsis*] by the Holy Spirit" (Acts 9:31).[22]

Sometime after this, Peter receives a vision. The Spirit directs him to
go to Cornelius, a Roman centurion (Acts 10:19). Peter tells him "how God
anointed Jesus of Nazareth with the Holy Spirit [cf. Luke 4:18] and with
power and how he went about doing good and healing all who were under
the tyranny of the devil, because God was with him. . . . They killed him by
hanging him on a tree. God raised up this man on the third day and caused
him to be seen" by many witnesses (Acts 10:38–41). Cornelius believes, and
while Peter was still testifying to Jesus, "the Holy Spirit came down on all
those who heard the message" (Acts 10:44; cf. vv. 45, 47).[23]

Later, Peter recounts this event to the church in Jerusalem. The Spirit
directed him to go to Cornelius's house (Acts 11:12), he reports, and while
Peter was still speaking, the Spirit "came down" on those present (Acts
11:15).[24] Peter adds that at that time he remembered Jesus's words that
John the Baptist baptized with water but believers would be baptized with
the Holy Spirit (Acts 11:16). This settled the matter. In the words of Peter,
"If, then, God gave them the same gift that he also gave to us when we

---

[21] The text does not explicitly identify the relationship between when Saul
believed and when he received the Spirit. But there is no indication that Saul believed
and then only later received the Spirit. If anything, the fact that Saul is not baptized
until Ananias comes to him is evidence that it is upon the arrival of Ananias and discussion with Saul that he believes. Luke's emphasis is that Saul has turned to Christ,
has received the Spirit, and will therefore serve as a witness. The Spirit here, as elsewhere in Acts (cf. 1:8), is thus connected with salvation (9:18) and empowerment to
witness (9:15–16, 19–20). See Bock, *Theology of Luke and Acts*, 143–44; Thompson,
Acts of the Risen Lord Jesus, 133, 142–43.

[22] Notice the connection between the "encouraged" or "counsel" (παράκλησις) of
the Spirit here and John's designation of the Spirit as the "Counselor" (παράκλητος)
in John 14:26; 15:26; 16:7.

[23] For a discussion of the connection between the giving of the Spirit and speaking in tongues (Acts 10:45–47), see the discussion earlier on Acts 2:1–13.

[24] Cf. Thiselton, *Holy Spirit*, 65: "The momentous event of the inclusion of the
Gentiles, represented by Cornelius, may be seen as a milestone of 'catching up' to
what Christian Jews had experienced. It is crucial that each radical new step in the
expansion of the Church to all the world is perceived as expressly initiated by the
Holy Spirit as the Spirit of Jesus Christ."

believed in the Lord Jesus Christ, how could I possibly hinder God?" (Acts
11:17; cf. 15:8, 28). In both cases, the Samaritans' and the Gentiles' reception of the Spirit serves as an indicator of inclusion into the eschatological
people of God.[25] What the Holy Spirit does, God initiates, directs, and
ordains. This shows that God the Father and the Holy Spirit are closely
and inextricably united in their saving mission, with Jesus at the heart of
God's redemptive plan.

Later, Barnabas is described as "a good man, full of the Holy Spirit
and of faith" (Acts 11:24). He goes to Tarsus to find Saul and bring him to
Antioch. This is true to Barnabas's character as a "Son of Encouragement"
(Acts 4:36). His initiative in recruiting Saul proves hugely significant, as
the two are soon set apart for their first missionary journey by the church
in Antioch (13:2), and Saul (also known as Paul) will turn out to be the
undisputed leader of the early Christian mission to the Gentiles. A prophet
named Agabus also comes down from Jerusalem to Antioch, and there by
the Spirit predicts a worldwide famine in the days of Emperor Claudius
(AD 41–54). The same prophet, Agabus, later predicts Paul's arrest in
Jerusalem (Acts 21:11).

From Antioch to Antioch: A Light to the Gentiles

In what follows, we read that while certain prophets and teachers in the
church at Antioch are worshipping the Lord and fasting, "the Holy Spirit
[presumably through the prophets mentioned in v. 1] said, 'Set apart for me
Barnabas and Saul for the work to which I have called them'" (Acts 13:2;
cf. v. 4). Thus the organized mission of the church to the Gentiles begins
in earnest, and the Holy Spirit himself is said to be the guiding impetus
behind the mission. "So being sent out by the Holy Spirit" on their first missionary journey (Acts 13:4), Paul and Barnabas go on their way.[26] In a place

---

[25] Wenk, "Acts," 121.

[26] Robert Banks, "The Role of Charismatic and Noncharismatic Factors in
Determining Paul's Movements in Acts," in Stanton, Longenecker, and Barton, *Holy
Spirit and Christian Origins*, 119, delineates four characteristics of the Spirit's word
here: (1) it gives direction ("set apart"); (2) it is specific ("Barnabas and Paul"); (3)
it is purposeful ("for the work"); (4) and it is evaluated ("Then after they had fasted,
prayed, and laid hands on them . . . ," v. 3). Finny Philip, *The Origins of Pauline*

called Paphos, Paul, "filled with the Holy Spirit," confronts a man named Elymas, a magician (Acts 13:9). This confrontation highlights the fact that the Christian mission is an exercise in spiritual warfare, carried out in the power of the Holy Spirit and doggedly opposed by evil supernatural forces every step of the way.

In due course, Paul and Barnabas arrive at Antioch of Pisidia. On the Sabbath, Paul delivers a homily in the local synagogue, only to return the following Sabbath to preach the gospel to a standing-room-only crowd. As part of this message, incredibly, Paul arrogates what is said about Jesus at the beginning of Luke's Gospel—that he has been made a "light for revelation to the Gentiles" (Luke 2:32)—to Barnabas and himself (and by extension other leaders of the Christian mission), asserting:

For this is what the Lord has commanded us:

I have made *you*
a light for the Gentiles
to bring salvation
to the end of the earth (Acts 13:47; cf. Isa 49:6).

This highlights just how much an "apostle" (specifically) and the church (more generally) represent Christ. It also fleshes out Acts 1:1, in that Luke's Gospel narrates what "Jesus *began* to do and teach," while Acts by implication narrates what Jesus *continued* to do and teach—via his Spirit and his church. As a result, the Gentiles hear, and many believe; the Word of God spreads through the entire region; the Jewish authorities resist the apostolic message and stir up persecution against Paul and Barnabas; and "the disciples were filled with joy and the Holy Spirit" (Acts 13:52).

Pneumatology: The Eschatological Bestowal of the Spirit upon Gentiles in Judaism and in the Early Development of Paul's Theology, WUNT 2/194 (Tübingen, DEU: Mohr Siebeck, 2005), 221–23, provides a helpful description of the development of Paul's understanding of the Spirit, especially concerning Paul's mission to the Gentiles. While one may not agree with all of his proposals, Philip rightly highlights the significance of Paul's time in Antioch for his mission to the Gentiles and his subsequent writing on the Spirit.

Jerusalem Council and Further Missionary Journeys: The Spirit Directing the Church's Mission

The Jerusalem Council follows, with the church ratifying the inclusion of the Gentiles in the new eschatological messianic community (Acts 15:1–35, see esp. vv. 8, 28; cf. 11:17). After this, Paul dispenses with Mark (who had left him and Barnabas on their first missionary journey) and replaces him first with Silas and later with Timothy (Acts 15:35–16:5), setting out on another missionary journey. The Spirit's active direction of Paul's mission is underscored when Luke writes that the Holy Spirit forbade Paul to preach in Asia and the "Spirit of Jesus" similarly thwarted mission work in Bithynia (Acts 16:6–7).[27] Conversely, Paul is redirected by a vision conveying the famous "Macedonian call" (v. 9) and crosses over into Greece.[28] In Philippi, the capital of Macedonia, Lydia the businesswoman and the Philippian jailer believe, together with their households. Paul subsequently carries the gospel to Thessalonica, then even to the intellectually sophisticated city of Athens (where he testifies to representatives of various philosophical schools), and then to Corinth (Acts 17:1–18:23).[29]

Ephesus to Jerusalem to Rome: To Jerusalem in the Spirit

Most of the remaining references to the Holy Spirit in the book of Acts are clustered around Paul's inexorable journey to Jerusalem, in striking parallel to the Lukan "travel narrative" depicting Jesus's similar journey (Luke 9:51–19:27). In Ephesus, Apollos is instructed in the way of the Lord (since he is said to have known only about John's baptism, we may infer that he was told about the baptism of the Holy Spirit; Acts 18:24–28). Similarly, a group of Ephesian disciples who likewise have heard only about John's baptism are

---

[27] Banks, "Role of Charismatic and Noncharismatic Factors," 123, suggests that this may have come through a prophetic utterance.

[28] Banks (124) notes that at this momentous occasion of Paul's moving from ministry in Asia to Greece there is a proliferation of divine activity in guiding Paul and his companions.

[29] See the discussion of references to the Spirit in 1–2 Thessalonians and 1–2 Corinthians in chap. 8.

told about the Holy Spirit and receive him when Paul lays hands on them; as an indication of their Spirit-filling, they promptly speak in tongues and prophesy (Acts 19:2, 6).[30] After a strange intermezzo with the sons of Sceva, a Jewish high priest, Paul resolves "by the Spirit" to go to Jerusalem by way of Macedonia and Achaia, planning to go to Rome also (Acts 19:21). Later he tells the Ephesians elders that he is going to Jerusalem, "compelled [lit., 'bound'] by the Spirit" (Acts 20:22), and that the Holy Spirit testifies that persecution awaits him in every town (v. 23). Paul exhorts the elders to pay careful attention to their own lives and to shepherd the flock of which the Holy Spirit has made them overseers (Acts 20:28).[31]

On Paul's way to Jerusalem, believers and the prophet Agabus warn him through the Spirit not to go to Jerusalem (Acts 21:4, 11), but he brushes aside their warnings, saying he is willing to die in Jerusalem for Christ's sake

---

[30] For a helpful discussion, see Wenk, "Acts," 121–22, who notes several gaps in the narrative and rightly points out that "what is at stake here is neither a 'conversion-initiation' paradigm, nor empowerment for missions or inspired speech, but the proper perspective regarding an eschatological fulfillment" (122). Similarly, see Turner, *Power from on High*, 391; Thompson, *Acts of the Risen Lord*, 139. However, while the emphasis in the text is not conversion, the disciples (whether of Jesus or John the Baptist) described in this passage most likely are not already believers but are coming to a saving faith at this point. Paul's initial question may well indicate he thinks they are believers, but their subsequent responses and Paul's further question reveal that in fact they are not. At the very least, their discipleship and faith are lacking in some of the most basic aspects of Christian understanding. For a nuanced discussion of this issue, see Craig S. Keener, *Acts: An Exegetical Commentary*, vol. 3, *15:1–23:15* (Grand Rapids: Baker, 2014), 2815–24. See also Thompson, *Acts of the Risen Lord*, 139–41; Dunn, *Baptism in the Holy Spirit*, 83–89. For the argument that the disciples were likely already believers, albeit with defective knowledge, see Darrell L. Bock, *Acts*, BECNT (Grand Rapids: Baker), 598–600; F. F. Bruce, *The Book of Acts*, NICNT (Grand Rapids: Eerdmans, 1988), 363. See also Conrad Gempf, "Apollos and the Ephesian Disciples: Befores and Afters (Acts 18:24–19:7)," in *Spirit and Christ in the New Testament and Christian Theology: Essays in Honor of Max Turner*, ed. I. Howard Marshall, Volker Rabens, and Cornelis Bennema (Grand Rapids: Eerdmans, 2012), 119–37, who contends that the Lukan treatment of Apollos and the Ephesian disciples is best viewed as a "before and after story."

[31] Regarding the Spirit's "appointing" (τίθημι) elders, Craig Keener notes, "That the Holy Spirit appointed the elders does not contradict the apostolic practice in Acts 14:23 ["When [Paul and Barnabas] had appointed [χειροτονέω] elders for them in every church . . ."] but throws the process farther back" (*Acts*, 3:3031).

if needed.[32] It is difficult to understand how the same Spirit who constrained Paul to go to Jerusalem (Acts 20:22) leads believers and Agabus to warn him against doing so (Acts 21:4, 11).[33] Upon arriving in Jerusalem, Paul is promptly arrested in the temple (Acts 21:27–36). He subsequently appeals to Caesar and is interrogated by various Roman officials, none of whom finds him guilty of any crime. In this way, Luke writes the entire book of Acts to Theophilus as a defense of the innocence of Christianity of any charges brought against the movement or its major protagonists, such as Paul. The book of Acts closes with Paul affirming that the Holy Spirit, through the prophet Isaiah, rightly indicted Israel for her unbelief (Acts 28:25–26; citing Isa 6:9) and with the apostle "proclaiming the kingdom of God and teaching about the Lord Jesus Christ with all boldness and without hindrance" in the capital of the empire, Rome (Acts 28:31).

Figure 14: References to the Spirit in the Book of Acts

Scripture Passage	Content
Acts 1:2	Jesus gave commands to the apostles through the Holy Spirit
Acts 1:4	Jesus tells believers to wait in Jerusalem for promised Holy Spirit
Acts 1:5	John baptized with water, but believers will soon be baptized with Spirit
Acts 1:8	Jesus's followers will receive power to be witnesses to the ends of the earth when the Holy Spirit comes upon them

---

[32] Other than the concluding reference in Acts 28:25 (see fig. 14), these are the final two references to the Spirit in Acts. There are no references to the Holy Spirit between Acts 21:11 and 28:25 (cf. the lack of references to the Holy Spirit between Luke 12:12 and 24:49).

[33] See the discussion in François Bovon, "Der Heilige Geist, die Kirche, und die menschlichen Beziehungen nach der Apostelgeschichte 20,36–21,16," in Bovon, *Lukas in neuer Sicht: Gesammelte Aufsätze* (Neukirchen-Vluyn, DEU: Neukirchener, 1985), 181–204, who points out that no one in the narrative completely understands God's will, including Paul; see also the discussion and summary in Wenk, "Acts," 126.

Acts 1:16	The Scripture had to be fulfilled which the Holy Spirit spoke beforehand
Acts 2:4	Believers are filled with Holy Spirit who is poured out at Pentecost
Acts 2:17–18	Fulfillment of prophecy: in the last days, God will pour out his Spirit (Joel 2:28–29)
Acts 2:33	Coming of Holy Spirit proves Jesus has been exalted to Father's right hand
Acts 2:38	All who repent and believe receive the Holy Spirit: 3,000 believers added
Acts 4:8–10	Peter, filled with the Holy Spirit, defending healing before the Sanhedrin
Acts 4:25–26	Holy Spirit predicted opposition to Lord's Messiah through David (cf. Psalm 2)
Acts 4:31	Early Christians are filled with the Holy Spirit to speak God's word boldly
Acts 5:3–5, 9	Ananias and Sapphira lie to the Holy Spirit, are struck dead; great fear
Acts 5:32	Holy Spirit bears witness to Jesus along with early believers
Acts 6:3	Administrators of the daily distribution to widows to be "full of the Spirit"
Acts 6:5, 10; 7:55, 59	Stephen, full of faith and of the Holy Spirit, becomes first Christian martyr
Acts 7:51	People of Israel have always resisted the Holy Spirit (OT prophets)
Acts 8:15, 17	Samaritans receive the Holy Spirit when Peter and John lay hands on them
Acts 8:19–20	Spirit is not for sale, nor can his distribution be licensed (Peter to Simon)
Acts 8:29, 39	Spirit sends Philip to evangelize Ethiopian eunuch, carries him away

Acts 9:17–18	Saul receives the Holy Spirit upon his conversion in Damascus
Acts 9:31	Church in Judea, Galilee, and Samaria in help of the Holy Spirit, grew
Acts 10:19; cf. 11:12	The Holy Spirit directs Peter to go to Cornelius
Acts 10:38	God anointed Jesus of Nazareth with the Holy Spirit and with power
Acts 10:44–47; cf. 11:15	Holy Spirit falls upon Cornelius and believing members of his household
Acts 11:16; cf. 1:5	Peter recounts Holy Spirit coming on Cornelius, remembers Jesus's words
Acts 11:17	God gives Spirit to all who believe; no one can resist (cf. 15:8, 28 below)
Acts 11:24	Barnabas is described as "a good man, full of the Holy Spirit and of faith"
Acts 11:28; cf. 21:11	Prophet Agabus by Spirit foretells a worldwide famine in days of Claudius
Acts 13:2, 4	Holy Spirit tells church to set apart Barnabas and Paul for mission work
Acts 13:9	Paul, "filled with the Holy Spirit," confronts Elymas the magician
Acts 13:52	The disciples were filled with joy and with the Holy Spirit
Acts 15:8, 28	Holy Spirit given also to Gentiles; Holy Spirit imposes no other burden
Acts 16:6–7	Holy Spirit forbids work in Asia; Spirit of Jesus thwarts work in Bithynia
Acts 19:2, 6	Paul tells ignorant Ephesian disciples about Holy Spirit; they receive him
Acts 19:21	Paul resolves "by the Spirit" to go to Jerusalem by way of Macedonia and Achaia; planning also to go to Rome

Acts 20:22	Paul says he is compelled by the Spirit to go to Jerusalem
Acts 20:23	Holy Spirit testifies to Paul that persecutions await him in every town
Acts 20:28	Paul's farewell to Ephesian elders, whom Holy Spirit made overseers
Acts 21:4, 11; cf. 11:28	Believers and prophet Agabus warn Paul not to go to Jerusalem
Acts 28:25	Holy Spirit spoke to ancient Israelites through Isaiah

Summary

The book of Acts highlights several distinct yet related roles of the Spirit of God. First, the Spirit is a *person* (not merely an impersonal force or power) and is clearly *divine*. To lie to him is to lie to God and to be subject to the severest punishment (Acts 5:3–5, 9). Also, the Spirit is intimately related to the Father and Jesus in both personhood and mission. He is the "Father's promise" (Acts 1:4; cf. Luke 24:49) and "the Spirit of Jesus" (Acts 16:7). He anointed Jesus for his messianic ministry (Acts 10:38), and it is through him that Jesus commands his apostles (Acts 1:2).

Second, the Spirit is shown to establish the *new eschatological messianic community* of the exalted Jesus, in keeping with OT prophetic prediction (Acts 2; cf. Joel 2:28–32). As such, the coming of the Spirit marks a new stage in the history of salvation. He is "what my Father promised" (Luke 24:49; cf. Acts 1:4) to be given subsequent to Jesus's resurrection, ascension, and exaltation with the Father. And just as John the Baptist baptized with water, so now the exalted Jesus *baptizes* with the Holy Spirit (Acts 1:5; 11:16; cf. Luke 3:16).

Third, throughout the book we see that the Spirit is a Spirit of *mission*. In particular, he provides the power for mission (see esp. Acts 1:8) and boldness for witness (Acts 4:31). Not only does he empower believers' witness; he himself is said to witness to the risen and exalted Jesus (Acts 5:32). He sends Philip to evangelize the Ethiopian eunuch (Acts 8:29). He sends Peter to the Gentile Cornelius (Acts 10:19; cf. 11:12). He sends out the first missionaries, Barnabas and Saul, from Antioch, where believers in Christ are first called

Christians (Acts 13:2, 4). He sends Paul to Macedonia by redirecting him twice, then giving him a vision (Acts 16:6–7, 16, 18).

Fourth, the Spirit *fills* all believers (Acts 2:4; 4:31; 13:52). In the book of Acts, the apostles and leaders of the early mission in particular are characterized as being full of the Spirit. This terminology is applied to the Seven, including Stephen (Acts 6:3, 5, 10; 7:55), Saul/Paul (Acts 9:17–18; 13:9), and Barnabas (Acts 11:24). The Spirit also fills his servants in order to engage and prevail in spiritual warfare against evil spirits and those controlled by them (Acts 13:9). Beyond this, an experience of the Spirit characterizes the community of believers generally, indicated by his inclusion in several vintage Lukan summary statements: the Spirit constitutes the believers as a witnessing community (Acts 5:32); the church in Judea, Galilee, and Samaria grows in the "help" of the Holy Spirit (a unique expression in this book; translated "encouraged by" in the CSB, Acts 9:31); they are filled with joy and with the Holy Spirit (Acts 13:52).[34]

Fifth, the Spirit is also a Spirit of *prophecy*. He is both the subject and the object of prophecy, inspiring prophecy and himself being prophesied about, most notably in Joel 2 (cf. Acts 2:17–18). The prophecy of John the Baptist that the Coming One would baptize with the Spirit (Matt 3:11, Mark 1:8, Luke 3:16) is taken up by the risen Christ (Acts 1:5) and fulfilled in Acts 2 (cf. 11:15–17). In the written Scriptures, through David, the Spirit (1) spoke beforehand of Judas's defection and the need to replace him (Acts 1:16; cf. Ps 69:25; 109:8) and (2) predicted the unholy alliance against the Lord's Messiah, resulting in Jesus's crucifixion, as Peter asserts (Acts 4:25–26; cf. Psalm 2). Through Isaiah, the Spirit predicted Israel's obduracy, as Paul affirms at the end of the book (Acts 28:25; Isa 6:9). The Holy Spirit also works through prophets such as Agabus, who predicts a worldwide famine in the days of Claudius (Acts 11:28) as well as Paul's arrest in Jerusalem (Acts 21:11).

Sixth, in keeping with his prophetic nature and mission, the Spirit also serves as one who *convicts* God's people and holds them to a moral standard.

---

[34] At times Luke emphasizes the Spirit's activity in relation to the *entire* church, not just a portion of it. From a biblical-theological perspective, this follows Moses's wish long before that the Lord would put his Spirit upon all his people (Num 11:29) and Joel's prophecy that this would indeed happen in the last days (Joel 2:28–29; cf. Acts 2:16–18).

Whoever lies to the Spirit is disciplined (Acts 5:3–5, 9). The Spirit spoke to God's people through the OT prophets, and when they resisted him, they resisted God and his will (Acts 7:51). Jesus's warning against blaspheming the Holy Spirit also comes to mind in this regard; attributing the work of God in him to the work of Satan draws severe consequences (Matt 12:31–32 and parallels). In this way, there is continuity between the Spirit's ministry in OT and NT times.

Seventh, the Holy Spirit is the one who *directs* the affairs of the church. He is sovereign and subject to no one's control (Acts 8:19–20; 11:17). He appoints missionaries and tells the church to set them apart (Acts 13:2); he appoints elders and gives them charge over the church (Acts 20:28). We may tend to think of the book of Acts as recording the acts of the apostles, but it is more accurate and in keeping with the spirit of this book to think of it as recording the *acts of the Holy Spirit in and through the apostles*, at times—even often—overriding their natural instincts and inclinations, overcoming their scruples and hesitations, and moving them boldly into areas where no one had ever gone before.

In this regard, it is intriguing to notice that the early Christians and their leaders seek to perceive the Spirit's work—primarily in opening a door for salvation to new groups of people, such as Samaritans or the Gentiles—and then simply accept the Spirit's work and leading, according to this premise: if God chooses to do a certain thing through his Spirit, who are we to say it is not legitimate (Acts 11:17; cf. 15:8, 28)? That said, in Peter's case it takes significant divine intervention—a vision—to break his resistance and open his mind to God's will. Similarly, the Spirit redirects Paul repeatedly (Acts 16:6–7), and he accepts such correction and is willing to follow the Spirit's leading even when it goes counter to his original purposes. Human planning is indeed necessary and appropriate, but we must always be open to being corrected or redirected as we set out on our journey (cf. Jas 4:13–17). Thus the Spirit commands submission to his authority and lordship over the church and the church's mission. As such, he may override a person's will, such as when Paul says he was "compelled" (lit., "bound") by the Spirit to go to Jerusalem (Acts 20:22), even when warned by other believers and a Spirit-led prophet against doing so! This need to submit to the Spirit unconditionally applies to the church collectively—as in the above-mentioned case of the inclusion of the Gentiles in the church—as well as to believers, whether leaders or ordinary believers, individually.

8

The Holy Spirit in Paul

The apostle Paul has been called the "theologian of the Spirit."[1] The following exploration of Paul's theology of the Spirit will consider each of his canonical letters with significant references to the Holy Spirit, in presumed order of writing: (1) Galatians; (2) 1–2 Thessalonians; (3) 1–2 Corinthians; (4) Romans; (5) Ephesians; and (6) 1–2 Timothy and Titus.[2] In each case, we will discuss the references to the Spirit in the order in which they appear in the respective letter and will seek to arrive at a progressive and cumulative understanding of Paul's theology of the Spirit.[3]

---

[1] C. Brown, "Spirit (NT)," *NIDNTT* 3:700, though the title could be applied with equal justification to Luke and John, the "evangelists of the Spirit."

[2] I will not discuss Philippians (except for briefly noting three relevant passages), Colossians, or Philemon due to the paucity of references to the Spirit in those writings.

[3] Fee, *God's Empowering Presence*, is substantial and particularly helpful for studying Paul's teachings on the Holy Spirit. In occasional footnotes below, we will refer readers to additional insights from Fee. For a helpful list of the roles of the Spirit in Paul, see Levison, *Filled with the Spirit*, 229. Philip, *Origins of Pauline Pneumatology*, espouses the thesis that "Paul's early Christian thinking on the Holy Spirit is based on the belief that God has bestowed the Spirit upon the Gentiles apart from Torah observance. This conviction in turn is rooted primarily in his own Damascus experience and secondarily in his experience with and as a missionary of the Hellenistic community in Antioch" (27). Thiselton, in chap. 5 of *The Holy Spirit in Biblical Teaching*, takes a thematic approach in synthesizing Paul's theology of the Holy Spirit. He lists eight basic themes: (1) the work of the Holy Spirit is Christ-centered; (2) every believer receives the Holy Spirit; (3) as in the OT, the Holy Spirit

103

Galatians

Galatians, the first of Paul's letters included in the NT canon, most likely written from Corinth, boasts a remarkable number of references to the Spirit: a total of seventeen, on average about three per chapter.[4] This makes Galatians one of the densest Spirit-oriented NT writings and emphatically underscores the importance of pneumatology in this epistle.[5] It is also note-worthy that Galatians anticipates many pneumatological themes struck later in Paul's letter to the Romans. James Dunn provides the following list in Figure 15 on page 105.[6]

Remarkably, however, the term *pneuma* is not found in the first two chapters of Galatians, which feature Paul's initial exhortation of the Galatians (1:6–10) and rehearse the apostle's personal background: his life before his conversion, his Damascus road experience, his interaction with the other apostles, and his climactic confrontation with Peter (1:11–2:21). The Spirit is absent from the epistolary introduction and the narrative portion of the letter until the beginning of chapter 3.[7]

---

constitutes both a special gift given to a chosen individual to perform particular tasks and a gift poured out over the community of God's people or within the framework of God's purposes for the whole community; (4) the Holy Spirit is the agent of resurrection; (5) the Spirit-empowered preaching of the gospel transcends the merely human; (6) the Holy Spirit imparts the power and presence of God; (7) the Holy Spirit has an eschatological dimension that transforms believers into their future destiny; and (8) as in the OT, the Holy Spirit is prophetic and revelatory.

[4] James D. G. Dunn, "Galatians," in Burke and Warrington, *Biblical Theology of the Holy Spirit*, 175. Remarkably, there is no reference to the Spirit as "the Holy Spirit." He is referred to consistently as "the Spirit" (πνεῦμα), perhaps to sustain a contrast with "the flesh" (σάρξ; e.g., 3:3).

[5] Fee notes that the Spirit is a necessary part of Paul's argument in Galatians: "The Spirit is an experienced reality providing evidence that righteousness is not by Torah (3:1–5, 14; 4:6) and is the effective agent for righteousness now that the time of Torah is past (5:13–6:10)" (*God's Empowering Presence*, 371). The experience of the Spirit by the Gentiles is proof that one's relationship with God is based not on Torah but on faith (378–80).

[6] Dunn, "Galatians," 175.

[7] See the discussion in Dunn, 175–76.

Figure 15: Comparison of References to the Spirit in Galatians and Romans

Content	Galatians	Romans
Christian life begins with reception of the Spirit	3:2, 14	8:15
The Spirit of God's Son cries, "*Abba, Father*"	4:6	8:15
Importance of being led by the Spirit	5:16, 25	8:4, 14
Opposition between Spirit and flesh	5:17	8:4–9, 12–13
The Spirit gives life	5:25; 6:8	8:2, 6, 10–11, 13

Proofs in Support of Paul's Argument (Probatio; 3:1–4:11)

Matters change dramatically in chapter 3, which features several important references to the Spirit, a pattern continued in the remainder of the letter. Addressing the Galatians, Paul presupposes that they "receive[d] the Spirit" (v. 2) and "beg[an] by the Spirit" (v. 3) when converted through his preaching of the crucified Christ (v. 1; cf. 2:16).[8] Even now, God "give[s] the Spirit" and "work[s] miracles" among them (v. 5). Paul's point is that the Galatians' reception of the Spirit at conversion was not merely an initial experience they could now leave behind. To the contrary, it was the foundational experience that grounded them in the reception of God's grace in Christ apart from any law keeping or personal merit. Thus Paul's concern in writing the letter—strikingly forgoing any opening pleasantries or thanksgiving—is that the Galatians are "turning away from" God, who had called them "by the grace of Christ," to, "a different gospel," which is really no gospel at all, on account of the intervention of some who are "troubling" them and want to "distort" the "gospel of Christ" (1:6–7). Paul is perturbed that in the case of

---

[8] See the study by Kendall H. Easley, "The Pauline Use of *Pneumati* as a Reference to the Spirit of God," *JETS* 27 (1984): 299–313, which, starting with Gal 3:3, covers all thirty-five instances of this phrase with reference to the Holy Spirit in Paul's writings (see table 2, p. 303).

the Galatians, his preaching may have been in vain (3:4) and they may have been "alienated from Christ" and have "fallen from grace" (5:4). As Dunn points out, the "experiential character of the Spirit's presence and activity in a life is one which Paul assumes in his further Spirit-talk in Galatians (4.6; 5.16–18, 22–23)."[9]

Still in chapter 3, Paul proceeds with the emphatic affirmation that "Christ redeemed us from the curse of the law by becoming a curse for us . . . [so] that the blessing of Abraham would come to the Gentiles by Christ Jesus, so that we could receive the promised Spirit through faith" (vv. 13–14).[10] In this way, Paul grounds the Galatians' reception of the Spirit at conversion in salvation history, maintaining that God's promise has *always* operated through faith—all the way back to Abraham "the believer" (v. 9). Thus the gospel, rather than being a novel invention or eccentric Pauline innovation, extends the reach of God's grace beyond the Jewish world and brings "the blessing of Abraham to Gentiles."[11] What is more, it was the reception of the Spirit by Gentiles that "proved to Paul that the promise to Abraham was now, at last, being fulfilled."[12] Significantly, Paul speaks of the reception of the Spirit in the same vein as he speaks of justification by faith (v. 7) and union with Christ (v. 14). This suggests that these phenomena are closely related and in fact inseparable.

In chapter 4 Paul then develops his affirmation at the end of chapter 3 that believers—including Gentiles—are heirs of the Abrahamic promise (3:28). In a salvation-historical illustration, Paul compares people before the

---

[9] Dunn, "Galatians," 179. Similarly, Fee notes that Paul reminds the Galatians of their experience of receiving the Spirit by faith before presenting them with the biblical argument as to who are Abraham's true children; the Spirit plays a central role both in conversion and as the defining marker of Christians (*God's Empowering Presence*, 381, 383).

[10] Fee observes that it is by the Spirit that the promised blessing to Abraham is received, not only justification through faith but also the new life in which Jews and Gentiles alike may share, and all of this through faith (394–95). Thomas R. Schreiner, *Galatians*, ZECNT (Grand Rapids: Zondervan, 2010), 218–19, appealing to the parallel terms "blessing" and "Spirit" in Isa 44:3, argues that the Spirit himself is the "blessing of Abraham" (v. 14) that here comes to the Gentiles.

[11] Dunn, "Galatians," 180.

[12] Dunn, 180.

coming of Christ to children under guardians who are not yet fit to receive their inheritance (vv. 1–3). He continues:

> When the time came to completion, God sent his Son, born of a woman, born under the law, to redeem those under the law, so that we might receive adoption as sons. And because you are sons, God sent the Spirit of his Son into our hearts, crying, *"Abba,* Father!" So you are no longer a slave but a son, and if a son, then God has made you an heir. (4:4–7)[13]

Along a salvation-historical continuum, therefore, the reign of the law is followed by God's sending of his Son, "born of a woman, born under the law, to redeem those under the law."[14] Those who trust Christ receive adoption into God's family, and God sends "the Spirit of his Son" (cf. Rom 8:9; Phil 1:19) into believers' hearts as an indication that they have now received their spiritual inheritance from God.[15] In this way, the coming of the Spirit serves as confirmation of believers' spiritual adoption and reception of all the rights that come with being adopted into God's family. Also, believers are God's "sons" by adoption in Christ, who is perennially God's Son; in this way, their

---

[13] Levison seems to miss Paul's point here when he claims that Paul's "dramatic protest that Torah and spirit do not mix is, to some extent, disingenuous" (*Filled with the Spirit*, 271), adducing several alleged parallels between the present passage and the *Community Rule* from Qumran (see 271–72). More likely, Paul's view of the Spirit differs from that of the *Community Rule* rather than aligning with it.

[14] Contra Dunn, "Galatians," 180n23, who unduly blurs the lines when he writes, "The implication [from the Greek] is not that the sending of the Spirit was subsequent to and consequent upon their having already become sons, but that the believing and the receiving were so closely related that the event of becoming Christian could be described by reference to either." Dunn is correct that there is a close relationship between the sending of the Son, believers' faith, and their reception of the Spirit, but he is on shaky ground when he speaks of the "uncertainty of the relation between faith and Spirit" in this passage.

[15] Dunn (181) rightly observes the varied terminology related to the Spirit thus far in Galatians—"received" (3:2, 14), "began with" (3:3), "gives" (3:5), and now "sent into our hearts" (4:6)—but is on more tenuous ground when he interprets this terminological diversity as indicating "the diverse character of the experience of the Spirit." While this is possible, it is not a necessary indication and could just as well reflect stylistic variation and various vantage points from which the *same* experience is described in the present epistle.

sonship is predicated upon their incorporation into Christ and their ongoing union with him.[16]

Again, we see a very close unity among God the Father, Son, and Spirit.[17] God the Father first sends his Son and subsequently his Spirit (note the parallel "sending" language in each case). The Spirit, for his part, is "the Spirit of his Son."[18] What is more, the Spirit, voicing the intimate relationship of the Son to the Father, cries out "*Abba*, Father!" in believers' hearts, as "the Spirit *of his Son*" is reminiscent of Jesus's own posture toward the Father.[19] Through the agency of the Spirit, therefore, whose ministry in turn is predicated upon the redemptive work of the Son, believers are intimately connected to none other than God himself in a seamless passing of the salvation-historical torch from Father to Son to Spirit.

Appeals (Exhortatio; 4:12–6:10)

In 4:21–31, Paul then adds a second illustration, the well-known allegory of Hagar and Sarah illustrating, respectively, the experience of those living

---

[16] Cf. Dunn, 181. Cf. Coulson, "Jesus and the Spirit in Paul's Theology," 94–95, who contends, "Through receiving 'the Spirit of Christ' (Rom 8:9), 'the Spirit of [God's] Son' (Gal 4:6), believers have been brought into relationship with God as God's children." As Fee points out, the reference to the Spirit as "the Spirit of his Son" connects the sonship of Christ to believers' sonship: "The same Son whose death effected redemption and secured 'sonship' for them, now indwells them by his Spirit, 'the Spirit *of the Son*,' whom God sent forth as he had the Son himself" (*God's Empowering Presence*, 405). God confirms experientially that we are sons through Christ by sending the Spirit to dwell in us, who cries out to God in the Son's intimate words (Fee, 406).

[17] Cf. Dunn, "Galatians," 182, who states that in the formulation "God sent the Spirit of his Son," "we see the theological thinking, and experience, which led to formulation of the Trinity."

[18] Dunn, *Jesus and the Spirit*, 318–26, provides an interesting examination of phrases such as "the Spirit of his Son" (cf. Rom 8:9; Phil 1:19) and concludes that for Paul, the truly distinctive mark of the Spirit in the lives of believers is his work of testifying to Jesus, of causing believers to share in Jesus's relationship as the Son, and in conforming believers to the image of Jesus.

[19] See, e.g., John 17:1, 5, 11, 24. In a later parallel, Rom 8:15–17, Paul invokes the Spirit's filial cry in believers' hearts as a sign of assurance that they are God's children and spiritual heirs.

under the law and those who inherit God's promise to Abraham.[20] In this allegory, Hagar's son, Ishmael, is characterized as having been "born as a result of the flesh" (i.e., being not only her physical child but also a child born of mere human effort and unbelief in God's promises) while Sarah's son, Isaac, is characterized as having been born "as a result of the Spirit" (i.e., as a spiritual son in the sense that Isaac was born by the power of the Spirit as a result of faith in God's promise).[21]

In chapter 5, Paul asserts that believers eagerly await "through the Spirit, by faith" the hope of righteousness (v. 5; cf. Rom 8:24–25).[22] This casts the Spirit as the "sustainer and enabler in the ongoing process" of living the Christian life.[23] Paul proceeds to state emphatically that circumcision (or lack thereof) is now irrelevant as a sign of covenant membership, for "only faith working through love" counts for anything (v. 6; cf. v. 14). In the Galatian context, where Judaizers have crept in, asserting that circumcision ought to continue as a requirement for covenant membership not only for Jews but also for Gentiles (cf. 2:1–14), Paul forcefully argues that faith in God's provision of Christ, coupled with the work of the Spirit, is the foundational operating principle of the new covenant community. Righteousness

---

[20] The OT source passage is Gen 21:1–14 (cf. Genesis 16–17).

[21] Note the parallelism in v. 23 ("as a result of the flesh . . . through *promise*") and v. 29 ("as a result of the flesh . . . as a result of the *Spirit*"). In addition, while most English versions capitalize "Spirit" in v. 29, it is possible that κατὰ σάρκα . . . κατὰ πνεῦμα should be understood as positing a contrast between "physical" and "spiritual." Dunn, "Galatians," 183, rightly notes that this is the only instance in Paul's writings where he speaks of believers' being "born as a result of the Spirit" (cf. John 1:12–13; 3:3, 5). Fee notes that this phrase is somewhat surprising, as Paul previously said that Isaac was born "through promise" (4:23) and called the Galatians "children of promise" (4:28). But here, as earlier in the letter (3:14), Paul connects the Spirit with the promise (*God's Empowering Presence*, 414–15).

[22] Dunn ("Galatians," 183–84) registers the interesting observation that Paul here adduces not believers' past experience of justification but their hope of future justification at the final judgment. Fee (*God's Empowering Presence*, 418–19) notes that Paul focuses here not on how people become right with God but on how those who are justified now live. Life lived according to the Spirit provides both hope for the future and enables us to live God-honoring lives now; life under the Torah can do neither (Dunn, 419).

[23] Dunn, 184.

is obtained by faith, not keeping the law; in fact, this is congruent with the way Abraham himself attained righteousness (3:6; cf. Gen 15:6).

The next section, vv. 16–26, features a veritable outburst of references to the Spirit—seven, to be exact—in a passage that contrasts living in "the Spirit" (*pneuma*) with living in "the flesh" (*sarx*; cf. v. 13; see also 4:23, 29).[24] The diversity of terminology related to the Spirit is striking: believers are to "walk" by the Spirit (v. 16), be "led" by the Spirit (v. 18), "live" by the Spirit, and "keep in step" with the Spirit (v. 25).[25] The Spirit has "desires" diametrically opposite to the flesh (v. 17) and produces "fruit" in the lives of believers that is likewise diametrically opposed to that brought about by fleshly, sinful desires (v. 22–23; cf. vv. 19–21).

"Walking" in (or "living" by) the Spirit—a Semitism—envisions a believer's way of life as guided by the Spirit (thus fulfilling the law's requirements; Rom 8:4);[26] being "led" by the Spirit may build on the prophetic vision of God's writing his law on people's hearts (Jer 31:33; Ezek 36:27; cf. 2 Cor 3:2–6). To "keep in step with" (*stoicheō*) means "being aligned with" in the sense of "walking in another's footsteps" (see Rom 4:12) or "living in accordance with a certain standard" (Gal 6:16; Phil 3:16).[27] Thus, Paul here encourages believers who claim to be controlled by and submitted to the Spirit to furnish evidence that this is in fact the case by the way they live, that is, by exhibiting the "fruit of the Spirit" (Gal 5:22–23).[28]

---

[24] Richard N. Longenecker, *Galatians*, WBC 41 (Dallas: Word, 1990), 245 (citing the work of W. D. Davies), calls this an "ethical dualism" attested also in John's writings and at Qumran. See also Harvey, *Anointed with the Spirit and Power*, 161.

[25] Longenecker (*Galatians*, 244) says all four terms are used synonymously in the present passage. Fee contends that the phrase "walk by the Spirit," though occurring only here in Paul's writings, is "Paul's basic ethical imperative," even more foundational than the command to love (*God's Empowering Presence*, 429).

[26] Fee, 433, observes, "Life in the Spirit is not passive submission to the Spirit to do a supernatural work in one's life; rather, it requires conscious effort, so that the indwelling Spirit may accomplish his ends in one's life."

[27] Longenecker, *Galatians*, 265–66.

[28] Dunn, *Jesus and the Spirit*, 295, aptly comments, "The spiritual man is not the one who insists on his liberty to indulge his own desires, but who limits his liberty by love of his neighbour and who expresses his liberty by serving his brother."

This "fruit," the results of the Spirit's continual work in a believer's life, is love, joy, peace, patience, kindness, goodness, faithfulness, gentleness (cf. 6:1), and self-control.[29] Paul trenchantly adds, "Against such things, there is no law" (v. 24). Only the Spirit is able to effect a lasting transformation of a person's character; the law is ultimately powerless to do so. In this process of spiritual growth, the Spirit and the believer work hand in glove: the Spirit leads, guides, and directs; the believer follows, trusts, and obeys. As is commonly the case in Paul's writings, there is a close connection between the Spirit's work and the believer's faith, though it is always the Spirit's enablement, not the believer's effort, that remains primary (cf., e.g., Phil 2:13).

In chapter 6, by way of final reminder Paul writes, "Do not be deceived: God is not mocked, for whatever one sows, that will he also reap. For the one who sows to his own flesh will from the flesh reap corruption, but the one who sows to the Spirit will from the Spirit reap eternal life" (v. 8).[30] Not only is the law of sowing and reaping an agricultural law; it is a spiritual law. In the original Galatian context, Paul here likely refers ominously to the Judaizers who "sow to the flesh" and thus will reap spiritual corruption. Conversely, believers must "sow to the Spirit." As Dunn observes, "Only by investing their being, values, priorities, time in the character-forming Spirit will the salvation process be completed in the resurrection of the body (Rom. 8.11) and eternal life."[31]

---

[29] The contrast between "works of the flesh" and "fruit of the Spirit" is one of human endeavor versus divine empowerment, though this does not indicate passivity on the part of the believer. In fact, most of these qualities are found elsewhere as imperatives (Fee, *God's Empowering Presence*, 443–44). The breadth of virtues shows that for Paul, the work of the Spirit in the Christian life (personally and corporately) is all-encompassing; what is more, he is concerned with the life of the believer in community, not simply Spirit-filled living in an individualistic sense (445).

[30] As Fee, 467, notes, Paul's concern is explicitly eschatological: "Paul's point is that the eschatological outcome is determined by whether one is living from the flesh or by the Spirit. . . . Those who persist in living from the flesh have de facto opted out of life in the Spirit." Living by the Spirit is not automatic, however; God's power is sufficient, but believers must sow.

[31] Dunn, "Galatians," 186, referring to Rom 8:23.

Figure 16: References to the Spirit in Galatians

Scripture Passage	Content
Gal 3:2	The Galatians received the Spirit at conversion, by hearing with faith
Gal 3:3	The Galatians began by the Spirit
Gal 3:5	God gives the Spirit and works miracles among the Galatians
Gal 3:14	Gentiles to receive the promise of the Spirit by faith
Gal 4:6	God sent the Spirit of his Son into believers' hearts, crying, "*Abba*, Father!"
Gal 4:29	In contrast to Ishmael, Isaac was born "as a result of the Spirit"
Gal 5:5	Through the Spirit, by faith, believers eagerly await the hope of righteousness
Gal 5:16	Believers are to "walk by the Spirit," and they will not gratify the flesh's desires
Gal 5:17	The desires of the flesh and of the Spirit are diametrically opposite
Gal 5:18	Those who are "led by the Spirit" are not under the law
Gal 5:22	The "fruit of the Spirit" is love, joy, peace, patience, kindness, etc.
Gal 5:25	If we "live by the Spirit," let us also "keep in step with the Spirit"
Gal 6:8	The one who sows to the Spirit will from the Spirit reap eternal life

Summary

Paul's references to the Spirit in Galatians are given in the context of the inclusion of Gentiles into the church on par with Jewish believers, over against the Judaizing heresy, which insisted that Gentiles must be circumcised if they were to be admitted into the church. Remarkably, the Spirit is absent from the first two chapters of Galatians. Equally remarkably, references to the Spirit are very frequent in the remainder of the book.

In chapter 3, Paul indicates that the Galatians began their Christian lives by receiving the Holy Spirit at conversion (vv. 2–3, 5); in this way, they inherited God's promise made to Abraham (v. 14). In chapter 4, Paul affirms that believers received the "Spirit of his [God's] Son," which attests to their filial relationship with God (v. 6). The allegory of Hagar and Sarah distinguishes between sons "born as a result of the flesh" with those "born as a result of the Spirit" (v. 29), contrasting the two respective experiences of living under the law and living in the Spirit.

In chapter 5, Paul then develops this contrast more fully, using several synonyms to describe this reality: "walking by," being "led by," "liv[ing] by," and "keep[ing] in step with" the Spirit (vv. 16, 18, 25). He also affirms that through the Spirit, by faith, believers eagerly await the hope of righteousness (v. 5) and emphatically states that the desires of the Spirit are diametrically opposite those of the flesh (v. 17), contrasting the "works of the flesh" with the "fruit of the Spirit" (vv. 19–23). In conclusion, believers are therefore exhorted to "sow to the Spirit" rather than to the flesh (6:8).

1–2 Thessalonians

In terms of Pauline chronology, the Thessalonian correspondence is most likely to be placed after the writing of Galatians and before the Corinthian correspondence and the letter to the Romans.[32] Indeed, noteworthy affinities may be noted between Paul's depiction of the reception of the Spirit in Galatians and 1 Thessalonians. In 1 Thess 1:4–6, Paul opens the letter by describing the coming of the gospel to the Thessalonians in the following way:

---

[32] Although Volker Rabens, "1 Thessalonians," in Burke and Warrington, *Biblical Theology of the Holy Spirit*, 198, citing a majority of scholars, believes 1 Thessalonians was Paul's earliest canonical epistle. But see the discussion on the date of Galatians (AD 48 or 49) and 1 Thessalonians (spring of AD 50) in Köstenberger, Kellum, and Quarles, *The Cradle, the Cross, and the Crown*, 491–94 and 516, 518, respectively.

We know, brothers and sisters loved by God, that he has chosen you, because our gospel did not come to you in word only, *but also in power, in the Holy Spirit, and with full assurance*. You know how we lived among you for your benefit, and you yourselves became imitators of us and of the Lord when, in spite of severe persecution, *you welcomed the message with joy from the Holy Spirit*.

There are obvious affinities between this passage and Paul's description of the Galatians' reception of the Spirit (though in Galatians this description is delayed until chapter 3):

I only want to learn this from you: Did you *receive the Spirit* by the works of the law or by believing what you heard? Are you so foolish? *After beginning by the Spirit*, are you now finishing by the flesh? Did you experience so much for nothing—if in fact it was for nothing? So then, does *God give you the Spirit and work miracles among you* by your doing the works of the law? Or is it by believing what you heard? (Gal 3:2–5)

The main difference between these two passages is that Paul in Galatians refers to the work of the Spirit in conjunction with the (sole) necessity of faith versus the performance of "works of the law" as part of his argument against the Judaizing heresy. In Thessalonians he takes a more affirming and encouraging posture. Notably, in both passages Paul refers to the suffering endured by believers as a result of embracing the gospel message (Gal 3:4: "experience so much"; 1 Thess 1:6: "severe persecution"). Thus persecution is cited in both instances as corroborating evidence that a genuine work of the Holy Spirit has taken place in the lives and hearts of believers in both locations.[33]

In the Thessalonian passage Paul cites the work of the Holy Spirit both in gospel proclamation and in the hearts of those who were its recipients. The gospel came in the power of the Holy Spirit (v. 4), and the Thessalonians received the word with the joy of the Holy Spirit (v. 6). This identifies the Holy Spirit as the powerful agent who made the gospel come to life (a possible

---

[33] Philip (*Origins of Pauline Pneumatology*, 168n10) adduces 1 Thess 1:4–6 to show how Paul often refers to the Holy Spirit to remind people of the reality of their conversion. Paul will then use this reference to believers' conversion to encourage them to live holy lives (see, e.g., Gal 3:1–5; 1 Cor 6:11).

reference to signs and wonders; cf. Rom 15:18–19; Heb 2:3–4) and who made Paul's gospel preaching effective ("not without result," 2:1), resulting in spiritual fruit in the form of repentance and faith, conversion, and regeneration.[34] It also sets Paul's message apart from other types of messages—Paul's message was undergirded by real spiritual power, evidenced by the spiritual fruit that resulted in transformed lives: these believers had turned "to God from idols to serve the living and true God" (1:9) and were eagerly awaiting the Lord's return (v. 10).

Significantly, the Spirit's power in Paul's gospel proclamation extended not merely to the *message* but also to the *messenger*: "You know how we lived among you for your benefit, and you yourselves became imitators [*mimētai*] of us and of the Lord" (vv. 5–6).[35] The believers in Thessalonica, in turn, "became an example [*typon*] to all the believers in Macedonia and in Achaia" (v. 7). Thus, in the case of the Thessalonians, the Spirit enabled them not only to bear up under persecution but also to bear witness to the gospel themselves, not only in Macedonia and Achaia but "in every place," so that Paul was able to move on to minister in other locales (v. 8).

The Spirit is thus presented as a vital, energizing, life-transforming, and missionary Spirit. Not only does he infuse the proclamation of the gospel with power; he also dynamically transforms those who respond to the message in faith so that they are able to "live worthy of God" (2:12; cf. 4:1). Embracing the gospel, therefore, entails more than "mere cognitive acquisition";[36] it involves an active and living faith that takes the Holy Spirit into a believer's life, which in turn has important character implications. The Spirit's work in initiation is thus of the same kind as his work in believers' lives as they continue in the faith. What is more, conversion entails a vital

---

[34] Dunn, *Jesus and the Spirit*, 226, suggests not only that the Spirit was the agent who made Paul's speaking effective but also that Paul is affirming that he had little or no choice in the words used, as these were also determined by the Spirit. This second assertion seems to exceed the evidence, however. Cf. Charles A. Wanamaker, *The Epistles to the Thessalonians*, NIGTC (Grand Rapids: Eerdmans, 1990), 79, who says that the reference to "not only" and "but also" indicates intensification, not contrast.

[35] Cf. 2:8–12; 4:1. See Rabens, "1 Thessalonians," 200, who observes that the "Spirit-empowering of Paul's gospel ministry" encompassed "the behaviour and character of the Apostles."

[36] Rabens, 201.

turning from idols to serve the living God (v. 9), which has real consequences
with regard to a person's spiritual ownership and that person's participation
in the spiritual warfare that is a constant reality in believers' lives.

Following the opening salvo in Paul's teaching on the Holy Spirit in 1
Thessalonians is a temporary hiatus, as Paul rehearses his previous ministry to the Thessalonians and lays out his future plans in chapters 2 and 3.
"Additionally," then, in chapter 4, Paul exhorts the Thessalonians to excel
even more in their Christian lives, especially in the pursuit of holiness,
which sets them apart from their pagan surroundings of which they had
once been a part (vv. 1–7). On the tail end of this exhortation, Paul reminds
the Thessalonian believers: "Consequently, anyone who rejects this does not
reject man, but God, who gives you his Holy Spirit" (v. 8).

This passage identifies God as the giver of the Holy Spirit. There is an
important link between God—who is holy—and his giving of the "Holy"
Spirit, issuing in the Holy Spirit's work in believers' lives in making them holy
and set apart from sexual immorality and other evils: "For this is God's will,
your sanctification" (v. 3; cf. 3:13; 5:23); "For God has not called us to impurity,
but to live in holiness" (v. 7).[37] If anyone among the Thessalonians disregards
the holiness to which God has called them and toward which Paul is exhorting them, they are disregarding God, who gives them his Spirit (v. 8; cf. v. 6).[38]

At the end of 1 Thessalonians, Paul provides in chapter 5 a concluding
list of various instructions (vv. 16–22), including the exhortation not to "stifle
the Spirit" (v. 19).[39] After issuing directives regarding prayer and thanksgiving (vv. 17–18), the apostle zeroes in on the injunction to refrain from

---

[37] For a detailed discussion of 1 Thess 4:8 and Paul's teaching on sanctification in 1 Thessalonians in interaction with recent scholarly literature (in particular, German scholarship), see Rabens, 201–9. Rabens adduces important parallels
between Ezekiel (esp. 11:19; 36:26–27; 37:6,14) and 1 Thess 4:8, defends the ethical
dimension of the passage, and contends that the "Thessalonians are thus called not to
resist this empowering dynamic in their midst." Cf. Victor Paul Furnish, "The Spirit
in 2 Thessalonians," in Stanton, Longenecker, and Barton, *Holy Spirit and Christian
Origins*, 231, who discusses the different roles the Spirit plays in 1 Thessalonians. In
chapter 1 he is connected with the Thessalonians coming to faith, whereas here in
chapter 4 he is focused on the ongoing sanctification of the community.

[38] Cf., e.g., John 13:16, 20; 15:18–25.

[39] As Fee, *God's Empowering Presence*, 53–55, observes, rejoicing, prayer, and thanksgiving are activities grounded in the presence of the Spirit; thus the presupposition

stifling the Spirit and from despising prophecies (vv. 19–20). He concludes the rapid-fire list by urging his readers to "test all things," to "hold on to what is good," and to "stay away from every form of evil" (vv. 21–22).

The connection between the Spirit in v. 19 and prophecy in v. 20 cannot be denied. "Stifle" may involve the metaphor of putting out a fire, perhaps because the Spirit was at times depicted in terms of fire.[40] In any case, in practical terms "stifling the Spirit" out of contempt for prophecy would mean not engaging in prophecy (as a spiritual gift in the NT sense) or prohibiting others from doing so (especially the latter). At the same time, such prophetic activity ought to be subject to congregational testing (v. 21).[41]

While the Spirit is not explicitly mentioned in v. 23 ("Now may the God of peace himself sanctify you completely. And may your whole spirit, soul, and body be kept sound and blameless at the coming of our Lord Jesus Christ"), he seems implied in the word "sanctify," as he is identified elsewhere in the letter as the primary agent of believers' sanctification.[42] As Paul closes his first letter to the believers in Thessalonica, he issues a prayer and benediction that God would sanctify them completely (*holoteleis*), building on the earlier references to the Spirit's work in believers' sanctification (esp. 4:1–8; cf. Jude vv. 24–25).

Paul adds, "He [God] who calls you is faithful; he will do it" (v. 24; cf. Phil 1:6). Thus believers' confidence with regard to the completion of their sanctification rests properly in the God who sanctifies, the God who "is faithful." This is a process that commences at conversion (1:5–6) and continues throughout believers' lives (4:1–8) but is not completed until "the coming of our Lord Jesus Christ" (v. 23).

---

of the Spirit in vv. 16–18 gives way to explicit references to the Spirit in vv. 19–22.

[40] Cf., e.g., Matt 3:11; Luke 3:16; Acts 2:3.

[41] Paul will develop this idea in much greater detail in his first letter to the Corinthians (see esp. chap. 14); see discussion in the next section below. Rabens, "1 Thessalonians," 211, registers the interesting observation that Paul does not ask believers to strengthen others in their own power. The Spirit will do his work; all that is needed is for believers not to suppress the Spirit's operation in their midst. Cf. Furnish, "Spirit in 2 Thessalonians," 232.

[42] Fee, *God's Empowering Presence*, 63–64, argues that vv. 23–24 are tied to the language of 4:3–8, presupposing the sanctifying work of the Spirit developed in the earlier passage.

The only explicit reference to the Holy Spirit in Paul's second letter to the Thessalonians harks back to his teaching on the Spirit's role in sanctification in the first letter, including at 1 Thess 5:23:

> But we ought to thank God always for you, brothers and sisters loved by the Lord, because from the beginning God has chosen you for salvation through sanctification by the Spirit and through belief in the truth. He called you to this through our gospel, so that you might obtain the glory of our Lord Jesus Christ. So then, brothers and sisters, stand firm and hold to the traditions you were taught, whether by what we said or what we wrote. (2 Thess 2:13–15)[43]

It appears that here reference is made primarily to the *initial* setting apart of believers by the Spirit at conversion upon their "belief in the truth" of the gospel.[44] At the same time, the reference is given in an eschatological orbit, which presents obtaining the "glory of our Lord Jesus Christ" as the final aim of the process of sanctification.[45] Toward that end, believers are urged to "stand firm and hold to the traditions" they were taught by Paul and his coworkers.

While in popular understanding "sanctification" is typically taken to refer to the *process* of Christian growth, in Paul and other NT writings sanctification *begins* at conversion (past), *continues* throughout a Christian's life (present), and is *completed* at the day of the Lord (future sanctification). Thus, when a person comes to saving faith in Christ through repentance and trust in Jesus's finished cross-work on his or her behalf, he or she is initially set

---

[43] Fee, 69–70, argues that the reference to "power" refers to the power of the Spirit.

[44] Furnish, "Spirit in 2 Thessalonians," 235–36, draws connections between Paul's language here and the language of God's election in the OT, pointing to Deut 33:12; Isa 41:8; 44:2; Hos 11:1 (LXX). The Spirit's work of sanctification, together with "belief in the truth," is "the means through which the elect are set apart for salvation." Furnish, however, says there is no indication as to how the Spirit's sanctification is related to belief. See also Dunn, *Baptism in the Holy Spirit*, 106, who agrees that the language specifies an order not of salvation but of importance.

[45] Contra Furnish, "Spirit in 2 Thessalonians," 236, 239, who writes, "In 2 Thessalonians the Spirit's sanctifying work is associated exclusively with God's choosing of the elect ('from the beginning') for future salvation (2:13). . . . Apart from the mention of ecstatic utterances as a possible source of doctrinal error (2:2), nothing in this letter suggests an understanding of the Spirit as present with and for the believing community."

apart spiritually for God and receives the Holy Spirit. This setting apart, while *positionally* realized, then becomes an increasing *progressive* reality as the Spirit continually does his work in a believer's life, although it is not completed until the future coming of Christ, when the believer's setting apart from sin will be completely realized in the final state.[46]

Figure 17: Past, Present, and Future Dimensions of Sanctification

Conversion	Christian growth	Consummation
Past	*Present*	*Future*

Figure 18: References to the Spirit in 1–2 Thessalonians

Scripture Passage	Content
1 Thess 1:5	Gospel came not only in word but also in power, the Holy Spirit, and conviction
1 Thess 1:6	Received the word in much affliction, with the joy of the Holy Spirit
1 Thess 4:8	Those who reject the gospel reject not man but God who gives the Holy Spirit
1 Thess 5:19	Do not stifle the Spirit
2 Thess 2:13	God chose you to be saved through sanctification by the Spirit (cf. 1 Thess 5:23)

---

[46] Cf., e.g., Rev 21:8, 27; and 22:15. See Andreas J. Köstenberger, *Excellence: The Character of God and the Pursuit of Scholarly Virtue* (Wheaton: Crossway, 2011), chap. 3, who speaks of believers' paradoxically "becoming [experientially] what they already are [positionally]," distinguishing between definitive or positional and progressive sanctification. Similarly, Harvey, *Anointed with the Spirit and Power*, 146n5, sees sanctification as consisting of three facets: initial (1 Cor 6:11; 2 Thess 2:13), progressive (Rom 6:19–22; 1 Thess 4:3), and final sanctification (Eph 5:25–27; 1 Thess 5:23–24). Fee, *God's Empowering Presence*, 79, likewise notes that sanctification is not primarily something that happens after conversion but refers to both being set apart for God's purposes and following God and reflecting his character.

In summary, in his Thessalonian letters Paul presents the Spirit as active in believers' lives both at the initial stage of conversion (1 Thess 1:5–6) and throughout their Christian lives. Particularly pronounced is Paul's emphasis on the role of the Holy Spirit in believers' sanctification (1 Thess 4:8; 5:23; 2 Thess 2:13). Not only does the Spirit's sanctifying work enable believers to abstain from sexual immorality and other kinds of evil; they are spiritually set apart from their pagan surroundings and thus empowered to engage in mission and witness to the God who saved them in Christ (1 Thess 4:1–8). Toward the end of his first letter, Paul identifies the Spirit as the Spirit of prophecy, who desires to be active in the Christian congregation and whom believers must not stifle (1 Thess 5:19).

1 Corinthians

As with the church in Thessalonica, Paul planted the church in Corinth and subsequently followed up with additional correspondence. According to a report from Chloe's people (1:11), there were divisions in the church that Paul sought to confront (chs. 1–4).[47] In addition, it appears that the Corinthians wrote to Paul with a series of questions (16:17), which he addresses in the second half of the letter (chs. 7–12). Notably, both portions of the epistle feature a prominent passage on the Spirit, in chapters 2 and 12 (continued in chapter 14), respectively.

Response to Reports from Chloe's People (chs. 1–6)

Apparently, what lay at the root of the divisions in the Corinthian church was that many considered Paul's rhetoric inferior to that of eloquent speakers such as Apollos (1:12; 3:4–6, 22).[48] In response, Paul asserts that he had preached the gospel in Corinth in such a way that nothing would detract

---

[47] On Chloe, see Andreas J. Köstenberger, "Women in the Pauline Mission," in *The Gospel for the Nations: Perspectives on Paul's Mission*, ed. Peter G. Bolt and Mark D. Thompson (Leicester, UK: InterVarsity, 2000), 330.

[48] See Corin Mihaila, *The Paul-Apollos Relationship and Paul's Stance toward Greco-Roman Rhetoric: An Exegetical and Socio-Historical Study of 1 Corinthians 1–4*, LNTS 402 (London: T&T Clark, 2009).

from the crucified Christ (2:1–2). His speech consisted not in mere human words of wisdom (as the rhetoric of Greek philosophers and sages might have done) but "with a demonstration of the Spirit's power" (v. 4; cf. 1 Thess 1:5: "in power, in the Holy Spirit, and with full assurance").[49]

In fact, Paul asserts that he *did* seek to impart a kind of wisdom, that is, "God's hidden wisdom in a mystery" (v. 7). Citing Isa 40:13 (LXX), he claims that "these things"—that is, the hidden wisdom of God, consisting in sending Christ to die for humanity's sins on the cross—"God has revealed . . . to us by the Spirit, since the Spirit searches everything, even the depths of God" (v. 10), for "no one knows the thoughts of God except the Spirit of God" (v. 11).[50]

For this reason, it is to be expected that worldly thinking would fail to appreciate *God's* wisdom as not measuring up to the wisdom of this world. Yet a truly spiritual person will be able to appreciate the difference between the wisdom of God displayed in the crucified Christ—Paul's gospel—and the wisdom of this world, which considers such to be foolishness.

In the end, it is not about the *messenger*—whether Paul or Apollos or any other human instrument—or the rhetoric they employ, but about the *message*. Thus, those who stir up divisions in the Corinthian church are shown to be guided by worldly perspectives on leadership and human speech. As Paul concludes:

---

[49] Fee, *God's Empowering Presence*, 92, notes that "Spirit" and "power" are virtually a hendiadys. Here Paul returns to his point from 1:18: the Holy Spirit works powerfully in people's lives to save, putting to shame the wise who trust themselves rather than God (93). Cf. Dunn, *Jesus and the Spirit*, 226, who says that the Corinthians' experience had nothing to do with Paul's rhetorical skill but was "rather of being grasped by divine power," with the result that they accepted Paul's message.

[50] See the discussion of this verse in Desta Heliso, "Divine Spirit and Human Spirit in Paul in the Light of Stoic and Biblical-Jewish Perspectives," in *Spirit and Christ in the New Testament: Essays in Honor of Max Turner*, ed. I. Howard Marshall, Volker Rabens, and Cornelis Bennema (Grand Rapids: Eerdmans, 2012), 171–75, who conjectures that Paul's Corinthian critics questioned his possession of the Spirit and cast doubt on his spirituality (174). For a study of Paul's pneumatology in 1 Cor 2:9–16 as grounded in his Christology in 1 Cor 1:18–2:8, see Cletus L. Hall, III, "The Grounding of Paul's Pneumatology in his Christology in 1 Corinthians 1:18–2:16" (PhD diss., Regent University, 2017).

Now we have not received the spirit of the world, but *the Spirit who comes from God*, so that we may understand what has been freely given to us by God. We also speak these things, not in words taught by human wisdom, but in those taught by the Spirit, explaining spiritual things to spiritual people. But the person without the Spirit does not receive *what comes from God's Spirit*, because it is foolishness to him; he is not able to understand it since it is evaluated spiritually. The spiritual person, however, can evaluate everything, and yet he himself cannot be evaluated by anyone. For

who has known the Lord's mind,
that he may instruct him?

But we have the mind of Christ. (vv. 12–16)

In other words, those who fail to appreciate Paul's message are unspiritual. It takes the work of the indwelling, illuminating Spirit to resonate with the spiritual nature of the gospel of the crucified Christ.[51] Thus Paul here affirms both the reality of divine revelation through the Holy Spirit and also the illumination of that revelation by the Holy Spirit.[52]

---

[51] André Munzinger, *Discerning the Spirits: Theological and Ethical Hermeneutics in Paul*, SNTSMS 140 (Cambridge, UK: Cambridge University Press, 2007), highlights Paul's use of Isa 40:13 in this passage ("Who has directed the Spirit of the Lord?"). To bring up Isaiah's question, here rendered "Who has known the Lord's mind?," is to expect the answer "No one" (see esp. *Wis* 9:13–14; *2 Bar* 14:8–9; *4 Ezra* 4:11; note that "mind" follows the LXX's νοῦς; the MT has רוּחַ, "S/spirit"). Yet Paul responds by saying "But we have the mind of Christ," meaning that knowledge of God's will is made possible through Christ. Thus, believers can discern the will of God (39–40). For an excellent survey of the comparison between Paul's theology and Stoic thought, see Munzinger, 121–138, 148. Menzies puts too much weight on a possible connection between 2 Cor 2:6–16 and *Wis* 9:9–18, which causes him to conclude that Christian communities before Paul did not view the Spirit as essential for salvation (*Development of Early Christian Pneumatology*, chap. 12). Turner rightly contends that if Paul alludes to any other writing, it is Isa 11:1–2, not *Wisdom of Solomon* (*Holy Spirit*, 109; see also Fee, *God's Empowering Presence*, 911–13).

[52] For a biblical-theological treatment see Michael X. Seaman, *Illumination and Interpretation: The Holy Spirit's Role in Hermeneutics* (Eugene: Wipf & Stock, 2013), who combines both initial and progressive illumination under the rubric of

Notably, 2:13–15 features multiple instances of *pneumatikos/ pneumatikōs*.[53] Paul's use of the term "spiritual" connects it not primarily with the human spirit but with being endowed with God's Spirit.[54] That Paul can use the term without special explanation not only in 1 Corinthians but also elsewhere suggests that the term had sufficient currency in the early church.[55] The use of the expression in the early church was unprecedented; while it occurs in secular literature before the NT, it is not used there to designate any kind of higher, spiritual existence.[56] As John Barclay observes, "The remarkable frequency of πνευματικός in the Pauline Epistles is not difficult to explain. Once the new and overwhelming experience of God in early Christianity was interpreted as the presence of 'the Spirit,' it was natural that this term, and its adjectival derivative, would play a prominent role in Christian discourse."[57]

---

transformative illumination (for a list of relevant passages see 6n17). For a summary of the debate and a proposal see David J. McKinley, "John Owen's View of Illumination: An Alternative to the Fuller-Erickson Dialogue," *BSac* 154, no. 613 (1997): 93–104.

[53] Note that, remarkably, over half of all NT references to πνευματικός are found in 1 Corinthians (eleven verses; no other Pauline writing features more than three), which may be explained by Paul's desire to contrast worldly or fleshly thinking with a way of looking at things that is spiritual (i.e., Spirit-illumined). For later references in 1 Corinthians see 3:1; 9:11; 10:3–4; 12:1; 14:1, 37; 15:44, 46 (see fig. 19). On the social and cultural embeddedness of the term, see esp. John M. G. Barclay, "Πνευματικός in the Social Dialect of Pauline Christianity," in Stanton, Longenecker, and Barton, *Holy Spirit and Christian Origins*, 157–67.

[54] Barclay, 161.

[55] See Barclay, 162. References elsewhere in Paul include Gal 6:1; Rom 1:11; 7:14; 15:27; Col 1:9; 3:16; Eph 1:3; 5:19; 6:12 (see fig. 19). Note that the adjective occurs elsewhere in the NT only in 1 Pet 2:5 and the adverb only in Rev 11:8.

[56] The use of the term in Gnostic literature is drawing on Pauline usage (see Barclay, 163).

[57] Barclay, 165. Cf. Dunn, *Jesus and the Spirit*, 207–9.

Figure 19: "Spiritual" (*Pneumatikos*) Terminology in Paul's Writings[58]

Scripture Passage	Content
Gal 6:1	You who are spiritual restore transgressor with a gentle spirit
1 Cor 2:13	We speak words taught by the Spirit, not by human wisdom, explaining spiritual things to those who are spiritual
1 Cor 2:14	The person without the Spirit does not understand the things of the Spirit of God, because they are evaluated spiritually
1 Cor 2:15	The spiritual person can evaluate everything but is evaluated by no one
1 Cor 3:1	The Corinthians are not spiritual but people of the flesh, mere babies in Christ
1 Cor 9:11	If one has sown spiritual things, is it too much to expect to reap material things?
1 Cor 10:3–4	All the Israelites ate the same spiritual food and drank the same spiritual drink in the wilderness
1 Cor 12:1	Now concerning spiritual gifts . . .
1 Cor 14:1	Earnestly desire spiritual gifts, especially prophecy
1 Cor 14:37	If anyone things he is a prophet, or spiritual, listen to me
1 Cor 15:44	Sown a natural body, raised a spiritual body; if natural, also spiritual body
1 Cor 15:46	First the natural, then the spiritual body

[58] Note that the Spirit is indirectly in view in many (if not most) of these passages, such as in the references to spiritual persons (the Spirit regenerates, illumines), gifts (the Spirit bestows), or bodies (the Spirit raises). Cf. the discussion in Fee, 28–32, who contends that πνευματικός is always related to the Spirit, never to the human spirit or generic spirituality.

Rom 1:11	Paul longs to see the Roman Christians to impart to them a spiritual gift
Rom 7:14	The law is spiritual, but people are sinful
Rom 15:27	Gentiles share in Jews' spiritual blessings; share material possessions too
Eph 1:3	God has blessed us in Christ with every spiritual blessing in the heavens
Eph 5:19	Speaking to one another in psalms, hymns, and spiritual songs
Eph 6:12	Our struggle is against the spiritual forces of evil in the heavens
Col 1:9	Prayer for knowledge of God's will in all wisdom and spiritual understanding
Col 3:16	Singing psalms, hymns, and spiritual songs

Following a lament that Paul could not address the Corinthians as spiritual people (3:1) and an affirmation of the partnership among God's servants—whether Paul or Apollos (3:2–15)—Paul asks rhetorically, "Don't you yourselves know that you are God's temple and that the Spirit of God lives in you? If anyone destroys God's temple, God will destroy him; for God's temple is holy, and that is what you are" (3:16–17).[59] Paul's temple analogy here builds on a rich trajectory of God's Spirit's manifesting the divine presence in the tabernacle and later the temple. After this, the Spirit had rested on the Messiah. Now he has taken up residence among God's people, and anyone who disrupts congregational unity is in effect attempting to destroy God's temple. This, Paul assures the Corinthians, is sure to draw severe divine judgment.

---

[59] This passage (3:16–17) is central to understanding Paul's view of the church, namely, that people are defined by their relationship to the Spirit (Fee, 115). Paul's purpose in chapter 3 has often been misconstrued to support distinctions between Christians, that is, between those who are truly spiritual and those who are not. However, "the gift of the Spirit does not lead to special status among believers; rather, it leads to special status vis-à-vis the world. But it should do so always in terms of the centrality of the message of our crucified/risen Savior" (Fee, 112).

A few chapters later,[60] Paul continues in the same vein, reminding the Corinthians that some of them had engaged in gross sexual or other immorality before their Christian conversion: "But you were washed, you were sanctified, you were justified in the name of the Lord Jesus Christ and by the Spirit of our God" (6:11). As is common in Paul and the NT, the Spirit is here presented as the agent in sanctification.[61] Notably, Paul here presents justification in Christ and sanctification by the Spirit in parallel terms (cf. 1:30). What is more, sanctification is mentioned before justification, in an apparent chiasm:

> A . . . you were sanctified,   A' and by the Spirit of our God.
>   B you were justified   B' in the name of the Lord Jesus Christ

Paul proceeds to clinch the argument as follows: "Don't you know that your body is a temple of the Holy Spirit who is in you, whom you have from God? You are not your own, for you were bought at a price. So glorify God with your body" (6:19–20).[62] Most likely, Paul's words are spoken in the first-century Corinthian context of church members' having sexual relations with temple prostitutes (6:16).[63] Paul's argument is that this is com-

---

[60] In keeping with his maximalist methodology throughout his work (seeing references to the person of the Holy Spirit in Paul's writings even where these are not explicit and in some cases likely not present at all), Fee (121, 123–25) argues that there are references to the Spirit in 4:21 ("spirit of gentleness," cf. Gal 6:1) and 5:3–5 (Paul is present with the Corinthians "in spirit"), but these are indirect at best.

[61] See the discussion of 1–2 Thessalonians, earlier in this chapter.

[62] Fee, *God's Empowering Presence*, 137, comments: "Sanctification includes the body, which through Christ's resurrection has been made his own possession and is thereby destined for resurrection. To be Spirit-ual, therefore, does not mean to deny the physical side of our human life; neither, of course, does it mean to indulge it. The presence of the Spirit means that God himself, who created us with bodies in the first place, has taken keen interest in our whole life, including the life of the body. The creation of the body was pronounced *good* in the beginning; it has now been purchased by Christ and is sanctified by the presence of God himself through his Holy Spirit. We must therefore 'sanctify' it as well ('therefore glorify God in your bodies'), by living the life of the Spirit, a life of holiness."

[63] Cf. Fee, 136: "Hence God not only dwells *among* his people, but is himself present, by his Spirit, *within* his people, sanctifying their present earthly existence and stamping it with his own eternity."

pletely unacceptable, for such sexual union unites one's body with another in a marriage-like fashion, while God intends sex to be pursued exclusively within the context of monogamous marriage (6:16; cf. Gen 2:24). Thus Paul uses temple imagery in both a corporate and an individual sense, referring to the church as a whole and to believers individually. Both are indwelt by the Spirit and must consequently refrain from sexual immorality, which would include sexual relations with temple prostitutes as well as every other sort of sexual behavior not in conformity with God's guidance.

Response to Corinthians' Queries (chs. 7–16)

Chapter 7 begins Paul's response to the queries addressed to him in the Corinthians' letter. First he tackles the question of whether sexual activity is somehow inferior to sexless spirituality. Is it more spiritual to remain single or, if a person is already married, to refrain from sex in marriage—or even to divorce one's spouse? In response, Paul provides a series of instructions, which he concludes, perhaps in a veiled reference to his opponents, by asserting, "And I think that I also have the Spirit of God" (7:40).[64] This reference builds on Paul's discourse on the work of the Spirit in chapter 2, where he asserted, "But we have the mind of Christ." This possession of and sensitivity to the Spirit enables him—and other mature believers like him—to make spiritual adjudication of various issues that arise in the Christian life and in the life of a congregation and allows others to recognize the Spirit's wisdom that led persons such as Paul to adjudicate matters with the "mind of Christ."

In chapter 12 Paul addresses yet another question: "Now concerning spiritual gifts . . ." (12:1). By way of introduction, Paul asserts, "No one speaking by the Spirit of God says 'Jesus is cursed,' and no one can say 'Jesus is Lord' except by the Holy Spirit" (v. 3). He continues:

> Now there are different gifts, *but the same Spirit*. There are different ministries, but the same Lord. And there are different activities, but the same God produces each gift in each person. A *manifestation of the Spirit* is given to each person *for the common good*: to one is given

---

[64] Dunn, *Jesus and the Spirit*, 260, notes that this is one of the rare times in which Paul speaks of the Spirit without reference to a "shared experience."

a message of wisdom *through the Spirit*, to another, a message of knowledge *by the same Spirit*, to another, faith *by the same Spirit*, to another, gifts of healing *by the one Spirit*, to another, the performing of miracles, to another, prophecy, to another, distinguishing between spirits, to another, different kinds of tongues, to another, interpretation of tongues. <u>One and the same Spirit</u> is active in all these, distributing to each person as he wills. (vv. 4–11)[65]

The repeated occurrences of "the same Spirit" (vv. 4, 8, 9, 11) and references to "the common good" (v. 7) and "the one Spirit" (v. 9)—culminating in the reference to "one and the same Spirit" (v. 11)—make clear that Paul's overriding concern continues to be congregational unity.[66] This is confirmed by Paul's concluding statement in chapter 14: "But everything is to be done decently and in order" (v. 40). As Paul writes earlier in chapter 12, "For just as *the body is one* and has many parts, and all the parts of that body, though many, are *one body*—so also is Christ. For we were all baptized with *one Spirit* into one body—whether Jews or Greeks, whether slaves or free—and we were all given *one Spirit* to drink" (vv. 12–13).

It is impossible to miss Paul's point: the church is *one body* because there is *one Spirit* into which all were baptized and of whom all, metaphorically speaking, were made to drink.[67] Congregational unity is thus grounded in

---

[65] The Spirit's choosing in v. 11 is a strong support for his personhood. Schnelle highlights the sovereign choices that in this verse the Spirit is said to make, observing, "The relation of the Spirit to God and Jesus Christ cannot be satisfactorily described in the categories of subordination, coordination, or identity, for the Spirit also has its own personal reality." Udo Schnelle, *Theology of the New Testament*, trans. M. Eugene Boring (Grand Rapids: Baker, 2009), 275.

[66] Alexander J. M. Wedderburn, "Pauline Pneumatology and Pauline Theology," in Stanton, Longenecker, and Barton, *Holy Spirit and Christian Origins*, 150, argues that the desire for congregational unity also stands behind the discussion of saying "Jesus is Lord" by the Spirit (v. 3): "All who confess Jesus as Lord . . . have the Spirit; it is the Spirit in them which enables them to recognize him as Lord. They *all* have the Spirit, and the possession of the Spirit is not limited to a small, elite group manifesting more spectacular and more overtly supernatural spiritual gifts." Contra Fee, *God's Empowering Presence*, 176, who argues that Paul's main desire here is to affirm not the unity of the body but its diversity in light of its unity.

[67] William P. Atkinson, "1 Corinthians," in Burke and Warrington, *Biblical Theology of the Holy Spirit*, 153–54, suggests that the metaphor "here is probably not so much that of a person drinking from a cup as that of parched ground drinking in

the fact that there is one and only one Spirit. Paul spends the remainder of chapter 12 and the next two chapters—including an ode to the supremacy of Christian love in chapter 13—to drive home his point that the diversity of spiritual gifts was given to believers in the church by God on the basis of its underlying unity in the Spirit. While Christ is thus the head of the church, and the church is his body, it is the Spirit who distributes the gifts and serves as the bond that binds the individual members of the church together in unity.[68] Not only chapters 1–4, therefore, but also chapters 12–14 are motivated by Paul's desire to promote unity in the church at Corinth.

Chapter 14 contains two final references to the Spirit.[69] Paul opens the chapter by commanding, "Pursue love and desire spiritual gifts, and especially that you may prophesy" (v. 1).[70] He affirms that speaking in tongues involves uttering "mysteries in the Spirit" (v. 2). Therefore, prophesying is to be preferred, and tongues must be interpreted (vv. 3–11). Paul concludes, "So also you—since you are zealous for spiritual gifts, seek to excel in building up the church" (v. 12). This suggests that the Corinthians were "eager for manifestations of the Spirit" but did not always exercise and control these manifestations in such a way that made for congregational unity.[71] True excellence,

---

rain" (citing James D. G. Dunn, *Baptism in the Holy Spirit: A Re-Examination of the New Testament Teaching on the Gift of the Spirit in Relation to Pentecostalism Today*, London: SCM, 1970, 131).

[68] Cf. Thiselton, *Holy Spirit*, 90: "In this special context we must bear in mind that none of the nine gifts of the Spirit in 1 Cor. 12:8–10 are primarily for the individual alone, but for the congregation."

[69] In addition, Richard B. Gaffin Jr., "'Life-Giving Spirit': Probing the Center of Paul's Pneumatology," *JETS* 41 (1998): 573–89, adducing 2 Cor 3:6 and Rom 8:11, suggests that 1 Cor 15:45 contains a reference to the Holy Spirit; not only this, he raises the bar when he says that "1 Cor 15:45 is not only central to Paul's Christology and pneumatology and his most pivotal pronouncement on the relationship between the exalted Christ and the Spirit. As such it is as well the cornerstone of his entire teaching on the Holy Spirit and the Christian life" (584). But see Fee, *God's Empowering Presence*, 16n13, who says the passage "does not refer to the Holy Spirit"; and all major English translations, which render "life-giving spirit" with a small *s*.

[70] Fee, 214, notes that Paul's overarching concern is that the desire for the Spirit should promote love in the gathered community. This picks up the themes of both chs. 12 and 13.

[71] Cf. Fee, 227, who notes that Paul's concern in 14:12 is for the Corinthians to redirect their zeal in corporate worship to the goal of building up one another in Christ.

however, lies not merely in extraordinary manifestations of the Spirit but in a desire for congregational unity and the "even better way" of love (12:31).

Figure 20: References to the Spirit in 1 Corinthians

Scripture Passage	Content
1 Cor 2:4	Paul's message came not with words of wisdom but in the power of the Spirit
1 Cor 2:10	The Spirit searches everything, even the depths of God
1 Cor 2:11	No one knows the thoughts of God except the Spirit of God
1 Cor 2:12	The Spirit from God helps believers understand the things of God
1 Cor 2:13	Believers are not taught by human wisdom but taught by the Spirit
1 Cor 2:14	The person without the Spirit does not accept the things of the Spirit of God
1 Cor 3:16	The Spirit of God dwells in believers, who are God's temple
1 Cor 6:11	Believers were sanctified by the Spirit of God
1 Cor 6:19	Believers' bodies are the temple of the Holy Spirit; they are not their own
1 Cor 7:40	Paul thinks that he also has the Spirit of God
1 Cor 12:3	No one can say "Jesus is Lord" except by the Holy Spirit
1 Cor 12:4	There are different gifts but the same Spirit
1 Cor 12:7	The manifestation of the Spirit is given to each person for the common good
1 Cor 12:8	The same Spirit gives wisdom and knowledge

1 Cor 12:9	The same Spirit, the one Spirit, gives faith and gifts of healing
1 Cor 12:11	One and the same Spirit sovereignly distributes spiritual gifts to each
1 Cor 12:13	Believers were baptized with one Spirit into one body
1 Cor 14:2	The person who speaks in tongues speaks mysteries in the Spirit
1 Cor 14:12	Zealous for manifestations of the Spirit, strive to excel in building others up

Summary

Paul's first letter to the Corinthians is particularly rich in its teaching on the Holy Spirit. Paul uses the term "Holy Spirit" only twice (6:19; 12:3); more commonly he refers simply to "the Spirit" or "the Spirit of God." First, close to half of the references to the Spirit (nine instances) are found in chapter 12, where Paul refers to the Spirit repeatedly as "the same Spirit" in conjunction with expressions such as "one Spirit," "the common good," and "one and the same Spirit." This underscores that in Paul's theology of the Spirit in 1 Corinthians, congregational *unity* takes center stage. This also highlights the fact that not only chapters 1–6 but also chapters 7–16, including Paul's teaching on spiritual gifts in chapters 12–14, are written primarily to promote unity in the church at Corinth, particularly in the harmonious and orderly exercise of spiritual gifts (14:40; cf. 14:33). The Corinthians are already "zealous for manifestations of the Spirit"; now they must "seek to excel in building up the church" (14:12).

Another vital, second aspect of Paul's teaching on the Spirit in 1 Corinthians pertains to his argument in chapter 2 (six instances). While some disparage Paul's persona, presence, or allegedly inferior rhetoric vis-à-vis skilled rhetoricians such as Apollos, Paul contends that his message did come "with a demonstration of the Spirit's power," so that the Corinthians' "faith might not be based on human wisdom but on God's power" (2:4–5).

He goes on to defend the divine wisdom expressed in God's plan of redemption in the crucified Christ, "God's hidden wisdom in a mystery" that "none of the rulers of this age knew" (2:7–8). Due to his close relationship with God, the Spirit serves as divine agent of *revelation* (2:10). He also serves as a teacher of divine *wisdom* to those who have received by the Spirit and are thus spiritual people—"taught by the Spirit, explaining spiritual things to spiritual people" (2:13). This divine, Spirit-imparted wisdom also enables Paul to adjudicate the Corinthians' queries (7:40).

A third, final aspect of Paul's teaching on the Spirit in 1 Corinthians is related to *temple* imagery. The Spirit's presence fills both the *corporate* church and the *individual* believers that constitute it. Thus whoever threatens the church's unity or seeks to cause a believer to stumble in effect endeavors to destroy God's temple (3:16). As Paul states emphatically, this will incur severe divine judgment (3:17). Also, an individual believer's body is a "temple of the Holy Spirit"; believers are not their own (6:19), so they must maintain sexual purity and not unite their bodies in sexual intercourse with a temple prostitute, as apparently some in the Corinthian church have done.

2 Corinthians

Paul writes 2 Corinthians in large part to defend his apostolic authority against detractors in the Corinthian church (see esp. chs. 10–13). In so doing, he highlights the significance of his new covenant ministry vis-à-vis the old covenant ministry of Moses, provides teaching on NT giving in conjunction with his collection among the Gentiles for the Jerusalem church (chs. 8–9), and gives additional glimpses into his understanding of his ministry and other topics.[72]

---

[72] As Fee, 365, notes, 2 Corinthians constitutes the first time in Paul's letters (though not the last) that the giving of the Spirit marks the end of the old covenant, because he is the fulfillment of the promised new covenant. In what follows, discussion will be limited to explicit references to the Spirit; other possible implicit references include those to a "new creation" (5:17), to "visions and revelations" (12:1), to "power . . . perfected in weakness" (12:9–10), and to "signs, wonders, and miracles" (12:12). For an exploration of these additional themes see Moyer Hubbard, "2 Corinthians," in Burke and Warrington, *Biblical Theology of the Holy Spirit*, 168–74.

Introduction

In the context of defending his change of travel plans, which has kept him from visiting Corinth (1:15–20, 23–24), Paul writes, "Now it is God who strengthens us together with you in Christ, and who has anointed us. He has also put his seal [*sphragisamenos*; cf. Eph 1:13] on us and given us the Spirit in our hearts as a down payment [*arrabōn*; cf. 5:5; Eph 1:14]" (2 Cor: 121–22).[73] By referring to God's gift of the Spirit as a "seal" and a "down payment," Paul highlights the fact that "God is faithful" (v. 18) and that the coming of "the Son of God, Jesus Christ," proves that God always keeps his promises (v. 19). Thus God's gospel is absolutely trustworthy even if the plans of his messengers may change.

Body of the Letter[74]

The bulk of Paul's references to the Spirit in 2 Corinthians (seven out of eleven) are found in chapter 3 in conjunction with Paul's depiction of his new covenant ministry in comparison to the old covenant ministry of Moses.[75] Along a salvation-historical trajectory, the OT account of the giving of the law at Mount Sinai serves as the antecedent frame of reference:[76]

---

[73] See Kurt Erlemann, "Der Geist als ἀρραβών (2 Kor 5, 5) im Kontext der paulinischen Eschatologie," *ZNW* 83 (1992): 202–23, who stresses the nature of the ἀρραβών as a legal promissory note. Fee, *God's Empowering Presence*, 294, notes that the passage indicates the eschatological nature of the Spirit. A new age has dawned, evidenced by the "down payment," but has not yet fully arrived. Yet the Spirit's presence is a guarantee that the full inheritance will come.

[74] Murray J. Harris, *The Second Epistle to the Corinthians*, NIGTC (Grand Rapids: Eerdmans, 2005), 13, identifies 2:14–7:4 as a "massive digression" featuring Paul's defense of his apostolic ministry. All the references to the Spirit in 2 Corinthians except for the opening reference in 1:22 and the concluding reference in 13:14 are found in this section.

[75] See table 13.1 contrasting "the letter" and the Spirit in Hubbard, "2 Corinthians," 166.

[76] Space does not permit an in-depth exploration of this passage and its OT background. See esp. Exod 31:18; 34:27–35; Deut 9:10–11; Jer 31:33; and Ezek 11:19; 36:26–27. See Scott J. Hafemann, *Paul, Moses, and the History of Israel: The Letter/Spirit Contrast and the Argument from Scripture in 2 Corinthians 3*, WUNT 81 (Tübingen: Mohr Siebeck, 1995); John W. Yates, *The Spirit and Creation in Paul*, WUNT 2/251 (Tübingen, DEU: Mohr Siebeck, 2008); and Richard B. Hays,

- Unlike others, Paul needs no letters of recommendation (vv. 1–2): "You show that you are Christ's letter, delivered by us, not written with ink but with *the Spirit of the living God*—not on tables of stone but on tablets of human *hearts*" (v. 3; cf. Exod 24:12; 31:18; Ezek 11:19; 36:26).
- In contrast to Paul's Jewish-Christian opponents (cf. chs. 10–13), God has made Paul and his coworkers "ministers of a new covenant, not of the letter, but of *the Spirit*. For the letter kills, but *the Spirit* gives *life*" (v. 6; cf. 5:17; Jer 31:31; Ezek 1:20; 36:1–14; 37:14; Gal 5:25).[77]
- If Moses's "ministry that brought death, chiseled in letters on stones," came with glory, "will the ministry of *the Spirit* not be *more glorious*?" (vv. 7–8; cf. Exod 34:27–35).
- When a person turns to the Lord (i.e., by conversion),[78] the spiritual "veil" is removed: "Now the Lord is *the Spirit*, and where *the Spirit* of the Lord is, there is *freedom*" (v. 17; cf. Exod 34:34).[79]
- Paul concludes: "We all, with unveiled faces, are looking as in a mirror at the glory of the Lord and are being *transformed* into the same image from glory to glory; this is from the Lord who is *the Spirit*" (v. 18; cf. v. 17).

Paul's points related to the Spirit are as follows: (1) the Spirit operates on the human *heart* (v. 3); (2) the Spirit gives *life* (v. 6); (3) the Spirit conveys *glory* (v. 8);[80] (4) the Spirit imparts *freedom* (v. 17); and (5) the Spirit effects

---

Echoes of Scripture in the Letters of Paul (New Haven: Yale University Press, 1989), 122–53.

[77] Fee, *God's Empowering Presence*, 305, points out that the Spirit marks points of continuity (God and his promises, specifically the promise of a new covenant) as well as discontinuity (the fulfillment of the promise with the Spirit's coming and the inclusion of the Gentiles) between NT believers and the OT people of God. Paul's point here is that there is no reason to return to the old covenant, as it is unable to bring life because of a lack of the Spirit (307–8).

[78] See Hubbard, "2 Corinthians," 167n23, and the additional bibliographic references cited there.

[79] For a survey of interpretations of the meaning of "the Lord who is the Spirit," see Turner, *Holy Spirit*, 127–31.

[80] Philip, *Origins of Pauline Pneumatology*, 183–84, provides a clear summary of the role of the Spirit in this passage. He notes that Paul draws a parallel between the

spiritual *transformation* (v. 18).[81] In all these ways, Paul's gospel ministry is superior to that of Moses and the law: (1) the law consisted of external regulations; (2) law observance could not impart life; (3) the giving of the law resulted only in veiled glory, which is reflected rather than lasting; (4) the law could not effect true freedom from sin; and (5) the law was unable to transform a person's inner being.

In what follows, Paul reiterates that God has given the Spirit as a "down payment" (*arrabōn*, 5:5; cf. 1:22).[82] He also commends himself and his coworkers as servants of God by, among other things, "kindness, by the Holy Spirit, [and] by sincere love" (6:6).[83] This is part of a long triadic list of experience, qualities, or attributes by which Paul commends his apostolic ministry to the Corinthians who seem to have rejected Paul, at least temporarily. Thus he appeals to them not to "receive the grace of God in vain"

---

glory Moses saw and the glory Paul saw. Paul claims that the giving of the covenant to Moses was legitimized by the appearance of God's glory (כָּבוֹד); in a similar manner, Paul's stewardship of the gospel was legitimized by the attending of God's glory (δόξα). Paul goes on to show that though the old and new covenants shared some affinities, there was also a key difference: the presence of the Spirit. The giving of the old covenant lacked the Spirit and thus led to death while the giving of the new covenant includes the Spirit and therefore leads to life.

[81] See Hubbard, "2 Corinthians," 166–68. See especially Fee, *God's Empowering Presence*, 309–10, who comments: "Thus several previous themes are tied together in the conclusion in vv. 17–18: the Spirit as the evidence of the new covenant; for those who have the Spirit the veil is now removed; such 'unveiling' therefore means 'freedom' (cf. v. 12: 'boldness, freedom'); the 'freedom' that comes with the removal of the veil means that people now have access to God's presence so as to behold the 'glory' which the veil kept them from seeing; the 'glory' turns out now to be that of the Lord himself. In beholding this glory God's people are thereby 'transformed into the same likeness, from glory to glory.' Thus, in the final analysis, the Spirit of the living God not only gives us the life of God, but serves for us as God's presence and enables us to behold God's glory so that we are being transformed into his likeness. That is 'glory' indeed!"

[82] Fee, 327, observes that Paul views the presence of the Spirit not as a means of present ecstasy or ease but as a source of power to endure suffering and afflictions in the hope of future glory. Levison also draws out the significance of the legal or commercial connotations of the word ἀρραβών. In addition, he discusses the possibility of the word having religious connotations (*Filled with the Spirit*, 255–56).

[83] As Fee, *God's Empowering Presence*, 333, notes, the presence of the Spirit in this list demonstrates that these qualities, which may seem to be based simply on attitude or experience, are in fact the gifts of the Spirit that he enables believers to have.

(6:1)—even writing that "now is the day of salvation" (6:2)—and urges them to open up their hearts to him (6:13). The inclusion of the Holy Spirit in the above-mentioned list is perhaps surprising, though he is associated in this list with Spirit-induced qualities (called "fruit of the Spirit" in Gal 5:22–23) such as patience, kindness, and love (6:6).

Conclusion

The final reference to the Spirit is found in the last verse of the letter, where Paul writes, employing a trinitarian formula:

> The grace of *the Lord Jesus Christ*
>   and the love of *God*
>   and the fellowship of *the Holy Spirit*
> be with you all. (13:14 ESV)[84]

Summary

In the context of Paul's defense of his apostolic ministry to the Corinthians, 2 Corinthians contributes to the NT theology of the Holy Spirit the sustained contrast between the OT ministry of Moses as epitomized by the giving of the law at Sinai and the NT ministry of Paul as epitomized by the giving of the Spirit by God. In contrasting the ministries of the old and new covenants, Paul accentuates the Spirit's work in the human heart, his impartation of life, his conveyance of glory, his procurement of freedom, and his agency of transformation.

Twice Paul also presents the Spirit as a guarantee of believers' future spiritual inheritance, affirming that God is always faithful to keep his promises (1:22) and pointing out that our present bodies are groaning in

---

[84] See Fee, 363: "To be Christian one must finally understand God in a Trinitarian way." This text serves as an entry point into Paul's theology proper. His understanding of God has been inexorably shaped by the death and resurrection of Jesus and the gift of the Spirit (Fee, 363). Except for Phil 2:1, this is the only instance in the NT where "fellowship" (κοινωνία) and "Spirit" are connected, ending the letter on a conciliatory note (note that the frequency of the term "fellowship" in 2 Corinthians [ESV: 4x] is second in the NT only to 1 John).

Figure 21: References to the Spirit in 2 Corinthians

Scripture Passage	Content
2 Cor 1:22	God gave believers his Spirit as a down payment
2 Cor 3:3	The Corinthians are a letter written by the Spirit of the living God
2 Cor 3:6	Paul is a minister of the new covenant of the Spirit; the Spirit gives life
2 Cor 3:8	The ministry of the Spirit is more glorious than the ministry of the letter
2 Cor 3:17	The Lord is the Spirit, and where the Spirit of the Lord is, there is freedom
2 Cor 3:18	The Lord who is the Spirit transforms believers into ever greater glory
2 Cor 5:5	God gave believers his Spirit as a down payment (cf. 1:22)
2 Cor 6:6	The Holy Spirit is one of several items commending servants of God
2 Cor 13:14	The fellowship of the Holy Spirit be with you all (ESV)

expectation of a permanent dwelling (the resurrection body, 2 Cor 5:1–5; cf. 1 Corinthians 15). Paul speaks of the Holy Spirit as characterizing his ministry and thus commending it to the Corinthians (6:6) and in his closing trinitarian benediction refers to the fellowship the Holy Spirit produces among believers (13:14 ESV).

Romans

Unlike Galatians, Romans is not written to confront a particular heresy (though Paul's concern for Jewish-Gentile unity pervades the entire letter). For this reason, Paul is able to set forth the gospel he preaches— which in fact is the "gospel of God" (1:1)—more programmatically. While the early portions of the letter are devoted primarily to showing that Jews

---

138   THE HOLY SPIRIT

and Gentiles are equally sinners (3:23) and thus both justified by faith, not works of the law (3:26; cf. 1:16–17), the letter moves inexorably to a depiction of the "newness of the Spirit" (7:6), which represents the essence of the Christian life now that "apart from the law, the righteousness of God has been revealed" in Christ (3:21).[85] The center of gravity in Paul's theology of the Spirit in Romans is indisputably chapter 8, where the vast majority of references to the Spirit are found.[86] In fact, there are only four references to the Spirit in the first seven chapters, and then none at all from 9:2 to 14:16, with four additional references in chapter 15 pertaining to Paul's mission to the Gentiles. The following discussion will trace these references in order.[87]

Introduction: The Gospel of Justification by Faith in Christ (chs. 1–4)

At the very outset of his letter to the Romans, Paul speaks of "the gospel of *God*—which he promised beforehand through his prophets in the Holy Scriptures—concerning his *Son*, Jesus Christ our Lord, who was a descendant of David according to the flesh and was appointed to be the powerful Son of God according to the *Spirit* of holiness by the resurrection of the dead" (1:1–4).[88] The trinitarian nature of the statement is apparent: "the gospel of

---

[85] Cf. Fee, 473–75, who observes that the role of the Spirit is focused not primarily on his role in sanctification but on the fulfillment of the new covenant God had promised, demonstrating that Torah observance has come to an end and that Jews and Gentiles are united as God's people.

[86] James D. G. Dunn, *The Theology of Paul the Apostle* (Grand Rapids: Eerdmans, 1998), 438, calls Romans 8 "Paul's great Spirit chapter"; Trevor J. Burke, "Romans," in Burke and Warrington, *Biblical Theology of the Holy Spirit*, 138, describes Romans 8 as "the pinnacle of Paul's pneumatological language."

[87] For a similar approach, see Burke, "Romans."

[88] As Fee notes, "flesh" and "Spirit" stand in contrast to each other, but not in the negative contrast that normally characterizes Paul's discussion of "flesh" and "Spirit." Rather, the contrast is between the earthly/present age (which is coming to an end) and the eschatological age Christ's resurrection has inaugurated (*God's Empowering Presence*, 481–82). Regarding the significance of 1:4 for Paul's argument in the letter see Burke, "Romans," 129–30, with further bibliography. According to Burke, "the *pneuma*, present at the resurrection of the Son of God, signals the ushering in of a new era of the Spirit, thereby eclipsing the old era of the law which could never be

God . . . concerning his Son . . . according to the Spirit." The expression "the Spirit of holiness [*hagiosunē*]" is unusual, replacing the more common phrase "the Holy Spirit."[89] The life-giving Spirit's *powerful role in Christ's resurrection* (cf. 8:11) is highlighted as part of the content of Paul's gospel.[90] Paul will return to the Spirit later in his epistle in chapter 8, where, as mentioned, the greatest concentration of Spirit references in this letter is found.

The only other reference to the Spirit in the first major section of Romans is found at 2:29, where Paul redefines being a Jew as being "one inwardly" and circumcision as being "of the heart—by the Spirit, not the letter" (cf. Lev 26:41; Deut 10:16; Jer 4:4; 31:31–34).[91] The "Spirit/letter" contrast is reminiscent of Paul's extensive discussion in 2 Corinthians 3, which has already been discussed.

Benefits Conferred by the Gospel on the Believer (chs. 5–8)

Building on his exposition of justification by faith in Christ in the first four chapters of his letter to the Romans, Paul opens chapter 5 by stating, "Therefore, since we have been declared righteous by faith, we have peace with God through our Lord Jesus Christ." Not only do believers have access to God's grace by faith; they also have hope in God's glory (v. 2), and this hope "will not disappoint us, because God's love has been poured out in our hearts through the Holy Spirit who was given to us" (v. 5). The Holy Spirit is

---

kept perfectly or give life" (130). See Burke's entire discussion of 1:4 (and 8:11) on 131–34.

[89] The phrase is Semitic; it is also attested in *T. Levi* 18.11. I owe this reference to Burke, "Romans," 132n17. Fee suggests that the phrase "Spirit of holiness" probably refers to the Spirit's role in producing holiness, which looks forward to later themes of the letter (*God's Empowering Presence*, 483).

[90] Coulson, "Jesus and the Spirit in Paul's Theology," 89, suggests that while the text does not explicitly mark the Spirit as the agent of Christ's resurrection, the text does imply his role.

[91] The reference to the Spirit here anticipates Paul's later argument of chs. 6–8, and the point made here is reaffirmed in 7:5–6 (Fee, *God's Empowering Presence*, 489). As Fee points out, Jesus Christ has inaugurated a new age through his resurrection in the Spirit (1:3–4). Just as the Spirit plays a role in ushering in this new age, he is also essential for working out the realities of this new age in the lives of believers (Fee, 489–90).

here presented as the *messenger of God's love* in Christ—the love God showed
when sending his Son to die for believers when they were still sinners (v. 8;
cf. John 3:16).[92]

Chapters 6 and 7 are devoted to a demonstration that the law is insuf-
ficient to deal effectively with the root problem of fallen humanity: the sin
nature with which every human being has been born since Adam. While
the Spirit is conspicuously absent from Paul's demonstration of humanity's
dilemma in Adam in 7:7–25, Paul does include a passing reference to the
Spirit in 7:6, where he asserts, "But now we have been released from the law,
since we have died to what held us, so that we may serve in the newness of
the Spirit and not in the old letter of the law" (cf. 2:29).[93] Paul will return
to this topic—the "newness of the Spirit"—in chapter 8 and develop it in
considerable detail.

It is hard to exaggerate the significance of the outburst of references
to the Spirit in chapter 8 of Paul's letter to the Romans.[94] Like a fireworks

---

[92] Burke, "Romans," 136: "The Spirit is the chief conduit by whom the believer
is made aware of the overwhelming love of God." Burke goes on to note that while
"the cross is, of course, the clearest, definable demonstration of God's love" for believers, Paul may also have in mind "the notion of God's love as an *experienced* reality"
(Burke, citing Douglas J. Moo, *The Epistle to the Romans*, NICNT [Grand Rapids:
Eerdmans, 1996], 305). Fee observes that God's love is not an abstract idea; it has
been demonstrated historically in Jesus's death and is experienced personally by every
believer. The Spirit both guarantees their future inheritance and strengthens them to
live as they wait for that inheritance to come to fruition (*God's Empowering Presence*,
496–97).

[93] Paul once again explicates that Christ's coming has brought one way of life
to an end (the old way, under the law) and begun a different way (the new way, by
the Spirit; Fee, 507–8). On the interpretation of Rom 7:13–25, see especially Ben
Witherington III, "'Almost Thou Persuadest Me . . .': The Importance of Greco-
Roman Rhetoric for the Understanding of the Text and Context of the NT," *JETS*
58 (2015): 83–87; but see the response by Stanley E. Porter, "'When It Was Clear
That We Could Not Persuade Him, We Gave Up and Said, "The Lord's Will Be
Done"' (Acts 21:14): Good Reasons to Stop Making Unproven Claims for Rhetorical
Criticism," *BBR* 26 (2016): 542–43.

[94] In Romans 8, Paul develops the idea he introduced in 7:5–6, that the Holy
Spirit is "God's alternative to Torah and antidote to the flesh"; the Spirit helps define
both believers' new relationship with God and their new way of living (Fee, *God's
Empowering Presence*, 515). The overarching concern of the letter should not be lost;
Fee describes it as follows: "(1) Jew and Gentile, equally disadvantaged through sin

grand finale, the Spirit is named eighteen times as Paul describes "the newness of the Spirit" (7:6) by those who have been justified by faith in Christ.[95]
The cumulative force of Paul's teaching on the Spirit in this chapter is perhaps best conveyed by a succinct successive listing of statements made by the
apostle regarding the Spirit's work in the believer's life:

- The law of the Spirit of life has set believers free from the law of sin
  and death (v. 2).[96]
- The law's requirements are fulfilled in those who walk according to
  the Spirit (v. 4).[97]
- Those who live according to the Spirit set their minds on the things
  of the Spirit (v. 5).[98]
- To set the mind on the Spirit is life and peace (v. 6).

---

and thus equally advantaged through Christ, form *one people of God*, which means (2)
that not only is there no advantage to Torah, but that the time of Torah has come
to an end with Christ; but (3) that does not mean that righteousness has come to
an end. To the contrary, *what the Law could not do because Sin was stronger than Law,
Christ and the Spirit have now done*" (515–16; emphasis original).

[95] Vv. 2, 4–6, 9–11, 13–16, 23, 26–27. Cf. Ben Witherington III and Laura M.
Ice, *The Shadow of the Almighty: Father, Son, and Holy Spirit in Biblical Perspective*
(Grand Rapids: Eerdmans, 2002), 130 (followed by Burke, "Romans," 139–40), who
observes that Paul emphasizes "the *personal* nature of the Holy Spirit" (emphasis
original) rather than describing his activity in impersonal terms (fire, water, wind,
etc.). Thus the Spirit leads believers (v. 14), bears witness (v. 16), helps believers in
their weakness, and intercedes for them (vv. 26,27).

[96] Note the possible connection with the reference to the "breath of life" in Gen
2:7. Fee calls the reference to the "Spirit of life" "perhaps the single most significant
designation of the Spirit in the Pauline corpus" (*God's Empowering Presence*, 525).
The Spirit is the Spirit of life because he is the Spirit of God who is the living God.
And he gives life to all who come to Christ (525–26).

[97] The verse does not indicate that believers, by their own efforts, fulfill the law
with the Spirit's help. Rather, it indicates that the law is fulfilled only in those who
have the Spirit (and therefore walk by the Spirit). The Spirit brings about righteousness in believers' lives, something the Torah was never able to do. This righteousness
is not Torah observance, however, but conformity to Christ and a life pleasing to
God (Fee, 534–37).

[98] In vv. 5–8 Paul is not describing the life of believers and the inner struggles
they face but contrasting two kinds of people—believers and unbelievers. Fee writes,
"Thus the absolutely basic description of Christian life, as Paul perceives it, begins
not with behavior as such, but with that which lies behind all life and behavior—a

- Believers are in the Spirit if the Spirit of God lives in them; whoever does not have the Spirit of Christ does not belong to him (v. 9).[99]
- The Spirit gives life because of righteousness (v. 10).[100]
- The Spirit of the one who raised Jesus from the dead lives in believers; his Spirit will also bring their mortal bodies to life (v. 11; cf. 1:4).[101]
- Believers will live if they put to death the deeds of the body by the Spirit (v. 13).
- All who are led by God's Spirit are God's sons (v. 14).[102]
- Believers have received the Spirit of adoption, crying out, "*Abba, Father!*" (v. 15).

---

mind set on God and his ways and that is intent upon what is in keeping with the Spirit" (541).

[99] Robert Jewett, "The Question of the 'Apportioned Spirit' in Paul's Letters," in Stanton, Longenecker, and Barton, *Holy Spirit and Christian Origins*, 197, notes the strong connection Paul draws between the presence of the Spirit in 8:9 and the presence of Christ in 8:10. For a Christian, having the Spirit is tantamount to having Christ.

[100] "Because of righteousness" is a reference to the righteousness of Christ he has given to believers. The idea is that the Spirit is the source of eternal life for believers because Christ has given them righteousness through his death and resurrection (Fee, *God's Empowering Presence*, 551–52).

[101] See the discussion of 8:11 in relation to 1:4 in Burke, "Romans," 132–34. Coulson, "Jesus and the Spirit in Paul's Theology," 91, suggests that while the verse may not explicitly connect Christ's resurrection to the agency of the Spirit, this is a theological implication supported by the verse. He goes on to highlight both the similarities and the differences between the role of the Spirit in Christ's and believers' resurrections: "Christ is the first human to be raised from the dead [never to rise again], but he is not the same as other humans. He is the divine human who makes it possible for all other humans to be raised. And now as the risen Lord he, together with God the Father, is the source of the Spirit (Rom 8:9; Gal 4:6) through whom God's people will ultimately be raised (Rom 8:11)" (94).

[102] Paul's emphasis in 8:14–17 is on encouragement. The Spirit who leads believers in the new life is the Spirit who caused them to become God's children: "True righteousness is not so much obedience to behavioral regulations as it is the living out of a new relationship with God—as his 'sons,' conformed to the likeness of his Son" (Fee, *God's Empowering Presence*, 561).

- The Spirit bears witness with believers' spirits that they are God's children (v. 16).[103]
- Believers have the firstfruits of the Spirit, eagerly awaiting adoption (v. 23).[104]
- The Spirit himself intercedes for believers with unspoken groans (v. 26).[105]
- God knows the mind of the Spirit; the Spirit intercedes according to God's will (v. 27).

By way of summary—and we can do little more than summarize the essence of Paul's teaching here—among the most important assertions made in this chapter are these:[106] (1) Possession of the Spirit is the fundamental prerequisite for being a Christian (v. 9). (2) The righteous requirements of the law are met by those who walk in the Spirit, yet believers are to put to

---

[103] See the discussion of this verse in Heliso, "Divine Spirit and Human Spirit in Paul," 168–71.

[104] Fee observes that this is the main point of vv. 18–27. While creation presently suffers, and believers suffer as well, the Spirit guarantees their final adoption (*God's Empowering Presence*, 572–73). The agricultural metaphor of firstfruits is found frequently in the OT, particularly in conjunction with the Feast of Firstfruits (e.g., Lev 23:10); fifty days later, the Feast of Pentecost marked the end of the grain harvest. Paul accounts for seven of the nine NT uses of the term "firstfruits" (ἀπαρχή), with the closest Pauline parallel to the present passage being 2 Thess 2:13.

[105] Thomas R. Schreiner, Romans, BECNT (Grand Rapids: Baker, 1998), 446, suggests: "God searches the hearts of believers and finds unutterable longings to conform their lives to the will of God. The Holy Spirit takes these groanings and presents them before God in an articulate form."

[106] For studies of Rom 8:1–17, see Gerald Bray, "The Work of the Spirit (Romans 8:1–17)," *Evangel* 19 (2001): 65–69; and J. Ayodeji Adewuya, "The Holy Spirit and Sanctification in Romans 8:1–17," *Journal of Pentecostal Theology* 9 (2001): 71–84. For a study of Rom 8:1–27, see John A. Bertone, "The Function of the Spirit in the Dialectic between God's Soteriological Plan Enacted but Not Yet Culminated," *Journal of Pentecostal Theology* 15 (1999): 75–97. For a study of Rom 8:12–27, see James D. G. Dunn, "Spirit Speech: Reflections on Romans 8:12–27," in *Romans and the People of God: Essays in Honor of Gordon D. Fee on the Occasion of His 65th Birthday*, ed. Sven K. Soderlund and N. T. Wright (Grand Rapids: Eerdmans, 1999), 82–91. For studies of Romans 8, see Richard J. Dillon, "The Spirit as Taskmaster and Troublemaker in Romans 8," *CBQ* 60 (1998): 682–702; and Roger L. Hahn, "Pneumatology in Romans 8: Its Historical and Theological Context," *Wesleyan Theological Journal* 21.1–2 (1986): 74–90.

death the deeds of the body by the Spirit (vv. 4, 13).[107] (3) Life in the Spirit
is freedom from bondage to sin—even though the sin nature remains—
as well as righteousness, life, and peace (vv. 2, 6, 10). (4) The same Spirit
who raised Jesus from the dead will also give life to believers' mortal bodies
(v. 11). (5) The Spirit conveys to believers their sense of spiritual adoption
and sonship, which entails not only a past and present, but also a future,
reality (vv. 14–16, 23).[108] (6) The Spirit intercedes for believers according to
God's will (vv. 26, 27).[109] Paul closes this section triumphantly as he sums up:

> We know that all things work together for the good of those who
> love God, who are called according to his purpose. For those he
> foreknew he also predestined to be conformed to the image of his
> Son, so that he would be the firstborn among many brothers and

---

[107] See the discussion of 8:13–14 in Burke, "Romans," 136–37. Burke notes that
it is the Spirit who enables believers to put to death the flesh. He also observes that
in the honor-shame culture of the Greco-Roman world of Paul's day, children were
expected not "to say or do anything that would have tarnished or besmirched the
father's name or that of the household." Cf. Wedderburn, "Pauline Pneumatology and
Pauline Theology," in Stanton, Longenecker, and Barton, *Holy Spirit and Christian
Origins*, 154, who writes that the theme of the Spirit in Romans 8 is related to Paul's
overall apologetic thrust in the letter and in part serves as a defense against the
charge of antinomianism.

[108] Paul's argument in vv. 18–30 is that the Spirit not only guarantees that God
will complete his redemption in believers but also enables them to live in the present,
interceding for them (Fee, *God's Empowering Presence*, 571).

[109] Burke ("Romans," 140) notes that while the Spirit is distinct from God or
Christ, he is not at cross-purposes with them but works in tandem with them. As
E. A. Obeng, "The Origin of the Spirit Intercession Motif in Rom. 8.26," *NTS*
32 (1986): 621–32, observes, Paul is "the first to clearly speak of the Spirit as an
intercessor" (cited in Burke, "Romans," 140). Later in the chapter Christ is also said
to intercede for believers (8:34). See also Kenneth Berding, "Who Searches Hearts
and What Does He Know in Romans 8:27?" *Journal of Biblical and Pneumatological
Research* 5 (2013): 94–108, who unpersuasively proposes that Rom 8:27 says not
that God knows the mind of the Spirit but that the Spirit knows that the mind of
the believer is set on the Spirit; and Timothy Wiarda, "What God Knows When
the Spirit Intercedes," *BBR* 17 (2007): 297–311, investigating "what Paul's teaching about the Spirit's intercession might contribute to theological discussion about
God's capacity to be touched by human suffering" (297).

sisters. And those he predestined, he also called; and those he called, he also justified; and those he justified, he also glorified. (vv. 28–30).

Paul follows this with the rhetorical question, "If God is for us, who is against us? He did not even spare his own Son but offered him up for us all. How will he not also with him grant us everything?" (vv. 31–32). Paul is convinced that nothing will be able to separate believers from God's love in Jesus Christ (v. 39). With this, we have reached a high point in Paul's, and the NT's, teaching on the Holy Spirit and his vital function in believers' lives.

Israel's Rejection of the Gospel and Practical Implications of the Gospel (9:1–15:13)

In introducing his lament concerning Israel's large-scale rejection of the gospel, Paul writes, "I speak the truth in Christ—I am not lying; my conscience testifies to me through the Holy Spirit" (9:1). In this brief reference, the Holy Spirit is presented as bearing witness to the truth in Christ.[110] The reference to the Holy Spirit in this context is remarkable, as it was customary to invoke God as one's witness; the inescapable conclusion is that the Spirit is here implied to be divine.

Remarkably, the Spirit is absent from Paul's salvation-historical and eschatological discussion of the Jew-Gentile relationship in chapters 9–11 and from his exposition of the practical implications of the gospel in 12:1–15:13, except for a reference to the Spirit in 14:17 and then again in the final verse of this exposition, 15:13.[111] In the context of Paul's discussion of not causing those who are weak in faith to stumble, he writes, "Therefore, do not let your good be slandered, for the kingdom of God is not eating and drinking, but righteousness, peace, and joy in the Holy

---

[110] Cf. Moo, *Romans*, 556 n. 7.

[111] Though Paul gives few explicit references to the Spirit after chapter 8, Munzinger makes a case for Paul's understanding of δοκιμάζω in Rom 12:1–2 as a Spirit-empowered activity as part of a renewed mind (cf. 1 Cor 2:16) within an eschatological framework (*Discerning the Spirits*, 21–44). Such a conclusion, if generally accurate, would place the entire unit 12:1–15:13 under the rubric of the Spirit's influence on the believer as seen in chap. 8. This observation would also be reinforced by the reference to the Spirit in 15:13, the concluding verse of this section.

Spirit" (14:16–17).[112] Similarly, Paul closes the body of his letter with the benediction, "Now may the God of hope fill you with all joy and peace as you believe so that you may overflow with hope by the power of the Holy Spirit" (15:13).[113] Thus in both passages the Holy Spirit is associated with peace and joy in believers' lives, with the additional reference to righteousness in 14:17.[114]

Conclusion (15:14–16:27)

As he moves toward a conclusion of his letter to the Romans, Paul identifies his calling as that of "a minister of Christ Jesus to the Gentiles, serving as a priest of the gospel of God. My purpose is that the Gentiles may be an acceptable offering, sanctified by the Holy Spirit" (15:16; cf. Isa 66:20).[115] "Sanctified by the Holy Spirit" here refers most likely to the Gentiles' being set apart at the moment of conversion as part of the progression of God's salvation-historical mission.[116] Paul proceeds by noting that he will not "say anything except *what Christ has accomplished through me* by word and

---

[112] Burke ("Romans," 138) invokes the way "biological siblings in antiquity were expected to behave by inculcating peaceable relations towards one another within the family." He adds, "The kingdom of God is not only about what you *eat* but also how you *treat* another brother or sister in Christ, where the transforming presence and power of the Holy Spirit is the means by which the Christian virtues of righteousness, peace and joy are exemplified in the lives of these end-time siblings" (Burke, 138).

[113] Fee notes that here Paul makes explicit what is often implicit: the Holy Spirit and power are intimately connected (*God's Empowering Presence*, 624).

[114] Fee points out that the peace in view here is not inner peace but the peace that should characterize believers' lives in community. In the present instance, the Spirit does not lead Gentiles to flaunt their freedom nor Jews to demand Torah observance but rather enables these two groups to live in peace. Peace and joy are intimately related, so that where there is peace in the Spirit, there also is joy (617–21).

[115] For a listing of cultic vocabulary in the context, see Burke, "Romans," 141 (see 141–42 for his discussion of 15:16). See also David J. Downs, "'The Offering of the Gentiles' in Romans 15.16," *JSNT* 29 (2006): 173–86, who unpersuasively argues for a subjective genitive in the present verse.

[116] David G. Peterson, *Possessed by God: A New Testament Theology of Sanctification and Holiness* (Leicester, UK: Apollos, 1995), 58–60.

deed for the obedience of the Gentiles, by the power of miraculous signs and wonders, and *by the power of God's Spirit.* As a result, I have fully proclaimed the gospel of Christ from Jerusalem all the way around to Illyricum" (15:18–19: cf. 1:4; see also 1 Thess 1:5; 1 Cor 2:4).[117] Paul's entire mission is what "Christ has accomplished" through him "by the power of the Spirit of God."[118]

The final reference in Romans to the Spirit forms part of a concluding appeal and a series of prayer requests: "Now I appeal to you, brothers and sisters, through our Lord Jesus Christ and through the love of the Spirit, to strive together with me in fervent prayers to God on my behalf. Pray that I may be rescued from the unbelievers in Judea, that my ministry to Jerusalem may be acceptable to the saints, and that, by God's will, I may come to you with joy and be refreshed together with you" (15:30–32). Notably, the Spirit is juxtaposed with the Lord Jesus Christ, and for the second time in the letter—though the phrasing "the love of the Spirit" is unusual—the Spirit is mentioned in conjunction with love (cf. 5:5).[119]

---

[117] Fee notes that the Spirit is the means Christ uses to accomplish his work, making it impossible to hold to any form of "Spirit Christology" (*God's Empowering Presence*, 630). See also the discussion of 15:18–19 in Burke, "Romans," 143–44.

[118] On Paul as a missionary, see Trevor J. Burke and Brian S. Rosner, *Paul as Missionary: Identity, Activity, Theology, and Practice* (London: T&T Clark, 2011); Robert L. Plummer, *Paul's Understanding of the Church's Mission: Did the Apostle Paul Expect the Early Christian Communities to Evangelize?* (Milton Keynes, UK: Paternoster, 2006); Eckhard J. Schnabel, *Early Christian Mission*, 2 vols. (Downers Grove: InterVarsity, 2004); though note that many studies of Paul's missionary activity neglect the role of the Spirit (as noted by Burke, "Romans," 143, who cites Thomas R. Schreiner, *Paul, Apostle of God's Glory in Christ: A Pauline Theology* [Downers Grove: InterVarsity, 2001]; and Eckhard J. Schnabel, *Paul the Missionary: Realities, Strategies, and Methods* [Downers Grove: InterVarsity, 2008]).

[119] "Love of the Spirit" likely refers to the Spirit's work in a believer's life in developing love for other believers (Fee, *God's Empowering Presence*, 633).

Figure 22: References to the Spirit in Romans

Scripture Passage	Content
Rom 1:4	Jesus was appointed to be the powerful Son of God according to the Spirit of holiness
Rom 2:29	Circumcision is of the heart, by the Spirit, not the letter
Rom 5:5	God's love poured into believers' hearts through the Holy Spirit
Rom 7:6	Believers serve in the newness of the Spirit, not the old letter of the law
Rom 8:2	The law of the Spirit of life has set believers free from the law of sin
Rom 8:4	Law's requirement fulfilled in those who walk according to the Spirit
Rom 8:5	Those who live according to the Spirit set minds on the things of the Spirit
Rom 8:6	The mindset of the Spirit is life and peace
Rom 8:9	Believers are in the Spirit if the Spirit of God lives in them; those devoid of the Spirit of Christ do not belong to him
Rom 8:10	The Spirit gives life because of righteousness
Rom 8:11	The Spirit of him who raised Jesus from the dead lives in believers; his Spirit will also bring your mortal bodies to life
Rom 8:13	Believers will live if they put to death the deeds of the body by the Spirit
Rom 8:14	All who are led by God's Spirit are God's sons
Rom 8:15	Believers have received the Spirit of adoption, crying out, "*Abba*, Father!"
Rom 8:16	The Spirit bears witness with our spirit that we are God's children

Rom 8:23	Believers have firstfruits of the Spirit, eagerly awaiting adoption
Rom 8:26	The Spirit himself intercedes for believers with unspoken groanings
Rom 8:27	God knows the mind of the Spirit; Spirit intercedes according to God's will
Rom 9:1	Paul's conscience testifies to him through the Holy Spirit
Rom 14:17	The kingdom of God is righteousness, peace, and joy in the Holy Spirit
Rom 15:13	May you overflow with hope by the power of the Holy Spirit
Rom 15:16	The offering of the Gentiles, sanctified by the Holy Spirit
Rom 15:19	By the power of signs and wonders, by the power of God's Spirit
Rom 15:30	Paul's appeal through our Lord Jesus Christ and by the love of the Spirit

Summary

It is hard to imagine Paul emphasizing the importance of the Spirit more strongly than he does in Romans.[120] At the outset he underscores the Spirit's powerful role in Christ's resurrection as an important part of God's gospel in his Son (1:4). Later, at the end of chapter 2, Paul affirms that circumcision is of the heart and that a Jew is one inwardly (2:29), asserting the Spirit/letter contrast familiar from 2 Corinthians 3. Building on his teaching on justification by faith in Christ in chapters 3–4, Paul opens chapter 5 by referring to

---

[120] Fee contends that Paul shows the Spirit as a central reality of almost every area of the Christian life: holy living (8:12–13); conversion (8:14–17); worship (12:3–8); community relationships (14:17); and gospel proclamation (15:18–19). The central areas of Christian doctrine are also intimately connected with the Spirit. Fee concludes, "Here is the certain evidence that one simply cannot have a truly Pauline theology without giving serious attention to the role of the Spirit in that theology" (634).

the Spirit as the messenger of God's love in believers' hearts, the very love that prompted God to send his Son to die for sins while we were still sinners (5:5; cf. v. 8). A rare reference to the Spirit in chapters 6–7 is found at 7:6, where Paul contrasts "the newness of the Spirit" with the letter of the law (cf. 2:29; chap. 8).

The climax of Paul's teaching on the Spirit is reached in chapter 8, which features as many as eighteen references. Among the points Paul makes are these: (1) Possession of the Spirit is essential for being a Christian (v. 9). (2) The requirements of the law are met by those who walk in the Spirit, but they must still put to death by the Spirit the deeds of the flesh (vv. 4, 13). (3) Life in the Spirit is a life of freedom, righteousness, life, and peace (vv. 2, 6, 10). (4) The same Spirit who raised Jesus from the dead will also bring believers' mortal bodies to live (v. 11). (5) The Spirit conveys the present and future reality of adoption and sonship (vv. 14, 15, 16, 23). (6) The Spirit intercedes for believers in keeping with God's will (vv. 26, 27). Thus the "newness of life in the Spirit" is qualitatively superior to life under the law.

In chapter 9 Paul invokes the Spirit as his witness (v. 1), thereby signaling his understanding that the Spirit is divine, and after a long hiatus mentions the Spirit twice more in the body of the letter in 14:17 and 15:13 in conjunction with the peace, joy, and righteousness the Spirit brings as part of life in the kingdom of God. The conclusion features three additional references to the Spirit in 15:16, 19, and 30, all related to Paul's ministry to the Gentiles: they are a priestly offering to the Lord (v. 16); Paul's ministry to the Gentiles is undergirded by signs and wonders and the power of God's Spirit (v. 19); and Paul asks for prayer as he prepares to come to Rome via Jerusalem, appealing to the Roman believers by the Lord Jesus Christ and "through the love of the Spirit" (v. 30). In this way Paul establishes a vital connection between himself and the recipients of his letter before his visit.

Ephesians

Among the Prison Epistles (Philippians, Ephesians, Colossians, and Philemon), it is only Ephesians that exhibits a full-orbed theology of the Spirit, a fact that is all the more remarkable when set in contrast to the paucity of references to the Spirit in the three other prison epistles. While references to the Spirit are virtually absent from Colossians and Philemon,[121] Philippians does refer to the Spirit in three places: "Yes, and I will continue to rejoice because I know this [my imprisonment] will lead to my salvation through your prayers and help from the Spirit of Jesus Christ" (1:19);[122] "If then there is any encouragement in Christ, . . . if any fellowship with [or participation in] the Spirit . . ." (2:1); and "We are the circumcision, the ones who worship by the Spirit of God, [and] boast in Christ Jesus" (3:3).[123]

References to the Holy Spirit pervade the book of Ephesians and are found in every chapter of the letter, with a frequency of about two references per chapter.[124] This frequency of references attests to the prominence of the Spirit in the theology of the book.[125] After pronouncing a blessing on God the Father, who in Christ has blessed believers with every spiritual blessing—including predestination, adoption, redemption, forgiveness, and inheritance—Paul writes that, in Christ, believers at conversion were also sealed (*sphragizō*) with the Holy Spirit, who is the down payment (*arrabōn*) of believers' inheritance (1:13–14; cf. 1:3–12).[126]

---

[121] The sole exception being Col 1:8: "your love in the Spirit."

[122] Fee, *God's Empowering Presence*, 738, notes that Paul is drawing on Job 13:16 here (see Hays, *Echoes of Scripture in the Letters of Paul*, 21–24). Fee writes, "His obvious concern is *not* that he will be 'delivered' from his imprisonment, but that no matter how his current circumstances are resolved . . . God will both 'save' Paul and vindicate Christ and the gospel." Paul describes the Spirit as "the Spirit of Jesus" because his focus throughout this section is on Jesus and the gospel. Jesus dwells within him by the Spirit and will cause both Paul and the gospel to be vindicated and not brought to shame (*God's Empowering Presence*, 742).

[123] Note that in all three passages in Philippians, the Spirit is closely aligned with Christ.

[124] Eph 1:13, 17; 2:18, 22; 3:5, 16; 4:3, 4, 30; 5:18; 6:17, 18 (see fig. 24). In addition, the Spirit may be referred to in 1:3; 4:7, 23; 5:19, 26. See Max Turner, "Ephesians," in Burke and Warrington, *Biblical Theology of the Holy Spirit*, 187.

[125] The twelve references to the Spirit in Ephesians compare with Paul's other letters (canonical order) as follows: Romans: 28; 1 Corinthians: 24; 2 Corinthians: 9; Galatians: 16; Philippians: 3; Colossians: 1; 1 Thessalonians: 4; 2 Thessalonians: 1; 1 Timothy: 2; 2 Timothy: 1; Titus: 1. Per fig. 23 below, Ephesians ranks second after only Galatians in frequency of references to the Spirit in Paul's writings, ahead of Romans and 1 Corinthians. For specific references, see the appendix.

[126] The Holy Spirit, promised to Israel, has now also been bestowed upon the Gentiles, sealing them as well as believing Jews. This sealing is also the reason they

In light of this spiritual reality, Paul proceeds to pray that God would give believers "the Spirit of wisdom and revelation" so that they would be able to fathom the hope to which they were called, the wealth of their glorious inheritance, and the greatness of his power that raised Christ from the dead and now lives in them (1:15–20; cf. 1:3–14; 4:23).[127] Most likely, the nature of Paul's intercession for believers here is that he is praying that the Spirit believers have received upon conversion would increasingly act as a wisdom-imparting and revelation-illuminating person in their lives.[128]

In chapter 2 Paul contrasts the Holy Spirit with another spirit at work in those who disobey the gospel (vv. 1–4). He continues, "But God . . . made us alive with Christ . . . and raised us up with him and seated us with him in the heavens in Christ Jesus" (vv. 4–6). As Gentiles, they were once far off from God's covenant community, but now, "through him," both believing Jews and

---

have confidence that they will receive their full inheritance (Fee, *God's Empowering Presence*, 669). Here Paul's already/not yet mindset is clearly on display, as the Spirit marks God's people as his own but also serves as the guarantee of what is yet to come. The Spirit is "certain evidence that the future has been set in motion" (671). On the Spirit as a seal (σφραγίζω) and as a guarantee or first installment (ἀρραβών), see Paul's previous use of both terms in 2 Cor 1:22; ἀρραβών is used also in 2 Cor 5:5. See also Rom 8:23; 1 Cor 15:45.

[127] Fee, *God's Empowering Presence*, 675–76, notes that many English translations (NKJV, NASB, NRSV; but see NIV, ESV) treat πνεῦμα here as referring to "a spirit" rather than the Holy Spirit. He offers five reasons the Holy Spirit is in view: (1) The lack of the definite article is not determinative, and its absence from the following two genitive nouns makes it fit. (2) The language, as in Col 1:9, is drawn from Isa 11:2, with "revelation" substituted for "understanding," as the focus here is on the Spirit as revealer. (3) While the ultimate concern of the prayer is that people come to know God, the focus is on the object of the verb, the Spirit. (4) Paul's understanding of wisdom and revelation in the life of the body are clearly connected with the Spirit (Eph 3:5; cf. 1 Cor 2:10–13; 12:8). (5) To speak of "a spirit" of revelation is "to speak near nonsense. What, one wonders, can 'a spirit of revelation' possibly mean in *any* sense in English?" (676).

[128] See the discussion in Turner, "Ephesians," 192, who adds that it is the Spirit of prophecy who "leads *all* believers deeper into the kind of relational knowledge of God that roots them in the new-covenant life of salvation (cf. esp. 1 Cor. 2:6–16), and fuels their passionate binitarian devotion to God and the Lord Jesus" (citing Chris Tilling, *Paul's Divine Christology*, WUNT 2/323 [Tübingen, DEU: Mohr Siebeck, 2012]; and Tilling, "Ephesians and Divine Christology," in Marshall et al., *Spirit and Christ in the New Testament*, 177–97).

Gentiles "have access in one Spirit to the Father" (v. 18).[129] While it is Jesus who through his substitutionary cross-death has opened access to God's grace (Rom 5:1–2; Heb 10:19–20), the Spirit now mediates this access in concert with God's salvation-historical work and provision in Christ. While this is true individually, it is also true corporately: The Holy Spirit is the one who engenders unity between previously separated groups of people— Jews and Gentiles—in the body of Christ. What is more, in Christ believers "are also being built together for God's dwelling in the Spirit" (v. 22). Here Paul refers to the temple as a precursor of a spiritual dwelling place for God among his people, as he has done previously in his letters to the Corinthians.[130] Specifically, this seems to imply that in every place a local church is planted, there is a manifestation of the presence of God as his Spirit dwells in the spiritual "temple" of a community of believers.[131]

In chapter 3 Paul develops further the thought of believing Jews and Gentiles dwelling together in the church by speaking of it as a former "mystery" (v. 4, i.e., a previously undisclosed salvation truth) now revealed "to his holy apostles and prophets by the Spirit" (v. 5).[132] What is this "mystery"? It is that "the Gentiles are coheirs, members of the same body, and partners in the promise in Christ Jesus through the gospel" (v. 6). This is an important part of God's eschatological purpose: to unite all things under the supreme

---

[129] As Fee, *God's Empowering Presence*, 683, notes: "The subject of the clause, 'we both,' which may simply mean 'we both *alike* have access,' more likely implies in this context that 'we both *together* have access.'"

[130] See 1 Cor 3:16–17; 2 Cor 6:16; cf. 2 Chr 7:1–3. Later in Ephesians, see 5:18; on temple imagery, see Köstenberger, "What Does It Mean?".

[131] Cf. Turner, "Ephesians," 196: "When [Paul] refers to churches as the body of Christ, or God's temple, he does not mean there is a multiplicity of bodies or temples: the *ekklēsia*, however multiple, is only one, as each is the local manifestation of the one heavenly 'congregation.'"

[132] See esp. Andreas J. Köstenberger, "The Mystery of Christ and the Church: Head and Body, 'One Flesh,'" *TrinJ* 12 NS (1991): 79–94; D. A. Carson, "Mystery and Fulfillment: Toward a More Comprehensive Paradigm of Paul's Understanding of the Old and New," in *Justification and Variegated Nomism*, vol. 2: *The Paradoxes of Paul*, ed. D. A. Carson, Peter T. O'Brien, and Mark A. Seifrid, WUNT 181 (Grand Rapids: Baker, 2004), 393–436; and G. K. Beale and Benjamin L. Gladd, *Hidden but Now Revealed: A Biblical Theology of Mystery* (Downers Grove: InterVarsity, 2014).

authority of the Lord Jesus Christ (1:10).[133] After a brief excursus on the nature of his gospel ministry, Paul again prays that God may grant believers "according to the riches of his glory, to be strengthened with power in your inner being through his Spirit, and that Christ may dwell in your hearts through faith. I pray that you, being rooted and firmly established in love, may be able to comprehend with all the saints what is the length and width, height and depth of God's love, and to know Christ's love that surpasses knowledge, so that you may be filled with all the fullness of God" (vv. 16–19).[134] In both passages the Spirit is depicted as an agent of revelation, both in God's apostles and prophets and also in all believers, with the purpose that they might "be filled with all the fullness of God." The Spirit thus provides illumination and insight into the spiritual riches believers have been given in Christ.

In chapter 4, then, Paul further drives home the important ecclesiastical implications of Spirit-induced unity among believers, urging them to make "every effort to keep the unity of the Spirit through the bond of peace" (v. 3; cf. 2:22). Fee elaborates:

> The phrase, "the unity of the Spirit," recalls in a very direct way 2:18, where Paul says that through Christ we both (Jew and Gentile) together in the one Spirit have access to God. That is, even though finally at the practical level this will have to do with personal relationships within the community, in its first instance it refers to the "union" of the two peoples into the one new humanity, the one new people of God. The "unity of the Spirit" does not refer to some sentimental or esoteric unity that believers should work toward. Rather, Paul is speaking of something that exists prior to the exhortation.

---

[133] See Max Turner, "Mission and Meaning in Terms of Unity in Ephesians," in *Mission and Meaning*, 138–66; Turner, "Human Reconciliation in the New Testament with Special Reference to Philemon, Colossians and Ephesians," *European Journal of Theology* 16, no. 1 (2007): 37–47.

[134] Note the paradox of being able to "comprehend" that which "surpasses knowledge." Believers' conformity to God's character, brought about by the Spirit's power, is what it means to have the fruit of the Spirit in one's life. As Fee writes, "Being filled to all the fullness of God means to have God's character reproduced in the life of the believer by the power of the Spirit" (*God's Empowering Presence*, 697). See also the discussion of 1:15–20, esp. v. 17, above.

Whether they like it or not, their lavish experience of the Spirit, which they have in common with all others who belong to Christ, has made them members of the one body of Christ, both on the larger scale and in its more immediate expression in the local community and in their own (believing) households. So they may as well get on with "liking it" and demonstrate as much by the way they live. All of this, then, underscores that for the unity of Jew and Gentile to happen on the larger scale, it must first of all happen among people who regularly rub elbows with one another. They *are* the one body of Christ by their common life in the Spirit; the exhortation is that they bend every effort to maintain this unity of which life together in the Spirit is the predicate.[135]

Even more, believers have one hope, "one Lord, one faith, one baptism, one God and Father of all, who is above all and through all and in all" (vv. 4–6). How, then, could the church be anything less than unified? What is more, God has given the church gifts in the form of apostles, prophets, evangelists, and shepherd-teachers to equip believers for the work of ministry (v. 11). Christ is the head, and the church is his body (vv. 13–16). Later, a series of exhortations includes the following reference to the Holy Spirit: "And don't grieve God's Holy Spirit. You were sealed by him for the day of redemption" (v. 30; cf. 1:13).[136] In context, this refers to sins such as lying, anger, stealing, slander, and malice (vv. 25–29, 31), which undercut the day-to-day unity of

---

[135] Fee, 700–1. Verse 2 mentions four qualities that are necessary for maintaining the unity of the Spirit, three of which (gentleness, patience, love) are also included in the fruit of the Spirit listed in Galatians 5. And Paul mentions peace in v. 3, which means that four of the five qualities listed here are directly connected with the fruit of the Spirit (Fee, 699). As Fee notes, "Only as humility, gentleness, and forbearance exist among them—those virtues that stand in such direct opposition to the flesh with its self-centeredness—do they have any hope for maintaining the unity of the Spirit" (700).

[136] Fee points out that this is one of many texts that demonstrate the personal nature of the Holy Spirit. The importance of grasping the personal nature of the Spirit is particularly poignant here, for it is far easier to dismiss our sins when God is viewed as transcendent and distant. But the Spirit within us is personal; he is God, he is present with us, and our sin grieves him (715–16). See also the discussion of 1 Thess 5:19 ("Do not quench the Spirit"), earlier in the chapter, under "1–2 Thessalonians."

the body.[137] The allusion is clearly to Isa 63:10, where the prophet says that the Israelites "grieved [God's] Holy Spirit" in the wilderness during the exodus (cf. Isa 63:11–12; cf. Num 11:25–26).[138] Similarly, God's new covenant people are urged not to grieve the Holy Spirit by avoiding activities that are displeasing to God—not in their own strength but in the strength God supplies (cf. 2:8–10; 4:23–24).

The sole—albeit strategic—reference to the Holy Spirit in chapter 5 is found in v. 18: "And don't get drunk with wine . . . but be filled by the Spirit."[139] This (corporate) Spirit-filling is to be evidenced in the church gathered for worship in the form of Spirit-filled congregational worship (vv. 19–20) as well as in the form of God-honoring, Christ-centered, and Spirit-transformed relationships. Fee explains:

> [I]n its immediate context the imperative has to do with community life. Here, perhaps, is an even greater need—that God's people collectively be so "full of God" by his Spirit that our worship and our homes give full evidence of the Spirit's presence: . . . So then, Paul urges the communities to whom the letter is written, be filled with the fullness of God by his Spirit, and let that be evidenced not by

---

[137] The material here is directed toward the injunction in v. 2 to maintain the unity of the Spirit—these sins undo that unity—and from the material in vv. 17–24; the list further develops what it means not to live like the Gentiles (Fee, 713).

[138] Frank Thielman, *Ephesians*, BECNT (Grand Rapids: Baker, 2010), 318. See also the discussion in Köstenberger, "What Does It Mean," 232.

[139] The comparison with being drunk is not meant to suggest that believers should be "drunk" on the Spirit but rather suggests that the filling of the Spirit should be evident to others, much like being drunk is manifest in one's behavior (Fee, *God's Empowering Presence*, 721). The contrast between the folly of intoxication with wine and sober-minded wisdom was commonplace in the ancient world (cf., e.g., Sir 39:6). Harvey, *Anointed with the Spirit and Power*, 165, concurs with Fee (*God's Empowering Presence*, 722) that 5:15–6:9 is "the ultimate imperative in the Pauline corpus" (presumably, the imperative that subsumes all others). He contends that the OT language of being "full" or "filled with" the Spirit (e.g., Bezalel, Joshua, Micah) stands behind Paul's command to "be filled by the Spirit" in 5:18; Köstenberger, "What Does It Mean," 230, 234, adduces parallels with OT references to God's glory filling the temple.

Spirit-inebriation, but by behavior and worship that give full evidence of God's empowering presence.[140]

Such body life is displayed in marriages between Spirit-filled, submitted wives and Spirit-filled, Christlike husbands who love their wives, lead them sacrificially, and nurture them devotedly (vv. 21–32).[141] In this way, the Spirit infuses the church and human relationships with divine life and restores the husband-wife relationship to its original, God-intended design.[142]

Finally, toward the end of his letter in chapter 6, in the context of his discussion of the "full armor of God," Paul references the Holy Spirit two more times. In v. 17 he mentions as the final piece of the armor "the sword of the Spirit," which is the Word of God. According to Turner, Paul here refers to the way the Spirit "enables the understanding and interpretation of the gospel (through gifts of wisdom and revelation) that serves the Church as a sword to fend off the enemy's attack" against its "inaugurated eschatological unity."[143] In v. 18 Paul urges believers to pray "at all times in the Spirit with every prayer and request."[144] Praying "in the Spirit" means praying "under the Spirit's guidance and influence,"[145] as the Spirit is united with God and Christ and is the Spirit of wisdom and revelation.[146] The "sword of

[140] Gordon D. Fee, *God's Empowering Presence*, 722.

[141] See on this passage Köstenberger, "Mystery of Christ and the Church." Fee notes that while the imperative to be filled with the Spirit can be obeyed only by individuals, Paul's focus is on the community. He wants God's people as a body to be filled with the Spirit so that the corporate body exhibits God's presence (*God's Empowering Presence*, 722).

[142] See on this Andreas J. Köstenberger and Margaret E. Köstenberger, *God's Design for Man and Woman: A Biblical-Theological Survey* (Wheaton: Crossway, 2014), esp. 180–86.

[143] Turner, "Ephesians," 193, citing Fee, *God's Empowering Presence*, 728–29.

[144] As Fee notes, the injunction to "pray in the Spirit" should be understood as governing the rest of vv. 18–20, so that we are to "pray in the Spirit" for all believers, with Spirit-fueled prayer serving as a key aspect of evangelism (*God's Empowering Presence*, 732).

[145] Turner, "Ephesians," 193.

[146] Turner, 194. Dunn, *Jesus and the Spirit*, 239, underplays the person's role in "praying in the Spirit," saying that Paul refers only to "praying which is determined wholly by the Spirit, where the words and sentiments come to the pray-er's lips as given from God-inspired utterance."

the Spirit," that is, the Word of God, is thus a spiritual weapon in a believer's armor. The Spirit is also the agent through whom prayer is to be offered.[147]

To summarize, the dozen or so references to the Holy Spirit in Paul's letter to the Ephesians span a considerable spectrum. There are several categories of usage, which, while distinct, also overlap to a certain extent. (1) *Eschatological*: Believers were sealed with the Holy Spirit at conversion as the down payment guaranteeing their end-time inheritance (1:13–14; 4:30). (2) *Salvation-historical*: The Spirit plays a key role in bringing about Jewish-Gentile unity (2:18). They are built up as a spiritual temple (2:22). The bringing together of believing Jews and Gentiles into one body is a salvation-historical mystery now disclosed to Paul and others by the Spirit (3:5). Salvation-historical in nature as well is the allusion to God's people not grieving the Spirit (4:30), as they did in the days of Moses and the exodus (cf. Isa 63:10). (3) *Ecclesiological*: More broadly, the Spirit engenders congregational unity (4:3, 4). Believers are urged to be filled with the Spirit, issuing in God-honoring congregational worship and praise (5:18) as well as God-honoring relationships in the household, which is being restored to God's original design (5:21–6:9). (4) *Related to the Word of God and prayer*: Paul repeatedly prays that believers—who already have received the Spirit at conversion—be given the Spirit of wisdom and revelation (1:17). Also, the Spirit helps believers wield the spiritual weapon of the Word of God (6:17), and believers are to pray in the Spirit (6:18), that is, guided and influenced by his prompting and direction. Thus the Spirit has an eschatological, salvation-historical, and ecclesiological sphere of involvement and is actively involved in bringing about wisdom and revelation in response to believing prayer and in the interpretation and proclamation of God's Word (including the combating of false teaching).

---

[147] Cf. Fee, *God's Empowering Presence*, 730, who notes that praying in the Spirit is not a separate idea disconnected from the imagery of warfare and armor but constitutes another weapon with which believers are to fight. He adds, "Prayer is not simply our cry of desperation or our 'grocery list' of requests that we bring before our heavenly *Abba*; prayer is an activity inspired by God himself, through his Holy Spirit. It is God siding with his people and, by his own empowering presence, the Spirit of God himself bringing forth prayer that is in keeping with God's will and his ways" (731).

Figure 23: References to the Spirit in Ephesians

Scripture Passage	Content
Eph 1:13–14	Believers sealed with the Holy Spirit, down payment of inheritance
Eph 1:17	Paul prays that God would give believers the Spirit of wisdom and revelation
Eph 2:18	Jews and Gentiles both have access to the Father through Jesus in one Spirit
Eph 2:22	Believers are built into one dwelling for God in Jesus in/by the Spirit
Eph 3:5	Mystery of one body made up of believing Jews and Gentiles revealed by Spirit
Eph 3:16	Paul prays that believers be strengthened with power through the Spirit
Eph 4:3	Paul urges believers to maintain the unity of the Spirit in the bond of peace
Eph 4:4	There is one body and one Spirit, just as believers were called to one hope
Eph 4:30	Don't grieve God's Holy Spirit, by whom you are sealed for day of redemption
Eph 5:18, 21	Be filled by the Spirit . . . , submitting to one another . . .
Eph 6:17	Full armor of God includes the sword of the Spirit, which is the word of God
Eph 6:18	Believers are to pray in the Spirit at all times, with every prayer and request

1–2 Timothy, Titus[148]

While the Holy Spirit does not play a very prominent role in the letters to Timothy and Titus, the teaching on the Spirit in these letters does make a contribution to their theological message, in particular their soteriology.[149] The letters to Timothy and Titus are often understood as having been written pseudonymously at a stage in the early church at which the regular, powerful, and visible work of the Spirit has faded and charismatic ministry has been replaced by institutionalization,[150] particularly in the realm of leader-

---

[148] This section is adapted from Andreas J. Köstenberger, *Commentary on 1–2 Timothy and Titus*, BTCP (Nashville: B&H, 2017), 427–31. In this commentary I defend the Pauline authorship of 1–2 Timothy and Titus and provide a survey of themes in these letters, including pneumatology.

[149] On the Spirit in the letters to Timothy and Titus, see especially Mark L. Bailey, "Theology of Paul's Pastoral Epistles," in *A Biblical Theology of the New Testament*, ed. Roy B. Zuck and Darrell L. Bock (Chicago: Moody, 1994), 347–49; Mathew Clark, "The Pastoral Epistles," in Burke and Warrington, *Biblical Theology of the Holy Spirit*, 213–25; Michael A. G. Haykin, "The Fading Vision? The Spirit and Freedom in the Pastoral Epistles," *EvQ* 57 (1985): 291–305; Haykin, "A High Pneumatology: Leaning on the Holy Spirit in 2 Timothy," in *The Empire of the Holy Spirit* (Mountain Home: BorderStone, 2010), 113–25; I. Howard Marshall, "The Holy Spirit in the Pastoral Epistles and the Apostolic Fathers," in Stanton, Longenecker, and Barton, *Holy Spirit and Christian Origins*, 257–69; Jerome D. Quinn, "The Holy Spirit in the Pastoral Epistles," in *Sin, Salvation, and the Spirit*, ed. Daniel Durken (Collegeville, MN: Liturgical Press, 1979), 35–68; Ceslas Spicq, *Les épîtres pastorales*, 2 vols., 4th ed., Études Bibliques 39 (Paris: Gabalda, 1969), 254–56; Philip H. Towner, *The Goal of Our Instruction: The Structure of Theology and Ethics in the Pastoral Epistles*, JSNTSup 34 (Sheffield, UK: Sheffield Academic Press, 1989), 56–58; Paul Trebilco, "The Significance and Relevance of the Spirit in the Pastoral Epistles," in Stanton, Longenecker, and Barton, *Holy Spirit and Christian Origins*, 241–56. Cf. John Brug, "A Rebirth-Washing and a Renewal-Holy Spirit," *Wisconsin Lutheran Quarterly* 92 (1995): 124–28; Robert W. Wall, "Salvation's Bath by the Spirit: A Study of Titus 3:5b–6 in Its Canonical Setting," in Marshall et al., *Spirit and Christ in the New Testament*, 198–212.

[150] Note, e.g., Dunn, *Jesus and the Spirit*, who discusses the letters to Timothy and Titus in §57.3 (347–50) and finds several contrasts between what he considers to be authentic Pauline pneumatology and that of 1–2 Timothy and Titus: "The vision of charismatic community has faded . . . *Spirit and charisma have become in effect subordinate to office, to ritual, to tradition*" (349, emphasis original). Trebilco, "Significance and Relevance," 241, strikes a sort of mediating position; he sees the

ship in the church. Yet, beyond a (liturgical) reference to Christ as having been "vindicated in the Spirit" at his resurrection (1 Tim 3:16), these letters highlight the connection between the Spirit and prophecy (1 Tim 1:18; 4:1, 14), affirm the Spirit's activity in gifting Timothy for ministry (1 Tim 4:14; 2 Tim 1:6), and speak of the rich outpouring of the Spirit upon the body of believers (Titus 3:6).[151] Since the Spirit is connected with the rebirth and transformation accompanying salvation (Titus 3:5), it is clear that his initial and ongoing activity in believers is presupposed.[152] What is more, the instruction to Timothy to guard "through the Holy Spirit who lives in us" the teaching of Christ passed down through Paul (2 Tim 1:13–14)—relying on the Spirit to empower him to cling tenaciously to the teaching given to him—also presumably applies to the faithful men who follow in Timothy's steps (2 Tim 2:2).[153] We might also mention Paul's reference to the Scripture as "God-breathed" (*theopneustos*, 2 Tim 3:16 NIV), which may refer implicitly to the Spirit's role in inspiring Scripture.[154] The Spirit thus continues to be active in the church in the letters to Timothy and Titus.

---

letters to Timothy and Titus as post-Pauline yet argues that the pseudonymous author does not neglect the work of the Spirit but "relates the Spirit to crucial issues he faces, makes connections between the Spirit and other facets of his theology, and understands the Spirit's activity to involve new and different areas."

[151] Marshall, "Holy Spirit in the Pastoral Epistles," 258, notes the connection between the language of the "pouring out" of the Spirit in Titus 3:5–6 and the description of Pentecost (Acts 2:17–18, 33; cf. 10:45); cf. Quinn, "Holy Spirit in the Pastoral Epistles," 351–52. Marshall also points out that from the earliest stages of the church there was a "system of leadership and oversight alongside the tasks of ministry (1 Thessalonians; 1 Corinthians), and there is overlap in that some leadership is more by appointment (e.g., apostleship and local eldership), whereas other leadership is more charismatic" (268).

[152] As to the believer's ongoing transformation, Trebilco, "Significance and Relevance," 252, connects the key soteriological role the Spirit plays in Titus 3:5 with the life of good deeds and Christian ethics enjoined in the context (vv. 1–8).

[153] See Köstenberger, *Commentary on 1–2 Timothy and Titus*, 220–21.

[154] Marshall, "Holy Spirit in the Pastoral Epistles," 258, points out that θεόπνευστος is a "term which might arouse echoes of πνεῦμα for readers"; cf. Quinn, "Holy Spirit in the Pastoral Epistles," 361–64. It is likely that under the rubric of "Scripture" Paul includes his own and other apostolic writings still being produced, thus pointing to the continuing work of the Spirit via the inspiration of Scripture in the church.

Arguably the most significant and sustained passage on the Holy Spirit in the letters to Timothy and Titus is Titus 3:4–7.[155] In this passage, Paul states the means by which salvation is applied: a washing that brings about regeneration and renewal, effected by the Holy Spirit, whom God has poured out on believers abundantly through Jesus Christ their Savior. Fee describes this as "the absolutely crucial event that effects both the washing away of the sins in which we all once walked [Titus 3:3] and the regeneration necessary for the good works now urged upon God's new people [Titus 3:1–2, 8]."[156]

The reference to the Holy Spirit in Titus 3 is part of the "trustworthy" saying in vv. 4–7, the only one of the five such sayings in the letters to Timothy and Titus that contains a reference to the Spirit. The saying, a concise summary of Pauline soteriology and trinitarian in nature, focuses on God's salvation of believers through Christ and his regenerating work through the Holy Spirit.[157] Paul states that God saved us "not by works of righteousness that we had done, but according to his mercy" (v. 5). This salvation was accomplished "through the washing of regeneration and renewal by the Holy Spirit," whom God poured out on us abundantly through Jesus Christ our Savior (vv. 5–6).[158] "Regeneration" and "renewal" are both tied to the metaphor of "washing" by the Holy Spirit (Ezek 36:25–27). The generous "pouring out" (*ekcheō*) of the Spirit evokes OT prophetic language (Zech 12:10; Joel 3:1–2 LXX).

One additional cluster of references to the Holy Spirit in the letters to Timothy and Titus pertains to Timothy's preservation of Paul's apostolic teaching.[159] In 1 Tim 6:20 Paul exhorts Timothy to guard (cf. 5:21) what has been entrusted to him (*parathēkē*) for careful preservation: the apostolic teaching. In his second letter Paul similarly urges Timothy to guard with the

---

[155] Harvey, *Anointed with the Spirit and Power*, 177–78, identifies six major ways the Spirit ministers to his people in the new birth: he regenerates (Titus 3:5), confirms our adoption (Rom 8:15), acts as a seal (Eph 1:13–14), indwells (Rom 8:9), baptizes (1 Cor 12:13), and bestows gifts (1 Cor 12:4).

[156] Fee, *God's Empowering Presence*, 779.

[157] See Fee, 779. Paul once again expresses God's salvation with a reference to the Trinity: God saved us in his love, which he accomplished historically through Christ's work and applies personally to individuals by the work of the Spirit.

[158] "Washing of renewal" and "regeneration of the Holy Spirit" are parallel, governed by a single preposition, referring to the same event (Fee, 781–82).

[159] See Clark, "Pastoral Epistles," 217–19.

help of the Holy Spirit the "good deposit" entrusted to him (2 Tim 1:14; cf. 1 Tim 5:21; 6:20; 2 Tim 4:15). Timothy must guard the deposit he has received from his apostolic mentor with the help of the indwelling (*enoik-ountos*) Holy Spirit, just as God will guard the deposit of Paul's life until the final day (2 Tim 1:12, 14). This underscores the importance not only of sustained and committed effort on the part of Timothy but also of the need for the enablement of the indwelling Holy Spirit.

The Holy Spirit is also mentioned repeatedly in conjunction with Timothy's appointment to ministry. In 1 Tim 4:14 reference is made to his ordination service, when the council of elders laid hands on him (cf. 1:18). Paul urges Timothy not to neglect his gift but to exercise it diligently. In context, "gift" may refer to Timothy's empowerment for ministry given by the Holy Spirit. The "gift of God" (*to charisma tou theou*; 2 Tim 1:6)[160] that is in Timothy through the laying on of Paul's hands may be the pastoral ministry assigned to Timothy at his ordination service. Alternatively, the Holy Spirit may be in view, or a combination of the two (i.e., the Spirit as the source of Timothy's ministry assignment). In the face of timidity (v. 7) or persecution (v. 8), the divine gift will help Timothy overcome and persevere.

Figure 24: References to the Spirit in the Letters to Timothy and Titus

Scripture Passage	Content
1 Tim 3:16	Jesus was vindicated in the Spirit
1 Tim 4:1	The Spirit predicts large-scale end-time apostasy
2 Tim 1:14	Timothy is to guard the good deposit by the indwelling Holy Spirit
Titus 3:4–7	God saved us by washing of regeneration and renewal of the Holy Spirit

---

[160] Haykin, "Fading Vision," 298, suggests that "2 Tim 1:6 and its wider context contain the richest pneumatological vein in the Pastoral Epistles." He notes the conceptual similarity between this verse and 1 Thess 5:19, where "the Thessalonian believers are admonished not to quench the fiery power and light of the Spirit either by refusing to allow the exercise of the gifts of the Spirit or by ignoring them" (299).

In sum, while the Holy Spirit is not referred to very often in the letters to Timothy and Titus—though the handful of above-mentioned references are hardly insignificant, clustering around soteriology, ecclesiology, and the teaching ministry of Paul's apostolic delegates—he is certainly not absent from these letters.[161] The work of the Spirit is bound up with other important themes in the letters to Timothy and Titus,[162] and the pneumatology of the letters is consistent with that of Paul elsewhere.[163] Especially through the remarkable "trustworthy" saying in the letter to Titus, these letters make a significant contribution to NT pneumatology in conjunction with the Holy Spirit's role in salvation, in particular his work of rebirth, regeneration, and renewal, which is mentioned only infrequently elsewhere in the NT.[164]

Summary of Paul

Together with Luke and John, the "evangelists of the Holy Spirit," Paul is the preeminent theologian of the Spirit in the NT. Particularly prominent is Paul's teaching on the Spirit in his letters to the Galatians, Thessalonians, Corinthians, Romans, and Ephesians. In Galatians, Paul makes the programmatic salvation-historical point that the Gentiles' reception of the Spirit constitutes the fulfillment of God's promises to Abraham. In the fullness of time, God sent his Son, then his Spirit of adoption and sonship (Gal 4:4–7). Practically, this means that believers ought to walk in, be led by, live by, and

---

[161] Contra Eckhard J. Schnabel, "Paul, Timothy, and Titus: The Assumption of a Pseudonymous Author and of Pseudonymous Recipients in the Light of Literary, Theological, and Historical Evidence," in *Do Historical Matters Matter to Faith?* ed. James K. Hoffmeier and Dennis R. Magary (Wheaton: Crossway, 2012), 392.

[162] Trebilco, "Significance and Relevance," 251–54, explores the connection of the pneumatology of 1–2 Timothy and Titus with the letters' teaching on salvation, the Christian life, and Christ.

[163] See especially Fee, *God's Empowering Presence*, 757, 794–95. Trebilco, "Meaning and Significance," 254, demurs but notes certain shared features of pneumatology of the letters to Timothy and Titus and that of Paul's letters elsewhere: "the importance of the Spirit at conversion, the concept of the indwelling Spirit, the Spirit and living the Christian life, the Spirit and power, the Spirit and love, the Spirit and eschatology, and the connection between Christ and the Spirit."

[164] See, e.g., John 1:13; 3:3, 5, 7; 1 Pet 1:23; cf. 2 Pet 1:4; 1 John 2:29; 3:9; 5:1, 4.

keep in step with the Holy Spirit and exhibit his characteristics in their lives (Gal 5:16, 18, 22–25).

In his Thessalonian letters, Paul particularly highlights the Spirit's role in sanctification (1 Thess 4:8; 5:23; 2 Thess 2:13). In his first letter to the Corinthians, especially chapters 12–14, Paul stresses the Spirit's role in fostering congregational unity, no doubt against the backdrop of divisions in the Corinthian church. He also emphasizes the Spirit's role as an agent of revelation, most prominently in chapter 2, against the backdrop of undue focus on rhetorical brilliance. The Spirit is also pressed into service in the context of temple imagery, both individual and corporate, to stress the need for purity and separation from idol worship. In his second letter to the Corinthians, Paul refers extensively to the Spirit as part of the contrast between his apostolic new covenant ministry and Moses's old covenant ministry (chap. 3). The Spirit works directly in the human heart, imparts spiritual life, conveys divine glory, procures true freedom, and effects inner transformation.

The pinnacle of Paul's teaching on the Spirit is doubtless found in his letter to the Romans, particularly chapter 8. There Paul notes that possession of the Spirit is essential for being a Christian (v. 9); the law's requirements are met by those who walk in the Spirit (vv. 4, 13); life in the Spirit is marked by freedom, righteousness, life, and peace (vv. 2, 6, 10); the same Spirit who raised Jesus from the dead will also raise the mortal bodies of believers (v. 11); the Spirit conveys the present and future realities of adoption and sonship (vv. 14–16, 23) and intercedes for believers in keeping with God's will (vv. 26–27). Thus the "newness of life in the Spirit" is qualitatively superior to life under the law. In Ephesians, Paul notes the Spirit's role pertaining to eschatology, salvation history, and ecclesiology and related to the Word of God and prayer.

Continuing through Paul's letters, we find in Philippians the Spirit closely associated with Jesus Christ in connection with believers' help (1:19), fellowship (2:1), and worship (3:3). In all its three references in Philippians, the Spirit is closely associated with Jesus Christ. The letter also contains the uncommon phrase "fellowship with [or participation in, ESV] the Spirit," which has a Pauline antecedent and parallel only in 2 Cor 13:14. Colossians' sole contribution is the phrase "love in the Spirit" (1:8). In 1 Timothy the Spirit is featured in a hymn (1 Tim 3:16) and as the source of end-time prophecy (1 Tim 4:1). The sole reference to the Spirit in 2 Timothy refers to his indwelling believers and his role in guarding the gospel (2 Tim 1:14). Titus, finally, presents the Spirit as the agent of "the washing of regeneration and renewal" (3:5), poured out by God "abundantly through Jesus Christ our Savior" (v. 6).

Figure 25: Frequency of References to the Spirit in Paul's Writings

Pauline Writing	Number of References	Word Total	Percentage
Galatians	16	2,230	0.72
1 Thessalonians	4	1,481	0.27
2 Thessalonians	1	823	0.12
1 Corinthians	24	6,830	0.35
2 Corinthians	9	4,477	0.20
Romans	28	7,111	0.39
Ephesians	12	2,422	0.50
Colossians	1	1,582	0.06
Philippians	3	1,629	0.18
1 Timothy	2	1,591	0.13
Titus	1	659	0.02
2 Timothy	2	1,238	0.02

9

The Holy Spirit in the General Epistles and in Revelation

H aving surveyed the Bible's teaching on the Spirit in the OT, the four Gospels, the book of Acts, and Paul's writings, we will conclude with a discussion of the teaching on the Spirit in the General Epistles and Revelation.[1] While the epistle of James does not feature a single reference to the Spirit,[2] the letter to the Hebrews contains several such

---

[1] For a study of the Spirit in the General Epistles see Larry L. Lichtenwalter, "The Person and Work of the Holy Spirit in the General Epistles and the Book of Hebrews," *Journal of the Adventist Theological Society* 23, no. 2 (2012): 72–111 (see esp. conclusion on 108–11).

[2] Πνεῦμα occurs twice in the book of James, at 2:26 and 4:5. James 2:26 quite plainly refers to the human spirit, while the reference in 4:5 is less certain. For a discussion and arguments against πνεῦμα in 4:5 as referring to the Holy Spirit, see the commentary literature, e.g., Peter H. Davids, *Commentary on James*, NIGTC (Grand Rapids: Eerdmans, 1982), 163–64; Martin Dibelius and Heinrich Greeven, *James*, trans. Michael A. Williams, Hermeneia (Philadelphia: Fortress, 1975), 223–25; cf. Luke Timothy Johnson, *The Letter of James*, AB 37A (New York: Doubleday, 1995), 280–81; Douglas J. Moo, *The Letter of James*, PNTC (Grand Rapids: Eerdmans, 2000), 188–90. For the opposing position see Richard Bauckham, "The Spirit of God in Us Loathes Envy: James 4:5," in Stanton, Longenecker, and Barton, *Holy Spirit and Christian Origins*, 270–81; Ralph P. Martin, *James*, WBC 48 (Waco: Word, 1988), 149–51; and Thiselton, *Holy Spirit*, 152. More broadly, see William R. Baker, "Searching for the Holy Spirit in the Epistle to James: Is 'Wisdom' Equivalent?" *TynBul* 59 (2008): 293–315. Similarly, Lichtenwalter, "Person and Work of the Holy Spirit," 77–80, says that wisdom in James functions "much like the Spirit does elsewhere in the New Testament" (80).

references.[3] All of the writings covered in this chapter were most likely penned by apostles (1–2 Peter, 1–3 John, Revelation), apostolic associates (Hebrews), or, in Jude's case, one of Jesus's brothers, and thus convey authoritative, inspired, and trustworthy teaching that complements and concludes the biblical-theological material on the Spirit already discussed.

Hebrews

H. B. Swete asserts, "In Hebrews there is no theology of the spirit [*sic*]." Similarly, Barnabas Lindars contends that "the Spirit plays no part in the argument" of Hebrews.[4] Yet, while the Spirit is not the primary focal point of the argument in the letter, the author does appear to have a working theology of the Spirit that undergirds his overall presentation.[5] Altogether, the book features seven references to the Holy Spirit, including three in "warning passages" and three in relation to the Spirit's authorship or interpretation of Scripture.[6]

---

[3] While some may question whether it is legitimate to include the book of Hebrews under the rubric "General Epistles," such technicalities will not deter us here. For a discussion, see Daniel B. Wallace, "Medieval Manuscripts and Modern Evangelicals: Lessons from the Past, Guidance for the Future," *JETS* 60 (2017): 11–14.

[4] H. B. Swete, *The Holy Spirit in the New Testament* (1909; repr., Eugene: Wipf & Stock, 1998), 248–49; Barnabas Lindars, *The Theology of the Letter to the Hebrews*, NT Theology (Cambridge, UK: Cambridge University Press, 1991), 56, both cited in Jack Levison, "A Theology of the Spirit in the Letter to the Hebrews," *CBQ* 78 (2016): 90.

[5] See Alan K. Hodson, "Hebrews," in Burke and Warrington, *Biblical Theology of the Holy Spirit*, 226 (see his entire chapter, 226–37); and Levison, "Theology of the Spirit in the Letter to the Hebrews," 90–110, who contends that "the pneumatology of Hebrews is coherent" and "integral to the letter's argument" (90; cf. 109). See also David M. Allen, "The Forgotten Spirit: A Pentecostal Reading of the Letter to the Hebrews," *JPT* 18 (2009): 51–66; Werner Bieder, "Pneumatologische Aspekte im Hebräerbrief," in *Neues Testament und Geschichte*, ed. Heinrich Baltensweiler and Bo Reicke (Tübingen, DEU: Mohr Siebeck, 1972), 251–60; Martin Emmrich, "*Pneuma* in Hebrews: Prophet and Interpreter," *WTJ* 63 (2002): 55–71; Lichtenwalter, "Person and Work of the Holy Spirit," 98–108; and Steve Motyer, "The Spirit in Hebrews: No Longer Forgotten," in *Spirit and Christ in the New Testament and Christian Theology: Essays in Honor of Max Turner*, ed. I. Howard Marshall, Volker Rabens, and Cornelis Bennema (Grand Rapids: Eerdmans, 2012), 213–27.

[6] Four of the references are articular (3:7; 9:8; 10:15, 29); three are anarthrous (2:4; 6:4; 9:14). Thiselton, *Holy Spirit*, 153–55, identifies four "clear" references to the Holy Spirit in 2:4; 6:4; 3:7 (cf. 10:15); and 10:29; he classifies 9:14 as ambiguous

Toward the beginning of the letter, the author speaks of the great salvation his hearers or readers must not neglect, which "had its beginning when it was spoken of by the Lord, and it was confirmed to us by those who heard him. At the same time, God also testified by signs and wonders, various miracles, and distributions of gifts from the Holy Spirit according to his will" (2:3–4). The passage refers to the apostolic witness in the early church (Acts 2 furnishes the closest NT parallel).[7] Together with 6:4 and 10:29 (on which later in this section), 2:4 constitutes a triad of warning passages linking rejection of the gospel, of Jesus's sacrifice, and of the new covenant with rejection of the Spirit.[8]

Figure 26: The Holy Spirit in Warning Passages in Hebrews

Scripture Passage	Content
Heb 2:4	Warning not to disregard testimony of God by sovereign gifts of Holy Spirit
Heb 6:4	Warning not to disregard manifestations of the Holy Spirit as did wilderness Israel
Heb 10:29	Warning not to disregard Son of God/blood of covenant, outraging Spirit of grace

and omits discussion of 9:8. For an excellent discussion and defense of the non-determinative nature of the use or non-use of the article in references to the Holy Spirit, see Hodson, "Hebrews," 227 (with additional bibliographic references); similarly, Motyer, "Spirit in Hebrews," 216–17. Hodson provides a topical discussion of the seven references to the Holy Spirit in Hebrews under the three headings "The Spirit and the need for the new covenant" (3:7; 9:8; 10:15–18), "The Spirit and the inauguration of the new covenant" (9:13–14; 10:29), and "The Spirit and the authentication of the new-covenant people" (2:4; 6:4–6; Hodson, 228–36).

[7] See esp. vv. 2–3, 17–22. Cf. Hodson, "Hebrews," 234–35; Motyer, "Spirit in Hebrews," 216–20.

[8] Cf. Motyer, "Spirit in Hebrews," 215, who cites Allen, "Forgotten Spirit," 59, as stating that the Spirit is mentioned in four out of five warning passages in Hebrews. Moyer speculates that the recipients are Jewish Christians who still belong to the synagogue but also meet as messianic believers and exercise the gifts of the Spirit (215).

At 3:7 the author attributes Psalm 95, a foundational passage for his argument, to the Holy Spirit. This citation is part of the author's larger premise that through his Word God still speaks "today," a premise he develops in chapters 3–4 of his letter. In other words, the warning of Psalm 95 (which in turns harks back to the Pentateuch), "Today, if you hear his voice, do not harden your hearts," is still applicable in his day (and in ours as well). Rest from one's sin can be found only in Jesus, the greater Joshua.

The second warning passage involving the Spirit is found at 6:1–5, where the author writes that "it is impossible to renew to repentance those who were once enlightened, who tasted the heavenly gift, who shared in the Holy Spirit, who tasted God's good word and the powers of the coming age," to be restored to repentance. In context, the analogy is between the wilderness generation and the hearers/readers of the letter. "Shared in the Holy Spirit" is not necessarily to be taken as actual reception of the Spirit but may refer merely to external observation of manifestations of the Spirit in the lives of others in the believing community.[9] Just as blasphemy of the Holy Spirit could not be forgiven in Jesus's day, so denying and rejecting the Spirit's work in those around us in the age of the church may have severe ramifications, as no path to salvation remains for those who do so.[10]

In 9:8 the author asserts, "The Holy Spirit was making it clear that the way into the most holy place had not yet been disclosed while the first tabernacle was still standing." The context of this pronouncement is the nature of the old covenant and its stipulations (9:1–5), including a sacrificial system that provides only external rituals but cannot effect true inner cleansing (9:9–10). While no specific Scripture passage is cited, the author asserts that the Holy Spirit has made clear that, before Christ's high-priestly

---

[9] See, e.g., Wayne A. Grudem, "Perseverance of the Saints: A Case Study from Hebrews 6:4–6 and the Other Warning Passages of Hebrews," in *The Grace of God, the Bondage of the Will*, vol. 1, *Biblical and Practical Perspectives on Calvinism*, ed. Thomas R. Schreiner and Bruce A. Ware (Grand Rapids: Baker, 1995), 133–82, esp. 139–50. See also R. Bruce Compton, "Persevering and Falling Away: Reexamination of Hebrews 6:4–6," *DBSJ* 1 (1996): 135–67. F. F. Bruce, *The Epistle to the Hebrews*, NICNT (Grand Rapids: Eerdmans, 2012), 146–47, adduces the possible parallel of Simon Magus in Acts 8:9–24. Contra Hodson, "Hebrews," 235–36, who speaks of "entering into a 'partnership for life'" (236).

[10] On 6:4 see also Motyer, "Spirit in Hebrews," 220–22, who stresses the close connection between the Spirit and Christ (cf. 10:29).

substitutionary sacrifice, sinful humans did not have permanent access to the presence of a holy God (cf. 9:15).

Later in the same context, specifically the Day of Atonement, the author, in an argument from the lesser to the greater, writes, "If the blood of goats and bulls and the ashes of a young cow, sprinkling those who are defiled, sanctify for the purification of the flesh, how much more will the blood of Christ, who through the eternal Spirit offered himself without blemish to God, cleanse our consciences from dead works so that we can serve the living God?" (9:13–14). In this trinitarian reference Jesus is said to have offered himself in a priestly sense as a sacrifice to God "through the eternal Spirit,"[11] an expression designating the Holy Spirit not found elsewhere in Scripture.[12] By using the epithet "eternal" for the Holy Spirit, the author appears to presuppose the Spirit's deity.[13] It is possible that the phrase "eternal Spirit" is used here to accentuate the abiding effect of the shedding of the blood of Christ in providing definitive atonement for sin.[14]

Another reference to the Holy Spirit is found in 10:15, where authorship of Jer 31:33, "'This is the covenant I will make with the house of Israel after those days'—the LORD's declaration. 'I will put my teaching within them and write it on their hearts,'" is attributed to the Holy Spirit (cf. 3:7 above), as in

---

[11] Cf. Hodson, "Hebrews," 232: "If these verses . . . are not overtly Trinitarian, they come very close." Similarly, Motyer, "Spirit in Hebrews," 227, who says the passage "begins to move us . . . in the direction of trinitarian theology."

[12] This reference to the Holy Spirit is disputed (see Thiselton, *Holy Spirit*, 155); some contend that the reference is to Jesus's spirit, though this is improbable. See Hodson, "Hebrews," 231; Gary L. Cockerill, *The Epistle to the Hebrews*, NICNT (Grand Rapids: Eerdmans, 2012), 398–400. Hawthorne notes that if the Spirit was central to Jesus throughout his ministry, then how much more should we expect the Spirit to be central at the culmination of his ministry. He connects the Spirit to Jesus's obedience, empowering him to submit himself to the Father at this moment (*The Presence and the Power: The Significance of the Holy Spirit in the Life and Ministry of Jesus*, [Dallas: Word, 1991], 182–84).

[13] Hodson, "Hebrews," 232.

[14] Cf. Hodson, 232: "The most logical assumption is that the title 'eternal Spirit' is used because the Holy Spirit was intimately involved in the 'Christ-event' that procured both eternal redemption and eternal inheritance." Motyer, "Spirit in Hebrews," 227, goes further by arguing that here the author states that "the *flesh* of Christ is offered by the *Spirit* to God, and thus lays the foundation for the kind of spiritual discipleship *in the flesh*" expounded in chapters 11–13.

v. 17, "I will never again remember their sins and their lawless acts" (cf. Jer 31:34).[15] The author has previously provided an even more extensive quote of the same passage, Jer 31:31–34 (Heb 8:8–12). The passage is adduced in support of the author's central premise that the establishment of the new covenant in Christ has rendered the old one obsolete (8:13). According to the author, the Holy Spirit is thus closely associated with the provision of forgiveness for sins and the inauguration of a new covenant. The fact that authorship of Scripture is attributed to the Holy Spirit in both 3:7 and 10:15 suggests that the author believes the Holy Spirit to be God, the very God who inspired the Scriptures and is thus able to interpret them (9:8).[16]

Figure 27: The Holy Spirit and Scripture in Hebrews

Scripture Passage	Content
Heb 3:7	Holy Spirit author of Psalm 95: past first covenant, need for new covenant
Heb 9:8	No specific Scripture passage cited: inadequacy of first (old) covenant
Heb 10:15 (cf. v. 17)	Holy Spirit author of Jeremiah 31: future establishment of new covenant

The third and final "warning passage" involving the Holy Spirit and the final reference to the Spirit in Hebrews is found at 10:29, where the Spirit

---

[15] Remarkably, the citation of Ps 95:7–11 in Heb 3:7–11 is the third-longest instance of a NT use of the OT (67 words), and the citation of Jer 31:31–34 in Heb 8:8–12 is the longest such instance (141 words). What is more, both passages are the subject of sustained discussion and cited repeatedly: Psalm 95 in 3:15 and 4:7 (38 words) and Jeremiah 31 in 10:16–17 (32 words). Cf. Hodson, "Hebrews," 230n19.

[16] See the discussion in Hodson, "Hebrews," 228–30, who points out that "Hebrews is the only NT book to suggest that the Holy Spirit is the author of the OT text" (229). See also the discussion of "the Spirit and Scripture" in Motyer, "Spirit in Hebrews," 222–26, who contends that the Spirit is active not only by speaking through Scripture but also by engendering "charismatic experience" in the lives of both the author and his readers (226). Thus, Motyer argues, "the Holy Spirit now only comes with Christ the Son of God," and "the 'Hebrews' cannot keep their charismatic gifts just as Jews, no longer attached to Jesus" (226–27).

again is part of an argument from the lesser to the greater: "How much worse punishment do you think one will deserve who has trampled on the Son of God, who has regarded as profane [lit. "regarded as common"] the blood of the covenant by which he was sanctified, and who has insulted [*enubrizō*, a NT hapax legomenon] the Spirit of grace?" "Spirit of grace" is an unusual way of referring to the Holy Spirit (only here in the NT; in the OT found only at Zech 12:10);[17] most likely the expression is chosen to communicate that the Spirit conveys God's gracious favor, in contrast to those who reject God's sacrifice of his Son.[18] Notably, "the Son of God" (amplified by "blood of the covenant") is parallel to "the Spirit of grace."[19] The close connection between the Son and the Spirit is striking: when the Son is rejected, the Spirit is outraged, because in this case people are rejecting not only God's grace but also the Son's blood by which he has established a new covenant with his people.[20]

The Holy Spirit is not the primary focal point of the book of Hebrews; the author sets out to further demonstrate that Jesus has instituted the new covenant, rendering the old covenant obsolete. As part of this argument, the author establishes a vital connection between Word and Spirit, between *Scripture* and the Holy Spirit as its divine *author*. In this vein, two of the most important scriptural passages quoted in the book—Psalm 95 and Jeremiah 31—are attributed to the Holy Spirit (Heb 3:7; 10:15).

---

[17] Post-NT references include *1 Clem* 46:4–7 and *T. Jud* 24:2.

[18] Cockerill, *Hebrews*, 490n42. Hodson, "Hebrews," 233, thinks subjective and adjectival senses are both in view: the Spirit gives grace and is himself gracious. Theologically significant instances of "grace" (χάρις) in Hebrews are found in 2:9 (". . . by God's grace [Jesus] might taste death for everyone"); 4:16 ("Let us approach the throne of grace with boldness"); 12:15 ("Make sure that no one falls short of the grace of God"); and 13:9 ("It is good for the heart to be established by grace").

[19] David J. A. Clines, "The Parallelism of Greater Precision: Notes from Isaiah 40 for a Theory of Hebrew Poetry," in *On the Way to the Postmodern: Old Testament Essays 1967–1998* (Sheffield, UK: Sheffield Academic Press, 1998), 1:314–36, calls the construction a "parallelism of greater precision."

[20] Cf. Thiselton, *Holy Spirit*, 155: "The verb expresses the *hubris* of apostasy, as an insult to the holy presence. Heb. 10:29 belongs with 6:4–6 in arguing for the logical impossibility of genuine Christian profaning 'the blood of the covenant' and outraging 'the Spirit of grace.'"

Figure 28: References to the Spirit in Hebrews

Scripture Passage	Content
Heb 2:(1–)4	Warning #1: Do not disregard God's witness borne by gifts of Holy Spirit
Heb 3:7	Holy Spirit's authorship of Psalm 95
Heb 6:4	Warning #2: Impossible for those who shared in Holy Spirit to be restored
Heb 9:8	Holy Spirit indicates that the way into the holy place is not yet open
Heb 9:14	Christ offered himself up through "the eternal Spirit"
Heb 10:15 (cf. v. 17)	Holy Spirit's authorship of Jeremiah 31
Heb 10:29	Warning #3: Severe punishment for those who insult "Spirit of grace"

Not only does this mean that God put his imprint on the truths contained in these passages in the *past*, nor does it merely validate the *prophetic fulfillment* inherent in these passages, but on a larger scale it reveals the author's all-important *hermeneutical axiom* that in Scripture God still speaks today. Thus, in an important sense, Scripture is not merely a repository of ancient writings; rather, in the words of the author:

> the word of God is living and effective and sharper than any double-edged sword, penetrating as far as the separation of soul and spirit, joints and marrow. It is able to judge the thoughts and intentions of the heart. No creature is hidden from him, but all things are naked and exposed to the eyes of him to whom we must give an account. (4:12–13)[21]

In addition, the Holy Spirit is said to have had an integral role in Christ's sacrifice (9:14), which, in turn, is associated with the *obsolescence* and

---

[21] See the related NT passages 2 Tim 3:16 and 2 Pet 1:21.

inadequacy of the *old covenant* (9:8) and the provision of forgiveness of sins and the *establishment* of a *new covenant* in and through the substitutionary sacrifice of Christ.[22] This links the Spirit integrally with these central aspects of God's redemptive plan and the gospel message of forgiveness and salvation through Jesus's death on the cross for sinful humanity.

Thus, rather than standing idly by or remaining obliquely in the background, the Spirit is presented as working in and through the saving sacrifice of Christ and the formation of the new messianic community. This reality is further underscored by the fact, mentioned earlier, that the Spirit is identified as the author of key Scriptures that anticipate and predict these events. In this regard the Holy Spirit's work and presence in God's Word convey the contemporary relevance of these saving events and of the new covenant for the first readers and all readers since then.

The book also contains repeated warnings against offending or rejecting the manifestations of the Spirit (2:4; 6:4; 10:29). In 2:4 God is said to have testified "by signs and wonders, various miracles and distributions of gifts from the Holy Spirit according to his will" and performed during the apostolic era (2:4). This affirmation is made in the context of the warning, "How will we escape if we neglect such a great salvation?" (2:3). Similarly, in 6:4 a severe warning is issued not to reject the manifestations of the Holy Spirit as the Israelites did in the wilderness, incurring severe divine punishment as a result.

In 10:29 we find a triplet indicting one who

> has trampled on the Son of God, who has regarded as profane the blood of the covenant by which he was sanctified, and who has insulted the Spirit of grace.[23]

The close association between the Spirit and Jesus the Son of God and the blood of the covenant again points to the integral part the Spirit plays in Jesus's death and the new covenant. What is more, "the parallelism—the Son

---

[22] See Hodson, "Hebrews," 232, who notes, "Hebrews 9:14 is the only place in the NT to explicitly link the Holy Spirit with the death of Christ, showing that there is a real and vital connection between Christology, soteriology and pneumatology."

[23] See the discussion in Hodson, 232–34, who likewise identifies the "triplet" in the present passage (234).

of God, the blood of the covenant, and the Spirit of grace—indicates a very high doctrine of the Spirit."[24] Whoever rejects the Son also rejects the Spirit. In fact, the Spirit is "insulted" when the Son of God is "trampled on" and the blood of the covenant is "regarded as profane." What all three warning passages seem to presuppose is that the readers (or listeners) have witnessed manifestations of the Spirit and are exhorted not to reject them in unbelief.

1–2 Peter, Jude

Peter's NT epistles contribute an interesting set of references to the biblical teaching on the Holy Spirit.[25] Most of those are found in Peter's first letter; one significant passage (2 Pet 1:21) is found in his second epistle. Due to its affinity with 2 Peter, Jude will be treated under the present heading as well. The book contains two references to the Spirit, in vv. 19 and 20.

1 Peter

First Peter begins with a trinitarian reference to "the foreknowledge of God the Father,[26] through the sanctifying work [*hagiasmos*] to be obedient and to be sprinkled with the blood of Jesus Christ" (1 Pet 1:2). The recipients are identified as "those chosen, living as exiles dispersed abroad" (1:1; cf. 2:11: "strangers and exiles"), and the Spirit is said to be the agent of sanctification, a topic developed more fully in 1:13–25 and 2:11–23. Just as the Jews were to live holy lives in the Diaspora following the Babylonian exile, believers in Christ must remain spiritually distinct and set apart from their worldly sur-roundings.[27] The readers are chosen

---

[24] See Hodson, 237.

[25] See Lichtenwalter, "Person and Work of the Holy Spirit," 80–87.

[26] The "trinitarian overtone" is noted by Verena Schafroth, "1 and 2 Peter," in Burke and Warrington, *Biblical Theology of the Holy Spirit*, 239, and most com-mentators. Schafroth provides a topical discussion under the rubrics "the Spirit of consecration," "the Spirit in times of suffering," "the Spirit of prophecy," and "the life-giving Spirit." However, it seems preferable to discuss the references to the Spirit in 1–2 Peter in chronological order.

[27] The connection between pneumatology and living in the Diaspora is noted by Joel B. Green, "Faithful Witness in the Diaspora: The Holy Spirit in 1 Peter," in Stanton, Longenecker, and Barton, *Holy Spirit and Christian Origins*, 290–95. He

- according to the foreknowledge of God the Father,
- in (ESV) or through the sanctifying work of the Spirit,[28] and
- for obedience to Jesus Christ and for sprinkling with his blood. (1:2)

On the basis of (*kata*) God the Father's foreknowledge and election, through (*en*) the sanctification of the Spirit, believers are chosen for the purpose (*eis*) of living a "sanctified and pure life of obedience and service to God."[29] This sanctification or setting apart is best understood as consecration, that is, as setting apart for a priestly or cultic service (cf. Ezek 45:4 LXX).[30] Not only does the Spirit set believers apart to be consecrated for God's service; he also sets them apart to be sprinkled with Jesus's blood.[31]

The fact that believers are said to be set apart for obedience first, and only subsequently for sprinkling with Jesus's blood, makes it likely that the latter phrase does not refer to Jesus's atonement, which forms the basis for believers' salvation (if so, the clauses would most likely be reversed: sprinkling with Jesus's blood first, then obedience). Rather, it refers to Jesus's blood being sprinkled on believers *following* salvation, perhaps in conjunction with their setting apart for priestly service in the hostile world surrounding them.[32] Like Jesus, they are called to suffer for doing what is right, and this righteous suffering is a call to sacrifice and taking up one's cross as Jesus did.

In an important excursus or digression on the nature of the believer's salvation, Peter later writes, "Concerning this salvation, the prophets . . . inquired

---

suggests that Peter's pneumatology addresses two particular concerns faced by those in the Diaspora: the problem of assimilation and the pursuit of holiness. The Holy Spirit as the agent of sanctification empowers Christians to live faithfully as exiles.

[28] The ESV translates the preposition ἐν as "in." However, ἐν might here be better understood as instrumental, i.e., "through" or "by" (NIV). Cf., e.g., Greg W. Forbes, *1 Peter*, EGGNT (Nashville: B&H, 2014), 13.

[29] Schafroth, "1 and 2 Peter," 239.

[30] Nijay K. Gupta, "A Spiritual House of Royal Priests, Chosen and Honoured: The Presence and Function of Cultic Imagery in 1 Peter," *Perspectives in Religious Studies* 1 (2009): 63.

[31] See the connection between the "blood of the covenant" by which a person was "sanctified" and the Spirit in Heb 10:29 (on which see our discussion earlier in the chapter).

[32] See Schafroth, "1 and 2 Peter," 240, who adduces Lev 8:30 as possible antecedent, where Moses sprinkles blood from the altar on his brother, Aaron, and his sons, to set them apart to serve as priests.

into what time or what circumstances the Spirit of Christ within them was indicating when he testified in advance to the sufferings of Christ and the glories that would follow" (1 Pet 1:10–11).[33] Peter proceeds to establish a connection between the OT prophetic message and "those who preached the gospel to you by the Holy Spirit sent from heaven" (1 Pet 1:12). Thus, Peter strikes an important note of continuity between OT and NT revelation before and following Christ's crucifixion and resurrection. By way of prophetic anticipation and by apostolic proclamation, the same saving message was proclaimed—and "angels long to catch a glimpse of these things" (1 Pet 1:12).[34] In context, it may be that Peter is seeking to reassure his readers that their salvation is assured notwithstanding their present suffering. The same Spirit who dwelt in the prophets and predicted the suffering of the Messiah also inspires the apostolic preaching of the cross.[35]

Later in the letter, still on the topic of righteous suffering, Peter writes, "For Christ also suffered for sins once for all, the righteous for the unrighteous, that he might bring you to God. He was put to death in the flesh but made alive by the Spirit, in which he also went and made proclamation to the spirits in prison" (1 Pet 3:18–19). While space does not permit a full discussion of this hotly debated passage, it seems reasonable to affirm that Christ's being "made alive by the Spirit" (cf. Rom 8:11) refers to his resurrection following his crucifixion (being "put to death in the flesh"), designating the Holy Spirit as the agent of Jesus's resurrection. Thus Christ's proclamation "to the spirits in prison" would most likely have taken place following the

---

[33] For a defense of the interpretation of this passage with reference to the Holy Spirit and to Jesus's sufferings see Schafroth, 244. The only other instance of the phrase "Spirit of Christ" is Rom 8:9 (there used in parallelism with "Spirit of God").

[34] Green, "Faithful Witness in the Diaspora," 292–93, shows that the Spirit here serves as the one who enables believers to understand rightly the OT. A proper reading of the OT prophets involves viewing them as pointing ahead to Christ's suffering and resurrection.

[35] See the discussion in Schafroth, "1 and 2 Peter," 243. Schafroth rightly notes the stress on continuity and Peter's encouragement that believers view their present sufferings in the light of the sufferings of Christ. The notion of the Spirit's "indwelling" the OT prophets is probably best taken as his inspiring the prophetic message rather than indicating a permanent indwelling.

resurrection.[36] In context, the function of 1 Pet 3:18–19 ("For Christ also suffered"), coming on the heels of the declaration, "For it is better to suffer for doing good, if that should be God's will, than for doing evil" (v. 17; cf. vv. 13–17), is to encourage believers that their own suffering, like Jesus's, is not a sign of defeat but will result in victory, just as Jesus was raised from the dead following the crucifixion and made proclamation to the evil spirit world (most likely to the spirits who disobeyed in the days of Noah, v. 20).[37] Thus, as the book of 1 Enoch (esp. chs. 6–16) affirms, "even rebellious angels will be judged in the end" (cf. Jude v. 6).[38]

In what follows, Peter makes the gospel proclamation the grounds of his exhortation to believers no longer to live as the Gentiles do—a fine irony, since the vast majority of them were likely Gentiles—writing, "For this reason the gospel was also preached to those who are now dead, so that, although they might be judged in the flesh according to human standards, they might live in the spirit according to God's standards" (4:6). "Those who are now dead" are most likely not the "spirits in prison" (3:19) but people who were alive when hearing the gospel but have since died.[39] Most likely, the expressions "in the flesh" and "in the spirit" are parallel and refer to the life of unbelievers and believers, respectively.[40]

The final mention of the Spirit is found in 1 Pet 4:14, where Peter makes a concluding reference to believers' suffering: "If you are ridiculed for the name of Christ, you are blessed, because the Spirit of glory and of God rests on you." Believers should not think it unusual (*xenizesthe*, v. 12) when they encounter the impending "fiery ordeal" (*pyrōsis*, v. 12) and suffer "as a Christian" (*Christianos*, v. 16). Peter's words here hark back to the train of thought of 2:21: "For you were called to this, because Christ also suffered for

---

[36] See William J. Dalton, *Christ's Proclamation to the Spirits: A Study of 1 Peter 3:18–4:6*, 2nd ed. (Rome: Pontifical Bible Institute, 1989), followed by a majority of recent commentators.

[37] Cf. Gen 6:1–6; see Karen H. Jobes, *1 Peter*, BECNT (Grand Rapids: Baker, 2005), 237.

[38] Schafroth, "1 and 2 Peter," 247, with reference to Lewis R. Donelson, *I & II Peter and Jude*, NT Library (Louisville: Westminster John Knox, 2010), 117.

[39] See, e.g., Andrew J. Bandstra, "Making Proclamation to the Spirits in Prison: Another Look at 1 Peter 3:19," *Calvin Theological Journal* 38 (2003): 123.

[40] The ESV translates πνεῦμα in both passages with lowercase "spirit," and there is some debate as to whether these two passages refer to the Holy Spirit.

you, leaving you an example, that you should follow in his steps." Therefore, Christians should expect to suffer as an inexorable consequence of their close identification with Christ in the hostile world that surrounds them. The phrase "the Spirit of glory and of God" appears to echo Isa 11:2 LXX, conveying the fulfillment of the OT prophetic vision of the universal outpouring of the Spirit on God's people in the last days (cf. Isa 32:15; Ezek 39:29; Joel 3:1–2; Zech 12:10).[41]

2 Peter

In his second letter, Peter defends his authority and his teaching—especially regarding the end times and Jesus's second coming—against challenges from false teachers, writing, "For we did not follow cleverly contrived myths when we made known to you the power and coming of our Lord Jesus Christ; instead, we were eyewitnesses of his majesty" (2 Pet 1:16). Most likely Peter is referring to witnessing the transfiguration (see the references to the "voice . . . from heaven" and "the holy mountain" in v. 18). Thus, his argument is that he has already seen Jesus in his glory, at the transfiguration, so when he is talking about Christ's glorious return, he literally knows what he is talking about—he is not following mere myths.[42] In this way, Peter's apostolic testimony stands in continuity with prophetic prediction:

> We also have the prophetic word strongly confirmed . . . Above all, you know this: No prophecy of Scripture comes from the prophet's own interpretation, because no prophecy ever came by the will of man; instead, men spoke from God as they were carried along by the Holy Spirit. (2 Pet 1:19–21)

Similar to 1 Pet 1:10–12, Peter here affirms the Spirit's work in the OT prophets, here using the expression "carried along" (*pheromenoi*) to convey the way the Spirit operated in those bearers of divine revelation—including himself, who engaged in prophecy during the NT era when proclaiming

---

[41] Cf. Mark Dubis, *Messianic Woes in First Peter: Suffering and Eschatology in 1 Peter 4:12–19* (New York: Peter Lang, 2002), 121.

[42] See esp. 1:12–15; 3:1–9. See Jerome H. Neyrey, "The Apologetic Use of the Transfiguration in 2 Peter 1:16–21," *CBQ* 42 (1980): 504–19.

the second coming of the Lord Jesus Christ (1 Pet 1:12–15; 3:1–9). Simply because Jesus's return was not immediate and apparently delayed—though "with the Lord one day is like a thousand years, and a thousand years like one day" (3:8)—does not mean Peter's prediction is of mere human origin and lacks divine inspiration; rather, God is patient and allows people time to repent (3:9).

Jude

Jude writes his letter to urge his readers "to contend for the faith that was delivered to the saints once for all" (v. 3).[43] Most of the epistle is devoted to a scathing denunciation of the false teachers (vv. 4–18). The two references to the Spirit in the letter occur toward the end as part of a contrast between the false teachers and the recipients of the letter:

> These people [false teachers] create divisions and are worldly, not
> having the Spirit. But you, dear friends, as you build yourselves up
> in your most holy faith, praying in the Holy Spirit, keep yourselves
> in the love of God. (vv. 19–21)

The false teachers in this passage are unregenerate. Earlier they were identified as "dangerous reefs at your love feasts as they eat with you without reverence. They are shepherds who only look after themselves" (v. 12). This seems to suggest that these false teachers take part in the church's love feasts (*agapē* community meals) and may even aspire to (or even occupy) a shepherding role in the congregation. However, their lack of the Spirit renders them divisive and worldly (*psychikoi*).[44]

Conversely, the believers in the congregation (those "loved by God") are urged to grow in their faith, to pray "in the Holy Spirit,"[45] and to remain in God's love (one of Jude's triadic formulations). By praying in the Holy Spirit, believers will act in stark contrast to the false teachers, who lack the Spirit. "Holy"

---

[43] For a discussion of the book of Jude, see Köstenberger, Kellum, and Quarles, *Cradle, the Cross, and the Crown*, 873–89. For a discussion of the Spirit in Jude, see Lichtenwalter, "Person and Work of the Holy Spirit," 95–98.

[44] See the discussion in Lichtenwalter, 97.

[45] Cf. Eph 6:18: "Pray at all times in the Spirit."

Spirit (rather than "the Spirit") may hint at a contrast with the false teachers, "ungodly" people, who "turn the grace of our God into sensuality" (v. 4); the recipients are urged to hate "even the garment defiled by the flesh" (v. 23).

Figure 29: References to the Spirit in 1–2 Peter and Jude

Scripture Passage	Content
1 Pet 1:2	Believers are chosen through the sanctifying work of the Spirit
1 Pet 1:11	The Spirit of Christ in OT prophets predicted Christ's sufferings and glories
1 Pet 1:12	Apostles preached gospel through the Holy Spirit sent from heaven
1 Pet 3:18	Christ was put to death in the flesh but made alive by the Spirit
1 Pet 4:14	Blessed are the persecuted: the "Spirit of glory and of God" rests on them
2 Pet 1:21	Prophets spoke from God as they were carried along by the Holy Spirit
Jude v. 19	False teachers are devoid of the Spirit
Jude v. 20	Believers are to pray in the Holy Spirit

Summary

The NT letters written by Peter and Jude make a significant contribution to the biblical teaching on the Spirit.

First, Peter in particular highlights the Spirit's role in sanctification, in the larger context of living as former Gentiles in an ungodly culture (1:2; cf. 1:13–25; 2:11–25).[46] Echoing Jesus (e.g., Matt 5:11–12), Peter reminds

---

[46] Green, "Faithful Witness in the Diaspora," 295, offers an apt summary of this point in 1 Peter: "Given the pressures of exilic living, holiness—engagement in the world of nations as the people belonging uniquely to Yahweh and therefore

believers that they are blessed when facing persecution: the Spirit of God rests upon them (1 Pet 4:14; cf. Gal 3:4; 1 Thess 1:6).

Second, Peter also underscores the Spirit's role in the ministry of the OT prophets and NT apostles (1 Pet 1:10–12; 2 Pet 1:21). To the OT prophets, the Spirit spoke regarding Christ's sufferings and glories to follow; to NT apostles such as Peter, the same Spirit bore witness regarding Christ's return.

Third, Peter testifies to the Spirit's role as an agent of Christ's resurrection (1 Pet 3:18). While Christ was put to death in the flesh, he was made alive by the Spirit.

Finally, Jude urges believers to pray "in the Holy Spirit," in contrast to the false teachers, "not having the Spirit" (vv. 19–20).

1–3 John

While the term *paraklētos*, a prominent designation of the Holy Spirit in John's Gospel, is conspicuously absent as a designation for the Holy Spirit from the Johannine epistles—the term refers to Jesus in 1 John 2:1—these letters make a significant contribution to Johannine and biblical pneumatology.[47] One important aspect is the letter's use of "anointing" language.

---

representing his character and ways—is possible through the agency of the Spirit. Christians making their lives in the diaspora thus find themselves living in the realm of holiness effected by the Spirit."

[47] This section adapts material from the section on the Spirit in 1 John in Köstenberger, *Theology of John's Gospel and Letters*, 400–402. John Christopher Thomas, "The Johannine Epistles," in Burke and Warrington, *Biblical Theology of the Holy Spirit*, 250, conjectures that the reason for this absence is that the opponents claimed possession of the παράκλητος in support of their teaching, which went beyond the teaching of Christ (2 John 9). Thomas's essay is largely self-referential (four of his six scholarly references are to his own work), however, and apparently based on a version of the "Johannine community hypothesis," leading to doubtful historical reconstructions. See also Lichtenwalter, "Person and Work of the Holy Spirit," 87–95, who believes the teaching on the Holy Spirit in 1 John provides evidence of a "pneumatological crisis" in the churches in John's community in the context of which the Holy Spirit testifies to the significance of Jesus's earthly life and sacrificial death (89, 94), citing Donald W. Mills, "The Holy Spirit in 1 John," *Detroit Baptist Seminary Journal* 4 (Fall 1999): 33–50; see also J. C. Coetzée, "The Holy Spirit in 1 John," *Neot* 13 (1979): 43–67; and Daniel R. Streett, *They Went Out from Us: The Identity of the Opponents in 1 John*, BZNW 177 (Berlin: de Gruyter, 2011), 328–33.

Immediately following the reference to the departure of the false teachers in
2:19, John writes, "But you have an anointing from the Holy One, and all of
you know the truth" (2:20). Together with the reference to the Father and the
Son in 2:22, this passage contains clear trinitarian teaching, with the three
persons of the Godhead working in tandem and the Spirit teaching believers about the Father's having sent the Son. This impression is reinforced by
the second reference to "anointing" in 2:27: "As for you, the anointing you
received from him remains in you, and you do not need anyone to teach you.
But as his anointing teaches you about all things and is true and is not a lie;
just as it has taught you, remain in him."

These are the only instances of the term "anointing" (*chrisma*) in the
NT, though the verb "anoint" (*chriō*) occurs in a handful of significant NT
passages.[48] What these passages make clear is that the anointing of Jesus
with the Holy Spirit at his baptism, which marks the beginning of his messianic mission, serves as the paradigm for believers' reception—or "anointing
with"—the Holy Spirit at conversion.[49] This marks them as "little anointed
ones," followers of Jesus the Messiah, who, like he, have the Holy Spirit resting on them.[50] This "anointing," in turn, provides accurate teaching regarding
Jesus (cf. John 14:26) and marks them as belonging to God as a seal of his
ownership of them. In this context, too, the reference to the Spirit as one of
the three witnesses to Jesus together with water and blood (5:6–7) is fitting,
especially if "water" refers to Jesus's baptism. There may also be a connection between true believers' affirming that Jesus is the Messiah (*christos*) and
their own receiving an anointing (*chrisma*), while those who reject Jesus's

---

[48] Luke 4:18 (citing Isa 61:1); Acts 4:27; 10:38; 2 Cor 1:21; Heb 1:9 (citing Ps
45:6–7).

[49] Dunn, *Baptism in the Holy Spirit*, 195–200, argues that John's reference to the
anointing of the Spirit refers neither to an event that happens when a Christian is
baptized in water nor to a secondary experience following salvation. Rather, John is
speaking of the reception of the Spirit by Christians in conjunction with the reception of the gospel at the beginning of their Christian lives.

[50] Cf. Dunn, 99, who states memorably, "One becomes a Christian by sharing
in the 'christing' of the Christ." Dunn elaborates that the proper connection to be
drawn between the life of a Christian and Jesus's baptism is not with Christian baptism as a rite but with receiving the Spirit at conversion.

messianic claim are instead infused by the "spirit of the antichrist" (*antichristos*; 4:3; see also 2:18, 22).

In 3:9, John writes, "Everyone who has been born of God does not sin, because his seed (*sperma*) remains in him; he is not able to sin, because he has been born of God." The passage is embedded in a context referring to the fall: "the devil has sinned from the beginning" (v. 8) and "This is how God's children and the devil's children become obvious. Whoever does not do what is right is not of God, especially the one who does not love his brother or sister" (v. 10). While the close parallel 1 Pet 1:23–25 refers to the imperishable "seed" (*spora*) of the word of God in allusion to Isaiah 40, in 1 John 3:9 a reference to the Holy Spirit is more likely, as in Johannine thought it is the Spirit who is the agent of the new birth (cf. 1:12–13; 3:3, 5).[51] As Colin Kruse rightly notes, "The author seems to be saying, within the wider context of a metaphor of God begetting, that the reason why those born of God cannot continue in sin is that God's 'sperm' remains in them; a most daring metaphor indeed."[52] Thus, people can be incorporated into the line of the woman's "seed," climaxing in Jesus the Messiah by receiving God's "seed," the Holy Spirit, in them.[53]

Another interesting contribution of John's first epistle to Johannine and biblical pneumatology is the explicit contrast between the "Spirit of truth" and the "spirit of deception" in 4:6, a contrast also attested in the DSS.[54] The treatment in 4:1–6 follows on the heels of John's affirmation in 3:24 that

---

[51] Cf. Brown, *The Gospel According to John XIII–XXI*, 411; Rudolf Schnackenburg, *The Johannine Epistles: A Commentary* (New York: Crossroad, 1992), 175 (adducing 2:20, 27); and Colin Kruse, *The Letters of John*, PNTC (Grand Rapids: Eerdmans, 2000), 124–25, esp. 125, n. 123. Judith M. Lieu, "What Was from the Beginning: Scripture and Tradition in the Johannine Epistles," *NTS* 39 (1993): 458–77 (cf. Lieu, *I, II & III John*, 137–40) argues for an allusion to Seth (cf. Gen 4:25).

[52] Kruse, *Letters of John*, 125.

[53] For the notion that the elect or those who are "spiritual" are possessed of a divine "seed," see Irenaeus, *Adv. Haer.* 1.6.1–2 (cited by Lieu, *I, II & III John*, 139, n. 78).

[54] See 1QS 3:18; cf. 1QS 4:23–26; see also 1 John 1:8. The CSB and the NIV (as well as the NLT and the ESV) here capitalizes "Spirit" and in the NIV reads, "the Spirit of truth and the spirit of falsehood" (noting the alternative "spirit" in a footnote), though here it is probably best to understand the reference as generic and

"the one who keeps [God's] commands lives in him, and he in them. And the way we know that he remains in us is from the Spirit he has given us." By drawing a stark contrast between the Holy Spirit and "every spirit," John urges that the spirits must be tested to determine whether they are "from God" (4:1).[55] The cardinal test, as in John's Gospel, is whether such spirits confess Jesus as Messiah (4:2–3).[56] The lack of proper christological confession divides between truth and error, as the then-recent departure of the false teachers had made clear (2:19). Anyone who listens to those who have the Spirit, therefore, proves to be a true believer, while those who do not, show themselves to be possessed by the spirit of error (4:6).

Also significant is John's teaching regarding the Spirit's external witness through water and the blood (i.e., Jesus's baptism and crucifixion, marking the beginning and end points of his ministry) in 5:6–8 and regarding the Spirit's internal witness in 5:10. The latter aspect of the Spirit's testimony is predicated upon his external witness as it is confirmed in the believer's heart ("within himself"; cf. Rom 8:16; 9:1).[57] Those who believe that Jesus is the Christ and Son of God receive God's "anointing" (2:20, 27), are cleansed from sin (1:7, 9), and have the Holy Spirit indwell and teach them all things regarding Christ (John 14:17–18; 16:13–15; 1 John 4:15).

---

read "spirit of truth" (so, e.g., the NASB, KJV, NKJV, NRSV). See the discussion in Robert W. Yarbrough, *1–3 John*, BECNT (Grand Rapids: Baker, 2008), 229.

[55] The rendering "of God" (ἐκ τοῦ θεοῦ) is preferable to the CSB's "from God," because the latter could convey a more direct descent from God, and in Johannine terminology "from God" corresponds to ἀπὸ τοῦ θεοῦ (see Yarbrough, *1–3 John*, 221n4).

[56] See Streett, *"They Went Out from Us,"* who contends, contra the conventional consensus (represented, e.g., by Yarbrough, *1–3 John*, 223–24, who speaks of a reference to "Jesus' full humanity as well as his full divinity," 223), that the reference in 4:2 "that Jesus Christ has come in the flesh" is a simple shorthand for acknowledging Jesus's messiahship (see the parallel in 4:3: "does not confess Jesus"; the same expression is found at 2 John 7).

[57] The internal witness of the Holy Spirit is recognized by translations such as the CSB, NIV, and NRSV (cf. RSV, ESV, HCSB) but not supported in the NLT or CEV. See also I. Howard Marshall, *The Epistles of John*, NICNT (Grand Rapids: Eerdmans, 1978), 241; Schnackenburg, *Johannine Epistles*, 239–40; and Kruse, *Letters of John*, 181; but see the discussion in Yarbrough, *1–3 John*, 287.

Figure 30: References to the Spirit in John's Letters

Scripture Passage	Content
1 John 2:20	Believers have an anointing from the Holy One (i.e., the Holy Spirit)
1 John 3:24	We know God remains in us by the Spirit whom he has given us
1 John 4:2	We know the Spirit by his confession that Jesus has come in the flesh
1 John 4:13	We know we remain in him and he in us because he has given us his Spirit
1 John 5:6–8	Because he is the truth, the Spirit—one of three witnesses—testifies to Jesus

To summarize: John's first letter adds to Johannine pneumatology references to the "anointing" of believers with the Holy Spirit; enjoins Christ's followers to test the spirits to see whether or not they are of God; and distinguishes between the Spirit's external and internal witness, that is, between his public and private testimony regarding Christ in the messianic mission of Jesus and the believer's heart, respectively.

John's first letter further develops the pneumatological teaching in his Gospel by showing various communal applications, especially in conjunction with the departure of the false teachers. Thus, while in John's Gospel the primary thrust of the Holy Spirit is related to mission, that is, believers' Spirit-aided witness to the world (e.g., John 15:26–27; 16:8–11; 20:21–23), in 1 John the primary application is to the testing of spirits in conjunction with the separation from the community of those who fail to confess Jesus as Messiah.[58]

---

[58] See Andreas J. Köstenberger, "The Contribution of the General Epistles and Revelation to a Biblical Theology of Religions," in *Christianity and the Religions: A*

Summary of General Epistles

The author of *Hebrews* asserts that the Holy Spirit is the divine author of Scripture, explicitly attributing two of the most important scriptural quotations in his book—Psalm 95 and Jeremiah 31—to the Spirit (Heb 3:7; 10:15). The Holy Spirit is also said to have had an integral role in Christ's sacrifice and in the provision of forgiveness of sins and the establishment of a new covenant (Heb 9:14). The Spirit is thus closely tied to the central aspects of God's redemptive plan. The book also contains repeated warnings against offending or rejecting the manifestations of the Spirit (2:4; 6:4; 10:29). Overall, the book exhibits a very high doctrine of the Spirit: whoever rejects the Son also rejects the Spirit.

Among the other writers, *Peter* highlights the Spirit's role in sanctification in the larger context of living as former Gentiles in an ungodly culture (1 Pet. 1:2; cf. 1:13–25; 2:11–25; 4:14). He also underscores the Spirit's role in the ministry of OT prophets and NT apostles (1 Pet 1:10–12; 2 Pet 1:21) and testifies to the Spirit's role as an agent of Christ's resurrection (1 Pet 3:18). *Jude* urges believers to pray "in the Holy Spirit," in contrast to the false teachers "not having the Spirit" (vv. 19–20). *John* speaks of believers' being "anoint[ed]" with the Spirit (1 John 2:20, 27) and urges them to test the spirits to see whether they are from God (1 John 4:1–6).

Revelation

Revelation is a prophetic-apocalyptic epistle aimed at encouraging suffering believers at the end of the first century. A large portion of the book is devoted to conveying God's judgment on the unbelieving world, vindicating believers who are currently subjected to righteous suffering. The book depicts God as sovereign Ruler on the throne and displays a rich, multifaceted Christology. In addition, the book includes several intriguing references to the Spirit that merit closer investigation.

The book starts with a greeting from him "who is, who was, and who is to come, and from the seven spirits before his throne, and from Jesus Christ,

---

Biblical Theology of World Religions, ed. Edward Rommen and Harold Netland, EMS Series 2 (Pasadena: William Carey Library, 1995), 124–27.

the faithful witness" (1:4–5). This appears to be a trinitarian reference to God the Father, the Holy Spirit, and the Lord Jesus Christ.[59]

First Vision

John's first vision takes place on the island of Patmos and commences in 1:10: "I was in the Spirit on the Lord's day." John sees "one like the Son of Man" (v. 13, cf. Dan 7:13), the resurrected Lord Jesus Christ, whose appearance is first described before his seven letters to the seven churches are recorded in chapters 2–3. This is the first of four major visions in the book, and John uses the phrase "in the Spirit" as he introduces each of them, designating the Spirit as the source of revelation.

The first vision comes from the risen Christ himself and is given to seven churches in the time of John, located along a circular road in the Roman province of Asia.[60] The visions uniformly close with the formula, "Let anyone who has ears to hear listen to what the Spirit says to the churches," reinforcing the notion that the Spirit is the source of the divine revelation contained in the respective letters to the seven churches (2:7, 11, 17, 29; 3:6,13,22; cf. 13:9).

In chapter 3 Jesus is identified as the one "who has the seven spirits of God and the seven stars" (3:1; cf. 4:5; 5:6), possibly denoting Jesus's full possession of the Holy Spirit (cf. John 3:34).[61] This establishes a close con-

---

[59] The book of Revelation features four instances of the phrase "seven spirits" ("before his throne," 1:4; "of God" 3:1; 4:5; 5:6; cf. Isa 11:2 LXX: πνεῦμα τοῦ θεοῦ, πνεῦμα σοφίας καὶ συνέσεως, πνεῦμα βουλῆς καὶ ἰσχύος, πνεῦμα γνώσεως καὶ εὐσεβείας ["the Spirit of the LORD . . . , the Spirit of wisdom and understanding, the Spirit of counsel and might, the Spirit of knowledge and the fear of the LORD"]; Zech 4:2: seven lamps; 4:10: seven eyes of the LORD). For an excellent summary and a defense of taking these as references to the person of the Holy Spirit, see Grant R. Osborne, *Revelation*, BECNT (Grand Rapids: Baker, 2002), 36–37, who notes the trinitarian nature of 1:4 and concludes, "In short, the sevenfold Spirit is sent both by the Father and the Son to be his eyes and his presence in the world" (37).

[60] For more information see Colin J. Hemer, *The Letters to the Seven Churches of Asia in Their Local Setting*, JSNTSup 11 (Sheffield, UK: JSOT, 1986).

[61] Contra David E. Aune, *Revelation 1–5*, WBC 52A (Dallas: Word, 1997), 34–35, who proposes that angels are in view. The epithet may echo Zech 4:2, where a golden, seven-channeled lampstand designates the Spirit (v. 6). See Richard

nection between Jesus's prophetic words to the churches and the Spirit as the one who inspires them.

Second Vision

The second vision, placed in the heavenly throne room and by far the longest in the book, commences in chapter 4 and is once again marked by the phrase "in the Spirit" (4:2). Around the throne are twenty-four elders in white garments, with golden crowns on their heads, and before the throne are the "seven spirits of God." Depicted as seven fiery torches (4:5), they evoke the imagery of the seven lamps in the tabernacle (Exod 25:31–40; cf. 40:4, 24–25; Zechariah 4).

In the following chapter the seven spirits of God are depicted as the seven eyes of the Lamb who are sent into all the earth (5:6). This is likely an allusion to "the seven eyes of the LORD, which scan throughout the whole earth" referred to in Zech 4:10. The symbolism is rich and multifaceted and may refer to the fullness of the Spirit's knowledge and his mission to the world through the "prophetic witness" of God's people.[62] The close identification between the Spirit and Jesus "the Lamb" is striking and underscores their unity in mission (cf. John 20:22). Thus there is a close connection between Jesus, the Holy Spirit, and the witness of the church, and even God himself.[63]

The church's prophetic witness is further described in 11:3–13 with reference to the two olive trees or branches featured in Zechariah 4. In the latter passage, "the word of the LORD" comes to Zerubbabel: "Not by strength or by might, but by my Spirit" (Zech 4:6); later in the same passage the two olive trees or branches are described as follows: "These are the two anointed ones . . . who stand by the Lord of the whole earth" (Zech 4:14). Similarly, the "two witnesses" in Rev 11:3–4 are pictured as the "two olive trees" and the "two lampstands" who "stand before the Lord of the earth" (cf. 1:20; 4:5). The authority of these two prophets is described in terms

---

Bauckham, *The Climax of Prophecy: Studies on the Book of Revelation* (Edinburgh: T&T Clark, 1993), 162–66.

[62] Cf. Thomas, "Revelation," 260, citing Bauckham, *Climax of Prophecy*, 162–66.

[63] Thomas, "Revelation," 261.

reminiscent of Moses and Elijah (11:6–7). The site of their activity, and eventual martyrdom, is the "great city"—figuratively identified as "Sodom" and "Egypt," here signifying the "old Jerusalem"—where "their Lord" (Jesus) was crucified (11:8).[64] When they are slain, and burial is denied them—in utter breach of ancient Near Eastern customs of hospitality and human decency—

> *a breath of life from God* entered them, and they stood on their feet. Great fear fell on those who saw them. Then they heard a loud voice from heaven saying to them, "Come up here." They went up to heaven in a cloud, while their enemies watched them. At that moment a violent earthquake took place, a tenth of the city fell, and seven thousand people were killed in the earthquake. The survivors were terrified and gave glory to the God of heaven. (11:11–13)

The same Spirit who empowered their witness now publicly vindicates the "two witnesses." The Spirit comes "from God" (cf. John 14:17) and is "a breath of life" (cf. Ezek 37:5 LXX), which underscores the Spirit's origin in God and indicates his life-giving nature and mission (cf. Gen 2:7). Remarkably, those who survive the massive earthquake "gave glory to the God of heaven," the possible sole instance of repentance in the book (11:13).

After a hiatus, the next reference to the Spirit is found toward the end of the second vision. Responding to a heavenly voice telling John to write, "Blessed are the dead who die in the Lord from now on," the Spirit echoes the beatitude and says, "Yes . . . so they will rest from their labors, since their works follow them" (14:13). This underscores the fact that the witness of those who died for their faith—the 144,000 blameless who were redeemed by God and are owned by him (14:1–5)—makes a lasting impact, continuing beyond their physical death.

---

[64] It is later equated with "Babylon" (16:19; 17:18; 18:10, 16, 18–19, 21), all of these place names serving as metaphorical descriptions of the immorality and oppression characterizing the sinful world persisting in rebellion against God. The "great city" is also identified as the site of the persecution of OT prophets and NT martyrs (18:24).

Third Vision

The third vision is introduced in 17:3: "Then he carried me away in the Spirit to a wilderness. I saw a woman sitting on a scarlet beast that was covered with blasphemous names and had seven heads and ten horns." The woman is identified as "Babylon the Great, the Mother of Prostitutes and of the Detestable Things of the Earth" (17:5) and later characterized as "a home for demons, a haunt for every unclean spirit" (18:2). Later in the same vision, the seer records the words of an angel urging him to worship God, "because the testimony of Jesus is the spirit of prophecy" (19:10).[65] This passage both identifies Jesus as the ultimate witness and associates him closely with the spirit of prophecy. The long string of witnesses in the book thus includes the following:

- John, the seer (1:2, 9)
- Antipas, Jesus's "faithful witness" (2:13)
- those martyred for their faith (6:9–11)
- the two witnesses (11:3, 7)
- ordinary believers (12:11, 17; 17:6)
- the 144,000 (14:4; cf. chap. 7)
- Jesus himself (19:10)

Fourth Vision

The fourth vision commences in 21:10: "He then carried me away in the Spirit to a great, high mountain, and showed me the holy city, Jerusalem, coming down out of heaven from God." This is the new Jerusalem, where God will forever dwell with his people. There will be no temple, because God himself and the Lamb will be there (21:22).

The final reference to the Spirit is found toward the end of the book, where both the Spirit and God's people are shown to long eagerly for Christ's return: "The Spirit and the bride say, 'Come'" (22:17). Jesus replies, "Yes, I am coming soon." And the response echoes longingly: "Amen! Come, Lord Jesus!" (22:20).

---

[65] A related reference is found in 22:6, where "the Lord" is identified as "the God of the spirits of the prophets."

Figure 31: References to the Spirit in the Book of Revelation (Visions in Bold)

Scripture Passage	Content
Rev 1:4	The seven spirits before God's throne
Rev 1:10	**The seer is "in the Spirit" (Vision #1)**
Rev 2:7, 11, 17, 29; 3:6, 13, 22	"Let anyone who has ears to hear listen to what the Spirit says to the churches"
Rev 3:1	Jesus has the seven spirits (depicted as seven stars)
Rev 4:2	**The seer is "in the Spirit" (Vision #2)**
Rev 4:5	The seven spirits of God (depicted as seven fiery torches)
Rev 5:6	The seven spirits of God sent into all the earth
Rev 11:11	A "breath of life from God" enters and revives the "two witnesses" of v. 3
Rev 14:13	Spirit echoes beatitude, calls believers at rest in the Lord blessed
Rev 17:3	**The seer is "in the Spirit" (Vision #3)**
Rev 21:10	**The seer is "in the Spirit" (Vision #4)**
Rev 22:17	The Spirit and the Bride say, "Come!"

Summary

Perhaps the most significant category of usage of "Spirit" in the book of Revelation is that of designating the four visions experienced by John the seer. While the location of the visions varies, in each case the vision is prefaced by the phrase "in the Spirit" (1:10; 4:2; 17:3; 21:10).

A second significant pattern of usage is the fourfold reference to the "seven spirits" of God/before his throne" concentrated toward the beginning of the book (1:4; 3:1; 4:5; 5:6).

Third is a sevenfold repetition of the declaration "Let anyone who has ears to hear listen to what the Spirit says to the churches" in the seven letters to the seven churches in chapters 2–3 (2:7, 11, 17, 29; 3:6, 13, 22). Throughout the book, the Spirit is shown to be prophetically involved in the church's witness and mission amid a hostile environment (see, e.g., the "two witnesses"; 11:1–13).

Finally, in 14:13 the Spirit echoes a blessing on those who are at rest in the Lord, and at the very end of the book, the Spirit and the bride (the church) longingly prod, "Come," expressing eager anticipation of the Lord's return (22:17).

10

The New Testament's Contribution to a Biblical Theology of the Spirit

The Fourfold Gospel[1]

The Synoptics feature the Spirit almost exclusively regarding his activity in Jesus's ministry,[2] and even when the Spirit is directly associated with someone else (e.g., Zechariah, Elizabeth, John the Baptist, Mary, Simeon), that person is related to (and often testifying to) the coming of Jesus. The Spirit conceives Jesus in Mary's womb (Matt 1:18, 20; Luke 1:35), descends on Jesus at his baptism, and leads him into the wilderness at the temptation (Mark 1:10, 12). He rests on Jesus throughout his ministry, designating him

---

[1] M. Wenk, "Holy Spirit," in *Dictionary of Jesus and the Gospels*, 2nd ed. (Downers Grove: InterVarsity, 2013), 393, observes, "Although each of the Gospels reflects its own particular outlook on the Spirit, their pneumatologies are in one way or another a corollary of the OT understanding of the Spirit as the creative and restoring power of God."

[2] This summary is adapted from Andreas J. Köstenberger, *Encountering John: The Gospel in Historical, Literary, and Theological Perspective*, 2nd ed. (Grand Rapids: Baker, 2013), 145. Cf. the summary in Thiselton, *Holy Spirit*, 47–48, who identifies four repeated themes: (1) the Spirit's anointing and equipping of Jesus; (2) the Gospels' restraint and relative silence regarding the Spirit, whether due to the primacy of the cross, the Spirit's "self-effacement" (Fison's term; see J. E. Fison, *The Blessing of the Holy Spirit* [London: Longmans, Green, 1950]), or the humility entailed by Jesus's messianic identity; (3) Jesus's practice of prayer and intimacy with God the Father and dependence upon the Spirit; and (4) the Gospels' narrative revelation of truth about the Holy Spirit and indirectly about the Trinity.

as God's Servant (Luke 4:18, citing Isa 61:1; Luke 10:21; Matt 12:18, citing Isa 42:1). Blasphemy against the Holy Spirit (i.e., attributing the work
of God to Satan and his demons), a sin unique to the time of Jesus's earthly
ministry, cannot be forgiven (Matt 12:31; Mark 3:29; Luke 12:10). In addition, John the Baptist tells the people that Jesus will baptize with the Holy
Spirit (Mark 1:8), and Jesus states that God will give the Spirit to those who
ask (Luke 11:13) and promises his followers that in times of persecution
the Spirit will give them words to say (Mark 13:11; Luke 12:12). Finally,
Luke records Jesus's promise that he will soon be sending the promise of his
Father, that is, the Spirit, clothing his followers with power "from on high," a
prediction fulfilled at Pentecost (Luke 24:49; cf. Acts 2:14–36).

John features the Spirit primarily in the Farewell Discourse under the
designations "the Spirit of truth," "the Holy Spirit," and "the *paraklētos*." John
records Jesus's intention to send to his disciples the Spirit as "another helping presence" (*paraklētos*) like Jesus; the Father is present with them through
Jesus, and both the Father and the Son will be present with them through
the Spirit. Jesus highlights various functions of the coming Spirit: bringing to recollection Jesus's teaching, testifying about Jesus, conviction of the
world, guidance of Jesus's followers in all truth, and disclosure of the future.
The Spirit will continue Jesus's ministry and extend it through the disciples'
mission. The reference to the Spirit at 20:22 conveys "new creation" theology
(cf. John 1:1) in anticipation of the giving of the Spirit at Pentecost.

The Book of Acts

The book of Acts portrays the promised Holy Spirit as divine and as a person
(not merely an impersonal force or power) who establishes a new eschatological community of the exalted Jesus in keeping with OT prophetic prediction
(Acts 2; cf. Joel 3:1–5; Luke 24:49; Acts 1:4). The Spirit is also shown to be
a Spirit of mission: he provides the power for the mission of the church and
gives boldness for witness. He sends out the first missionaries from Antioch
as well as others, such as Philip, Peter, and Paul. Further, the Spirit fills all
believers and renders leaders, in particular, to be full of the Spirit, including
Stephen, Paul, and Barnabas. The Spirit is a Spirit of prophecy who serves as
both the subject and the object of prophecy. He also directs the affairs of the
church as one who is sovereign and subject to no one's control.

The Pauline Corpus

The pneumatological teaching in the Pauline corpus commences with references to the Spirit in chapter 4 of his letter to the Galatians. There Paul affirms that the Christian life starts with the reception of the Spirit and enables believers to address God as *Abba*, "Father" (v. 6). Important from a biblical-theological perspective, Paul indicates that this reception of the Spirit means that the Gentiles have inherited God's promise made to Abraham. In contrast to the Judaizers, Paul affirms the importance of walking by, being led by, and keeping in step with the Spirit. Paul consistently presents the Spirit as being opposed to the flesh.

In 1–2 Thessalonians Paul stresses the Spirit's power in gospel proclamation as well as in believers' sanctification, calling on them not to quench the Spirit but to allow those with the gift of prophecy to exercise that gift.

In 1 Corinthians, likewise, Paul stresses that his message came in the power of the Spirit and affirms that only the spiritual person can understand spiritual truth; consequently, Paul is able to adjudicate the Corinthians' questions (7:40). In addressing spiritual gifts, Paul stresses that, while there are diverse gifts, they are distributed by "one and the same Spirit" (12:11); thus believers should be unified in exercising those gifts for the common good (12:7; cf. 14:12). Using temple imagery, Paul highlights the Spirit's presence in the new eschatological community of Jesus, both in the church corporately (3:16–17) and in believers individually (6:19).

In 2 Corinthians Paul affirms that God has given his Spirit to believers as a down payment of things to come (1:22; 5:5). Over against his Jewish opponents, Paul asserts that his new covenant ministry "of the Spirit" is far superior to the old covenant ministry "of the letter" (i.e., of the law; 3:6). He highlights the Spirit's work in the human heart, his impartation of life, his conveyance of glory, his procurement of freedom, and his agency of transformation.

The book of Romans affirms the Spirit as an agent of Christ's resurrection (1:4), and that of believers as well (8:11). Paul speaks of "the newness of the Spirit" (7:6) and explicates what he means by this rather extensively in chapter 8. The Spirit is the distinguishing and essential mark of the Christian (8:9); he brings freedom from the bondage to sin, as well as love, life, peace, righteousness, hope, and joy (5:5; 8:2, 6, 10; 14:17; 15:13). He also conveys to believers the reality of their spiritual adoption (8:14–16, 23) and intercedes for them in their weakness (8:26–27). Walking in the Spirit allows believers to meet the requirements of the law (8:4, 13). The Spirit is also active in Paul's mission to the Gentiles, setting them apart through conversion.

In the book of Ephesians, Paul portrays the Spirit as sealing believers at conversion, being given to them as a guarantee of their eschatological inheritance (1:13–14; 4:30). He prays that the Spirit would convey wisdom and revelation to believers, strengthen them with power in their inner being, and instill in them an appreciation for the knowledge-surpassing love of Christ (1:16–17; 3:16, 19). The Spirit is instrumental in joining Jews and Gentiles together into Jesus's eschatological community (2:18, 22), fostering unity among its members (4:3–4). Negatively, believers are not to grieve him by engaging in sin (4:30). Positively, Paul calls on believers to be filled with the Spirit, resulting in heartfelt worship, thankfulness, and rightly ordered household relationships (5:18–21). The full armor of God includes the "sword of the Spirit," which is the Word of God (6:17), and believers are to pray "in the Spirit" in all their prayers (6:18; cf. Jude v. 20).

In his letters to Timothy and Titus, Paul says that the Spirit has predicted a large-scale end-time apostasy (1 Tim 4:1). Paul's injunction to Timothy to guard the "good deposit" (i.e., the gospel) by the indwelling Holy Spirit highlights the role of the Spirit in defending and propagating God's truth (2 Tim 1:14). In Titus 3:4–7 Paul affirms that God has saved believers by the washing of regeneration and renewal of the Holy Spirit.

The General Epistles and Revelation

The Holy Spirit is featured in three warning passages in the letter to the Hebrews. The unknown author issues warnings not to disregard the witness borne by God through the Holy Spirit; not to disregard manifestations of the Holy Spirit, as wilderness Israel did in their day; and not to disregard the Son of God and the blood of the covenant, thus insulting the Spirit of grace (2:1–4; 6:1–4; 10:29). The Spirit is also featured as the author of Scripture, who through Scripture still speaks today (3:7; 9:8; 10:15).

Peter in his first letter highlights the Spirit's role in sanctification (1:2). He reminds his readers that they are blessed when persecuted, because the Spirit of God rests on them (4:14). He also underscores the Spirit's role in the ministry of OT prophets and NT apostles (1 Pet 1:10–12; 2 Pet 1:21) and features the Spirit's role as an agent of Christ's resurrection. John in his first letter speaks of believers' having an "anointing from the Holy One," that is, the Holy Spirit (2:20, 27). The Spirit is also one of three witnesses to Jesus, along with his baptism ("the water") and crucifixion ("the blood," 5:6–8), and bears internal witness to believers (5:10).

In the book of Revelation, the Spirit is associated with each of John's four visions (1:10; 4:2; 17:3; 21:10). He is also repeatedly featured as the "seven spirits" of God/before his throne (1:4; 3:1; 4:5; 5:6), and the letters to the seven churches contain the consistent refrain, "Let anyone who has ears to hear listen to what the Spirit says to the churches" (2:7 et al.) The Spirit is shown to be actively involved in the church's witness and mission amid persecution. At the end of the book, the Spirit and the church longingly plead with Jesus to return soon (22:17).

Figure 32: Major NT Quotations of OT Passages on the Spirit

NT Passage	OT Passage Cited	Summary of Content
Matt 12:18–21	Isa 42:1–4	God will put his Spirit on his servant, the Messiah; the Gentiles will hope in his name
Luke 4:18–19	Isa 61:1–2	The Spirit of the Lord is on the Messiah and has anointed him to proclaim good news to the poor
Acts 2:17–21	Joel 2:28–32	In the last days, God will pour out his Spirit on all people, and they will prophesy

11

A Biblical-Theological Synthesis of the Holy Spirit in Scripture

From Genesis to Revelation, from creation to new creation, the Spirit of God is an active participant in the story of Scripture. He is life-giving, empowering, and transforming. While closely aligned with God, the Spirit operates as a distinct person along the salvation-historical continuum. He is at God's side at creation (Gen 1:2; cf. "wisdom" in Proverbs 8). He empowers divinely appointed leaders, whether national deliverers, craftsmen constructing the tabernacle, or royalty such as King David. In keeping with prophetic vision, the Spirit anoints and rests on the Messiah (Luke 4:18–19; cf. Isa 61:1–2).

In this way, the Spirit is not only integrally involved in God's work throughout salvation history; he increasingly steps into the foreground. While his activity during Jesus's earthly ministry is accomplished in and through the Messiah, particularly in Jesus's healings and other miracles, he bursts onto the scene even more spectacularly on the day of Pentecost, following Jesus's exaltation, again in fulfillment of the prophetic vision as well as the words of Jesus (Acts 2; cf. Joel 3; Acts 1:5, 8). In fact, the acts of the apostles are the acts of the Holy Spirit in and through the apostles.

The church age, as well, may accurately be described as the age of the Holy Spirit, inaugurating the last days. Thus the Holy Spirit serves as Jesus's successor on the earth, the "Counselor," or "other helping Presence" sent jointly by God the Father and God the Son (John 14:26; 15:26), empowering the church's mission and witness and providing the energizing dynamic underlying the proclamation of Jesus's resurrection and triumph over Satan, the demonic forces, sickness, and even death. The book of Revelation, in keeping with Isaiah's portrayal, depicts the Spirit as the seven spirits of God before God's throne (Rev 3:1; 4:5; 5:6; cf. Isa 11:2–3). In this way the Spirit is presented as intimately associated with God and his sovereign rule and yet distinct in personhood.

The Bible, in both Testaments, provides a fascinating and intriguing conglomeration of pieces that make up the mosaic sketching the contours of a biblical theology of the Spirit. D. A. Carson has rightly said that the measure of any biblical-theological proposal is the way it deals with the question of the Bible's unity and diversity.[1] Regarding a biblical theology of the Spirit, one detects a measure of both unity and diversity, continuity and discontinuity. On the one hand, the same Spirit is operative throughout the full orbit and canvas of Scripture. On the other hand, the day of Pentecost marks a watershed with the outpouring of the Spirit on all believers.[2]

The NT writers provide a multifaceted portrayal of the roles and ministries of the Spirit. He regenerates, renews, transforms, guides, convicts, teaches, sovereignly distributes spiritual gifts, and fulfills many other functions in the corporate life of the church and in the lives of individual believers. He also sustains an intimate and integral relationship with God the Father and God the Son throughout salvation history past, present, and future.

We may here profitably trace several prominent pneumatological themes as they unfold in Scripture. First, and perhaps most foundational, is

---

[1] D. A. Carson, "New Testament Theology," in *Dictionary of the Later New Testament and Its Development*, ed. R. P. Martin and P. H. Davids (Downers Grove: InterVarsity, 1997), 810. "The most pressing of these [issues] is how simultaneously to expound the unity of NT theology (and of the larger canon of which it is a part) while doing justice to the manifest diversity while doing justice to the manifest diversity; or, to put it the other way, how simultaneously to trace the diversity and peculiar emphases and historical developments inherent in the various NT (and biblical) books while doing justice to their unifying thrusts."

[2] Hawthorne provides a helpful contrast: "The OT primarily focuses attention upon the presence and power of the Spirit in periods of national crisis and in the lives of select individuals. The NT, however, primarily focuses attention upon the presence and power of the Holy Spirit in the life of Jesus and then through him in the lives of all his followers." G. F. Hawthorne, "Holy Spirit," in Martin and Davids, 492.

the developing understanding of the Spirit's identity. Throughout Scripture, the Spirit is tightly identified with God; Scobie rightly notes, for instance, that "the OT can speak of God and his spirit virtually interchangeably."[3] However, the Spirit is also portrayed in terms of personal identity and agency that distinguish him at some level from God (or, as the NT eventually specifies, from "the Father"), in both the OT and—especially and more explicitly—the NT. Indeed, in the very first verses of Genesis, immediately after God is said to create the heavens and the earth, the Spirit of God is said to be hovering over the waters—poised for creative action, as it were (Gen 1:1–2). At various points in the OT, we find the Spirit coming "powerfully upon," "rushing upon" (ESV) or "stir[ring]" various leaders of God's people;[4] "depart[ing]" from Saul (1 Sam 16:14 ESV); speaking through David (2 Sam 23:2); giving rest to God's people (Isa 63:14), and so forth. This is not to say that Yahweh is not involved in any of these things—other passages suggest that he is—but the Spirit is often portrayed as an independent actor, not simply as an impersonal extension of God's activity. This portrayal only intensifies in the NT.[5]

---

[3] Scobie, *The Ways of Our God*, 270. George Ladd goes so far as to say that the "*rûaḥ Yahweh* in the Old Testament is not a separate, distinct entity; it is God's power—the personal activity in God's will achieving a moral and religious object." *A Theology of the New Testament*, rev. ed (Grand Rapids: Eerdmans, 1993), 323. Max Turner avers that "in the OT, the Spirit is 'personal' only in the sense that *rûaḥ* is the self-manifesting activity of God himself, the extension of his personal vitality. The phrase 'Spirit of the Lord' is thus a synecdoche for *God himself* in action." "Holy Spirit," in *New Dictionary of Biblical Theology*, ed. T. Desmond Alexander and Brian S. Rosner. Leicester, UK: InterVarsity, 2000]), 558.

[4] E.g., judges: Judg 13:25; 14:6, 19; 15:14; kings: 1 Sam 10:10; 11:6; 16:13.

[5] This is seen in the following representative list: the Spirit leads/drives Jesus into the wilderness (Matt 4:1/Mark 1:12/Luke 4:1); speaks through the disciples when they must defend themselves, teaching them what to say (Mark 13:11; Luke 12:12); gives life (John 6:63); speaks by the mouth of David (Acts 1:16); bestows ability to speak in different languages (Acts 2:4); speaks to Philip and later carries him away (Acts 8:29, 39); speaks to Peter (Acts 10:19; 11:12) and to prophets and teachers in the Antioch church (Acts 13:2); prohibits Paul and Timothy from gospelizing in certain areas (Acts 16:6–7); intercedes for believers (Rom 8:26–27); gives life (2 Cor 3:6); reveals the mystery of Christ (Eph 3:4–5); vindicates Jesus (1 Tim 3:16); and speaks to churches (Rev 2:7, 11, 17, 29; 3:6, 13, 22). In addition, the Spirit is a *paraclete* of the same sort as Jesus (John 14:16), which indicates his personal character (Guthrie, *New Testament Theology*, 531. Using narrative criticism,

At the same time, biblical revelation makes clear that the Spirit is not entirely independent but moves at the behest of God. This is evident in the OT, where Yahweh is said to fill craftsmen with his Spirit (Exod 31:1–3; 35:30–31), to distribute some of the S/spirit that is on Moses to the seventy elders (Num 11:17, 25), to put his Spirit upon his chosen Servant (Isa 42:1; cf. Matt 12:18) and in the midst of his people (Isa 63:11), and to promise to pour his Spirit upon his people and their offspring (Isa 39:29; 44:3; Joel 2:28–29; cf. Acts 2:17–18). Moving into the NT, we see that the Father gives the Spirit to those who ask him (Luke 11:13) and to Jesus to an unlimited extent (John 3:34; cf. Acts 10:38), sends the Spirit in Jesus's name (John 14:26), gives the Spirit to those who obey him (Acts 5:32), gives the gift of the Spirit to Cornelius and other Gentiles (Acts 11:16–17; 15:8–9), gives the Spirit to believers (Gal 3:5; 1 Thess 4:8; 1 John 4:13), and sends the Spirit of his Son into the hearts of believers (Gal 4:6).[6] The Spirit is specified as an agent by whom God works in the world: God gives his good Spirit to instruct and to warn his people (Neh 9:20, 30), sends forth his Spirit (or "breath" in the CSB) in creation (Ps 104:30), promises to put his Spirit within his people and to cause them to obey him (Ezek 36:27), communicates by his Spirit through prophets (Zech 7:12; cf. 2 Pet 1:21), reveals truth to NT believers through the Spirit (1 Cor 2:9–10), gives believers his Spirit in their hearts as a down payment (2 Cor 1:22; 5:5), strengthens believers with power by his Spirit (Eph 3:16), and abides in believers through his Spirit (1 John 3:24).

Thus, pertaining to his identity we see that the Spirit is portrayed as an individual and acting as such, but in conjunction with God, and eventually in conjunction with Jesus as well. This culminates in several passages in the NT in which the Father, the Son, and the Spirit are spoken of in strikingly parallel fashion, and this not just by one author but by several (Matt 28:19; 1 Cor 12:4–6; 2 Cor 13:14; Eph 4:4–6; 1 Pet 1:2; Rev 1:4–5). This parallelism demonstrates that the NT authors think of the Spirit as a divine person

---

Ju Hur demonstrates that the Spirit is portrayed by Luke as both a "person-like" and "person-unlike" character in the narrative of Luke-Acts, and thus to be understood as a "divine character." Hur, *A Dynamic Reading of the Holy Spirit in Luke-Acts* (London/ New York: T&T Clark, 2004), 129–30.

[6] As well, in conjunction with the Father, Jesus himself promises to send the Spirit (John 15:26) and does indeed pour out the Spirit upon his people (Acts 2:33).

in his own right, a conclusion bolstered by passages that speak of the Spirit in such a way as to indicate his divine nature: the Spirit can be blasphemed (Matt 12:31/Mark 3:29/Luke 12:10); lying to the Spirit is equivalent to lying to God (Acts 5:3–4); divine gifts are distributed by the Spirit as the Spirit wills (1 Cor 12:11; Heb 2:4); the Spirit "proceeds from the Father" (John 15:26), which "suggests that the Spirit shares the same nature as the Father"[7]; and the Spirit is said to be "eternal" (Heb 9:14).

We should consider the biblical presentation of the Spirit not only in terms of his *identity* but also in terms of his *activity*. Here we may for convenience's sake speak of the Spirit's activity under six interrelated headings: The Spirit (1) mediates God's presence and, in doing so, (2) imparts life, (3) reveals truth, (4) fosters holiness, (5) supplies power, and (6) effects unity.

The Spirit Mediates God's Presence

Adam and Eve's sin prevents them and their descendants from experiencing the presence of God in the same way as had been the case in Eden. As the OT progresses, however, we find God graciously providing his presence through his Spirit to leaders of his people, and occasionally others: the Spirit fills Bezalel for his work as a craftsman (Exod 31:2–5; 35:30–33); rests on Moses and eventually the seventy elders (Num 11:17, 25); is present with various prophets (Num 24:2; 2 Chr 24:20; Ezek 2:2; 3:12, 14, 24; 8:3; 11:1, 5, 24; 37:1; 43:5; Mic 3:8; Zech 7:12); is said to be in Joshua (Num 27:18; Deut 34:9); and comes upon various judges, such as Othniel (Judg 3:10), Gideon (Judg 6:34), Jephthah (Judg 11:29), and Samson (Judg 13:25; 14:6, 19; 15:14). Saul experiences the presence of God through his Spirit (1 Sam 10:6, 10; 11:6), but due to Saul's disobedience, the Spirit leaves him (1 Sam 16:14, though note the episode in 19:19–24). The Spirit mediates God's presence to David once he is anointed to be king (1 Sam 16:13), such that David can say that the Spirit has spoken through him (2 Sam 23:2), can ask for God's Spirit to lead him (Ps 143:10), and can pray that God would not take his Holy Spirit from him due to his sin (Ps 51:11). God's presence with the coming Messiah is emphasized by noting that the Spirit of Yahweh will rest on him (Isa 11:2; 42:1; 61:1).

---

[7] Guthrie, *New Testament Theology*, 531.

As far as the OT data is concerned, then, we find that God's Spirit is present in all places in a general way (Ps 139:7) and present among his people in a general way as well (Isa 63:10–11, 14; Hag 2:5). In addition, we have seen that the special presence of God via his Spirit seems to have been limited to key individuals and as a rule is temporary or removable.[8] Moses expresses his wish that all the Lord's people could be prophets, with his Spirit on them (Num 11:29), but does not seem to expect this could be the case. However, God reveals to his prophets that a time is coming when the presence of the Spirit among God's people will be more widespread (Isa 32:15; 44:3; 59:21; Ezek 36:25–27; 37:12–14; 39:28–29; Joel 2:28–29).

This time arrives in the NT. The Spirit is active in key individuals— John the Baptist (Luke 1:15), Mary (Luke 1:35), Elizabeth (Luke 1:41), Zechariah (Luke 1:67), Simeon (Luke 2:25–27)—in preparation for the coming of Jesus, the promised Immanuel, by whom God is present with his people. In Jesus himself, the Spirit is prominently present, at Jesus's baptism specially gracing Jesus with his continuing presence (Matt 3:16/Mark 1:10/Luke 3:22/John 1:32–33) and resting upon Jesus to an unlimited degree (John 3:32).

However, more extensive pneumatological developments are in store for God's people. John the Baptist speaks of Jesus as the one who will baptize with the Holy Spirit (Matt 3:11/Mark 1:8/Luke 3:16/John 1:33). Jesus refers to this future giving of the Spirit in John 7:38: "The one who believes in me, as the Scripture has said, will have streams of living water flow from deep within him," and the apostle John appends a key explanation to this assertion: "He said this about the Spirit. Those who believed in Jesus were going to receive the Spirit, for the Spirit had not yet been given because Jesus had not yet been glorified" (v. 39). As Jesus prepares to return to his Father, he assures his disciples that both will make their home with those who love him (John 14:21); this promised presence will be mediated by the soon-to-be-sent Spirit, who will be with them forever (John 14:16–17). Jesus speaks

---

[8] "Temporary": note the several times the Spirit comes upon Samson in Judg 13:25; 14:6, 19; 15:14. "Removable": as with Saul in 1 Sam 16:14. Ju Hur suggests that the bestowal of the Spirit upon David is "presumably permanent" on the basis of 1 Sam 30:25; 2 Sam 23:2 (*A Dynamic Reading of the Holy Spirit in Luke-Acts*, 44n17), but this would seem to ignore Ps 51:11.

specifically of sending "what my Father promised," the Spirit, upon his disciples (Luke 24:49), reiterating this assurance after his resurrection: "John baptized with water, but you will be baptized with the Holy Spirit in a few days" (Acts 1:5).[9]

This pneumatological bestowal occurs at Pentecost, where believers are "all filled with the Holy Spirit" (Acts 2:4) and speak in tongues, and Peter announces that the Lord has fulfilled the promise of Joel 2 regarding the outpouring of the Spirit "on all people" (Acts 2:16–21). Having ascended to his Father, the glorified Jesus has obtained the promise of the Holy Spirit and sent him to his followers as promised (Acts 2:33), so that now it is not only the leaders of God's people who experience the special presence of the Spirit but all of God's people who call on the name of the Lord.[10] Later it will be evident that the same special presence of the Spirit is available to Gentiles who believe in Jesus (Acts 10, esp. vv. 44–47), and Peter subsequently engages John the Baptist's Spirit-baptism prophecy to conclude that the Gentiles are to be incorporated into the nascent church (Acts 11:15–17).[11]

---

[9] A. J. Thompson, *The Acts of the Risen Lord Jesus: Luke's Account of God's Unfolding Plan*, NSBT 27 (Downers Grove: InterVarsity, 2011), 126–27, helpfully points out that Jesus's reference to the Spirit as the "promise of the Father" in Acts 1:4 (ESV) reaches back further than Luke 24:49 to OT prophecy; lexical links bring Thompson to find Isa 32:15 to be the specific OT "promise of the Father," but it may well be that multiple OT passages underlie Jesus's reference.

[10] In this we may see one of many ways Jesus fulfills his role as a "prophet like" Moses (Deut 18:18; Acts 3:22) who is greater than Moses (cf. Heb 3:1–6). Uniquely in the OT, God distributed the Spirit who was upon Moses to seventy elders (with prophecy as evidence) in order to extend his ministry (Num 11:16–17, 24–25); in Acts, Jesus himself bestows the Spirit who has empowered him in his ministry not just to seventy leaders but to all who follow him (with prophecy as evidence) in order to extend his ministry. Moses expressed his wish that "all the LORD's people [would be] prophets and the LORD would place his Spirit on them" (Num 11:29), and at Pentecost this becomes a reality.

[11] Various terminology is used of the giving of the Spirit at Pentecost, its prior predictions, and subsequent events said to be equivalent. "Baptize" is the key descriptor of this action of the Spirit (Matt 3:16/Mark 1:9–10/Luke 3:21–22/John 1:33; Acts 1:5; 11:16), but we also find "come on" (Acts 1:8), "fill" (Acts 2:4), "pour out" (Acts 2:17–18, 33; 10:45), "receive" (Acts 2:38; cf. 8:15, 17, 19; 10:47; cf. Gal 3:14), "give" (Acts 5:32; cf. 8:18), and "fall" (ESV: Acts 10:44; 11:15; cf. 8:16). In addition, Jesus speaks of the Spirit's bestowal at Pentecost in terms of the disciples' being "empowered from on high" (Luke 24:49). This spectrum of language suggests

The NT epistles reinforce the understanding that every believer now has the Spirit's presence. Believers have "received" the Spirit whom God "gives" or has "given to us" (Rom 5:5; 8:15; 1 Cor 2:12; Gal 3:2; 1 Thess 4:8; 1 John 4:13). The Spirit is "in" believers (1 Cor 6:19) and can be said to "live in" believers (Rom 8:9, 11; 1 Cor 3:16; 2 Tim 1:14) and to be in their very hearts (Gal 4:6; cf. Eph 3:16). They possess the Spirit as "firstfruits" (Rom 8:23) and a "down payment" (2 Cor 1:22; 5:5). Indeed, "if anyone does not have the Spirit of Christ, he does not belong to him" (Rom 8:9), and "the way we know that [God] remains in us is from the Spirit he has given us" (1 John 3:24).

The Spirit Imparts Life

Life is divinely sourced, a gift from God, as the opening chapters of Scripture make clear. It is no surprise, then, that the Spirit of God is portrayed as imparting life. Although the "breath" (*ruach*) of God in Gen 2:7 is likely not a direct reference to the Spirit, it does gesture toward the life-giving Spirit (*ruach*) portrayed elsewhere, and (as we saw in OT Wisdom literature) the Spirit of Gen 1:2 has an active part in the creation of the world and its living inhabitants. Elihu asserts that "the Spirit of God has made me, and the breath of the Almighty gives me life" (Job 33:4), likely a reference to the creation of his life in the womb. Ezekiel's vision of the valley of dry bones culminates with Yahweh's promise of restoration to exiled and "dead" Israel:

> This is what the Lord GOD says: I am going to open your graves and bring you up from them, my people, and lead you into the land of Israel. You will know that I am the LORD, my people, when I open your graves and bring you up from them. I will put my Spirit in you, and you will live, and I will settle you in your own land." (Ezek 37:12–14)

Carson rightly notes that "one of the clearest characteristics of the Spirit in the Old Testament is the giving of life."[12]

---

that hard-and-fast lines may not always be drawn between different terms used in Scripture of the Spirit's activity in a believer's life.

[12] Carson, *Gospel according to John*, 301.

As the NT opens, we find life being created in Mary's womb "from the Holy Spirit" (Matt 1:18, 20; cf. Luke 1:35) as Jesus is conceived in his humanity. Among the mighty works of Jesus's Spirit-empowered ministry, we find him raising the dead to life (John 11). Jesus states plainly to his disciples that "the Spirit is the one who gives life," not the flesh (John 6:63). Perhaps this dominical saying informs Paul's great Spirit chapter, Romans 8, which opens by speaking of the "Spirit of life" (v. 2). This appellation underlies the great contrast of the chapter: on the one hand is the old way of the written code of the law, and the flesh, and sin, and death; on the other hand is the new way of the Spirit, and life. Paul notes that on the physical plane the body is dead because of sin, but the Spirit is life because of the righteousness that Christ in us provides (v. 10); the same God who raised up Jesus will by his Spirit bring our mortal bodies to life (v. 11).[13] Moreover, from a spiritual perspective a Spirit-oriented way of living yields life and peace, over against the death that characterizes a flesh-oriented manner of life (vv. 5–6; cf. Gal 6:8); if by the Spirit we put to death the deeds of the body, we will live (Rom 8:13). With a similar contrast, Paul notes in 2 Cor 3:6 that whereas the "letter" of the old covenant kills, the Spirit associated with the new covenant gives life.

The Spirit Reveals Truth

The Spirit performs the vital function of mediating divine truth to humankind, and this occurs in two major related ways: through spoken prophecy and through written Scripture. In a seminal passage, God takes some of the Spirit that is on Moses (a prophet himself; cf. Deut 18:15, 18; 34:10) and distributes it to seventy elders, who prophesy for a time as a result (Num 11:16–17, 25). In this context, Moses expresses his desire that all of God's people would be prophets with the Spirit on them (Num 11:29). Throughout the OT, the Spirit leads various individuals to prophesy God's truth; Neh 9:30 (and later, 1 Pet 1:11 and 2 Pet 1:21) states this in general terms,[14] and we find specific

---

[13] On the Spirit as an agent of Christ's resurrection, see also Rom 1:4; 1 Pet 3:18.

[14] Guthrie aptly notes the claim in Zech 7:12 that God's revelation had been sent "by his Spirit through the former prophets" (ESV) and observes, "This implies that those prophets who do not specifically link their work with the Spirit nevertheless

examples in Balaam (Num 24:2), Saul (1 Sam 10:1–13; 19:22–24) and his
messengers (1 Sam 19:20–21), David (2 Sam 23:2), Azariah (2 Chr 15:1),
Jahaziel (2 Chr 20:14), Zechariah (2 Chr 24:20), Ezekiel (esp. Ezek 11:5),
and Micah (Mic 3:8). Hosea uses "prophet" and "man of the Spirit" (ESV)
as parallel terms (Hos 9:7). The prophesied Servant of Isa 61:1 proclaims
God's truth as a result of having the Spirit upon him, a scenario fulfilled in
the ministry of Jesus (Luke 4:16–21). Joel prophesies of the time when God
would pour out his Spirit and reveal truth to his people through prophecy
and other means (Joel 2:28), and we have seen that Peter looks to this passage to explain Pentecost.

The NT sets forth more explicit teaching regarding the Spirit as the
revealer of divine truth. The greatest of prophets, John the Baptist, is ener-
gized by the Spirit (Luke 1:15) and boldly proclaims God's truth, prophesying of the coming Messiah. Elizabeth seems to have God's truth revealed to
her regarding Mary as a result of the Spirit's filling her (Luke 1:41–45), and
her husband, Zechariah, prophesies regarding his son, John, and the coming
Messiah after being filled with the Spirit (1:67–79). Similarly, the Spirit-
filled Simeon prophesies about Jesus after encountering him with his parents
in the temple (2:25–35). As the "prophet like" Moses (cf. Acts 3:22), Jesus
authoritatively speaks divine truth through the Spirit.[15] Later, once Jesus has
poured out the Spirit upon the church at Pentecost, all the followers of Jesus
gathered in Jerusalem prophesy in foreign languages of the "magnificent acts
of God" (Acts 2:1–18); similarly, some disciples of John later prophesy in
foreign languages after receiving the Spirit (Acts 19:6). After Pentecost, we
find Agabus prophesying "by the Spirit" (Acts 11:28; cf. 21:10).

---

were recognized as giving the Word of the Lord through the Spirit"; he also highlights the "close connection between the Word and the Spirit in OT thought" (*New
Testament Theology*, 512).

[15] Moisés Silva observes that since Jesus thinks of himself as a prophet (Matt
13:57 et al.), and "since the Spirit was regarded by contemporary Jud[aism] mainly
as the source of prophecy, Jesus is in effect claiming to be inspired by the Spirit"
("πνεῦμα," *NIDNTTE* 3:810). Note Luke 4:18–19, where Jesus appropriates the
prophecy of Isa 61:1–2, claiming that the Spirit is upon him to fulfill prophet-like
functions. Note also John 3:34, where the Spirit's resting on Christ "without measure" is tied to Jesus' "utter[ing] the words of God."

Jesus himself calls the Spirit "the Spirit of truth" (John 14:17; 15:26; 16:13) and speaks of his ministry of teaching the disciples all things and of bringing his teaching to their remembrance after his departure (John 14:26). To put it another way, the Spirit will "guide them into all truth," including revelation about the future (John 16:13).[16] Paul understands this role of the Spirit, speaking of it most extensively in 1 Corinthians 2; there he asserts that God has revealed his "hidden wisdom" to him and other believers through the Spirit (vv. 6–10), who provides understanding of divine truth (v. 12). He is the "Spirit of wisdom and revelation" (Eph 1:17), and once-hidden truths have now been revealed by the Spirit to the apostles and prophets (Eph 3:4–5). What is more, though it is difficult to be certain about the specific nature of all of the spiritual gifts to which Paul refers (see Rom 12:6–8; 1 Cor 12:8–10, 28), a number of these manifestations of the Spirit in the early church, such as prophecy (cf. 1 Cor 14:29–32), seem to involve the revelation of divine truth to God's people.

In addition, importantly, in the NT we have several occasions where the Spirit is connected with the revelation of God's truth in Scripture.[17] Jesus himself quotes from Psalm 110 and notes that in it David had spoken "by the Spirit" (Matt 22:43/Mark 12:36). Peter follows suit: like Jesus, he observes that David spoke (here, in Psalm 2) "through the Holy Spirit" (Acts 4:25–26), but—apparently giving the Spirit more prominence—also affirms that "the Holy Spirit through the mouth of David foretold" in the book of Psalms (Acts 1:16, 20). Similarly, Paul cites Isa 6:9–10 and says that in this passage the Holy Spirit spoke through Isaiah the prophet (Acts 28:25–27). The author of Hebrews dispenses with the human author altogether, so to speak, when he straightforwardly attributes Ps 95:7b–11 to the Holy Spirit (Heb. 3:7–11) and does the same with Jer 31:33–34b (Heb. 10:15–17). The same Spirit who is operative in revealing God's truth, and is now present with believers is able to illumine the meaning of Scripture to God's people (1 Cor 2:12–16; Eph 1:15–20).

---

[16] The things that are "to come" that would be shown to the disciples (John 16:13) include, perhaps most notably, John's visions in Revelation. Turner, "Holy Spirit," 558, lists four aspects in Revelation of the Spirit as a Spirit of prophecy.

[17] Although the Spirit is not mentioned directly in 2 Tim 3:16, the term θεόπνευστος may allude to his activity in the writing of Scripture.

The Spirit Fosters Holiness

It is not for nothing that Scripture associates the Spirit more with holiness than with any other characteristic, such that his most common appellation is simply "Holy Spirit."[18] "Holy" does distinguish the Spirit as "the Spirit which is separate or different from that of humans"[19] but in doing so also points to the moral excellence of God toward which the Spirit actively transforms believers in Jesus.[20] The Spirit convicts people of their sin when they fall short of that moral excellence (Gen 6:3; John 16:8–11). Strikingly, in one of only two OT passages that refer to the "Holy Spirit," we find David repenting from his sin and asking God not to take his Holy Spirit from him (Ps 51:11).[21] We might also make a connection between the Spirit's holy nature and his energizing of OT prophets to call people away from their sin and back to their God. And within their prophecies we find anticipation of the time when God's bestowed Spirit will bring about transformation and obedience on the part of God's people (Ezek 36:27).

In the NT we find the Spirit to be a key factor in the sanctification of believers. How could it be otherwise? As we have seen, the very presence of God the Father and God the Son is mediated to the believer through the Spirit. Indeed, upon believing the truth of the gospel, believers are set apart by the Spirit to God in initial sanctification (2 Thess 2:13; cf. Rom 15:16). Paul speaks of the "Spirit of holiness" in Rom 1:4 in anticipation of his discussion of the Spirit's sanctifying work later in Romans, especially Romans 8: believers are set free from the law of sin and death by the law of the Spirit of life (8:2),[22] are to live their lives according to the Spirit (vv. 4–5), and can by the Spirit put to death the deeds of the body (v. 13). The believer who

---

[18] See discussion in C. F. D. Moule, *The Holy Spirit* (1978; repr., London: Continuum, 2000), 22–23.

[19] Scobie, *Ways of Our God*, 270.

[20] See, helpfully, Hawthorne, "Holy Spirit," 490–91.

[21] In this connection, it will be recalled that Saul's sin eventuated in the Spirit's being removed from him.

[22] In discussing the Spirit's role in the life of believers, Guthrie engages the category of "liberation," noting that "it is an important function of the Spirit to break shackles which have been carried over from pre-conversion days" and that spiritual liberty "is one of the most characteristic functions of the Spirit" (*New Testament Theology*, 557).

insists on living in impurity rather than holiness disregards God, who has given believers the Holy Spirit (1 Thess 4:7–8; cf. 5:23); the sin of God's people grieves the Holy Spirit (Isa 63:10; Eph 4:30). Such impure behavior belongs to the old life, while in their new life believers have been sanctified by the Spirit (1 Cor 6:11) and, indeed, are the very temple of the Holy Spirit, both individually (1 Cor 6:19) and collectively (3:16–17)—and "God's temple is holy" (3:17).

The Spirit Supplies Power

Given what we have seen in our biblical survey, we may immediately acknowledge the aptness of "God's empowering presence" as a description for the Spirit.[23] In the OT the Spirit is said to come upon various leaders of God's people—Saul, David, the judges—and, as a result, they are empowered in various ways for their leadership roles. Micah—and other prophets by extension—is filled "with power by the Spirit of the LORD" in order to prophesy against the sin of God's people (Mic 3:8).

In the NT the virgin Mary is told by the angel, "The Holy Spirit will come upon you, and the power of the Most High will overshadow you" (Luke 1:35), and, as a result, she miraculously conceives. Given that the evangelists consistently take note of the Spirit's coming upon Jesus at his baptism (Matt 3:16/Mark 1:10/Luke 3:22/John 1:32–33), we are doubtless to understand that the Spirit empowers Jesus for the earthly ministry, which his baptism inaugurates. In a key text, Luke tells us that after Jesus's wilderness temptation subsequent to his baptism, he "returned to Galilee in the power of the Spirit" (Luke 4:14), and immediately thereafter in Luke's narrative, Jesus publicly appropriates the messianic text in Isa 61:1–2a as being fulfilled in him: "The Spirit of the Lord is on me, because he has anointed me to preach good news to the poor. He has sent me to proclaim release to the captives and recovery of sight to the blind, to set free the oppressed, to proclaim the year of the Lord's favor" (Luke 4:18–19). Luke then goes on to note the Spirit's power in action in Jesus's healing (see esp. Luke 5:17; 6:19) and exorcisms

---

[23] Fee, *God's Empowering Presence*, passim. At times, Scripture parallels "power" with the Spirit, practically equating the two in some contexts. See, e.g., Mic 3:8; Luke 1:35; 24:49; Acts 1:8; 10:38; 1 Cor 2:4; 1 Thess 1:5.

(see esp. Luke 4:36; 11:20). Later, Luke records Peter's speaking of "how God anointed Jesus of Nazareth with the Holy Spirit and with power, and how he went about doing good and healing all who were under the tyranny of the devil, because God was with him" (Acts 10:38).[24] Regarding John's presentation of Jesus's ministry, "the continual abiding of the Spirit on Jesus Christ is explicitly emphasized (John 1:32–33), so that his whole public life, his words and deeds, are understood as an event in the power of the Spirit."[25]

The Spirit empowerment energizing Jesus's ministry is mirrored in the early church. Jesus describes his gift of the Spirit to the early church in terms of "power" (Acts 1:8; cf. Luke 24:49) and links the reception of that gift to the church's witness to him, a witness that involves not only powerful proclamation (e.g., Acts 4:31, 33; cf. 1 Cor 2:4; 1 Thess 1:5) but also validation, such signs as tongues and prophecy (e.g., Acts 2:4, 17–18; 10:44–46; 19:6; cf. Rom 15:19; 1 Cor 12:11; Heb 2:3–4). Other results of the Spirit's power in the church include believers' overcoming sin (Rom 8:1–13), abounding in hope (Rom 15:13), and being strengthened in their inner being (Eph 3:16).

The Spirit Effects Unity

We have seen in the NT in particular that the Spirit ministers in such a way as to bring God and believers into a unified family relationship. This relationship is, on the one hand, a vertical one: the Spirit brings all who trust in Christ into a new relationship with God. He becomes their Father, and they become his children. In this regard, Paul speaks of the "Spirit of adoption," who provides the ground for believers to refer to God as "Father" and bears witness to believers that they are God's children, indeed, his heirs (Rom 8:14–17; Gal 4:4–7). This adoption via the Spirit was planned long ago (Eph 1:5) and made possible "when the time came to completion" (Gal 4:4–5).

This vertical familial relationship effected by the Spirit implies and grounds a horizontal one. All who have God as their Father are by definition siblings, participating in the "unity of the Spirit" (Eph 4:1–3; cf. Phil 2:1–4; 2 Cor 13:14). This is perhaps of greatest import when it comes to the inclusion

---

[24] Note 9.4, "Spirit and Power," in Bock, *Theology of Luke and Acts*, 225.
[25] Schnelle, *Theology of the New Testament*, 705.

of the Gentiles into the church on equal footing as Jews.[26] Paul presents Gentiles and Jews as being joined together into "one new man," both having "access in one Spirit to the Father" (Eph 2:15, 18); shifting metaphors, he presents Jews and Gentiles as "being built together for God's dwelling in the Spirit" (Eph 2:22; cf. 1 Cor 3:16). This teaching is doubtless grounded in the experience of the early church as portrayed in the book of Acts, where God clearly indicates that the Gentiles are to be included in the church, not least by sending the Spirit upon the Gentile Cornelius and company; Peter's vision is a prelude to Gentile inclusion (Acts 10:9–16, 28; 11:5–10), but it is the bestowal of the Spirit that clinches matters for the early church (Acts 10:44–48, esp. v. 47; 11:15–18, esp. v. 17; 15:7–9). Paul appeals to the objective unity provided by the Spirit when he challenges believers to live harmoniously (1 Cor 12:4–13; Eph 4:1–6; Phil 2:1–4).

We have seen how, from Genesis to Revelation, from creation to new creation, the Spirit of God is an active participant in the story of Scripture— life-giving, empowering, and transforming.[27] While closely aligned with God, he has been shown to operate as a distinct person along the salvation-historical continuum. On the basis of the above biblical-theological investigation, it will now be helpful to systematize the biblical teaching on these matters and to survey how the church has historically understood and developed its teaching on the person and work of the Holy Spirit.

---

[26] See on this point esp. Thompson, *Acts of the Risen Lord Jesus*, 137–41.

[27] Thanks are due Chuck Bumgardner for his help with the biblical-theological synthesis provided in this chapter.

APPENDIX: REFERENCES TO
THE SPIRIT IN SCRIPTURE

Passage	Term	Passage	Term
Gen 1:2	the Spirit of God	Job 32:8	the breath from the
Gen 6:3	my Spirit		Almighty
Gen 41:38	God's Spirit	Job 33:4	the Spirit of God
Exod 31:3	God's Spirit	Ps 33:6	the breath of his mouth
Exod 35:31	God's Spirit	Ps 51:11	Holy Spirit/desire for
Num 11:17	the Spirit		holiness
Num 11:25	the Spirit (2x)	Ps 104:30	your breath
Num 11:26	the Spirit	Ps 139:7	your Spirit
Num 11:29	his Spirit	Ps 143:10	your gracious Spirit
Num 24:2	the Spirit of God	Prov 20:27	the LORD's lamp
Num 27:18	the Spirit	Isa 11:2	the Spirit of the LORD
Deut 34:9	the spirit of wisdom	Isa 30:1	my Spirit (ESV)
Judg 3:10	the Spirit of the LORD	Isa 32:15	the Spirit
Judg 6:34	the Spirit of the LORD	Isa 34:16	his Spirit
Judg 11:29	the Spirit of the LORD	Isa 40:7	the breath of the LORD
Judg 13:25	the Spirit of the LORD	Isa 40:13	the Spirit of the LORD
Judg 14:6	the Spirit of the LORD	Isa 42:1	my Spirit
Judg 14:19	the Spirit of the LORD	Isa 44:3	my Spirit
Judg 15:14	the Spirit of the LORD	Isa 48:16	his Spirit
1 Sam 10:6	the Spirit of the LORD	Isa 59:19	the wind/breath (NIV) of
1 Sam 10:10	the Spirit of God		the LORD
1 Sam 11:6	the Spirit of God	Isa 59:21	my Spirit
1 Sam 16:13	the Spirit of the LORD	Isa 61:1	the Spirit of the Lord GOD
1 Sam 16:14	the Spirit of the LORD	Isa 63:10	his Holy Spirit
1 Sam 19:20	the Spirit of God	Isa 63:11	his Holy Spirit
1 Sam 19:23	the Spirit of God	Isa 63:14	the Spirit of the LORD
2 Sam 23:2	the Spirit of the LORD	Ezek 11:5	the Spirit of the LORD
1 Kgs 18:12	the Spirit of the LORD	Ezek 11:24	the Spirit; the Spirit of God
2 Kgs 2:16	the Spirit of the LORD	Ezek 36:27	my Spirit
1 Chr 12:18	the Spirit	Ezek 37:1	his Spirit
2 Chr 15:1	the Spirit of God	Ezek 37:14	my Spirit
2 Chr 20:14	the Spirit of the LORD	Ezek 39:29	my Spirit
2 Chr 24:20	the Spirit of God	Dan 4:8, 9, 18	spirit of the holy gods (3x)
Neh 9:20	your good Spirit	Dan 5:11	a spirit of the holy gods
Neh 9:30	your Spirit	Dan 5:14	a spirit of the gods
Job 4:9	the breath of God (ESV)	Joel 2:28–29	my Spirit (2x)
Job 15:30	the breath of God's mouth	Mic 2:7	the Spirit of the LORD
Job 27:3	the breath from God	Mic 3:8	the Spirit of the LORD

Passage	Term	Passage	Term
Hag 2:5	my Spirit	John 3:5–8	the Spirit (3x)
Zech 4:6	my Spirit	John 3:34	the Spirit
Zech 6:8	my Spirit	John 6:63	the Spirit
Zech 7:12	his Spirit	John 7:39	the Spirit (2x)
Zech 12:10	a spirit of grace	John 14:16	another Counselor
Matt 1:18	the Holy Spirit	John 14:17	the Spirit of truth
Matt 1:20	the Holy Spirit	John 14:26	the Counselor, the Holy
Matt 3:11	the Holy Spirit		Spirit
Matt 3:16	the Spirit of God	John 15:26	the Counselor, the Spirit of
Matt 4:1	the Spirit		truth
Matt 10:20	the Spirit of your Father	John 16:7	the Counselor
Matt 12:18	my Spirit	John 16:13	the Spirit of truth
Matt 12:28	the Spirit of God	John 20:22	the Holy Spirit
Matt 12:31	the Spirit	Acts 1:2	the Holy Spirit
Matt 12:32	the Holy Spirit	Acts 1:4	the Father's promise
Matt 22:43	the Spirit	Acts 1:5	the Holy Spirit
Matt 28:19	the Holy Spirit	Acts 1:8	the Holy Spirit
Mark 1:8	the Holy Spirit	Acts 1:16	the Holy Spirit
Mark 1:10	the Spirit	Acts 2:4	the Holy Spirit; the Spirit
Mark 1:12	the Spirit	Acts 2:17–18	my Spirit (2x)
Mark 3:29	the Holy Spirit	Acts 2:33	the promised Holy Spirit
Mark 12:36	the Holy Spirit	Acts 2:38	the Holy Spirit
Mark 13:11	the Holy Spirit	Acts 4:8	the Holy Spirit
Luke 1:15	the Holy Spirit	Acts 4:25	the Holy Spirit
Luke 1:35	the Holy Spirit	Acts 4:31	the Holy Spirit
Luke 1:41	the Holy Spirit	Acts 5:3	the Holy Spirit
Luke 1:67	the Holy Spirit	Acts 5:9	the Spirit of the Lord
Luke 2:25	the Holy Spirit	Acts 5:32	the Holy Spirit
Luke 2:26	the Holy Spirit	Acts 6:3	the Spirit
Luke 2:27	the Spirit	Acts 6:5	the Holy Spirit
Luke 3:16	the Holy Spirit	Acts 6:10	the Spirit
Luke 3:22	the Holy Spirit	Acts 7:51	the Holy Spirit
Luke 4:1	the Holy Spirit	Acts 7:55	the Holy Spirit
Luke 4:14	the Spirit	Acts 8:15	the Holy Spirit
Luke 4:18	the Spirit of the Lord	Acts 8:17	the Holy Spirit
Luke 10:21	the Holy Spirit	Acts 8:18	the Spirit
Luke 11:13	the Holy Spirit	Acts 8:19	the Holy Spirit
Luke 12:10	the Holy Spirit	Acts 8:20	the gift of God
Luke 12:12	the Holy Spirit	Acts 8:29	the Spirit
Luke 24:49	power from on high (ESV)	Acts 8:39	the Spirit of the Lord
John 1:32	the Spirit	Acts 9:17	the Holy Spirit
John 1:33	the Spirit, the Holy Spirit	Acts 9:31	the Holy Spirit

Passage	Term	Passage	Term
Acts 10:19	the Spirit	1 Thess 1:6	the Holy Spirit
Acts 10:38	the Holy Spirit	1 Thess 4:8	his Holy Spirit
Acts 10:44	the Holy Spirit	1 Thess 5:19	the Spirit
Acts 10:45	the gift of the Holy Spirit	2 Thess 2:13	the Spirit
Acts 10:47	the Holy Spirit	1 Cor 2:4	the Spirit
Acts 11:12	the Spirit	1 Cor 2:10	the Spirit (2x)
Acts 11:15	the Holy Spirit	1 Cor 2:11	the Spirit
Acts 11:16	the Holy Spirit	1 Cor 2:12	the Spirit who comes from God
Acts 11:17	the same gift		
Acts 11:24	the Holy Spirit	1 Cor 2:13	the Spirit
Acts 11:28	the Spirit	1 Cor 2:14	the Spirit; God's Spirit
Acts 13:2	the Holy Spirit	1 Cor 3:16	the Spirit of God
Acts 13:4	the Holy Spirit	1 Cor 6:11	the Spirit of our God
Acts 13:9	the Holy Spirit	1 Cor 6:19	the Holy Spirit
Acts 13:52	the Holy Spirit	1 Cor 7:40	the Spirit of God
Acts 15:8	the Holy Spirit	1 Cor 12:3	the Holy Spirit
Acts 15:28	the Holy Spirit	1 Cor 12:4	the same Spirit
Acts 16:6	the Holy Spirit	1 Cor 12:7	the Spirit
Acts 16:7	the Spirit of Jesus	1 Cor 12:8	the Spirit, the same Spirit
Acts 19:2	the (or, a) Holy Spirit (2x)	1 Cor 12:9	the same Spirit, the one Spirit
Acts 19:6	the Holy Spirit		
Acts 19:21	the Spirit	1 Cor 12:11	the same Spirit
Acts 20:22	the Spirit	1 Cor 12:13	one Spirit (2x)
Acts 20:23	the Holy Spirit	1 Cor 14:2	the Spirit
Acts 20:28	the Holy Spirit	2 Cor 1:22	his Spirit
Acts 21:4	the Spirit	2 Cor 3:3	the Spirit of the living God
Acts 21:11	the Holy Spirit	2 Cor 3:6	the Spirit (2x)
Acts 28:25	the Holy Spirit	2 Cor 3:8	the Spirit
Gal 3:2	the Spirit	2 Cor 3:17	the Spirit, the Spirit of the Lord
Gal 3:3	the Spirit		
Gal 3:5	the Spirit	2 Cor 3:18	the Spirit
Gal 3:14	the promised Spirit	2 Cor 5:5	the Spirit
Gal 4:6	the Spirit of his Son	2 Cor 6:6	the Holy Spirit
Gal 4:29	the Spirit	2 Cor 13:14	the Holy Spirit (ESV)
Gal 5:5	the Spirit	Rom 1:4	the Spirit of holiness
Gal 5:16	the Spirit	Rom 2:29	the Spirit
Gal 5:17	the Spirit (2x)	Rom 5:5	the Holy Spirit
Gal 5:18	the Spirit	Rom 7:6	the Spirit
Gal 5:22	the Spirit	Rom 8:2	the Spirit of life
Gal 5:25	the Spirit (2x)	Rom 8:4	the Spirit
Gal 6:8	the Spirit (2x)	Rom 8:5	the Spirit (2x)
1 Thess 1:5	the Holy Spirit	Rom 8:6	the Spirit

Passage	Term	Passage	Term
Rom 8:9	the Spirit, the Spirit of God, the Spirit of Christ	Heb 3:7	the Holy Spirit
		Heb 6:4	the Holy Spirit
Rom 8:10	the Spirit	Heb 9:8	the Holy Spirit
Rom 8:11	the Spirit of him who raised Jesus from the dead, his Spirit	Heb 9:14	the eternal Spirit
		Heb 10:15	the Holy Spirit
		Heb 10:29	the Spirit of grace
Rom 8:13	the Spirit	1 Pet 1:2	the Spirit
Rom 8:14	God's Spirit	1 Pet 1:11	the Spirit of Christ
Rom 8:15	the Spirit of adoption	1 Pet 1:12	the Holy Spirit sent from heaven
Rom 8:16	the Spirit		
Rom 8:23	the Spirit	1 Pet 3:18	the Spirit
Rom 8:26	the Spirit (2x)	1 Pet 4:14	the Spirit of glory and of God
Rom 8:27	the Spirit		
Rom 9:1	the Holy Spirit	2 Pet 1:21	the Holy Spirit
Rom 14:17	the Holy Spirit	1 John 2:20	anointing from the Holy One
Rom 15:13	the Holy Spirit		
Rom 15:16	the Holy Spirit	1 John 3:24	the Spirit
Rom 15:19	God's Spirit	1 John 4:2	the Spirit of God
Rom 15:30	the Spirit	1 John 4:13	his Spirit
Eph 1:13	the promised Holy Spirit	1 John 5:6	the Spirit (2x)
Eph 1:17	the Spirit of wisdom and revelation	1 John 5:8	the Spirit
		Jude v. 19	the Spirit
Eph 2:18	one Spirit	Jude v. 20	the Holy Spirit
Eph 2:22	the Spirit	Rev 1:4	the seven spirits
Eph 3:5	the Spirit	Rev 1:10	the Spirit
Eph 3:16	his Spirit	Rev 2:7	the Spirit
Eph 4:3	the Spirit	Rev 2:11	the Spirit
Eph 4:4	one Spirit	Rev 2:17	the Spirit
Eph 4:30	God's Holy Spirit	Rev 2:29	the Spirit
Eph 5:18	the Spirit	Rev 3:1	the seven spirits of God
Eph 6:17	the Spirit	Rev 3:6	the Spirit
Eph 6:18	the Spirit	Rev 3:13	the Spirit
Phil 1:19	the Spirit of Jesus Christ	Rev 3:22	the Spirit
Phil 2:1	the Spirit	Rev 4:2	the Spirit
Phil 3:3	the Spirit of God	Rev 4:5	the seven spirits of God
Col 1:8	the Spirit	Rev 5:6	the seven spirits of God
1 Tim 3:16	the Spirit	Rev 11:11	the breath of life from God
1 Tim 4:1	the Spirit	Rev 14:13	the Spirit
2 Tim 1:14	the Holy Spirit	Rev 17:3	the Spirit
Titus 3:5	the Holy Spirit	Rev 21:10	the Spirit
Heb 2:4	the Holy Spirit	Rev 22:17	the Spirit

Note that references to the Spirit in Paul's writings are given in likely chronological order of writing.

PART II
SYSTEMATIC THEOLOGY

12

Introduction, Methodology, Central Themes, and Assumptions of a Systematic Theology of the Holy Spirit

Introduction

In the past, the Holy Spirit gave birth to the church as the body of Jesus Christ. In the future, the Holy Spirit will perfect the church as the bride, the wife of the Lamb. In the present, the church lives, grows, ministers, and multiplies in the age of the Holy Spirit.[1]

Despite this critical and sustained activity, for much of its history the church has largely and lamentably overlooked the doctrine of the Holy Spirit. As Gerald Bray highlights, theology of the first three centuries developed the doctrine of the person and work of the Father. As the Gnostic

---

[1] Accordingly, Owen did not engage in overstatement when he warned, "Take away the dispensation of the Spirit, and his effectual operations in all the intercourse that is between God and man; be ashamed to avow or profess the work attributed unto him in the gospel—and Christianity is plucked up by the roots." Similarly, he averred, "No dispensation of the Spirit, no Church," because "on [the Spirit's] presence the being of the church, the success of the ministry, and the edification of the whole, do absolutely depend." John Owen, *Pneumatologia: A Discourse concerning the Holy Spirit*, in *The Works of John Owen*, vol. 3, ed. William H. Goold (Edinburgh: Banner of Truth Trust, 1965), 8, 192, 194.

threat that challenged the doctrine of the Father waned, new threats, such as Arianism, arose in the later third century and throughout the fourth century, now directed toward the person of Jesus Christ. Christian theology responsibly turned its attention to articulating and defending the doctrine of the Son.[2]

After its first millennium, and having suffered a major division into East and West, the church's western part—originally the Roman Catholic Church and, after a second divide, now including Protestant churches—focused on the work of Christ.[3] Christian theology addressed two related matters. The first issue was the atonement, that is, what the death of Christ accomplished; possible answers included, for example, the satisfaction model, Christ as example, the governmental theory, penal substitution, and so forth. The second issue was salvation, that is, how the work of Christ is applied and appropriated. On the one hand, Protestant churches championed justification as both the forgiveness of sin and the imputation of Christ's righteousness, received by grace alone through faith alone in Christ alone. On the other hand, the Roman Catholic Church defined justification as forgiveness, regeneration, and sanctification together, received by the infusion of grace through the sacraments, by which human merit may be achieved, leading to eternal life.[4]

It is certainly not the case that throughout these theological developments of the person and work of the Father and the person and work of the Son the church completely ignored the person and work of the other member of the Trinity. Still, Christian theology has only of late placed the doctrine of the Holy Spirit at the forefront of reflection and practice.[5] Beginning in the twentieth century with the rise of Pentecostal theology and the new

---

[2] Gerald Bray, *God Has Spoken: A History of Christian Theology* (Wheaton: Crossway, 2014), 206–8.

[3] Bray, 398–402.

[4] Gregg R. Allison, *Roman Catholic Theology and Practice: An Evangelical Assessment* (Wheaton: Crossway, 2014), chap. 13.

[5] In the nineteenth century, Adolf von Harnack called pneumatology the "orphan doctrine" of systematic theology. Adolf von Harnack, *History of Dogma*, 7 vols. (Boston: Roberts Brothers, Little, Brown, 1895–1900), 4:108–34. In 1984, Frederick Bruner and William Hordern used the word "shy" in conjunction with the Holy Spirit. Frederick Dale Bruner and William Hordern, *The Holy Spirit: The Shy Member of the Trinity* (Minneapolis: Augsburg, 1984).

churches it birthed, and continuing with the incorporation of that theology into already existing (e.g., Roman Catholic, Anglican, Methodist, Lutheran, Baptist) churches through the Charismatic movement, the person and work of the Holy Spirit has taken center stage.[6]

Accordingly, whereas even fifty years ago some voices in the church lamented the plight of "the forgotten person of the Trinity," Christian theology's interest in the Holy Spirit today is unmatched and here to stay.[7] We may happily disagree with the following perspective, expressed in 1964: "It is true, beyond a doubt, that pneumatology is a neglected field of systematic

---

[6] Though most everyone attributes the contemporary renaissance in pneumatology to the twentieth century developments just mentioned, we would like to imagine that it is also (primarily?) due to a discovery of Owen's centuries-old affirmation about the Holy Spirit: "The doctrine concerning his person, his work, his grace, is the most peculiar and principal subject of the Scriptures of the New Testament, and a most eminent immediate object of the faith of them that do believe" (*Pneumatologia*, 23).

[7] This overly brief and excessively general sketch of the development of the doctrine of the Holy Spirit requires qualification (with some discussion to follow later). The early church defended both the deity and the personhood of the Holy Spirit against detractors (e.g., the Pneumatomachians; literally, "Spirit fighters"). Even in his pre-Montanist writings, Tertullian underscored the work of the Spirit in the inspiration of Scripture, the anointing of Christ and the church, and the empowerment of believers to stand firm against paganism. Augustine devoted significant attention to the proper names of "Love" and "Gift" in his trinitarian-focused treatment of the Third Person. Thomas Aquinas reflected on and advanced the early church's pneumatology. The theology of the Reformers had much to say in this regard, to the extent that John Calvin is often referred to as the "theologian of the Holy Spirit." From the post-Reformation period, John Owen's *Pneumatologia* still stands as the singular most extensive exposition of this doctrine. In particular, Hesselink takes pains to demonstrate that the Reformed tradition has made a significant contribution to the doctrine, if not the experience, of the Holy Spirit. I. John Hesselink, "The Charismatic Movement and the Reformed Tradition," in Donald K. McKim, ed., *Major Themes in the Reformed Tradition* (Eugene: Wipf & Stock, 1998), 377–85 (esp. 380–82). For further discussion see Michael Horton, *Rediscovering the Holy Spirit: God's Perfecting Presence in Creation, Redemption, and Everyday Life* (Grand Rapids: Zondervan, 2017), 17–20; and Sinclair B. Ferguson, *The Holy Spirit*, Contours of Christian Theology (Downers Grove: InterVarsity, 1996), 11. My thanks to Jordan Edwards for his work on the pre-Montanist pneumatology of Tertullian.

development."[8] Indeed, "one of the most exciting developments in theology has been an unprecedented interest in the Holy Spirit."[9]

Methodology

In terms of a methodology for developing our doctrine of the Holy Spirit, we must avoid two extremes: last-minute addition and first-order priority.[10] The former extreme approaches this doctrine by first taking all of the other systematic theological categories—for example, providence and salvation—and then, having developed them fully, "in a second, non-constitutive moment, . . . decorat[ing] the already constructed system with pneumatological baubles, a little Spirit tinsel."[11] It should be evident why we must avoid this "last-minute addition" method.

The latter extreme is the approach that gives first-order priority to the doctrine of the Holy Spirit. An example is the rather recent "third article theology." The numerical adjective "third" refers to the order of the "articles," or topics, that are treated in the earliest Christian creeds. Specifically, the Creed of Nicaea, the Nicene-Constantinopolitan Creed, and the Apostles' Creed address, in order, the "first article," which is the confession of belief

---

[8] Hendrikus Berkhof, *The Doctrine of the Holy Spirit*, 2nd ed. (Richmond: John Knox, 1967), 10. This book was the publication of Berkhof's Warfield Lectures at Princeton in 1964. Similarly, writing in 1962, Arthur Wainwright, *The Trinity in the New Testament* (London: SPCK, 1962), 199, lamented that the "doctrine of the Holy Spirit has long been a Cinderella of theology. It has suffered from much neglect and has always been one of the most difficult doctrines to discuss." For those unfamiliar with the story, Cinderella was the stepsister of two young women; when they went to the prince's ball, she was forced to stay at home.

[9] Veli-Matti Kärkkäinen, ed. *Holy Spirit and Salvation: The Sources of Christian Theology* (Louisville: Westminster John Knox, 2010), xi. Elsewhere Kärkkäinen describes this development as "a pneumatological renaissance"; see his *Pneumatology: The Holy Spirit in Ecumenical, International, and Contextual Perspective*, 2nd ed. (Grand Rapids: Baker Academic, 2018), 1.

[10] For a brief treatment of contemporary approaches to pneumatology see Kärkkäinen, 10–12. For a brief treatment of historical approaches to pneumatology see Graham A. Cole, *He Who Gives Life: The Theology of the Holy Spirit*, Foundations of Evangelical Theology (Wheaton: Crossway, 2007), 28–31.

[11] Killian P. McDonnell, "The Determinative Doctrine of the Holy Spirit," *Theology Today* 39, no. 2 (July 1, 1982): 142.

in God the Father; the "second article," which is the confession of belief in Jesus Christ the Son of God; and the "third article," which is the confession of belief in the Holy Spirit.

According to this third article approach, "Christian theology should begin its task . . . with an account of the Spirit; and thus that should now be *first* which has traditionally been *last*."[12] Specifically, third article theology "is not simply a study of pneumatology but is, rather, a conscious and considered approach to conceiving of theology and witnessing to God's self-revelation in Word and works, from the perspective of the Spirit where questions of pneumatology set the agenda and control the trajectory of the dogmatic enterprise, rather than pneumatology being the sole focus."[13] Out of respect to the traditional taxis or order of the divine persons—the Father is the First Person, the Son is the Second Person, and the Holy Spirit is the Third Person[14]—and the codification of this taxis in the order of the early creeds' articles—first article, Father; second article, Son; third article, Holy Spirit—we will not adopt this approach.[15]

The method that we use prioritizes biblical revelation as it presents the person and work of the Holy Spirit; this God-breathed Scripture possesses ultimate authority in the construction of our pneumatology. Moreover, our approach respects and incorporates the church's traditional formulation of the doctrine of the Holy Spirit, considering such theological consensus to

---

[12] D. Lyle Dabney, "Why Should the Last be First? The Priority of Pneumatology in Recent Theological Discussions," in *Advents of the Spirit: An Introduction to the Current Study of Pneumatology*, ed. Bradford E. Hinze and D. Lyle Dabney (Milwaukee: Marquette University Press, 2001), 4.

[13] Myk Habets, "Prolegomenon: On Starting with the Spirit," in *Third Article Theology: A Pneumatological Dogmatics*, ed. Myk Habets (Minneapolis: Fortress, 2016), 3. See also Myk Habets, *The Progressive Mystery: Tracing the Elusive Spirit in Scripture and Tradition* (Bellingham: Lexham Press, 2019), 4. For a critique of third article theology, see Christopher R. J. Holmes, *The Holy Spirit*, New Studies in Dogmatics (Grand Rapids: Zondervan, 2015), 123–30.

[14] The term *taxis* refers to order, and the church, following Scripture, has traditionally affirmed the eternal ordering of the three persons as first, the Father; second, the Son; and third, the Holy Spirit.

[15] Another approach that will not be adopted is that of Sarah Coakley, *God, Sexuality, and the Self: An Essay 'On the Trinity'* (Cambridge: Cambridge University Press, 2013). For an interaction with her "Spirit-leading approach," see Holmes, *The Holy Spirit*, 33–42.

enjoy presumptive authority.[16] Thus, building on the biblical theology of the first part of this book, this second part interacts with common theological topics in dialogue with pneumatology, as well as the Spirit-provided wisdom from the church of the past, to present a systematic theology of the Holy Spirit.

Central Themes and Assumptions

Our approach is further shaped by eight central themes, key assumptions that will appear at various junctures in our pneumatology:

(1) A Traditional/Catholic Trinitarian Orientation

Specifically, this orientation embraces the eternal trinitarian processions of the Son and the Spirit, that is, the eternal generation of the Son and the eternal procession of the Holy Spirit. Additionally, it affirms the inseparable operations of the three divine persons in all external works of the triune God, the appropriations of particular works by one of the persons without excluding the participation of the other two persons, and perichoresis, that is, the mutual indwelling of the three persons in one another.[17]

---

[16] For the idea of presumptive authority and theological formulation, see Gregg R. Allison, "The *Corpus Theologicum* of the Church and Presumptive Authority," in *Revisioning, Renewing, Rediscovering the Triune Center: Essays in Honor of Stanley J. Grenz*, ed. Derek J. Tidball, Brian S. Harris, and Jason S. Sexton (Eugene: Wipf & Stock, 2014), 323.

[17] By the term *catholic* (small *c*), the reference is not to the Roman *Catholic* Church but to the (largely) universal theological consensus on many doctrines in general and on the doctrine of the Trinity in particular. In making this move we join ourselves to the recent evangelical project of *resourcement*, or retrieval of the church's tradition that is well established in its history, well-grounded on Scripture, and widely embraced by the three branches of Christendom (Roman Catholicism, Eastern Orthodoxy, and Protestantism). For a sampling of this retrieval, see Michael Allen and Scott R. Swain, *Reformed Catholicity: The Promise of Retrieval for Theology and Biblical Interpretation* (Grand Rapids: Baker Academic, 2015); and the books in the Zondervan series New Studies in Dogmatics, with Allen and Swain as general editors: Christopher R. J. Holmes, *The Holy Spirit* (2015); Fred Sanders, *The Triune God* (2016); Michael Allen, *Sanctification* (2017); and Michael Horton, *Justification* (2 vols., 2018).

(2) A Canonical Reading of Scripture

This interpretive strategy seeks to understand the biblical affirmations about the Holy Spirit in light of the whole Bible without flattening the diverse emphases of the biblical groupings (e.g., Pentateuch, Synoptic Gospels, the Pauline corpus), by appreciating the different accents of the biblical genres (e.g., poetry, prophecy, narrative), and by taking into consideration the progress of revelation. This interpretative approach will be particularly important in the matter of continuity and discontinuity between the OT and the NT, especially with respect to its impact on our understanding of the experience of the Holy Spirit by the people of God.

(3) A Covenantal Framework to Theological Formulation

Scripture presents a progression of covenants as the divinely established, structured ways by which God relates to his people.[18] A proper understanding of these covenants and their relationship to one another is crucial for theological formulation in general and pneumatology in particular. Specifically, while we note the commonalities and diversities between the old and new covenants, our understanding of the covenantal framework means that particular attention will be given to the new covenant reality of the Spirit as what believers and the church live today. Thus, for example, while consideration of whether old covenant saints were regenerated is an interesting matter, what is most important to understand is the Spirit's work of regeneration in new covenant believers in Jesus Christ.

(4) A Focus on the Outpouring of the Holy Spirit[19]

This emphasis has firm biblical warrant, as the metaphor appears in many scriptural affirmations about the Holy Spirit. Specifically, Scripture presents

---

[18] This covenantal framework has been particularly developed by two of our colleagues: Peter J. Gentry and Stephen J. Wellum, *Kingdom through Covenant: A Biblical-Theological Understanding of the Covenants*, 2nd ed. (Wheaton: Crossway, 2018).

[19] During the writing of the rough draft of this book, Abilene Christian University Press released an excellent book whose title reinforced our emphasis on

the outpouring of the Spirit in contrast with the devastation of Israel (Isa 32:15; 44:3), as a promise of future renewal (Ezek 36:27; 37:14; Joel 2:28, fulfilled in Acts 2:17), as a description of what occurs on the day of Pentecost (Acts 2:33) and to Cornelius and his family (Acts 10:45), and as the experience of Christians (Rom 5:5) as part of their salvation (Titus 3:5–6).[20] The reasons for focusing on the outpouring of the Spirit, given the context in which pneumatology must be constructed today, are:[21]

(a) The metaphor offers a corrective to the problem of an overintellectualization of the Holy Spirit. In some churches and denominations, pneumatology focuses largely on the Spirit's role in transforming an individual believer's mentality or thinking. Certainly, Scripture calls for the renewal of a believer's mind (e.g., Rom 12:1–2), a process fostered by the tandem working of the Word of God and the Spirit of God. But such intellectual renewal is only part of the vast transformation that God effects individually in a believer's life and, as importantly, corporately among his people living in community.

> The problem is not the use of reason in faith and in the church. The decisive problem is the reduction of the human spirit and even the works of the divine Spirit to powers of intellect and reason. . . . A biblically oriented alternative . . . has to start from a different perspective than the self-referential cognitive and mental power. It should start, as I propose, with the great biblical image of the "outpouring of the Spirit." Talking about the outpouring of the Spirit forces us to focus on a wealth and plenitude of relations, on the constitution of a spiritual community with many interrelations, mutual effects and radiations.[22]

---

this metaphor: Leonard Allen, *Poured Out: The Spirit of God Empowering the Mission of God* (Abilene: Abilene Christian University Press, 2018). Allen presents the biblical support for this metaphor on 30–33.

[20] For the considerable variety in which the role of the Holy Spirit is portrayed in the New Testament (thus bolstering the case for our emphasis on the Spirit's outpouring), see pp. 53-54.

[21] Levison, *Filled with the Spirit*, xxv, comes close to listing some of these reasons for his choice of the metaphor "filling with the spirit."

[22] Michael Welker, "Rooted and Established in Love: The Holy Spirit and Salvation," in *Spirit of God: Christian Renewal in the Community of Faith*,

Following this proposal in the hope of correcting this overintellectualization, our pneumatology emphasizes the outpouring of the Spirit.[23]

(b) This metaphor highlights the Spirit's presence and work in keeping with the oft-neglected biblical emphases of divine control, savage judgment, and invasion. Three examples—Saul, Samson, and Cornelius—from our biblical theology section suffice as warrant. The Spirit "rush[ed] upon" Saul, who, being empowered to prophesy, was "turn[ed] into another man" (1 Sam 10:6, 10 ESV). As Samson grew, "the Spirit of the LORD began to stir him" (Judg 13:24–25). This stirring manifested itself in savage ways: as "the Spirit of LORD came powerfully on him," Samson ripped apart a lion (14:6), killed thirty men (14:19), and later "killed a thousand men" with the "jawbone of a donkey" (15:14–15). Finally, the Holy Spirit invaded the room in which Cornelius, together with his family and friends, were listening to Peter's announcement of the gospel: "The Holy Spirit came down on all those who heard the message. The circumcised believers who had come with Peter were amazed because the gift of the Holy Spirit had been poured out even on the Gentiles. For they heard them speaking in other tongues and declaring the greatness of God" (Acts 10:44–46).

Our biblical theology reminds us that the presence and work of the Holy Spirit is according to his sovereign will and not under human control and hence is at times unexpected, even shocking.[24] As Jesus underscores, the

---

ed. Jeffrey W. Barbeau and Beth Felker Jones (Downers Grove: IVP Academic, 2015), 185.

[23] In a personal conversation with Craig Keener (April 28, 2018), Keener noted that the theological tradition of which he is a part—Pentecostalism—has the opposite problem of underappreciating the role of the Spirit in cognitive renewal. Indeed, his book *The Mind of the Spirit: Paul's Approach to Transformed Thinking* (Grand Rapids: Baker Academic, 2016) addresses his tradition's oversight.

[24] A brief note about the use of masculine pronouns ("he," "his," "him") to refer to the Holy Spirit. By using this convention, we follow standard procedure, finding the use of neuter pronouns ("it," "its") to run the risk of depersonalizing the Holy Spirit and the use of feminine pronouns ("she," "her") to foist gender issues inappropriately to the forefront. The key point is that the Holy Spirit (as is true of the triune God, and as is true of both the Father and the Son) is non-gendered; gender does not apply to the Spirit, who is neither male nor female. We must avoid confusing gendered *language* (e.g., referring to the Spirit with masculine pronouns such as "he") with gendered *beings* (e.g., thinking the Holy Spirit is masculine). For further discussion see Gregg R. Allison, "What's the Difference between a Pansexual Miley Cyrus

coming and going of the Spirit is like the blowing of the wind (John 3:8). The metaphor of outpouring emphasizes this reality.

(c) This metaphor positions the Holy Spirit front and center while correcting the common caricature of him as "bashful," "deferential," or "always in the shadow of Christ" (based on a misunderstanding of John 16:14).[25] While the three divine persons work inseparably together in creation, providence, salvation, and consummation, each one appropriates specific divine works such as, in the case of the Third Person, speaking, creating/re-creating/perfecting, and filling with the divine presence.[26] To move the Holy Spirit into the background of trinitarian operations is surely to (dis)miss the prominent roles he exercises in communicating divine revelation, applying and perfecting the salvation purposed by the Father and accomplished by the Son, and rendering the presence of the triune God to believers and the church. Highlighting the Spirit's outpouring will ensure that we avoid this oversight.

(d) This metaphor underscores the church's long-overdue focus on the person and work of the Holy Spirit inaugurated with the turn-to-the-Spirit Pentecostal renewal beginning in 1906 and continued in the charismatic renewal inaugurated in the 1960s/1970s.[27] Moreover, it is in step with the powerful renewals taking place through the Holy Spirit in contemporary contexts outside of the North American context in which this book is written.[28] At the same time, this emphasis on his outpouring does not give

---

and a Non-Gendered God?" *Gospel Taboo* (blog) September 8, 2015, http://gospel-taboo.com/home/pansexual-miley-cyrus-and-non-gendered-god. Bloesch provides a brief overview of the debate in Donald G. Bloesch, *The Holy Spirit: Works and Gifts*, Christian Foundations (Downers Grove: InterVarsity Press, 2000), 60–62.

[25] Horton shares this concern in *Rediscovering the Holy Spirit*, 16–17.

[26] These appropriations will be developed in due course.

[27] Indeed, the metaphor of the outpouring of the Spirit will be quite familiar to Pentecostal and charismatic readers.

[28] Estimates of the number of Pentecostal and charismatic Christians worldwide hover between 650 and 700 million. Churches influenced by the pneumatology of these movements are by far the fastest-growing and -multiplying churches in the world. Projections for the year 2050 are of about one billion Pentecostal and charismatic Christians.

quarter to claims of patently absurd manifestations and dubious miracles attributed to the Holy Spirit in fringe movements.

For these reasons, our pneumatology will focus on the outpouring of the Spirit while not overlooking or minimizing other metaphors that emphasize his creative activity (the Spirit as a hovering bird), his setting apart for mission (the Spirit like a dove), his revitalizing ministry (the Spirit as water), his sovereign empowerment (the Spirit as the finger of God), and more.

(5) A Revitalizing Experience of the Holy Spirit

This emphasis on both personal and corporate/ecclesial experience of the Spirit is to encourage the growth of believers and their churches in being filled with, walking by, and keeping in step with the Spirit (Eph 5:18; Gal 5:16, 25). The presupposition is that, far too often, we settle for and suffer "parched lives, in need of renewal and refreshment."[29]

Tragically, some believers and churches are skeptical about and even afraid of the presence and work of the Spirit. Their mistrust and dread are often due to poor or absent teaching about the Holy Spirit and/or bizarre experiences with extreme forms of Pentecostalism and/or the Charismatic movement. Such suspicion and trepidation, even when properly held, too often result in a suspicion of rightful experiences of the Spirit. Our pneumatology, with its emphasis on a renewing experience of the Spirit, seeks to prompt believers and churches to move beyond cynicism and fear. Indeed, it affirms, "Without the active presence of the Spirit of God there must be a desperate vacuum at the heart of the Christian life."[30]

For believers and churches who find themselves on the opposite end of the spectrum, our doctrine of the Holy Spirit cautions them against overly emphasizing the Spirit's "bold" or "miraculous" manifestations but to expect with joy and thanksgiving the Spirit's "mundane" or "normal" works. From a simple prayer like "Spirit, fill me!" as they tumble out of bed in the morning to their daily reading of Scripture, and from their trust in and obedience to the

---

[29] J. Todd Billings, *Remembrance, Communion and Hope* (Grand Rapids: Baker, 2018), 138.

[30] Alasdair I. C. Heron, *The Holy Spirit* (Philadelphia: Westminster, 1983), 107.

Spirit-breathed Word of God to going about their work as spouses, singles, parents, educators, small-business owners, carpenters, farmers, homemakers, and more, they should be renewed by the Spirit in the routines of life.[31]

(6) A Theology Filled with Thanksgiving

In Matthew's Gospel Jesus promises that "your Father who is in heaven [will] give *good things* to those who ask him" (Matt 7:11). Luke's Gospel expresses the promise a bit differently: "The heavenly Father [will] give *the Holy Spirit* to those who ask him" (Luke 11:13). If the Spirit is a good thing—indeed, *the* good gift—of God, then our pneumatology must be an expression of thanksgiving.[32] The Spirit is the greatest free and undeserved favor conferred on the people of God from the Father in Christ alone, through grace alone, received by faith alone, and leading to the glory of God alone as expressed in thanksgiving for the Holy Spirit.

(7) A Missional Pneumatology

Anointed with the Holy Spirit in fulfillment of Old Testament prophecies about Messiah's Spirit-directed mission (see e.g., Isa 42:1–9; 61:1–11), Jesus carries out his mission of announcing the gospel, healing the sick, exorcising demons, making disciples, confronting enemies, and inaugurating the kingdom of God. Upon the eleven apostles on the day of his resurrection, Jesus breathes the Holy Spirit as an enacted parable or harbinger of the outpouring of the Spirit on the day of Pentecost (John 20:19–23; Acts 2:1–4, 33). This outpouring has a missional emphasis, as foretold by Jesus: the Spirit will testify of Christ, as will the disciples (John 15:26–27) through empowerment by the Spirit (Luke 24:48–49; Acts 1:4–5, 8). Indeed, from its inception the church has been a missional community because it is directed and

---

[31] Horton also emphasizes this point (*Rediscovering the Holy Spirit*, 14, 29).

[32] As Moltmann expresses it, "The gift and the presence of the Holy Spirit is the greatest and most wonderful thing which we can experience." Jürgen Moltmann, *The Source of Life: The Holy Spirit and the Theology of Life*, trans. Margaret Kohl (Minneapolis: Fortress, 1997), 10.

emboldened by the Holy Spirit. Thus our pneumatology will focus on the mission of the church to make disciples in all the nations (Matt 28:18–20).

(8) A Framework of Three "Ages": the Spirit of the Age, the Age of the Spirit, and the Spiritual Age

It is common in theologies of the Holy Spirit to make a distinction between the "spirit of the age" and the "age of the Spirit."[33] The first era refers to the context in which we live (the North American context and, in some cases, beyond) as characterized by autonomy, the collapse of authority, the disparagement of truth, the relativity of moral standards, self-constructed reality, and the like. Contemporary "idols" of the spirit of the age include money, sex, power, security, status, comfort, political prowess, and more. These are the concrete idols after which citizens of this age chase.

The "age of the Spirit" refers to the period between the first and second comings of Christ. Scripture calls this era "the last days" (Acts 2:17; 2 Tim 3:1; Heb 1:2; Jas 5:3; 2 Pet 3:3). Inaugurated by the incarnation, crucifixion, resurrection, and ascension of the Son of God, as well as the outpouring of the Spirit of God on Pentecost, "the last days" for the people of God means being incorporated into the new covenant, which is characterized by the presence and power of the Holy Spirit. Thus it is the age of the Spirit.

Additionally, the particular context in which this pneumatology finds itself is a spiritual age. While characterized by autonomy, the rejection of traditional beliefs and practices, and self-constructed reality, the majority of its people consider themselves to be spiritual, in some sense of that word.[34] One example is Oprah Winfrey's "spirituality,"[35] which believes that people

---

[33] For example, Horton, *Rediscovering the Holy Spirit*, chap. 6 (entitled "The Age of the Spirit"), 300, 319.

[34] Recent Pew research bears out this affirmation. See Michael Lipka and Claire Gecewicz, "More Americans Now Say They're Spiritual but Not Religious, *Fact Tank* (blog), September 6, 2017, http://www.pewresearch.org/fact-tank/2017/09/06/more -americans-now-say-theyre-spiritual-but-not-religious.

[35] See David Cloud, "Oprah Winfrey, The New Age High Priestess," Way of Life Literature, last updated September 3, 2019, https://www.wayoflife.org/reports /oprah_winfrey_new_age_priestess.html, excerpted from Cloud, *The New Age Tower of Babel*, 4th ed. (Port Huron: Way of Life Literature, 2010).

are more than their physical selves and that there are millions of ways to find and please God. The spiritual age is also exemplified by our friends and neighbors "getting in touch with their spiritual side" through the selective integration of various "spiritualities," such as centering prayers, meditation, labyrinth walking, yoga, and more, often in an attempt to counter the physical demands of their workplaces and the life-consuming materialistic orientation of our culture. Other means of seeking a sense of a religious or transcendent state of being include the use of hallucinogen drugs and believing that loved ones who have died are with us, watching over, helping, and protecting us.[36] In a sense, this spiritual age is a subset of the spirit of the age, but as it is such a pronounced phenomenon, it deserves its own category.

With these eight central themes and assumptions, we begin our systematic theology of the Holy Spirit.

---

[36] The popularity of dimethyltryptamine (DMT, or "the Spirit Molecule"), the active hallucinogenic compound of ayahuasca, is on the rise as a means of obtaining a spiritual experience. As an example of the latter belief that deceased loved ones are with the living, see Jenny McCoy, "Never Forgotten: This Man's GPS Routes Honor Children Battling Cancer," *Runner's World*, January 10, 2018, https://www.runners world.com/runners-stories/a20864977/gps-routes-to-honor-kids.

13

The Deity and Personhood of the Holy Spirit

O ur pneumatology affirms that the Holy Spirit is God, a personal divine being, and not a creature or an impersonal force.

The Nicene-Constantinopolitan Creedal Affirmation

With the affirmation of the Nicene-Constantinopolitan Creed (AD 381), including the addition of the *filioque* ("and the Son") clause from the Synod of Toledo (589), the (Western) Christian church has historically confessed the following with respect to the Holy Spirit:

> We believe in the Holy Spirit, the Lord, and Giver of life, who proceeds from the Father and the Son, who with the Father and the Son together is worshipped and glorified, who spoke by the prophets.

The key affirmations are: (1) The Holy Spirit is God, being called "the Lord" and, together with God the Father and God the Son, being the object of worship and adoration. (2) The Holy Spirit is a divine Person, the Third Person of the Trinity, proceeding from both the person of the Father and the person of the Son. (3) Two major works in which the Holy Spirit (without separation from the Father and the Son) is involved are as the "Giver of life"—creation/re-creation/perfection—and as the one who spoke by the prophets—revelation—with particular reference to Scripture, the written

Word of the triune God. These works also demonstrate the divine person-hood of the Spirit, which the church confesses.

This confession means that the Holy Spirit is characterized by all the attributes that characterize the Father and all the attributes that characterize the Son.

whatever we can say of the Father, who is	we can likewise say of the Son, who is	and can likewise say of the Holy Spirit, who is
independent (exists of himself)	independent (exists of himself)	independent (exists of himself)
immutable (unchanging)	immutable (unchanging)	immutable (unchanging)
eternal	eternal	eternal
omnipresent (every-where present)	omnipresent (every-where present)	omnipresent (every-where present)
simple (not composed of parts)	simple (not composed of parts)	simple (not composed of parts)
spiritual (immaterial)	spiritual (immaterial)	spiritual (immaterial)
omniscient (knows all things)	omniscient (knows all things)	omniscient (knows all things)
wise	wise	wise
truthful	truthful	truthful
omnipotent (all-powerful)	omnipotent (all-powerful)	omnipotent (all-powerful)
faithful	faithful	faithful
good	good	good
loving	loving	loving
gracious	gracious	gracious
merciful	merciful	merciful
patient	patient	patient
holy	holy	holy
righteous/just	righteous/just	righteous/just
jealous	jealous	jealous
wrathful	wrathful	wrathful

In summary, as the Father is a divine Person, characterized by the afore-mentioned attributes, so the Son is a divine Person, characterized by these exact same attributes, and so is the Holy Spirit a divine Person, characterized by these very same attributes. Technically, the Father, the Son, and the Holy Spirit are ὁμοούσιος (*homoousios*), of the same nature or essence.[1]

We confess the deity of the Holy Spirit because of the following.

Scriptural Warrant and Historical Consensus of the Spirit's Deity

Biblical Affirmations

In many discussions of the deity of the Holy Spirit, the point is made that there are no direct biblical affirmations of his divine nature. The most straightforward evidence—though, admittedly, even this passage appeals to grammatical parallelism and OT background—is Luke's narrative of the sin of Ananias and Sapphira. Peter confronts the former with this charge: "Ananias, . . . why has Satan filled your heart to *lie to the Holy Spirit* and keep back part of the proceeds of the land? Wasn't it yours while you possessed it? And after it was sold, wasn't it at your disposal? Why is it that you planned this thing in your heart? You have not *lied* to people but *to God*" (Acts 5:3–4). The parallelism is striking: "lie to the Holy Spirit" parallels "lied . . . to God"; the conclusion is that the Holy Spirit is God. Later in the narrative, Peter confronts the deceased Ananias's wife, Sapphira: "Why did you agree to *test the Spirit of the Lord*? Look, the feet of those who have buried your husband are at the door, and they will carry you out" (5:9). "Test the Spirit of the

---

[1] The word ὁμοούσιος (*homoousios*) was part of the central debate during the Arian controversy of the fourth century. Initially applied to the Son to affirm that he is of the same nature as the Father, it was later extended to the Holy Spirit to affirm that he is of the same nature as the Father and the Son. For example, Athanasius argued for the application of *homoousios* to the Holy Spirit in his *Letter to Serapion* 1:21. H. B. Swete, *The Holy Spirit in the Ancient Church: A Study of Christian Teaching in the Age of the Father* (London: MacMillan and Co., 1912), 213–19. For further discussion see Gregg R. Allison, *Historical Theology: An Introduction to Christian Doctrine* (Grand Rapids: Zondervan, 2011), 366–77.

Lord" is an OT expression for sinning against Yahweh (see e.g., Exod 17:2, 7; Deut 6:16; Ps 78:18, 41, 56); the conclusion is that the Holy Spirit is God.

Whatever we make of this passage as straightforward evidence of the deity of the Spirit, the biblical warrant for his divinity is certainly not confined to this instance. Arguing deductively from the divine attributes—for example, omnipresence, omniscience, omnipotence, and eternality are characteristics of deity—we rightly conclude that the Holy Spirit is divine, for he exhibits the divine attributes. He is everywhere present (Ps 139:7–10). He knows all things (Isa 40:13–14), including the future (John 16:13) and the depths of the mystery of the triune God (1 Cor 2:10–11). He is all-powerful, capable, for example, of effecting the incarnation of the Son of God in the womb of the virgin Mary (Luke 1:34–37). And he is ever-existing (Heb 9:14). The conclusion, therefore, is that the Holy Spirit is divine.

Moreover, arguing deductively from the divine works—for example, creation, providence, redemption, and consummation are divine actions—we rightly conclude that the Holy Spirit is divine. He was active in the original creation (Gen 1:2) and continues his creative work in the ongoing creation of living beings (Job 33:4). He providentially cares for what has been created (Ps 104:27–30). He saves fallen human beings through, for example, regeneration (John 3:5–6; Titus 3:5), union with Christ (Rom 8:9–10), justification, and sanctification (1 Cor 6:11; 2 Thess 2:13–14; 1 Pet 1:1–2). He will ultimately effect the consummation of all things through, for example, the resurrection of the body (Rom 8:11). The conclusion, therefore, is that the Holy Spirit is divine.

In addition to these arguments—and in keeping with the traditional/ catholic trinitarian orientation to our pneumatology—we begin with Scripture's presupposition of the doctrine of the Trinity and, together with this trinitarian framework, its presupposition of the deity of the Third Person. Given this approach, we read the opening chapter of Scripture as a narrative of the triune God's creative action: God the Father speaks the universe and everything it contains into existence through his Word, the Son of God, while "the Spirit of God was hovering over the surface of the waters" (Gen 1:2). From the very beginning, then, the divine Spirit is at work in the divine act of creation. Of course, this reading of Genesis 1 is confirmed by later Scripture, which affirms the participation of the three persons in creation (e.g., Gen 2:7;[2] Job 33:4; Pss 33:6, 9; 104:30; John 1:1–3; Col 1:15–20; Heb 1:1–3).

In fact, we continually find references to the triune God—some more implicit, other more explicit—as we read Scripture with this traditional/catholic trinitarian orientation. Some "hints" of the Trinity include:

- the divine deliberation about the creation of humanity: "Let *us* make man in *our* image, according to *our* likeness" (Gen 1:26)
- the divine address of "God" by "God:" "Your throne, *God*, is forever and ever; the scepter of your kingdom is a scepter of justice. You love righteousness and hate wickedness; therefore, *God, your God*, has anointed you with the oil of joy more than your companions" (Ps 45:6–7; cited in Heb 1:8–9)
- the similar divine address of "the Lᴏʀᴅ" by "my Lord:" "This is the declaration of the Lᴏʀᴅ to *my Lord*: 'Sit at my right hand until I make your enemies your footstool'" (Ps 110:1; cited in Matt 22:44–45)

More explicit references include:

- the baptism of Jesus, in which the Father speaks words of commendation about the Son being baptized as the Holy Spirit descends upon him (Matt 3:16–17)
- the divine work of adoption by the Father, who sends the Son to redeem adopted sons, into whose hearts he has sent the Spirit of his Son (Gal 4:4–6)
- Jesus's authoritative instruction about baptizing disciples "in the name of the Father and of the Son and of the Holy Spirit" (Matt 28:19)
- the divine enablement of the church: "There are different gifts, but the same Spirit. There are different ministries, but the same Lord. And there are different activities, but the same God produces each gift in each person" (1 Cor 12:4–6)

---

[2] As will be discussed later, "the breath [*neshamah*] of life" is associated with the "Spirit" (*ruach*) of the life-giving God.

- the apostolic benediction: "The grace of the Lord Jesus Christ, and the love of God, and the fellowship of the Holy Spirit be with you all" (2 Cor 13:13)

This traditional/catholic trinitarian scaffolding, which is both the presupposition of Scripture and the framework that itself emerges from Scripture, links the Father, the Son, and the Holy Spirit, thereby underscoring the deity of the Third Person.[3]

Two final points in support of the Spirit's divine nature emerge when Scripture rehearses the awful plight of those who sin in relation to the Holy Spirit. First, blasphemy against the Spirit (Matt 12:22–32) is in such a grievous category of sin that Jesus warns, "People will be forgiven every sin and blasphemy, but the blasphemy against the Spirit will not be forgiven. Whoever speaks a word against the Son of Man, it will be forgiven him; but whoever speaks against the Holy Spirit, it will not be forgiven him, either in this age or in the one to come" (vv. 31–32). Blasphemy is speech that insults or shows contempt for God; in the Old Testament it is punishable by death (Lev 24:10–16), and Jesus is executed for blasphemy as he is alleged to be a mere man who claims to be God (Matt 26:63–65).[4] For the Spirit to be blasphemed, he must be God.

---

[3] Commenting on 2 Cor 13:13 (cited above), Gordon Fee underscores the apostolic benediction's support for the deity of the Third Person: "That Paul would include the Holy Spirit as an equal member of this triadic formula, and that he would pray to the Spirit in their behalf, says as much about his understanding of the Spirit both as person and as deity as any direct statement of this kind ever could"; Gordon Fee, *God's Empowering Presence*, 364–65. Note also John's triadic greeting in Revelation: "Grace and peace to you from the one who is, who was, and who is to come, and from the seven spirits before his throne, and from Jesus Christ, the faithful witness, the firstborn from the dead and the ruler of the kings of the earth" (Rev 1:4–5). This greeting associates the Holy Spirit ("the seven spirits") with the Father (named triadically as "the one who is, who was, and who is to come") and the Son ("Jesus Christ," described triadically as witness, firstborn, and king). For further discussion see Malcolm B. Yarnell III, *God the Trinity: Biblical Portraits* (Nashville: B&H Academic, 2016).

[4] See Gregg R. Allison, *The Baker Compact Dictionary of Theological Terms* (Grand Rapids: Baker, 2016), s.v. "blasphemy."

Second, people who continue to sin grievously after hearing the gospel should heed this warning: "How much worse punishment do you think one will deserve who has trampled on the Son of God, who has regarded as profane the blood of the covenant by which he was sanctified, and who has insulted the Spirit of grace?" (Heb 10:29). Divine judgment awaits those who heinously reject the salvation accomplished by the Son of God and the accompanying grace of the Spirit, who himself is God.

Accordingly, we rightly presuppose and conclude the deity of the Holy Spirit. In so doing, we confess this truth along with the church throughout its history. This confession is in keeping with the Nicene-Constantinopolitan Creed, with which we began our discussion.

Historical Development

Of course, this creed was the product of much theological reflection in the early church about the nature of the Holy Spirit.[5] A half century earlier, the Council of Nicaea (325) had confessed in the third article of its creed, "We believe in the Holy Spirit," a confession that was a good initial step. Much more reflection and a more robust confession were necessary, however, in the face of heresies denying the Spirit's deity. One group that opposed the growing church consensus was the Pneumatomachians, or Spirit-fighters.

Gregory of Nyssa,[6] in his *On the Holy Spirit against the Followers of Macedonius*, denounced these opponents who asserted an essential difference between the Holy Spirit and the other two persons, the Father and the Son. These adversaries maintained that the Holy Spirit is inferior to and less than the other two persons in every point—in power, glory, dignity. The Holy Spirit does not share in the glory and honor of the Father and the Son and,

---

[5] For surveys of the early church's discussion of the Holy Spirit, see Swete, *The Holy Spirit in the Ancient Church*; Myk Habets, *The Progressive Mystery: Tracing the Elusive Spirit in Scripture and Tradition* (Bellington: Lexham Press, 2019), part 3.

[6] In the following discussion, the fourth-century contributions of the three Cappadocian Fathers—Gregory of Nyssa, Gregory of Nazianzus, and Basil the Great—are summarized as examples of early church affirmation of the deity of the Holy Spirit.

in terms of power, possesses "only so much of it as is sufficient for the partial activity assigned to him," which is thus a denial of creative power—and deity—to the Spirit.[7]

To counter this error, Gregory outlined a case for the deity of the Spirit from Scripture: he is absolutely good, omnipotent, wise, glorious, eternal, immutable, beautiful, independent of human ascriptions, sovereign, and holy, being himself goodness, wisdom, power, sanctification/holiness, righteousness, eternality, and immortality. Moreover, Gregory confronted the alleged evidence against the deity of Holy Spirit on the basis of his lack of creative power. According to the Pneumatomachians, Scripture affirms that the Father is Creator and that creation came about through the Son, but it says nothing about the Holy Spirit in relation to the creation; thus, they concluded, the Spirit is not divine. Gregory countered that such an idea imagines that the Holy Spirit was not always with the Father and the Son, and it raises the question of what the Spirit was doing at creation. Perhaps he was engaged in some other work? Maybe he was resting easy? Gregory's response set forth the inseparable operations (see later discussion) of the three persons. It is not as though God created through the Son because the Father needed help. Likewise, it is not as though the Son lacked the necessary power and needed the Holy Spirit's help to work. Rather, "the fountain of power is the Father, and the power of the Father is the Son, and the spirit of that power is the Holy Spirit; and creation entirely, in all its visible and spiritual extent, is the finished work of that divine power."[8] In other words, creation came about through the one will, impulse, and power of the triune God, "beginning from the Father, advancing through the Son, and completed in the Holy Spirit."[9]

Furthermore, Gregory countered the charge that the Holy Spirit is of lesser glory than the Father and the Son. The one who gives glory to another must himself possess superabundant glory; otherwise it would be impossible for him, devoid of glory, to give glory. From all eternity, the three persons have been engaged in mutual glory-giving. The Father eternally glorifies the

---

[7] Gregory of Nyssa, *On the Holy Spirit against the Followers of Macedonius; Nicene- and Post-Nicene Fathers*, ed. Alexander Roberts, James Donaldson, Philip Schaff, and Henry Wace, 2nd ser., 14 vols. (Peabody: Hendrickson, 1994), 5:316.

[8] Nyssa, 5:320.

[9] Nyssa, 5:320.

Son and the Spirit. The Son eternally glorifies the Father and the Spirit. The Spirit eternally glorifies the Father and the Son. The conclusion from this last affirmation must be that the Holy Spirit is himself glorious; this is "the revolving circle of the glory moving from Like to Like."[10] The Father, the Son, and the Holy Spirit are alike in their glory. Accordingly, the Holy Spirit is divine.

In his *On the Holy Trinity, and of the Godhead of the Holy Spirit*, Gregory of Nyssa further demonstrated the deity of the Spirit from the fact that the three persons always act together in every divine work or operation. He noted that if the operations of the Father, the Son, and the Holy Spirit were to differ from one another, we would rightly conclude that the natures that operated these different works were also different. In this scenario, the three persons would possess different natures. However, if the work of the Father, the Son, and the Holy Spirit is one, we rightly infer the oneness of their nature from the identity of their operation. In this scenario, the three persons possess one divine nature, meaning that the Holy Spirit is divine. According to Scripture, the Father, the Son, and the Holy Spirit work together to give sanctification, life, light, comfort, and other such graces. Thus the identity of operations indicates a commonality of nature, that is, one Godhead, with the three persons sharing in that one divine nature. Accordingly, the Holy Spirit is divine.[11]

A second contributor, Gregory of Nazianzus, in his *Fifth Theological Oration: On the Holy Spirit*, proposed a complex argument for the deity of the Spirit based on the difference between a *substance*—something that exists in itself—and an *accident*—something that exists in something else.[12] Gregory offered two options: either the Holy Spirit is (1) a substance, thus existing in himself; or (2) an accident, existing in and dependent on something else. Beginning with option (2), there are two possibilities: either the Holy Spirit is (2a) an activity of God or (2b) part of God. This latter option (2b) is impossible, for God is not composed of parts. But the former option (2a) is also impossible, for God (not the Holy Spirit) will engage in the activity,

---

[10] Nyssa, 5:324.

[11] Nyssa, 5:328–29.

[12] For example, a human being is a substance, whereas blue eyes and blond hair are accidents.

and once God has engaged in the activity, it will cease to exist. But Scripture emphasizes that the Holy Spirit himself acts, which is not possible for an activity (an activity does not act, but an agent acts); thus the Holy Spirit must be an agent, not an activity. Therefore Gregory eliminated the second option, that the Holy Spirit is an accident. As for option (1), there are two possibilities: either the Holy Spirit is (1a) a creature of God or (1b) God. The former option (1a) is impossible, for Christians believe in the Holy Spirit and are perfected by him, something that would be blasphemous and unattainable if he were a creature.[13] This leaves the latter option (1b) as true: the Holy Spirit is God.[14]

Basil the Great made a third important contribution to this development. In response to the position that the Holy Spirit is third in dignity and rank and therefore different in nature from the Father and the Son, he admitted the trinitarian order—the Father is the First Person, the Son is the Second Person, and the Spirit is the Third Person. He dissented, however, from the conclusion that third in dignity and rank means third—thus, inferior—in nature.[15] Moreover, Basil pointed to the baptismal formula in the Great Commission (Matt 28:19), in which the Father, the Son, and the

---

[13] Later, Augustine argued against viewing the Holy Spirit as a creature. Appealing to Paul's statement that a believer's body "is a temple of the Holy Spirit" (1 Cor 6:19) and combining it with the apostle's earlier statement that "your bodies are members of Christ" (v. 15 ESV), Augustine reasoned, "What can be more senseless or profane than that anyone should dare to say that the members of Christ are the temple of one who, in their opinion, is a creature inferior to Christ?" Augustine rejected the creatureliness of the Holy Spirit by means of this parallel: Christians are members of Christ. Christians are the temple of the Holy Spirit. Consequently, there is a parallel between Christ and the Holy Spirit. Christ is not a creature; therefore, the Holy Spirit is not a creature. Augustine, *On the Trinity*, bk. 1, chap. 13; *Nicene-and Post-Nicene Fathers*, ed. Alexander Roberts, James Donaldson, Philip Schaff, and Henry Wace, 1st ser., 14 vols. (Peabody: Hendrickson, 1994), 3:23.

[14] Gregory of Nazianzus, *Fifth Theological Oration: On the Holy Spirit*, 6; NPNF² 7:319.

[15] Basil, *St. Basil of Caesarea against Eunomius*, 3.1, trans. Mark Delcogliano and Andrew Radde-Gallwitz (Washington, DC: Catholic University Press of America, 2011), 186. Basil reasoned, "The Son is second to the Father in rank because he is from him. He is second to the Father in dignity because the Father is the principle and cause by virtue of which he is the Son's Father and because we approach and access the God and Father through the Son. Even so, the Son is not second in nature, since there is one divinity in both of them." Basil concluded that though the Spirit is

Holy Spirit are conjoined. Clearly there is a trinitarian order in the succession of the three persons, but "we have never learned from anywhere that the Holy Spirit is cast out into some sort of nature third from the Son and the Father."[16]

Continuing his case for the Spirit's deity, Basil appealed to many of the reasons already presented here, including the parallelism between lying to the Holy Spirit and lying to God (Acts 5:3–4); his exalted title ("Holy Spirit");[17] his works, including creation, the incarnation of the Son, Jesus's exorcisms, remission of sins, the resurrection, intercession for believers; the Spirit's divine nature; and much more.[18] Basil underscored the difference between creatures, whose holiness may be augmented or diminished, and the Spirit, who is holy by nature and the source of creaturely holiness. Such consideration proves that the Spirit is a divine person and not a human creature.[19] Further proofs include the many benefits bestowed on Christians by the Spirit: adoption as sons, teaching truth, distributing spiritual gifts (which demonstrates that the Spirit "has nothing other than authoritative and sovereign power"), scrutinizing the depths of God (only a divine being can know the divine being), granting eternal life, rendering believers the dwelling place of God, and perfecting the saints.[20] Indeed, Basil presented the Spirit as the divine person who will actualize the consummation of the divine blessings in the age to come:

> Through the Holy Spirit comes our restoration to paradise, our ascension into the kingdom of heaven, our return to the adoption of

---

third in rank and dignity in relation to the Father and the Son, he is not of a different (that is, inferior) nature; rather, he is God.

[16] Basil, 3.2, 187. Basil added, "Baptism is the seal of faith, and faith is an assent to divinity. For one must first believe, then be sealed with baptism." Accordingly, Christians acknowledge the deity of the Spirit when they are baptized (3.5, 192).

[17] Basil, 3.6, 194, worked hard to distinguish the Son, who is "the Only-Begotten," from the Third Person: "What should we call him? Holy Spirit, Spirit of God, Spirit of truth sent from God and bestowed through the Son, not a servant, but a holy, good, and guiding Spirit that gives life, Spirit of adopted sonship, the one who knows all that is God's."

[18] Basil, *On the Holy Spirit*, 15.36–16.37, 19.48–50, 22.53; *NPNF*[2] 8:22–23, 30–32, 34.

[19] Basil, *St. Basil of Caesarea against Eunomius*, 3.2, 188.

[20] Basil, 3.4–5, 190–92.

sons, our liberty to call God our Father, our being made partakers of the grace of Christ, our being called children of light, our sharing in eternal glory, and, in a word, our being brought into a state of all "fullness of blessing" (Rom 15:29), both in this world and in the world to come, of all the good gifts that are in store for us, by promise hereof, through faith, beholding the reflection of their grace as though they were already present, we await the full enjoyment. If such is the earnest, what the perfection?[21]

Accordingly, the Holy Spirit is God.

In summary, through the theological leadership of these fourth-century stalwart Christians, the early church countered attacks against the deity of the Holy Spirit and mounted a convincing case for his deity.[22] From the Creed of Nicaea's simple affirmation, "We believe in the Holy Spirit," a robust confession arose in the Nicene-Constantinopolitan Creed that established the church's abiding belief in the deity of the Holy Spirit.

The Holy Spirit is a divine person.[23]

---

[21] Basil, *On the Holy Spirit*, 16:36; *NPNF*[2] 8:22.

[22] For treatment of the historical development of the doctrine of the Holy Spirit, see Anthony C. Thiselton, *The Holy Spirit in Biblical Teaching through the Centuries and Today* (Grand Rapids: Eerdmans, 2013), 163–467; Stanley M. Burgess, "Holy Spirit, Doctrine of: The Ancient Fathers"; Burgess, "Holy Spirit, Doctrine of: The Medieval Church"; and Burgess, "Holy Spirit, Doctrine of: Reformation Traditions"; in *The New International Dictionary of Pentecostal and Charismatic Movements*, rev. and expanded ed., ed. Stanley M. Burgess and Eduard M. van der Maas (Grand Rapids: Zondervan, 2002), 730–69; Veli-Matti Kärkkäinen, *The Holy Spirit: A Guide to Christian Theology* (Louisville: John Knox, 2012); Kärkkäinen, *Pneumatology*, 27–96; Cecil M. Robeck and Amos Yong, eds., *The Cambridge Companion to Pentecostalism* (New York: Cambridge University Press, 2014), 1–72; Yves Congar, *I Believe in the Holy Spirit*, trans. David Smith, 3 vols. (New York: Crossroad/Herder & Herder, 2015), 1:65–158; 3:19–127; F. LeRon Shults and Andrea Hollingsworth, *The Holy Spirit*, Guides to Theology (Grand Rapids: Eerdmans, 2008); Heron, *The Holy Spirit*, 63–117; Gary Badcock, *Light of Truth and Fire of Love: A Theology of the Holy Spirit* (Grand Rapids: Eerdmans, 1997), 35–124; Bloesch, *The Holy Spirit*, 78–143; Christopher R. J. Holmes, *The Holy Spirit, (New Studies in Dogmatics)* (Grand Rapids: Zondervan, 2015), 45–79 (Augustine), 83–130 (Thomas Aquinas), 133–64 (Karl Barth); Allison, *Historical Theology*, 430–49.

[23] For a classical defense of the deity and personhood of the Spirit see Owen, *Pneumatologia*, 64–92.

Scriptural Warrant and Historical Consensus of the Spirit's Personhood

As to the personhood of the Holy Spirit, we begin with an ongoing difficulty. Given the names "Father" and "Son," we have little problem affirming the personhood of the first two members of the Trinity. With the name "Holy Spirit," however, we do not so readily understand the third member to be a person. Matters can be complicated by the common English moniker "Holy Ghost," an expression that conjures up the idea of a phantom, phantasm, or poltergeist—perhaps even Casper the friendly ghost![24] Moreover, the contemporary emphasis on the power of the Holy Spirit has confused some people so that they imagine the Spirit to be a compelling force, a source of supernatural energy, or a mighty influence—a potency rather than a person.

Wisdom from the church's past helps us in recognizing that the expression "Holy Spirit" is not a vague reference to some ethereal force but instead the proper name of the Third Person.[25] Speaking of the Trinity, Augustine noted that the terms "holy" (the attribute of exaltedness above creation and absolute moral purity) and "spirit" (the attribute of immateriality rather than embodiment) apply alike to all three persons: the First Person is both holy and spirit, the Second Person is both holy and spirit, and the Third Person is both holy and spirit. In anticipation of a later discussion, we note here that the Holy Spirit proceeds from both the Father and the Son and as the Third Person is the bond of love between the first two persons and the gift of them both. Accordingly, his proper name is *Holy Spirit*, because "he is referred both to the Father and the Son."[26] Diagrammatically:

---

[24] Karl Barth remarked, "In English the word should certainly not be reproduced by 'Ghost' with its frightening proximity to 'spooks.'" Karl Barth, *Evangelical Theology: An Introduction* (New York: Holt, Rinehart, and Winston, 1963), 53.

[25] For further discussion, see Owen, *Pneumatologia*, 47–64.

[26] Augustine, *On the Trinity*, 5.12; *NPNF*[1] 93. Basil of Caesarea, *St. Basil of Caesarea against Eunomius*, 3.3, 189, made a similar argument but employed it in defense of the Spirit's deity: "Not only does the Spirit have the name 'holy' in common with the Father and the Son, but he also has the very designation 'Spirit' in common with them. [Basil cites John 4:24; Lam 4:20, and 2 Cor 3:17 in support.] These testimonies make it clear to everyone that the communion of the names does not communicate the Spirit's estrangement [difference] of nature, but rather his affinity with the Father and the Son."

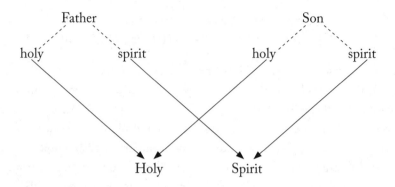

Once again, for Augustine, "the Holy Spirit is a certain unutterable communion of the Father and the Son." Therefore he is properly named "Holy
Spirit," "because the same name is suitable to both the Father and the Son.
For he himself is called especially that which they are called in common,
because both the Father is a spirit and the Son is a spirit, both the Father
is holy and the Son is holy. In order, therefore, that the communion of both
may be signified by a name that is suitable to both,"[27] the Third Person is
properly called "Holy Spirit." Understood in this way, as a term that expresses
the relation of the Third Person to the first two persons, his very name "Holy
Spirit" helps us recognize his personhood.

Gregory of Nazianzus aids in this regard, noting the relationship
between the Holy Spirit and the incarnate Son: "Christ is born; the Spirit is
his forerunner. He is baptized; the Spirit bears witness. He is tempted; the
Spirit leads him up. He works miracles; the Spirit accompanies them. He
ascends; the Spirit takes his place."[28] With a bit of reasoning, the conclusion
to be drawn is that as the incarnate Son is a person, so also is the Holy Spirit,
who stands in relationship to him.

Moreover, from our earlier discussion we have already established the
ground for affirming the personhood of the Holy Spirit. Characterized by
independence, immutability, omnipresence, truthfulness, holiness, love, and
the like, and sharing in the exact same nature as that of the Father (the First
Person) and the Son (the Second Person), the Holy Spirit is clearly a divine
person, the Third Person of the Trinity.

---

[27] Augustine, *On the Trinity*, 5.12; *NPNF*[1] 93.
[28] Gregory of Nazianzus, *Fifth Theological Oration*, 29; *NPNF*[2] 7:327.

Biblical Affirmations

We have biblical warrant for such an affirmation. According to Scripture, the Holy Spirit exhibits personal characteristics: (1) intelligence: he knows all things; (2) emotions: in ways that are true for a divine person and in some ways analogous to human persons, the Holy Spirit can be grieved (Isa 63:10; Eph 4:30)[29] and even insulted (Heb 10:29 CSB), or outraged (Heb 10:29 ESV); and (3) will: as the sovereign Lord, the Holy Spirit's volition is expressed, for example, in the distribution of believers' spiritual gifts (1 Cor 12:11) and in appointing specific missionary personnel and directing them on their mission (e.g., Acts 13:1–4; 16:6–8). Moreover, according to Scripture the Spirit engages in personal activities: testifying (about Christ, John 15:26; to believers, Rom 8:16), teaching (John 14:26), leading (Ps 143:10; Rom 8:14), and praying (Rom 8:26–27). Accordingly, "the Holy Spirit is not only an *action* but also an *actor*, that is, a principle endowed with will and intelligence who acts consciously and freely."[30]

Certainly, the Holy Spirit is all-powerful, as evidenced in his works of creating ex nihilo, sustaining the universe in existence, effecting the incarnation of the Son in the womb of the virgin Mary, raising the crucified Jesus from the dead, and much more. But it is a *person* who engages in such actions, not an impersonal force or energy. In this case, he is an all-powerful divine person who effects these realities: the Third Person of the Trinity, the Holy Spirit.

Historical Development

Historically, as we have seen, opponents of the deity of the Holy Spirit maintained that he is something other than God. Thus the early church debate was pitched not in terms of the personhood of the Spirit but in terms of his inferiority in nature. According to von Harnack, "When the question as to the personality of the Spirit emerged, it was as quickly settled that it

---

[29] Gordon Fee notes the importance of this passage for affirming the personal nature of the Holy Spirit (*God's Empowering Presence*, 715–16). [AK 176fn340]

[30] Raniero Cantalamessa, *The Mystery of Pentecost*, trans. Glen S. Davis (Collegeville: Liturgical Press, 2001), 52. Cf. Witherington and Ice, *Shadow of the Almighty*, 130.

must be a *persona*, for the nature of God is not so poor that his Spirit cannot be a person."[31]

This position was rarely challenged until, in the sixteenth century, the heretical Socinianism denied the Trinity and considered the Holy Spirit to be the power of God.[32] Pantheism, panentheism, the German idealism of Hegel and Schelling, and similar philosophies considered God and the world to be intricately connected, even identified, such that in some versions a world spirit courses through all that exists. Within a religious context, confusion arose about the personhood of the Holy Spirit among some cults. The Jehovah Witnesses, for example, believe that "the holy spirit is the active force of God. It is not a person but a powerful force that God causes to emanate from himself to accomplish his holy will."[33] Mary Baker Eddy, founder of Christian Science, defined "Holy Ghost" as "Divine Science; the development of eternal Life, Truth, and Love."[34] Mormonism teaches that the Holy Ghost, as the third member of the Godhead, "is a personage of Spirit, not having a body of flesh and bones," as do the Father and the Son.[35]

In both its historical and contemporary forms, the denial of the personhood of the Holy Spirit stands in stark contrast to the church's insistence, based on Scripture, that he is the Third Person of the Trinity.

Conclusion

As the church confesses the divine personhood of the Holy Spirit, it is compelled to worship and glorify him together with the Father and the Son. In our weekly gatherings, we sing songs of praise and thanksgiving to the triune God, honoring the Spirit for his works of creation/re-creation/perfection

---

[31] Von Harnack, *History of Dogma*, 4:117.

[32] Owen briefly treated this Socinian heresy in *Pneumatologia*, 68–72.

[33] Watch Tower Bible and Tract Society of Pennsylvania, *Reasoning from the Scriptures* (Brooklyn: Watch Tower Bible and Tract Society of Pennsylvania, 1985), 381.

[34] Mary Baker Eddy, *Science and Health with Key to the Scriptures* (Boston: Christian Science Board of Directors, 2006), 588.

[35] The Church of Jesus Christ of Latter-Day Saints, Guide to the Scriptures, accessed August 20, 2019, https://www.churchofjesuschrist.org/study/scriptures/gs/holy-ghost?lang=eng&clang=eng#title2.

(e.g., regeneration, adoption, and resurrection). We confess our sins, aided by the Spirit's conviction, acknowledging that we have grieved him by our rebellion. We receive the forgiveness of our sins with thankfulness for the Father's sovereign plan of redemption through the Son's curse-reversing work applied through the Holy Spirit's action. As Scripture is read and preached, we recognize the Spirit's work of inspiration and depend on his work of illumination to understand rightly and live obediently the Word of God. Together we pray in step with the Spirit for the concerns of our church, its missional engagement with our neighbors near and far, its hurting and suffering members, and much more. We rejoice as new people are baptized and believers celebrate the Lord's Supper, trusting the Spirit's work of uniting our church with Christ through identification with his death, burial, and resurrection and participation in and nourishment with his body and blood. As the gathering concludes, we enter into our mission field, refreshed by the Lord and dependent on the Spirit's empowerment for holy living and fruitful witness.

Furthermore, because the Holy Spirit is a divine person, we treat him accordingly. We obey him as he speaks to us through the Word of God. Specifically, we yield to the one who commands us to "be filled by the Spirit" (Eph 5:18). As we walk in the Spirit, we submit consciously and continually to his leading. We depend on him for both life and new life. We honor and respect him as the Spirit who provides access to the Father and the Son and who renders the triune God present in our life and our church.

14

The Holy Spirit and the Holy Trinity: Intratrinitarian Relations

Our pneumatology explores more deeply what it means to confess that the Holy Spirit is the Third Person of the Trinity, equal to the Father and the Son in terms of his divine nature yet distinct from the First Person and the Second Person. We begin with a discussion of the *ontological* (also called the *immanent*, or *essential*) Trinity: "ontology" has to do with the *being* (Gr. ὄντος [*ontos*] = being) of God. Technically, this discussion is about God *ad intra*, God as he is in himself, rather than God *ad extra*, God as he is toward the world.

The doctrine of the Trinity affirms that God eternally exists as the Father, the Son, and the Holy Spirit, three distinct divine persons, each of whom is fully God; yet there is only one God. The reality to which this doctrine refers is infinitely and ultimately mysterious, yet on the basis of Scriptural warrant, and in keeping with a traditional/catholic trinitarian orientation, our pneumatology affirms the following.

The Notion of a Trinitarian "Person"

Technically, the notion of a trinitarian person is a *subsisting relation*: the Father, the Son, and the Holy Spirit are three persons existing as eternal

relations.[1] It is not as though the relations *exist between* the three persons (we may think of our relationship with our spouse or with one of our
friends); rather, the persons *are* the relations.[2] The three are defined and
distinguished from one another as the eternal relations. These relations are
also called *relations of origin* because they express the three persons in terms
of their origination.[3] However, we should think in terms not of a *temporal*
beginning but of an *eternal* relation of origin. Thus we have the following
trinitarian "grammar":

- The Father is characterized by *paternity*: he is eternally the Father
  of the Son.
- The Son is characterized by *eternal generation* (also called *eternal
  begottenness*, but for simplicity's sake we will only use the term *generation*): the Son is eternally generated by the Father, or, put another
  way, the Father eternally generates the Son.
- The Holy Spirit is characterized by *eternal procession* or *eternal spiration*: the Holy Spirit eternally proceeds from the Father and the
  Son or, put another way, the Father and the Son eternally spirate the
  Holy Spirit.[4]

Now that we have the grammar of paternity, generation, procession, and
spiration, we can say a bit more about the three persons as subsisting relations or relations of origin.

---

[1] Thus, to affirm "God is" makes a statement about the divine essence, which is
common to the three persons. To affirm "God subsists" makes a statement about the
subsisting relations, which are different for the three persons. See Holmes's discussion of Augustine on this point in Christopher R. J. Holmes, *The Holy Spirit*, New
Studies in Dogmatics (Grand Rapids: Zondervan, 2015), 65–67.

[2] Thomas Aquinas affirmed that the relations are the persons and are the essence
of the Godhead: "Since relation, considered as really existing in God, is the divine
essence itself, and the essence is the same as person . . . relation must necessarily be
the same as person." Aquinas, *Summa Theologica*, pt. 1, q. 40, art. 1.

[3] Aquinas, pt. 1, q. 40, art. 2, distinguished relation and origin, but for the sake
of simplicity we will not nuance the discussion in this way.

[4] *Spiration*, the noun, and *spirate*, the verb, have to do with *breath* and *breathing*.
Our biblical theology section makes the connection between *breath* and *spirit/Spirit*.
See especially Ezek 37:1–14.

- The Father is eternally characterized by paternity, which is his eternal relation of origin in respect to the Son. The Father is not generated (generation belongs to the Son only), nor does he proceed (procession belongs to the Holy Spirit only). The Father is unoriginate, being instead the eternal source of the divine Person of the Son and, together with the Son, the eternal source of the divine Person of the Holy Spirit.[5]

- The Son is characterized by eternal generation, which is his eternal relation of origin in respect to the Father. "Eternal generation does not mean that the Son was created by the Father, or that the Son's divine nature is derived from his, or that the Son is inferior, but it means that the Son is eternally dependent on the Father for his person-of-the-Son. Affirmations that the Father grants the Son to have life in himself (John 5:26) and that the Son has been born of God (1 John 5:18) point to his eternal generation by the Father."[6]

- The Holy Spirit is characterized by eternal procession, which is his eternal relation of origin in respect to the Father and the Son. "This does not mean that he was created by them, or that his divine nature is derived from theirs, or that he is inferior, but it means that he is eternally dependent on them for his person-of-the-Spirit."[7] To put it another way, the Father and the Son eternally spirate the Holy Spirit, granting him his person-of-the-Spirit.[8]

---

[5] The divine being (the Godhead) cannot generate or spirate. Rather, only a divine person can generate (the Father eternally generates the Son), and only a divine person or persons can spirate (the Father and the Son eternally spirate the Holy Spirit); see Holmes, *The Holy Spirit*, 65–67.

[6] Allison, *The Baker Compact Dictionary of Theological Terms*, s.v. "eternal generation."

[7] Allison, *The Baker Compact Dictionary of Theological Terms*, s.v. "eternal procession."

[8] Our pneumatology does not support the idea that eternal procession (and, likewise, eternal generation) has to do with the Father and the Son granting to the Spirit his divine nature. As Holmes, *The Holy Spirit*, 95–97, notes, "the Spirit does not receive divine status from the Son (or the Father). The Spirit is God from eternity, as are Father and Son: God the Holy Trinity." Indeed, following Calvin, we affirm that the Holy Spirit is *autotheos*: God of himself; thus, he does not and cannot derive his deity from the Father and the Son through eternal procession; see John Calvin, *Institutes of the Christian Religion*, 1.13.25, LCC (Philadelphia: Westminster,

Though we have noted biblical support for the eternal generation of the Son (John 5:26; 1 John 5:18), the biblical case for the eternal procession of the Holy Spirit requires more development.

The Eternal Procession of the Holy Spirit

In his Upper Room Discourse (John 14–16), Jesus pledges a future coming of the Holy Spirit:

- "The Counselor, the Holy Spirit, *whom the Father will send in my name*, will teach you all things and remind you of everything I have told you." (14:26)
- "When the Counselor comes, *the one I will send to you from the Father*—the Spirit of truth who proceeds from the Father—he will testify about me." (15:26)
- "I am telling you the truth. It is for your benefit that I go away, because if I don't go away the Counselor will not come to you. If I go, *I will send him to you*." (16:7)

In these words of promise we hear a tandem sending (the italicized sections) of the Holy Spirit: the Father, from whom the Spirit proceeds, will send the Holy Spirit (in Jesus's name), and Jesus himself will send the Holy Spirit (from the Father).[9] This promise of sending points forward to the day of Pentecost, when the promise is fulfilled. As Peter, speaking of Jesus, explains, "Therefore, since he has been exalted to the right hand of God and has received from the Father the promised Holy Spirit, [Jesus] has poured out what you both see and hear" (Acts 2:33).[10]

1960), 21:153–54. For further discussion of Calvin's idea of *autotheos* see Paul Helm, *John Calvin's Ideas* (Oxford, UK: Oxford University Press, 2004), 35–57.

[9] Jesus did not indicate that the Spirit proceeds from the Father *alone* (15:26). Thus, when the church formulated the doctrine of the eternal procession of the Holy Spirit from the Father *and* the Son, the church *added to* the biblical affirmation of John 15:26 but *did not contradict* it.

[10] Thus, at Pentecost "Jesus transitions from being the Spirit-bearer, the promised one who was filled with the Spirit, to the Spirit-sender. Now he becomes the one who gives the Spirit." Allen, *Poured Out*, 81.

Seeking to understand this event, we rightly raise the question of why the Father and the Son send the Holy Spirit on the day of Pentecost. Why does the Father alone, or the Son alone, not send the Spirit? Or why does the Holy Spirit not send the Father? The church has historically answered with an appeal to the Spirit's eternal relation of origin: the Holy Spirit is characterized by eternal procession from the Father and the Son.[11] Being eternally dependent on them for his person-of-the-Spirit, he comes when sent by the Father and the Son on the day of Pentecost.

The eternal procession of the Spirit from the Father and the Son is confirmed by other biblical passages. On the day of his resurrection, Jesus appears to his disciples and, after commissioning them to continue the mission he has inaugurated, engages in an enacted parable: "*He breathed* on them and said to them, '*Receive the Holy Spirit*'" (John 20:22). In this harbinger of his forthcoming sending of the Spirit on the day of Pentecost, Jesus imparts the Spirit to his disciples. Moreover, the Holy Spirit is referred to as "the Spirit of your Father" (Matt 10:20) and "the Spirit of Jesus Christ" (Phil 1:19) as well as "the Spirit of his Son" (Gal 4:6). Indeed, Paul joins the two expressions, calling him "the Spirit of God [the Father]" and "the Spirit of Christ" (Rom 8:9). As the Spirit of the Father and the Spirit of the Son, the Holy Spirit is sent by both on the day of Pentecost and now dwells in Christians. And this missional reality derives from the eternal relation of origin: the Holy Spirit eternally proceeds from the Father and the Son.

Support for this double procession of the Holy Spirit also comes from the Western church—Roman Catholic and Protestant—but not the Eastern church.[12] For example, while Basil the Great affirmed that the Holy Spirit proceeds from the Father, he also noted that the Spirit is joined "to the one Father *through* the one Son" and that "the natural goodness and the inherent holiness and the royal dignity extend *from* the Father *through*

---

[11] For further discussion see Thomas Smail, *The Giving Gift: The Holy Spirit in Person* (London: Hodder and Stoughton, 1988), 116–43.

[12] Someone may object that my following two examples—Basil the Great and Gregory of Nyssa—are *Eastern* theologians and thus cannot be cited as *Western* church support for the double procession of the Spirit. However, my distinction between Western and Eastern churches refers to the decisive break over the issue of double procession that occurred in 1054, long after Basil and Gregory addressed the matter.

the only-begotten [Son] to the Spirit."[13] Similarly, Gregory of Nyssa maintained that "the Holy Spirit is indeed *from* God, and *of* the Christ, according to Scripture," such that he could speak of the Spirit as "proceeding from the Father, receiving from the Son."[14]

Augustine clarified the double procession of the Holy Spirit, underscoring that the Father and the Son are not "two agents as the source of the Holy Spirit. Rather, through the one action of the Father and the Son together, the Spirit proceeds. Indeed, in begetting the Son, the Father made it such that the Spirit would proceed from both of them":[15]

> It is not to no purpose that in this Trinity the Son and none other is called the Word of God, and the Holy Spirit and none other is called the Gift of God, and God the Father alone is he from whom the Word is born [begotten or generated], and from whom the Holy Spirit principally proceeds. And therefore I have added the word *principally*, because we find that the Holy Spirit proceeds from the Son also. But the Father gave [the Son] this too, not as to one already existing, and not yet having it; but whatever he gave to the only-begotten Word, he gave by begetting him. Therefore he so begat him as that the common Gift should proceed from him also, and the Holy Spirit should be the Spirit of both.[16]

That is, an element of the Father's eternal generation of the Son is the Son's participation with the Father in the eternal spiration of the Holy Spirit: he proceeds from both the Father and the Son. Again, according to Augustine: "The Son is from the Father, the Spirit is also from the Father. But the former is begotten, the latter proceeds. So the former is the Son of the Father from whom he is begotten, but the latter is the Spirit of both since he proceeds from both. . . . The Father is the author of the Spirit's procession

---

[13] Basil, *On the Holy Spirit*, 18:45, *NPNF²* 8:28–29.
[14] Gregory of Nyssa, *On the Holy Spirit against the Followers of Macedonius*; *NPNF²* 5:314–15.
[15] Allison, *Historical Theology*, 438.
[16] Augustine, *On the Trinity*, 15.17/29; *NPNF¹* 3:216.

because he begot such a Son, and in begetting him made him also the source from which the Spirit proceeds."[17]

In 589 the Third Council of Toledo (Spain) officially sanctioned the doctrine of the double procession of the Holy Spirit. It did so by modifying the Nicene-Constantinopolitan Creed (written in Latin) by the addition of one word: *filioque* ("and the Son"). Thus, the creed reads in part: "I believe in the Holy Spirit, the Lord and giver of life, who proceeds from the Father and the Son." Accordingly, the Holy Spirit in his intratrinitarian relation, or relation of origin, is the Third Person, characterized by eternal procession from the First Person and the Second Person.[18]

Thomas Aquinas maintained that without the *filioque*—and hence without the double procession of the Spirit from the Father and the Son—there would be no way of distinguishing the Son from the Holy Spirit. He explained the nature of the eternal relations of origin: they must be "opposite relations," that is, different relations. Diagrammatically:

relation type 1

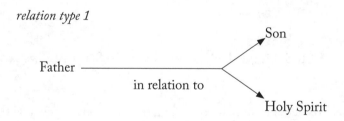

For Aquinas, these two relations are not opposite relations and thus do not constitute two distinct persons, as they belong only to the one person of the Father.

---

[17] Augustine, *Collattio cum Maximino Arianorum episcopo*, 2.14.1, cited in J. N. D. Kelly, *Early Christian Doctrines*, rev. ed. (San Francisco: Harper San Francisco, 1978), 275–76.

[18] In terms of the early doctrine of double procession, Leo I (the Great), in his *Letter* 15 to Turribius in 447, referred to the Holy Spirit as "the Other who proceeds from both [the Father and the Son]" (*qui de utroque processerit*). Swete, *The Holy Spirit in the Ancient Church*, 340–41. According to the Athanasian Creed, "the Holy Spirit is from the Father and the Son, neither made, nor created, nor begotten, but proceeding."

relation type 2

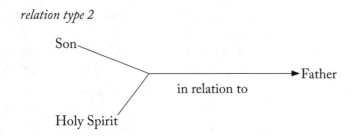

Again, for Aquinas these two relations are not opposite relations and thus do not make two distinct persons, as each is related to the Father; they belong only to the one person of the Son and of the Holy Spirit, which is heresy. Therefore the Son and the Holy Spirit must be related to each other by opposite relations; either:

Holy Spirit ⟶ Son (the Son is from the Holy Spirit, which nobody says)
       in relation to

or

Son ⟶ Holy Spirit (the Holy Spirit is from the Son, which we say)
  in relation to

We can also diagram this matter by using the traditional equilateral triangle (with all three sides being equal) to represent the three persons of the triune God:

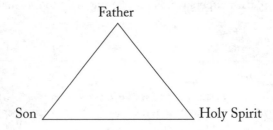

If the Father-Son relation of eternal generation is represented by a solid bold line, and the Father-Spirit relation of eternal procession is represented by a dashed line, then the two relations are equal (as the two sides of the triangle are equal); there is no distinction between the Son and the Spirit:

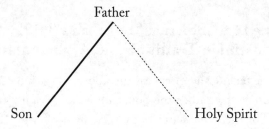

However, if the Father-Son relation of eternal generation is represented by a solid bold line and the Father + Son-Spirit relation of eternal double procession is represented by a dashed line, then the two relations are not equal; there is a clear distinction between the Son and the Spirit:

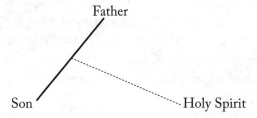

Thus, to return to the original equilateral triangle:

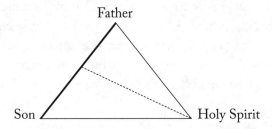

The relation of eternal generation is represented by the solid bold line between the Father and the Son, and the relation of eternal double procession is represented by the mid-triangular dashed line between the Father + Son and the Holy Spirit. Thus, affirming the *filioque*—and hence affirming the double procession of the Spirit from the Father and the Son—provides a way of distinguishing between the Son and the Holy Spirit.[19]

The Holy Spirit as "Love" and "Gift": The Augustinian Tradition and Argumentation[20]

So far we have technically discussed the notion of a trinitarian person as a *subsisting relation*: the Father, the Son, and the Holy Spirit are defined and distinguished by their eternal relations or relations of origin. But we can say more about the notion of a trinitarian person by following the church's rich trinitarian tradition of referring to the Holy Spirit by the names "Love" and "Gift." Accordingly, we can define and distinguish the three divine persons not only in terms of the Father, the Son, and the Holy Spirit but also in terms of the Father, the Son who is "Word," and the Holy Spirit who is "Love" and "Gift." Augustine originated this tradition and developed it in accordance with his faith-oriented approach to the interpretation of Scripture, his view of the Holy Spirit as the bond of love between the Father and the Son, and a particular exegesis of two key biblical passages.[21]

In terms of his hermeneutical approach, Augustine interpreted the Bible with the assumption

> that the Triune God wills to teach us about himself through Scripture, so that we might come to know and to love the living God. The faith-based expectation that God in Scripture is teaching us about his triunity leads Augustine to be alert for clues to the identity of the Holy Spirit, clues that Augustine employs to build his case that the Spirit is properly (i.e., distinctively among the three persons) named not only "Holy Spirit" but also "Love" and "Gift."[22]

---

[19] Thomas Aquinas, *Summa Theologica*, pt. 1, q. 36, art. 2–3.

[20] Much of the following discussion reflects the insights of Matthew Levering, *Engaging the Doctrine of the Holy Spirit: Love and Gift in the Trinity and the Church* (Grand Rapids: Baker, 2016), 51–70.

[21] Though this is a venerable tradition, it is not without its difficulties, as will become apparent in the following discussion. Though it lacks the strong biblical support we wish it possessed, because it expresses a near theological consensus in the church, we embrace it with caution.

[22] Levering, *Engaging the Doctrine of the Holy Spirit*, 54.

As Augustine approached Scripture with the expectation that it reveals that the Holy Spirit is also named "Love" and "Gift," his expectation was confirmed.

Augustine also warranted the name "Love" on the basis of his view that the Third Person is the bond of love between the other two persons: "The Holy Spirit . . . is something common both to the Father and the Son. But that communion itself is consubstantial and co-eternal; and if it may fittingly be called friendship, let it be so called. But it is more aptly called love." Detailing this bond of love, Augustine presented the Father as "one who loves him who is from himself" (i.e., the Son, who is from the Father), the Son as "one who loves him from whom he is" (i.e., the Father, from whom the Son is), and the Holy Spirit as "love itself."[23] Thus the Father loves the Son, the Son loves the Father, and the Holy Spirit is the love between the two. Or, the Father is the lover, the Son is the one who is loved, and the Spirit is the bond of love.

As for Augustine's particular interpretation of two key biblical passages relevant to naming the Holy Spirit "Love," he linked 1 John 4:7–13 with Rom 5:5. The apostle John urges:

> Dear friends, let us love one another, because love is from [or "of"] God, and everyone who loves has been born of God and knows God. The one who does not love does not know God, because God is love. God's love was revealed among us in this way: God sent his one and only Son into the world so that we might live through him. Love consists in this: not that we loved God, but that he loved us and sent his Son to be the atoning sacrifice for our sins. Dear friends, if God loved us in this way, we also must love one another. No one has ever seen God. If we love one another, God remains in us and his love is made complete in us. This is how we know that we remain in him and he in us: He has given us of his Spirit. (1 John 4:7–13)

Augustine's interpretation of this passage can be summarized as follows:

- Love is of God (v. 7).
- Love is God (v. 8).

---

[23] Augustine, *On the Trinity*, 6.5/7, *NPNF*[1] 3:100.

- Therefore, love is "God of God."
- Two divine persons can be called "God of God": the Son and the Holy Spirit.[24]
- God manifested his love by sending his Son as the atonement for our sins (vv. 9–10).
- In turn, we should love one another (v. 11).
- In so doing, God dwells in us and his love matures in us (v. 12).
- We can know that God dwells in us when we love one another, and the way we love is by God's gift of the Holy Spirit (v. 13).
- Therefore, the "God of God" is the Holy Spirit whom God has given.[25]
- Conclusion: the Holy Spirit "is the gift of God who is love," and the two names "Love" and "Gift," implying each other, are proper names of the Holy Spirit.

But there is more, as John continues in this letter: "And we have come to know and to believe the love that God has for us" (1 John 4:16). So Augustine continued: as we can know that God dwells in us when we love one another, and the way we love is by God's gift of the Holy Spirit (v. 13), so can we know that when we abide in love, we abide in God. Thus Augustine equated the Holy Spirit abiding in us with love abiding in us. He concluded, "The Holy Spirit, whom [God] has given us, makes us abide in God, and God in us; and this it is that love does. Therefore [the Holy Spirit] is the God who is love."[26]

With appeal to another passage in Scripture, Augustine drew his argument to a close: "Hope does not put us to shame, because *the love of God* has been poured into our hearts through the Holy Spirit who has been given to us" (Rom 5:5 ESV). Key to Augustine's argument is his interpretation of Paul's phrase "the love of God." Exegetically, this can refer either to *God's love*

---

[24] Augustine means that the expression "God of God" can be applied to the Son, as he is "God of God" in virtue of his eternal generation from the Father, and to the Holy Spirit, as he is "God of God" in virtue of his eternal procession from the Father and the Son.

[25] Thus, whereas before the expression "God of God" could refer to either the Son or the Holy Spirit, Augustine concludes that it refers to the Holy Spirit.

[26] Augustine, *On the Trinity*, 15.31; *NPNF¹* 217.

for us or to *our love for God.* Most modern interpreters take the expression in the first way: *God's love for us* has been poured out in our hearts through the gift of the Holy Spirit. As noted in chapter 8, in the section titled "Benefits Conferred by the Gospel on the Believer ([Romans] chs. 5–8)," "The Holy Spirit is here presented as *the messenger of God's love* in Christ—the love God showed when sending his Son to die for believers when they were still sinners" (Rom 5:8).[27] Augustine, by contrast, took it in the second way: *our love for God* is made possible through the gift of the Holy Spirit who has been poured out into our hearts.[28] Furthermore, he maintained that the love we are able to express for God through the Holy Spirit is due only to the fact that "the Holy Spirit *is* the love of God."[29] Accordingly, a proper name for the Holy Spirit is "Love."[30]

In addition to naming the Holy Spirit "Love," Augustine also named him "Gift," arguing for this moniker both theologically and biblically.[31] Theologically, he moved from the fact that the Holy Spirit's name is "Love"

---

[27] See the discussion of Romans 5:5 pp. 139–40.

[28] That is, in the phrase ἡ ἀγαπη του θεου (*hē agapē tou theou*), most modern interpreters take the genitive as a subjective genitive, but Augustine took it as an objective genitive. This point is a key reason our pneumatology is cautious about embracing this Augustinian tradition.

[29] Levering, *Engaging the Doctrine of the Holy Spirit*, 58.

[30] Thomas Aquinas contributed further to this discussion in *Summa Theologica*, pt. 1, q. 37. For Aquinas, the name of the Holy Spirit is "Love proceeding." In God, there are two processions, one by way of intellect and a second by way of will. The procession by way of intellect is the Word, while the procession by way of will is love. By this second procession, God loves himself. Such love is not the attribute shared commonly among the three persons in terms of the divine nature ("God is love;" 1 John 4:8). Rather, it is love in terms of "the relation to its principle" (*Summa Theologica*, pt. 1, q. 37, art. 1, answers that). As the Holy Spirit proceeds from both the Father and the Son (they are the one principle of his procession), he is "Love proceeding" in relation to his principle. Thus, he is the bond of love of the Father and the Son. Moreover, because the eternal procession of the Holy Spirit is a subsisting relation, "the Spirit is not a mere bond, but Love in person"; Levering, *Engaging the Doctrine of the Holy Spirit*, 98–101 (101); cf. Holmes, *The Holy Spirit*, 106–10. Our pneumatology has strong reservations about this distinction between procession by way of intellect and procession by way of will, finding inadequate biblical support for such a distinction.

[31] Thomas Aquinas expanded on Augustine's presentation in *Summa Theologica*, pt. 1, q. 38.

to the additional fact that the Spirit's name is "Gift." His reason was that "there is no gift of God more excellent than this [love]."[32]

Biblically, Augustine noted Jesus's promise of the Holy Spirit using the metaphors of drinking and water: "On the last and most important day of the festival, Jesus stood up and cried out, 'If anyone is thirsty, let him come to me and *drink*. The one who believes in me, as the Scripture has said, will have *streams of living water flow from deep within him*.' He said this about *the Spirit*" (John 7:37–38). Augustine further noted that Paul employs a similar metaphor: "We were all *given one Spirit to drink*" (1 Cor 12:13).

In answer to his own inquiry—"The question then is whether that water is called the gift of God, who is the Holy Spirit"—Augustine appealed to Jesus's conversation with the woman at the well of Samaria (John 4:7–14). Exhausted from his journey, Jesus says to her, "Give me a drink" (4:7), to which she replies with reluctance due to cultural factors between Jews and Samaritans. Jesus's response links the water under discussion with the gift of God: "If you knew *the gift of God*, and who is saying to you, 'Give me a drink,' you would ask him, and he would give you *living water*" (4:10). After some discussion on the woman's part, Jesus responds, "Everyone who drinks from this water will get thirsty again. But whoever drinks from *the water that I will give him* will never get thirsty again. In fact, the water that I will give him will become *a well of water springing up in him* for eternal life" (4:13–14). Combining the earlier affirmation—"streams of living water [will] flow from deep within him" (7:38)—with the expression "will become a well of water springing up in him to eternal life" (4:14), Augustine concluded that the reference is to the Holy Spirit, who is "the gift of God" (4:10). Accordingly, the proper name of the Holy Spirit is "Gift."[33]

Augustine appealed to other biblical passages to support his contention. From Paul's affirmation that "grace was given to each one of us according to the measure of *Christ's gift*" (Eph 4:7), Augustine explained that the gift is none other than the Holy Spirit.[34] In the book of Acts, Augustine highlighted

---

[32] Augustine, *On the Trinity*, 15.32; *NPNF*¹ 217.

[33] Augustine, 15.33; *NPNF*¹ 217–18.

[34] Augustine, 15.34; *NPNF*¹ 218–19. To arrive at his conclusion, Augustine riffed on Eph 4:8; Ps 68:18; Acts 9:4; Matt 25:40; 1 Cor 12:11; Heb 2:4; Eph 4:7–12; and Ps 127:1.

the several times Luke refers to the Holy Spirit as a gift. Peter's call to repentance offers the promise, "You will receive *the gift of the Holy Spirit*" (Acts 2:38). To Simon Magus's ploy to purchase the power of the Holy Spirit, Peter issues this rebuke: "May your silver be destroyed with you, because you thought you could obtain *the gift of God* with money!" (8:20). When the Holy Spirit falls on Cornelius and his family and friends, Peter and the Jewish believers with him are "amazed because *the gift of the Holy Spirit* had been poured out even on the Gentiles" (10:45). In Luke's second narrative of that event, Peter underscores the same point about the Holy Spirit: "God gave them *the same gift* as he also gave to us when we believed in the Lord Jesus Christ" (11:17). Augustine concluded, "And there are many other testimonies of the Scriptures, which unanimously attest that the Holy Spirit is the gift of God, in so far as he is given to those who by him love God."[35] Thus the Holy Spirit is also properly named both "Love" and "Gift."[36]

Our pneumatological view on the use of the names "Love" and "Gift" (1) affirms the Augustinian faith-oriented approach to biblical interpretation but (2) encounters difficulty with his exegesis of Scripture (particularly 1 John 4:7–13 with Rom 5:5) as biblical warrant for the name "Love," yet (3) embraces the name "Gift" on the basis of the several passages noted above.

With the names "Love" and "Gift," the Holy Spirit's work among the new covenant people of God gains a certain clarity: "If the action of the Holy Spirit in the economy is that of hypostatized [personalized] 'Love' and 'Gift,' this opens up plenty of theo-drama, as indeed we find in Scripture."[37] As "Love," the Holy Spirit is appropriately the person of the Trinity through whom "God's love has been poured out in our hearts" (Rom 5:5).[38] As "Gift," the Holy Spirit is appropriately the highest of the "good gifts" whom the heavenly Father gives to his children (Matt 7:11; Luke 11:13). Specifically, he is the promised "gift" whom the Father and the Son pour out on the Jews on the day of Pentecost (Acts 2:1–4, 33, 38), later on the Samaritans (Acts 8:14–20), and still later on the Gentiles (Act 10:45–47; 11:16–17).

---

[35] Augustine, 15.35; *NPNF*[1] 219.

[36] For further discussion of the Holy Spirit as "Giving Gift" see Smail, *The Giving Gift*, 14–22.

[37] Levering, *Engaging the Doctrine of the Holy Spirit*, 35.

[38] This interpretation takes the genitive "of God" as a subjective genitive, in agreement with most modern interpreters and against Augustine.

Moreover, as "Gift" he is the source of all "spiritual gifts" (1 Corinthians 12–14; Heb 2:4) and "gifted" people—"the apostles, the prophets, the evangelists, the shepherds and teachers"—whom Christ has given to lead his church (Eph 4:7–16 ESV).

Furthermore, the first letter of John makes an important distinction between the Son and the Spirit: the Son is *sent*, while the Spirit is *given*. In terms of the Son's being sent, John affirms, "God's love was revealed among us in this way: *God sent* his one and only Son into the world so that we might live through him. Love consists in this: not that we loved *God*, but that he loved us and *sent his Son* to be the atoning sacrifice for our sins. . . . And we have seen and we testify that *the Father has sent his Son* as the world's Savior" (1 John 4:9–10, 14). As for the Holy Spirit's being given, John affirms, "The way we know that [God] remains in us is from *the Spirit he has given us*. . . . This is how we know that we remain in him and he in us: *He has given us of his Spirit*" (1 John 3:24; 4:13).[39] The apostle John's distinction between the sending of the Son and the giving of the Spirit underscores the propriety of calling the Holy Spirit by the name "Gift."

Conclusion

In this section, our pneumatology has faced the great mystery of the Holy Spirit in the Holy Trinity. Because the reality to which this discussion points is shrouded in mystery, many people avoid talking about it altogether. However, given the hints in Scripture and the explorations of historical theology, our pneumatology embraces the eternal procession of the Holy Spirit from the Father and the Son as appropriately expressing the eternal relation of origin of the Third Person. Before and apart from the distinction in roles in relation to the *ad extra* works of the triune God, the Holy Spirit is eternally distinguished from the other two persons in virtue of receiving his person-of-the-Spirit from both the Father and the Son. We rightly praise God for his oneness and threeness, holding the two truths together: "No

---

[39] Thanks to Gregg's friend and colleague Oren Martin for pointing out this distinction. In terms of the Son's sending, John uses the verb ἀποστέλλω (*apostellō*), while he addresses the Spirit's being given using the verb δίδωμι (*didōmi*).

sooner do I conceive of the one than I am illumined by the splendor of the three; no sooner do I distinguish them than I am carried back to the one."[40]

Moreover, the discussion of eternal procession and the naming of the Holy Spirit as "Love" and "Gift" highlight the co-eminence of the Third Person in relation to the First Person and Second Person of the Trinity: the Holy Spirit is fully God and thus "with the Father and the Son together is worshipped and glorified." It may be that some people are hesitant to praise the Spirit, honor and adore him, obey and trust him, or give him thanks; indeed, some may even recoil at the thought. But such hesitation and adverse reaction are out of place. Our pneumatology challenges those who are suspicious of the propriety of reverencing and loving the Spirit. Such apprehension may be due to bad experiences with extreme manifestations of certain Spirit-emphasizing movements or to a church culture that undervalues or ignores the person and work of the Spirit, but it does not find biblical and theological support. Rather, though our worship of, love for, trust in, and thanksgiving to the Holy Spirit may be expressed differently than in those same activities with respect to the Father and the Son (for example, we thank the Son, and not the Father and the Holy Spirit, for becoming incarnate and dying on the cross for our sins), they are not different in essence from those same activities directed toward the Father and the Son (for example, we do not fear the Father, love the Son, or obey the Holy Spirit differently than we fear, love, or obey the other two persons).

Furthermore, the Holy Spirit as "Love" is the one through whom "God's love has been poured out in our hearts" (Rom 5:5). Believers and the church cannot know the divine love apart from the outpoured Holy Spirit. Additionally, the Spirit as "Gift" is the highest of the "good gifts" the heavenly Father gives to Christians and the church. In turn, their hearts should overflow with joy and thanksgiving for God's wonderful favor—the Spirit himself!

---

[40] Gregory of Nazianzus, *Oration* 40, "On Holy Baptism," 41; *NPNF*² 7:375.

15

The Holy Spirit and the Holy Trinity: Trinitarian Processions and Missions

A s our pneumatology confesses that the Holy Spirit is the Third Person of the Trinity, equal to the Father and the Son in terms of his divine nature yet distinct from the First Person and the Second Person, we began with a discussion of the *ontological* (also called the *immanent*, or *essential*) Trinity. Up to this point, then, our discussion has been about God *ad intra*, God as he is in himself, God in his divine nature and intratrinitarian relations of origin.

This chapter turns to a discussion of the *economic* Trinity. While the word *economy* (Gr. οἰκονόμια [*oikonomia*]) conjures up several connotations—financial systems, frugality, home management—in this case it refers to divine operations. This discussion is about God *ad extra*, God as he is toward the world—God in his works of creation, providence, redemption, and consummation. Rather than being about intratrinitarian life and relations, the economy is about trinitarian activity and works.

While the distinction we are making between the ontological Trinity and the economic Trinity is a standard approach toward this discussion, our pneumatology will follow another traditional approach that makes the distinction between trinitarian processions and trinitarian missions. As for the relationship between these two approaches, "trinitarian processions" approximates the ontological Trinity, whereas "trinitarian missions" approximates the economic Trinity. Because the terms used in this discussion are technical, we start with some trinitarian grammar.

Definition of Trinitarian Processions

The term "procession" means *coming forth*, such that one thing originates from another thing. In terms of a "trinitarian procession," the coming forth is an eternal origination. There are two trinitarian processions. The first is the *eternal generation of the Son* from the Father. The Father eternally generates the Son, such that the Son eternally *comes forth* from the Father in terms of his divine sonship or person-of-the-Son. The second procession is the *eternal procession of the Holy Spirit* from the Father and the Son. The Father and the Son eternally spirate the Holy Spirit, such that the Spirit eternally *comes forth* from the Father and the Son in terms of his divine person-of-the-Spirit.[1] To avoid misunderstanding, the eternal action that God is, "is the single, simple, unrepeatable, eternal generation-of-the-Son-and-procession-of-the Spirit." This single eternal divine operation is the divine life and not something separable from it.[2]

As is true of the essence, persons, and relations of origin of the triune God, the two processions are *necessary*: God necessarily exists as the Father, the Son, and the Holy Spirit. Moreover, the two processions are *incommunicable*: The Father alone is eternally characterized by paternity, is not generated, and does not proceed. The Son alone is eternally characterized by sonship/filiation and is eternally generated. The Holy Spirit alone eternally proceeds. These relations of origin are both necessary and incommunicable.

Definition of Trinitarian Missions

The term "mission" means *a temporal sending*, such that one thing embarks on a specific task or operation on behalf of another thing. In terms of a

---

[1] The wording can be confusing, because the one term "procession" refers to both the Son with respect to his generation and the Spirit with respect to his procession.

[2] Stephen R. Holmes, "Trinitarian Action and Inseparable Operations," in *Advancing Trinitarian Theology: Explorations in Constructive Dogmatics*, ed. Oliver D. Crisp and Fred Sanders (Grand Rapids: Zondervan, 2014), 71.

"trinitarian mission," the temporal sending is a new relationship with created beings.[3] There are two trinitarian missions. The first is the *sending of the Son* by the Father, actualized by Jesus's incarnation, sinless life, passion, death, burial, resurrection, and ascension. The second mission is the *sending of the Holy Spirit* by the Father and the Son, actualized by the Spirit's outpouring on the day of Pentecost and continuing in his ongoing work (e.g., indwelling believers) in the world.

By contrast with the necessity of the two divine processions, the trinitarian missions are not necessary but *contingent*: the triune God, while necessarily existing as the Father, the Son, and the Holy Spirit, did not have to create, redeem, or engage in other *ad extra* works but was free to engage or not engage in mission. Trinitarian missions are dependent on the divine will to create, save, and more. Moreover, though it is common to speak of two missions, one related to the Son and another related to the Holy Spirit, because of the inseparable operations of the triune God, these two missions are ultimately the one divine mission. "Indeed, the mission of the Holy Spirit is coextensive with the mission of the Word (the Lord Jesus Christ)."[4]

The Relationship of Trinitarian Processions and Trinitarian Missions

If we conceptualize (1) the trinitarian processions as the inner life and eternal relations of the Father, the Son, and the Holy Spirit, and (2) the

---

[3] When we affirm the temporal sending of the Son, we do not mean that the divine Second Person, who is omnipresent, began to exist at the time of his incarnation. Similarly, when we affirm the temporal sending of the Spirit, we do not mean that the divine Third Person, who is omnipresent, began to exist at the time of his outpouring on the day of Pentecost. As Thomas Aquinas, *Summa Theologica*, pt. 1, q. 43, art. 1, ad. 2, noted, such movement "has no place in the mission of a divine person; for the divine person sent neither begins to exist where he did not previously exist, nor ceases to exist where he was [with the Father]." As Levering, *Engaging the Doctrine of the Holy Spirit*, 189, explains, "Instead, the change described by a divine 'mission' consists in a creature gaining a new real relation to the Son or Holy Spirit, a relation of intimacy that elevates the creature into a participation in the trinitarian communion." Cf. Christopher R. J. Holmes, *The Holy Spirit*, 116–18.

[4] Holmes, 21; cf. 26–28.

trinitarian missions as the external activity and temporal works of the triune
God, then we can consider (3) the trinitarian missions to be the trinitarian processions turned outside and in time.[5] Processions fittingly express
themselves as missions. The connection between the two is important: "The
processions enable us to distinguish the persons [the Father, the Son, and
the Holy Spirit] without eviscerating the divine unity, while the missions
add 'a specific relationship to the creature' without conflating the economy
of salvation with the intratrinitarian life."[6] To unite the processions and the
missions even more intimately, we can think of (1) the one twin procession
of the Son, consisting of an eternal procession (eternal generation from the
Father) and a temporal procession (mission or sending for incarnation and
salvation); and (2) the one twin procession of the Holy Spirit, consisting of
an eternal procession (eternal procession from the Father and the Son) and
a temporal procession (mission or sending for outpouring and indwelling).[7]
Diagrammatically:

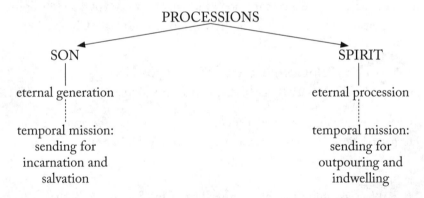

PROCESSIONS

SON

eternal generation

temporal mission:
sending for
incarnation and
salvation

SPIRIT

eternal procession

temporal mission:
sending for
outpouring and
indwelling

Moreover, the temporal missions of the Son and the Spirit express and
are reflective of their eternal processions. There is an appropriateness to the
incarnation and salvation as the particular mission of the Son as eternally

---

[5] Thomas Aquinas addressed the relationship between the processions and the
missions in *Summa Theologica*, pt. 1, q. 43, art. 2, ad. 3. In my discussion I lean on
Levering, *Engaging the Doctrine of the Holy Spirit*, 189–90.

[6] Levering, *Engaging the Doctrine of the Holy Spirit*, 169, citing Bruce D.
Marshall, "The Unity of the Triune God: Reviving an Ancient Question," *Thomist*
74 (2010): 8.

[7] Levering, 190.

generated by the Father. And there is an appropriateness to the outpouring and indwelling as the particular mission of the Holy Spirit as eternally proceeding from the Father and the Son.[8]

Before exploring the specific works of the Holy Spirit in his trinitarian mission, however, our pneumatology must first address the inseparable operations of the three persons.

Inseparable Operations

As Adonis Vidu explains, "The doctrine of the inseparable operations of the Trinity affirms that the trinitarian persons act as a single agent in the economy, such that each trinitarian person is co-agent in each other's action tokens [works; e.g., creation and providence]."[9] More specifically, for the operations to be inseparable means that in every *ad extra* work the Father, the

---

[8] See Michael Horton, *Rediscovering the Holy Spirit: God's Perfecting Presence in Creation, Redemption, and Everyday Life* (Grand Rapids: Zondervan, 2017), 34–35; Levering, *Engaging the Doctrine of the Holy Spirit*, 182n50. This "appropriateness" has nothing to do with the proposal that the Father is in an eternal relation of authority with the Son, who eternally submits to him (an eternal relation of authority-submission manifested temporally in the mission of the Son), and that the Father and the Son are in an eternal relation of authority with the Holy Spirit, who eternally submits to them (an eternal relation of authority-submission manifested temporally in the mission of the Spirit). This proposal is unconvincing and does not enjoy the support of the church's trinitarian tradition. Rather, we think in terms of "correspondence" between (1) the eternal paternity of the Father and the eternal filiation/generation of the Son, expressed correspondingly in the mission of the Son (beginning with the incarnation) and characterized by temporal obedience (to the Father, along with dependence on the Holy Spirit); and (2) the Holy Spirit's eternal relation of procession from the Father and the Son, expressed correspondingly in the mission of the Spirit (beginning with his outpouring on Pentecost) and characterized by temporal fulfillment (of the Father's will centered on the gospel of the Son). On this latter point Owen offered, "The Holy Ghost doth immediately work and effect whatever was to be done in reference unto the person of the Son or the sons of men, for the perfecting and accomplishment of the Father's counsel and the Son's work, in an especial application of both unto their especial effects and ends," *Pneumatologia*, 159.

[9] Adonis Vidu, "Trinitarian Inseparable Operations and the Incarnation," *Journal of Analytic Theology* 4 (May 2016): 106. See his extensive treatment in Adonis Vidu, *The Same God Who Works All Things: An Exposition and Defense of the Doctrine of Inseparable Operations* (Grand Rapids: Eerdmans, forthcoming).

Son, and the Holy Spirit act in common or indivisibly with one will and one power, with the power to bring forth coming from the Father, the power to arrange from the Son, and the power to perfect from the Holy Spirit.[10] Paul expresses this operation in his blessing of God: "For him and through him and to him are all things" (Rom 11:36). Accordingly, this threefold operation is "first, that by which all things are originated (*of him*); second, that by which all things consist (*through him*); third, that by which all things attain their final destiny (*to him*)."[11]

Theological support for inseparable trinitarian operations includes the unity of the Father, the Son, and the Holy Spirit in the one divine nature; the mutual indwelling of the three persons (perichoresis); and their possession of one will, knowledge, and power.[12] First, in terms of unity, God is one, and it is as the one God that the Father, the Son, and the Holy Spirit act. Thus, there are not three actors but one, with the three persons acting inseparably together as the one God with one will and one power. "The three persons act in the same action, but each of them performs this act in the distinct mode of his personal relation. . . . The Father acts as the source of the Son and Spirit, the Son acts as Word of the Father, the Holy Spirit acts as Love and Gift of the Father and the Son."[13]

Second, in terms of indwelling, "*perichoresis* (from Gk. *perichōrēsis*, 'rotation') refers to the mutual indwelling of the Father, the Son, and the Holy Spirit. This interpenetration of divine persons is affirmed in Jesus's prayer for his disciples, 'that they may all be one, just as you, Father, are in me, and I in you, that they also may be in us' (John 17:21). This mutual indwelling of the Father and the Son (including the Spirit also) is the ground for the perfect

---

[10] Abraham Kuyper, *The Work of the Holy Spirit* (Grand Rapids: Eerdmans, 1946), 19.

[11] Kuyper, 20.

[12] In reference to the divine operations, Yves Congar, *I Believe in the Holy Spirit*, trans. David Smith, 3 vols. (New York: Crossroad/Herder & Herder, 2015), 2.85, notes, "All such activity is performed by those Persons according to and through a divinity that is common to all three, not only because they are consubstantial, but also because they are inside one another. (The latter is known as perichoresis or circumincession. . . .)."

[13] Giles Emery, *The Trinitarian Theology of Thomas Aquinas*, trans. Francesca A. Murphy (Oxford, UK: Oxford University Press, 2007), 72.

unity of the three persons."[14]Accordingly, the mutually indwelling persons operate inseparably as the one God in all the divine works.

Third, it is God—who possesses one will, knowledge, and power—who acts. These divine attributes belong to the one divine nature, not separately to the three persons. Accordingly, there is in the Godhead one will, one knowledge, and one power, not three wills, three centers of knowing, or three powers. The Father, the Son, and the Spirit, possessing one will, knowledge, and power, operate inseparably in all *ad extra* works.

Biblically, three examples of inseparable operations suffice for support. The first example is creation: the Father speaks through his Son the Word by the Holy Spirit, thereby creating the universe and everything in it ex nihilo. The role of the Father is detailed in terms of the ten "words" of Genesis 1. The role of the Son, the Word, is affirmed in John 1:3; Col 3:16; and Heb 1:2. The role of the Spirit is narrated in Gen 1:2. It is not as though each of the three persons does his own part, with the Father being responsible for a third of the creation, the Son being responsible for another third of the creation, and the Holy Spirit being responsible for the final third of the creation. Rather, the three persons operate inseparably in the divine act of creation.

The second example is the ministry of the incarnate Son. Jesus constantly insists that his work is nothing other than the work of the Father: not two works in which the two cooperate but one work in which the two operate inseparably. For example, Jesus affirms, "My Father is still working, and I am working also. . . . Truly I tell you, the Son is not able to do anything on his own, but only what he sees the Father doing. For whatever the Father does, the Son likewise does these things. For the Father loves the Son and shows him everything he is doing" (John 5:17, 19–20). As the Son sees the Father working, the Son works that one work; indeed, the Son does the Father's will and accomplishes the Father's work (4:34; 5:36; 9:4; 17:4). Tragically, doing the good works of the Father places Jesus at odds with the religious establishment, who seek to execute him for making himself out to be God (10:30–39). This harsh response flows from the fact that the works in which Jesus engages demonstrate the perichoresis of the two divine persons, "that the Father is in me and I in the Father" (10:38). The mutual indwelling of the Father and the Son means that the Son works nothing other than the

---

[14] Allison, *The Baker Compact Dictionary of Theological Terms*, s.v. *"perichoresis."*

work of the Father. Indeed, because of perichoresis, Jesus can affirm that "the Father who lives in me does his works" (14:10). Importantly, the interchangeability of affirming that Jesus works and affirming that the Father works underscores the inseparable operations of the two divine persons. To be added to this discussion is the fact that Jesus never operates apart from the Holy Spirit, whom the Father has poured out on his Son without measure (John 3:34). Accordingly, as the incarnate Son engages in his works, he operates always and inseparably with the Father and the Holy Spirit.

The third example of inseparable operations is redemption, with several points. The three persons operate inseparably in the divine mission: "When the time came to completion, *God* sent his *Son*, born of a woman, born under the law, to redeem those under the law, so that we might receive adoption as sons. And because you are sons, God sent *the Spirit of his Son* into our hearts, crying, '*Abba*, Father!'" (Gal 4:4–6). Thus the Father sends both the Son and the Spirit to redeem us, and the three engage together in the divine mission.[15] Moreover, focusing on the atonement, the letter to the Hebrews emphasizes "how much more will the blood of *Christ*, who through the *eternal Spirit* offered himself without blemish to *God*, cleanse our consciences from dead works so that we can serve the living God" (Heb 9:14). While we often think of the atonement with reference to the Son alone, his work of accomplishing salvation through his sacrificial death is the inseparable operation of all three persons.[16]

Furthermore, in terms of the application of this salvation, such gracious activity is another indivisible work, as Paul underscores: "When the kindness of *God our Savior* and his love for mankind appeared, he saved us—not by works of righteousness that we had done, but according to his

---

[15] Indeed, as will be discussed, the Holy Spirit prompts two cries from believers: "Abba, Father!" in recognition of the Fatherhood of the First Person, who has adopted them into his family, and "Jesus is Lord" (1 Cor. 12:3), in recognition of the lordship of the Second Person, who has rescued them. Smail's comment about these two confessions is important: "Before the Spirit relates us to one another in love or to the world in missionary outreach, he relates us to God the Father and God the Son in worshipping acknowledgement of who they are for us." Smail, *The Giving Gift*, 13.

[16] Gregg Allison, "No Holy Spirit, No Penal Substitutionary Atonement," Gospel Coalition (June 25, 2019), https://www.thegospelcoalition.org/article/role-holy-spirit-penal-substitutionary-atonement/

mercy—through the washing of regeneration and renewal by *the Holy Spirit*. He poured out his Spirit on us abundantly through *Jesus Christ our Savior*" (Titus 3:4–6). Additionally, the persevering and preserving nature of this gracious salvation is the inseparable operation of the three persons: "Now it is *God* who strengthens us together with you in *Christ*, and who has anointed us. He has also put his seal on us and given us the *Spirit* in our hearts as a down payment" (2 Cor 1:21–22). Finally, as the church engages in its ministry centered on the good news, such church activity arises from the inseparable activity of the triune God: "Now there are different gifts, but the same *Spirit*. There are different ministries, but the same *Lord*. And there are different activities, but the same *God* produces each gift in each person" (1 Cor 12:4–6).

Creation, Christ's ministry, and redemption are three examples of the inseparable operations of the Father, the Son, and the Holy Spirit.

Historically, the church has affirmed inseparable operations. Gregory of Nyssa set the stage for what was to come by articulating the inseparable unity of the three divine persons in the Godhead. Speaking of the Holy Spirit, he noted, "While his place is counted third in mere sequence after the Father and Son, third in the order of the transmission, in all other respects we acknowledge his inseparable union with them, both in nature, honor, deity, glory, majesty, and omnipotence, and in all devout belief."[17] Gregory's point, as we have already discussed, is that the three persons are not of different natures but share in one divine nature. Of what importance is this truth for the doctrine of inseparable operations? Gregory employs a basic syllogistic (*modus tollens*) argument:[18]

- If the operations of the triune God are separable (different) between the three Persons, then the natures of the Father, the Son, and the Holy Spirit are different;
- but the natures of the Father, the Son, and the Holy Spirit are not different (rather, they are of one nature);
- therefore, the operations of the triune God are inseparable.[19]

---

[17] Gregory of Nyssa, *On the Holy Spirit against the Followers of Macedonius*, *NPNF*² 5:320.

[18] A *modus tollens* argument is: if p, then q; not q; therefore, not p.

[19] Gregory of Nyssa, *On the Holy Trinity, and of the Godhead of the Holy Spirit*, *NPNF*² 5:328.

Basil of Caesarea, in *Against Eunomius*, articulated the inseparable operations of the three persons in his defense of the deity of the Holy Spirit. Appealing to Ps 32:6, Basil noted that the one work of creation is the indivisible action of the Word as the "creator of the heavens" and the Holy Spirit who "bestows firmness and steadfastness upon the heavenly powers." Citing 1 Cor 12:4–6 (noted earlier), Basil underscored the inseparable operation of the ministries of church members, with the Father distributing activities, the Son distributing services, and the Spirit distributing gifts.[20]

Augustine later applied the finishing touches to this doctrine, affirming, "Just as Father and Son and Holy Spirit are inseparable, so do they work inseparably."[21]

Appropriations

At the same time that our pneumatology upholds the inseparable operations of the Father, the Son, and the Holy Spirit, it also affirms divine "appropriations." The notion of appropriations is that the various operations of the triune God have specific, but not exclusive, reference to one of the three persons. Moreover, these appropriations are particularly expressive or reflective of the eternal relations of the three persons, that is, the unbegottenness of the Father, the eternal generation of the Son, and the eternal procession of the Holy Spirit.[22] As Thomas Aquinas explained:

To appropriate simply means to connect a thing that is common to something particular. Now, what is common to the entire Trinity

[20] *St. Basil of Caesarea against Eunomius*, 3.4, 190.

[21] Augustine, *On the Trinity*, 1.7; *NPNF*[1] 20. The translation is from John E. Rotelle, ed., Edmond Hill, trans., *The Trinity*, The Works of Saint Augustine: A Translation for the 21st Century (n.p.: New City Press, 1991), 70.

[22] Congar, *I Believe in the Holy Spirit*, 2.85, explains: "Certain essential attributes or activities that are really common to the three Persons are appropriated to one of those Persons, even though they may not be peculiar to that Person in a sense that would exclude the other Persons. This is because of their resemblance to the personal property characterizing that Person. . . . There is really something in that Person to justify the appropriation, but we cannot clarify it or say with certainty that there is an attribute peculiar to that one Person that would exclude the other Persons from what is appropriated to the one." Cf. Keith Johnson, "Penal Substitution as an Undivided Work of the Triune God," *TrinJ* 36 NS, no. 1 (2015): 56–57.

cannot be appropriated to a single Person on the grounds that this belongs more to this Person than it does to another. Such an action would deny the equality of the Persons. However, appropriation may be made on the grounds that what is common nevertheless has a greater resemblance to what is proper to one Person than it has to what is proper to another.[23]

This discussion may also use the term "termination" (or "terminus"). The notion of termination is that a work appropriated to one of the three persons terminates in that person in the sense of reaching the goal or end of that work.[24] As an example, the incarnation is a divine operation *appropriated* to the Son; or, to use our other term, the incarnation *terminates* in the Son. He is the one divine person who became incarnate. Still, while having specific reference to the Son, the incarnation is not exclusively his work. Given inseparable operations, the Father, who planned the incarnation and sent his Son to become incarnate, and the Holy Spirit, by whom the Son was conceived in the womb of the virgin Mary, were indivisibly engaged along with the Son in that work.[25] Moreover, it was fitting for the Second Person to become incarnate because of his eternal trinitarian relation: by eternal

---

[23] Thomas Aquinas, *Truth* (*Questiones Disputatae de Veritate*), q. 1, art. 3. The translation combines that of Robert W. Mulligan and the adaptation by Yves Congar of the French translation by C. Journet. See Robert W. Mulligan, *Truth*, ed. R. W. Schmidt (Indianapolis: Hackett, 1994); and Congar, *I Believe in the Holy Spirit*, 2.95n25.

[24] Vidu, "Trinitarian Inseparable Operations," 115, defines *terminus* as "the appropriation of various actions to distinct persons. In this case the personal property of one of the persons has a special affinity to the end that is brought about by the action of all." Moreover, "appropriation" and "terminus" are interchangeable terms: "An action is appropriated to one divine person if that action terminates in that person. Conversely, an action which is appropriated to a person (in view of an affinity between that person's *propria* and the created effect) is also said to terminate in that person."

[25] Dominic Legge summarizes Thomas Aquinas's position on inseparable operations and terminus: "All three divine persons are a single efficient *principle* . . . while a single divine person can be, on the side of God, its *terminus*. . . . (For example, all three divine persons efficiently cause Christ's human nature to be united to the Son in person.) [But the effect] . . . 'terminates to' the one divine person who is sent—and *not* to the others." Dominic Legge, *The Trinitarian Christology of St Thomas Aquinas* (Oxford: Oxford University Press, 2017), 24–25.

generation, he is the Son of the Father. Thus, because of his personal property of sonship, he has a special affinity for this work.[26] The incarnation is appropriated to, or terminates in, the Son.[27]

As we turn from this example of the incarnation to our pneumatology, the obvious question asks what work or works are appropriated to, or terminate in, the Holy Spirit. On the one hand, in relation to the divine works in general, as we now live in the age of the Spirit it is possible to affirm that the triune God *acts in all things,* yet the Father and the Son do so not directly but *specifically in/through the Holy Spirit.* In accord with inseparable operations, our pneumatology maintains that all of the divine works are common to the three persons, yet, in accord with divine appropriations, it also holds that they are common with distinctions, with the terminus of all of the divine works being the Spirit. Indeed, "it is the Holy Spirit that seems to invariably serve as the terminus of divine actions, since he is the perfecting cause, in addition to the originating (or efficient) cause (Father) and 'moulding' (or formal) cause (Son). As perfecting cause, the Spirit applies the agency of the three persons, and is thus in a certain sense, most proximal to its terminus."[28]

On the other hand, in relation to particular divine works appropriated to, or terminating in, the Holy Spirit, there are three: (1) speaking; (2) creating, re-creating, and perfecting; and (3) filling with the presence of the triune God. Why these three works? Acknowledging that the question is ultimately unanswerable because the matter is ultimately mysterious, we engage in a

---

[26] Legge, chap. 3. Legge explains Aquinas's reasoning for "Why the *Son* became Incarnate" (the title of this chapter).

[27] As Congar, *I Believe in the Holy Spirit,* 2.85, explains, "The fact that every action performed by God is common to all three Persons of the Trinity has given rise to the idea that an activity in creatures can only be *appropriated* to one Person, but is not peculiar to him, or his own. This clearly does not apply to the incarnation insofar as it is a personal union of a humanity with the Person of the Son, within that Person's being. If, however, it is seen as a work that has been actively caused, even the incarnation is common to the three Persons."

[28] Vidu, "Trinitarian Inseparable Operations," 115. Owen, *Pneumatologia,* 57, described the Spirit as "the immediate operator of all divine works that outwardly are of God." Elsewhere, Owen used the terminology "the immediate, peculiar, efficient cause of all external divine operations" (161) and "the immediate efficacy and power of the Holy Ghost" (162).

bit of speculation.[29] First, these three works have a particular affinity for the Holy Spirit because he proceeds from the Father and the Son. The eternal procession of the Spirit is an eternal coming forth expressed in the Spirit's temporal mission upon which he is sent by the Father and the Son. One senses an appropriateness for the Holy Spirit's mission to express itself as speaking, that is, communicating divine revelation to human creatures, that they may know the words, ways, and works of the triune God in whose image they are made.[30] Second, these three works have a particular affinity for the Holy Spirit because he is "Love." Out of the overflow of divine love, the triune God created a world distinct from himself. Permitting his human image bearers to fall, the triune God purposed to rescue some sinners through his re-creating love and to restore them fully to the status of eminent image bearers through his perfecting love. This creating, re-creating, and perfecting work, being an expression of divine love, is specifically appropriated to the Holy Spirit, who is "Love."[31] Third, this particular affinity is related to the Holy Spirit because he is "Gift." As the highest of the divine gifts, the Spirit is received by believers, welling up and flowing from them like streams of living water. The express purpose of his indwelling and filling Christians is to render the presence of the Father and Son, and he does so as "Gift."[32]

---

[29] Thanks to Gregg's friend Keith Johnson for pushing him to write this paragraph. All errors of speculation are Gregg's, not his.

[30] As explained earlier, in John 14–16 Jesus promises the Holy Spirit as the one who proceeds from the Father, who will be sent by the Father in Jesus's name, and who will be sent by Jesus (from the Father). In conjunction with this trinitarian-shaped promise, Jesus highlights the role of "the Spirit of truth" in teaching, reminding the apostles of Jesus's teaching and guiding them into all truth, bearing testimony to Jesus, and taking the words of Jesus and declaring them to the apostles. The conjunction of Jesus's presentation of trinitarian activity in relation to the Spirit with the Spirit's revelatory role supports our speculation that one of the works that terminates in the Spirit is appropriately that of speaking.

[31] To underscore the divine love in the work of re-creation and to tie this love to the following point about gift, we consider Paul's exhortation that "God's love has been poured out in our hearts through the Holy Spirit who was given to us" (Rom 5:5).

[32] In discussing Augustine's notion of the Spirit as "Gift," Holmes, *The Holy Spirit*, 76–77, concludes that "the revelation of this gift is the Spirit's mission. . . . [which is] the immediate transforming presence of God."

Keeping in mind the following counsel—"we should be looking not for the *works that are done uniquely by the Holy Spirit* but for the *unique role of the Holy Spirit in every work*"—each of these three works is explored in turn.[33]

Speaking

From the opening pages of Scripture, the Lord appears as the speaking God: he speaks creation into existence, he deliberates about the creation of human beings in his image (a deliberation expressed in written words), he blesses and commands the first image bearers, he curses the fallen world, he promises through covenant making, and more. Particularly, according to scores of biblical passages, when the Spirit comes upon people, they speak. Select Old Testament examples include the following:

- *The seventy elders with Moses.* As promised, the Lord "took some of the Spirit that was on Moses and placed the Spirit on the seventy elders. As the Spirit rested on them, they prophesied" (Num 11:25).
- *The two men with the seventy elders.* Moses responds to his people's complaints that the Spirit has rested on Eldad and Medad, so that these two prophesy in the camp, by asking, "Are you jealous on my account? If only all the LORD's people were prophets and the LORD would place his Spirit on them!" (Num 11:29).
- *The Balaam narratives* (Numbers 22–24). When the Spirit of God comes upon (the non-Israelite) Balaam, he prophesies as one "whose eyes are opened," "who hears the sayings of God," and "who sees a vision from the Almighty" (24:3–4).
- *The fulfillment of Samuel's three prophecies concerning Saul* (1 Sam 10:1–13). "All the signs came about that day. When Saul and his servant arrived at Gibeah, a group of prophets met him. Then the Spirit of God came powerfully on him, and he prophesied along with them. Everyone who knew him previously and saw him prophesy with the prophets asked each other, 'What has happened to the son of Kish? Is Saul also among the prophets?' Then a man who was

---

[33] Horton, *Rediscovering the Holy Spirit*, 41 (emphasis original). Elsewhere, he urges, "It is not different *works* but different *roles* in *every work* that the divine persons perform" (38).

from there asked, 'And who is their father?' As a result, 'Is Saul also among the prophets?' became a popular saying. Then Saul finished prophesying and went to the high place." (10:9–13).

- *Joel's prophecy of a fresh, unprecedented outpouring of the Holy Spirit.* "After this I will pour out my Spirit on all humanity; then your sons and your daughters will prophesy, your old men will have dreams, and your young men will see visions. I will even pour out my Spirit on the male and female slaves in those days" (Joel 2:28–29).

Select New Testament examples include:

- *The Gospel of Luke.* Elizabeth is filled with the Holy Spirit and pronounces a blessing on Mary (1:41–42); Zechariah is filled with the Holy Spirit and prophesies (1:67); "the Holy Spirit was on" Simeon who, "guided by the Spirit, . . . entered the temple" to bless God (2:25–32); and Anna, "a prophetess, . . . began to thank God and to speak about him to all who were looking forward to the redemption of Jerusalem" (2:36–38).
- *John the Baptist's description of the Son of God.* "The one whom God sent speaks God's words, since he gives the Spirit without measure. The Father loves the Son and has given all things into his hands" (John 3:34–35). Thus, the unlimited presence of the Spirit in the Son explains why the Son speaks the words of the Father.
- *Jesus, filled with the Holy Spirit without measure, proclaiming the gospel and the arrival of the kingdom of God* (e.g., Mark 1:14–15).
- *Jesus's awareness of being a prophet* (e.g., Mark 6:4; Luke 13:33). Appropriately, the people who know Jesus view him as a prophet (e.g., Matt 13:57; 16:14; 21:11, 46; Mark 11:32; Luke 7:16; 24:19; John 4:19; 6:14; 7:40; 9:17). Following Jesus's resurrection, the heralds of the gospel explain that the prophet Jesus has fulfilled the ancient promise that God would raise up a prophet like Moses (Deut 18:15–19; Acts 3:22–23; 7:37). Thus, anointed with the Holy Spirit, Jesus speaks authoritatively as a prophet in fulfillment of Isaiah's prophecy (Luke 4:18–19).
- *Acts.* Luke narrates various outpourings or fillings of the Holy Spirit, almost all of which are closely associated with some type of speaking: the disciples speak in tongues, rehearsing the mighty acts

of God (2:1–4); the community prays for and receives boldness to proclaim the gospel (4:29–31); the apostles boldly proclaim the gospel in the face of persecution (5:27–32); Paul proclaims in the synagogues that Jesus is the Son of God (9:17–20); Cornelius and his family and friends speak in tongues (10:44–45); Paul pronounces a rebuke (13:9–10); the disciples of John the Baptist speak in tongues and prophesy (19:1–7); the Holy Spirit prophesies to Paul, Agabus, the disciples in Tyre, and the people of Caesarea (20:22–23; 21:4, 10–14).

• *Revelation.* John speaks "in the Spirit" (1:10; 4:2; 17:3; 21:10) and, at the end of each of the seven letters, urges, "Let anyone who has ears to hear listen to what the Spirit says to the churches" (2:7, 11, 17, 29; 3:6, 13, 22).

This significant sampling of biblical passages underscores that one of the divine works appropriated to the Holy Spirit is speaking. God is a speaking God (Heb 1:1), with the terminus of the divine speech in the Holy Spirit (Heb 3:7; 10:15).[34]

This affirmation is confirmed by the Holy Spirit's inspiration and illumination of Scripture (a topic to be discussed in detail later). The church has historically acknowledged this point in the Nicene-Constantinopolitan Creed, which confesses belief in "the Holy Spirit the Lord, and Giver of life, . . . *who spoke by the prophets.*"[35] The fourth century creed of Epiphanius agrees:

---

[34] In light of inseparable operations, this general affirmation acknowledges that both the Father and the Son work together with the Spirit in all divine communications, and that at times those communicative acts are ascribed to the Father or to the Son. For example, at the baptism of Jesus, the Father speaks words of commendation about his beloved Son (Luke 3:21–22). Furthermore, Jesus explains to Peter that his confession of the Son of Man's identity flows from the Father's revelation (Matt 16:17). Moreover, Jesus himself engages in his ministry of proclamation and teaching; though much of this communication is not inscripturated, at the time it is spoken it is divine revelation from the mouth of the Son incarnate. But, as we will develop later, the Spirit's particular speaking role is identified with his inspiration of written Scripture (2 Pet 1:16–21).

[35] Before this creedal affirmation, the second century theologian Irenaeus (*Against Heresies*, 1.10.1; *Ante-Nicene-Fathers*, ed. Alexander Roberts, James Donaldson, Philip Schaff, and Henry Wace, 10 vols. [Peabody: Hendrickson, 1994],

We believe in the Holy Spirit who
spoke in the law
and *taught* by the prophets
and descended to the Jordan,
spoke by the apostles,
and lives in the saints;
thus, we believe in him: that he is the Holy Spirit,
the Spirit of God,
the perfect Paraclete,
uncreated, proceeding from the Father
and receiving of the Son, in whom we believe.
Amen.[36]

Speaking is one of the works of the triune God that terminates in the Holy Spirit.[37]

Creating, Re-creating, and Perfecting

To return to the Nicene-Constantinopolitan Creed, in addition to its confession of the Holy Spirit as speaking, the church also confesses belief in "the Holy Spirit, the Lord, and *Giver of life*." This life-giving divine work, in which the three persons inseparably operate, yet which terminates in the Holy Spirit, is all-encompassing, starting with creation, moving through re-creation in terms of redemption, and concluding with the consummation,

---

1:330), in his "rule of faith," or short confession of Christian doctrine, had expressed belief "in the Holy Spirit, who proclaimed through the prophets the dispensations of God, and the advents, and the birth from a virgin, and the passion, and the resurrection from the dead, and the ascension into heaven in the flesh of the beloved Christ Jesus, our Lord, and his [future] manifestation from heaven in the glory of the Father."

[36] Philip Schaff, *Creeds of Christendom*, 3 vols. (New York: Harper, 1877–1905), 2:37–38.

[37] Perhaps the analogy is poor, but could we consider the trinitarian communication to consist of Speaker (the Father), Speech (the Son), and Speakerphone (the Holy Spirit), with the latter term playing off the Greek word φωνη (*phōnē* = sound/voice)?

the perfecting of the new heaven and new earth. Thus, a second divine work appropriated to the Holy Spirit is creating, re-creating, and perfecting.[38]

In the original creation, the Holy Spirit's role was that of protecting and preparing the formless and void, dark and watery earth for the upcoming divine work of fashioning this space into a place hospitable for human beings as the divine image bearers (Gen 1:2). Indeed, the expression "the breath (*nephesh*) of life" is probably associated with the "Spirit" (*ruach*) of the life-giving God.[39] As the energizing principle that courses through all living creatures (Gen 1:30; as for its opposite, death, see Gen 7:22), this breath is imparted by God himself into the "dust from the ground" that he formed. The result of this divine action, closely associated with the "Spirit" (*ruach*), is that "the man became a living being" (Gen 2:7). This is the Spirit's work of creation. More will be said later about the creative activity of the Spirit.

Due to the fall into sin of the first image bearers and the ongoing, tragic reality of desperate sinfulness of all subsequent image bearers, God plans, executes, and carries out a redemptive work of re-creation, again with particular appropriation to the Holy Spirit. In terms of the accomplishment of salvation, the Holy Spirit works the incarnation of the Son (Matt 1:18–25; Luke 1:26–38), marks him for his messianic work (Mark 1:9–11), indwells and empowers him throughout his life and for his mission (e.g., Luke 4:1, 14, 18–19), undergirds his sacrificial death by crucifixion (Heb 9:14), raises him from the dead (Rom 8:11), and effects his ascension (Acts 2:32–36). As for the application of salvation, the Spirit's work is all-encompassing and includes conviction of sin, regeneration, union with Christ, justification, adoption, conversion (repentance, faith, and confession of Christ), sealing, assurance of salvation, guidance, filling, sanctification, and resurrection/glorification.[40] To sum it up, all of the benefits of Jesus Christ come to Christians and the church through the Holy Spirit, who unites us to Christ and his saving work.[41]

---

[38] Though he does not address creation, re-creation, and perfection in the context of appropriations, Smail, *The Giving Gift*, 166–81, links the three activities under the confession of the Holy Spirit as "the Lord and giver of life."

[39] See the earlier discussion pp. 11–12.

[40] All of these aspects of redemption will be explored later in the book.

[41] For further discussion, see John Calvin, *Institutes of the Christian Religion*, LCC (Philadelphia: Westminster, 1960), 3.1.1.

As this present world will one day come to an end, the consummation of all things will be the climax of the Spirit's perfecting work. He is the eschatological Spirit whose orientation is always toward the future. As the Spirit of adoption, he "himself testifies together with our spirit that we are God's children, and if children, also heirs—heirs of God and coheirs with Christ—if indeed we suffer with him so that we may also be glorified with him" (Rom 8:16–17; cf. Gal 4:4–6). With regard to our future existence, Paul underscores that the one "who has prepared us for this very purpose is God, who gave us the Spirit as a down payment" (2 Cor 5:5). Indeed, he is the down payment, the firstfruits, the one who seals believers for the day of redemption; his saving work always has future reference. The Holy Spirit is preparing a people for an upcoming salvation, in which the church will be presented as the perfected, beautiful "bride, the wife of the Lamb" (Rev 21:9).

Creating, re-creating, and perfecting is the second work terminating in the Holy Spirit.

Filling with the Presence of the Triune God[42]

A third divine work appropriated to the Holy Spirit is the filling of believers and the church with the presence of the Father, the Son, and the Holy Spirit. "Through the Spirit's operation, all three persons come near to us and bring us into their fellowship."[43] Such personal manifestation of the triune God is brought by the Holy Spirit on the divine side and through faith on the human side.

As for the divine aspect, "Through his Spirit, God the Father makes Christ dwell in our hearts, that is, in the depths of our being where our lives are oriented (see Eph 3:14–17)."[44] Indeed, Jesus pledges, "If anyone loves me, he will keep my word. My Father will love him, and we will come to him and make our home with him" (John 14:23). Immediately before this part of his promise, Jesus assures his disciples: "I will ask the Father, and he will give

---

[42] As he discusses the work of the Holy Spirit, Packer highlights the idea of presence in J. I. Packer, *Keep in Step with the Spirit: Finding Fullness in Our Walk with God*, rev. and enl. ed. (Grand Rapids: Baker, 2005).

[43] Horton, *Rediscovering the Holy Spirit*, 28.

[44] Congar, *I Believe in the Holy Spirit*, 2.101.

you another Counselor to be with you forever. He is the Spirit of truth. . . . You . . . know him, because he remains with you and will be in you" (John 14:16–17).[45] Thus the abiding of the Father and the Son in believers is connected to the dwelling of the Holy Spirit in them. Moreover, this promise finds an ecclesiological orientation in Paul's prayer (referenced above) that God may grant believers a powerful and inner strengthening "through his Spirit, and that Christ may dwell in your hearts through faith . . . [so that you may] know Christ's love that surpasses knowledge, so that you may be filled with all the fullness of God" (Eph 3:16–19).[46] Through the Holy Spirit, the triune God dwells in his people. Appropriately, then, Thomas Aquinas refers to the Spirit as the divine Person "next/nearest to us" (*nobis propinquior*).[47]

On the human side, Paul underscores the posture of faith. The way to receive the promised Spirit is not by the works of the law but by hearing with faith (Gal 3:2, 5). Indeed, we were "sealed with the promised Holy Spirit when [we] believed" (Eph 1:13). Narrative examples of receiving the Spirit by faith include the Gentiles as well as the Jews (Acts 15:8–9) and the peculiar case of the disciples of John the Baptist (Acts 19:1–7).

Accordingly, as Christians believe in the gospel, Christ baptizes them with the Holy Spirit, they are incorporated into Christ's body, and they are filled with the Holy Spirit. Indeed, they form the temple of the Holy Spirit, meaning that the triune God dwells in the church through the Spirit.

Importantly, this is the fulfillment of promises made long ago. In terms of Old Testament background, God's design for created human beings is emplacement, a physical space in which he might dwell with his image bearers. After forming the first man, Adam, from the dust of the ground and creating him in the divine image, "the LORD God planted a garden in Eden, in the east, and there he placed the man he had formed" (Gen 2:8). Next comes

---

[45] Raymond Brown notes this, as discussed p. 73n52.

[46] The context of Paul's discussion is the church. Thus, while individual application is certainly proper (Paul even prays that the Spirit would indwell one's inner being; Eph 3:16), one must not lose sight of the fact that Paul's concern is for the corporate entity, the church.

[47] Thomas Aquinas, *Commentary on the Sentences*, III, d. 2, q. 2, a.2, qla 2, 119.2. As Legge notes, Aquinas names Augustine and Hillary of Poiters (without references) as his source for this affirmation. Legge, *Trinitarian Christology of St Thomas Aquinas*, 16 fn. 32.

the creation of the first woman, Eve (Gen 2:18–25). Thus, God dwells with his image bearers in the garden, and the three enjoy a full and transparent relationship.

Tragedy strikes, resulting in expulsion from the place of God's presence. As Adam and Eve transgress, God punishes them for their heinous sin by expelling them from the garden: "So the LORD God sent him away from the garden of Eden to work the ground from which he was taken. He drove the man out and stationed the cherubim and the flaming, whirling sword east of the garden of Eden to guard the way to the tree of life" (Gen 3:23–24). The garden in which Adam and Eve had been placed and where God dwelt with them becomes shuttered to them. They are banished to a wasteland of their own making.

Graciously, a note of expectation is sounded: God will dwell once again with his people. He himself accomplishes this feat through the liberation of his people from enslavement in Egypt. Then, after giving instructions to Moses about the consecration of the tabernacle and the priesthood, God promises: "I will dwell among the Israelites and be their God. And they will know that I am the LORD their God, who brought them out of the land of Egypt, so that I might dwell among them. I am the LORD their God" (Exod 29:45–46). If his people will obey the old covenant, God pledges, "I will place my residence among you, and I will not reject you. I will walk among you and be your God, and you will be my people" (Lev 26:11–12).

In the New Testament's realization of this promise, "the Word became flesh and dwelt among us" (John 1:14), the Son of God fulfills the Old Testament expectation through incarnation and emplacement. Referring to the mutual indwelling of the Father and the Son (perichoresis), Jesus prays that believers may "all be one, as you, Father, are in me and I am in you. May they also be in us, so that the world may believe you sent me. I have given them the glory you have given me, so that they may be one as we are one. I am in them and you are in me, so that they may be made completely one" (John 17:21–23). Thus, the divine perichoresis is the ground of the unity of Christians, in whom the triune God dwells.

Paul confirms that the church, as the temple of the Holy Spirit, is this dwelling place of God:

> What agreement does the temple of God have with idols? For we
> are the temple of the living God, as God said: "I will dwell and walk

among them, and I will be their God, and they will be my people. Therefore, come out from among them and be separate," says the Lord; "do not touch any unclean thing, and I will welcome you. And I will be a Father to you, and you will be sons and daughters to me," says the Lord Almighty." (2 Cor 6:16–18)

Paul's appeal is to the Old Testament expectation and promise, now fulfilled in the church: God dwells in his people, just as he promised long ago. Again, this divine indwelling transpires through the Holy Spirit, as Paul concludes in his warning to the church of Corinth: "Don't you yourselves know that you are God's temple and that the Spirit of God lives in you?" (1 Cor 3:16). Accordingly, by his creation of a spiritual temple, the Holy Spirit creates space for the presence of the triune God to dwell with his new covenant people.

The filling of believers and the church with the presence of the triune God is the third divine work terminating in the Holy Spirit.

Thus, while our pneumatology embraces the inseparable operation of the three persons, it also affirms three particular divine works appropriated to, or terminating in, the Holy Spirit: speaking; creating, re-creating, and perfecting; and filling with the presence of the triune God.

Conclusion

With appreciation for both the inseparable operations of the Father, the Son, and the Holy Spirit, believers and the church also properly praise and give thanks to the Spirit for his particular works. Indeed, the church should specifically rely on the Spirit's presence and power as it engages in its proclamation of the gospel and teaching of Scripture, its missional expansion throughout the world, its discipleship for growth in Christlikeness, and much more that will be detailed in the following chapters of this book.

16

The Holy Spirit and Creation and Providence

Having set forth the deity and personhood of the Holy Spirit, followed by a presentation of the Holy Spirit in relation to the Holy Trinity, we now turn to articulating pneumatology in relation to the other topics of systematic theology. The purpose of these chapters is to highlight the role of the Spirit in creation and providence, Scripture, the angelic/demonic realm, humanity, sin, the person and work of Christ, salvation, the church, and future matters. We begin with the doctrines of creation and providence.

The doctrines of creation and providence express Christian belief about the origin and continuing existence of the universe and all it contains. Creation, as held by the church from its inception, is "the divine work to bring this universe into existence out of nothing (Lat. *ex*, 'out of"; *nihilo*, 'nothing')."[1] Providence is "the continuing work of God to sustain this created universe in existence and to direct it toward its end."[2] Our pneumatology explores the relation of the Holy Spirit to both creation and providence.

---

[1] Allison, *The Baker Compact Dictionary of Theological Terms*, s.v. "creation *ex nihilo*."

[2] Allison, s.v. "providence."

Creation[3]

Following the opening general statement of the divine act of creation—"In the beginning God created the heavens and the earth" (Gen 1:1)—Scripture immediately shifts to focus on the latter part of that created reality: "Now the earth was formless and empty, darkness covered the surface of the watery depths, and the Spirit of God was hovering over the surface of the waters" (1:2). Narratively, this description of the original state of the earth sets the stage for what is to follow; that is, it presents the context for what is to unfold over the course of the six days of creation (1:3–31). As God initially creates it, the earth is formless and empty, a dark, watery chaos. Some interpreters consider this description to indicate some type of devastation: from its original pristine condition and order, the earth had devolved into confusion and disorder. What had been formed and full had fallen into a chaos without form and void. Other interpreters understand this description to designate the as-yet unprepared, crude start-up supply—the raw materials that would eventually become the ordered world. But "raw" does not mean "sinful" or "fallen," only "natural" or "not developed."

Either or both of these interpretations can find a home in the recent understanding of Genesis 1 as a polemic against ancient Near Eastern creation mythologies. According to this diatribe view, Hebrew Scripture is a polemic against other cosmologies that present the creation as arising from a battle between a god or gods and the forces of evil and destruction. In contrast to these creation myths, Genesis 1 recounts Yahweh's victory over ruinous powers as he triumphantly ushers the earth out of chaos and into order.[4]

---

[3] For further study see Cole, *He Who Gives Life*, 95–114; Kuyper, *The Work of the Holy Spirit*, 22–31.

[4] Examples of these various interpretations include Hermann Gunkel, "Influence of Babylonian Mythology upon the Biblical Creation Story," in *Creation in the Old Testament*, ed. B. W. Anderson (Philadelphia: Fortress, 1984); Brevard S. Childs, *Old Testament Theology in Canonical Context* (London: SCM, 1985); Bruce K. Waltke, *Genesis: A Commentary* (Grand Rapids: Zondervan, 2001); John N. Oswalt, *The Bible among the Myths* (Grand Rapids: Zondervan, 2009); John H. Walton and Brent Sandy, *The Lost World of Scripture: Ancient Literary Culture and Biblical Authority* (Downers Grove: IVP Academic, 2013); JoAnn Scurlock and Richard H. Beal, eds. *Creation and Chaos: A Reconsideration of Hermann Gunkel's* Chaoskampf *Hypothesis* (Winona Lake: Eisenbrauns, 2013).

Whatever one's view may be of the polemical nature of Genesis 1, the interpretation of Gen 1:2 as expressing not the fallen condition but the original state of the earth makes much sense with the final clause of the verse: "The Spirit of God was hovering over the surface of the waters."[5] The notion of "hovering" as "readying" or "preparing" underscores the work of the Spirit in turning an original space that is "formless and empty" into a place formed and full, a hospitable home for the plant world, animal kingdom, and, as the crown of creation, the human race. One may wonder why "the Spirit of God was hovering over the surface of the waters." Readying the earth, which was formless and empty, for what? Preparing the dark, watery chaos for what? For the creative days of forming—days one, two, and three—and the creative days of filling—days four, five, and six. As he floats preparedly over the raw materials, the Spirit intends to form and fill a "very good" creation, an intention he does indeed actualize.[6]

In the narrative of the actualization of the divine intention (1:3–31), two types of accounts of God's creative activity are placed side by side.[7] The first type begins with the words "Let there be." For example: "Then God said, '*Let there be an expanse* between the waters, separating water from water.' *So God made the expanse* and separated the water under the expanse from the water above the expanse. And it was so'" (1:6–7). The second type begins with the words "Let the earth produce." For example: "Then God said, '*Let the earth produce vegetation*: seed-bearing plants and fruit trees on the earth bearing fruit with seed in it according to their kinds.' And it was so. *The earth produced vegetation*: seed-bearing plants according to their kinds and trees bearing fruit with seed in it according to their kinds" (1:11–12). The difference in expression is striking: "Let there be . . . So God made" and "Let the earth produce . . . The earth produced." Focusing on the second type of

---

[5] "The phrase *tōhû wābōhû* has nothing to do with the idea of a chaotic state of the earth. It simply refers to a desolate and empty earth. Genesis 1:2 provides the SETTING information before the actual creation ACTION is narrated"; David Tsumura, *Creation and Destruction: A Reappraisal of the* Chaoskampf *Theory in the Old Testament* (Winona Lake: Eisenbrauns, 2005), 196.

[6] For further discussion see Malcolm B. Yarnell III, *Who is the Holy Spirit? Biblical Insights into His Divine Person* (Nashville: B&H Academic, 2019), 10–11.

[7] The following discussion is adapted from Horton, *Rediscovering the Holy Spirit*, 51–54.

expression, one could consign the earth's ability to produce in accordance with the divine command to some immanent force within nature itself. However, the alternative—which our pneumatology embraces—is to assign the earth's ability to produce to the creative activity of the Holy Spirit. As introduced in v. 2, the Spirit of God is carrying out his intention to form and fill the earth as it is being created.

Further support for this view is found in the two parallel statements concerning the divine blessing of/purpose for creatures. First is the divine blessing/purpose with respect to water creatures and winged birds:

> Then God said, "Let the water swarm with living creatures, and let birds fly above the earth across the expanse of the sky." So God created the large sea-creatures and every living creature that moves and swarms in the water, according to their kinds. He also created every winged creature according to its kind. And God saw that it was good. God blessed them: "*Be fruitful, multiply, and fill* the waters of the seas, and let the birds multiply on the earth." (1:20–22)

Second is the parallel divine blessing/purpose with respect to human creatures: "God blessed them, and God said to them, '*Be fruitful, multiply, fill* the earth, *and subdue* it. *Rule* the fish of the sea, the birds of the sky, and every creature that crawls on the earth'" (1:28). One wonders if water creatures and winged birds have the ability to fulfill God's blessing/purpose. Yes, obviously, but why and how? Unless one is ready to consign their ability to be fruitful, multiply, and fill the earth to some imminent force within nature itself, the alternative is to assign their ability to the creative activity of the Holy Spirit. Not to be pedantic, but one wonders if human creatures have the ability to fulfill God's blessing/purpose. Yes, obviously, but why and how? Unless one is ready to consign their ability to be fruitful, multiply, fill, and subdue/rule the earth to some immanent force within nature itself, the alternative is to assign their ability to the creative activity of the Holy Spirit. Indeed, his work is to fructify the creation, that is, to render it productive in accordance with its divine design.

This pneumatological interpretation of the creation account takes its context-setting passage (1:2) not as a mere mention of the Spirit at the start of the narrative. Rather, it understands that verse as indicating what "the Spirit of God," who "was hovering over the surface of the waters," intended to, and did indeed, actualize. Beginning with the raw materials of an earth that "was formless and empty, [while] darkness covered the surface of the watery depths," the Spirit formed and filled that space so that it would become a hospitable place for living creatures: seed-bearing plants and fruit trees, water creatures and winged birds, and human beings.

Of course, this creative activity of the Holy Spirit was not carried out apart from the inseparable operations of the Father and the Son. According to the Genesis 1 narrative, God (the Father) spoke the creation into existence through his Word (God the Son).[8] The divine speech act (e.g., "Let there be light"; 1:3) is an utterance of the Father through the agency of the Son. As the psalmist rehearses, "The heavens were made by the word of the LORD, and all the stars, by the breath of his mouth. . . . For he spoke, and it came into being; he commanded, and it came into existence" (Ps 33:6, 9; cf. John 1:1–3; Col 1:15–20). Inseparably joined to this creative utterance is the work of the Spirit of God "to bring about the intended effect of the Father's command, in the Son."[9]

This pneumatological interpretation of the creation account stands against all non-creationist views of the origin and development of the world. As introduced here, it rejects the idea that the universe and everything it contains came into existence and evolved through an immanent process, or in accordance with an impersonal property, of nature. Accordingly, it rules out secular, or nontheistic, evolutionary theory, "the idea that the natural selection/mutation mechanism has the *creative power* to produce fundamental innovations in the history of life. . . . The mechanism of natural selection and random variation/mutation represents a causal *process* that can allegedly generate . . . large-scale macroevolutionary change."[10] This secular, or nontheistic, evolutionary view is incorrect. Moreover, our pneumatology rejects theistic evolution, "the view that God created matter and after that did not guide or intervene to cause any empirically detectable change in the natural behavior of matter until all living things had evolved by purely natural

---

[8] In parallel with the Ten Commandments, there are ten words of creation ("God said;" Gen 1:3, 6, 9, 11, 14, 20, 24, 26, 28, 29).

[9] Horton, *Rediscovering the Holy Spirit*, 51.

[10] Stephen C. Meyer, "Scientific and Philosophical Introduction: Defining Theistic Evolution," in J. P. Moreland et al., eds., *Theistic Evolution: A Scientific, Philosophical, and Theological Critique* (Wheaton: Crossway, 2017), 37.

processes."[11] This theistic evolutionary view is incorrect. The world did not originate and evolve through an immanent process or in accordance with an impersonal property of nature; rather, it was created by the triune God.

Over the course of the six-day creation, the divine assessment of what emerges is "good" (six times; 1:4, 10, 12, 18, 21, 25). At the conclusion of his creative activity, "God saw all that he had made, and it was very good indeed" (1:31). This good/very good evaluation is not a moral judgment; after all, there is not as yet evil in the earthly realm. Only moral goodness exists at this point, so a divine assessment of good/very good in terms of moral goodness would be a tautology.[12] More appropriately, the good/very good evaluation is a judgment with regard to correspondence: the creation corresponds exactly to the divine design for it. As God planned to form and fill the earth, so he forms and fills it. In the sense of correspondence, the creation is good/very good. We may go a step further: the good/very good assessment is a judgment of beauty.[13] In addition to, or perhaps because of, the perfect correspondence of the creation to the divine design, the creation as coming from the hands of its Creator is beautiful.[14] The beauty of the initial creation is underscored as the opening narrative projects a *telos*, or future fulfillment, in the beautiful new heaven and new earth (Revelation 21–22): as it was in the beginning, so it will be in the end—a beautiful creation/re-creation. Moreover, this idea is hinted at in the description of one aspect of creation, the fruit trees placed in the garden of Eden: "The LORD God caused to grow out of the ground

---

[11] Gregg R. Allison, "Theistic Evolution is Incompatible with Historical Christian Doctrine," in Moreland et. al, 946.

[12] Still, as readers of this affirmation "very good" live in a post-fall world and thus are very familiar with the reality of evil, they are reminded of the original goodness of the now tainted creation and long for its renewal.

[13] Thanks to Gregg's friend Brian Lilly for suggesting this line of thought.

[14] As Walter Brueggemann, *Theology of the Old Testament: Testimony, Dispute, Advocacy* (Minneapolis: Fortress, 1997), 339 offers, "In Gen 1:31, at the conclusion of the sixth day of creation, Yahweh exclaimed, 'It was very good.' Most probably this is an aesthetic judgment and response to a brilliant act of creation. The sense of beauty, or loveliness evokes on Yahweh's part a doxological response to the created order, a sense of satisfaction on the part of the artist, a glad acknowledgment of success. Here and in some other places a glad affirmation of creation is moved more by awe and delight than by ethical insistence or command. Thus Prov 8:30–31, in speaking of creation, culminates in a statement of 'delight' and 'rejoicing.'"

every tree pleasing in appearance and good for food" (Gen 2:9). Not merely utilitarian—they supply nourishment for Adam and Eve—but pleasing to the sight as well: such are the lush trees in the garden. They are beautiful, as (we suspect) is the rest of creation. And the divine assessment of good/very good underscores this beauty.

This dual notion of goodness in terms of correspondence to divine design and beauty reappears later in Scripture. The tabernacle and the temple, built according to a divine blueprint and featuring precious jewels for its building materials and elaborate furnishings, are beautiful.[15] Importantly, Bezalel is filled with the Spirit of God (along with Oholiab) in order to design and build the tabernacle with beauty in accordance with divine instructions (Exod 31:1–11; 35:30–35). The new Jerusalem, prepared like a bride adorned for her husband, is depicted in terms of perfect measurement and will feature precious jewels for its building materials. It will be a glorious, radiant, light-filled city—stunningly beautiful (Revelation 21–22)! If, as we will see, the Holy Spirit, as the one who perfects the divine works, will actualize this eschatological vision of the new heaven and new earth, then that new world flows from the fact that the one responsible for creating the original earth made it good/very good—corresponding to divine design and beautiful.

Providence[16]

Providence is "the continuing work of God to sustain this created universe in existence and to direct it toward its end. Providence (from Lat. *providere*, 'to provide beforehand') includes (1) preservation, God's work to maintain the creation in existence and functioning as he designed it; (2) cooperation, God's work of collaborating with all created realities as they act and occur; and (3) government, God's work of directing the creation toward its divinely purposed end."[17]

---

[15] For example, gold and onyx, which are found in "the whole land of Havilah" (Gen 2:11–12), are incorporated into the ephod and the breastplate, the ark, the mercy seat, and the lampstand in the tabernacle (Exod 25:1–31).

[16] For the Spirit's work in providence, see Horton, *Rediscovering the Holy Spirit*, 57–64.

[17] Allison, *The Baker Compact Dictionary of Theological Terms*, s.v. "providence."

The psalmist expresses the preserving aspect of divine providence as he presents the dependence of living creatures upon God's supply of nourishment: "All of them wait for you to give them their food at the right time. When you give it to them, they gather it; when you open your hand, they are satisfied with good things. When you hide your face, they are terrified; when you take away their breath [*ruach*], they die and return to the dust. When you send your breath [*ruach*], they are created, and you renew the surface of the ground" (Ps 104:27–30). God both sends his breath and takes it away. With the first divine action comes the communication of life; with the second, the demise of death. Again, the close connection of creaturely life with divine breath (*ruach*) prompts remembrance of Gen 1:2 and underscores the Holy Spirit's sustaining role in divine providence.

The aspect of providential government involves the original design for, and *telos* of, creation. As already discussed, its original design unfolds in the progressive stages of creation from inorganic/inanimate realities (water, light, air, and dry land) to organic/biotic realities, such as the plant world (seed-bearing plants and fruit trees) and the animal kingdom (water creatures, birds, wildlife, livestock, and crawling creatures), culminating in the apex of creation, human beings. To his divine image bearers, God gives the mandate to build civilization by Edenizing the created order.[18]

At the same time, this earthly drama emerges out of the backdrop of an eternal divine purpose, revealed in several New Testament affirmations centered on the person and work of God the Son incarnate. The first affirmation expresses the eternal plan in relation to believers in Christ: "Those [God the Father] foreknew he also predestined to be conformed to the image of his Son, so that he would be the firstborn among many brothers and sisters. And those he predestined, he also called; and those he called, he also justified; and those he justified, he also glorified" (Rom 8:29–30). Foreknowledge and predestination indicate that God's good purpose for Christians extends back into eternity past. Calling and justification speak of God's goodness to believers in the present. Glorification announces that the continuation of God's goodwill to Christians extends forward into eternity future. This divine purpose is "for the good of those who love God, who are

---

[18] The idea of this Edenic task is noted by William J. Dumbrell, *The Search for Order: Eschatology in Focus* (Eugene: Wipf & Stock, 2001), 11.

called according to his purpose" (8:28), a good that is detailed as full conformity to the image of the Son of God. Thus, the future of believers is one of eminence. Yet, as glorious as that future may be, it pales in comparison with the future of the one to whose image believers will one day be conformed: Christ will "be the firstborn among many brothers and sisters" (8:29). He will shine with radiant glory and magnificent splendor, the preeminent one among his eminent people.

For this exalted purpose for the Son and his followers to be realized, Christ had to first endure humiliation. Other New Testament passages disclose this aspect of the eternal plan. Speaking of "the precious blood of Christ, like that of an unblemished and spotless lamb," Peter explains that this sacrificial Lamb of God "was foreknown before the foundation of the world but was revealed in these last times for you" (1 Pet 1:20; cf. Acts 2:23; 4:27–28). The centrality of Jesus Christ in this eternal purpose is summed up as "the mystery of [God's] will, according to his good pleasure that he purposed in Christ as a plan for the right time—to bring everything together in Christ, both things in heaven and things on earth in him" (Eph 1:9–10). Scripture reveals the *telos* of creation to be the uniting of all created realities in Christ. As the one who inspired this scriptural revelation, the Holy Spirit providentially directs the creation toward its divinely purposed end.

This providential work of the Holy Spirit does not in any way minimize the importance of secondary causes in (most) everything that comes to pass in creation.[19] Through scientific research, we understand the production of ova and sperm through the process of meiosis, the effect of the moon's gravity on the earth's tides, the formation of chemical bonds through electrostatic force of attraction or the sharing of electrons, the relationship between energy and mass ($E = mc^2$), and much more. Such discoveries enable us to

---

[19] The qualification "most" acknowledges that God's miraculous activity may circumvent secondary causes. For example, the miracle of changing water into wine (John 2:1–11) entailed the transformation of H_2O into a compound substance of water and ethyl alcohol, or CH_3CH_2OH (along with a few grams of glycerine, pectins, acids, and polyphenols). The introduction of carbon atoms, to focus on that aspect alone, did not entail any secondary causes. In contrast, the miracle by which Jesus restored sight to the blind man by applying mud made from dirt and spit, which was then washed off in the pool of Siloam, involved secondary causes (John 9:6–7).

grasp and appreciate divine providence, particularly its cooperative aspect—
God's work of collaborating with all created realities as they act and occur. As
has been emphasized, our pneumatology refuses to consign meiosis, gravita-
tional fields, chemical bonding, the interchangeability of energy and mass, or
the other biological, chemical, physical, genetic, electrical, thermodynamic,
and hydrological structures of the creation to an immanent process or an
impersonal property of nature. The Holy Spirit cooperates providentially in
all that comes to pass.

Conclusion

From its inception, the church has voiced prayers of praise and sung hymns
of thanksgiving to God as the Creator and providential Provider. In its
expression of adoration of the Maker and Sustainer of all that exists, the
church follows Scripture:

> You, Lord, are the only God.
> You created the heavens,
> the highest heavens with all their stars,
> the earth and all that is on it,
> the seas and all that is in them.
> You give life to all of them,
> and all the stars of heaven worship you. (Neh 9:6)

Similarly,

> Our Lord and God,
> you are worthy to receive
> glory and honor and power,
> because you have created all things,
> and by your will
> they exist and were created. (Rev 4:11)

Rightfully so, the early creeds assign the primary role of Creator to
the First Person of the Trinity: "We believe in one God, the Father, the
Almighty, maker of heaven and earth, of all that is, seen and unseen" (Nicene-
Constantinopolitan Creed). The origination of the creation belongs to God
the Father. Still, in accordance with inseparable operations, the church has

acknowledged the concurrent work of the Son and the Spirit. To the Word belongs divine agency; indeed, the second article of the creed confesses belief in the "Lord Jesus Christ . . . by whom all things were made." As for the Holy Spirit, the creed's third article acknowledges that he is "the Giver of life"; to him particularly belongs fruition and completion. As the church praises and gives thanks to the triune God for creation and providence, it confesses the fructifying and perfecting work of the Spirit.

17

The Holy Spirit and Scripture

A s speaking is one of the works of the triune God that terminates in the Holy Spirit, the relationship between the Holy Spirit and Scripture is evident.[1] Once again, turning to the Nicene-Constantinopolitan Creed, our pneumatology confesses belief in "the Holy Spirit . . . *who spoke by the prophets.*" This creedal affirmation has particular reference to what we now call the Old Testament. In keeping with the expansion of the canon of Scripture, which was undergoing its final stages of development in the fourth century (and in the midst of the theological debates that gave rise to this creed), the prophets referenced now include the apostles. Thus, the Holy Spirit spoke by Scripture, the Word of God.

Scripture, Inseparable Operations, and Appropriations

In keeping with inseparable operations, the triune God is ultimately the author of the Word of God. At the same time, the inspiration of Scripture terminates in the Holy Spirit.

Looking at the first piece, the Bible is trinitarian communication. In the Gospel of John, Jesus himself presents a trinitarian structure of divine revelation.[2] In regard to the Father and himself (the Son), Jesus affirms, "I do noth-

---

[1] For further discussion see Kuyper, *The Work of the Holy Spirit*, 56–78, 164–78.

[2] The following discussion is adapted from Gregg R. Allison, "The Word of God and the People of God: The Mutual Relationship between Scripture and the Church," in *Scripture and the People of God: Essays in Honor of Wayne Grudem*,

ing on my own authority, but speak just as the Father taught me" (John 8:28 ESV). Additionally, he explains, "For I have not spoken on my own authority, but the Father who sent me has himself given me a commandment—what to say and what to speak. . . . What I say, therefore, I say as the Father has told me" (12:49–50 ESV). Moreover, appealing to divine perichoresis, Jesus presents an implication: "The words that I say to you I do not speak on my own authority, but the Father who dwells in me does his works" (14:10 ESV). Thus, Jesus emphasizes the initiatory role of the Father in revelation and the responsive role of the Son. Specifically, the Son does not speak on his own authority but, communicating what he has heard/learned from the Father, speaks what the Father has taught him to say.

Next, in giving his disciples the promise of the Holy Spirit, Jesus adds the second piece of revelation terminating in the Spirit: "I still have many things to say to you, but you cannot bear them now. When the Spirit of truth comes, he will guide you into all the truth, for he will not speak on his own authority, but whatever he hears he will speak, and he will declare to you the things that are to come. He will glorify me, for he will take what is mine and declare it to you. All that the Father has is mine; therefore I said that he will take what is mine and declare it to you" (16:12–15 ESV).[3] Thus, as the Father initiates the work of revelation and the Son responds, not speaking on his own authority but communicating what he has heard/learned from the Father, so also does the Holy Spirit. Specifically, not speaking on his

---

ed. John DelHousaye, John J. Hughes, and Jeff T. Purswell (Wheaton: Crossway, 2018), 27–46.

[3] The Spirit does not speak on his own authority and does not seek his own glory. The same is true of the Son in relation to the Father (John 7:18). Yet elsewhere we understand that the Father glorifies the Son in a mutual giving of glory (e.g., John 17:1). Why would we not affirm the same mutual glory-giving between the Son and the Spirit—indeed, between the Father, the Son, and the Spirit? In the words of the Nicene-Constantinopolitan Creed, the Spirit is he "who with the Father and the Son together is worshipped and glorified." The glory that redeemed humanity gives to the triune God is reflective of, and in response to, the eternal mutual glory-giving among the Father, the Son, and the Holy Spirit. The Third Person does not take a back seat to, or act demurely toward, the other two Persons. For the Spirit's work of receiving from and giving to the Son and the Father based on John 16:14, see Smail, *The Giving Gift*, 64–66, 84–87.

own authority, the Spirit hears from the Son and, in turn, speaks what the Son has taught him to say. And the Holy Spirit directs this divine speech to the apostles, the final link in the trinitarian communicative chain (1 Cor 2:10–13): "We [apostles] also speak these things [divine revelation, freely given to us by God; vv. 10, 12], not in words taught by human wisdom, but in those taught by the Spirit, explaining spiritual things to spiritual people" (v. 13). The Holy Spirit is the one by whom Scripture is inspired.

Accordingly, as an inseparable operation, divine revelation is trinitarian: The Father spoke and the Son heard. The Son spoke and the Holy Spirit heard. The Holy Spirit spoke and the apostles heard.[4] At the same time, divine revelation is appropriated to the Holy Spirit, as the biblical authors, "carried along by the Holy Spirit[,] . . . spoke from God" (2 Pet 1:21). Written Scripture is trinitarian revelation, initiated by the Father, expressed through the Son, and terminating in the Holy Spirit, who inspired it.

Scripture, Speech-Act Theory, and Trinitarian Communicative Agency

Recently, theologians have adapted a philosophy of language—speech-act theory—to explain in part the doctrine of Scripture.[5] Briefly, speech-act theory maintains that every communication between people consists of three aspects:[6] (1) a *locution*, the content of the communication; (2) an *illocution*,

---

[4] Later, to this trinitarian structure of divine revelation, our pneumatology will add the inspiration of Scripture by the Holy Spirit, through which the apostolic hearing and oral teaching were written down for people to hear and read.

[5] Nicholas Wolterstorff, *Divine Discourse: Philosophical Reflections on the Claim that God Speaks* (Cambridge, UK: Cambridge University Press, 1995); Kevin Vanhoozer, *Is There a Meaning in This Text? The Bible, the Reader, and the Morality of Literary Knowledge* (Grand Rapids: Zondervan, 1998); Anthony C. Thiselton, *New Horizons in Hermeneutics: The Theory and Practice of Transforming Biblical Reading* (Grand Rapids: Zondervan, 1992); Richard S. Briggs, *Words in Action: Speech Act Theory and Biblical Interpretation* (London: T&T Clark, 2001); Timothy Ward, *Word and Supplement: Speech Acts, Biblical Texts, and the Sufficiency of Scripture* (Oxford, UK: Oxford University Press, 2002). Our pneumatology does not concur with all the applications of speech-act theory made by these proponents.

[6] J. L. Austin, *How to Do Things with Words* (Cambridge: Harvard University Press, 1962); John R. Searle, *Speech Acts: An Essay in the Philosophy of Language*

the type of communication (assertion, command, promise, declaration, exclamation, warning); and (3) a *perlocution*, the response or effect of the communication (for an assertion, acknowledgment or belief; for a command, obedience; for a promise, trust; for a declaration, a new state of affairs; for an exclamation, joy or fear; for a warning, action or avoidance).

Given this speech-act framework, two key points arise. First, similar to the fact that people do things with words, God does things with his words. For example, beyond giving assertions, people make promises, issue commands, express warnings, and more. In an analogous way, beyond asserting, God promises, commands, warns, and more. "Accordingly, speech-act theory emphasizes the divine agency associated with the many-faceted utterances of Scripture: God himself is the agent who communicates through his Word, and God does more than merely state things, that is, make propositional statements."[7] Indeed, this theory holds that the nature of the relationship between God and his Word is that Scripture is a divine speech act: "The words of the Bible are a significant aspect of *God's action* in the world."[8]

The second key point is that the Holy Spirit is especially associated with the perlocutionary aspect of a divine speech act.[9] The Spirit plays a particularly crucial role in helping the hearers/readers of Scripture understand it correctly and respond rightly to God's Word. The Spirit stirs up obedience to its commands, ignites faith in its promises, prompts a sense of dread to its warnings, and the like. The perlocutionary action of the Holy Spirit dovetails nicely with the traditional doctrine of the Spirit's illumination of Scripture.

To what end is the Word of God given? Speech-act theory underscores that Scripture is trinitarian communicative agency for the purpose of

---

(Cambridge, UK: Cambridge University Press, 1974); Searle, *Expression and Meaning: Studies in the Theory of Speech Acts* (Cambridge, UK: Cambridge University Press, 1986).

[7] Allison, "The Word of God and the People of God," 4. This affirmation should not be (mis)understood to be a criticism of the traditional evangelical insistence on the propositional nature of divine revelation.

[8] Timothy Ward, *Words of Life: Scripture as the Living and Active Word of God* (Downers Grove: InterVarsity, 2009), 12.

[9] Kevin Vanhoozer, *First Theology: God, Scripture, and Hermeneutics* (Downers Grove: IVP Academic, 2002), 155.

redeeming God's people.[10] Examples of the divine saving activity through Scripture include conviction of sin (Acts 2:37), effective calling (2 Thess 2:13–14), regeneration (1 Pet 1:22–25), repentance from sin (Acts 19:18–20), faith in Christ (Rom 10:17), sanctification (John 17:17), and assurance of salvation (1 John 5:11–13). As will be presented later, the Holy Spirit plays an accompanying and equally important role in these mighty acts of God. To anticipate that discussion, the letter to the Hebrews captures well the Holy Spirit's speaking in Scripture:[11] "As the Holy Spirit says: 'Today, if you hear his voice, do not harden your hearts as in the rebellion'" (Heb 3:7–8). The Holy Spirit himself, through written Scripture (the text of Ps 95:7–11), commands believers today to respond properly to God and thereby enter his rest (cf. Heb 10:15–18).

Thus, through his Word as trinitarian communicative agency, God saves his people from distress: "Then they cried out to the LORD in their trouble; he saved them from their distress. He sent his word and healed them; he rescued them from the Pit" (Ps 107:19–20). His people's response to Scripture should correspond appropriately to this purpose, including answering the divine call summoning them to salvation, imploring the Lord for mercy, repenting of their sins and trusting in Jesus Christ, submitting to his transforming work in their lives, counting on the promise of assurance, and the like. To summarize, God's people should respond to his rescuing word by fleeing to him for salvation. "Through his speech act the triune God savingly engages his people through assertions, commands, promises, exclamations, declarations, and warnings, and their response must be fitting to this inscripturated trinitarian communication."[12]

Accordingly, Scripture as divine speech act and trinitarian communicative agency has particular reference to the Holy Spirit.

In the following, our pneumatology explores this specific work of the Spirit with reference to three important areas: inspiration, truthfulness and inerrancy, and illumination and interpretation.

---

[10] John Webster, *Holy Scripture: A Dogmatic Approach*, Current Issues in Theology (Cambridge, UK: Cambridge University Press, 2003), chap. 1.

[11] The expression "the Holy Spirit speaking in the Scripture" is found in the Westminster Confession of Faith, 1.10.

[12] Allison, "The Word of God and the People of God," 7.

The Inspiration of Scripture

Inspiration is "the special work of the Holy Spirit by which he superintended the human authors as they composed their writings. While these authors employed their own personalities, theological perspectives, writing styles, and so forth, the Spirit ensured that what they wrote was what God wanted them to write: the Word of God, fully truthful and divinely authoritative."[13] Specifically, inspiration is (1) *plenary*: all Scripture, not part of it, is inspired;[14] (2) *verbal*: inspiration extends to the words of Scripture, not merely to the concepts and thoughts in the minds of the biblical authors as they wrote; and (3) *confluent* or *concursive*: the Holy Spirit and the biblical authors wrote together.

Scripture itself affirms the Spirit's work of inspiration in its composition. Paul underscores this point in encouraging Timothy: "You know that from infancy you have known the sacred Scriptures, which are able to give you wisdom for salvation through faith in Christ Jesus. All Scripture is inspired by God and is profitable for teaching, for rebuking, for correcting, for training in righteousness, so that the man of God may be complete, equipped for every good work" (2 Tim 3:15–17). While "inspiration" is the traditional word used to name this divine activity, the concept is more that of "expiration": Scripture is the result not so much of inspiration—breathing *in*—but of expiration—breathing *out*. Scripture is the product of the creative breath of God. Thus, Scripture is *God-breathed* (2 Tim 3:16 NIV). Such divine activity applies to *all* Scripture, not to some of its parts; thus inspiration is *plenary*. Furthermore, given the connotation of the term "Scripture" (Gr. γραφη [graphē] = "word"), this divine activity extends to the very *words* themselves; thus inspiration is *verbal*.[15] Moreover, the usefulness of Scripture

---

[13] Allison, *The Baker Compact Dictionary of Theological Terms*, s.v. "inspiration of Scripture."

[14] Inspiration is not confined to the "important" parts of Scripture, those passages that guide people to salvation or instruct about faith and obedience for pleasing God. Rather, its historical references (e.g., Adam and Eve, Noah's ark, Jonah and the great fish), its affirmations about the world (e.g., creation out of nothing, the sun and the moon appearing as two great lights), its genealogies, and the rest are inspired by the Spirit such that all Scripture is God-breathed.

[15] Inspiration is not just an influence of providential care or guidance extending to a heightened religious consciousness or extending only to the thoughts or

is tied to its inspiration: Scripture is profitable for communicating sound doctrine, warning of the misdirection in which people are walking, pointing out the right direction in which they should walk, and conforming them to the divine image so they may please God fully as they carry out his will.

Peter focuses specifically on the Holy Spirit's concursive role in the production of Scripture (2 Pet 1:16–21). He begins with his own experience on the Mount of Transfiguration, in which Jesus appeared in majesty and was commended by God the Father, who spoke from heaven (1:16–18). Surely nothing could be more certain than such direct divine speech! Peter disagrees: "We also have the prophetic word strongly confirmed, and you will do well to pay attention to it, as to a lamp shining in a dark place, until the day dawns and the morning star rises in your hearts. Above all, you know this: No prophecy of Scripture comes from the prophet's own interpretation, because no prophecy ever came by the will of man; instead, men spoke from God as they were carried along by the Holy Spirit" (2 Peter 1:19–21). The referent of the similar expressions "the prophetic word," "prophecy of Scripture," and "prophecy" is not limited to the particular writings of the prophets (for example, Isaiah, Jeremiah, Daniel, and Amos) but is the entirety of the Old Testament.[16] In this regard, nothing written in the Old Testament is the writer's own interpretation. The biblical authors do not express their own understanding of the mighty acts of God (e.g., the divine liberation of the people of Israel from enslavement in Egypt through the plagues, the Passover, and the crossing of the Red Sea). Nor do they present their own human wisdom (e.g., the proverbial literature) or establish the laws by which the people of God related to him (e.g., the old covenant regulations regarding dietary restrictions and prescriptions of appropriate sacrifices for sin). The explanation for this denial of human interpretation is another denial: the biblical authors did not take the initiative to invent their writings. By contrast, they "spoke from God as they were carried along by the Holy Spirit." The metaphor of a strong wind catching the sails of a boat

---

ideas in the minds of the human authors. Rather, inspiration is verbal. See Millard J. Erickson, *Christian Theology*, 3rd ed. (Grand Rapids: Baker Academic, 2013), 180–82. Cf. John S. Feinberg, *Light in a Dark Place: The Doctrine of Scripture*, Foundations of Evangelical Theology (Wheaton: Crossway, 2017), 208–15.

[16] For a similar expression, which also has the entirety of Old Testament Scripture as its referent, see Rom 16:26.

and moving it across a lake signifies the superintending work of the Spirit in the writing of Scripture. Importantly, it was a collaborative effort of the human authors and the Holy Spirit that produced Scripture: the biblical writers "spoke from God"—they truly composed their narratives, prophecies, poems, letters, and the like—as the Spirit directed the writing process to ensure its outcome as the inspired Word of God.[17]

Thus, our doctrine of inspiration (1) upholds divine authorship of Scripture, with particular attention to the Holy Spirit's superintending role; (2) affirms human authorship, with the correlative denial of a docetic Scripture (which holds that the Bible only appears [Gr. δοκεω (dokeō) = "to appear"] to have been written by human authors);[18] and (3) rejects the mechanical dictation theory of inspiration (which holds that Scripture came about as God dictated the words to the biblical authors, whose participation was like that of passive secretaries rather than willful engagement in writing).[19] Inspiration is *confluent* or *concursive*.[20] A "confluence" is the flowing together of two streams, or the body of water that is formed. In regard to this doctrine, inspiration is confluent in the sense that the biblical writers

---

[17] On the dual authorship of Scripture see Henri A. G. Blocher, "God and the Scripture Writers: The Question of Double Authorship," in *The Enduring Authority of the Christian Scriptures*, ed. D. A. Carson (Grand Rapids: Eerdmans, 2016), 497–541.

[18] We should acknowledge that some of the early church leaders tended toward a docetic view of inspiration, accentuating the divine activity in the writing of Scripture over the human element. For example, Justin Martyr, *Hortatory Address to the Greeks*, 8; *ANF* 1:276, used the image of the Holy Spirit as a musician plucking a harp or strumming a lyre—that is, the biblical author was a mere instrument in the Spirit's work of inspiration. Athenagoras, *A Plea for the Christians*, 7, 9; *ANF* 2:132–33, likened the Spirit to a flautist playing a flute—again, the biblical writer was the instrument of inspiration.

[19] Non-evangelicals often accuse evangelicals of holding to the mechanical dictation theory of inspiration, but it is nearly impossible to find actual cases of evangelicals who hold it. We should acknowledge that some of the early church fathers seemed to embrace mechanical dictation. For example, Irenaeus and Caius described Scripture as "dictated by the Holy Spirit." Irenaeus, *Against Heresies*, 2.28.2; *ANF* 1:399; Caius, *Against the Heresy of Artemon*, 3. Preserved in Eusebius, *Ecclesiastical History*, 5:28, in *Eusebius' Ecclesiastical History*, trans. Christian Frederick Cruse (Grand Rapids: Baker, 1962), 216.

[20] B. B. Warfield, *The Inspiration and Authority of the Bible* (Phillipsburg: Presbyterian & Reformed, 1948), 83.

and the Holy Spirit came together to produce Scripture. "Concursive" is writing together. In regard to this doctrine, inspiration is concursive as the biblical authors and the Holy Spirit together wrote Scripture. Not to be overlooked in this discussion is the Spirit's prevenient work in the biblical authors, preparing them throughout their experiences of life for their future task of writing Scripture.

Scripture is God-breathed, inspired by the Holy Spirit.

The Truthfulness or Inerrancy of Scripture

The church has historically believed in the truthfulness of Scripture:

> It would be pointless to call into question that Biblical inerrancy in a rather absolute form was a common persuasion from the beginning of Christian times, and from Jewish times before that. For both the Fathers and the rabbis generally, the ascription of any error to the Bible was unthinkable. . . . If the word was God's it must be true, regardless of whether it made known a mystery of divine revelation or commented on a datum of natural science, whether it derived from human observation or chronicled an event of history.[21]

As this summary highlights, it was a *theological argument* that grounded the church's belief in Scripture's truthfulness. Given our framework of Scripture as trinitarian revelation, we reprise that theological argument—first biblically, then historically.

As noted earlier, according to trinitarian order, first the Father spoke; then the Son heard and spoke the words of the Father. In addressing this sequence, the Son (at least) implies the truthfulness of those words: "The one [the Father] who sent me is true, and what I have heard from him—these things I tell the world" (John 8:26). More directly, Jesus affirms, "[I] told you the truth that I heard from God" (John 8:40; cf. 7:18). Furthermore, trinitarian order of revelation passed from the Son to the Holy Spirit: what the Son heard from the Father, the Son spoke to the Holy Spirit, who thus heard the words of the Son and the Father. Jesus underscores the truthfulness of these divine words: "When the Spirit of truth comes, he will guide you into all

[21] Bruce Vawter, *Biblical Inspiration* (Philadelphia: Westminster, 1972), 132–33.

the truth, for he will not speak on his own authority, but whatever he hears he will speak, and he will declare to you the things that are to come" (John 16:13 ESV; cf. 15:26). John, the writer of the Gospel, was one of the disciples of the truth-hearing and truth-speaking Spirit and, appropriately, concluded his testimony, "This is the disciple who testifies to these things and who wrote them down. We know that his testimony is true" (John 21:24). This is the theological argument at the heart of Scripture's inerrancy: "The triune God is the true God, which means his revelation is true as well: The words the Father speaks and the Son hears are true words. The words the Son hears and speaks are true words. The words the Holy Spirit hears and speaks are true words. The words the apostles hear and speak are true words. And the words the people of God read and heed are the true words of Scripture. As Jesus himself expressed, 'Your word is truth' (John 17:17)."[22]

Historically, the early church defended the truthfulness of Scripture by appealing to this theological argument. Clement of Rome, focusing on the Spirit's role, noted, "You have searched the Scriptures, which are true, which were given by the Holy Spirit; you know that nothing unrighteous or counterfeit is written in them."[23] Irenaeus, highlighting the speech act of the Son and the Spirit, explained, "The Scriptures are indeed perfect, since they were spoken by the Word of God and his Spirit."[24] Athanasius, underscoring the work of the Father, denied internal contradictions in Scripture and any falsehood in God: "But there is no disagreement at all. Far from it! Neither can the Father, who is truth, lie; 'for it is impossible that God should lie' [Heb 6:18]."[25] The one true God speaks the truth; thus Scripture, as trinitarian

---

[22] Allison, "The Word of God and the People of God," 8. Of course, this discussion does not engage with the phenomenon of the human authorship of Scripture and its impact on the inerrancy of Scripture. For the classic article on inerrancy see Paul D. Feinberg, "The Meaning of Inerrancy," in *Inerrancy*, ed. Norm Geisler (Grand Rapids: Zondervan, 1982), 268ff. Also helpful is Paul Helm, "The Idea of Inerrancy," in *The Enduring Authority of the Christian Scriptures*, ed. D. A. Carson, 899–919. For an extended treatment see Feinberg, *Light in a Dark Place*, chs. 7–9.

[23] Clement of Rome, *Letter of the Romans to the Corinthians*, 45, in Michael W. Holmes, *Apostolic Fathers: Greek Texts and English Translations*, 3rd ed. (Grand Rapids: Baker Academic, 2007), 79; *ANF*, 1:17.

[24] Irenaeus, *Against Heresies*, 2.28.2; *ANF* 1:399.

[25] Athanasius, *Easter Letter*, 19.3; *NPNF*² 4.546.

revelation from the Father through the Son and terminating in the Holy Spirit, is wholly true.

The Illumination and Interpretation of Scripture

Inspiration and inerrancy treat the nature of Scripture as God-breathed and wholly true. Illumination and interpretation address the understanding of Scripture. Our pneumatology affirms that as the Holy Spirit superintended the biblical authors as they wrote Scripture, thereby guaranteeing its truthfulness, so he engages the hearers/readers of Scripture through his work of illumination as they seek to understand and enact it.

Illumination is "the work of the Holy Spirit by which he enables the understanding of Scripture by enlightening its readers. Illumination is needed because of the spiritual blindness and stubborn ignorance of sinful people. For this insensitivity to divine truth to be overcome, the same Spirit who inspired Scripture opens up its comprehension."[26] The details of this operation of the Spirit are uncertain. "Debate centers on whether the Spirit's work supplies knowledge (an external impartation of the Word) or is a subjective stimulation—an internal enlightening—of the interpreter's mind, will, or both, through the Word."[27]

Scripture conjoins inspiration with illumination and links both to the Holy Spirit. To pick up our earlier discussion, as the Spirit heard the words of the Son (and, originally, the speech of the Father), the Spirit spoke those words to the apostles, the final link in the trinitarian communicative chain: "We [apostles] also speak these things, not in words taught by human wisdom, but in those taught by the Spirit, explaining spiritual things to spiritual people" (1 Cor 2:13). To this work of inspiration is attached the

---

[26] Allison, *The Baker Compact Dictionary of Theological Terms*, s.v. "illumination."

[27] Allison. For further discussion see Feinberg, *Light in a Dark Place*, chap. 15; Daniel Fuller, "The Holy Spirit's Role in Biblical Interpretation," in *Scripture, Tradition, and Interpretation: Festschrift in Honor of Everett F. Harrison*, ed. W. Ward Gasque and William Sanford La Sor (Grand Rapids: Eerdmans, 1979), 189–98; Fred H. Klooster, "The Role of the Holy Spirit in the Hermeneutic Process: The Relationship of the Spirit's Illumination to Biblical Interpretation," in *Hermeneutics, Inerrancy, and the Bible*, ed. Earl D. Radmacher and Robert D. Preus (Grand Rapids: Zondervan, 1984), 451–72.

illuminating work of the same Spirit in interpretation. In regard to understanding Scripture, Paul comments on the status of two types of people. The first category consists of nonbelievers: "The natural person does not accept the things of the Spirit of God, for they are folly to him, and he is not able to understand them because they are spiritually discerned" (2:14 ESV). Due to the absence of the Holy Spirit and the illumination he provides, non-Christians do not—indeed, cannot—grasp the Word of God. The second category consists of believers: "The spiritual person judges all things, but is himself to be judged by no one. 'For who has understood the mind of the Lord so as to instruct him?' But we have the mind of Christ" (2:15–16 ESV). Due to the indwelling of the Holy Spirit and the illumination that he supplies, Christians can understand Scripture. Indeed, as the Word and the Spirit renew them, it may be said that they have the "mind of Christ."

Elsewhere, Paul accentuates this enabling effect of the Spirit with reference to grasping the gospel:

> If our gospel is veiled, it is veiled to those who are perishing. In their case, the god of this age has blinded the minds of the unbelievers to keep them from seeing the light of the gospel of the glory of Christ, who is the image of God. For we are not proclaiming ourselves but Jesus Christ as Lord, and ourselves as your servants for Jesus's sake. For God who said, "Let light shine out of darkness," has shone in our hearts to give the light of the knowledge of God's glory in the face of Jesus Christ. (2 Cor 4:3–6)

In this case, the Spirit's illumination is needed to overcome the debilitating blindness that nonbelievers experience due to the wiles of Satan.[28]

---

[28] Given the broader context in which this discussion occurs, we should see this illumination as the work of the Holy Spirit. Immediately preceding this passage, Paul contrasts the old covenant with the new, which is the covenant especially associated with the Holy Spirit (2 Cor 3:1–18). Indeed, the Lord (Yahweh) of the old covenant is now the Spirit of the new covenant (v. 18). Moreover, in its original context, the divine command "Let light shine out of darkness," cited here from Gen 1:3, follows closely this description: "Now the earth was formless and empty, darkness covered the surface of the watery depths, and the Spirit of God was hovering over the surface of the waters" (Gen 1:2). The replacement of darkness with light, both in the original creation and in the illumination of satanically darkened nonbelievers, is the work of the Spirit of God.

Additionally, Peter orients the hearers/readers of Scripture to the Spirit's role in understanding the Bible canonically:

> Concerning this salvation, the prophets, who prophesied about the grace that would come to you, searched and carefully investigated. They inquired into what time or what circumstances the Spirit of Christ within them was indicating when he testified in advance to the sufferings of Christ and the glories that would follow. It was revealed to them that they were not serving themselves but you. These things have now been announced to you through those who preached the gospel to you by the Holy Spirit sent from heaven. (1 Pet 1:10–12)

The Holy Spirit revealed to the prophets who foretold the future work of Christ that their God-breathed writings would serve a future generation of the people of God. Christians, as the recipients of these prophetic writings— that future generation[29]—read them properly, in line with what Jesus taught his disciples: "He opened their minds to understand the Scriptures. He also said to them, 'This is what is written: The Messiah would suffer and rise from the dead the third day, and repentance for forgiveness of sins would be proclaimed in his name to all the nations, beginning at Jerusalem'" (Luke 24:45–47).

Accordingly, in step with the Holy Spirit, who inspired the Old Testament as anticipatory revelation, Christians interpret it canonically, that is, as finding its fulfillment in Christ and his saving work. Thus, for example, Adam (Gen 2:7) was the first Adam, foreshadowing the second Adam, Jesus Christ (1 Cor 15:45–49; Rom 5:12–21). Moreover, Adam was the son of God (Gen 1:26–28), anticipating the Son of God, the incarnate God-man (Luke 3:38; Rom 1:4). Melchizedek (Gen 14:18–20; Ps 110:4) presaged Jesus the eternal High Priest after the order of Melchizedek (Heb 5:6; 7:11–22). Israel was the firstborn son of God (Exod 4:22–23), foreshadowing Jesus the first-born Son (Heb 1:6; Rom 8:29). David was the king of Israel (2 Samuel 7; Ps 2:7), prefiguring David's kingly son, Jesus Christ (Matt 1:1; Acts 13:33; Heb

---

[29] This "generation" stretches from the first coming of Christ to his second coming, that is, Christians "on whom the ends of the ages has come" (1 Cor 10:11; cf. Rom 15:4).

1:5; 5:5). The Suffering Servant (Isaiah 53) anticipated the healing ministry (Matt 8:14–17) and crucifixion (1 Pet 2:22–25) of Jesus Christ.[30]

In line, therefore, with his inspiration of Scripture, the Holy Spirit through his work of illumination "encourages pneumatological attentiveness to the Old Testament," such that Christians rightly interpret it canonically as pointing to Jesus Christ and his work of salvation.[31]

To recall the earlier discussion of speech-act theory and its application to the doctrine of Scripture, the illumination of the Spirit is particularly associated with the perlocutionary aspect of a divine speech act. "The Holy Spirit is largely involved at the perlocutionary level as we are enabled to understand the truthfulness of the text, recognize what it requires from us and then actually take the appropriate steps to actualize the intentions that the Holy Spirit initially delivered to the human instrument."[32]

Historically, the doctrine of illumination is especially associated with Protestantism. Martin Luther, rejecting an allegorical approach to biblical interpretation and proposing instead a grammatical-historical hermeneutic, insisted on the necessity of the Holy Spirit to understand the Bible: "The truth is that nobody who has not the Spirit of God sees a jot [bit] of what is in the Scriptures. . . . The Spirit is needed for the understanding of all Scripture and every part of Scripture."[33] In a similar vein, John Calvin rehearsed the importance of the Spirit's illuminating ministry: "The Spirit of God, from whom the doctrine of the gospel comes, is its only true interpreter, to open it up to us. Hence, in judging of it, men's minds must of necessity be in blindness until they are enlightened by the Spirit of God."[34] This enlightenment affects the soul's faculty of understanding: "The soul, illumined by [the Spirit

---

[30] Stephen J. Wellum, *God the Son Incarnate: The Doctrine of Christ*, Foundations of Evangelical Theology (Wheaton: Crossway, 2016), 117–19.

[31] Keith A. Quan, "A Pneumatological Retrieval of Neglected Dimensions of the Doctrine of Scripture," in *Third Article Theology: A Pneumatological Dogmatics*, ed. Myk Habets (Minneapolis: Fortress, 2016), 136.

[32] John H. Walton and Brent Sandy, *The Lost World of Scripture: Ancient Literary Culture and Biblical Authority* (Downers Grove: IVP Academic, 2013), 289; cf. Horton, *Rediscovering the Holy Spirit*, 29, 36.

[33] Martin Luther, *The Bondage of the Will*, trans. James I. Packer and O. R. Johnston (Old Tappan: Revell, 1957), 73–74; cf. Martin Luther, *Luther's Works*, eds., Jaroslav Pelikan, Hilton C. Oswald, and Helmut T. Lehmann, 55 vols. (St. Louis: Concordia, 1955-1986), 33:28.

[34] John Calvin, *Commentaries on the Epistles of Paul to the Corinthians*, 1:117.

of God], takes on a new keenness, as it were, to contemplate the heavenly mysteries, whose splendor had previously blinded it. And man's understanding, thus beamed by the light of the Holy Spirit, then at last truly begins to taste of those things which belong to the Kingdom of God."[35]

A recent development on the interface of the Holy Spirit and biblical interpretation is pneumatological hermeneutics.[36] Such an approach considers "how the experience of the Spirit that empowered the church on the day of Pentecost can and should dynamically shape our reading of Scripture [today]."[37] Specifically, Scripture should be read experientially, missionally, and eschatologically. An experiential reading does not mean interpreting the Bible purely subjectively, only in light of one's own personal experience. Rather, it approaches Scripture as setting forth the people of God's experiences with him and, in turn, reading one's own experience analogously, seeking to grasp what the Bible says to one's own particular situation.[38] Reading the Bible missionally emphasizes Jesus's promise of the Spirit being poured out at Pentecost to empower the church for mission (Luke 24:48–49; Acts 1:1–8). In light of the Spirit's missional task, a missional reading of the Word that the Spirit inspired is proper.[39] An eschatological reading of Scripture is in keeping with our pneumatology's emphasis on the church existing in the age of the Spirit. In the "last days" between Jesus's first and second comings, this age dominated by the Spirit, who is preparing the people of God for what is still to come, an eschatological reading of Scripture views contemporary experiences as a foretaste of the future and anticipates ongoing renewal until that future arrives in full rather than in part.[40]

---

[35] John Calvin, *Institutes*, 3.2.34, LCC 1:582.

[36] Craig S. Keener, *Spirit Hermeneutics: Reading Scripture in Light of Pentecost* (Grand Rapids: Eerdmans, 2016); cf. Kenneth J. Archer, *A Pentecostal Hermeneutic: Spirit, Scripture, and Community* (Cleveland: CPT Press, 2009); Kevin L. Spawn and Archie T. Wright, eds., *Spirit and Scripture: Exploring a Pneumatic Hermeneutic* (London: T&T Clark, 2012); Leulseged Philemon, *Pneumatic Hermeneutics: The Role of the Holy Spirit in the Theological Interpretation of Scripture* (Cleveland: Centre for Pentecostal Theology, 2019); Kevin J. Vanhoozer, "Reforming Pneumatic Hermeneutics," in *Holy Spirit: Unfinished Agenda*, ed. Johnson T. K. Lim (Singapore: Genesis Books and Word N Works, 2015): 18–24.

[37] Keener, *Spirit Hermeneutics*, 4.

[38] Keener, 21–38.

[39] Keener, 42–43.

[40] Keener, 49–53.

Conclusion

Our pneumatology concludes this chapter with an admonition to read the Bible in line with "the Holy Spirit speaking in the Scripture."[41] He is the one responsible for its God-breathed quality (inspiration). He is the one who leads to its proper interpretation through his work of illumination. And he is the one who prompts a canonical reading of Scripture.[42]

Such a reading of Scripture may begin with a prayer for illumination by the Holy Spirit. An example is one that Huldrych Zwingli prayed each day that the pastors and theological students in Zurich met for an hour of intense exegesis of Scripture: "Almighty, eternal and merciful God, whose Word is a lamp unto our feet and a light unto our path, open and illuminate our minds, that we may purely and perfectly understand your Word and that our lives may be conformed to what we have rightly understood, that in nothing we may be displeasing unto your majesty, through Jesus Christ our Lord. Amen."[43] Accordingly, a prayer for illumination requests the Spirit's aid both in rightly understanding the meaning of Scripture and in enacting its properly understood meaning, whether that is obedience to a command, trust in a promise, confession of sin, praising God, or the like.

Moreover, such a reading should heed Jesus's words, "Let anyone who has ears to hear listen to what the Spirit says to the churches" (Rev 2:7). Accordingly, reading Scripture involves listening for and to the voice of the Spirit as he—the divine person who guides into all truth (John 16:13)—illumines the Word of God. The Spirit is not the light itself, nor does he merely provide help, for understanding Scripture. He himself is present and active in the reading, studying, meditating on, memorizing, and applying the Word of God. His personal presence demands acknowledgement.

Finally, the proper disposition toward reading the Bible in line with "the Holy Spirit speaking in the Scripture" is thanksgiving. Karl Barth

---

[41] Westminster Confession of Faith, 1.10.

[42] Space constraints prevent further development of the sufficiency, necessity, transformative power, and authority of Scripture. For the latter attribute, Calvin's work on the "secret testimony of the Spirit" is unsurpassed. See Calvin, *Institutes*, 1.7.4–5, LCC 20:74–81.

[43] Gottfried W. Locher, *Zwingli's Thought: New Perspectives* (Leiden, NL: Brill, 1981), 28.

underscored the desperate situation of sinful people—even believers—in coming face-to-face with divine revelation: "The hearing of the Word of God the Creator . . . is not man's work but God's: the Holy Spirit's work. Just as our spirit cannot produce the Word of God, so too it cannot receive it. . . . It is incapable, unassisted, of hearing God's Word. . . . The spirit of man . . . is a spirit that evades what God has really said to it." Still, it must be a human "hearing of God's Word," a human taking in of the Word, but it is not a man's possession, says Barth; rather "it must simply *be conveyed* to him all along. A sheer miracle must happen to him. . . . This miracle is the office of the Holy Spirit.[44]

In light of this incapacity for hearing the Word of God, we should express thanksgiving for the illumination and piercing voice of the Holy Spirit.

---

[44] Karl Barth, *The Holy Spirit and the Christian Life: The Theological Basis of Ethics* (Louisville: Westminster John Knox, 1993), 10–11, emphasis original. Though what Barth meant by the Word of God and what we understand to be the Word of God are different, his insights on the miraculous work of the Holy Spirit in overcoming human resistance to the Word are appreciated.

18

The Holy Spirit and Angelic Beings

W hile it is rather uncommon to consider the relationship of the Holy Spirit with the angelic realm, our pneumatology notes biblical and historical presentations in which the two are joined.[1]

Angels

Angels are the "category of creatures that have been created as immaterial (without a body) beings. . . . They are highly intelligent, moral creatures who wield significant power and authority, and they both worship and serve God, especially providing help for believers."[2] The only commonalities angels share with the Holy Spirit are their immaterial nature and their messaging. Still, Scripture occasionally relates angels and the Holy Spirit.

For example, at the annunciation, the angel Gabriel gives directions to Mary concerning Jesus's conception, which will be a miracle wrought by the Holy Spirit (Matt 1:18–25; Luke 1:26–38). Why this message comes through an angel and not by a human being (for example, a prophet through whom the Holy Spirit could speak) is a mystery. Also, many angels are present at Jesus's birth, announcing to the shepherds the good news of the Savior's arrival and forthcoming work of salvation. Thus, what the Holy

---

[1] For a helpful discussion on angels and demons see Graham A. Cole, *Against the Darkness: The Doctrine of Angels, Satan, and Demons*, Foundations of Evangelical Theology (Wheaton: Crossway, 2019).

[2] Allison, *The Baker Compact Dictionary of Theological Terms*, s.v. "angels."

Spirit accomplishes in effecting the incarnation of the eternal Son as the God-man, Jesus of Nazareth, is attested by an angelic host (Luke 2:8–20). Furthermore, after being led by the Holy Spirit into the wilderness to be tempted by Satan, the victorious Christ is cared for by angels (Matt 4:11; Mark 1:13).

While the church has historically engaged in wild speculation about angels, John Calvin called the church to think biblically and theologically about them. One issue he raised was why God ever employs angels to carry out his will: "Surely he does not do this out of necessity as if he could not do without them. For as often as he pleases, he disregards them and carries out his work through his will alone."[3] For our purposes, Calvin implied that the powerful working of the Holy Spirit is always sufficient for God's will to be done; thus, the role of angels is at best a subsidiary one and never necessary for God's purposes to be actualized. Appealing to divine accommodation, Calvin imagined that angels provide extra assurance for weak and doubting Christians: "When we see ourselves surrounded by so many dangers . . . we would sometimes be filled with fear or yield to despair if the Lord did not make us realize the presence of his grace according to our capacity. For this reason, he not only promises to take care of us, but tells us he has innumerable guardians whom he has commanded to look after our safety."[4] In other words, though the Holy Spirit as divine comforter should suffice for believers' support and consolation, at times God employs angels as concrete messengers of his aid.

Accordingly, the Holy Spirit must not be confused with angels. They are never to be worshipped, as is the Holy Spirit, nor are they necessary, as is the Holy Spirit. Still, at times God employs angels to announce and accomplish his will, provide aid for his people, and guard them against danger (e.g., Acts 12:6–11)—ministries that approximate the work of the Holy Spirit.

Satan and Demons

Tragically, there is another dimension of immaterial beings. "As 'the prince of this world' (John 12:31 [NIV]) and 'the god of this age' (2 Cor. 4:4 [NIV]),

---

[3] Calvin, *Institutes*, 1.14.11, LCC 20:171.
[4] Calvin, 1.14.11.

Satan is the head of the realm of demons. Though originally created good with all the angels, Satan fell from his lofty position as the supreme angel by rebelling against God, being cast down to earth, on which he now opposes God as the 'evil one.'"[5] The names of Satan,[6] indicative of his evil activities in relation to human beings, contrast strongly with the Holy Spirit and his good works in support of believers. As Satan, he is the "adversary" (Heb *satan*; see 1 Pet 5:8); the Holy Spirit is the "Advocate" (John 14:26 NIV). As the devil, he is the "slanderer" (Gk. *diabolos*); the Holy Spirit glorifies Christ. As Apollyon, he is the "destroyer" (Gk. *Apollyon*; see Rev 9:11); the Holy Spirit is the Creator. As the "ancient serpent" (Rev 12:9), he is the liar and the slayer of life; the Holy Spirit is the Spirit of truth and the "Giver of life." We should not understand this oppositional reality as some type of metaphysical dualism, as if Satan and the Holy Spirit have been locked eternally in a battle between the powers of evil and the powers of good. Still, the two are opposed to one another.

Though originally created upright, demons are angels who "followed their head, Satan, in rebelling against God, lost their original goodness, and seek to oppose God and his work. Their evil activities with reference to human beings include temptation, deception, lying, false belief, torment, sickness, and even possession leading to self-destructive activity, mental instability, pronounced strength to harm others, and anguish."[7] Again, the strong contrast between demons and the Holy Spirit is not one of cosmic dualism but underscores the reality of the spiritual battle between demons, who are led by Satan, and believers, who are led by the Holy Spirit.

Scripture occasionally relates Satan and/or demons and the Holy Spirit. For example, immediately after Christ's baptism, the Holy Spirit leads Jesus "into the wilderness to be tempted by the devil" (Matt 4:1/Luke 4:1/Mark 1:12). After these fierce satanic temptations toward which the Holy Spirit directed Jesus, "the angels came and began to serve him" (Matt 4:11/Mark 1:13). Moreover, Jesus casts out demons by the Holy Spirit. The Gospels narrate demonic activity in the following passages:

---

[5] Allison, *The Baker Compact Dictionary of Theological Terms*, s.v. "Satan."
[6] The following discussion relies in part on Allison, s.v. "Satan."
[7] Allison, s.v. "demons."

- *General statements*: Jesus casts out demons from many people (Matt 8:16; Mark 1:32–35; Luke 4:40–41).
- *Specific narratives* of Jesus's casting out demons:

  — multiple demons from the two men/one man of the Gadarenes/ Gerasenes (Matt 8:28–34; Mark 5:1–20; Luke 8:26–39)
  — a single demon from a mute man (Matt 9:32–33; Luke 11:14)
  — one or more demons from a blind and mute man (Matt 12:22–23)
  — a demon from the Canaanite/Syrophoenician woman's daughter (Matt 15:22–28; Mark 7:24–30)
  — a demon from a boy suffering from seizures (Matt 17:14–20; Mark 9:14–29; Luke 9:37–43)
  — a demon from a man in the synagogue (Mark 1:23–27; Luke 4:31–37)
  — the seven demons from Mary Magdalene (Luke 8:2)

Of particular importance is the account of Jesus's casting out demons from the blind and mute man. In his narrative, Matthew emphasizes that Jesus does his work by the Holy Spirit (Matt 12:22–32); in the parallel account, Luke underscores that it is "by the finger of God" that Jesus casts out the demons (Luke 11:14–23).[8] Assuming the programmatic nature of this narrative, we affirm that in all the incidences of Jesus's rescuing people from demonic oppression or possession, he casts out the demon(s) by the Holy Spirit.

The Spirit's role in freeing demonically influenced people is proper. In the Old Testament, when enemies of the people of God conquer and enslave them, the Holy Spirit raises up judges to defeat Israel's tormentors and grant

---

[8] Narratively, the close conjunction of Jesus's promise that "the heavenly Father give[s] the Holy Spirit to those who ask him" (Luke 11:13) with Jesus's reference to "the finger of God" (11:20) supports the interpretation that the latter expression is a reference to the powerful Holy Spirit. Canonically, the one other place in Scripture in which the metaphor "the finger of God" is used to express divine power in contrast to opposition is the third plague of gnats at the time of the exodus. When the Egyptian magicians attempt and fail to reproduce this plague, they express their resignation with the admission, "This is the finger of God" (Exod 8:16–19).

peace to the nation. Moreover, the Old Testament prophesies of freedom from oppression for the people of God in association with the Messiah. With the Spirit of the Lord resting upon him, the Messiah would execute justice for the oppressed of the land (Isa 11:1–4). With the Spirit on him, he would "open blind eyes, to bring out prisoners from the dungeon, and those sitting in darkness from the prison house" (Isa 42:7). With the anointing of the Spirit of the Lord upon him, the Messiah would "bring good news to the poor . . . heal the brokenhearted . . . proclaim liberty to the captives and freedom to the prisoners . . . proclaim the year of the LORD's favor and the day of our God's vengeance . . . [and] comfort all who mourn" (Isa 61:1–2). Such activity, prophesied in Scripture, finds its fulfillment in the Spirit-anointed Son incarnate, Jesus Christ, who casts out demons by the Holy Spirit. As the New Testament affirms, "God anointed Jesus of Nazareth with the Holy Spirit and with power, and . . . he went about doing good and healing all who were under the tyranny of the devil, because God was with him" (Acts 10:38).

Moreover, this role is proper because the Holy Spirit accompanies Jesus as he is being tempted by Satan. Though it could not be described as the Spirit's freeing Jesus from these satanic temptations, the Spirit's work of sustaining Jesus during this time is crucial. Importantly, the temptation narrative begins with the affirmation that "Jesus, full of the Holy Spirit, . . . was led by the Spirit in the wilderness for forty days to be tempted by the devil" (Luke 4:1–2). The temptation narrative flows into the next story by noting that "Jesus returned to Galilee in the power of the Spirit" (Luke 4:14). It would be wrong to conclude that the Holy Spirit abandons Jesus to his wilderness plight, then reconnects with him after Jesus has successfully completed his sufferings. On the contrary, Jesus is full of the Holy Spirit as he faces down Satan's wiles. Fittingly, then, having defeated the evil one in his own tormented period, Jesus casts out the evil one and his minions from others tormented by them.

Furthermore, this fittingness can be detected from the oppositional nature of Satan and demons and the Holy Spirit. Through oppression and possession, Satan and demons seek to kill, destroy, oppose, soil, and pervert. The Holy Spirit does the exact opposite: he seeks to restore life, prompt flourishing, advocate, cleanse, and render holy.

In summary, the Spirit's role in freeing demonically influenced people is proper.

Moreover, the Spirit's role in liberating demonically tormented people is good. While our reading of Jesus's exorcisms often focuses on their miraculous nature and the power of the Spirit that the exorcisms engage, our attention should also move to the impact of these liberating experiences on those who are oppressed or possessed by the demons. They are released from savage torment. They begin to see, hear, and speak. They are restored to their families. They are (re)introduced into society as productive people. They can enter the synagogue and the temple to worship God. They proclaim the miraculous work of Jesus. These exorcisms accomplish much good, and they are the powerful work of the one whose name is Love and Gift.

Birthed and empowered by this Spirit, the church is to engage Satan and demons in spiritual warfare for the good of others, which involves many elements:

> Finally, be strengthened by the Lord and by his vast strength. Put on the full armor of God so that you can stand against the schemes of the devil. For our struggle is not against flesh and blood, but against the rulers, against the authorities, against the cosmic powers of this darkness, against evil, spiritual forces in the heavens. For this reason take up the full armor of God, so that you may be able to resist in the evil day, and having prepared everything, to take your stand. Stand, therefore, with *truth* like a belt around your waist, *righteousness* like armor on your chest, and your feet sandaled with *readiness for the gospel* of peace. In every situation take up the shield of *faith* with which you can extinguish all the flaming arrows of the evil one. Take the helmet of *salvation* and the sword of the Spirit—which is the *word of God*. Pray at all times in the Spirit with every *prayer and request*, and stay alert with all perseverance and intercession for all the saints. (Eph 6:10–18)

The Holy Spirit's role in spiritual warfare is striking. He is the Spirit of *truth* (John 14:17; 15:26; 16:13). He renders the church holy and *righteous* (1 Cor 3:16–17). He is the empowerment for *evangelism* (Acts 1:8). He is the one through whom Christians confess *faith* in Christ (1 Cor 12:3). He is the one who applies *salvation*—regeneration, justification, adoption, sanctification, and the like (John 3:1–8; 1 Cor 6:11; Gal 4:4–7; Titus 3:4–7; 1 Pet 1:2). He is the one who inspires *Scripture* and illumines its understanding (1 Cor 2:10–16; 2 Tim 3:16–16; 2 Pet 1:19–21). He is the one by whom and in whom believers are to *pray*, following his guidance, relying on his intercession (Rom 8:26–27; Eph 2:18; Jude v. 20).

The Holy Spirit equips the church, which is to be full of the Spirit, to battle Satan and demons, similar to how the church's head, who was always full of the Spirit, warred against those same evil powers.

Conclusion

Accordingly, our pneumatology returns to one of its central themes and assumptions: the contrast between the spirit of the age and the age of the Spirit. These two epochs, which are contemporaneous, stand in strong contrast with each other. The New Testament explains, "We know that we are of God, and the whole world is under the sway of the evil one" (1 John 5:19). The contrast is between those who know God—Christ's followers, who have been "born of God" (5:18)—and the world. Vividly, all people who have not yet been rescued by the regenerating work of the Holy Spirit are certainly not in a good position, nor are they merely in a neutral position; rather, they lie in the power of Satan. Devoid of the Spirit and held in the clutches of the evil one, the world is in dire straits before God. Indeed, Jesus prophesies about the coming of "the Spirit of truth. The world is unable to receive him because it doesn't see him or know him. But you do know him, because he remains with you and will be in you" (John 14:17).

On the one hand, then, we have the spirit of this age, also known as the kingdom of darkness, the world, the realm of Satan, who is "the god of this age" and "the ruler of this world" (2 Cor 4:4; John 12:31). On the other hand, we have the age of the Spirit, also called the kingdom of God, (in part) the church, the realm of Holy Spirit. The former is not to be ignored, toyed with, or underestimated; "the whole world is under the sway of the evil one" (1 John 5:19). Such evil manifests itself in more or less heinous ways, the list of which could go on interminably: war, rape, murder, caustic speech, racism, lying, indifference, child molestation, sexism, idolatry, abortion, divorce, ageism, sloth, systemic corruption, poverty, and much more. Scripture envisions the desacralization of all earthly powers and the sacralization of Jesus as

Lord—"sanctify Christ as Lord in your hearts" (1 Pet 3:15 NASB)[9]—a hallowing that comes only through the Holy Spirit (1 Cor 12:3).[10]

The church is called to stand firm against the evil one and his minions. It does so by living in the fullness of the Holy Spirit.

---

[9] Cornelis van der Kooi, *This Incredibly Benevolent Force: The Holy Spirit in Reformed Theology and Spirituality* (Grand Rapids: Eerdmans, 2018), 110.

[10] In the early church, this renunciation of Satan as one's old master, and the enthronement of Jesus as Lord, was an element in the ceremony of baptism: "When entering the water, we make profession of the Christian faith in the words of its rule: we bear public testimony that we have renounced the devil, his pomp, and his angels [demons]" (Tertullian, *The Shows*, 4, *ANF* 3:81; cf. Tertullian, *The Chaplet* [*Crown*], 3, *ANF* 3:94).

19

The Holy Spirit and Human Beings and Sin

Human Creation[1]

Similar to the context-setting passage of Gen 1:2, which highlights the original state of the earth, the account of the creation of the first human being starts with a lengthy description of the original state of the place of Adam's creation (2:4–7). In both cases, the presence of "spirit" or "breath" is an important feature of the narrative. Specifically:

- *The context of the original creation*: "Now the earth was formless and empty, darkness covered the surface of the watery depths. . . ." (Gen 1:2a)
- *The role of spirit/breath*: "and the Spirit [*ruach*] of God was hovering over the surface of the waters." (Gen 1:2a)
- *The context of human creation*: "At the time that the LORD God made the earth and the heavens, no shrub of the field had yet grown on the land, and no plant of the field had yet sprouted, for the LORD God had not made it rain on the land, and there was no man to work the ground. But mist would come up from the earth and water all the ground." (Gen 2:4–6)

---

[1] For further discussion see Kuyper, *The Work of the Holy Spirit*, 32–38, 203–51.

- *The role of spirit/breath*: "Then the LORD God formed the man out of the dust from the ground and breathed the breath [*neshamah*] of life into his nostrils, and the man became a living being." (Gen 2:7)

This striking parallelism prompts three points.

First, in both cases the context is one of lack or absence. In the case of the original creation, the earth lacks form, fullness, light, and land. In the case of human creation, the space lacks shrubs, plants of the field,[2] rain (though there is mist), and a caretaker. Second, in both cases divine activity is decisive. In the case of the original creation, the Spirit (*ruach*) of God hovers preparedly, readying the dark, watery chaos for the life-giving form and fullness in a lighted land that will soon be created. In the case of human creation, God communicates the breath (*neshamah*) of life into the first man's nostrils, by which Adam becomes a living creature. Third, a strong case can be made for the interchangeability of the Hebrew words *ruach* and *neshamah* (Job 12:10; 27:3; 32:8; 33:4; 34:14–15; Isa 42:5). Indeed, in most cases they are used in tandem to refer to the same thing: the spirit or breath of life, the energizing principle that courses through all living creatures.[3]

While caution is to be exercised, it is not a stretch to see a parallelism between the Spirit of God in the account of the original creation and the breath of life in the account of human creation. What is not being said is that the infusion of the breath of life into Adam is an impartation of the Holy Spirit. Rather, "This infusion of the breath of life constitutes the impartation of the energizing principle, or spark of life, that actualizes the material reality of Adam (of the dust of the ground) so that he became a living being."[4] Moreover, this breath of life must be seen in conjunction with the Spirit of God. Though the two are distinct, they are not unconnected, in that the Holy Spirit, as "the Lord and Giver of life," gives the spark of life to the previously formed "dust of the ground," and Adam becomes a living

---

[2] Though vegetation had been created on the third day, this type of vegetation was not the domesticated crops and plants that require the presence of a human farmer or gardener to care for them.

[3] Accordingly, death is the loss of this spirit or breath of life (e.g., Gen 7:22; Eccl 12:7; Zech 12:1).

[4] P. 12.

creature. The impartation of life to the first human creature is linked to the Holy Spirit.

Adam becomes a living being, thus setting the stage for God to rectify the original context of lack or absence. Indeed, the narrative continues: "The LORD God planted a garden in Eden, in the east, and there he placed the man he had formed. The LORD God caused to grow out of the ground every tree pleasing in appearance and good for food. . . . The LORD God took the man and placed him in the garden of Eden to work it and watch over it" (Gen 2:8–9, 15). What had been a space lacking shrubs, plants of the field, rain (though there was mist), and a caretaker becomes a place containing the missing components. Through divine action, the garden in Eden is the launching site for human beings created in the divine image to embark on their cultural mandate (Gen 1:28) by ruling over the rest of creation. In other words, the human responsibility is to build civilization[5] or to "Edenize" the world[6] by the procreation of godly offspring ("be fruitful, multiply, fill the earth") and by the extension of the boundaries of the garden to encompass the still uncivilized and undomesticated space outside of Eden ("subdue it").

Thus, parallel to the Spirit's initial work of transforming the original creation from formlessness and emptiness, the Spirit begins to transform the pre-Edenic space into a place of beauty and flourishing that will be enlarged through the good work of Adam and Eve.

As in the case of the creation in general, this actualization of God's design for his human image bearers does not come about through an immanent process or in accordance with an impersonal property of nature. Yes, the first humans, to whom the mandate "be fruitful, multiply, fill the earth, and subdue it" is given, have the ability to obey the command. But this capacity is not independent of the Designer. As discussed earlier, the Holy Spirit's work is to fructify the creation, that is, to render it productive in accordance with its divine design. Accordingly, it is the Spirit who renders human beings fruitful in relation to their divinely mandated purpose.

---

[5] Gregg R. Allison, *Sojourners and Strangers: The Doctrine of the Church*, Foundations of Evangelical Theology (Wheaton: Crossway, 2012), 459–63.

[6] Dumbrell, *The Search for Order*, 11.

Creation Mandate

Simply put, the divine mandate entails both procreation ("be fruitful, multiply, fill the earth") and vocation ("subdue it" by exercising dominion over the created order). This is the dual nature of the human task, and the first steps to fulfill the mandate are narrated almost immediately:

> The fruitful multiplication of the human species is clearly seen in the subsequent chapters of Genesis, beginning with the union of Adam and Eve that produces the first human offspring, Cain and Abel (Gen. 4:1–2), and continuing with the list of descendants, first of Adam, then of Noah, and finally of Shem (Genesis 5; 10; 11). The exercise of dominion is also clearly noted in these chapters: shepherding and farming (Gen. 4:2), building cities (vv. 16-17), tending livestock, musical artistry, and fashioning tools (vv. 2-22)—these human endeavors were the beginning of the fulfillment of the cultural mandate for all human beings to engage in civilization building.[7]

The first human beings engage fruitfully in their divinely designed mandate not through their own independent capacities but through the abilities given to them by the Holy Spirit.

Moreover, the Spirit seems to be responsible for the characteristics that are proper and unique to human beings.[8] Scripture specifically mentions discernment, wisdom, understanding, and craftsmanship (Gen 41:38–39; Exod 28:3; 31:3–5; 35:30–35; Job 32:7–8) as endowments from the Holy Spirit.[9] At times it is difficult to know if such abilities are the Spirit's gifts to the people of God only or to all human beings. Given the above discussion about the Spirit's work rendering the creation productive in line with the divine design for it, our pneumatology opts for the latter: the Spirit is responsible for the fecundity of human beings in general, enabling all people to be productive, inventive, creative, resourceful—in some cases, prolifically so.[10] Still, the Spirit gives specific endowments to Christians: the spiritual

---

[7] Allison, *Sojourners and Strangers*, 460.

[8] For further discussion see Kuyper, *The Work of the Holy Spirit*, 38–42.

[9] For further discussion see Owen, *Pneumatologia*, 146–50.

[10] Could it be that the prolific nature of the Spirit's "natural" endowments is reflected in the acknowledgments of winning athletes as they exclaim, "I just want to give thanks to God for giving me the victory today"?

gifts of apostleship, prophecy, teaching, administration, exhortation, faith, speaking in tongues, and more. We will address these particular gifts of the Spirit to believers later on.

This discussion of the Holy Spirit's endowments and abilities in relation to humans prompts a return to an earlier topic: providence. Applying that earlier presentation to anthropology, we see that the providential work of the Holy Spirit does not in any way minimize the importance of secondary causes in (most) everything that occurs in the human realm.[11] Human beings rightly believe, obey, love, serve, hope, work, reproduce, and much more. Tragically, they wrongly mistrust, rebel, hate, overconsume, doubt, loaf, abort, and so on. As has been emphasized, our pneumatology refuses to consign these attitudes and actions of humans to an immanent process or an impersonal property of human nature. The Holy Spirit cooperates providentially in all that takes place in the human realm, and this divine activity by no means minimizes or destroys secondary human causes.

Historically, in relation to God's creation of human beings in his image, Irenaeus proposed the metaphor of "the hands of the Father": "by the Son and the Holy Spirit," the Father created people in the divine image.[12] Though not a biblical metaphor, the "two hands" motif underscores the inseparable operations of the three persons: the Father, the Son, and the Holy Spirit together create human beings in the divine image. Additionally, the motif highlights that human creatures as divine images are reflective of the archetypal Image, the Son (Col 1:15; 2 Cor 4:4), and properly display the character of the One whom they image through the Spirit and his fruit of Christlikeness (Gal 5:22–23; cf. 2 Cor 3:18).

Conclusion on the Doctrine of Human Creation

God's work of creating human beings in his image is not confined to the original pair of Adam and Eve. Not just historically but individually, ever since that initial human creation, God has created people as his image bearers. The reality of being divinely created evokes great praise to God. Indeed,

---

[11] As before, the qualification "most" acknowledges that God's miraculous activity may circumvent secondary causes.

[12] Irenaeus, *Against Heresies*, 5.6.1. *ANF* 1:531–32.

when the psalmist considers the vastness of the created universe, he ponders with amazement that God would remember human creatures and even install them as his vice-regents, ruling over the rest of creation. The psalmist then praises the wonder-working God: "LORD, our Lord, how magnificent is your name throughout the earth!" (Ps 8:3–9). Again, as he considers the fact that the Spirit of God is everywhere present ("Where can I go to escape your Spirit? Where can I flee from your presence?" Ps 139:7), the psalmist extols God for personally creating him:

> For it was you who created my inward parts;
> you knit me together in my mother's womb.
> I will praise you
> because I have been remarkably and wondrously made.
> Your works are wondrous,
> and I know this very well.
> My bones were not hidden from you
> when I was made in secret,
> when I was formed in the depths of the earth.
> Your eyes saw me when I was formless;
> all my days were written in your book and planned
> before a single one of them began.
> God, how precious your thoughts are to me;
> how vast their sum is! (Ps 139:13–17)

These psalms direct believers and the church to engage in praise and thanksgiving to the triune God for his creation of human beings in his image. In so doing, the Holy Spirit as "the Lord and Giver of life" is honored.

Human Sin[13]

The proper background to the understanding of sin is the very name "*Holy Spirit.*" Much different from a violation of community norms or of self-imposed standards of social behavior, sin must be seen in relationship to the character of God: he is "holy, holy, holy" (Isa 6:3). Indeed, it is not as though

---

[13] For further discussion see Kuyper, *The Work of the Holy Spirit*, 252–82.

sin is lawbreaking in the sense that the law is something external to God. On the contrary, the law is an expression of the very nature of God, who is holy.[14] Thus, all sin has ultimate reference to the holiness of God.[15]

Intriguingly, the Old Testament uses the full name "Holy Spirit" (instead of, for example, "the Spirit" or "the Spirit of the Lord") only three times, and in each occurrence the theme is sin. The first occasion (with two uses) is Isaiah's rehearsal of God's deliverance of his people from horrific enslavement in Egypt: "In all their suffering, he suffered, and the angel of his presence saved them. He redeemed them because of his love and compassion; he lifted them up and carried them all the days of the past" (Isa 63:9). Tragically, God's newly liberated people did not live obediently in response: "But they rebelled and grieved his Holy Spirit. So he became their enemy and fought against them" (v. 10). Thankfully, though, God acted mercifully toward his covenant people despite their sin. "Then he remembered the days of the past, the days of Moses and his people. Where is he who brought them out of the sea with the shepherds of his flock? Where is he who put his Holy Spirit among the flock?" (v. 11). Twice Isaiah highlights the role of the Holy Spirit: though he dwelt among the rescued people of Israel, who thus were expected to obey the Lord, the Spirit became grieved and thus warred against the rebellious Israelites. In the absence of expected holiness, the Holy Spirit presented himself as an enemy combatant.

The second occasion (and third use) is David's prayer of confession following his adulterous and murderous debacle. As he acknowledges his sin and begs God for mercy, he also pleads, "Do not banish me from your presence or take your Holy Spirit from me" (Ps 51:11). Having witnessed the complete undoing of his predecessor, King Saul, a calamity that included the withdrawal of the Spirit's anointing for effective kingship (contrast 1 Sam 16:13 with 16:14), David entreats God to spare him from the same end. In the presence of heinous sin, the retreating absence of the Holy Spirit is threatened.

---

[14] Thomas Aquinas, *Summa Theologica*, pt. 1 of pt. 2, q. 91, art. 1.

[15] For further discussion see Thomas H. McCall, *Against God and Nature: The Doctrine of Sin*, Foundations of Evangelical Theology (Wheaton: Crossway, 2019).

With appropriate differences for the change of covenants, the New Testament reinforces a similar idea.[16] Stephen rebukes his Jewish listeners in his rehearsal of the tragic, rebellious history of Israel: "You stiff-necked people with uncircumcised hearts and ears! You are always resisting the Holy Spirit. As your ancestors did, you do also" (Acts 7:51).[17] Moreover, in the midst of his warning against a plethora of sins—lying, anger, stealing, foul language, bitterness, wrath, shouting, slander, and malice (Eph 4:25–32)—Paul urges, "And don't grieve God's Holy Spirit. You were sealed by him for the day of redemption" (v. 30). Sinful words, attitudes, and behavior sadden the Holy Spirit, courting the displeasure of the one who has particular reference to the ultimate overcoming of sin at the time of Jesus Christ's return.

Conviction of Sin by the Holy Spirit

Until then, and to actualize that "day of redemption," Jesus Christ has sent the Holy Spirit to carry out a particular work in relation to sin: "When [the Holy Spirit] comes, he will convict the world about sin, righteousness, and judgment: About sin, because they do not believe in me; about righteousness, because I am going to the Father and you will no longer see me; and about judgment, because the ruler of this world has been judged" (John 16:8–11).[18] "Conviction" in relation to negative matters (e.g., sin) means convincing a person of error, persuading a person of being in the wrong, declaring a person to be guilty. Accordingly, the Holy Spirit's work is that of exposing error and wrongdoing. This work has specific reference to "the world." In Johannine literature, "the world" commonly refers to people who are hostile to God.

---

[16] As will be argued later, the new covenant ministry of the Holy Spirit includes his permanent indwelling in believers. Therefore, Christians never have to repeat David's prayer that God not take the Spirit from them.

[17] Similarly, the final reference to the Holy Spirit in Acts reinforces the idea that the Spirit, speaking through Isaiah the prophet, indicted the people of Israel for their unbelief (Acts 28:25).

[18] The following interpretation of John 16:8–11 reflects that of Carson, *The Gospel according to John*, 536–39. Alternative interpretations may understand "righteousness" to refer to that of Christ (hence, the Spirit confronts the world with Christ's righteousness, of which it has need) and "judgment" to refer to the condemnation coming upon the world because of its sin of unbelief and lack of righteousness.

Thus, Jesus promises that the Holy Spirit will convict people who are hostile to God.

The Spirit's convicting work is in relation to three major faults. The first is "sin," specifically "unbelief." Given that John is the "Gospel of Belief,"[19] "written so that you may believe that Jesus is the Messiah, the Son of God, and that by believing you may have life in his name" (John 20:31), the convicting work of the Spirit in regard to unbelief is particularly crucial. He persuades people that they have not trusted in Jesus Christ, who is the only way of salvation (14:6). The second error is "righteousness," or, to keep with the negative emphasis of the controlling verb "convict," the fault is "self-righteousness." An error thematized in the Gospel, self-righteousness characterizes Jesus's Jewish opponents, who rely on their lineage, Sabbath keeping, attendance at the temple, and possession of the law of Moses to become righteous before the Lord.[20] As Jesus during his earthly ministry exposed the futility of such self-righteousness, so the Spirit today continues that work of conviction. The third fault is "judgment," or, again keeping with the notion of "convict," the error is "worldly judgment." Again, thematized in this Gospel, judgment of the worldly type—focused on appearance and status—stands in stark contrast with Jesus's judgment, which is right and true (7:24; 8:16). Because all worldly judgment finds its source in "the ruler of this world" (12:31), the Spirit's convicting work has specific reference to Satan, who "has been judged" already (16:11). The Spirit exposes the faulty judgment of the world.

This work of the Spirit in making people aware of and sorry for their sin prompts them to confess and repent of it. As Barth underscored, "Man, even the Christian man, is not aware that he is a sinner, particularly a sinner against God." Citing Luther, Barth continued, "The name Comforter . . . means that he must discharge his office at no place [except] where there is *no* comfort to be found and where comfort is needed and longed for. Therefore he cannot comfort hard heads and haughty hearts, for they

---

[19] Merrill C. Tenney appropriately entitled his commentary on the Fourth Gospel *John: The Gospel of Belief* (Grand Rapids: Eerdmans, 1997).

[20] John 8:33; 5:1–18; 2:13–22; 5:45–47; 7:19–24; 9:28–29. Alternatively, the Spirit's work of conviction applies to the lack of righteousness on the part of people who are hostile toward God. See p. 74.

have never suffered flounderings or rejections." It is these sufferings that become—unexpectedly, in the Holy Spirit—salutary: "These very 'flounderings' and rejections, this very lack of comfort when felt, are signs of the Holy Spirit's work as Comforter."[21]

Thus, being disturbed and distressed by the Spirit, and consequently longing for and needing his comfort, a person becomes aware of his sin. Barth linked the Word and the Spirit in this revelation of sin: "In other words, he can learn the condemnation that is pronounced over him only through the Word of the cross of Christ, only through the Holy Spirit." Again, citing Luther, Barth emphasized, "'*Spiritually*, for it is not naturally, must man be made out to be a sinner.'. . . His word alone convicts us of sin, and his Spirit alone can make this word become truth to us."[22] Such conviction has particular reference to "the most critical sins of all sins," that is, unbelief: "But who will accuse himself of this sin? . . . Who will admit that the very best and purest efforts, by which we want to assure ourselves against this accusation, are idolatry, paganism within Christendom . . . ? This too is not man's work; namely, to understand that our relying on what man does is unbelief and that it is indeed sin and paganism."[23]

Such conviction of the Holy Spirit stirs up hope as Christians communicate the gospel of Jesus Christ. Through believers' words and life, the Spirit works in ways appropriate to his divine agency to effect a salutary dissatisfaction and expose guilt and shame, prompting confession, repentance, and faith in Christ.[24] Such conversion is the fruit of the Spirit's action. Beyond this hope for others, Christians seek the Spirit's work to awaken them to their own unintentional sins (Lev 5:17–18; Num 15:27–31), hidden faults (Ps 19:12–13), unconfessed sins, functional idols, insensitivities to others,

---

[21] Barth, *The Holy Spirit and the Christian Life*, 27. The citation is from Martin Luther, *Sermon* on John 14:23–31. Though Barth did not use it, an English edition in which the sermon is found is *The Sermons of Martin Luther*, ed. John Nicholas Lenker, 7 vols. (Grand Rapids: Baker, 2000), 3:273–87.

[22] Barth, 27–28. The citation is from Martin Luther, *Römerbrief, Ficher's Edition*, 2:71.

[23] Barth, 28.

[24] Such activity is appropriate for the Third Person, whose name expresses something fitting about his mission: he is the *Holy* Spirit, the παρακλητος (*paraklētos*), the attorney whose responsibility it is to prosecute the divine case against unbelievers. See Horton, *Rediscovering the Holy Spirit*, chap. 4.

unacknowledged broken relationships, and more. Such hope encourages a posture of humility in which Christians implore the Spirit to reveal sin of which they cannot be aware apart from his "comforting" action.

Blasphemy against the Holy Spirit

At the apex of this discussion of sin and the Holy Spirit, blasphemy against the Spirit stands dangerously as the unpardonable sin. The identity of this sin is highly debated, with at least four views proposed.[25] One view is that blasphemy against the Spirit is persistent unbelief, the failure to embrace Jesus Christ for salvation that endures throughout one's life to the moment of death. One cannot be saved apart from belief in Christ, so this tenacious unbelief means one is unforgiven.

A second position is that such blasphemy is the sin of apostasy that a Christian commits, thereby forfeiting his salvation. Biblical support for this position is a particular interpretation of Heb 6:4–6: "It is impossible to renew to repentance those who were once enlightened, who tasted the heavenly gift, who shared in the Holy Spirit, who tasted God's good word and the powers of the coming age, and who have fallen away. This is because, to their own harm, they are recrucifying the Son of God and holding him up to contempt." According to this interpretation, the writer is describing the tragic cases of actual Christians who abandon their salvation, a reality presented as enlightenment, a taste of the divine gift, a participation in the Spirit, and a taste of the goodness and power of the Lord. As they have fallen away from their redemption through heinous crimes against their Redeemer, it is impossible for them to be re-redeemed.

A third view is that blasphemy against the Holy Spirit is malicious, irrational rejection and slander against the work of the Spirit in bearing testimony to Jesus Christ, attributing that work to Satan instead.[26] This position follows closely the narrative in which Jesus heals "a demon-possessed man

---

[25] For a presentation of these views see Wayne Grudem, *Systematic Theology: An Introduction to Biblical Doctrine* (Grand Rapids: Zondervan, 1994, 2006), 506–9. Grudem follows the discussion in Louis Berkhof, *Systematic Theology*, 4th ed. (Grand Rapids: Eerdmans, 1939), 252–53; cf. Cole, *He Who Gives Life*, 176–77.

[26] The definition is developed from Berkhof, *Systematic Theology*, 253.

who was blind and unable to speak" (Matt 12:22). Against Jesus's power-ful restoration of this man, the Pharisees attribute it to Satan: "This man drives out demons only by Beelzebul, the ruler of the demons" (v. 24). But Jesus exposes the irrationality of this pharisaical attribution: for one thing to be divided against itself is the height of absurdity (vv. 25–27). Rather than casting out demons by Satan, Jesus claims to exorcise them by the Holy Spirit. The narrative comes to a close with Jesus's warning, "Whoever speaks against the Holy Spirit, it will not be forgiven him, either in this age or in the age to come" (v. 32). This, then, is blasphemy against the Spirit: heinous, absurd rejection and slander of the work of the Holy Spirit testifying to Christ, assigning that work to Satan instead. This position agrees with the first view that persistent unbelief spells unforgiveness, but does not consider this truth to be the point of the narrative of Matthew 12. Furthermore, this third position may or may not agree with the aforesaid interpretation of Hebrew 6, but in either case it does not consider this section of Hebrews to be addressing blasphemy against the Holy Spirit.[27]

The fourth view follows the third one, with this modification: because Jesus no longer engages in his ministry of casting out demons, blasphemy against the Holy Spirit, which is inextricably tied to exorcisms, can no longer be committed today. It is a particular sin associated only with the work of Jesus Christ during his earthly ministry.

Whatever one's position (one of us holds the third view, the other, the fourth view), blasphemy against the Holy Spirit is the most serious sin of all: it is unforgivable. Though unlikely, the unforgivable nature of this sin may be due to its being beyond the pale of the atoning sacrifice of Christ: he did not die to forgive this particular sin against the Spirit, with whom he insepa-rably works to effect salvation. A still less likely reason is that the character

---

[27] Herman Bavinck, after presenting this sin in accordance with the third posi-tion, continues with an affirmation that "this act of blaspheming the Holy Spirit can be committed in various circumstances." These circumstances include "falling back into Judaism" (a version of the second position, with appeal to Hebrews 6:4–6) and "a firm and deliberate denial of the Christ as the incarnate Son of God" (a version of the first position, based on 1 John 5:16). See Bavinck, *Reformed Dogmatics*, vol. 3, *Sin and Salvation in Christ*, ed. John Bolt, trans. John Vriend (Grand Rapids: Baker Academic, 2006), 155–57.

of this sin is "no longer human but demonic."[28] More likely, its unpardonable nature is due to the callousness of the heart of the person who commits this sin. Having denounced the divine Person by whom redemption from sin is applied, one who blasphemes the Holy Spirit cuts off all hope of embracing the announcement of the gospel with repentance and faith in the Savior/Son to whom it points.

While Christians are aware of the biblical warnings about blasphemy against the Holy Spirit, the foreboding anxiety that grips those who fear that they have committed this sin should subside. Such sensitivity and concern signals that they have not become irrationally and defiantly calloused to the Holy Spirit such that they have blasphemed him. At the same time, it cautions Christians to be circumspect in their assessment of what is of God and what is of Satan.[29] The tendency to attribute to the evil one doctrines and practices with which one disagrees may run the risk of being not only naive, presumptuous, foolish, or wrong, but blasphemous against the Holy Spirit.

Conclusion on the Doctrine of Human Sin

The issue of what constitutes sin, the dawning and development of an awareness and repudiation of sin, and the resources to overcome sin are all matters related to the Holy Spirit. As his name indicates, the *Holy* Spirit is opposed to the unholiness of sin, thereby defining what sin is. In conjunction with the Word of God, Christians and the church should seek the direction of the Spirit of God in discerning what constitutes sin and what is mere human judgment, opinion, or preference in terms of what is displeasing to the Lord. Moreover, as nonbelievers are moving toward salvation, one of the gracious divine acts in that process is the Spirit's work of conviction—exposing sin, self-righteousness, and worldly judgment. As they engage in sharing the good news, Christians and the church should rely on this oft-hidden work of the Spirit, trusting that his convicting activity will prompt repentance and faith.

---

[28] Bavinck, 3:156.

[29] This is not a plea to be gullible, tolerant of clearly inadequate or wrong views, unconcerned about truth, or the like. It is a call for Christians to be thoughtful about their assessments of divine (or demonic) activity.

20

The Holy Spirit and Christ

Processions and Missions Revisited

With the interface of the doctrines of the Holy Spirit and of Jesus Christ, our pneumatology brings together the two processions and two missions of the triune God. As rehearsed earlier, in terms of the two processions, the first procession is the eternal generation of the Son from the Father. The second procession is the eternal procession of the Holy Spirit from the Father and the Son. As for the two trinitarian missions, the first mission is the sending of the Son by the Father, actualized by Jesus's incarnation, sinless life, passion, death, burial, resurrection, and ascension. The second mission is the sending of the Holy Spirit by the Father and the Son, actualized by the Spirit's outpouring on the day of Pentecost and continuing in his ongoing work (e.g., indwelling believers) in the world. The relationship between processions and missions is crucial. The trinitarian processions concern the inner life and relations of the Father, the Son, and the Holy Spirit; the trinitarian missions concern the external activity and temporal works of the triune God. Accordingly, the trinitarian missions are the trinitarian processions turned outside and in time.

A quandary arises: If the mission of the Son, which is linked to the procession (generation) of the Son from the Father, precedes the mission of the Holy Spirit, which is linked to the procession of the Spirit from the Father and the Son, then how do we account for the work of the Holy Spirit in effecting the incarnation of the Son? This matter appears to wreak havoc with the traditional trinitarian order: first, the Father; second, the Son; and

347

third, the Holy Spirit. When it comes to the incarnation, the order appears to be first, the Father; second, the Holy Spirit; and third, the Son. To complicate matters, if the mission of the Holy Spirit precedes and inaugurates the mission of the Son in terms of effecting the Son's incarnation, then the order of missions appears to be first, the mission of the Holy Spirit (to effect the Son's incarnation); second, the mission of the Son (sinless life, passion, death, burial, resurrection, and ascension); and third, the mission of the Holy Spirit (outpouring on the day of Pentecost and ongoing work in the world).[1]

To avoid such confusion, our pneumatology reserves the term "mission" to refer to, in regard to the Son, his incarnation, sinless life, passion, death, burial, resurrection, and ascension; and, in regard to the Spirit, his outpouring on the day of Pentecost and his ongoing work in the world.[2] To speak about their activities before these two missions, our pneumatology proposes to use the term "prolepsis." By definition, a prolepsis is a "representation or assumption of a future act or development as if presently existing or accomplished."[3] Accordingly, a trinitarian prolepsis is a biblical representation of a future mission of either the Son or the Spirit as if occurring before the coming of Christ. Thus, for example, a prolepsis of the Son was his Christophanies, appearances in which he temporarily took on a human-like nature (e.g., to Jacob, Gen 32:22–32; to Joshua, Josh 5:13–15). Another prolepsis was his accompaniment of the people of Israel as the "spiritual rock" (1 Cor 10:1–4). As for examples of the prolepsis of the Spirit, he came upon judges to empower them to lead the people of Israel in victory over

---

[1] The discussion is further complicated by Thomas Aquinas's terminology for the miraculous work of the Holy Spirit, at the moment of Christ's conception, such that the Spirit began to be present in Christ as habitual grace: Aquinas labels it an "invisible mission" of the Spirit (*Summa Theologica*, pt. 1, q. 43, art. 5, art. 7). This invisible mission of the Spirit is different from the visible mission of the Son, which accounts for his personal union with a human nature, and the visible mission of the Holy Spirit to Christ at his baptism, his transfiguration, his breathing on the apostles in the upper room, and at Pentecost. For detailed discussion, see Legge, *Trinitarian Christology of St Thomas Aquinas*, 50–51, 132–34, 142–43, 147–53, 153–55, 161–64, 178, 186, 234.

[2] For further discussion of this "mission" see Köstenberger, *The Missions of Jesus and the Disciples according to the Fourth Gospel*.

[3] Merriam-Webster Dictionary, s.v. "prolepsis," accessed August 22, 2019, https://www.merriam-webster.com/dictionary/prolepsis.

their enemies (e.g., Othniel, Judg 3:7–11; Gideon, 6:34; Jephthah, 11:29–33) and anointed kings to enable them to rule the people of Israel (e.g., 1 Sam 16:13–14). These prolepses, as representations of the future missions of the Son and of the Spirit, bear some resemblance to those missions, yet are significantly different from them.

Accordingly, with regard to Christology, the miraculous work of the Holy Spirit to effect the virginal conception of the Son is a prolepsis of the Spirit rather than an aspect of his mission. These proposals enable our pneumatology (1) to affirm the traditional trinitarian order: first, the Father; second, the Son; and third, the Holy Spirit; and (2) to avoid confusion in the order of the missions: the (pre-mission) prolepsis of the Holy Spirit (to effect the Son's incarnation); then the mission of the Son (sinless life, passion, death, burial, resurrection, and ascension); then the mission of the Holy Spirit (outpouring on the day of Pentecost and ongoing work in the world).

These two missions are foretold in the Hebrew Bible inspired by the Holy Spirit. The entire Old Testament points to the coming of one who will be the ideal Son, Prophet, Priest, King, Messiah, and Suffering Servant. Additionally, even while being written, the Old Testament warns of the upcoming failure of the old covenant and its replacement with a new covenant, which will feature a fresh, unprecedented outpouring of the Holy Spirit.

Additionally, specific prophesies link the Messiah/Suffering Servant with the Spirit (e.g., Isa 42:1–9; 61:1–11). It is the Spirit as inspirer of those prophecies who predicts this joint salvific venture (1 Pet 1:10–12). Closer to the time of the actual fulfillment of this anticipation, fresh prophecies further rehearse the Spirit's role in the coming events. First, John the Baptist, the son of Zechariah and Elizabeth, will "be filled with the Holy Spirit while still in his mother's womb" (Luke 1:15). He will go before the Lord "in the spirit and power of Elijah, to turn the hearts of fathers to their children, and the disobedient to the understanding of the righteous, to make ready for the Lord a prepared people" (1:17). This prophecy acknowledges the forerunner of the Messiah and the important mission in which the forebearer will engage.

Second, Elizabeth herself, "filled with the Holy Spirit," meets Mary and exclaims, "Blessed are you among women, and your child will be blessed! How could this happen to me, that the mother of my Lord should come to me?" (1:41–43). The Spirit prompts Elizabeth to recognize the still in utero Son incarnate, whom the Spirit will fill without measure. Third, Zechariah, "filled with the Holy Spirit," prophesies about his own son, John: "You, child, will be called a prophet of the Most High, for you will go before the Lord to prepare his ways, to give his people knowledge of salvation through the forgiveness of their sins" (1:76–77). The Spirit stimulates Zechariah to acknowledge the preparatory role of John the Baptist for the mission of the Messiah. Accordingly, the missions of the Son and of the Spirit, along with the interconnection between the missions, are predicted long before they are enacted and as they are being actualized.[4]

The Virginal Conception

The beginning of the fulfillment of both the general trajectory of the Old Testament and these specific prophecies takes place with the Spirit's proleptic work of effecting the incarnation of the Son.[5] The Gospel of Luke provides one of the New Testament's two narratives of the virginal conception. At the annunciation, the angel Gabriel declares to Mary, "Now listen: You will conceive and give birth to a son, and you will name him Jesus. He will be great and will be called the Son of the Most High, and the Lord God will give him the throne of his father David. He will reign over the house of Jacob forever, and his kingdom will have no end" (Luke 1:31–33). The long-awaited mission of the Son/Davidic King is about to be inaugurated. But it gives pause to the one through whom the incarnation will take place: "Mary

---

[4] As the birth of Jesus takes place, and thus the fulfillment of these prophecies occurs, the Spirit stirs up still more prophetic activity about the newborn Son and his mission yet to come. Simeon experiences intense activity of the Holy Spirit: "the Holy Spirit was on him," "it had been revealed to him by the Holy Spirit that he would not see death before he saw the Lord's Messiah," and he enters the temple "guided by the Spirit." Moved by the Spirit, Simeon describes the salvation of the Lord in terms of "a light for revelation to the Gentiles and glory to your people Israel" (Luke 2:25–32). Although Luke makes no direct mention of the Holy Spirit in relation to Anna, as a prophetess the assumption should be that the Spirit regularly spoke through her. Accordingly, her "speak[ing] about him [God] to all who were looking forward to the redemption of Jerusalem" should be interpreted as Spirit-given prophetic activity about the Messiah's mission of salvation (Luke 2:38). For further discussion see Cole, *He Who Gives Life*, 151.

[5] For further discussion see Cole, 153–56; Ferguson, *The Holy Spirit*, 38–45; Kuyper, *The Work of the Holy Spirit*, 79–92; Owen, *Pneumatologia*, 160–71.

asked the angel, 'How can this be, since I have not had sexual relations with a man?'" (1:34). What is physically impossible will be divinely possible: "The angel replied to her: 'The Holy Spirit will come upon you, and the power of the Most High will overshadow you. Therefore, the holy one to be born will be called the Son of God'" (1:35). The Holy Spirit will be the one to effect the virginal conception.

To assure her that such a future miracle will happen, Gabriel refers Mary to another miracle that has recently occurred: "And consider your relative Elizabeth—even she has conceived a son in her old age, and this is the sixth month for her who was called childless. For nothing will be impossible with God" (1:36–37). Convinced and believing, Mary expresses her wish: "'I am the Lord's servant,' she said. 'May it be done to me according to your word.' Then the angel left her" (1:38).[6] Submitting to the word of God through the angel's annunciation, Mary becomes *theotokos*: the one who bears the one who is God.

The other narrative of the virginal conception appears in the Gospel of Matthew. Like Luke's account, Matthew's narrative underscores that Mary's conception of Jesus is not through ordinary means:

> The birth of Jesus Christ came about this way: After his mother Mary had been engaged to Joseph, it was discovered before they came together that she was pregnant from the Holy Spirit. So her husband Joseph, being a righteous man, and not wanting to disgrace her publicly, decided to divorce her secretly. But after he had considered these things, an angel of the Lord appeared to him in a

---

[6] The Roman Catholic interpretation of Mary's response—"May it be done to me according to your word"—considers γένοιτό μοι (*genoito moi*) to be her fiat, or command. However, the Greek verb is in the optative mood, expressing a wish. Mary does not engage in the incarnation of the Son through her active, sinless participation, for which she was prepared by an immaculate conception. Rather, her obedience of faith is a consent to the Lord's will through a passive posture of yieldedness. The Holy Spirit accomplishes the miracle. For a Roman Catholic biblical theology of Mary, see Pope John Paul II, *Redemptoris Mater* (March 25, 1987), http://w2.vatican.va/content/john-paul-ii/en/encyclicals/documents/hf_jp-ii_enc_25031987_redemptoris-mater.html. For a response see Allison, *Roman Catholic Theology and Practice*, 134–43; cf. Smail, *The Giving Gift*, 22–29.

dream, saying, "Joseph, son of David, don't be afraid to take Mary as your wife, because what has been conceived in her is from the Holy Spirit. She will give birth to a son, and you are to name him Jesus, because he will save his people from their sins." (Matt 1:18–21)

After noting that the virginal conception of Jesus is a fulfillment of Isaiah's prophecy (1:22–23; citing Isa 7:14), Matthew concludes his account: "When Joseph woke up, he did as the Lord's angel had commanded him. He married her but did not have sexual relations with her until she gave birth to a son. And he named him Jesus" (1:24–25). As he does at the beginning, so also at the end of his narrative Matthew emphasizes that Mary's conception of Jesus is not through sexual relations with Joseph (or any other man, for that matter). On the contrary, the proleptic activity of the Holy Spirit effects the virginal conception.

On the basis of these two biblical narratives,[7] the virginal conception has been a pillar of Christian belief from the very outset of the church. Ignatius, who was martyred early in the second century, made the first mention of it in extant literature outside of the New Testament in his *Epistle to the Ephesians* (18:2–19:1). Three of the early church creeds—Nicene-Constantinopolitan, Apostles', and Chalcedonian—affirm it. Thus, the church has historically believed that Jesus "was conceived by the power of the Holy Spirit and born of the virgin Mary."[8]

The Spirit's Outpouring on the Son

Conceived by the Holy Spirit, Jesus as the Christ—literally, "Anointed One"—is anointed not with oil but with the Holy Spirit. Indeed, God the

---

[7] Other New Testament passages that may hint at the virginal conception are Matt 13:55/Mark 6:3/Luke 4:22; Gal 4:4; and Phil 2:7.

[8] For a response to the recent challenge to the doctrine of the virgin birth by Andrew Lincoln, *Born of a Virgin? Reconceiving Jesus in the Bible, Tradition, and Theology* (Grand Rapids: Eerdmans, 2013), see the review and critique by Andreas Köstenberger: "Born of a Virgin?," Gospel Coalition, February 17, 2014, https://www.thegospelcoalition.org/reviews/born_of_a_virgin.

Father pours out the Spirit on his Son "without measure" (John 3:34).[9] This trinitarian sharing recalls our earlier discussion of inseparable operations of the three persons. Yet, in the incarnation, we must account for something new: the Father pours out the Spirit on his Son, who is now the God-man. It is God the Son incarnate who is enriched without measure with the Holy Spirit. On the one hand, the Son was never apart from the Holy Spirit; this intratrinitarian relation never changes. On the other hand, the incarnate Son is filled with the Holy Spirit from the moment of conception and lives the entirety of his earthly life in dependence on the Holy Spirit indwelling him. Indeed, in summarizing Aquinas's thought, Legge offers, "Christ can never be without his Spirit. What is more, Christ as man relies on—indeed, cannot do without—the Holy Spirit in accomplishing the work given to him by the Father."[10] This relationship of reliance is new at the incarnation. To be discussed later, this view is not Spirit Christology: the Holy Spirit does not become the acting agent in the incarnation. On the contrary, the incarnate Son, the God-man, is the acting agent who engages in all things—obeying the Father who sent him, resisting temptations, communicating divine words, loving his disciples, preaching the gospel, suffering, and dying—through the "indwelling, empowering, and anointing work" of the Holy Spirit.[11] The intratrinitarian relation of perichoresis—the mutual indwelling of the Son and the Spirit—takes on a new reality as the incarnate Son, upon whom the Spirit is poured out without measure, lives in the power of that indwelling Spirit.

As Jesus himself notes, the Spirit's anointing of the Messiah is part of predictive Hebrew Scripture:

> [Jesus] came to Nazareth, where he had been brought up. As usual, he entered the synagogue on the Sabbath day and stood up to read. The scroll of the prophet Isaiah was given to him, and unrolling the scroll, he found the place where it was written:

---

[9] For further discussion of the Holy Spirit and the Son's incarnation see Horton, *Rediscovering the Holy Spirit*, 95–104.

[10] Legge, *Trinitarian Christology of St Thomas Aquinas*, 132.

[11] Wellum, *God the Son Incarnate*, 327.

> The Spirit of the Lord is on me,
> because he has anointed me
> to preach good news to the poor.
> He has sent me
> to proclaim release to the captives
> and recovery of sight to the blind,
> to set free the oppressed,
> to proclaim the year of the Lord's favor.

He then rolled up the scroll, gave it back to the attendant, and sat down. And the eyes of everyone in the synagogue were fixed on him. He began by saying to them, "Today as you listen, this Scripture has been fulfilled." (Luke 4:16–21; citing Isa 61:1–2).

In fulfillment of Old Testament prophecy, the God-man Jesus Christ is anointed by the Holy Spirit, not partially but immeasurably.[12] This inundation corresponds appropriately to the Messianic mission upon which the Son was sent by the Father.[13]

The Spirit's Activity in Jesus: Baptism, Temptations, Proclamation, Exorcisms, Miracles[14]

The inauguration of this mission and the public reception of this boundless anointing by the Spirit occur at Jesus's baptism.[15] Again, the three persons operate inseparably, yet the action terminates in one of them: "When Jesus was baptized, he went up immediately from the water. The heavens suddenly opened for him, and he saw the Spirit of God descending like a

---

[12] Summarizing Aquinas, Legge describes "three marks of Christ's 'fullness' of the Holy Spirit that distinguishes him from all others. First, . . . he receives the full *extent* of the Spirit's gifts. . . . Second, . . . unlike other saints and prophets, Christ *always* has this fullness. . . . Christ is not like a prophet who must wait for the Spirit to come to him. . . . Finally, Christ has the infinite capacity to pour out the Spirit's gifts—and the Holy Spirit himself—on others." Legge, *Trinitarian Christology of St Thomas Aquinas*, 162–63.

[13] For further discussion see Kuyper, *The Work of the Holy Spirit*, 91–102.

[14] For further discussion see Ferguson, *The Holy Spirit*, 45–52.

[15] For further discussion see Cole, *He Who Gives Life*, 156–59; Owen, *Pneumatologia*, 171–75.

dove and coming down on him. And a voice from heaven said: 'This is my beloved Son, with whom I am well-pleased'" (Matt 3:16–17). The Father speaks words of commendation about the baptized Son upon whom the Holy Spirit descends and remains. This final note of the abiding presence of the Spirit is also emphasized in the Gospel of John: twice John underscores the fact that the Spirit descended and rested on Jesus (John 1:32–33). As anointed/baptized, the God-man is fully empowered by the Holy Spirit dwelling within him.[16]

The empowering presence of the Spirit first manifests itself to Jesus in an unexpected manner: "Immediately the Spirit drove him into the wilderness. He was in the wilderness forty days, being tempted by Satan" (Mark 1:12–13).[17] Propelled by the Spirit to face the onslaughts of the evil one, Jesus does not resist temptation by virtue of his divine nature: a nature does not act; rather, a person acts. Neither does Jesus repulse temptation by virtue of his human nature:[18] again, a nature does not act, and at no time is the human nature of the Son alone, apart from the divine nature. Yet again, Jesus does

---

[16] Dunn addresses the consciousness of Jesus with respect to the fullness of the Spirit, proposing that Jesus possessed "an *awareness* of an *otherly* power working through him, together with the *conviction* that this power was *God's* power." It is probably safe to affirm something like Dunn posits, as long as we avoid overly speculating what the consciousness of Jesus must have been. Dunn, *Jesus and the Spirit*, 47 (emphasis original).

[17] For further discussion see Cole, *He Who Gives Life*, 159–60.

[18] It is important to understand the distinction between "person" and "nature." (1) "Person" is about the *who*; "nature" is about the *what*. (2) "Person" is about an acting subject; "I wrote this footnote." "Nature" is about what someone is; "I am a complex being, consisting of a body and a soul." (3) Thinking about God, he is three persons sharing the one divine nature; the Father, the Son, and the Holy Spirit (the three Persons) share the identically same properties of omnipotence, omnipresence, omniscience, eternality, love, holiness, and more (the divine nature). (4) Thinking of a human being, I (the person) decide and act through my mind, emotions, motivations, purposing, will, and body (my nature). (5) Importantly, the divine nature does not act; "knowing everything" does not act; rather, a divine person—the Father, who is all-knowing—acts. Similarly, a human nature does not act; "feeling anger" does not act; rather, I—a human person who feels anger—act. (6) Thus, the Son's holy nature did not face temptations; a nature does not face temptations; rather, God the Son incarnate, being holy, faced temptations. Likewise, Jesus's upright human nature did not face temptations; a nature does not face temptations; rather, God the Son incarnate, being upright, faced temptations.

not repel temptations as the Son incarnate apart from the Holy Spirit, who indwells Jesus without measure. Rather, it is the God-man filled with the Holy Spirit who faces down Satan and defeats all the temptations thrust at him. By means of these temptations victoriously resisted, as well as the trials and tribulations that dog him throughout his life (the chief example being the struggle with the issue of life and death in the garden of Gethsemane), the Spirit-filled Jesus is well prepared for his mission: "Although he was the Son, he learned obedience from what he suffered. After he was perfected, he became the source of eternal salvation for all who obey him" (Heb 5:8–9).

It is within this all-encompassing framework of the Spirit's enablement of the Son that particular expressions of such empowerment are properly understood.[19] The first and most obvious is Jesus's ministry of proclamation. Jesus himself links his ministry of preaching with his anointing by the Spirit, as prophesied by Isaiah: "The Spirit of the Lord is on me, because he has anointed me to preach good news to the poor. He has sent me to proclaim release to the captives and recovery of sight to the blind, to set free the oppressed, to proclaim the year of the Lord's favor" (Luke 4:18–19, citing Isa 61:1–2). Filled with and dependent upon the Holy Spirit, Jesus proclaims the good news of the kingdom of God (Luke 4:43), teaches in parables (Matthew 13), calls his listeners to repentance and faith (Mark 1:15), commands them to love God and others (Matt 22:34–40), directs them to deny themselves for the sake of his name (Mark 8:34), and the like. His listeners' reaction reflects the excellency of Jesus's message empowered by the Holy Spirit: "When Jesus had finished saying these things, the crowds were astonished at his teaching, because he was teaching them like one who had authority, and not like their scribes" (Matt 7:28–29; cf. John 7:46; Luke 4:22).

A second category of particular expressions of the Spirit's enablement is Jesus's ministry of exorcism. As discussed earlier, Jesus exorcises demons by the power of the Holy Spirit (Matt 12:22–32). In these pitched battles, Jesus does not act by virtue of his human nature while calling upon the Spirit to put an end to demonic oppression in others. Nor does Jesus act by virtue of his divine nature that in some strange way needs augmentation by the Spirit.[20] Rather, as the God-man, Jesus exorcises demons through an

---

[19] For further discussion see Cole, *He Who Gives Life*, 160–62.

[20] See the discussion about "person" and "nature" in n. 18.

appropriation of the power of the Holy Spirit. Jesus's conversations with the demon/demons, his words of expulsion, and the restoration of the formerly tormented people evidence the enablement of the Spirit. To take the Gerasene demoniac as an example of the Spirit's work through Jesus: Jesus asks the demon's name, which turns out to be Legion, "because we are many," and permits the demons to enter a herd of pigs. Jesus commands the unclean spirit to come out of the man. And the man is "dressed and in his right mind," eager and able to proclaim "how much Jesus had done for him" (Mark 5:1–20). Jesus exorcises demons by the power of the Holy Spirit.

A third category of particular expressions of the Spirit's enablement is Jesus's miracles. It is generally assumed that Jesus performs his miracles by virtue of his divine nature. Support for this assumption comes from John's use of particular miracles as confirmation of Jesus's divine Sonship. Specifically, John selects seven "signs"—changing water into wine (2:1–11), cleansing the temple (2:13–22), healing the official's son (4:46–54), healing the paralytic (5:1–15), feeding the 5,000 (6:5–14), walking on water (6:16–24), healing the blind man (9:1–7), and raising Lazarus (11:1–45)—and writes them in his Gospel "so that you may believe that Jesus is the Messiah, the Son of God, and that by believing you may have life in his name" (20:30–31).[21] John's point seems to be that Jesus performs miracles by virtue of his deity.[22]

Others challenge this assumption by referencing part of Peter's gospel message to Cornelius: "You know . . . how God anointed Jesus of Nazareth with the Holy Spirit and with power, and how he went about doing good and healing all who were under the tyranny of the devil, because God was with him" (Acts 10:37–38).[23] The point underscored is that Jesus performed

---

[21] This list of eight "signs" reflects a disagreement about two of them. Traditionally, Jesus's walking on water has been considered a sign, but Andreas Köstenberger challenges this action as being a private matter and thus not constituting a sign. In its place he proposes Jesus's cleansing of the temple. See Köstenberger, "The Seventh Johannine Sign: A Study in John's Christology," *Bulletin of Biblical Research* 5 (1995): 87–103.

[22] Interestingly, none of the seven signs or miracles is an exorcism. If Jesus casts out demons by the Holy Spirit rather than by virtue of his divine nature, then John's selection of an exorcism would not support his point that Jesus's miracles are confirmation of his deity. But this explanation severely and illegitimately separates Jesus's divine nature and the power of the Holy Spirit at work in him as the God-man.

[23] Another passage cited in this regard is Acts 2:22.

miraculous healings and exorcisms through the power of the Holy Spirit, with whom God the Father had anointed Jesus. Accordingly, it was not because he was the fully divine Son of God that Jesus worked miracles, but due to the enablement of the Spirit: "God was with him," empowering Jesus to perform miraculous acts. This emphasis has come to the forefront in Spirit Christology, which will be treated later.

Our pneumatology dissents from such dichotomizing of the person and work of Christ in relation to the Holy Spirit. It is the God-man, anointed without measure by, and constantly filled with, the Holy Spirit, who restores sight to the blind, hearing to the deaf, speech to the mute, mobility to the paralyzed, wholeness of body to the lepers, and life to the dead. In accordance with inseparable operations, all three persons work together in Jesus's miraculous activity. This intratrinitarian relation does not change in the incarnation but is manifested in the Son's miracles. At the same time, the incarnate Son, filled with and dependent on the Holy Spirit, performs miracles as God is with him. This economic relationship of reliance on the Spirit is new at the incarnation and expressed in the Son's miraculous works.

The Spirit's Activity in Jesus: Death, Resurrection, Ascension[24]

Guided and empowered by the Holy Spirit throughout his three-year ministry, at its close Jesus is compelled by the Spirit to "set his face to go to Jerusalem" (Luke 9:51 ESV) to face death, burial, and resurrection—as Jesus himself had predicted through the Spirit (Mark 8:31; 9:30–31; 10:33–34; John 2:18–22). By these culminating events, Jesus will complete his mission. The intensity of his sufferings increases exponentially as his "hour" draws near (John 12:23, 27; 13:1; 17:1), and Jesus becomes "troubled in his spirit" (John 13:21; cf. 12:27). Now more than ever Jesus feels the necessity of the Holy Spirit's enablement. Through the Spirit, Jesus hands a morsel of bread to Judas (John 13:26–27); submits to Judas the betrayer's kiss (Luke 22:48–50); reprimands Peter for his futile combative tactic (John 18:10–11);

---

[24] For further discussion see Ferguson, *The Holy Spirit*, 53–56; Kuyper, *The Work of the Holy Spirit*, 102–11; Cole, *He Who Gives Life*, 164–67; Owen, *Pneumatologia*, 176–83.

looks at Peter, who has denied him (Luke 22:54–62); responds forthrightly to Annas the high priest (John 18:19–24); engages Pilate in a conversation about kingship and truth (18:33–38); remains silent before Herod (Luke 23:8–9); carries his cross partway to Golgotha (John 19:17); comforts weeping daughters of Jerusalem (Luke 23:27–31); promises paradise to a repentant thief (Luke 23:39–43); and yields himself up to death (John 19:30). Jesus's crucifixion is enabled by the Holy Spirit: "Christ . . . through the eternal Spirit offered himself without blemish to God" (Heb 9:14).[25] As in life, so in death, God the Son incarnate, anointed with the Spirit without measure, depends on the Spirit to carry out his mission of salvation.

But death does not have the last word; crucifixion is followed necessarily by resurrection, as Peter rehearses: "God raised him up, ending the pains of death, because it was not possible for him to be held by death" (Acts 2:24).[26] It was impossible for death to triumph because of the divine promise spoken by David through the Holy Spirit. Indeed, it is Jesus as the Messiah who confidently affirms, "I saw the Lord ever before me; because he is at my right hand, I will not be shaken. Therefore my heart is glad and my tongue rejoices. Moreover, my flesh will rest in hope, because you will not abandon me in Hades or allow your holy one to see decay. You have revealed the paths of life to me; you will fill me with gladness in your presence" (Acts 2:25–28, citing Ps 16:8–11). Following this citation, Peter explains that even though David wrote the words of that psalm, their referent was not the psalmist but the Messiah. David spoke in this manner because he prophesied through the Holy Spirit, as Peter explains:

> "Brothers and sisters, I can confidently speak to you about the patriarch David: He is both dead and buried, and his tomb is with us to this day. Since he was a prophet, he knew that God had sworn an oath to him to seat one of his descendants on his throne. Seeing what was to come, he spoke concerning the resurrection of the Messiah: He was not abandoned in Hades, and his flesh did not experience decay: God has raised this Jesus; we are all witnesses of this." (Acts 2:29, 30)

---

[25] On the Spirit's enablement of the crucifixion, see Gregg Allison, "No Holy Spirit, No Penal Substitutionary Atonement."

[26] For further discussion see Cole, *He Who Gives Life*, 167–69.

Jesus is raised from the dead in accordance with prophetic Scripture. Other prophecies of the Messiah's resurrection include Jonah in the great fish (Jonah 1:17; referenced in Matt 12:40; 16:4; Luke 11:30) and Isaiah 53, in which are found expressions of hope: "he will see his seed, he will prolong his days"; "he will see light and be satisfied"; "he will receive the mighty as spoil" (Isa 53:10–12). These expressions articulate the hope of Messiah's resurrection. In light of this hope, Jesus as the Messiah predicts his own resurrection (John 2:18–22; Matt 16:21; 17:22–23; 20:17–19).

Not only is the resurrection foretold through the prophetic work of the Holy Spirit; it is effected by the Spirit himself. Again, in accordance with the inseparable operations of the triune God, we affirm the collaborative work of the three persons in raising the second person. The Father raises the Son (Acts 2:24; 2 Cor 4:14). The Son raises himself (John 2:19; 10:18). And the Holy Spirit raises the Son (Rom 1:4). Paul's explanation—"If the Spirit of [the Father] who raised Jesus from the dead lives in you, then [the Father] who raised Christ from the dead will also bring your mortal bodies to life through his Spirit who lives in you" (Rom 8:11)—emphasizes the Father's initiatory work carried out through the Holy Spirit to raise the Son. Given Paul's focus on the resurrection of believers "through the [Father's] Spirit who lives in you," it seems appropriate to highlight the Spirit's role in the resurrection of the Son, a resurrection to which believers will be conformed (1 Cor 15:20–22, 47–49).[27]

Beyond resurrection, the Son also ascended into heaven and "sat down at the right hand of the Majesty on high" (Heb 1:3).[28] Our pneumatology links Jesus's ascension to the work of the Holy Spirit. As has been emphasized throughout this discussion, the inseparable operations of the three persons demands that the ascension of the Son involve the operation of the Holy Spirit. Specifically, God the Father sends God the Son on his earthly mission, which begins with God the Holy Spirit's effecting the incarnation and ends with the Spirit's effecting the ascension. In Paul's words of descent and ascent, the Son "descended to the lower parts of the earth" (Eph 4:9), that is,

---

[27] Indeed, a further argument may be made from Paul's description of the resurrection body as "spiritual" (1 Cor. 15:44). By "spiritual" Paul means not "immaterial" but "dominated by the Spirit." The Spirit's full control of resurrected believers is due to the fact that he is the one who will effect the resurrection of their bodies.

[28] For further discussion see Cole, *He Who Gives Life*, 169–71.

became incarnate. And "the one who descended is also the one who ascended far above all the heavens, to fill all things" (v. 10). As the Holy Spirit works the descent of the Son into the earthly womb of the virgin Mary, so the Spirit works the ascent of the Son to the heavenly throne room. From heaven to earth and back again: the work of the Holy Spirit.

Furthermore, Luke repeatedly emphasizes the Holy Spirit in his narrative of Acts 2: the Spirit is poured out at the beginning of the day of Pentecost (vv. 1–4) in fulfillment of Joel's prophecy (vv. 14–21); the Spirit gives the disciples the ability to speak in tongues (vv. 5–13); the Spirit prompts prophetic activity in predicting the Messiah's resurrection (vv. 25–32); and the Spirit is poured out on the newly inaugurated church (vv. 37–41). In the midst of this emphasis on the Holy Spirit, Luke also narrates Peter's presentation of the ascension of the resurrected Jesus:

> God has raised this Jesus; we are all witnesses of this. Therefore, since he has been exalted to the right hand of God and has received from the Father the promised Holy Spirit, he has poured out what you both see and hear. For it was not David who ascended into the heavens, but he himself says:
>
> > "The Lord declared to my Lord,
> > 'Sit at my right hand
> > until I make your enemies your footstool.'"
>
> Therefore let all the house of Israel know with certainty that God has made this Jesus, whom you crucified, both Lord and Messiah. (vv. 32–36)

It is hard not to see the work of the Holy Spirit in the ascension. The Spirit, through David, prophesies the Messiah's ascension. Following his ascension, Jesus as "both Lord and Messiah" pours out the Holy Spirit upon the church. If the Spirit points to and is poured out by the ascended Son, it is reasonable to conclude that the Spirit effects the ascension of Jesus, exalting him to the right hand of the Father.[29]

---

[29] We may wonder why the Spirit's outpouring awaits Jesus's ascension or, to put it another way, why the mission of the Spirit is subsequent to the mission of the Son.

Thus, from the beginning of the Son's incarnation as Jesus of Nazareth, continuing throughout Jesus's entire earthly life, and culminating in Jesus's death, resurrection, and ascension, the Holy Spirit fills and enriches the God-man without measure.

Spirit Christology: An Improper Approach[30]

Our pneumatology affirms a view of the Christ-Spirit relationship that differs significantly from a certain type of Spirit Christology, an approach to the incarnation that maintains that "in becoming a human being, the Son of God willed to renounce the exercise of his divine powers, attributes, prerogatives, so that he might live fully within those limitations which inhere in being truly human."[31] This approach (rightly) distinguishes itself from traditional (and heretical) kenotic Christology, which affirms that in becoming incarnate, God the Son "gave up" or "laid aside" (Phil 2:7; Gr. ἐκένωσεν [ekenōsen = "emptied"]; hence kenosis) certain divine attributes—for example, omnipotence, omniscience, and omnipresence.[32] Rather, this version of Spirit

---

Jesus's mission encompasses his incarnation, holy life, suffering, death, burial resurrection, and ascension. It is through this entire work of salvation that Jesus provides atonement, forgiveness, cleansing, justification, and the like. This saving work *had* to precede the outpouring of the Spirit, leading to his indwelling and filling of believers, for it renders them a holy dwelling place for the Holy Spirit. For further discussion see Vidu, *The Same God Who Works All Things.*

[30] This discussion follows the excellent treatment of Spirit Christology in Wellum, *God the Son Incarnate*, 380–93, 404–11.

[31] Gerald F. Hawthorne, *The Presence and the Power: The Significance of the Holy Spirit in the Life and Ministry of Jesus* (Eugene: Wipf & Stock, 2003), 208. Other proponents of a type of Spirit Christology include Garrett J. DeWeese, "One Person, Two Natures: Two Metaphysical Models of the Incarnation," in *Jesus in Trinitarian Perspective: An Introductory Christology*, ed. Fred Sanders and Klaus D. Issler (Nashville: B&H Academic, 2007), 114–53; Klaus Issler, "Jesus' Example: Prototype of the Dependent, Spirit-Filled Life," in *Jesus in Trinitarian Perspective*, 189–225; and Issler, *Living into the Life of Jesus: The Formation of Christian Character* (Downers Grove: InterVarsity, 2012).

[32] For proponents of this historical position see Gottfried Thomasius, *Christi Person und Werk*, 3 vols. (Erlangen, DEU: Theodore Bläsing, 1852–1861); W. F. Gess, *Das Dogma von Christi Person und Werk*, 3 vols. (vol. 1: Calw, DEU: Verlag der Vereinsbuchhandlung, 1870; vols. 2–3: Basel, CH: Buchhandlung, 1887). For a summary of Thomasius's view see Gottfried Thomasius, "Christ's Person and Work,"

Christology maintains that these attributes become "potential or latent within this incarnate One—present in Jesus in all their fulness, but no longer in exercise."[33] Any and all attributes "incompatible with [Jesus's] humiliation and redemption," which would eliminate "any possibility of his really experiencing those temptations, testings, frustrations, and disappointments that belong to a truly human life," become inactive rather than operative in the incarnate Son.[34] Accordingly, "Jesus fulfills his specifically human vocation from conception to glory through the power of the Spirit. In this Jesus shows his likeness to us, since for every human being it is the gift of the Spirit that both constitutes (in creation) and completes (in glory) a person's human nature."[35] Accordingly, this form of Spirit Christology maintains that the classical view of the incarnation fails to account adequately for the humanity of the Son of God by overly emphasizing his deity.

The importance of this view for our discussion is that "the miracles that [Jesus] performed and the prescience he displayed can be accounted for by the power and illumination of the Spirit that was in him. . . . Jesus was . . . a human being commissioned to do the will of God in this world, and filled and empowered by the Holy Spirit to bring it all to a successful completion."[36]Accordingly, it is argued that everything Jesus does during his earthly ministry, from resisting temptation, being conscious of God the Father's work through him, performing miracles, exorcising demons, suffering, and more, does not involve his divine nature but flows from the empowerment of the Spirit dwelling in him. Some proponents of Spirit Christology modify this approach by conceding that while the incarnate Son is usually dependent on the Holy Spirit for his life and ministry, at times the Son relies on his divine nature to do some things, for example, some of his miracles.[37]

in *God and Incarnation in Mid-Nineteenth Century German Theology*, ed. and trans. Claude Welch (New York: Oxford University Press, 1965).

[33] Hawthorne, *Presence and Power*, 208.

[34] Hawthorne, 210, 209.

[35] Ian A. McFarland, "Spirit and Incarnation: Toward a Pneumatic Chalcedonianism," *International Journal of Systematic Theology* 16 (2014): 158.

[36] Hawthorne, *Presence and Power*, 211, 219.

[37] Issler, *Living into the Life of Jesus*, 204. Issler provides five examples of Jesus's relying on his divine nature: his forgiveness of sin (Mark 2:1–12); the transfiguration (Matt 17:1–13); the miracle of changing water into wine, by which Jesus displays his glory (John 2:11); his use of the phrase "I am" as an expression of his deity (John

This version of Spirit Christology is an improper approach to the incarnation, for several reasons. First, the idea that the divine attributes were latent in the incarnate Son cannot account for biblical affirmations that, during his incarnation, he continued to sustain the universe in existence (Heb 1:3; Col 1:17). Moreover, whatever one may think about the attributes of omnipresence, omnipotence, and omniscience becoming temporarily potential in the incarnate Son,[38] it is impossible for the Son's independence and eternal existence, for example, to become latent. Spirit Christology of this variety evidences a misunderstanding of the incarnate Son and his divine nature.

Second, this type of Spirit Christology risks minimizing the agency of the Son in most or all of his actions. For example, if Jesus performed the following "signs" or miracles exclusively or even predominantly by the Holy Spirit—changing water into wine (John 2:1–11), cleansing the temple (2:13–22), healing an official's son (4:46–54), healing a paralytic (5:1–15), feeding the 5,000 (6:5–14), walking on water (6:16–24), healing a blind man (9:1-7), and raising Lazarus (11:1-45)[39]—then it was not as a divine agent that he engaged in such actions. Rather, the Spirit as agent performed those miracles through him. Such a view contradicts John's purpose for including those seven signs in his Gospel to demonstrate, not that the Son was a man full of the Spirit, but that he was the divine Son of God (20:30–31).

Moreover, Jesus as the incarnate Son always acknowledges his dependence on God the Father (John 5:19; 8:28; 10:25, 37–38; 12:49–50; 14:10) while being filled with the Holy Spirit without measure. Accordingly, "a proper understanding of Trinitarian relations and agency never views the Son as 'merely a spectator, looking on whilst his human nature is manipulated by the Holy Spirit.'. . . The agency of the Son never disappears, even

---

18:6); and Jesus's desire for the preexistent glory that he shared with the Father (John 17:5).

[38] In regard to these attributes, Issler, *Living into the Life of Jesus*, 125n31, considers that the incarnate Son "temporarily delegated to the other members of the Trinity his usual divine duties, such as sustaining the universe (Col 1:17; Heb 1:3)." The doctrine of inseparable operations contradicts the idea of a period of time in which only the Father and the Holy Spirit operated together in certain works and apart from the (incarnate) Son.

[39] See n. 21 in this chapter, which discusses why eight signs are included in this list.

as incarnate, so that all of his actions are *his* actions, but always in relation to the Father and the Spirit."[40] It is as the incarnate Son of God, fully divine and fully human, completely and always dependent on God the Father and completely and always filled with God the Holy Spirit, that Jesus proclaims the gospel of the kingdom, resists temptation, disciples the Twelve, confronts his enemies, performs miracles, suffers, is crucified, rises again, and ascends into heaven. While seeking to emphasize the genuine humanity of the incarnate Son and his likeness with believers (for example, he serves as the paradigm for Christians facing temptations and suffering), this type of Spirit Christology is an improper approach to the Christ-Spirit relationship. It suffers from misunderstandings of the divine nature, trinitarian relations, inseparable operations, and divine agency.[41]

Aware of the deep problems with this version, other forms of Spirit Christology offer a nuanced approach in keeping with classical Christology as expressed in the Chalcedonian Creed. For example, in his formulation (and reflective of similar approaches like those of Ralph Del Colle[42] and Gary Badcock[43]), Myk Habets develops a Spirit Christology in keeping with several criteria, including: faithfulness to the biblical testimony to Jesus, affirmation of both the full deity and full humanity of Jesus, coherence with other doctrines, and consistency with the creeds of Nicaea and Chalcedon (thus, an acceptable Spirit Christology must not contradict or replace classical Logos Christology, but supplement it).[44] Such a pneumatological Christology rejects the elements of the Spirit Christology critiqued

---

[40] Wellum, *God the Son Incarnate*, 410. He quotes Oliver Crisp, *Revisioning Christology: Theology in the Reformed Tradition* (Surrey, UK: Ashgate, 2011), 102.

[41] While some consider John Owen to be a proponent of Spirit Christology, his view differs significantly from those just criticized. For a discussion see Kyle David Claunch, *The Son and the Spirit: The Promise of Spirit Christology in Traditional Trinitarian and Christological Perspective* (PhD diss., The Southern Baptist Theological Seminary, 2017).

[42] Ralph Del Colle, *Christ and the Spirit: Spirit Christology in Trinitarian Perspective* (New York: Oxford University Press, 1994).

[43] Gary Badcock, *Light of Truth and Fire of Love: A Theology of the Holy Spirit* (Grand Rapids: Eerdmans, 1997).

[44] Myk Habets, *The Anointed Son: A Trinitarian Spirit Christology*, Princeton Theological Monograph Series (Eugene: Pickwick, 2010). My thanks to Myk for his suggestions about this section.

above, finding them to be either unbiblical, or a departure from classical Christology, or both.

Conclusion

It is impossible to understand and experience the person and work of Christ apart from the presence and power of the Holy Spirit. This conclusion should not be surprising, as our pneumatology has emphasized the inseparable operations of the Trinity. Moreover, the conclusion has extensive and sound biblical support. Through the Spirit's inspiration, the Old Testament writers predict a coming Messiah/Suffering Servant who will be filled with the Holy Spirit, rescue the people of God from their sins, and establish a new covenant with the redeemed. Through the Spirit's coming upon the virgin Mary, the Son of God becomes incarnate and filled with the Spirit without measure. Accordingly, throughout his earthly ministry—including his baptism, temptations, proclamation, exorcisms, miracles, death, resurrection, and ascension—Jesus relies upon and is empowered by the Spirit.

The proper response to this Christ-Spirit relationship is for Christians and the church to be both Christ-centered and Spirit-dependent. Certainly, the trinitarian relations and the immeasurable fullness of the Spirit with respect to the Son are irreproducible for the people of God. Still, believers and the church are directed to look to their merciful, faithful, and sympathetic High Priest to find mercy and grace when suffering and being tempted (Heb 2:14–18; 4:14–16). They are to imitate him in being self-sacrificial, suffering for his sake, forgiving others, and more. They are also directed to be filled with the Spirit, walk in the Spirit, and keep in step with the Spirit (see the next section) so as to be Christlike (e.g., Gal 5:22–23) and to walk as Christ himself walked (1 John 2:6), taking into account the differences between his sonship and theirs. Through their prayers of adoration for, and their desperate cries of dependence on, both the Son of God and the Spirit of God, the people of God rightly acknowledge and acclaim the Christ-Spirit relationship.

21

The Holy Spirit and Salvation

O ur pneumatology focuses on the biblical metaphor of the outpouring of the Holy Spirit, and the vividness of this metaphor is particularly manifested in the work of the Spirit to save fallen human beings. The
Spirit's outpouring is seen in both the extensiveness and the intensiveness
of salvation. The mighty divine work of rescuing sinful people is extensive, a multifaceted operation that runs the gamut from conviction of sin
to incorporation into the body of Christ to resurrection. It is also intensive,
as it includes subjective, transformative aspects such as regeneration, guidance, and assurance of salvation. When the Holy Spirit is poured out, sinful
human beings experience a rich and profound salvation.[1]

As Wolfhart Pannenberg offered, "One might expect nothing to be more
familiar to every Christian than the reality of the Spirit."[2] This familiarity is
due to the fact that, from beginning to end, salvation is the work of the Holy
Spirit. For Calvin the key question, reflective of the inseparable operations
of the triune God, is, "How do we receive those benefits which the Father
bestowed on his only-begotten Son—not for Christ's own private use, but
that he might enrich poor and needy men?" His answer: "the secret energy
[Lat. and Fr. "effective operation"] of the Spirit, by which we come to enjoy

---

[1] For a reader on pneumatology and soteriology see Kärkkäinen, ed., *Holy Spirit and Salvation*.

[2] Wolfhart Pannenberg, "The Working of the Spirit in the Creation and in the People of God," in *Spirit, Faith, and Church*, ed. Wolfhart Pannenberg, Avery Dulles, and Carl E. Braaten (Philadelphia: Westminster, 1970), 13.

Christ and all his benefits."[3] Following a traditional order of the application of salvation, our pneumatology will connect this secret work of the Holy Spirit to conviction of sin, regeneration, union with Christ, justification, adoption, conversion (repentance, faith, and confession of Christ), baptism with the Spirit, sealing, assurance of salvation, guidance, filling, sanctification, and resurrection/glorification.

Conviction of Sin

As discussed earlier, even before people become Christians, the Holy Spirit engages with them through the conviction of sin.[4] Jesus foretells this work of the Spirit: "When [the Holy Spirit] comes, he will convict the world about sin, righteousness, and judgment: About sin, because they do not believe in me; about righteousness, because I am going to the Father and you will no longer see me; and about judgment, because the ruler of this world has been judged" (John 16:8–11). The Holy Spirit's work of exposing error and wrongdoing has particular reference to "the world," or people who are hostile to God. Specifically, Jesus promises that the Holy Spirit will convict unreceptive people of their failure to believe in Christ, their futile reliance on their self-righteous efforts to please God, and their faulty judgment based on mere appearance. By unsettling people who are antagonistic or indifferent to salvation, the Spirit moves them toward their only hope, the gospel.[5]

---

[3] John Calvin, *Institutes*, 3.1.1, LCC 20:537. Owen, *Pneumatologia*, 27, picked up on this theme: "There is not any spiritual or *saving good* from first to last communicated unto us, or that we are from and by the grace of God made partakers of, but it is revealed to us and bestowed on us by the Holy Ghost" (cf. 157).

[4] See pp. 340–43.

[5] This hope for conviction of sin is voiced in Robert Seagrave's "Come, Holy Spirit, Heavenly Power":

Visit a formal, dead mankind,
And lift them from their graves of sin.
Amongst the tombs Thy circuit take,
Bring Sinai's wakening thunders there, [an appeal for the law to bring conviction of sin]
Followed by Grace's softer voice:
But give the slumberers ears to hear.

Regeneration[6]

In conjunction with the announcement of the gospel,[7] the Spirit effects regeneration, the "mighty work of God by which unbelievers are given a new nature, being born again. . . . It is both (1) the removal of one's old self, and (2) the imparting of a new self that is responsive to God. Unlike conversion, which is the human response to the gospel, regeneration is completely a divine work, to which human beings contribute nothing."[8]

Jesus himself addresses the absolute necessity of regeneration and regards it as a work of the Holy Spirit:

> There was a man from the Pharisees named Nicodemus, a ruler of the Jews. This man came to him at night and said, "Rabbi, we know that you are a teacher who has come from God, for no one could perform these signs you do unless God were with him."
>
> Jesus replied, "Truly I tell you, unless someone is born again, he cannot see the kingdom of God."
>
> "How can anyone be born when he is old?" Nicodemus asked him. "Can he enter his mother's womb a second time and be born?"
>
> Jesus answered, "Truly I tell you, unless someone is born of water and the Spirit, he cannot enter the kingdom of God. Whatever is

Cited in Esther Rothenbusch, "'Is Not This the Land of Beulah?' The Search for the Holy Spirit in American Gospel Hymns," *Review and Expositor* 94, no. 1 (Winter 1997): 55.

[6] On the role of the Holy Spirit in regeneration see Kuyper, *The Work of the Holy Spirit*, 293–332; Owen, *Pneumatologia*, bk. 3.

[7] Biblical passages that present the instrumentality of the gospel, or Word of God, for regeneration are Jas 1:18 and 1 Pet 1:22–23. As for the relationship between the Word and the Spirit, Calvin, *Institutes*, 2.5.5, LCC 20:322, proposed, "God works in his elect in two ways: within, through his Spirit; without [i.e., externally], through his Word. By his Spirit, illuminating their minds and forming their hearts to the love and cultivation of righteousness, he makes them a new creation (*nova creatio*). By his Word, he arouses them to desire, to seek after, and to attain that same renewal."

[8] Allison, *The Baker Compact Dictionary of Theological Terms*, s.v. "regeneration." Anthony A. Hoekema, *Saved by Grace* (Grand Rapids: Eerdmans, 1989), 94, offered this definition: "Regeneration may be defined as that work of the Holy Spirit whereby he initially brings persons into living union with Christ, changing their hearts so that they who were spiritually dead become spiritually alive, now able and willing to repent of sin, believe the gospel, and serve the Lord."

born of the flesh is flesh, and whatever is born of the Spirit is spirit. Do not be amazed that I told you that you must be born again. The wind blows where it pleases, and you hear its sound, but you don't know where it comes from or where it is going. So it is with everyone born of the Spirit." (John 3:1–8)

Jesus describes regeneration as being "born again" or being "born of water and the Spirit"; apart from this regenerative work, no one can see or enter the kingdom of God.[9]

Two incorrect interpretations of regeneration, particularly tied to misunderstandings of the phrase "born of water and the Spirit," are these: (1) Baptism is the means of regeneration and thus necessary for salvation. As baptismal regeneration developed in the early church, the ground for this belief was original sin and the consequent need for cleansing from guilt and corruption if salvation is to occur. As Origen explained, "No one is clean of filth, not even if his life on earth has only been for one day. . . . Because the filth of birth is removed by the sacrament of baptism, for that reason infants, too, are baptized."[10] Cyprian also advanced this view: "This recently born infant has not sinned except that—being born physically according to Adam—he has contracted the contagion [infection] of the ancient death by his first birth. Thus, he more easily approaches the reception of the forgiveness of sins, because the sins forgiven are not his own but those of another."[11] Appealing to John 3:5 and interpreting the expression "born of water" as referring to water baptism, the church officially adopted the practice of infant baptism based on the doctrine of baptismal regeneration.

(2) Both water baptism and Spirit baptism are involved in regeneration. This view distinguishes two elements in regeneration: the new birth by water and the new birth by the Holy Spirit. Thus, the Spirit effects regeneration,

---

[9] Using Pauline language, "the body is dead because of sin, but the Spirit gives life because of righteousness" (Rom 8:10). From spiritual death, people are brought to spiritual life through the Holy Spirit.

[10] Origen, *Homilies on the Gospel of Luke* 14.5; cited in Jaroslav Pelikan, *The Christian Tradition: A History of the Development of Doctrine*, 5 vols. (Chicago: University of Chicago Press, 1971–1991), 1:291.

[11] Cyprian, *Letter* 58.5; *ANF* 5:354 (the text has been rendered clearer).

which is attested through water baptism. And both elements are necessary for renewal to take place.

Both positions on regeneration err because of their misunderstandings of the phrase "born of water and the Spirit." The first position is incorrect because it anachronistically takes Jesus's reference to water to refer to water baptism, a reference Nicodemus could not have understood. Moreover, if the referent in John 3:5 were baptism, it would be the only place in the Gospel of John where this topic would appear. Though such a singularity does not categorically preclude the idea of baptism being introduced here without further development elsewhere, it renders it highly unlikely. Furthermore, Jesus's likening of the Spirit's regeneration to the mysterious action of the wind would be an inappropriate metaphor. If the Spirit's work of the new birth is tied to baptism, then there is nothing mysterious about what occurs when a person (who, in most cases, is an infant) is baptized: she is regenerated. There is no secret or enigma; rather, the effect is known.

The second position errs because it understands Jesus's phrase as referring to two elements: one must be born of water—that is, water baptism—and one must be born of the Spirit—that is, Spirit baptism. Grammatically, however, the phrase "born of water and the Spirit" has not two referents but one.[12] It is one action or event that Jesus enjoins on sinful people: they must be "born of water-and-the-Spirit." In the Old Testament, water occurs as an image for cleansing. For example, the Aaronic priests are consecrated with water before engaging in their vocation (Exod 29:4), and priests ceremonially wash their hands and feet (30:17–21; 40:30–32).[13] Moreover, water functions as a metaphor for renewal, a signal of the end of a period of aridity and the beginning of flourishing (Isa 27:2–3; 35:6; 58:11; Ezek 47:1–12; Joel 3:18; Zech 14:8).

On occasion, the Old Testament links water and the Holy Spirit (Isa 44:3–4; cf. 32:15); the passage that is germane for our discussion is a prophecy of Ezekiel: "I will also sprinkle clean water on you, and you will be clean. I will cleanse you from all your impurities and all your idols. I will give you a

---

[12] Linda L. Belleville, "'Born of Water and Spirit': John 3:5," *Trinity Journal 1* NS (Fall 1980): 125–41. Ferguson, *The Holy Spirit*, 122.

[13] Robert V. McCabe, "The Meaning of 'Born of Water and the Spirit' in John 3:5," *DBSJ* 4 (Fall 1999): 88.

new heart and put a new spirit within you; I will remove your heart of stone and give you a heart of flesh. I will place my Spirit within you and cause you to follow my statutes and carefully observe my ordinances" (Ezek 36:25–27).

This link of divine sprinkling with water, symbolic of cleansing from sin and idolatry, and the indwelling of the Spirit, effecting a renovation of the heart and enabling covenantal obedience, appears to be the Old Testament passage Jesus has in mind when discussing the new birth with Nicodemus. After all, Jesus fully expects this leading Jew to grasp the need for regeneration: "'How can these things be?' asked Nicodemus. 'Are you a teacher of Israel and don't know these things?' Jesus replied" (John 3:9–10). Jesus's chagrin at Nicodemus's lack of understanding is due to Jesus's expectation that Nicodemus would know the biblical background for the teaching about the new birth. And what Ezekiel prophesied has nothing to do with Christian baptism and its regenerative power, nor does it have to do with a two-step process of water baptism and Spirit baptism. On the contrary, the prophecy is of the divine work of regeneration that involves cleansing from sin and new birth by the Spirit—one divine action that concerns purification and renewal.

Accordingly, Jesus's exhortation about regeneration emphasizes the work of the Holy Spirit to effect this action. It involves both a life-transformative cleansing and an identity-transferring change from being characterized by one's old self to being a new creation (2 Cor 5:17).

Regeneration is depicted in Titus 3, again with a link between water and renewal. The passage begins with an exhortation to engage in good works, an encouragement set against the dismal reality of life before the new birth: "Remind them to submit to rulers and authorities, to obey, to be ready for every good work, to slander no one, to avoid fighting, and to be kind, always showing gentleness to all people" (vv. 1–2). Christians, to whom this exhortation is directed, are expected to engage in good works, exemplified by submission to leaders, obedience, kindness, and gentleness. Their new life-style should stand in stark contrast with their former manner of life, which was characterized by evil speech, quarreling, foolish behavior, disobedience, deception, enslavement to sin, and more. The question arises: By what means or by whom does this new life of good works take place?

The answer focuses on the action of the triune God: "But when the kindness of God our Savior and his love for mankind appeared, he saved us—not by works of righteousness that we had done, but according to his mercy—through the washing of regeneration and renewal by the Holy Spirit. He poured out his Spirit on us abundantly through Jesus Christ our Savior so that, having been justified by his grace, we may become heirs with the hope of eternal life" (vv. 4–7). Expressing kindness, love, mercy, and grace, the triune God—the Father, the Son, and the Holy Spirit—operates inseparably to save sinful people. For our purposes, we attend to the regenerative work of the Spirit. Reflective of Ezek 36:25–27, the outpoured Spirit cleanses from sin and transforms sinful people who, incapable of performing works of righteousness by which they could merit salvation, are renewed in their nature. In light of believers' new identity, the earlier exhortation to engage in good works resounds expectantly: "This saying is trustworthy. I want you to insist on these things, so that those who have believed God might be careful to devote themselves to good works. These are good and profitable for everyone" (Titus 3:8). Regeneration is not by good works but expresses itself in good works. And it is the work of the Holy Spirit, who is poured out on sinful people to transform them into good people.[14]

---

[14] Because of ongoing interest in the topic, our pneumatology briefly treats the issue of the regeneration of followers of Yahweh before the coming of Christ. Several approaches lead to different positions: (1) From a continuity approach—that of Reformed theology, for example—there is one covenant of grace for all the people of God. Thus, the experience of salvation for believers before Christ is essentially the same as that of Christians. The people of God before Christ experienced circumcision of the heart (the Old Testament metaphor for regeneration); the people of God after Christ experience the new birth (the New Testament metaphor for regeneration). But both groups were/are regenerated. (2) According to Jim Hamilton, regeneration is "God's work of granting to humans the ability to hear, understand, believe, obey, and enter the kingdom. The New Testament's metaphor of 'new birth' matches the Old Testament's metaphor of 'heart circumcision.'" James M. Hamilton Jr., *God's Indwelling Presence: The Holy Spirit in the Old and New Testaments*, NAC Studies in Bible and Theology (Nashville: B&H Academic, 2006), 2. (3) From a discontinuity approach—that of dispensational theology, for example—while *the way of salvation* is the same for all the people of God—justification by divine grace through faith (Rom 4:22–25)—*the experience of salvation* differs for the people of God before Christ and those after Christ. One of those differences is regeneration: the people of Israel were not regenerated, while Christians are regenerated. This difference has to do with the history of salvation and the different covenants to which people before and after Christ belonged/belong. Just as people before Christ could not belong to his body, the church—as that phenomenon awaited the death, resurrection, and

Union with Christ

Union with Christ is "the mighty work of God to join his people in eternal covenant with the Son, who accomplished their salvation. Through union, believers are identified with Christ's death, burial, resurrection, and ascension (Rom. 6:1–11; Eph. 2:6), and God communicates all his blessings of salvation: grace, regeneration, redemption, eternal life, justification, sanctification, and glorification. Christ dwells in those with whom he is united, and they in turn dwell in him (John 15:1–5; Gal. 2:20)."[15]

This union is closely associated with the Holy Spirit.[16] Scripture affirms of believers: "You, however, are not in the flesh, but in the Spirit, if indeed *the Spirit of God lives in you*. If anyone does not have the Spirit of Christ, he does not belong to him. Now if *Christ is in you*, the body is dead because of sin, but the Spirit gives life because of righteousness" (Rom 8:9–10). The parallelism is striking: "the Spirit of God lives in you" and "Christ is in you." As developed earlier, the indwelling of the Son is effected by the Holy Spirit's dwelling in believers; the Spirit renders the presence of Christ in this union. Moreover, as will be discussed, Christ baptizes new Christians with the Holy Spirit, thereby incorporating them into his body, the church (1 Cor 12:13).

---

ascension of Christ, together with the outpouring of the Holy Spirit and his inauguration of the new covenant to replace the old covenant—so the people of God before Christ were not, indeed, could not be, regenerated. Regeneration is dependent on the new covenant reality of the Holy Spirit. As for Hamilton's notion, if one grants his definition of regeneration, then of course all the people of God of all times were/are regenerated. But one questions if his definition is the correct one, given the progress of revelation (for example, the Old Testament's circumcision of the heart seems to look forward to a future reality, one that would not be available for the people of Israel) and especially the New Testament's presentation of regeneration. For further discussions see Cole, *He Who Gives Life*, 143–45; Horton, *Rediscovering the Holy Spirit*, 146–58.

[15] Allison, *The Baker Compact Dictionary of Theological Terms*, s.v. "union with Christ."

[16] For a brief treatment of the Holy Spirit and union with Christ see Oliver D. Crisp, "Uniting Us to God: Toward a Reformed Pneumatology," in *Spirit of God: Christian Renewal in the Community of Faith*, ed. Jeffrey W. Barbeau and Beth Felker Jones (Downers Grove: IVP Academic, 2015), 92–109; Kuyper, *The Work of the Holy Spirit*, 333–37.

Again, the tandem working of the Son and the Holy Spirit associates the two in union with Christ.

The consequences of this union are all the blessings of salvation. To focus on one aspect, Christians are to consider themselves dead to sin and alive unto Christ (Rom 6:1–14). As for the aspect of mortification, Paul personifies sin: it is an active agent, seizes opportunity, produces coveting and death, springs to life, and performs evil deeds (Rom 7:7–25). The solution to such aggressive, life-destroying sin must be seen not just as a power but as a holy, divine person who counteracts such sin and enables believers to mortify it. As for the aspect of reckoning oneself alive to Christ, such faith comes from the Holy Spirit, as already rehearsed. As the Westminster Confession of Faith affirms, "All saints that are united to Jesus Christ the Head, by his Spirit and by faith, have fellowship with him" (26:1).

Justification[17]

Justification is the "mighty act of God by which he declares sinful people not guilty but righteous instead. He does so by imputing, or crediting, the perfect righteousness of Christ to them. Thus, while they are not actually righteous, God views them as being so because of Christ's righteousness." Thus, justification is a forensic act, a legal declaration, consisting of two elements. "The first aspect is the forgiveness of sins, resulting from Christ's substitutionary death (Rom. 3:25; 5:9). The second is imputation, resulting from Christ's obedience that makes people righteous (5:18–29)."[18]

The New Testament ties justification to the Holy Spirit in one passage, in which an absolute contrast is made between "the unrighteous, [who] will not inherit God's kingdom" (1 Cor 6:9), and believers: "And some of you used to be like this. But you were washed, you were sanctified, you were justified in the name of the Lord Jesus Christ and *by the Spirit of our God*" (6:11). In what sense is justification by the Holy Spirit? Justification is by faith; that is, its appropriation is by faith alone in Christ alone and not through works (Rom 3:21–31; 4:1–25; Gal 3:1–14). Moreover, faith, while a human

---

[17] For discussion of the role of the Holy Spirit in justification see Kuyper, 354–77.

[18] Allison, *The Baker Compact Dictionary of Theological Terms*, s.v. "justification."

response to the gospel, is not *merely* a human response but is aided by the Holy Spirit. Therefore, justification is ascribed to the Spirit, who prompts faith by which sinful people are declared not guilty but righteous instead.[19]

Justification may be indirectly tied to the Spirit in Galatians:

> I only want to learn this from you: Did you receive the Spirit by the works of the law or by believing what you heard? Are you so foolish? After beginning by the Spirit, are you now finishing by the flesh? Did you experience so much for nothing—if in fact it was for nothing? So then, does God give you the Spirit and work miracles among you by your doing the works of the law? Or is it by believing what you heard—just like Abraham who believed God, and it was credited to him for righteousness? (Gal 3:2–6)

It appears that the mighty divine act of justification should underscore the fact that one's righteous standing before God has relationship not to the works of the law but only to faith in the gospel, which is closely tied to one's reception of the Spirit. Again, the conjunction of justification, faith, and the Holy Spirit comes to the forefront.

Adoption

Adoption is "the mighty work of God to take sinful people—enemies who are alienated and separated from him—and embrace them as beloved children into his family forever. Redemption through the Son of God results in their adoption as sons and daughters, together with the reception of the Spirit of adoption, by whom God is called '*Abba*, Father!'"[20] Continuing our emphasis on the inseparable operations of the triune God, we see that adoption exhibits the collaborative work of the Father, the Son, and the Holy Spirit. The key New Testament passage setting forth this trinitarian work affirms, "When the time came to completion, God sent his Son, born of a woman, born under the law, to redeem those under the law, so that we might receive adoption as sons. And because you are sons, God sent the Spirit of his Son into our hearts, crying, '*Abba*, Father!' So you are no longer

---

[19] Horton, *Rediscovering the Holy Spirit*, 44, concurs.
[20] Allison, *The Baker Compact Dictionary of Theological Terms*, s.v. "adoption."

a slave but a son, and if a son, then God has made you an heir" (Gal 4:4–7; cf. Rom 8:14–15).

The language of "sonship" is important in terms of a canonical and covenantal reading of Scripture. While to contemporary sensibilities the gender-specific term "sonship" may seem sexist or exclusionary, its rich canonical and covenantal context (1) underscores its importance in terms of the inheritance of divine blessings and (2) indicates that both male and female believers are included in the inheritance. That is, as Scripture unfolds canonically and its covenants develop progressively, the theme of sonship progresses exponentially.[21] Adam, the divine image bearer, is the first son of God (Gen 1:26–28; Luke 3:38). As the image of God, Adam is to reflect and represent God and thus enjoy the privileges of the covenant of creation. Next, Israel is the "firstborn son" of God (Exod 4:22), followed by those identified with David: King David himself; David's sons as kings, beginning with Solomon; and the eternal Davidic king, Jesus Christ (2 Samuel 7; Psalm 2). Like Adam before them, Israel and "David" are to reflect and represent God as his sons in old-covenant and Davidic-covenant relationship with him. Sonship, therefore, is the status of divine favor, bestowing a rich inheritance of covenantal blessing and privilege.

Accordingly, when the New Testament speaks of the bestowal of sonship on Christians, it offers the promise of divine favor to all who follow Jesus Christ—male and female Christ-followers alike are heirs. As members of the new covenant, men and women together receive its blessing and are one in sharing its privileges (Gal 3:26–28).

There is one more exemplification of sonship in Scripture, and it is more important than those already presented: the sonship of the Second Person. He is the *eternal* Son, the everlasting Son of the Father, distinguished from the Father by the relation of origin of eternal generation. As the Galatians passage cited earlier highlights (4:4–7), in the fullness of time (about 2,000 years ago) the Father sent forth the *eternal* Son. He was "born of a woman, born under the law"; that is, he became the *incarnate* Son, born of the virgin Mary as a first-century Jew. By taking on the fullness of human nature, through his life, sufferings, death, burial, resurrection, and ascension God the Son incarnate rescues sinful people so they "might receive adoption as

---

[21] For further discussion see Wellum, *God the Son Incarnate*, 118–19.

sons." Such sonship language relates Christians to the archetypal Son. The *eternal* Son, who became the *incarnate* Son, stands in covenantal relationship with *human* sons whom he has redeemed. Redemption comes about through the work of the Spirit, who applies the work of the Son to those sons. Accordingly, "because you are sons, God sent the Spirit of his Son into our hearts, crying, '*Abba*, Father!'" Related as sons in new covenant relationship with God the Father through God the Son by God the Holy Spirit, Christians—both male and female—are heirs, receiving the divine blessing and covenantal privileges.[22]

It is "the Spirit of adoption, by whom we cry out, *Abba*, Father'" (Rom 8:15), who confers on Christians a status mirroring the sonship of Adam, Israel, and David yet progressing exponentially beyond it by joining them to the sonship of the archetypal Son.

What is the nature of the cry of adoption? John Owen contrasted the desperate screams of unbelievers with the voice of the Holy Spirit by which believers call out "*Abba*, Father": "Take an instance of the prayers of wicked men under their convictions, or their fears, troubles, and dangers, and the prayers of believers. The former is merely . . . an outcry that distressed nature makes to the God of it, and as such alone it considers him. But the other is . . . the voice of the Spirit of adoption addressing itself in the hearts of believers unto God as a Father."[23]

An example of the first is Eric Clapton, who recounted his first prayers:

I was absolutely terrified, in complete despair. . . . In the privacy of my room, I begged for help. I had no notion who I thought I was

---

[22] This discussion is deeply influenced by Fred Sanders, *The Deep Things of God: How the Trinity Changes Everything*, 2nd ed. (Wheaton: Crossway, 2017), 162–63: "Adoption is a central biblical description of how God saves. It emphasizes the quality of the new relationship that God brings us into, a relationship of having been made into his children. In explicitly Trinitarian terms, this means that God brings us into the relationship of sonship that has always been a part of his divine life. When we become sons of God, we are joined to the sonship of the incarnate Son, which is in turn the human enactment of the eternal sonship of the second person of the Trinity. Sonship was always with God, and it came to be on earth as it is in heaven, in the person of the incarnate Christ."

[23] Owen, *Pneumatologia*, 192.

talking to, I just knew that I had come to the end of my tether . . . and, getting down on my knees, I surrendered. Within a few days I realized that something had happened for me. . . . I had found a place to turn to, a place I'd always known was there but never really wanted, or needed, to believe in. From that day until this, I have never failed to pray in the morning, on my knees, asking for help, and at night, to express gratitude for my life and, most of all, for my sobriety. I choose to kneel because I feel I need to humble myself when I pray, and with my ego, this is the most I can do. If you are asking why I do all this, I will tell you . . . because it works, as simple as that.[24]

Clapton's outcry exemplifies the first type of cry of adoption.

The second is exemplified by *"Abba*, Father!" as by the Holy Spirit believers voice this cry of sonship. This is not a generic prayer, addressed to some vague being or force. Nor is it merely an acknowledgment of someone or something because such recognition works. Rather, it is a cry of dependence born out of a relationship of son to Father, a reliance on the fatherhood of the only good, wise, and loving God. Such a cry is the fruit of "the Spirit of adoption."

Conversion (Repentance, Faith, and Confession of Christ)[25]

Conversion is "the human response to the gospel. It consists of two aspects: (1) repentance, or sorrow for sin, hatred of it, and resolve to turn from it, and (2) faith, or belief in God's provision of forgiveness and trust in Christ for salvation."[26] Emerging from conversion is a confession of the lordship of Christ, an acknowledgment by the new convert that she is no longer under the mastery of sin, law, Satan, death, and condemnation but is under the rulership of Jesus Christ. Though conversion "is a thoroughly human response,

---

[24] Eric Clapton, *Clapton: The Autobiography* (New York: Random House, 2007), 235–36.

[25] On regeneration, faith, and repentance see Ferguson, *The Holy Spirit*, 116–38.

[26] Allison, *The Baker Compact Dictionary of Theological Terms*, s.v. "conversion."

it is not merely human, because it is gospel prompted (Rom 10:17) and grace stirred (Acts 18:27)."[27] This divine aid in conversion has particular reference to the Holy Spirit.[28]

Repentance[29]

Repentance is the first "aspect of conversion (the other being faith), which is the human response to the gospel. Repentance is changing one's mind and life. It involves an acknowledgment that one's thoughts, words, and actions are sinful and thus grievous to God; a sorrow for one's sin; and a decision to break with sin."[30] Given the dreadful situation of sinful human beings (e.g., Eph 2:1–3), divine aid is desperately needed. Fallen human nature is characterized not only by "its lack of openness" to God but also "its unbelief . . . stubbornness . . . meek self-righteousness"; "this is the spirit of hostility toward grace and is sin in its proper nature and its total seriousness." As part of his re-creating work, and through the gospel that is sounded, the Spirit graciously prompts repentance. "Being the Spirit of grace, the Holy Spirit strikes against man's hostility to grace,"[31] opposing the human resistance to the divine call to salvation. The response to the Holy Spirit's action is a human response, but not a mere human response.

Repentance expresses itself concretely. John the Baptist instructs his audience to "produce fruit consistent with repentance" (Luke 3:8); this exhortation has specific application for different groups of penitents:

---

[27] Allison.

[28] A biblical example is Nicodemus (John 3:1–13). He is resistant to Jesus and his teaching on the new birth and, as the text implies, will continue to resist until the Holy Spirit regenerates him. Then, and only then, can he turn from his obstinacy and believe in Jesus for eternal life (Holmes, *The Holy Spirit*, 55).

[29] For the role of the Holy Spirit in repentance see Kuyper, *The Work of the Holy Spirit*, 338–53.

[30] Allison, *The Baker Compact Dictionary of Theological Terms*, s.v. "repentance."

[31] Barth, *The Holy Spirit and the Christian Life*, 1, 2, 25. As to the efficacy of the Spirit's operation, Owen, *Pneumatologia*, 202, affirmed, "When [the Spirit] exerts his power in and by the word, to the creation of a new heart and the opening of blind eyes, he so removes the principle of resistance, that he is not, cannot be resisted."

"What then should we do?" the crowds were asking him.

He replied to them, "The one who has two shirts must share with someone who has none, and the one who has food must do the same."

Tax collectors also came to be baptized, and they asked him, "Teacher, what should we do?"

He told them, "Don't collect any more than what you have been authorized."

Some soldiers also questioned him, "What should we do?"

He said to them, "Don't take money from anyone by force or false accusation, and be satisfied with your wages." (Luke 3:10–14)

In the case of one particular tax collector, his repentance is shocking: "Zacchaeus stood there and said to the Lord, 'Look, I'll give half of my possessions to the poor, Lord. And if I have extorted anything from anyone, I'll pay back four times as much'" (Luke 19:8). And in terms of Ephesian converts in Acts: "Many who had become believers came confessing and disclosing their practices, while many of those who had practiced magic collected their books and burned them in front of everyone. So they calculated their value and found it to be fifty thousand pieces of silver" (Acts 19:18–19).

Sharing with those who have need. Engaging ethically in one's profession. Renouncing bribery, extortion, and lying. Living contentedly. Restoring what one has illegitimately taken from others. Denouncing idolatry, sorcery, and magic. These manifestations of repentance, prompted and aided by the Holy Spirit, are examples of the fruit of repentance.

Faith[32]

Faith is the second "aspect of conversion (the other being repentance), which is the human response to the gospel. Faith is belief and personal trust. It involves an understanding of the person and work of Christ to provide salvation; an assent to one's need for forgiveness; and a decision to trust Christ to

---

[32] For the role of the Holy Spirit and faith see Kuyper, *The Work of the Holy Spirit*, 402–27.

personally save."[33] Just as "repentance is not an affair that we can accomplish
in our own resources" but "is left to the Holy Spirit," so is faith: "Shall we
be able to say anything different, when we turn now to example what constitutes the other phase of the Christian life, namely, faith?" Indeed, fallen
human beings who are characterized by unbelief are "made open," or believe,
"through the Holy Spirit."[34]

Similarly, Martin Luther framed this confession in his Small Catechism:
"I believe that I cannot by my own reason or strength believe in Jesus Christ,
my Lord, or come to him; but the Holy Spirit has called me by the gospel,
enlightened me with his gifts, sanctified and kept me in the true faith."[35]
Luther underscored the role of the Holy Spirit in igniting faith and maintaining the individual believer in the Christian faith. Still, the Spirit's prompting
and preserving work of the individual Christian is a subset of a broader work
of the Spirit, as Luther continued: the Holy Spirit "calls, gathers, enlightens,
and sanctifies the whole Christian church on earth, and keeps it with Jesus
Christ in the one true faith."[36] In other words, in response to Jesus's piercing
question, "When the Son of Man comes, will he find faith on earth?" (Luke
18:8), the answer is yes, because the Holy Spirit kindles faith in both individuals and the church.

The Holy Spirit ignites faith in conjunction with the hearing of the
gospel. After rehearsing the necessity of communicating the good news, Paul
appeals to Scripture: "As it is written: How beautiful are the feet of those
who bring good news. But not all obeyed the gospel. For Isaiah says, Lord,
who has believed our message? So faith comes from what is heard, and what
is heard comes through the message about Christ" (Rom 10:15–17; citing
Isa 52:7 and 53:1). The tragic case of Israel and its unbelief is contrasted
with the joyful case of the Gentiles and their belief. Like Israel, the Gentiles
heard the good news but, unlike Israel, embraced the gospel by faith. Such
faith leading to salvation comes by divine grace and is thus a gift of God

---

[33] Allison, *The Baker Compact Dictionary of Theological Terms*, s.v. "faith."
[34] Barth, *The Holy Spirit and the Christian Life*, 29, 30.
[35] Martin Luther, *Small Catechism*, III. The Creed; Third Article; Of
Sanctification; What Does This Mean?—Answer.
[36] Luther.

(Eph. 2:8–9). Specifically, this mighty act of grace-salvation-faith is part of the re-creating work of the Holy Spirit.

Confession of Christ

Such faith expresses itself in confession: "You know that when you were pagans, you used to be enticed and led astray by mute idols. Therefore I want you to know that no one speaking by the Spirit of God says, 'Jesus is cursed,' and no one can say, 'Jesus is Lord,' except by the Holy Spirit" (1 Cor 12:2–3). The confession of belief stands in stark contrast with the silence of idolatry: whereas idols are mute, Christians speak by the Holy Spirit and proclaim the lordship of Jesus Christ. Once again, we see speaking as one of the works terminating in the Holy Spirit. In this case, it is the Christian's confession of faith that is spoken through the Spirit. To say "Jesus is Lord" is an expression of faith and thus a confession of conversion wrought by the Spirit. Moreover, such confession of the lordship of Christ entails the renunciation of idols or false gods and goddesses that have been, up to the point of conversion, the object of one's faith.[37]

Accordingly, the Holy Spirit engages actively with sinful people to prompt repentance and faith: "The Son has created a redeemed community, and the Spirit is creating a repentant and believing community, with the fruit of love and hope."[38]

Baptism with the Spirit

Along with regeneration, union with Christ, justification, and the like, another mighty work of God in saving sinful people is baptism with the Holy Spirit. This work of Christ to pour out the Spirit on new believers has both a historical and an ongoing dimension. We begin with the historical framework for baptism with the Spirit.

---

[37] In a power-fear culture, for example, this denunciation may express itself by one's removing an amulet that has the power of idols/gods/goddesses.
[38] Michael S. Horton, *People and Place: A Covenant Ecclesiology* (Louisville: Westminster John Knox, 2008), 28.

Historical Development of Baptism with the Spirit throughout Scripture

As he peered into the future, Moses predicted the demise of the old covenant:

> When all these things happen to you—the blessings and curses I have set before you—and you come to your senses while you are in all the nations where the LORD your God has driven you, and you and your children return to the LORD your God and obey him with all your heart and all your soul by doing everything I am command- ing you today, then he will restore your fortunes, have compassion on you, and gather you again from all the peoples where the LORD your God has scattered you. Even if your exiles are at the farthest horizon, he will gather you and bring you back from there. The LORD your God will bring you into the land your fathers possessed, and you will take possession of it. He will cause you to prosper and multiply you more than he did your fathers. The LORD your God will circumcise your heart and the hearts of your descendants, and you will love him with all your heart and all your soul so that you will live. (Deut 30:1–6)

As he was finishing the document of the old covenant, Moses envisioned that its element of cursing would prevail: the people of Israel would be scat- tered to the far ends of the world. This exile would not be due to the failure of the old covenant itself but would be traced to the failure of the old cov- enant people to obey their obligations as covenant partners. Still, the faith- ful God promised to regather his dispersed people, bring them back to the Promised Land, and cause them to flourish. The means of bringing about this salvation would be the circumcision of their hearts, by which the people of God would love him fully and live for him faithfully.

Centuries later, Jeremiah offers a prophecy spelling out in greater detail this divine rescue scheme:

> "Look, the days are coming"—this is the LORD's declaration— "when I will make a new covenant with the house of Israel and with the house of Judah. This one will not be like the covenant I made with their ancestors on the day I took them by the hand to

lead them out of the land of Egypt—my covenant that they broke even though I am their master"—the LORD's declaration. "Instead, this is the covenant I will make with the house of Israel after those days"—the LORD's declaration. "I will put my teaching within them and write it on their hearts. I will be their God, and they will be my people. No longer will one teach his neighbor or his brother, saying, 'Know the LORD,' for they will all know me, from the least to the greatest of them"—this is the LORD's declaration. "For I will forgive their iniquity and never again remember their sin." (Jer 31:31–34)

Jeremiah explains what we earlier noted, that the demise of the old covenant would not be due to any intrinsic defect in the covenant itself. Rather, the disobedience of the people to the old covenant would make them the covenantal party at fault. Still, the old covenant itself had a built-in obsolescence. From the beginning of his creation of, and covenanting with, his people, God had designed the old covenant to be replaced by a second and better covenant: a new covenant.[39]

Features of this new pact will include, first, an interiority of the divine law: it will be written on the hearts of the new covenant people. Second, it will include the fulfillment of the earlier divine promise, "I will be their God, and they will be my people" (cf. Exod 29:45–46; Lev 26:11–12). Third, in distinction from the old covenant community, with its mixed membership (both believers and unbelievers), the community of the new covenant will consist of believers only. Fourth, the new covenant will deal decisively with the problem of sin and offer forgiveness for all iniquities.

Both Ezekiel and Joel underscore that this new covenant will be associated with the Holy Spirit. According to the prophecy of Ezekiel: "I will also sprinkle clean water on you, and you will be clean. I will cleanse you from all

---

[39] The letter to the Hebrews uses the language of "first covenant" and "second covenant" to describe these two arrangements. Moreover, it emphasizes that God found fault with his old covenant people; they were to blame for the failure of the first covenant. Furthermore, Hebrews describes the second covenant as a "better covenant, which has been established on better promises." Finally, by Jeremiah's prophecy of a new covenant, God "has declared that the first is obsolete. And what is obsolete and growing old is about to pass away" (Heb 8:6–13).

your impurities and all your idols. I will give you a new heart and put a new spirit within you; I will remove your heart of stone and give you a heart of flesh. I will place my Spirit within you and cause you to follow my statutes and carefully observe my ordinances" (Ezek 36:25–27). Elements of the new covenant revealed in earlier prophecies include the forgiveness of sin (now portrayed with the powerful image of washing with water) and the gift of a new heart (recalling circumcision of the heart). The new element is the promise of the indwelling of the Holy Spirit, who will prompt and empower the new covenant people's obedience to their covenantal obligations, a feature the old covenant lacked.

Joel's prophecy focuses on this last aspect of the dynamic presence of the Spirit in the new covenant: "After this I will pour out my Spirit on all humanity; then your sons and your daughters will prophesy, your old men will have dreams, and your young men will see visions. I will even pour out my Spirit on the male and female slaves in those days" (Joel 2:28–29). According to Joel, the work of the Holy Spirit will no longer be confined to a powerful activity among the leaders of the people of Israel. Rather, a fresh, unprecedented outpouring of the Spirit will target all kinds of people: men and women, young and old, slaves and free. Indeed, "in the last days" (Acts 2:17, citing Joel 2:28) salvation will go out to the ends of the earth as the Holy Spirit is poured out on all humanity. In fact, "everyone who calls on the name of the LORD will be saved" (Joel 2:32).

This Old Testament expectation of a new covenant associated with a fresh, unprecedented outpouring of the Holy Spirit carries into the New Testament. John the Baptist continues and heightens this anticipation as he announces to the crowds, "I baptize you with water, but one who is more powerful than I am is coming. I am not worthy to untie the strap of his sandals. He will baptize you with the Holy Spirit and fire" (Luke 3:16). Unbeknownst to John, the Messiah of whom he speaks is already in his midst. Still, John the Baptist prophesies that this Coming One will baptize his followers with the Holy Spirit. In a similar note, John refers to the Messiah as "the Lamb of God, who takes away the sin of the world" (John 1:29) and testifies, "I saw the Spirit descending from heaven like a dove, and he rested on him. I didn't know him, but he who sent me to baptize with water told me, 'The one you see the Spirit descending and resting on—he is the one who baptizes with the Holy Spirit'" (vv. 32–33). The Holy Spirit rests on the Messiah, who will in turn baptize his followers with that same Spirit.

As this long-awaited Messiah, Jesus himself continues and intensifies the expectation of a new covenant associated with a fresh, unprecedented outpouring of the Holy Spirit:

> On the last and most important day of the festival, Jesus stood up and cried out, "If anyone is thirsty, let him come to me and drink. The one who believes in me, as the Scripture has said, will have streams of living water flow from deep within him." He said this about the Spirit. Those who believed in Jesus were going to receive the Spirit, for the Spirit had not yet been given because Jesus had not yet been glorified. (John 7:37–39)

"The hour" for which Jesus had come into this world had not yet arrived (John 2:4; 4:21, 23; 7:30; 8:20).[40] Thus, at the time Jesus utters these words, they constitute a promise for all of his disciples following his death, resurrection, ascension, and outpouring of the Holy Spirit on the day of Pentecost. That fresh, unprecedented pouring out of the Spirit will result in Jesus's followers experiencing an abundance of life, a fullness that Jesus compares to the flowing of rivers within them.

Moreover, as Jesus's hour for him to depart draws nearer, he comforts the apostles with this promise: "I will ask the Father, and he will give you another Counselor to be with you forever. He is the Spirit of truth. The world is unable to receive him because it doesn't see him or know him. But you do know him, because he remains with you and will be in you" (John 14:16–17). It is not as though Jesus's followers are unacquainted with the Holy Spirit; indeed, he is *with them*. At the same time, Jesus promises his disciples a more intimate relationship with the Spirit: in the future, the Spirit will be *in them*.

Following his death, burial, and resurrection, Jesus continues and heightens the expectation of a new, unprecedented outpouring of the Holy Spirit. Luke underscores the preparation for this event at the end of his Gospel and the beginning of his second volume, Acts. In the Gospel, Jesus appears to his

---

[40] The Gospel of John also affirms the arrival of Jesus's "hour" (12:23, 27; 13:1; 17:1).

disciples and instructs them, "This is what is written: The Messiah would suffer and rise from the dead the third day, and repentance for forgiveness of sins would be proclaimed in his name to all the nations, beginning at Jerusalem. You are witnesses of these things. And look, I am sending you what my Father promised. As for you, stay in the city until you are empowered from on high" (Luke 24:46–49). In order for the apostles to be witnesses to the Messiah's suffering, death, resurrection, and promise of the forgiveness of sin, they have to wait in Jerusalem for the promise of the Father, a divine empowerment for their mission of proclaiming the gospel.

Luke begins his second book with similar instructions from Jesus to his disciples: "While he was with them, he commanded them not to leave Jerusalem, but to wait for the Father's promise. 'Which,' he said, 'you have heard me speak about; for John baptized with water, but you will be baptized with the Holy Spirit in a few days'" (Acts 1:4–5). Jesus heightens the expectation by tying it to an event that is poised to occur: in just a few days, Jesus will baptize his disciples with the promised Holy Spirit. This is a promise with Old Testament roots, amplified by John the Baptist and announced and ultimately fulfilled by Jesus, who, along with the Father, will pour out the Spirit in a fresh, unprecedented way.

Just as he promised, Jesus pours out the Holy Spirit within that short time frame: "When the day of Pentecost had arrived, they were all together in one place. Suddenly a sound like that of a violent rushing wind came from heaven, and it filled the whole house where they were staying. They saw tongues like flames of fire that separated and rested on each one of them. Then they were all filled with the Holy Spirit and began to speak in different tongues, as the Spirit enabled them" (Acts 2:1–4). Two expressions— "baptized with the Holy Spirit" and "filled with the Holy Spirit"—describe the beginning of the fulfillment of that long-awaited promise of a new, unprecedented outpouring of the Spirit on Pentecost. As the narrative continues, Peter explains the source of this inundation: "Since [Jesus] has been exalted to the right hand of God and has received from the Father the promised Holy Spirit, he has poured out what you both see and hear" (Acts 2:33).

This baptism with the Holy Spirit occurs, first, historically on the day of Pentecost and, second and derivatively, as an initial experience of salvation for all Christians. It is "the mighty work of Jesus Christ by which he inundates people with the Holy Spirit for incorporation into his body. Jesus is the baptizer (John 1:33), the Christian is the one baptized, the Spirit is the element, and the purpose is incorporation into the church (1 Cor. 12:12–13)."[41]

The Experience of Baptism with the Spirit

Our pneumatology locates this mighty work of Christ at the beginning of salvation, coinciding with, yet distinct from, the other mighty acts of regeneration, union with Christ, justification, and more.[42] Several reasons can be offered for considering baptism with the Spirit to be a part of the initial experiences of salvation: (1) According to Paul, "just as the body is one and has many parts, and all the parts of that body, though many, are one body—so also is Christ. For we were all baptized with one Spirit into one body—whether Jews or Greeks, whether slaves or free—and we were all given one Spirit to drink" (1 Cor 12:12–13). "In the midst of his discussion of spiritual gifts and before he talks about the diversity of spiritually-gifted Christians, Paul underscores a point of commonality for them: all are baptized in the same Spirit into one body."[43] This common experience, universal for all Christians, implies that baptism with the Spirit is an initial experience, inaugural for all Christians.[44]

---

[41] Allison, *The Baker Compact Dictionary of Theological Terms*, s.v. "baptism with/in/by the Holy Spirit." For a similar idea see Ferguson, *The Holy Spirit*, 193–94.

[42] For a similar view see Horton, *Rediscovering the Holy Spirit*, 170–201; John R. W. Stott, *The Baptism and Fullness of the Holy Spirit* (Downers Grove: Inter-Varsity Press, 1964); Ferguson, *The Holy Spirit*, 87–89. For other views on baptism with the Spirit see J. Rodman Williams, *Renewal Theology*, 3 vols. (Grand Rapids: Zondervan, 1996), 2:137–409; Gary McGee, ed., *Initial Evidence: Historical and Biblical Perspectives on the Pentecostal Doctrine of Spirit Baptism* (Eugene: Wipf & Stock, 1991); Kilian McDonnell and George T. Montague, eds., *Christian Initiation and Baptism in the Holy Spirit: Evidence from the First Eight Centuries* (Collegeville: Liturgical Press, 1991); Frank D. Macchia, "The Kingdom and the Power: Spirit Baptism in Pentecostal and Ecumenical Perspective," in *The Work of the Spirit: Pneumatology and Pentecostalism*, ed. Michael Welker (Grand Rapids: Eerdmans, 2006), 109–25; Chad Owen Brand, ed., *Perspectives on Spirit Baptism: Five Views* (Nashville: B&H, 2004).

[43] Gregg R. Allison, "Baptism with and Filling of the Holy Spirit," *Southern Baptist Journal of Theology* 16, no. 4 (Winter 2012): 6; available online at http://equip .sbts.edu/wp-content/uploads/2014/02/SBJT-16.4-Allison-p-4-21.pdf.

[44] Stott, *The Baptism and Fullness of the Holy Spirit*, 21.

(2) In his Pentecost message, Peter locates baptism with the Spirit at the moment of salvation. As his listeners are "pierced to the heart" by the gospel, Peter instructs them:

> "Repent and be baptized, each of you, in the name of Jesus Christ for the forgiveness of your sins, and you will receive the gift of the Holy Spirit. For the promise is for you and for your children, and for all who are far off, as many as the Lord our God will call." With many other words he testified and strongly urged them, saying, "Be saved from this corrupt generation!" So those who accepted his message were baptized, and that day about three thousand people were added to them. (Acts 2:37–41)

Among the constellation of activities narrated—hearing and accepting the gospel message, being convicted and repenting of sin, believing in Jesus Christ (v. 44 calls those who respond to Peter "believers"), experiencing forgiveness of sin, and obeying by being baptized—is the focus of our attention: receiving the gift of the Holy Spirit. This expression is just another way of referring to what Jesus had previously promised the disciples ("You will be baptized with the Holy Spirit in a few days," 1:5), what Luke had previously narrated about the disciples ("They were all filled with the Holy Spirit," 2:4), and what Peter had previously explained (concerning "the promised Holy Spirit, [Jesus] has poured out what you both see and hear," 2:33). Thus, the opening of Acts narrates the pattern of salvation as involving adherence to the gospel, repentance from sin, belief in Christ, forgiveness of sins, water baptism, and baptism with the Holy Spirit. While distinct activities, these are united as part of the one constellation of initiatory events that effect salvation.

(3) In Luke's two narratives of the salvation of Cornelius, together with Cornelius's family and friends, baptism with the Spirit occurs as Cornelius and company are listening to Peter's message of the gospel. In the first account, Luke narrates the saving events:

> While Peter was still speaking these words, the Holy Spirit came down on all those who heard the message. The circumcised believers who had come with Peter were amazed because the gift of the Holy Spirit had been poured out even on the Gentiles. For they

heard them speaking in other tongues and declaring the greatness of God.

Then Peter responded, "Can anyone withhold water and prevent these people from being baptized, who have received the Holy Spirit just as we have?" He commanded them to be baptized in the name of Jesus Christ. (Acts 10:44–48)

"While the falling of the Holy Spirit upon these Gentiles was certainly unexpected and unprecedented, the fact that this event was Jesus baptizing them with the Holy Spirit was unmistakable. Peter and those with him heard the proof: now, even the Gentiles were rehearsing the mighty acts of God in unusual utterances, as the Jewish disciples had done on the day of Pentecost when they were baptized with the Spirit."[45] Moreover, Peter describes this event as the outpouring of "the gift of the Holy Spirit" (10:45; cf. 2:33, 38). This baptism with the Spirit occurs together with the message of the gospel and water baptism.

Luke's second narrative about Cornelius offers Peter's reminiscence of the saving events: "As I began to speak, the Holy Spirit came down on them, just as on us at the beginning. I remembered the word of the Lord, how he said, 'John baptized with water, but you will be baptized with the Holy Spirit.' If, then, God gave them the same gift that he also gave to us when we believed in the Lord Jesus Christ, how could I possibly hinder God?" (Acts 11:15–17).

The startling experience of his Gentile audience reminded Peter of the startling experience of the 120 disciples—among which he himself was included—on the day of Pentecost. The parallelism is striking:

- The Holy Spirit had fallen on the Jewish disciples; the Holy Spirit fell on the Gentiles.
- The Jewish disciples had been baptized with the Spirit; the Gentiles were baptized with the Holy Spirit.
- God gave the gift of the Holy Spirit to the Jewish disciples when they believed in Christ, who had promised them such a

---

[45] Allison, "Baptism with and Filling of the Holy Spirit," 7.

baptism (Luke 3:15–17; Acts 1:4–5); God gave "the same gift [of the Holy Spirit]" to the Gentiles when they believed.[46]

The parallelism between the experience of the Jewish disciples on the day of Pentecost and the experience of the Gentiles confirms that baptism with the Spirit occurred as the Gentiles believed in Jesus Christ for salvation. Of particular note is Peter's identification of the day of Pentecost with the coming of the Spirit as the occasion "when we [the disciples and himself] believed in the Lord Jesus Christ." Even for the disciples of the Lord, baptism with the Spirit and faith in Christ were contemporaneous.[47]

These passages affirm that baptism with the Holy Spirit is (1) initiatory; that is, it takes place at the beginning of salvation and occurs in conjunction with hearing the gospel, repentance from sin, belief in Christ, forgiveness of sins, and water baptism. Moreover, baptism with the Spirit is (2) universal; that is, it is true for all Christians and not just for some; (3) purposeful; that is, it incorporates believers into the body of Christ, the church; and (4) indelible; that is, it effects a permanent membership in the body of Christ, from which no genuine believer may fall away.[48]

Pentecostal and Charismatic Understanding of Baptism with the Spirit

Pentecostal and charismatic theology dissents from this view and locates baptism with the Spirit as either logically or temporally subsequent to the initial experience of salvation. In terms of logical subsequence, the notion is that baptism with the Spirit and salvation occur at the same time but that Spirit baptism is logically dependent on salvation: salvation is the necessary ground for baptism with the Spirit. In terms of temporal subsequence, the idea is that baptism with the Spirit occurs sometime after salvation:

---

[46] At the Council of Jerusalem, Peter makes the same point when he recounts the experience of the Gentiles as he preached to them: "And God, who knows the heart, bore witness to them by giving them the Holy Spirit, just as he also did to us" (Acts 15:8).

[47] Allison, "Baptism with and Filling of the Holy Spirit," 7–8.

[48] See the later discussion in this chapter on assurance of salvation.

seconds, minutes, hours, days, weeks, years, or even decades after a person experiences salvation, she is baptized with the Spirit. In terms of a description of this event, it is "a profoundly internal experience of the Spirit of God moving throughout like wind or fire until all barriers are breached and the Holy Spirit pervades everything."[49] In this view such an experience is different from salvation, which includes the work of the Holy Spirit for conviction of sin, regeneration, and other mighty divine acts. Indeed, according to some Pentecostal and charismatic theologians, the experience of salvation includes Jesus's baptizing new believers with the Spirit, in accordance with 1 Cor 12:13. Still, such salvation is not the reception of the gift of the Spirit, which is believed to logically or temporally follow it. Indeed, "the purpose of this Spirit baptism is not soteriological—that is, to save nonbelievers—but missional—that is, to empower Christians for effective evangelism and ministry."[50]

While the case for this Pentecostal/charismatic view is rather extensive, two key biblical passages deserve treatment. Proponents commonly appeal to these passages, which appear at first glance to support their position. The first is the delay in the reception of the Holy Spirit by the new believers in Samaria: "When the apostles who were at Jerusalem heard that Samaria had received the word of God, they sent Peter and John to them. After they went down there, they prayed for them so the Samaritans might receive the Holy Spirit because he had not yet come down on any of them. (They had only been baptized in the name of the Lord Jesus.) Then Peter and John laid their hands on them, and they received the Holy Spirit" (Acts 8:14–17). According to the Pentecostal/charismatic interpretation, this narrative recounts the conversion of a large number of Samaritans ("When they believed Philip, as he proclaimed the good news about the kingdom of God and the name of Jesus Christ, both men and women were baptized," 8:12), yet none of them are baptized in the Holy Spirit when they are saved. Only when Peter and John pray for and lay hands on them do the Samaritans receive the Holy Spirit. The conclusion is that baptism with the Spirit is subsequent to salvation.

---

[49] Williams, *Renewal Theology*, 2:203.
[50] Allison, "Baptism with and Filling of the Holy Spirit," 8.

On closer examination, Luke's narrative actually highlights this delay as an unusual experience of the Spirit. Verse 15—"because he had not yet come down on any of them"—is an explanation "indicating the reason why the Samaritans still needed to receive the Holy Spirit. This explanatory comment points to an unusual experience; delay is not normative. Indeed, if it were the case that this delay portrays the normal reality of experiencing the Holy Spirit, there would be no need for an explanation."[51] When we Christians read Luke's narrative and compare our experience of receiving the Holy Spirit at salvation with the Samaritans' experience of receiving the Spirit after salvation, we would be confused if not for Luke's highlighting their experience as abnormal. Accordingly, the Samaritans' delayed reception of the Spirit is not normative for Christians; baptism with the Spirit subsequent to salvation is not supported by this narrative.

The second key passage to which Pentecostal and charismatic theologians point in support of their position is Acts 19:1–7:

> While Apollos was in Corinth, Paul traveled through the interior regions and came to Ephesus. He found some disciples and asked them, "Did you receive the Holy Spirit when you believed?"
>
> "No," they told him, "we haven't even heard that there is a Holy Spirit."
>
> "Into what then were you baptized?" he asked them.
>
> "Into John's baptism," they replied.
>
> Paul said, "John baptized with a baptism of repentance, telling the people that they should believe in the one who would come after him, that is, in Jesus."
>
> When they heard this, they were baptized into the name of the Lord Jesus. And when Paul had laid his hands on them, the Holy Spirit came on them, and they began to speak in other tongues and to prophesy. Now there were about twelve men in all.

According to the Pentecostal/charismatic interpretation, this narrative may describe either Christians—the term "disciples" is used of them—who much later are baptized in the Spirit, or these "disciples" of John the Baptist becoming Christians through Paul's presentation of the gospel yet subsequently

---

[51] Allison, 12.

being baptized in the Spirit. In either case, salvation is the ground for their reception of the Holy Spirit.

On closer examination, Luke's narrative actually highlights baptism with the Spirit as part and parcel of salvation. Paul's question—"Did you receive the Holy Spirit when you believed?" (19:2)—"underscores the normal experience of Christians; we receive the Holy Spirit upon embracing the gospel. Thus, the lack of receiving the Spirit pointed to an abnormal experience on the part of these disciples of John the Baptist. Indeed, these twelve men were not even believers in Jesus Christ, as the rest of the narrative demonstrates."[52] Thus, Paul preaches the gospel, the men believe in Christ and are baptized into his name, Paul lays his hands on them, they receive the Holy Spirit, and they speak in tongues and prophesy as evidence of their baptism with the Spirit—all elements of their experience of salvation through Christ. Accordingly, baptism with the Spirit as an essential part of believing in Christ for salvation is normative for Christians.

Accordingly, our pneumatology considers baptism with the Holy Spirit to be one of the mighty divine acts that takes place at the beginning of salvation, in conjunction with, yet different from, regeneration, union with Christ, adoption, and more.

Sealing/Down Payment/Guarantee/Firstfruits

All those who embrace the gospel and confess the lordship of Jesus Christ by means of the Holy Spirit are in turn marked by the Spirit: "In [Christ] you also were sealed with the promised Holy Spirit when you heard the word of truth, the gospel of your salvation, and when you believed. The Holy Spirit is the down payment of our inheritance, until the redemption of the possession, to the praise of his glory" (Eph 1:13–14; cf. 2 Cor 1:22; 5:5). This work of the Spirit underscores the partial nature of salvation: during their earthly life, Christians are truly redeemed, yet their redemption is incomplete. In this age of the Spirit, they enjoy his presence, empowerment, victory over sin, growth in Christlikeness, and the like—but only in part. Christians yearn for the day when their redemption will be completed. In the age that is still to come, at Jesus's return, then and only then will believers experience the

---

[52] Allison, 13.

divine presence face-to-face, indefatigable power, total victory over sin, full conformity to the image of Christ, and much more.

In the meantime—in this age—the Spirit serves as the seal of this future work of fulfillment. He is the divine down payment, a type of earnest money paid with the promise of the remainder still to be remunerated. The Holy Spirit is the firstfruits, the initial portion of the harvest gathered in anticipation of the rest still to be reaped. He is the guarantee for believers that "he who started a good work in you will carry it on to completion until the day of Christ Jesus" (Phil 1:6).[53]

In light of bearing the Spirit's mark, Christians adopt two postures. The first is an avoidance of sin, in accordance with the biblical command: "Don't grieve God's Holy Spirit. You were sealed by him for the day of redemption" (Eph 4:30). How nonsensical would it be for Christians to sadden the Spirit, whose mark of redemption they bear, by rebelling against him! The second posture is an anticipation of salvation in its fullness: like the creation itself yearns for renewal from decay, "we ourselves who have the Spirit as the firstfruits—we also groan within ourselves, eagerly waiting for adoption, the redemption of our bodies" (Rom 8:23). Believers and the church wait for the return of Christ (1 Thess 1:10) and the resurrection that the Spirit will effect upon the Son's return. The "already-not yet" framework, rehearsed above, demands that Christians long for the partial salvation they enjoy *now* to give way to the fullness of salvation they will enjoy *then*.

Assurance of Salvation

Assurance of salvation is "the subjective confidence that is the privilege of all genuine believers that they will remain Christians throughout their life. This doctrine is dependent on the doctrine of perseverance, which is God's mighty act to preserve true Christians by his power through their ongoing faith, until their salvation is complete (1 Pet. 1:5)."[54] To take the latter aspect first: God preserves his people for ultimate salvation. Through his presence, inspired Scripture, discipline, protection from the evil one, and more, God conserves those who belong to him (1 Cor 1:8–9; Rom 8:31–39). On this

---

[53] For further discussion of these three metaphors see Allen, *Poured Out*, 89–90.
[54] Allison, *The Baker Compact Dictionary of Theological Terms*, 27.

basis, the former aspect applies: Christians are privileged to know that they will remain believers throughout their life and will enjoy eternal life. Though various reasons exist for why Christians lack assurance of salvation—lack of or poor teaching about it, depression, persistent sin, demonic attack—such assurance is not reserved for some but available to all who genuinely know Jesus Christ.

Assurance of salvation is a work of the Holy Spirit. As Scripture guarantees Christians, "You did not receive a spirit of slavery to fall back into fear. Instead, you received the Spirit of adoption, by whom we cry out, '*Abba*, Father!' The Spirit himself testifies together with our spirit that we are God's children, and if children, also heirs—heirs of God and coheirs with Christ—if indeed we suffer with him so that we may also be glorified with him" (Rom 8:15–17). The Spirit of adoption, by whom enslaving fear is cast out and recognition of the fatherhood of God is voiced, provides assurance. Called the "inner witness" or "secret testimony" of the Spirit, this subjective confidence derives from the Spirit's bearing witness to the believer's spirit, or inner core.[55] And the message is that of adoption: Christians are and will continue to be children of God, now and forever; they will be fully conformed to the image of Christ and be glorified with him (Rom 8:29). Again, this assurance is not for those who merely profess faith in him; rather, it is promised to genuine believers, those who suffer with Christ. His pattern was first humiliation, then exaltation. So is the pattern of his followers: first suffering, then glorification. For those who follow the pattern, the assurance of salvation accompanies, comforts, cheers, and motivates them along the way.[56]

Through the Holy Spirit, the cry "*Abba*, Father!" continues to resound alongside the cry "Jesus is Lord!" (1 Cor 12:3) when Christians are faced with a degree of persecution that, without divine aid, would lead to their abandoning the faith. Genuine believers do not recant but continue to confess Christ even as they are being led to their death. Stephen is the quintessential model

---

[55] Among others, John Wesley developed this aspect of the witness of the Spirit. See John Wesley, "The Witness of the Spirit" (1746). For further development of Wesley's position see Winfield H. Bevins, "The Historical Development of Wesley's Doctrine of the Spirit," *Wesleyan Theological Journal* 41/2 (Fall 2006): 161–81.

[56] Gregg R. Allison, "Assurance of Salvation," in *Evangelical Dictionary of World Missions*, ed. Scott Moreau (Grand Rapids: Baker, 2000), 92; cf. Allison, "Eternal Security," *EDWM*, 318–19.

as he, "full of the Holy Spirit" (Acts 7:55), continued to bear witness to Jesus Christ as he was martyred. Such perseverance is promised to persecuted believers and comes through the Holy Spirit (Matt 10:20).

While the testimony of the Spirit often seems mysterious and can even create confusion in some quarters, the assurance to which he bears witness is quite straightforward: "This is how we know that we remain in him and he in us: He has given us of his Spirit" (1 John 4:13). Assurance becomes a matter of believing the divine promise that God has given the Spirit of adoption to his children. That Spirit bears witness that these children belong to God now and forever.[57]

Guidance

Statements such as "The Holy Spirit is leading me to do such and such" or "The Spirit told me to say such and such" have become so commonplace that a tendency has developed in some circles to avoid discussion of the guidance of the Spirit. However, this work of the Spirit is well supported biblically and confirmed in genuine experiences of his guidance in the lives of both individual Christians and churches.

Guidance in Fulfilling the Moral Law

To sample biblical affirmations of Spirit guidance, we see that the New Testament emphasizes:

---

[57] It is with this hope of the Spirit's bearing witness of adoption that Isaac Watts expressed in his hymn "Why Should the Children of a King [Go Mourning All Their Day?]" the following two stanzas:

> Assure my conscience of her part
> In the Redeemer's Blood;
> And bear Thy witness with my heart
> That I am born of God.

> Thou art the Earnest of His Love,
> The Pledge of joys to come;
> And Thy soft wings, celestial Dove,
> Will safe convey me home.

Cited in Rothenbusch, "'Is Not This the Land of Beulah?'," 55.

What the law could not do since it was weakened by the flesh, God did. He condemned sin in the flesh by sending his own Son in the likeness of sinful flesh as a sin offering, in order that the law's requirement would be fulfilled in us who do not walk according to the flesh but according to the Spirit. (Rom 8:3–4)

An extended discussion of the conflict between living according to the flesh and living according to the Spirit ensues, highlighting this point about moral guidance of the Spirit: when believers walk in step with the Spirit, they fulfill the righteous requirements of the divine law (8:4), experience life and peace (8:6), and please God (8:8). Thus, anyone claiming to be guided by the Spirit should bear the fruit of holiness, love God and others, obey the commands and trust the promises of Scripture, repent when sin occurs, resist temptation and the wiles of the evil one, and more. Being led by God's Spirit as sons (8:14–15) means living as true, righteous heirs of God.

A point of clarification is needed. The Spirit's guidance has nothing to do with moralism, behaviorism, legalism, or the like. Moralism is an approach to Christianity that focuses on keeping the moral law or adhering to moral standards in an effort to earn salvation (e.g., Rom 3:20). Behaviorism in a Christian context underscores obedience to God in terms of right conduct, with little or no concern for matters of pleasing God from the heart—with one's whole being and not just one's actions (e.g., Isa 29:13; Matt 15:8). Legalism is "the approach that advocates obeying additional commands and prohibitions beyond biblical norms, for the increase in holiness and/or to merit favor with God. Legalism flows from the human tendency to seek to work for everything one receives, including salvation and God's blessings" (e.g., Col 2:16–23).[58] Moralism, behaviorism, and legalism contradict the gospel of Christ and the sanctifying guidance of the Holy Spirit.

Indeed, instead of these three subtle and dangerous counterfeits, Scripture urges believers to follow the Holy Spirit in order to make progress in Christlikeness and to overcome temptation and sin:

I say then, walk by the Spirit and you will certainly not carry out the desire of the flesh. For the flesh desires what is against the Spirit, and the Spirit desires what is against the flesh; these are opposed to

---

[58] Allison, *The Baker Compact Dictionary of Theological Terms*, s.v. "legalism."

each other, so that you don't do what you want. But if you are led by
the Spirit, you are not under the law. Now the works of the flesh are
obvious. . . . But the fruit of the Spirit is love, joy, peace, patience,
kindness, goodness, faithfulness, gentleness, and self-control. (Gal
5:16–19, 22–23)

Not moralism, behaviorism, or legalism but being guided by and walking
in the Spirit is Scripture's prescription for pleasing God and doing his will,
which in turn is ultimately satisfying for those who so live.

Guidance in Personal Matters

In addition to moral guidance, the Spirit also set the course for believers
and churches by giving specific guidance as to the where, when, how, and
whom of career, ministry, marriage or singleness, family, and more. While
controversial in some circles, such guidance is well supported by Scripture
and derives from the fact that this is the age of the Spirit. As he has led
Christians and churches in the past, so he continues to guide them today.

The presence and power of the Holy Spirit has directed the expansion
of the church from Jerusalem to Judea and Samaria and ultimately to all the
corners of the globe (Acts 1:8). This general direction has been accompanied by the Spirit's specific guidance of the church to encounter particular
people and plant itself in particular places.[59] Two biblical examples serve as
illustrations. The first regards Philip, fresh off his fruitful evangelization of
the Samaritans (8:4–25). At first, an angel directs Philip to travel along a
particular road in the middle of a desert (8:26). Traveling on the same road
as a eunuch from Ethiopia, Philip is commanded by the Holy Spirit to join
the eunuch's caravan (8:29). After leading the eunuch to Christ and baptizing him (8:30–39), Philip is whisked away by the Spirit and continues
his preaching ministry elsewhere (8:40). This encounter is no mere chance
meeting in the middle of nowhere but is orchestrated by the specific guidance of the Spirit.

---

[59] The following section is condensed from Gregg R. Allison, "Holy God and
Holy People: The Intersection of Pneumatology and Ecclesiology," in *Building on the
Foundations of Evangelical Theology: Essays in Honor of John S. Feinberg*, ed. Gregg R.
Allison and Stephen J. Wellum (Wheaton: Crossway, 2015), 243–47.

The second example regards Paul, Silas, and Timothy (later joined by Luke) at the outset of Paul's so-called second missionary journey (Acts 16:6–18:22). As missionaries, their calling and responsibility is to preach the gospel while they travel; however, something unusual occurs: the Holy Spirit forbids them to announce the good news in Phrygia or Galatia/Asia (Acts 16:6), then prevents them from evangelizing Bithynia (16:7). Through a night vision, Paul and the team are redirected toward Macedonia (16:9–10). They travel 400 miles without engaging in the missionary task for which they have been sent, until they reach Philippi (16:11–12). Finding some women at prayer alongside a river, Paul preaches the gospel and leads Lydia to the Lord; she and her household are baptized as the first converts in Asia (16:13–15). These conversions are followed by the exorcism of a demon who preys upon a young fortune-teller (16:16-18) and the salvation of a jailer and his family (16:25–34). Accordingly, through the specific guidance of the Holy Spirit, the church of Philippi is founded.

These clear examples of specific guidance by the Holy Spirit should not mask the difficulties that Christians sometimes encounter in discerning the direction of the Holy Spirit. Even Scripture narrates such complicatedness. In Acts 19–21, Luke narrates four episodes of the leading of the Spirit. In the first, Paul resolves in the Holy Spirit to go to Rome via Jerusalem (19:21). Luke highlights that the apostle's personal determination comes through the guidance of the Spirit. According to the second narrative, Paul is constrained by the Holy Spirit to travel first to Jerusalem, where the apostle will encounter imprisonment and suffering (20:22–24). Luke underscores the definitive nature of the Spirit's leading of Paul ("I am on my way to Jerusalem, compelled by the Spirit") as well as a certain vagueness about what awaits Paul in Jerusalem ("not knowing what I will encounter there, except that in every town the Holy Spirit warns me that chains and afflictions are waiting for me").[60]

---

[60] As John B. F. Miller, "Not Knowing What Will Happen to Me There," in *The Unrelenting God: God's Action in Scripture: Essays in Honor of Beverly Roberts Gaventa*, ed. David J. Downs and Matthew L. Skinner (Grand Rapids: Eerdmans, 2013), 55, explains, "The Spirit's testimony leaves Paul with an awareness that chains and suffering await him—an awareness that apparently lacks any detail. Paul's certainty that he understands the direction in which the Spirit leads is offset by an amorphous image of what he will find when he gets there."

Third, as Paul travels and intentionally visits the Christians in Tyre, they plead with him "through the Spirit" not to go to Jerusalem (Acts 21:4–5). Luke does not resolve the obvious narrative tension between the apostle's Spirit-prompted resolve that he must go to Jerusalem and these disciples' Spirit-prompted entreaty that he must not travel to Jerusalem.[61] The fourth episode features a warning from the prophet Agabus, who "took Paul's belt, tied his own feet and hands, and said, 'This is what the Holy Spirit says: "In this way the Jews in Jerusalem will bind the man who owns this belt and deliver him over to the Gentiles."' When we heard this, both we and the local people pleaded with him not to go up to Jerusalem" (21:11–12). Once again, the narrative tension is not resolved: Agabus prophesies by the Spirit that the Jews would seize Paul if he traveled to Jerusalem. The Christians in Caesarea consider the prophet's message to be a word from the Holy Spirit and, expressing their deep love for the apostle, urge Paul to desist from his intention—prompted by the same Spirit—to go to Jerusalem and thus avoid capture. Ultimately, the Caesarean disciples yield to whatever the Lord wills for Paul.[62]

In conclusion,

> not only does the Holy Spirit in a general sense propel the church on its missional movement; he also specifically guides the announcement of the gospel to particular people and the planting of the church in particular places. At the same time, such guidance may be interpreted differently by different people, without such tension necessarily being resolved. The church today is called to follow such Spirit-given guidance while being open to differing understandings of such direction.[63]

As believers and the church live in the age of the Spirit, they rightly expect him to guide them to accomplish both the moral will of God and his specific

---

[61] "The passage would be rather unremarkable if it did not indicate a dramatic tension between characters who express two very different understandings of direction from the same Spirit." Miller, 56.

[62] "These passages feature anything but straightforward experiences of the Spirit. Different characters are guided by the same Spirit in different directions, with little or no explanation." Miller, 57.

[63] Allison, "Holy God and Holy People," 246–47.

will for them. Without waiting for or depending on dramatic guidance from the Spirit, they keep in step with the Spirit moment by moment through even the most mundane matters of life.

Affirming the Spirit's guidance raises the practical question of how one is to discern whether it is the Spirit who is directing a particular course of action or if such an idea is simply the product of one's imagination—or worse. On the one hand, one must be "in the Spirit" to discern the leading of the Holy Spirit. Certainly, this subjective element may frighten or worry others, because it can lead to questions about personal understanding of the Spirit's guidance. Still, this subjectivity is inescapable. On the other hand, several "objective" criteria help in the process of discerning the leading of the Holy Spirit: (1) Scripture: Is such guidance in accordance with the Word of God? Though a specific passage may not be invoked, is there biblical precedent or a biblical pattern for such a course of action? (2) Christology: Does such direction exalt Jesus Christ? Or will the alleged guidance wrongly foster one's own reputation and/or promote one's own fame? (3) Sanctification: Does such guidance stimulate progress in holiness? Does it lead to walking in the way that Christ walked? (4) Missionality: Is such guidance directed at engaging others with the gospel so that they may become disciples of Jesus Christ? (5) Ecclesiology: Does the church community—especially those members who know the person well—confirm this direction of the Spirit? Though the tendency is to dismiss the church's authority in such matters (and ready examples exist of carnal churches being obstacles to the Lord's will), is such rejection not due more to personal frustration of not getting one's (wrong-headed) way? (6) Pneumatology: Does such direction bear the fruit of the Spirit, which clearly consists of "love, joy, peace, patience, kindness, goodness, faithfulness, gentleness, and self-control" (Gal 5:22–23); "righteousness, peace, . . . and joy" (Rom 14:17) and "hope" (Rom 15:13); and submitting to one another in the fear of Christ" (Eph 5:19–21)?

This fruit is the result of being filled with/walking in the Spirit, the next topic in our discussion of the Holy Spirit and salvation.

Filling with/Walking in the Holy Spirit

Christians and the church consciously seek the Spirit's guidance by relying on his filling and walking in him. With proper consideration for the difference between Jesus Christ and Christians, our pneumatology affirms that, as the fullness or plenitude of the Holy Spirit pertains to Jesus the Son of God incarnate, the filling or sufficiency of the Spirit pertains analogously to Christ's followers. Two major differences are important to consider. First, while the Son and the Spirit are divine persons eternally related, Christians are not so connected with the Spirit. They are *adopted* sons of God, not *the* Son of God; thus, their relationship to the Spirit is not and cannot be one of *perichoresis* (mutual indwelling of the Son and the Spirit) but is one of *presence* (indwelling by the Spirit). Second, while Jesus the Son is filled with the Holy Spirit *without measure*, Christians are filled with the Spirit *with a limited measure*, one that is adequate for their lives in the age of the Spirit. Diagrammatically:

the one in relationship to the Spirit:	the Son	a son
the kind of relationship:	fullness of the Spirit	filling with the Spirit
the intensity of relationship:	immeasurable	measured

Instructions to believers about the filling of the Spirit are given in Eph 5:18–21:[64]

> Don't get drunk with wine, which leads to reckless living, but be filled by [with] the Spirit: speaking to one another in psalms, hymns, and spiritual songs, singing and making music with your heart to the Lord, giving thanks always for everything to God the Father in the name of our Lord Jesus Christ, submitting to one another in the fear of Christ.

This instruction appears in (1) the imperatival mood; thus it is a command to be obeyed: "be filled by the Spirit"; (2) the present tense; thus it is an ongoing command: to paraphrase, "keep on being filled with the Spirit"; (3) the passive voice; thus it is not an imperative to do something or to engage in some action (e.g., "transform this equation") but a command that

---

[64] The following is adapted from Allison, "Baptism with and Filling of the Holy Spirit," 4–20.

calls for receptivity or submission (e.g., "be transformed"). "The expected or intended response to this command is for Christians to yield to the Holy Spirit, to be controlled—pervaded or permeated—by the Spirit in all their ways, to consciously place themselves under the guidance of the Spirit moment by moment."[65]

Given much confusion about the results or manifestations of being filled with the Spirit, we draw attention to the four phrases that follow the command to submit to the Spirit. Importantly, these phrases (gerunds in English, participles in Greek) portray the Spirit at work among Christians in the gatherings of the church. Indeed, the individualism that is the focus of much contemporary consideration of this passage takes a back seat to the Spirit's activity in the corporate assembly. When church members are filled with the Spirit, their yieldedness will be evidenced by their (1) "speaking to one another in psalms, hymns, and spiritual songs"; that is, genuine community; (2) "singing and making music from your heart to the Lord"; that is, God-honoring worship; (3) "giving thanks always for everything to God the Father in the name of our Lord Jesus Christ"; that is, gratitude expressed in every circumstance; and (4) "submitting to one another in the fear of Christ"; that is, love for one another through mutual submission.[66]

Moreover, beyond underscoring the manifestations of the Spirit's filling in the church, these phrases also provide a mandate for the church. They

> not only indicate the results that flow from Christians obeying the Pauline command and thus being filled with the Spirit; they also absorb some of the imperatival force of the main verb ("be filled") and are thereby constituted concrete activities in which Christians filled with the Spirit are to be engaged. Accordingly, Spirit filled Christians [1] develop authentic community by rebuking, admonishing, correcting, encouraging, and edifying one another; [2] worship the Lord

---

[65] Allison, 15.

[66] See also Köstenberger, "What Does It Mean to Be Filled with the Spirit?", 229–50, who argues that filling with the Spirit in Scripture (Luke-Acts) is always at God's sovereign initiative and discretion, often equipping or strengthening believers to speak God's Word boldly in times of persecution or, in the case of Eph 5:18, to pursue worship and right relationships in keeping with God's creational design.

together with great delight; [3] live intentionally with gratitude; and [4] show preference for and serve one another for Christ's sake.[67]

This is what it means to "be filled with the Spirit."

Such yielding to the Spirit is expressed also as "walking in the Spirit": "I say then, walk by [in] the Spirit and you will certainly not carry out the desire of the flesh. For the flesh desires what is against the Spirit, and the Spirit desires what is against the flesh; these are opposed to each other, so that you don't do what you want" (Gal 5:16–17). Rather than yielding to the promptings of their "flesh," Christians are to yield to the Spirit by walking in him. It is the Spirit who leads them according to the will of God, which is the very thing they desire to do. Their fallen nature wants to drag them away from doing God's will; if they yield to their fleshly desires, they will end up doing the exact opposite of what they truly want to do.[68]

Following a negative list of the fruit of the flesh (e.g., immorality, impurity, idolatry)—iniquities that disqualify people from inheriting the kingdom of God (5:19–21)—a positive list of the fruit of the Spirit appears: "love, joy, peace, patience, kindness, goodness, faithfulness, gentleness, self-control" (5:22–23). Christians filled with the Spirit, who walk in the Spirit, bear the pleasant fruit of Christlikeness. Accordingly, if death results from yielding to sin, "those who belong to Christ Jesus have crucified the flesh with its passions and desires" (5:24). Furthermore, if life abounds as "we live by the Spirit, let us also keep in step with the Spirit" (5:25; cf. Rom 8:4–13).[69]

---

[67] Allison, "Baptism with and Filling of the Holy Spirit," 15.

[68] For a Roman Catholic perspective on the struggle between the Spirit and the flesh, with the promise of freedom, see Congar, *I Believe in the Holy Spirit*, 2.119–33.

[69] Being filled with/walking in/keeping in step with the Spirit is crucial for navigating the rough waters of *adiaphora*, that is, indifferent matters or "activities that are neither moral nor immoral"; Allison, *The Baker Compact Dictionary of Theological Terms*, s.v. "*adiaphora*." Legalism errs on the side of overregulation of such matters; antinomianism errs on the side of laissez-faire or unchecked freedom. Neither solution is proper; rather, following the direction of the Spirit for how he desires individual believers to conduct themselves in these matters is the key. As examples, for some believers and Christian families, the Spirit grants permission to celebrate Christmas and Easter; for others, the Spirit prohibits such celebrations. Also, for some believers and Christian families, the Spirit prompts them to homeschool their children and eat only organic food; for others, the Spirit leads them to send their

Sanctification[70]

Being filled with the Spirit, walking in the Spirit, and keeping in step with the Spirit express one of two aspects of the ongoing reality of sanctification, which is "the cooperative work of God and Christians (Phil. 2:12–13) by which ongoing transformation into greater Christlikeness occurs. . . . Unlike other divine works, which are monergistic (God alone works), sanctification is synergistic. God operates in ways that are proper to his divine agency . . . and Christians work in ways that are proper to their human agency."[71]

Sanctification, therefore, consists of two aspects—one divine, the other human. The divine operation in sanctification encompasses some of the roles of the Holy Spirit: his conviction of sin, exposure of hidden faults, comfort in times of trouble, rebuke in periods of stagnation, empowerment to overcome temptation, and development of a willingness and effort to accomplish God's good pleasure.

One particular aspect is the Spirit's intercession for believers: "In the same way the Spirit also helps us in our weakness, because we do not know what to pray for as we should, but the Spirit himself intercedes for us with unspoken groanings. And he who searches our hearts knows the mind of the Spirit, because he intercedes for the saints according to the will of God" (Rom 8:26–27).[72] Such intercession is born out of the "already–not yet" reality in which Christians live. In anticipation of the arrival of the age to come, believers, like the rest of the created order, are hard-pressed in the present age. Indeed, the creation "groan[s] together with labor pains" in anticipation that it will one day "be set free from the bondage to decay" (8:21–22).

---

children to Christian or public schools and eat nonorganic food. Cf. Romans 14; 1 Corinthians 8.

[70] For the role of the Holy Spirit in sanctification see Ferguson, *The Holy Spirit*, 139–73; Kuyper, *The Work of the Holy Spirit*, 432–507; Owen, *Pneumatologia*, book 4; Michael Horton, "'Let the Earth Bring Forth . . .' The Spirit and Human Agency in Sanctification," in *Sanctification: Explorations in Theology and Practice*, ed. Kelly M. Kapic (Downers Grove: InterVarsity, 2014), 127–49 (though Horton's treatment is broader than what the word "sanctification" usually connotes).

[71] Allison, *The Baker Compact Dictionary of Theological Terms*, s.v. "sanctification."

[72] For a Roman Catholic perspective on the Spirit and prayer see Congar, *I Believe in the Holy Spirit*, 2.112–18.

Similarly, for Christians, "we ourselves who have the Spirit as the firstfruits—we also groan within ourselves, eagerly waiting for adoption, the redemption of our bodies" (8:23). In the meantime, as those who live with the reality of sin and in a sinful world, believers are weak, especially in prayer. In the midst of sufferings, trials, and temptations, they stumble in not knowing how and what to pray for; indeed, with their backs against the wall, they lapse into silence. Scripture encouragingly points them to the Spirit's work of praying on their behalf.[73] An eternal conversation, in which the Father invites and listens to the intercession of the Spirit (as he does as well with the Son; Rom 8:32), is already occurring, and believers trust the effectiveness of the Father-Spirit communication on their behalf, drawing comfort from it.[74]

The human operation in sanctification has both an active and a passive element, both of which engage with the Holy Spirit. Christians exercise their active role by reading Spirit-inspired Scripture, praying in the Spirit, and mortifying sin by the Spirit. They implement their passive role by yielding to the Spirit, consciously being filled with the Spirit, and walking the path on which he leads them. Indeed, pilgrims' progress is wrought by the Holy Spirit.[75]

---

[73] The fact that the Spirit intercedes with "unspoken groanings" (8:26) or "groanings too deep for words" (ESV) does not indicate any kind of private prayer language or speaking in tongues. It simply refers to the type of conversation between the Father and the Spirit: given that they are divine persons, they do not communicate through words, as do human persons. Nonetheless, and as one might expect, the divine communication is completely effective: the Father perfectly understands and responds to the Spirit's intercession, to the benefit of weak-in-prayer believers.

[74] Sanders, *The Deep Things of God*, 212–13.

[75] This synergy does not render the Holy Spirit a mere potentiator for human effort. In the pharmacological world, a potentiator is a substance (for example, a drug) that intensifies the effect of another drug. Grapefruit juice, for example, is a potentiator for oxycodone. In sanctification, which is a synergistic reality, the Holy Spirit does not merely enhance the effort put forth by believers in pursuing greater Christlikeness. Rather, the Holy Spirit is the active divine agent who is the ground for, and the initiator of, all human activity in growing in Christian maturity. Still, in most cases the Holy Spirit's sanctifying work does not operate apart from human agents. Thanks to Gregg's friend Bryan Lopina for his explanation of a potentiator.

For the past several centuries, a recurring emphasis on sanctification in some evangelical circles has been on the power of the Holy Spirit.[76] As J. I. Packer expressed this focus:

> To start with, some people see the doctrine of the Spirit as essentially about *power*, in the sense of God-given ability to do what you know you ought to do and indeed want to do, but feel you lack the strength for. Examples include saying no to cravings (for sex, drink, drugs, tobacco, money, kicks, luxury, promotion, power, reputation, adulation, or whatever), being patient with folks who try your patience, loving the unlovable, controlling your temper, standing firm under pressure, speaking out boldly for Christ, trusting God in face of trouble. In thought and speech, preaching and prayer, the Spirit's enabling power for action of this kind is the theme on which these people constantly harp.

As Packer duly notes, this emphasis is not wrong; indeed, the New Testament often rehearses the power of the Holy Spirit. Some examples include the Spirit's power for evangelism (Luke 24:49; Acts 1:8), his bestowal of abundant hope (Rom 15:13), his work among Paul's ministry among the Gentiles in general (Rom 15:18–19) and the Corinthians in particular (1 Cor 2:4–5), and his granting of fruitfulness to the gospel message (1 Thess 1:5). Clearly, Scripture enjoins believers and the church to rely upon and minister through the power of the Holy Spirit. "Evangelical stress, therefore, on supernatural

---

[76] Recent books include Kathryn Kuhlman, *The Greatest Power in the World* (n.p.: Bridge-Logos, 2007); Billy Graham, *The Holy Spirit: Activating God's Power in Your Life* (Nashville: Thomas Nelson, 2000); Timothy Gracie, *Holy Spirit: Unlocking the Power of the Holy Spirit* (n.p.: CreateSpace, 2017); Charles Stanley, *Living in the Power of the Holy Spirit* (Nashville: Thomas Nelson, 2005); Joyce Meyer, *Filled with the Spirit: Understanding God's Power in Your Life* (Fenton: Life in the Word, 2001); John D. Harvey, *Anointed with the Spirit and Power: The Holy Spirit's Empowering Presence* (Phillipsburg: P&R, 2008); William W. and Robert P. Menzies, *Spirit and Power: Foundations of Pentecostal Experience* (Grand Rapids: Zondervan, 2000). The titles underscore our point of the emphasis on the power of the Holy Spirit, though the contents may or may not emphasize such empowerment for selfish gain.

sanctity through the Spirit as something real and necessary has been and always will be timely teaching."[77]

Tragically, however, a fundamental misunderstanding of the biblical notion of power taints this rightful emphasis on the Spirit's empowerment.[78] The distortion is seen in the aching for power for selfish reasons: to enhance one's reputation, to build numerically bigger ministries, to promote one's personal platform, to elevate one's spirituality beyond the progress of others, to avoid suffering by accumulating money and other creaturely comforts, and more. By contrast, the biblical notion of empowerment by the Spirit is always associated with accomplishing the will of God, humility, mercy for the distressed, love for God and love for others, ministry to and for the sake of unbelievers, doing good—ultimately so that glory may redound to God through human weakness. Rather than serving self-aggrandizement, the power of the Holy Spirit is to be appropriated for selfless motives and God-honoring ends. Such appropriation furthers sanctification according to the will of God.

Sanctification encompasses various aspects, traditionally named *positional* sanctification, *progressive* sanctification, and *perfected* sanctification. As for the first, positional sanctification is God's consecration of all who embrace Jesus Christ through repentance and faith. All Christians, from the newest believer to the most mature disciple, are set apart for God's particular concern and use; as such, they are called "saints" (1 Cor 1:2; Rom 1:7). Clearly, the *Holy* Spirit is the one who positions believers as *holy* people.[79] Progressive sanctification is the second and most familiar type. This is the ongoing maturation by which believers become more conformed to the image of Jesus Christ: "We all, with unveiled faces, are looking as in a mirror at the glory of the Lord and are being transformed into the same image from glory to glory"; such progressive sanctification "is from the Lord who is the Spirit" (2 Cor 3:18).[80]

---

[77] Packer, *Keep in Step with the Spirit*, 21–24.

[78] A recent book that addresses this misguided notion of power is Jamin Goggin and Kyle Strobel, *The Way of the Dragon or the Way of the Lamb: Searching for Jesus' Path of Power in a Church That Has Abandoned It* (Nashville: Thomas Nelson, 2017).

[79] Peterson, *Possessed by God.*

[80] The Holy Spirit, in conjunction with Scripture, effects sanctification. Jesus himself prayed that his followers would be sanctified by the truth, the Word of God

As for the third type, perfected sanctification is the final stage of the divine operation in Christians by which they are conformed fully to the image of Christ as his resurrected disciples. It is for this finished work that Paul prays: "Now may the God of peace himself sanctify you completely. And may your whole spirit, soul, and body be kept sound and blameless at the coming of our Lord Jesus Christ. He who calls you is faithful; he will do it" (1 Thess 5:23–24). The Holy Spirit, who at the outset positions believers as holy people and who continues to work in such a way that they progress in holiness, will one day perfect their holiness. It is the Holy Spirit who sanctifies thoroughly, from beginning to end (1 Pet 1:2).

The Spirit's sanctifying work expresses itself in a great variety of ways in individual Christians as well as in the church. One of these is the way of restriction: the Spirit acts so as to bridle the human proclivity to sin. In conjunction with the Word of God and its prohibitions, the Spirit prompts believers to limit their thoughts, words, feelings, impulses, and activities as these realities move toward sinful expression. This way of restriction cuts across the grain of our sinful tendency toward autonomy and self-determinism, vices that are urged on by the spirit of the age in which we live. For Christians, antinomianism and its accompanying excesses are not an option. Neither is legalism an option, however, as Scripture exposes the futility of over-restriction, going beyond what Scripture commands or prohibits (Col 2:20–23). Indeed, the Word of God condemns both excesses, antinomianism and legalism. Thankfully, the Spirit helps believers avoid both extremes, aiding them to walk in a bridled and life-giving freedom. Through the Spirit's enabling presence, believers curb their appetites, contain their desires, curtail their actions, check their words. Indeed, self-control is a fruit of the Spirit (Gal 5:22–23).

Another of these sanctifying ways is expansion: the Spirit pushes believers and churches outward to engage with the disenfranchised and marginalized of society. Jesus himself, filled with the Spirit, sought out prostitutes, tax collectors, and other such "sinners" (Matt 9:11; 11:19; Luke 15:2; 19:7). The early church, filled with the Spirit, provided support for its struggling

---

being that truth (John 17:17). This is the Word of God's grace, "which is able to build you up and to give you an inheritance among all who are being sanctified" (Acts 20:32).

members such that "there was not a needy person among them" (Acts 4:34). The apostle Paul, agreeing with the wisdom of his fellow apostles, was eager to "remember the poor" (Gal 2:10). Yet many Christians and churches readily admit the difficulty they find in such merciful engagement; failure in this area is commonplace. The Spirit's way of expansion enables believers and churches to do what is not within their own ability: engage with the excluded and disregarded around them.

Examples of both the way of restriction and the way of extension abound. One example from the mid-second century demonstrates that Christians lived these ways from the very beginning of the church's existence:

> Those who once rejoiced in fornication now delight in continence alone. Those who made use of magic arts have dedicated themselves to the good and unbegotten God. We who once took most pleasure in the means of increasing our wealth and property now bring what we have into a common fund and share with everyone in need. We who hated and killed one another and would not associate with people of different tribes because of [their different] customs, now after the manifestation of Christ live together and pray for our enemies and try to persuade those who unjustly hate us, so that they, living according to the fair commands of Christ, may share with us the good hope of receiving the same things [that we will] from God, the master of all.[81]

A noticeable emphasis in this example is that part and parcel of sanctification is the earnest desire that unbelievers, including those who hate Christians, will embrace the gospel of Christ and join in eternal life those whom they are persecuting.[82] Such faithful pursuit of sanctification bears fruit in leading others to Christ: "This we can show in the case of many who were once on your [evil] side and have turned from the ways of violence and tyranny, overcome by observing the consistent lives of their neighbors, or noting the strange patience of their injured acquaintances, or experiencing the way they

---

[81] Justin Martyr, *First Apology*, 14; *ANF* 1:249–50.

[82] Scripture underscores the connection between the proclamation of the gospel and the Holy Spirit (e.g., Acts 1:8; 4:7–12; 5:29–32; 9:17–20; Rom 15:18–19).

did business with them."[83] As Christians and the church exhibit consistent sanctification through the work of the Holy Spirit, and as they love, pray for, and share the gospel with those around them—even their detractors and persecutors—the fruit of the Spirit is manifested in transformed lives.

Thus, the Spirit's work of sanctification expresses itself in a variety of ways, including the way of restriction and the way of expansion. James underscores these two ways, in reverse order, in his appeal to believers: "Pure and undefiled religion before God the Father is this: to look after orphans and widows in their distress and to keep oneself unstained from the world" (Jas 1:27). Love and concern for those on the margins of society exemplify the way of expansion; walking in a bridled and life-giving freedom embodies the way of restriction.

Resurrection/Glorification

The completion of sanctification awaits the resurrection of the body, another mighty work of the Holy Spirit. Paul underscores the Spirit's life-giving action in resurrection: "If the Spirit of him who raised Jesus from the dead lives in you, then he who raised Christ from the dead will also bring your mortal bodies to life through his Spirit who lives in you" (Rom 8:11). The connection between the Spirit and the resurrection begins with the resurrection of the Son: Jesus was raised from the dead by the Father's initiation through the Holy Spirit. The connection continues with the resurrection of believers: Christians will be resurrected through the Father's Spirit who lives in them and gives life to their mortal bodies. In both cases, Paul emphasizes the Spirit's role: as in the resurrection of the Son, so in the resurrection of believers. Indeed, it is the resurrection of the Son to which believers will be conformed (1 Cor 15:20–22, 47–49).

Conclusion

As "the Lord and Giver of life," the Holy Spirit is engaged not only in creation but in re-creation as well. He operates from the beginning of salvation (e.g., conviction of sin and regeneration), throughout the advancement of

---

[83] Justin Martyr, 16; *ANF* 1:252.

salvation (e.g., assurance of salvation and sanctification), and to the end of salvation (resurrection and glorification). As "Love" and "Gift," it is said of the Spirit that "God's love has been poured out in our hearts through the Holy Spirit who was given to us" (Rom 5:5). The proper response to such saving activity is to express continual thanksgiving to the Holy Spirit and to desire earnestly that those who have not yet experienced salvation would do so through the witness of Christians and the church. As Peter proclaims in the midst of fierce persecution, "We are witnesses of these things, and so is the Holy Spirit whom God has given to those who obey him" (Acts 5:32).

By his re-creating work, the Holy Spirit effects salvation.

22

The Holy Spirit and the Church

O ur pneumatology has emphasized the person and work of the Holy Spirit not only for individual Christians but also for the church. In this chapter, the Spirit's particular presence and role in the church comes to the forefront.[1]

Definition of the Church

To present the role of the Holy Spirit in relation to the church, our pneumatology will use the following definition of the church:

> The church is the people of God who have been saved through repentance and faith in Jesus Christ and have been incorporated into his body through baptism with the Holy Spirit. It consists of two interrelated elements: the universal church is the fellowship of all Christians that extends from the day of Pentecost until the

---

[1] Thomas Smail, *The Giving Gift*, 13, succinctly sums up this chapter: "The importance of a mature understanding of the Holy Spirit is that it will help to produce a more mature Church." He treats the topic of pneumatology and ecclesiology on 182–98. White introduces this topic like this: "The church is above all else the locus of the Spirit; her origin, direction, authority, expansion, and development are directly the Spirit's concern, and her members are those upon whom the Spirit has 'fallen' or 'been poured.'" In R. E. O. White, *The Biblical Doctrine of Initiation* (Grand Rapids: Eerdmans, 1960), 189, cited in Allen, *Poured Out*, 106. For further discussion see Cole, *He Who Gives Life*, 209–24.

second coming, incorporating both the deceased believers who are presently in heaven and the living believers from all over the world. This universal church becomes manifested in local churches characterized by being doxological, logocentric, pneumadynamic, covenantal, confessional, missional, and spatio-temporal/eschatological. Local churches are led by pastors (also called elders) and served by deacons and deaconesses, possess and pursue purity and unity, exercise church discipline, develop strong connections with other churches, and celebrate the ordinances of baptism and the Lord's Supper. Equipped by the Holy Spirit with spiritual gifts for ministry, these communities regularly gather to worship the triune God, proclaim his Word, engage non-Christians with the gospel, disciple their members, care for people through prayer and giving, and stand both for and against the world.[2]

This definition of the church will guide the discussion of the intersection of pneumatology and ecclesiology.

The members of the church are redeemed people who, upon hearing the good news of Jesus Christ, repent of their sins and trust him for salvation. Throughout the movement from death and condemnation to life and salvation, the Holy Spirit is active. Specifically, as rehearsed earlier, his works in effecting redemption include conviction of sin, regeneration, union with Christ, and more. One important mighty act of God that comes to the forefront in discussion of ecclesiology is baptism with the Holy Spirit. As we have seen, this is the mighty work of Jesus Christ to pour out the Holy Spirit on new believers, thereby incorporating them into the body of Christ, the church. Moreover, this Spirit baptism is attested to by water baptism: the church baptizes those who offer a credible profession of faith in Christ, engendered by the Holy Spirit. As united both to Christ and with one another, Spirit- and water-baptized believers constitute the members of the church.

Clearly, this definition of the church reflects a baptistic ecclesiology: the church consists of people who have responded to the gospel with repentance and faith and have been baptized by Christ with the Spirit and baptized

---

[2] Allison, *Sojourners and Strangers*, 29–30.

by the church with water. For those whose ecclesiology differs from this theology, proper adjustments can be made to benefit from the following discussion. For those in churches that practice infant baptism—Presbyterian, Reformed, and Methodist churches, for example—while they maintain some type of incorporation of baptized infants into the covenant community, they also emphasize the necessity of embracing the gospel at some point in adolescence or adulthood. By focusing on these activated members of the church, they should find the subsequent presentation to be helpful.

The church consists of two interrelated elements: the universal church and local churches.[3] The universal church came into existence on the day of Pentecost and will endure in its current expression until the Second Coming. This position on the inauguration of the church does not deny that the people of God have always existed, but it does distinguish between the old covenant people of Israel, for example, and the new covenant people of the church:[4] one people of God; two covenantal expressions. While not totally discontinuous, these two expressions reflect the canonical and covenantal framework of Scripture. As presented earlier, the Old Testament rehearses the demise of the old covenant (Deut 30:1–6; Jer 31:31–34), emphasizes the anointing of the Messiah with the Spirit (Isaiah 42; 61), and anticipates a fresh, unprecedented outpouring of the Holy Spirit in association with the new covenant and its Messiah (Ezek 36:25–27; Joel 2:28–32). The New Testament confirms the end of the old covenant (Matt 26:26–20; 2 Corinthians 3; Hebrews 8), underscores that Jesus the Messiah experiences the fullness of the Spirit (John 3:34), and narrates the fulfillment of the expectation of the outpouring of the Spirit (Luke 3:15–17; John 1:33; John 7:37–39; Acts 2:33). Importantly, this fulfillment of the long-awaited baptism with the Spirit takes place on the day of Pentecost and corresponds with the inauguration of the church of Jesus Christ (Acts 2:1–4). Given this, our pneumatology affirms that the Holy Spirit is the "co-instituting principle" of the church, along with the incarnate Son.[5] Indeed, our pneumatology considers Jesus's hour (e.g., John

---

[3] The following paragraphs reflect the discussion in Allison, 28–31.

[4] For the sake of simplicity and space constraints, we will not discuss the other biblical covenants. For an excellent treatment of that topic, see Gentry and Wellum, *Kingdom through Covenant*.

[5] Congar, *I Believe in the Holy Spirit*, 2.9.

12:23,27; 13:1; 17:1) to consist not only of his suffering, death, burial, resurrection, and ascension. It also includes the outpouring of the Holy Spirit on the day of Pentecost. Consequently, the church is called into, and made part of, Jesus's hour as the community of the Holy Spirit.

The universal church incorporates both the deceased believers who are presently in heaven and the living believers from all over the world. The first company is the "heavenly" church, "the assembly of the firstborn whose names have been written in heaven" (Heb 12:23).[6] These disembodied Christians experience the immediate and joyful presence of the Lord, rest from their earthly labors, join in the heavenly chorus of unending praise to the one who is worthy of all glory and honor, and await the return of Christ and the resurrection of their bodies. Contrary to popular opinion, their heavenly existence is not their final destination, for disembodiment is an abnormal state. Human beings were designed to be embodied creatures, and the company of disembodied believers in heaven longs for the completion of their salvation. This fullness of redemption includes their reestablishment as embodied worshippers of the triune God in the millennial kingdom and/or the new heavens and the new earth (depending on one's eschatology).

The second company that constitutes the universal church is believers who are presently alive throughout the world. As described in the New Testament, they are the ones "sanctified in Christ Jesus, called as saints, with all those in every place who call on the name of Jesus Christ our Lord" (1 Cor 1:2). This aspect of the universal church "does not assemble, does not possess a structure or organization, does not have human leaders, and does not have a specific space-time address. These intangibles do not render the universal church any less real."[7]

---

[6] Heb 12:23 presents a second group of human worshippers in its heavenly scene (12:22–24): "the spirits of righteous people made perfect." "This expression most likely refers to the whole company of old covenant followers of Yahweh, who are listed in chapter 11 and described there (Heb. 11:39–40) as people who, 'though approved through their faith, . . . did not receive what was promised, since God had provided something better for us, so that they would not be made perfect without us.'" Allison, *Sojourners and Strangers*, 154n112. If this interpretation is correct, the heavenly scene of Heb 12:22–24 presents both the recipients of worship—God, Jesus—and the givers of worship—angels, new covenant believers in Jesus, and old covenant followers of Yahweh.

[7] Allison, 31.

Seven Identity Markers of the Church

This universal church expresses itself in local churches characterized by seven identity markers.[8] Indeed, the church is manifested by both Jesus Christ, its head and baptizer, and the Holy Spirit, the one with whom Christians are baptized and thus incorporated into the church (John 1:33; 1 Cor 12:13). In response to this divine initiative, Christians commit themselves to one another in local churches, which are manifestations of the universal church. The seven identity markers of these churches, and their relationship to the Holy Spirit, are as follows:

First, the church is *doxological*, that is, oriented to the *doxa*, or glory, of God. The church, as a community turned toward honoring, praising, and adoring the Lord in all that it is and does, "worship[s] by the Spirit" (Phil 3:3).

Second, the church is *logocentric*, that is, centered on the *logos*, or Word of God, in two senses: the incarnate Word, Jesus Christ, and the inspired Word, Scripture. As discussed earlier, both the incarnation and empowerment of God the Son and the inspiration and illumination of Scripture are wrought by the Holy Spirit. Indeed, through both the Word of God and the Spirit of God, Jesus is building his church (Matt 16:18). Indeed, the church is "built on the foundation of the apostles and prophets, with Christ Jesus himself as the cornerstone. In him the whole building, being put together, grows into a holy temple in the Lord. In him you are also being built together for God's dwelling in the Spirit" (Eph 2:20–22).

Third, the church is *pneumadynamic*, that is, activated by the *pneuma*, or Spirit. As already mentioned, the church was birthed by the Spirit and, as the following presentation will emphasize, grows and multiplies by the Spirit.

Fourth, the church is *covenantal*, that is, gathered as members in new covenant relationship with God and in covenantal relationship with each other. Again, the Old Testament prophesies the termination of the old covenant and its replacement with the new covenant. Importantly, the inauguration of the new covenant will be associated with the Spirit-anointed Messiah and a fresh, unprecedented outpouring of the Holy Spirit upon the new people of God. Accordingly, the new covenant as the church's structured relationship with God has particular reference to the Holy Spirit.

---

[8] The following paragraphs reflect the discussion in Allison, chs. 3–4.

Moreover, the members of the church associate with one another in a covenantal relationship. Ephesians 4 portrays the nature, and commands the attitudes and deeds, of this new covenant community:

> Putting away lying, speak the truth, each one to his neighbor, because we are members of one another. Be angry and do not sin. Don't let the sun go down on your anger, and don't give the devil an opportunity. Let the thief no longer steal. Instead, he is to do honest work with his own hands, so that he has something to share with anyone in need. No foul language should come from your mouth, but only what is good for building up someone in need, so that it gives grace to those who hear. And don't grieve God's Holy Spirit. You were sealed by him for the day of redemption. Let all bitterness, anger and wrath, shouting and slander be removed from you, along with all malice. And be kind and compassionate to one another, forgiving one another, just as God also forgave you in Christ. (Eph 4:25–32)

At the heart of this charter of the new covenant community is "God's Holy Spirit," who must be obeyed and depended upon for genuine community living. As discussed earlier, Paul again emphasizes the need for the covenant community to "be filled with the Spirit" so that intimate fellowship, genuine worship, continuous thanksgiving, and mutual submission will characterize it (Eph 5:18–21). As church members obey the command to yield to the Spirit, their endeavors to relate deeply to one another, praise God corporately, thank him continually, and submit to one another will flourish in genuine community living.

Fifth, the church is *confessional*, that is, united by both personal confession of faith in Christ and common confession of the historic Christian faith. Membership in the church is dependent upon a proper response to the gospel. As Paul explains, "This is the message of faith that we proclaim: If you confess with your mouth, 'Jesus is Lord,' and believe in your heart that God raised him from the dead, you will be saved" (Rom 10:8–9). As noted earlier, such confession of faith comes only through the Holy Spirit. Indeed, "no one can say, 'Jesus is Lord,' except by the Holy Spirit" (1 Cor 12:3).

Additionally, the church expresses its confessional nature through a common, corporate profession of what it believes. The Holy Spirit saw fit to include snippets of early church confessions of faith in the emerging New

Testament. One example rehearses the entire career of Jesus Christ, the great "mystery of godliness":

He was manifested in the flesh,
vindicated in the Spirit,
seen by angels,
preached among the nations,
believed on in the world,
taken up in glory. (1 Tim 3:16)[9]

Other extracts from early church confessions of faith incorporated in the New Testament include Phil 2:5–11 and Col 1:15–20.

The Spirit's role in the inspiration of the Bible, by which inclusion of these public professions of faith or hymns in Scripture was prompted, suggests that corporate confessions of the faith are proper to the identity of the church. Unsurprisingly, then, the church throughout its history has written and recited creeds and confessions—for example, the Nicene Creed, the Nicene-Constantinopolitan Creed, the Apostles' Creed, the Chalcedonian Creed, the Schleitheim Confession, the Augsburg Confession, the Belgic Confession, the Thirty-nine Articles, the Westminster Confession, the First and Second London Confessions—with the conviction that the Holy Spirit has guided these corporate declarations of what the church believes.[10]

---

[9] Many biblical scholars consider this short composition to be a citation of (part of) an actual confession of faith recited by Christians or a hymn they sang when assembled together as the church for worship. Two principal interpretations are offered: (1) The confession/hymn expresses the career of Jesus in terms of six acts or elements: incarnation, resurrection, display of victory before the angels, proclamation of the gospel, the faith of Christ's followers, and ascension. (2) It consists of two parts: "The first strophe (lines 1–3) refers to the events in the life of Jesus, and the second strophe (lines 4–6) refers to the early church. The phrase 'taken up in glory' (line 6) would then refer not to Jesus but to the raising up of the church into the realm of the divine." See Matthew E. Gordley, *New Testament Christology Hymns: Exploring Texts, Contexts, and Significance* (Downers Grove: IVP Academic, 2018), 187. The book is a recent and thorough treatment of the Christological hymns such as Phil 2:5–11; Col 1:15–20; John 1:1–18; and others.

[10] For a good summary of the creedal impulse of the church from its earliest days, see Donald Fairbairn and Ryan M. Reeves, *The Story of Creeds and Confessions: Tracing the Development of the Christian Faith* (Grand Rapids: Baker Academic, 2019).

Sixth, the church is *missional*, that is, the body of divinely called and sent ministers proclaiming the gospel and advancing the kingdom of God. Jesus himself expresses the missionality of the church and associates it with the Holy Spirit: "Jesus said to [the Eleven] again, 'Peace be with you. As the Father has sent me, I also send you.' After saying this, he breathed on them and said, 'Receive the Holy Spirit. If you forgive the sins of any, they are forgiven them; if you retain the sins of any, they are retained'" (John 20:21–23). There is one mission of the triune God, and it is given to the church as its witness empowered by the Holy Spirit.[11] The Father commissions the Son with the mission of becoming incarnate, living a holy life, dying, resurrecting, and ascending to accomplish salvation for sinful human beings. In turn, the Son commissions his disciples with the same mission, with this modification: the church is sent not to accomplish salvation but to announce the salvation accomplished by the Son and how to appropriate it. The mission is all of a piece. It is not two missions but one, from the Father to the Son and from the Son to the church.[12]

But how could it be possible for the church to engage in such a lofty, sacred enterprise? As an enacted parable, Jesus breathes and commands the apostles to receive the Holy Spirit. This harbinger looks forward to the day of Pentecost, when the Son, together with the Father, will pour out the Holy Spirit on those men, thus inaugurating the church and its mission.[13] Then, and only then, are the disciples in a position to engage in the mission, which

---

[11] This point does not contradict what was expressed earlier, that there are two sendings or two missions, one of the Son and one of the Spirit. Those two commissions are ultimately part of the one mission of the triune God, which also engages the church. For further discussion see Allen, *Poured Out*, 28–30; Köstenberger and Swain, *Father, Son, and Spirit*, chap. 9; and Köstenberger, *John*, chap. 15.

[12] We also note that the mission of the Messiah as connected to the Holy Spirit is to be "a light for the nations" (Isa 49:6). Thus, the missionality of the Spirit-anointed Messiah points to and continues through the missionality of the Spirit-empowered body of Christ, which has a worldwide orientation (Matt 28:18–20).

[13] We return to the earlier discussion of the sending of the Son and the giving of the Spirit: just as the Son, who is *sent* by the Father, *sends* his church, so the Son (along with the Father) promises that he will *give* the Holy Spirit to his church to accomplish its commission. Thus, the church experiences both a sending (*apostellō*) and a giving (*didōmi*)—it is constituted by both Son and Spirit—because the missions of both the Son and the Spirit target the church.

is still today the proclamation of the gospel.[14] For all who embrace this good news, the church proclaims the forgiveness of sins. For all who rebuff this good news, the church tearfully issues a warning of continued, impending judgment. Importantly, for this missional task the Holy Spirit is absolutely necessary, as expressed in the Amsterdam Declaration (2000):

> The fullness of the ministry of the Holy Spirit in relation to the knowledge of Christ and the enjoyment of new life in him dates from the Pentecostal outpouring recorded in Acts 2. As the divine inspirer and interpreter of the Bible, the Spirit empowers God's people to set forth accurate, searching, life-transforming presentations of the gospel of Jesus Christ, and makes their communication a fruitful means of grace to their hearers. The New Testament shows us the supernatural power of the Spirit working miracles, signs and wonders, bestowing gifts of many kinds, and overcoming the power of Satan in human lives for the advancement of the gospel. Christians agree that the power of the Holy Spirit is vitally necessary for evangelism and that openness to his ministry should mark all believers.[15]

Similarly, the Third Lausanne Congress on World Evangelization (2010) confessed:

> We love the Holy Spirit within the unity of the Trinity, along with God the Father and God the Son. He is the missionary Spirit sent by the missionary Father and the missionary Son, breathing life and power into God's missionary Church. We love and pray for the presence of the Holy Spirit because without the witness of the Spirit to Christ, our own witness is futile. Without the convicting work of the Spirit, our preaching is in vain. Without the gifts, guidance and

---

[14] As Horton, *People and Place*, 295, observes, "Even in the moments leading to the ascension the disciples could still gather to inquire of Jesus, 'Lord, is this the time when you will restore the kingdom to Israel?' (Acts 1:6). Only after Pentecost is this question no longer asked, while the disciples are empowered as apostles of the Word to the ends of the earth."

[15] "Definition of Key Terms: 3. Holy Spirit," in "The Amsterdam Declaration: A Charter for Evangelism in the 21st Century," *Christianity Today*, August 1, 2000, https://www.christianitytoday.com/ct/2000/augustweb-only/13.0.html.

power of the Spirit, our mission is mere human effort. And without the fruit of the Spirit, our unattractive lives cannot reflect the beauty of the gospel.[16]

Accordingly, the missional church can fulfill its divinely given mandate to make disciples of all the nations only through the direction and empowerment of the Holy Spirit.[17] Indeed, the contemporary rediscovery of the person and work of the Holy Spirit has coincided with a spectacular missional movement global in its reach.[18]

Seventh and last, the church is *spatio-temporal/eschatological*, that is, here, but not here; already, but not yet. On the day of Pentecost, the Spirit descends in a particular location and gives birth to the church in Jerusalem. Decades later, as the leaders of the church in Antioch are worshipping the Lord, "the Holy Spirit said, 'Set apart for me Barnabas and Saul for the work to which I have called them.' Then after they had fasted, prayed, and laid hands on them, they sent them off" (Acts 13:1–3) to Cyprus and eventually to Antioch of Psidia, Iconium, Lystra, and Derbe (Acts 13:4–14:28). During this "first missionary journey," Paul plants churches in these regions. Years later, though Paul and his missionary band seek to evangelize in Phrygia and Galatia, then Bithynia, the Holy Spirit forbids entrance to those districts. Instead, he directs them to go to Macedonia, where the church in Philippi is formed (Acts 16:6–40).

---

[16] The Cape Town Commitment (2010): Part 1: "For the Lord We Love: The Cape Town Confession of Faith," 5, We Love God the Holy Spirit, https://www.lausanne.org/content/ctc/ctcommitment#p1-5.

[17] The connection between the Spirit and the church's mission is fitting when one thinks of the roles of the Spirit: he convicts, regenerates, justifies, stimulates repentance and faith, prompts confession of Christ, adopts, seals, assures, fills, sanctifies, unites with the triune God, and adds "living stones" to "the . . . building . . . a holy temple in the Lord . . . God's dwelling in the Spirit" (1 Pet 2:5; Eph 2:20–22). In turn, he thrusts out and empowers the church for more mission.

[18] Leonard Allen, *Poured Out*, 28, who traces the demise of the church's missionality to its neglect of the person and work of the Holy Spirit beginning with Constantinianism, or the rise of Christendom, underscores: "The diminishment of mission and of the Spirit's work in the Christendom centuries went hand in hand; so it is that after (neo-)Christendom the recovery of mission and of the Spirit go hand in hand" (original italics removed).

This pattern suggests that the Holy Spirit establishes churches in particular sites, according to his sovereign will. These local assemblies have specific addresses: "the church of God at Corinth" (1 Cor 1:2; 2 Cor 1:1), "the churches of Galatia" (Gal 1:2), "the church of the Thessalonians" (1 Thess 1:1; 2 Thess 1:2), Calvin Presbyterian Church, St. Mark's Lutheran Church, First Baptist Church, Sojourn Community Church. The locations of the seven golden lampstands (Rev 1:12, 20; 2:1) are not accidental; churches exist in particular places, not haphazardly or accidentally but providentially. "God called the churches *there* for his purposes—and the *there* was not inconsequential, seeing God's providential ordering of peoples, times, and places (Acts 17:26)."[19] Certainly, Jesus rebuffs the notion that worship must take place on Mount Gerizim or in the temple in Jerusalem (John 4:20). Still, the church must worship *somewhere*: "The church is not geographically bound to one place . . . but it is not geographically agnostic, in that it lives, moves, and has its being in some spatiotemporal reality. It can be anywhere, but always is 'somewherealso.'"[20] Accordingly, the Holy Spirit births and develops churches in certain places at certain times. By the Spirit, the church is a spatio-temporal reality.

Beyond this reality, the church is eschatological, composed of sojourners and strangers, a people on the way to something greater. With its foundation of the apostles and prophets, and with its cornerstone of Jesus Christ, "the whole building, being put together, grows into a holy temple in the Lord. In him you are also being built together for God's dwelling in the Spirit" (Eph 2:20–22). The church is a work in progress, moving from impurity to purity, from immaturity to maturity, from being spotted and wrinkled to being holy and without blemish (Eph 5:27). As individual believers encounter the tension of the "already-not yet," so the church is an eschatological assembly that already experiences salvation, sanctification, growth, and multiplication—but only in part. It longs for the fullness of those blessings—the not yet, which is still to come. Only then will the Holy Spirit, one of whose roles is that of perfecting the divine works, finish his work of transformation.

[19] Reid Monaghan, personal correspondence.
[20] Monaghan.

The Growth of the Church: Spiritual Gifts[21]

As churches are initiated and developed by the Holy Spirit, they grow through a synergism of divine operation and human cooperation. Such a dynamic is particularly seen in a church's growth through the Spirit's endowment and empowerment of spiritual gifts.[22]

Purposes of Spiritual Gifts

The primary purpose of spiritual gifts is to promote this growth, which is manifested in two areas: (1) The church progresses in maturity as spiritual gifts serve to deepen its conformity to the image of Christ, safeguard its doctrinal soundness, foster the genuineness of its community life, and more. (2) The church expands its mission as spiritual gifts serve the proclamation of the gospel and the making of disciples throughout the world in obedience to the Great Commission.

Spiritual gifts serve other purposes as well. In the early decades of the church, God "testified by signs and wonders, various miracles, and distributions of gifts from the Holy Spirit according to his will" (Heb 2:4) to confirm the message and messengers of the gospel. As the church's leaders—apostles like Peter and Paul, servants like Stephen and Philip—preach the good news, their hearers can know their message is true and delivered by its God-ordained messengers because of the miraculous activity and powerful spiritual gifts accompanying their mission. As an example, Peter raises Tabitha

---

[21] Much of this discussion is adapted from Gregg R. Allison, *50 Core Truths of the Christian Faith: A Guide to Understanding and Teaching Theology* (Grand Rapids: Baker, 2018), 194–97.

[22] For resources on spiritual gifts see Max Turner, *The Holy Spirit and Spiritual Gifts in the New Testament Church and Today*, rev. ed. (Grand Rapids: Baker Academic, 2012); D. A. Carson, *Showing the Spirit: A Theological Exposition of 1 Corinthians 12-14* (Grand Rapids: Baker, 1987); Frederick Dale Bruner, *A Theology of the Holy Spirit* (Grand Rapids: Eerdmans, 1970), 130–49; Kenneth Berding, *What Are Spiritual Gifts: Rethinking the Conventional View* (Grand Rapids: Kregel, 2006); Thomas R. Schreiner, *Spiritual Gifts: What They Are and Why They Matter* (Nashville: B&H 2018); Sam Storms, *Practicing the Power: Welcoming the Gifts of the Holy Spirit in Your Life* (Grand Rapids: Zondervan, 2017).

(or Dorcas) from the dead, and her resurrection "became known throughout Joppa, and many believed in the Lord" (Acts 9:36–42).

Additionally, spiritual gifts are a harbinger of things still to come. As a small sample of the abundant, future work of the Spirit, they offer a taste of life in the Spirit in the age to come. Moreover, spiritual gifts attest to Christ's victory over his enemies. As Paul notes, "When [Christ] ascended on high, he took the captives captive; he gave gifts to people" (Eph 4:8). The ascension signals a resounding defeat of Christ's enemies. As the exalted head over all creation, Christ is the head of his body, the church. It is upon the church that Christ (together with the Father) pours out the Holy Spirit, through whom he gives gifts to his followers. As Paul details later, these gifts are actually gifted people—apostles, prophets, evangelists, pastor-teachers (4:11)—who display his victory.

Finally, spiritual gifts underscore the church's role in the accomplishment of its own growth and multiplication. As discussed earlier in regard to God's providence both in creation in general and in the human realm in particular, divine activity (almost always) engages with secondary causes to accomplish the eternal purpose.[23] The next section addresses the reality of this human dimension through the church's exercise of spiritual gifts.

Biblical Affirmations about Spiritual Gifts

The New Testament addresses the gifts of the Spirit in four major passages. Ephesians 4:7–16 emphasizes that the ascended Christ gave gifts to his church, thereby exhibiting his triumph over his enemies (vv. 7–10). These gifts are particularly associated with gifted leaders: apostles, prophets, evangelists, and pastors and teachers (v. 11). Their specific role in the church is to equip its members for ministry and thus contribute to the maturity of the church (vv. 12–14). As already noted, there is a dual dimensionality to this growth. Foundationally, a divine dimension is at work: Christ "promotes the growth of the body." Flowing from this divine foundation, a human dimension is at work: the church is to "grow in every way into him who is the

---

[23] Horton carefully labors to press home the important link between the work of the Spirit and the means of grace. Though this is a repeated theme of his entire book, see especially Horton, *Rediscovering the Holy Spirit*, 244–83.

428

head—Christ. From him the whole body . . . [builds] up itself in love by the proper working of each individual part" (vv. 15–16). The divine and human dimensions, operating synergistically, foster the growth of the church.

According to 1 Corinthians 12–14, the Spirit is responsible for the distribution of spiritual gifts, which are to be used purposefully. Specifically, at least one "manifestation of the Spirit is given to each person for the common good" (12:7). Indeed, it is the Spirit who is active in these gifts, "distributing to each person as he wills" and empowering church members as they exercise their gifts (12:11).

> Here, again, the dual dimensionality of spiritual gifts comes into focus. The Spirit sovereignly distributes and empowers spiritual gifts. This is the divine dimension. Correspondingly, there is a human dimension: spiritual gifts are endowments for believers. As the gospel is communicated, it is the evangelist who shares it. As a meeting is directed, it is by one who has the gift of leadership. As a revelation is given, it is spoken by a prophet. Moreover, the church is to "earnestly desire the higher gifts" (12:31 [ESV]), those that, like prophecy, have the greatest potential to build up the greatest number of people (14:1–5). Thus, the exercise of the gifts is a fully human activity "for the common good." But it is not a merely human activity, because of the Spirit's work.[24]

As it is the Holy Spirit who distributes and empowers his gifts, believers' suffering from a sense of inferiority or boasting out of a sense of superiority is precluded. Certainly, there are less noticeable gifts, such as administration and helping, and more visible gifts, such as leading, teaching, and prophecy. But both behind-the-scene gifts and out-in-the-public-eye gifts are essential for the proper growth of the church. Thus, rather than an atmosphere in which disappointment and pride flourish, the proper environment for the use of spiritual gifts is love (1 Corinthians 13).

Romans 12:4–8 provides specific instructions about seven gifts and how Christians with those gifts should exercise them: "If prophecy, use it according to the proportion of one's faith; if service, use it in service; if teaching, in teaching; if exhorting, in exhortation; giving, with generosity; leading, with

---

[24] Allison, *50 Core Truths of the Christian Faith*, 196.

diligence; showing mercy, with cheerfulness" (vv. 6–8). Implied in this exhortation is that believers recognize what gifts they have so they can heed these instructions. First Peter 4:10–11 is similar: "Just as each one has received a gift, use it to serve others, as good stewards of the varied grace of God. If anyone speaks, let it be as one who speaks God's words; if anyone serves, let it be from the strength God provides, so that God may be glorified through Jesus Christ in everything." When the church attends to these instructions, it lives as a community that uses the gifts of the Spirit to serve one another and glorify God.

The Current Debate: Continuationism versus Cessationism[25]

With the rise of Pentecostalism in the early twentieth century and the development of the charismatic movement in the 1960s/1970s, spiritual gifts became one of the most discussed and divisive practices in the church. Indeed, an important debate arose, framed in terms of two questions:

> Does the Holy Spirit continue to distribute all the spiritual gifts to the church, including the "sign gifts" of prophecy, speaking in tongues, interpretation of tongues, word of knowledge, word of wisdom, miracles, and healings? This view is called continuationism. Or has the Holy Spirit ceased to distribute these sign gifts while

---

[25] For resources on the debate see B. B. Warfield, *Counterfeit Miracles* (New York: Scribner's, 1918); Wayne Grudem, ed., *Are Miraculous Gifts for Today?: Four Views* (Leicester, UK: IVP, 1988); Vern S. Poythress, "Modern Spiritual Gifts as Analogous to Apostolic Gifts: Affirming Extraordinary Works of the Spirit within Cessationist Theology," *JETS* 39 (1996): 71–101; Jack Deere, *Surprised by the Power of the Spirit* (Eastbourne, UK: Kingsway, 1994); John MacArthur, *Charismatic Chaos* (Grand Rapids: Zondervan, 1992); MacArthur, *Strange Fire: The Danger of Offending the Holy Spirit with Counterfeit Worship* (Nashville: Thomas Nelson, 2013); Robert W. Graves, ed., *Strangers to Fire: When Tradition Trumps Scripture* (n.p.: The Foundation for Pentecostal Scholarship, 2014); John Ruthven, *On the Cessation of the Charismata: The Protestant Polemic on Postbiblical Miracles* (Sheffield, UK: SAP, 1993); Iain M. Duguid, "What Kind of Prophecy Continues? Defining the Difference between Continuationism and Cessationism," in *Redeeming the Life of the Mind: Essays in Honor of Vern Poythress*, ed. John M. Frame, Wayne Grudem, and John J. Hughes (Wheaton: Crossway, 2017), 112–28; Cole, *He Who Gives Life*, 248–58; Ferguson, *The Holy Spirit*, 208–39; Horton, *Rediscovering the Holy Spirit*, 226–43; Congar, *I Believe in the Holy Spirit*, 2.149–88.

still giving the other gifts such as teaching, leading, serving, giving, and more? This view is called cessationism.[26]

To be clear, both positions agree that most gifts—for example, teaching, leading, service, and giving—are given by the Spirit and thus are activated in the church today. The divergence comes over the sign gifts. Continuationism holds that they are given by the Spirit and thus operate today, while cessationism maintains that they are no longer given by the Spirit and thus are inactive in the church.[27]

Both sides offer important support, appealing to both Scripture and church history to demonstrate their correctness. Continuationism marshals the following points in its favor:

(1) Because the primary purpose for spiritual gifts is to foster the church's maturity and mission, the church, which is still maturing and has not completed its mission, continues to need all of the gifts. (2) First Corinthians 13:8–13 (also 1:7–8) places the cessation of spiritual gifts at the return of Christ, not before that event. (3) Over against cessationism, which specifically links sign gifts with the apostles, continuationism notes that many nonapostles exercised the gifts of prophecy, speaking in tongues, miracles, and healing (1:7; Gal. 3:5; Acts 8:4–8; 10:44–48). Thus, it is wrong to argue that because there are no more apostles, there can be no more sign gifts. (4) Historical evidence points to the continuation of sign gifts in the post-first-century church.[28]

---

[26] Allison, *50 Core Truths of the Christian Faith*, 195.

[27] Sam Storms makes an important point that Scripture itself does not have a special category of "sign gifts" that distinguishes prophecy, speaking in tongues, healing, and more from other spiritual gifts. To make this distinction is, for Storms, to favor the cessationist position that confines these "sign gifts" to the apostles in the early church while promoting the continuation of all other gifts of the Spirit such as teaching, administration, and exhortation. Storms concludes that "to speak of certain spiritual gifts as 'sign' gifts does not serve us well. It tends to suggest a narrow and temporary purpose for some gifts, something not corroborated elsewhere in the NT." Sam Storms, "Enjoying God" blog (December 16, 2019). https://www.samstorms.org/enjoying-god-blog/post/is-there-such-a-thing-as--sign--gifts.

[28] Allison, 196.

Continuationism is a characteristic element of Pentecostalism, the charismatic movement, third-wave evangelicalism, and other Christians and churches that embrace the Spirit's ongoing distribution of all the spiritual gifts.

Cessationism points to the following support in its favor:

(1) First Corinthians 13:8–13 associates the cessation of sign gifts such as prophecy and speaking in tongues with the completion of the New Testament canon. It is this fullness of revelation to which the phrase "when the perfect comes" refers (13:10). Sign gifts were the means God used to provide his revelation to the early church. When the perfect came—when God's provision of revelation was finished with the completion of the New Testament—these revelatory gifts no longer had a function and have ceased. (2) A modification of point 1 is that 1 Corinthians 13:8–13 does not specify the time of the cessation of these spiritual gifts. Thus, the determination of this issue must be made on the basis of other passages. (3) Sign gifts were specifically associated with the apostles (2 Cor. 12:12). Because apostles no longer exist, the sign gifts associated with them are no longer being given to the church. (4) Because the sign gifts have to do with the giving of revelation, their continuation would challenge the sufficiency of Scripture. (5) Historical evidence points to the cessation of sign gifts in the post-first-century church.[29]

Cessationism is a characteristic element of Reformed and Presbyterian denominations and churches, most Baptist denominations and churches, dispensationalism, and other Christians and churches that deny the Spirit's ongoing distribution of the sign gifts of prophecy, speaking in tongues, interpretation of tongues, word of knowledge, word of wisdom, miracles, and healings.

Expanding on the above case for this position, advocates of continuationism advance the following reasons:[30]

---

[29] Allison, 196–97.

[30] This discussion broadly follows the case for continuationism in Andrew Wilson, *Spirit and Sacrament: An Invitation to Eucharismatic Worship* (Grand Rapids: Zondervan, 2018), 89–120.

First, Paul's apostolic instructions are quite clear:

Pursue love and desire spiritual gifts, and especially that you may prophesy. (1 Cor 14:1)

So then, my brothers and sisters, be eager to prophesy, and do not forbid speaking in other tongues. (1 Cor 14:39)

According to the grace given to us, we have different gifts: If prophecy, use it according to the proportion of one's faith. (Rom 12:6)

Don't stifle the Spirit. Don't despise prophecies, but test all things. Hold on to what is good. (1 Thess 5:19–21)

As the early churches read these passages, and as church leaders preached and taught them, what would have signaled to them that these apostolic instructions no longer apply and thus should not be obeyed? No such signal appears in the texts themselves. These instructions were delivered to several churches—those in Corinth, Rome, and Thessalonica—and thus do not concern parochial matters but churches generally.[31] If the cessationist view ties the disappearance of these gifts with the closing of the New Testament canon, as it sometimes does, at what point and in what manner did the early churches and their leaders know to suspend the operation of the gifts of prophecy, speaking in tongues, and the other sign gifts? Appropriately, "the burden of proof should always be on the person who says we don't have to obey an apostolic instruction, rather than on the person who says we do."[32]

Second, advocates of continuationism point to the historical record of the continuation of signs gifts in the early centuries.[33] They claim that it is simply not the fact that these gifts died out after the apostolic age was over or that their continuation was confined to marginal, even heretical, groups.

---

[31] Examples of parochial instructions include: "And tell Archippus, 'Pay attention to the ministry you have received in the Lord, so that you can accomplish it'" (Col 4:17); "Bring Mark with you, for he is useful to me in the ministry" (2 Tim 4:11); "When you come, bring the cloak I left in Troas with Carpus, as well as the scrolls, especially the parchments" (2 Tim 4:13). No reader of Scripture today mistakes these instructions as pertaining to him or her.

[32] Wilson, *Spirit and Sacrament*, 108.

[33] Burgess, *The New International Dictionary of Pentecostal and Charismatic Movements*, 730–69.

Third, in addition to the above-cited argument that Paul places the cessation of spiritual gifts at the return of Christ (1 Cor 1:7–8; 13:8–13), continuationism advocates point to the "Magna Carta" of the Spirit's activity in "the last days":

> And it will be in the last days, says God,
> that I will pour out my Spirit on all people;
> then your sons and your daughters will prophesy,
> your young men will see visions,
> and your old men will dream dreams.
> I will even pour out my Spirit
> on my servants in those days, both men and women
> and they will prophesy. (Acts 2:17–18; citing Joel 2:28–29)

"The last days" is the period of time that was inaugurated by the first coming of Christ, as well as the outpouring of the Holy Spirit on Pentecost, and that will extend until the second coming of Christ. This period—all of it—is the age of the Spirit, the time of the new covenant, the era of the church. And it is characterized from beginning to end by Spirit-given prophetic and visionary activity—the continuation of the sign gifts—as illustrated by the ongoing narrative of Acts in which Luke recounts healings, miracles, speaking in tongues, prophecies, and the like. Accordingly, continuationism affirms this ongoing activity of the Spirit in the church today.[34]

---

[34] As for criticisms of continuationism: (1) Some cessationists argue that prophecy undermines the authority and sufficiency of Scripture. It only does so, however, if it possesses Scripture-level authority; responsible continuationists deny that it does. Indeed, it can be demonstrated that both the Old Testament and the New Testament have two categories for prophetic activity: one is authoritative or foundational prophecy (e.g., "Thus says the Lord"; the church is "built on the foundation of the apostles and prophets," Eph 2:20), the second is non-authoritative or non-foundational prophecy (e.g., that which was communicated by the unclothed, seemingly mad Saul, 1 Sam 19:24; that which was communicated by the four virgin daughters of Philip, Acts 21:9). None of the second type of prophecy undermines the authority and sufficiency of Scripture. For further discussion, see Duguid, "What Kind of Prophecy Continues?", 112–28. (2) Some cessationists dismiss the sign gifts because they have not experienced them personally or seen them operate (at least, in the estimation of those cessationists, according to scriptural instructions). While often used against continuationism, this appeal is not an argument. (3) Building off the last point, some cessationists dismiss the sign gifts because prophetic activity, healings, miracles, speaking in tongues, and the rest do not operate as powerfully and effectively today as they did in the early church (as presented in the New Testament). Wilson replies,

Whatever one's position may be, two major errors must be avoided: neglecting biblical instruction about, and the use of, spiritual gifts, and over-emphasizing spiritual gifts and/or expressing them in ways that contradict biblical instruction. After all, if the progress of the gospel and the growth of the church are inextricably linked to its members' recognizing and exercising their gifts as the Spirit distributes and empowers them, the church will stagnate and die in their absence or abuse.[35] As the Third Lausanne Congress on World Evangelization (2010) underscored:

> There is no true or whole gospel, and no authentic biblical mission, without the Person, work and power of the Holy Spirit. We pray for a greater awakening to this biblical truth, and for its experience to be reality in all parts of the worldwide body of Christ. However, we are aware of the many abuses that masquerade under the name of the Holy Spirit, the many ways in which all kinds of phenomena are practiced and praised which are not the gifts of the Holy Spirit as clearly taught in the New Testament. There is great need for more profound discernment, for clear warnings against delusion, for the exposure of fraudulent and self-serving manipulators who abuse spiritual power for their own ungodly enrichment. Above all there is a great need for sustained biblical teaching and preaching, soaked in humble prayer, that will equip ordinary believers to understand and rejoice in the true gospel and to recognize and reject false gospels.[36]

"Yes, the apostles were more successful at healing and prophecy than we are. There is, indeed, a discrepancy between our experience and what is described in the New Testament. But the apostles were also far more successful at evangelism. And church planting. And leadership. And cross-cultural mission. And church discipline. And teaching. And standing firm under persecution. And handling disappointment. Yet in none of these cases do we conclude that the gulf is so wide, their 'success' so much greater than ours, that to tell people how to share the gospel or teach or lead more effectively, is to encourage people to be satisfied with sub-biblical Christianity. Rather, we acknowledge the disparity and seek to learn from it. . . . The same, surely, should apply to the miraculous gifts." Wilson, *Spirit and Sacrament*, 110–11.

[35] Wilson, 197.

[36] Cape Town Commitment: "For the Lord We Love: The Cape Town Confession of Faith," 5.

Unity and Purity

Just as spiritual gifts are given by the Holy Spirit for the building up of the body of Christ, so the growth of the church involves both unity and purity. These two elements correspond to two of the core attributes of the church confessed in the early creeds: the church is "*one, holy,* catholic, and apostolic."[37] The Spirit's activity in the oneness, or unity, and the holiness, or purity, of the church is essential.

Unity

The unity of the church "signifies that the church is united in oneness. [Such] unity comes from the two marks of the church: 'it is sufficient to agree concerning the doctrine of the gospel and the administration of the sacraments [baptism and the Lord's Supper].'"[38] To true churches characterized by these two marks, the Holy Spirit grants unity. Moreover, such unity comes through "fellowship with the Spirit" and is actualized in the church "by thinking the same way, having the same love, [being] united in spirit, [and] intent on one purpose" (Phil 2:1–2).

The unity of the church is grounded on, and patterned after, the unity of the three persons in the one Godhead. Indeed, Jesus the Son prays to the Father for the church, "that they [church members] may be one as we are one" (John 17:11, 22). More specifically, Jesus prays, "May they all be one, as you, Father, are in me and I am in you. May they also be in us, so that the world may believe you sent me" (John 17:21). The perichoresis of the three persons is the pattern and goal for the church's oneness. Not that the church's unity could ever be the sharing of one essence among its members; such ontological oneness and mutual indwelling is characteristic of the triune God alone. Rather, through the Holy Spirit's dwelling in the church, such unity is possible. Accordingly, the following clarification is necessary:

> Because human persons cannot be internal to one another as subjects, their unity cannot be conceived in a strictly perichoretic fashion. . . .

---

[37] Nicene-Constantinopolitan Creed.

[38] Allison, *The Baker Compact Dictionary of Theological Terms,* s.v. "unity," citing Augsburg Confession, 7.

The statement "as you, Father, are in me and I am in you" is continued not by "may they also be *in one another*," but rather by "may they also be *in us*." Human beings can be in the triune God only insofar as the Son is in them (John 17:23; 14:20); and if the Son is in them, then so also is the love with which the Father loves the Son (John 17:26). Because the Son indwells human beings through the Spirit, however, *the unity of the church is grounded in the interiority of the Spirit*—and with the Spirit also the interiority of the other divine persons—*in Christians*. . . . It is not the mutual perichoresis of human beings, but rather the indwelling of the Spirit common to everyone that makes the church into a communion corresponding to the Trinity.[39]

Thus, it is the Holy Spirit who fosters the unity of the church.

Given this reality, the church may be complacent and assume that the experience of oneness in the Spirit will be easy and constant; however, due to the sinfulness of its members, the church's unity is constantly threatened. Thus, Paul exhorts the church:

I, the prisoner in the Lord, urge you to live worthy of the calling you have received, with all humility and gentleness, with patience, bearing with one another in love, making every effort to keep the unity of the Spirit through the bond of peace. There is one body and one Spirit—just as you were called to one hope at your calling—one Lord, one faith, one baptism, one God and Father of all, who is above all and through all and in all. (Eph 4:1–6)

The gift of the Spirit to the church is unity, but the church must strive eagerly to maintain that unity, a oneness too easily damaged or destroyed by its members' sin. In step with the Spirit of oneness, they must exhibit certain requisite attitudes and engage in certain required activities to preserve the church's unity.[40] They are exhorted to humility, eschewing both an overestimation of themselves, expressed as arrogance and pride, and an underestimation of themselves, expressed as false Christian humility (Phil 2:1–5). They are to yield their rights in preference for others (1 Cor 9:3–18). They are called to gentleness, "a

---

[39] Miroslav Volf, *After Our Likeness: The Church as the Image of the Trinity* (Grand Rapids: Eerdmans, 1998), 212–13, emphasis original.

[40] Allison, *Sojourners and Strangers*, 173–74.

meekness of disposition that eschews combativeness; with a leading cause of divisiveness set aside, church unity is maintained by this virtue."[41] Patience is to reign in their midst, a refusal to give up in the face of difficulty and a commitment to work through matters that would otherwise result in division. And church members are to bear with one another in love by making allowances for one another's faults, enduring one another's failures, and forgiving one another as God in Christ has forgiven them (Eph 4:32). These attitudes and actions recall the fruit of the Spirit (Gal 5:22–23); thus, though church members labor to maintain the oneness of the church by exhibiting such fruit, the Spirit's work provides the divine help needed for unity to flourish.

The unity of the church is also fostered by seven commonalities shared by all its members (Eph 4:4–6).[42] There is "one body," that is, one church rather than many churches, though the one church consists of many diverse members united under one head, Jesus Christ (Eph 1:22–23). The "one Spirit" is the Holy Spirit (2:18), who unites Jews and Gentiles, men and women, rich and poor, slave and free (Gal 3:26–28; Acts 2:17–18). The "one hope at your calling" is "the hope of eternal life" (Titus 1:2; 3:7) through Jesus Christ (Eph 1:2). He is the "one Lord," the mediator of salvation through the ransom of himself to accomplish salvation (1 Tim 2:5–6; 4:10). The "one faith" is the sound doctrine of Christian belief—the triune God, the one person of Jesus Christ, who is both fully God and fully man, salvation through divine grace alone by faith alone in Christ alone, and more. As the church lives in unity, it contends for "the faith that was delivered to the saints once for all" (Jude v. 3). All those who embrace this one faith share "one baptism," the initiatory rite of the church. "Because all Christians have been baptized, portraying their identification with the death and resurrection of Christ and their cleansing from all sins, this common rite demonstrates their unity."[43] Finally, there is "one God and Father of all," who has created all people in his image; thus, in the sense of creation, the entire human race is one family under the fatherhood of God. Moreover, God the Father has redeemed all those whom he has elected, called, and saved through the powerful work of the Holy Spirit and belief in Jesus Christ (2 Thess 2:13–14).

---

[41] Allison, 174.

[42] Allison, 171–73.

[43] Allison, 172.

To conclude, "these seven items are part of the 'givens' of Christianity. Unity is already provided by God in the most important things. Sharing these fundamental things gives a broad and strong basis for unity."[44] Relying on the Holy Spirit, who has already granted oneness to the church, its members are to exhibit the right attitudes and engage in the proper activities, within the framework of the seven commonalities. "The human task is not to achieve unity among themselves, but to keep the unity already created. . . . 'United and pursuing unity' describes the situation of members of Christ's body, the church."[45] They engage in their responsibility with the aid of the Holy Spirit, the creator and sustainer of church unity.[46]

Purity

The purity or holiness of the church "signifies that the church is already sanctified, though imperfectly. [Such holiness] is threefold: positionally, the church is already set apart from sin for God's use; purposively, the church aims at perfect purity; and instrumentally, the church fosters greater purity by pursuing the holiness of its members."[47] As was developed more fully under the topic of sanctification, the Holy Spirit is characteristically associated with

---

[44] Everett Ferguson, *The Church of Christ: A Biblical Ecclesiology for Today* (Grand Rapids: Eerdmans, 1996), 403.

[45] Ferguson, 406.

[46] This unity is reflected of "the fellowship of the Holy Spirit" (2 Cor 13:14 ESV). Additionally, though the letter of James is often excluded from discussions of the Holy Spirit, one section indirectly links the Spirit with community cohesiveness and peace. James 3:13–18 contrasts two types of wisdom. Wisdom that "does not come down from above" is described as "earthly, unspiritual, demonic." Wisdom "from above" is characterized as "first pure, then peace-loving, gentle, compliant, full of mercy and good fruits, unwavering, without pretense." As the first variety is "unspiritual," it is disconnected from the Holy Spirit. The second variety, while not called "spiritual," still bears all the marks of the work of the Spirit. The fruit of the first type is "bitter envy and selfish ambition . . . disorder and every evil practice," which stands in stark contrast with the "fruit of righteousness . . . sown in peace by those who cultivate peace" as expressed by the second type of wisdom. A church that depends on and acts out of wisdom from above experiences unity, or, in Paul's words, "righteousness, peace, and joy in the Holy Spirit" (Rom 14:17); sadly, the converse is also true.

[47] Allison, *The Baker Compact Dictionary of Theological Terms*, s.v. "holiness of the church."

the church's purity, or holiness. Specifically, Scripture underscores that the will of God is that the church be sanctified, and he himself gives the Holy Spirit to the church for this express purpose (1 Thess 4:3, 8). Within a broader trinitarian context, the church consists of believers who are "chosen according to the foreknowledge of God the Father, through the sanctifying work of the Spirit, to be obedient and to be sprinkled with the blood of Jesus Christ" (1 Pet 1:1–2). The goal of the Holy Spirit's purifying operation is for the church always to obey the will of God. Yet, when the church goes astray, the Spirit's sanctifying work is to cleanse the church from its sin with Christ's blood.

The Spirit particularly stimulates the purity of the church in times of spiritual renewal:

> The power of the Holy Spirit continues to be manifested in special ways during times of spiritual revival which occur periodically in the life of the church. These times of awakening and spiritual refreshing further the expansion of God's kingdom by making people more conscious of their sinfulness and turning them to Christ in a new and deeper way. At such times, believers are reminded of the presence of the Holy Spirit as they become more aware of his working in their lives and of his gifts to them. Spiritual revival is especially effective in bringing God's people back to him by reforming the church, which is constantly in danger of going astray. Nevertheless, the work of the Holy Spirit which is evident at times of spiritual revival is always present in the church and believers must eagerly pray for his fruits and his gifts at all times.[48]

Accordingly, whether in times of spiritual refreshment or during the prolonged periods of normal progress, the church relies on the presence and power of the Holy Spirit for its advancement in purity.

Church Discipline

Church discipline is "the process of rebuking and correcting sinful members of the church. It consists of four steps (Matt. 18:15–20): a personal

---

[48] Statement of Faith of the World Reformed Fellowship (2011), IV, The Person and Work of the Holy Spirit, 4, The Holy Spirit and Spiritual Revival, http://wrfnet .org/about/statement-of-faith#spirit.

confrontation; rebuke by two or three people; admonition by the whole church; and excommunication, or removal from membership. Whenever repentance occurs, the process is terminated and the member is restored."[49]

At no place does Scripture directly address the role of the Holy Spirit in the church's exercise of discipline against its persistently sinful and unrepentant members. Briefly, then, we extrapolate the following points. First, in the four steps of church discipline, the Holy Spirit intersects with several actions. He is the one who brings conviction of sin and prompts repentance; thus, throughout the stages of applying discipline, the church prays for the Spirit to bring an acknowledgment of sin and stir up confession and repentance. Additionally, Jesus's promise of his presence with the church as it engages in discipline is fulfilled by the Holy Spirit: he is the one who renders the Son present among the people of God.[50]

Second, when the drastic step of expulsion from the church occurs, the "action entails removal from church membership and ministry, exclusion from the Lord's Supper, and rupture of relationship with the church and with God."[51] As severe as these undertakings may seem to our contemporary sensibilities, they are fitting, given the presence and work of the Spirit. If the church is God's holy temple because of the Spirit's dwelling in it, then the sinful member in rebellion against the Spirit cannot remain in the temple. If the member is engaged in ministry, he must be removed from his service so as to rid the church of one who is building with wood, hay, and straw, thereby destroying the church (1 Cor 3:10–17). If the Spirit is the one who bridges the space between Christ and his church as it celebrates the Lord's Supper, then the sinful member who is not in fellowship with the Lord cannot be permitted to participate in his blood and body (1 Cor 10:16). If the Spirit is the one who creates and sustains unity among the body, then any member who lives in such a way as to belie such unity cannot remain in the body (1 Cor 10:17).

---

[49] Allison, *The Baker Compact Dictionary of Theological Terms*, s.v. "church discipline."

[50] This point is an application of our earlier discussion that the Holy Spirit renders the presence of the triune God.

[51] Allison.

Third, such excommunication is designed ultimately to prompt the expelled member to repentance, restoration, and reinstatement. Excommunication functions as a handing over of the sinful member "to Satan for the destruction of the flesh, so that his spirit may be saved in the day of the Lord" (1 Cor 5:5). As discussed earlier, the two realms reappear: one of the kingdom of darkness, the world, the dominion of "the god of this age" (2 Cor 4:4); the other of the kingdom of light, (in part) the church, the age of the Spirit.

> Removal from membership in the church involves the loss of divine protection, power, compassion, forgiveness, joy, and comfort—the exhibits of divine grace that are found in the church. Furthermore, it results in the disciplined person's being exposed to the exact opposite reality: Satanic attack, corruption, temptation, deception, accusation, sorrow, and torment. This transfer from the one to the other realm underscores the seriousness of church discipline and highlights the supportive, beneficial environment of the church.[52]

By excommunicating persistently sinful and unrepentant members, the church casts them into the severe realm of the evil one and out of the soothing realm of the Holy Spirit, not for vengeance or out of hatred but for repentance, restoration, and reinstitution.

Personal sin committed by one member against another member (Matt 18:15–20) and egregious/public moral failures (1 Cor 5:1–13, with 2 Cor 2:5–11) are two categories of sin that demand that a church exercise discipline. Scripture proscribes certain other sins that also warrant the exercise of church discipline.[53] These sins are closely attached to the Holy Spirit. Heretical teaching is one such sin. As Paul alerts, "Now the Spirit explicitly says that in later times some will depart from the faith, paying attention to deceitful spirits and the teachings of demons, through the hypocrisy of liars whose consciences are seared. They forbid marriage and demand abstinence from foods that God created" (1 Tim 4:1–3). The Holy Spirit

---

[52] Allison, *Sojourners and Strangers*, 192.

[53] This section advances on the discussion in Allison, 195–99.

warns the church between the two advents of Christ ("in later times") about heretical teaching and even traces its source to deceitful spirits and demons. Again, the stark opposition appears: On the one hand is the Holy Spirit, who inspired Scripture and guides the church as it establishes its doctrine based on Scripture. On the other hand are Satan and his minions, who seek to draw the church away from sound doctrine so as to embrace heresy. Thus, the church is to discipline its members who affirm and spread false doctrine (1 Tim 1:3–4; Titus 1:9–14; 2 John 9–11).

Likewise, divisiveness is a sin that calls for church discipline: "Reject a divisive person after a first and second warning. For you know that such a person has gone astray and is sinning; he is self-condemned" (Titus 3:10–11). This action is fitting, seeing that the Holy Spirit is the creator and sustainer of church unity. In the face of persistent factionalism, which is an attack against the foundation of unity granted by the Spirit, the church is to remove its provocateurs of division (Rom 16:17–18; 1 John 2:18–19).

Idleness, which Scripture denounces in the case of able-bodied people who are lazy and refuse to work, is another sin that leads to church discipline: "Now we command you, brothers and sisters, in the name of our Lord Jesus Christ, to keep away from every brother or sister who is idle and does not live according to the tradition received from us. . . . For we hear that there are some among you who are idle. They are not busy but busybodies. Now we command and exhort such people by the Lord Jesus Christ to work quietly and provide for themselves" (2 Thess 3:6, 11–12). Such industriousness, which enables workers to provide for themselves, their families, the church, and the poor (1 Tim 5:8; 6:17–19; Jas 1:27), is the way the Holy Spirit designed human beings and which he enhances in the case of believers. Accordingly, where idleness, sloth, and busybody activity are found, the church exercises discipline.

Finally, Scripture provides specific instructions about discipline in the case of leadership failures (1 Tim 5:19–21). This is fitting in light of the fact that the Holy Spirit establishes leaders in the church. For their sake and for the sake of the church, when their leadership breaks down, leaders are to be disciplined. More about the role of the Holy Spirit and church leadership follows in the next section.

The Leadership of the Church[54]

From its outset, the church has been led (for a time) by the apostles and (permanently) by pastors/elders and deacons and deaconesses. These offices—apostleship, pastorate/eldership, and diaconate—have specific reference to the Holy Spirit.[55]

Apostleship[56]

The first (nonpermanent) leadership office in the early church was apostleship: "Apostles are the disciples chosen by Jesus to be the foundation of his church. Foremost among these leaders were the original apostles—'the Twelve'—whom Jesus called to follow him. They were Spirit-empowered eyewitnesses of his life, death, and resurrection. Additionally, *apostle* (Gk. *apostolos*, 'messenger') is used to refer to a few other leaders—Paul, Barnabas, and James."[57] The relationship of these leaders to the Holy Spirit is very significant. As part of the old covenant people of God, they traveled with Jesus while being accompanied by the Holy Spirit, who "remain[ed] with" them, with the promise that he would one day "be in" them (John 14:17). Indeed, throughout his ministry Jesus prepared the apostles by teaching them about the fresh, unprecedented outpouring of the Spirit that awaited Christ's departure from the world (e.g., John 7:37–39; 16:8–11).

Specifically, during his post-resurrection and pre-ascension period, Jesus gave "instructions through the Holy Spirit to the apostles he had chosen" (Acts 1:2). One particular command was "not to leave Jerusalem, but to wait for the Father's promise" with the further detail that the apostles would "be

---

[54] For a discussion of the authority of the Holy Spirit and the structure and leadership of the church, see John A. Studebaker Jr., *The Lord Is the Spirit: The Authority of the Holy Spirit in Contemporary Theology and Church Practice*, Evangelical Theological Society Monograph Series (Eugene: Pickwick, 2008), 277–314.

[55] Many denominations and churches also include a third permanent office of bishops, the bishopric.

[56] For discussion of the Holy Spirit and the apostolate see Kuyper, *The Work of the Holy Spirit*, 139–65.

[57] Allison, *The Baker Compact Dictionary of Theological Terms*, s.v. "apostle."

baptized with the Holy Spirit in a few days" (1:4–5; cf. Luke 24:49). That promise is fulfilled on the day of Pentecost, as the newly constituted "Twelve" (with Matthias replacing Judas Iscariot, according to God's will; 1:15–26) are "filled with the Holy Spirit" (2:4). Peter announces this Pentecost event as the fulfillment of Joel's prophecy (Joel 2:28–29) that "it will be in the last days, says God, that I will pour out my Spirit on all people; then your sons and your daughters will prophesy, your young men will see visions, and your old men will dream dreams. I will even pour out my Spirit on my servants in those days, both men and women and they will prophesy" (Acts 2:17–18). Baptized with the Spirit on Pentecost, the apostles continue to be filled with the Spirit for bold proclamation of the gospel (e.g., 4:8, 31), exorcisms of demons (e.g., 13:9), courage in the face of persecution (13:50–52), discernment of the divine will for the church (15:28–29), missional direction (16:6–10; 19–21), and more.

Accordingly, the apostles are the first installment of the outpouring of the Holy Spirit; with their baptism with the Spirit, the age of the Spirit commences. "The apostles were the first to preach the gospel, and they led the church in Jerusalem, from which they established churches in other places. They performed signs and wonders, which confirmed their message; they established authoritative doctrine and practice for the church; and some wrote Scripture."[58] It is by the Spirit that they preach, govern, plant churches, work miracles, institute sound theology and ecclesial practice, and author Scripture. Because of the particular qualifications required of apostles (Acts 1:21–22) and due to their foundational role (Eph 2:20), their office of apostleship came to a close at the death of the last apostle.

This termination means that two offices—eldership/pastorate and diaconate—continue in churches today.

Eldership/Pastorate

The word "elder" refers to "one who ministers in the office of oversight, or eldership. . . . The qualifications for elders are listed in 1 Timothy 3:1–7 and Titus 1:5–9. Elders are entrusted with four responsibilities: teaching, or communicating sound doctrine; leading, or providing overall direction;

---

[58] Allison.

praying, especially for the sick; and shepherding, or guiding, nourishing, and protecting the church."[59] Church members who meet the qualifications for eldership and, once established as elders, carry out weighty responsibilities of their office can be and function as elders only through the calling, equipping, and empowering of the Holy Spirit. Indeed, the apostle Paul, addressing the elders of the church of Ephesus, exhorts them, "Be on guard for yourselves and for all the flock of which the Holy Spirit has appointed you as overseers, to shepherd the church of God, which he purchased with his own blood" (Acts 20:28). Only by appointment of the Holy Spirit and his ongoing endowment can elders faithfully and fruitfully care for their church.

Diaconate

With regard to the second office, "Deacons are those who serve in the office of service. From the Greek (*diakonia*, 'service'; *diakonos*, 'servant'), these terms are used generically to refer to anyone who engages in service and used technically for a person who is a publicly recognized officer serving in a church. . . . The qualifications for men and women to serve are listed in 1 Timothy 3:8–13. Deacon responsibilities do not include leading and teaching but consist of serving in ministries."[60] Still, a key distinction between church members, all of whom are expected to serve, and deacons is that the latter lead the various (non-elder level) ministries in which church members serve. Thus, deacons are leading servants. Church members who meet the qualifications for the diaconate and, once established as deacons and deaconesses, carry out weighty responsibilities of their office can be and function as leading servants only through the calling, equipping, and empowering of the Holy Spirit. Indeed, the apostles' instructions to the church of Jerusalem to search among its members for servants to care for its widows is very focused: "Select from among you seven men of good reputation, full of the Spirit and wisdom, whom we can appoint to this duty" (Acts 6:3). The first of this

---

[59] Allison, s.v. "elder/eldership." Allison adds, "The Greek term *presbyteros* ('presbyter, elder') is used interchangeably in Scripture with *episkopos* ('bishop') and *poimēn* ('pastor'); thus, *elder*, *bishop*, and *pastor* refer to the same office. However, some denominations distinguish between elder and bishop and elevate the latter office above the former."

[60] Allison, s.v. "deacon/deaconess/diaconate."

select group of servants is Stephen, who is described as a "man full of faith and the Holy Spirit" (6:5). For his condemnation of the Jews' crucifixion of Jesus, Stephen becomes the church's first martyr as he, "full of the Spirit," is stoned to death (7:54–60). The second of this select group is Philip, who, through the Spirit, carries out the evangelization of the Samaritans, of the Ethiopian eunuch, and in the towns from Azotus to Caesarea (Acts 8). Though some today overlook the importance of deacons and deaconesses, these leading servants must be full of the Spirit and empowered by him as they engage in ministry.[61]

The Worship of the Church

In one sense worship is any "act of acknowledging and acclaiming the majestic greatness of God in ways that he prescribes."[62] As such, it is "the all-encompassing passion and purpose of the church"[63] in its acts of faithfulness and obedience, discipleship and mercy ministries, evangelism, children and youth programs, and much more. In a more restricted sense,

> Christians gather regularly for a service of worship. This corporate act consists of ascribing honor to God through praise of his nature and mighty works by singing and praying; reading, preaching, and hearing the Word of God, with responses of obedience and faithfulness to covenant responsibilities (e.g., giving money, confessing sin, edifying one another, sending missionaries); and the administration of the new covenant ordinances of baptism and the Lord's Supper.[64]

To focus on this restricted sense, corporate worship of God is made possible by the Holy Spirit. As Jesus himself expresses to the woman of Samaria:

---

[61] For further discussion, see Gregg Allison and Ryan Welsch, *Raising the Dust: How to Equip Deacons to Serve the Church* (Louisville: Sojourn Network Press, 2019).

[62] Allison, *The Baker Compact Dictionary of Theological Terms*, s.v. "worship."

[63] Allison, *Sojourners and Strangers*, 424. For further discussion see David Peterson, *Engaging with God: A Biblical Theology of Worship* (Downers Grove: InterVarsity, 2002).

[64] Allison, *The Baker Compact Dictionary of Theological Terms*, s.v. "worship."

> Believe me, woman, an hour is coming when you will worship the Father neither on this mountain nor in Jerusalem. You Samaritans worship what you do not know. We worship what we do know, because salvation is from the Jews. But an hour is coming, and is now here, when the true worshipers will worship the Father in Spirit and in truth. Yes, the Father wants such people to worship him. God is spirit, and those who worship him must worship in Spirit and in truth. (John 4:21–24)

Jesus emphasizes that new covenant worship represents a change from previous arrangements for corporate worship. The "hour" to which Jesus refers is his death, burial, and resurrection but extends beyond that event to include his ascension, exaltation to the right hand of the Father, and outpouring of the Holy Spirit. Inaugurated in part in the person of Jesus himself, genuine worship is no longer preoccupied with location. Indeed, gone are the days when the Samaritans (ignorantly) worshipped on Mount Gerizim and the Jews (rightly) worshipped in the temple in Jerusalem. In place of location, worship is a matter of approach, a genuineness for which true worshippers must be qualified: the new covenant people of God "worship the Father in Spirit and truth." "These are not two separable characteristics of the worship that must be offered: it must be 'in spirit and truth', i.e., essentially God-centered, made possible by the gift of the Holy Spirit, and in personal knowledge of and conformity to God's Word-made-flesh, the one who is God's 'truth.'"[65] Through the regenerating work of the Holy Spirit, sinful people are "born of water and the Spirit" and thus have a new identity and exist in a new realm: "Whatever is born of the Spirit is spirit" (John 3:5–6). Their new birth through the Spirit of truth (John 14:17; 15:26; 16:13) establishes them in a relationship with the true God (John 17:3; 1 John 5:20) through Jesus Christ, who is "the way, the truth, and the life" (John 14:6) and "full of grace and truth" (John 1:14; cf. v. 17).

Accordingly, Christians, as born again through the Spirit into the identity and realm of "spirit," are qualified to worship God through Jesus Christ according to new covenant directions for genuine worship. Similarly, Paul underscores that believers, in contrast to those who merely circumcise the

---

[65] Carson, *The Gospel according to John*, 196.

flesh, "are the circumcision, the ones who worship by the Spirit of God, boast in Christ Jesus, and do not put confidence in the flesh" (Phil 3:3).

The Ordinances or Sacraments of the Church: Baptism and the Lord's Supper

General Considerations[66]

As has been done with the doctrine of Scripture, we may view the sacraments or ordinances in terms of speech acts. After all, the heritage of the Protestant Reformation closely connects the Word and the sacraments, the two serving as marks of a true church. Thus, if we consider the Word of God in terms of speech acts, we may likewise consider the sacraments or ordinances as speech acts. In the case of baptism and the Lord's Supper, an additional element is included: in the first case the sign of water and in the second case the signs of bread and wine (or grape juice). Thus, these two rites are more properly called "signed speech acts," as the communicative method is not *verba* but *res*, not words but things—not a preached word but a visible word;[67] not sermon but *semeion*/sign. As with speech acts, signed speech acts have three aspects: (1) that which is signed, (2) the force of that which is signed, and (3) the effect of that which is signed.

Baptism

In the case of baptism, (1) that which is signed is multifaceted: association with the triune God, into whose name the person is baptized (Matt 28:19); identification with the death and resurrection of Jesus Christ, who by these events has accomplished the salvation of the person being baptized (Rom 6:3–5); cleansing from sin (Acts 22:16; prophesied in Ezek 36:25); and escape from divine judgment, paralleling rescue from the waters of the condemning Noahic flood (1 Pet 3:20–21).

---

[66] For a Roman Catholic perspective on the Holy Spirit and the sacraments, see Congar, *I Believe in the Holy Spirit*, 3.217–74.

[67] Augustine, *Against Faustus*, 19, considered a sacrament to be a visible word.

(2) The force of that which is signed is both command and promise. As for the imperatival aspect, the pattern of baptism in association with hearing the gospel, repentance from sin, and belief in Jesus Christ leads to the obligation of the person being saved to be baptized. The promissory aspect is that whatever is signed becomes true of the baptized person: she becomes associated with the triune God, identified with the death and resurrection of Christ, cleansed from her sins, and rescued from divine judgment. What is portrayed and thus promised in baptism is to become true of the one who is baptized.

As for (3) the effect, obedience and faith are the proper responses on the part of the person being baptized. As an example, on the day of Pentecost Peter's baptismal command and promise is to "repent and be baptized, each of you, in the name of Jesus Christ for the forgiveness of your sins" (Acts 2:38). His imperative demands that his hearers submit obediently to baptism and believe that their sins are forgiven. In terms of our contemporary administration of this rite, the imperatival and promissory aspects of the signed speech act of baptism lead to people's obeying the command and being baptized, trusting the promise that the triune God, into whose name they are baptized, has saved them through Jesus Christ. As argued earlier, the Holy Spirit is particularly engaged in the perlocutionary aspect of divine speech acts. Similarly, the Holy Spirit is specifically engaged in the third aspect of the signed speech act of baptism, prompting obedience and faith.

Moreover, the presence and work of the Holy Spirit coordinates well with the various meanings of baptism. Baptism associates believers with the triune God, into whose name they are baptized (Matt 28:19), and it is by the indwelling of the Spirit that the Father and the Son dwell in them as well. Baptism vividly portrays Christians' identification with the death and resurrection of Jesus Christ (Rom 6:3–5), and it is by the Holy Spirit that they are united with Christ. Baptism also tangibly depicts cleansing from sin (Acts 22:16), and one of the metaphors for renewal by the Holy Spirit is sprinkling with water (Ezek 36:25; John 3:1–8; Titus 3:4–7). Finally, baptism strikingly pictures escape from divine judgment (1 Pet 3:20–21), and the work of the Spirit to convict of sin and effect the new birth and to serve as advocate and intercessor makes that escape a reality.

The Lord's Supper

In the case of the Lord's Supper, (1) that which is signed is multifaceted as well: the broken body of Jesus Christ, given to accomplish salvation; his shed blood as atoning sacrifice; the gospel itself, proclaimed not by words but by the actions just listed; the presence of Christ, through participation in his blood and body; and the unity of the church, all of whose members share in the sacred meal.

(2) The force of that which is signed is, similar to baptism, both command and promise. As for the imperatival aspect, the one administering the Lord's Supper takes one loaf of bread and breaks it in two, elevates one cup of wine, gives thanks for the blessing of Christ's saving work, and distributes the elements to the members. Participating together and in a worthy manner as a united body, the church eats the bread and drinks the cup of wine. That is, the church obediently observes the Lord's Supper in accordance with the commands of Scripture for its celebration. The promissory aspect is that whatever is signed is true of the members who partake: "The cup of blessing that we bless, is it not a sharing in the blood of Christ? The bread that we break, is it not a sharing in the body of Christ? Because there is one bread, we who are many are one body, since all of us share the one bread" (1 Cor 10:16–17). Church members enjoy fellowship with Christ and his saving benefits, as well as fellowship with one another in the unity of one body.

As for (3) the effect, obedience and faith are the proper responses on the part of the church as it celebrates the Lord's Supper.[68] From Paul's account (1 Cor 11:23–26), one command is to engage in this rite in remembrance of Christ. This commemorative aspect is nurtured through the actions of breaking the loaf of bread, elevating the cup of wine, giving thanks/blessing, and inviting the entire church to eat and drink the elements in remembrance of Christ. A second command is to observe the Lord's Supper in hope, in expectation of his second coming. This eschatological framework is fostered by the church's celebrating Christ's victory over sin, Satan, and death through his first coming and anticipating its celebration of Christ's future victorious return in glory.

---

[68] Some of the following discussion is adapted from Allison, *Sojourners and Strangers*, 406–9.

A third command is for members to ensure, through self-examination, that they eat the bread and drink the cup in a worthy manner. As argued elsewhere, Paul's instruction is not applied by giving church members fifteen seconds to confess all known sins before the Supper is administered. Personal confession should be an ongoing practice and not stored up for the moment before celebrating this rite. Moreover, Paul does not demand that those who partake be *worthy persons*; rather, they are to participate in *a worthy manner*.[69] That is, eschewing all divisions and moving quickly to repair factions, church members should celebrate the Lord's Supper and not their own. The Corinthian supper was reprehensibly characterized by social stratification, disrespect for the poor in its midst, and gluttonous and drunken conduct. In terms of our contemporary administration of this rite, the members must ensure that there are no divisions among themselves; if there are, they move quickly and earnestly to repair them before celebrating this ordinance that portrays the church's unity.

Accordingly, the imperatival and promissory aspects of the signed speech act of the Lord's Supper lead to the church's obeying the command and celebrating it in accordance with biblical instruction, trusting the promise that Christ and his saving benefits move them toward greater Christlikeness. As argued earlier, the Holy Spirit is particularly engaged in the perlocutionary aspect of divine speech acts. Similarly, the Holy Spirit is specifically engaged in the third aspect of the signed speech act of the Lord's Supper, prompting obedience and faith.

Historical Theology: John Calvin on the Sacraments

John Calvin contributed much to the church's consideration of the Holy Spirit and these two sacraments. Briefly, for Calvin a sacrament "is an outward sign by which the Lord seals on our consciences the promises of his good will toward us in order to sustain the weakness of our faith; and we in turn attest our piety toward him."[70] Several elements are involved in a sacrament. First is God's accommodation to human frailty. Certainly, "God's truth

---

[69] Allison, 406–7.

[70] Calvin, *Institutes*, 4.14.1, LCC 21:1277. Calvin expressed his dependence on Augustine's notion of a sacrament as "a visible sign of a sacred thing" or "a visible

is of itself firm and sure enough, and it cannot receive better confirmation from any other source than from itself." Still, because human faith is "slight and feeble," God "condescends to lead us to himself even by these earthly elements, and to set before us in the flesh a mirror of spiritual blessings."[71]

The second element is the Word of God, which ignites faith in the divine promises at the heart of baptism and the Lord's Supper. Indeed, for Calvin, "The sacraments have the same office as the Word of God: to offer and set forth Christ to us, and in him the treasures of heavenly grace. But they avail and profit nothing unless received in faith."[72] The third element is the covenant: these two sacraments are signs of the new covenant that, while "first conceived, established, and decreed in words," is ratified by the signs of water, bread, and wine. Thus a sacrament "represents God's promises as painted in a picture and sets them before our sight, portrayed graphically and in the manner of images."[73]

Calvin carefully distanced his view from any magical power at work in the sacraments, emphasizing instead the power of the Holy Spirit at work in them. He specified that baptism and the Lord's Supper "do not bestow any grace of themselves, but announce and tell us, and (as they are guarantees and tokens) ratify among us, those things given us by divine bounty. The Holy Spirit . . . is he who brings the graces of God with him, gives a place for the sacraments among us, and makes them bear fruit."[74] Specifically, Calvin underscored the work of the Spirit as the one who powerfully engages believers through both Word and sacrament: "That the Word may not beat your ears in vain, and that the sacraments may not strike your eyes in vain, the Spirit shows us that in them it is God speaking to us, softening the stubbornness of our heart, and composing [settling] it to that obedience it owes the Word of the Lord."[75]

---

form of an invisible grace." Augustine developed this idea in his *On the Catechizing of the Uninstructed*, 26.50.

   [71] Calvin, *Institutes*, 4.14.3, LCC 21:1278.
   [72] Calvin, 4.14.17, LCC 21:1292.
   [73] Calvin, 4.14.6, LCC 21:1281.
   [74] Calvin, 4.14.9, LCC 21:1284.
   [75] Calvin, 4.14.10, LCC 21:1285–86.

With respect to the Lord's Supper, Calvin is well known for his "spiritual presence" view in terms of Christ's relationship with this sacrament.[76] While agreeing that the elements of bread and wine are signs, Calvin insisted that in the Lord's Supper, God does not present "a vain and empty sign but manifests there the effectiveness of his Spirit to fulfill what he promises."[77] Accordingly, the once-humiliated-and-crucified-but-now-resurrected-and-ascended-and-exalted God-man, Jesus Christ, who sits triumphantly (as to his human nature) at the right hand of the throne of God the Father in heaven, is present spiritually with the church as it celebrates this sacrament. Such presence is certainly not physical, as transubstantiation and consubstantiation maintain, yet it is more than a mere remembrance or memorial of Christ and his saving work.[78] Rather, Christ, together with his saving benefits, is spiritually present in the Lord's Supper, specifically through the Holy Spirit: "Even if it seems unbelievable that Christ's flesh, separated from us by such great distance, penetrates to us, so that it becomes our food, let us remember how far the secret power of the Holy Spirit towers above all our senses, and how foolish it is to wish to measure his unmeasurableness by our measure. What, then, our mind does not comprehend, let faith conceive: that the Spirit truly unites things separated in space."[79]

So how is the presence of Christ in the Lord's Supper to be conceived? Two axioms function in Calvin's answer to his own question: nothing may be allowed to detract from Christ's glorious deity (such as locating him in the elements), and nothing inappropriate may be ascribed to his humanity (such as considering it to be present everywhere rather than located in heaven).[80] Admitting that Christ's presence in the sacrament is ultimately a mystery, Calvin appealed to the Holy Spirit, who, as just noted, "unites things separated in space."[81] Perhaps the Spirit makes it such that the church "soars up

[76] Allison, *Sojourners and Strangers*, 381–83.

[77] Calvin, *Institutes*, 4.17.10, LCC 21:1370.

[78] Calvin distinguished his view from Roman Catholic transubstantiation (4.17.12, LCC 21:1372–73), Luther's consubstantiation (4.17.16–17, LCC 21:1379–80), and Zwingli's memorialist view (4.17.5, LCC 21:1365); cf. Allison, *Sojourners and Strangers*, 372–81.

[79] Calvin, *Institutes*, 4.17.10, LCC 21:1370.

[80] Calvin, 4.17.19, LCC 21:1382.

[81] Calvin, 4.17.10, LCC 21:1370.

to heaven" to commune with Christ there.[82] Perhaps "Christ descends to us
both by the outward symbol and by his Spirit, that he may truly quicken our
souls by the substance of his flesh and of his blood."[83] In either case, participation in the blood and body of Christ (1 Cor 10:16) is "a secret too lofty
for either my mind to comprehend or my words to declare. And, so to speak
more plainly, I rather experience than understand it."[84]

Our pneumatology reflects Calvin's spiritual presence view of the Lord's
Supper in large measure.[85] Its specific points include: (1) "Divine omnipresence as *ontological presence* means that 'God is present in the totality of his
being at each point of space.'" (2) "Divine omnipresence as *spiritual or moral
presence* means that God is present in different ways at different times and
places to bless his obedient people and judge those who are against him." (3)
In the new covenant celebration of the Lord's Supper, both the ontological
presence of Christ as well as the particular manifestation of his covenantal
presence through the Holy Spirit mean that Christ is present either to bless
proper celebrations of the ordinance or to judge improper celebrations of it
(e.g., divine judgment on the Corinthians' abuse of the Lord's Supper; 1 Cor
11:29–31).

(4) The church participates in Christ and his saving benefits, and its
members are united as his body. As Paul rehearses, "The cup of blessing that
we bless, is it not a sharing in the blood of Christ? The bread that we break,
is it not a sharing in the body of Christ? Because there is one bread, we who
are many are one body, since all of us share the one bread" (1 Cor 10:16–17).
While affirming the commemorative aspect of this ordinance, we recognize
that it is more than mere remembrance of Christ and his death, more than a
memorial of his saving work. Church members enjoy fellowship with Christ
and his saving benefits, as well as fellowship with one another in the unity of
one body. (5) While agreeing with Calvin about the crucial role of the Holy
Spirit in rendering the presence of Christ in the Lord's Supper, the specula-
tive nature of his discussion—the church ascends to Christ, or he descends

---

[82] Calvin, 4.17.24, LCC 21:1390. In such case, Christ acts so as to "lift us to
himself . . . [to] enjoy his presence" (Calvin, 4.17.31, LCC 21:1403).

[83] Calvin, 4.17.24, LCC 21:1390.

[84] Calvin, 4.17.31, LCC 21:1403.

[85] The following discussion is adopted from Allison, *Sojourners and Strangers*,
395–98.

to the church—urges caution. What is affirmed is the presence of Christ by the Holy Spirit when the church administers this new covenant ordinance. The *how* of this presence remains largely mysterious.

Conclusion

Three biblical metaphors for the church are the church as the people of God, as the body of Christ, and as the temple of the Holy Spirit. While distinct metaphors, these remind us of the inseparable operations of the triune God in inaugurating and developing the church. This united ecclesial framework finds emphasis in Eph 2:19–22: "You are no longer foreigners and strangers, but fellow citizens with the saints, and members of God's household, built on the foundation of the apostles and prophets, with Christ Jesus himself as the cornerstone. In him the whole building, being put together, grows into a holy temple in the Lord. In him you are also being built together for God's dwelling in the Spirit." The Father, the Son, and the Holy Spirit initiate and build the church.

Our pneumatology focuses on the third metaphor, the church as the temple of the Holy Spirit. His outpouring on the day of Pentecost gave birth to the church, whose identity markers express the presence and work of the Spirit. For the church's growth and multiplication, the Spirit gives spiritual gifts, grants unity, and prompts purity. When failures in holiness occur, the Spirit operates throughout the process of church discipline. To guide the church toward greater Christlikeness and missional engagement, the Spirit establishes and empowers leaders. As the church convenes its service of worship, the Holy Spirit qualifies members to "worship in Spirit and truth." As the church celebrates baptism and the Lord's Supper, the Holy Spirit brings a reality to what is portrayed and promised in these new covenant ordinances.

Accordingly, the church offers praise and thanksgiving for the Spirit's presence and work, earnestly desires and prays for an increase in his filling and empowerment, engages with unbelievers in expectation of the Spirit's saving operation, and awaits the return of its Savior and its own glorious future through the action of the eschatological Spirit.

23

The Holy Spirit and the Future

The eschatological Spirit is presented in Scripture and affirmed in the church's doctrine and confession.[1] Given our pneumatology's emphasis on the outpouring of the Spirit, it is fitting that the prophecy of Joel appears first in this discussion of the Holy Spirit and the future (Joel 2:28–32). On occasion, we have cited the first part of Joel's prophetic message: "After this I will pour out my Spirit on all humanity; then your sons and your daughters will prophesy, your old men will have dreams, and your young men will see visions. I will even pour out my Spirit on the male and female slaves in those days" (2:28–29). Seamlessly, Joel continues his prophecy: "I will display wonders in the heavens and on the earth: blood, fire, and columns of smoke. The sun will be turned to darkness and the moon to blood before the great and terrible day of the LORD comes. Then everyone who calls on the name of the LORD will be saved" (2:30–32; cited with minor variation in Acts 2:17–21).

---

[1] It may sound strange to refer to him as "the eschatological Spirit," but such he has been and continues to be. As we have rehearsed, the Old Testament predicts a future outpouring of the Spirit in association with the Messiah and the new covenant. Thus, from the beginning, he has been the eschatological Spirit. Jesus refers to him as "what my Father promised" (Luke 24:49; cf. Acts 1:4; cf. 2:33). Thus, from Jesus's standpoint, he is the eschatological Spirit. Paul highlights the fact that, having heard and believed the gospel, believers are "sealed with the promised Holy Spirit . . . [who] is the down payment of our inheritance" (Eph 1:13–14). Thus, from the perspective of our current age between the first and second comings, he continues to be the eschatological Spirit. For further discussion see Congar, *I Believe in the Holy Spirit*, 2.69.

As we have rehearsed, Joel's prophecy begins to be inaugurated with the outpouring of the Spirit on the day of Pentecost. As significant as that event is, however, it is only the beginning. Certainly, the apocalyptic imagery—blood, fire, smoke, darkness—underscores the cataclysmic nature of this long-anticipated day. But it also foreshadows a second aspect of this "day," "the great and terrible day of the LORD," "the future climactic event encompassing Christ's return; universal judgment, including condemnation and salvation; and ultimately the new heaven and new earth."[2] That day has dawned with the outpouring of the Spirit, and it hastens to its conclusion.[3] And from beginning to end, the day is associated with the Holy Spirit; indeed, to use our terminology, it is the age of the Spirit. That day, that age, is drawing to a close, and the presence and work of the Holy Spirit is now oriented to bringing about that eschatological ending. Indeed, "The Spirit who filled and directed the life of Jesus and who was present at creation is also determinative for our life horizon. . . . The Spirit embodies the eschaton, the end-point, the completion."[4]

Peter, who cites Joel's prophecy of the eschatological Spirit at Pentecost, returns to this theme in his first letter: "Dear friends, don't be surprised when the fiery ordeal comes among you to test you as if something unusual were happening to you. Instead, rejoice as you share in the sufferings of Christ, so that you may also rejoice with great joy when his glory is revealed. If you are ridiculed for the name of Christ, you are blessed, because the Spirit of glory and of God rests on you" (1 Pet 4:12–14). The apostle, whose letter is directed at encouraging Christians as they suffer trials and persecutions in this fallen world, exhorts them not to be surprised at the fiery trial but to rejoice because their experience of suffering means they share in Christ's sufferings. But Peter underscores that there is more to their current rejoicing in suffering: it will lead to glad rejoicing (intensified, as it were) when Christ returns in glory, a strong encouragement in light of the fact that Christians will be glorified when Christ's glory is revealed. Furthermore, their present

---

[2] Allison, *The Baker Compact Dictionary of Theological Terms*, s.v. "day of the Lord."

[3] For the role of the Holy Spirit in the final judgment, see Rustin Umstattd, *The Spirit and the Lake of Fire: Pneumatology and Judgment* (Eugene: Wipf & Stock, 2017).

[4] Van der Kooi, *This Incredibly Benevolent Force*, 5.

suffering for Christ indicates that the Holy Spirit—"the Spirit of glory and of God"—rests on them. As the Spirit of glory, he is the one who will bring them to glory by accomplishing their glorification. When Christ is revealed in glory, so also will Christians be revealed in glory because of the Spirit of glory resting on them now, with future implications.[5]

Peter's exhortation comports well with Paul's discussion of the present suffering of the fallen creation (Rom 8:18–21).[6] Paul ends on a note of hope, again linked to the Spirit: "We know that the whole creation has been groaning together with labor pains until now. Not only that, but we ourselves who have the Spirit as the firstfruits—we also groan within ourselves, eagerly waiting for adoption, the redemption of our bodies" (8:22–23). Masterfully, the apostle connects the future of the cursed creation, which will be redeemed, with the future of Christians, who are now redeemed in part and will be redeemed fully, even bodily. Importantly for our discussion, this hope is centered on the firstfruits of the Spirit, whom Christians currently possess. The conjunction of the Holy Spirit with believers' future (completed) adoption, described in terms of bodily resurrection, and the future restoration of the entire created order underscores the work of the Spirit in both personal and cosmic eschatology. Indeed, as it was in the beginning, so it will be in the end. The opening chapters of Genesis narrate the original creation, in which the Holy Spirit plays a crucial role (Gen 1:2). With its teleological orientation, Genesis 1–3 sets the entire Bible and its account of the redeeming action of the triune God on the trajectory that culminates in consummation: the new heavens and the new earth (Rev 21–22), actualized through the work of the Holy Spirit.[7]

---

[5] This passage underscores the link between Christ and the Holy Spirit in eschatological realities. It is Christ for whom Christians and the church wait while the Holy Spirit rests on them; the Spirit will effect their glorious resurrection in conformity with the resurrection body of Christ. Indeed, both Christ and the Holy Spirit are called "the firstfruits" (Christ, 1 Cor 15:20; Holy Spirit: Rom 8:23); thus, together they direct believers and the church toward the future.

[6] For a discussion of Pauline pneumatology and eschatology see T. David Beck, *The Holy Spirit and the Renewal of All Things: Pneumatology in Paul and Jürgen Moltmann*, Princeton Theological Monograph Series (Eugene: Pickwick, 2007), 25–83.

[7] "The telos of the garden of Eden in its consummative fulfillment for redeemed humanity is depicted in terms of the Edenic imagery in Revelation 22:1–2, which, at

Building on this biblical foundation for the eschatological Spirit, the church has historically confessed that eschatology flows from pneumatology: "I believe in the Holy Spirit; . . . the resurrection of the body; and the life everlasting" (Apostles' Creed). This foundation also undergirds the church's traditional emphasis on the perfecting work of the Holy Spirit.[8] In its affirmation of the inseparable operations of the triune God, the church notes that the Father, the Son, and the Holy Spirit act indivisibly, with the power to bring forth coming from the Father, the power to arrange from the Son, and the *power to perfect* from the Holy Spirit.[9] Indeed, the work of completion terminates in the Spirit.

Accordingly, and with the realization of existing in "the last days," Christians live a liminal or transitional existence in which the eschatological Spirit has invaded this world, with the kingdom inaugurated, the new covenant installed, and the church launched and multiplying.[10] As sojourners and strangers "on whom the ends of the ages have come" (1 Cor 10:11), they travel on a pilgrimage to something greater. Indeed, "every coming of the Spirit is an eschatological act, because in it the ultimate future to which God is leading us invades, touches, and transforms our temporal lives."[11] Realistic expectations must be set for their progress; over-realized pneumatological

---

the macro level, represents what the garden of Eden in Genesis 2:8–17 represents at the micro level as part of God's creational intention for humanity." Jonathan King, *The Beauty of the Lord: Theology as Aesthetics*, Studies in Historical and Systematic Theology (Bellingham: Lexham, 2018), 105. To the objection that the work of the Holy Spirit is not explicitly mentioned in the narrative of the consummation, the reply is to note the teleological orientation of the narrative of the creation and underscore that what was in the beginning—the creative work of the Spirit—will be also in the end—the consummative work of the Spirit.

[8] For an emphasis of the Spirit's perfecting work in relation to the future of human beings, see Stephen R. Guthrie, *Creator Spirit: The Holy Spirit and the Art of Becoming Human* (Grand Rapids: Baker Academic, 2011).

[9] Kuyper, *The Work of the Holy Spirit*, 19. Basil the Great made a similar distinction in the work of creation, assigning the original cause of all things to the Father, the creative cause to the Son, and the perfecting cause to the Spirit. See Basil, *On the Holy Spirit*, 16.38; *NPNF*² 8:23.

[10] Worth noting is the subtitle of Michael Horton's *Rediscovering the Holy Spirit: God's Perfecting Presence in Creation, Redemption, and Everyday Life.*

[11] Smail, *The Giving Gift*, 29.

eschatology must be avoided.[12] The betrothed bride will one day be without spot or wrinkle, but she has a long way to go in preparation for her bridegroom. Any progress that she makes, she makes by the Holy Spirit, who, together with her, yearns for the consummation: "Both the Spirit and the bride say, 'Come!'" (Rev 22:17).

---

[12] Barbeau and Jones, "Come, Holy Spirit: Reflections on Faith and Practice," in *Spirit of God: Christian Renewal in the Community of Faith*, 248–49. Examples of over-realized eschatology are legion, but a contemporary manifestation is Bill Johnson and the Bethel Church movement. Working off a poorly developed view of divine sovereignty, Johnson maintains that anything on earth that is different from what it is in heaven is a perversion of God's will. Accordingly, sickness, suffering, and evil are not according to the divine design and are to be resisted through the power of the Holy Spirit. Moreover, because Jesus performed his miracles as a man empowered by the Spirit (without any reliance on his divine nature), believers who are filled with the power of the Spirit can perform similar miracles. Any failure on their part is due to lack of faith. See Bill Johnson, *Hosting the Presence: Unveiling Heaven's Agenda* (Shippensburg, PA: Destiny Image, 2012).

24

Contemporary Issues in Pneumatology

Given the many options that we could treat in this section, and the fact that we have treated various contemporary issues already in this work, our pneumatology will restrict itself to brief comments on a few selected issues.

The Three Ages

In keeping with the distinctives of our pneumatology, what does "the age of the Spirit" have to offer to "the spirit of the age" and "the spiritual age"? (1) The virtues of humility and deference to others, as the Spirit stirs up meekness and fosters submission. (2) An other-centered life oriented to a pursuing love for, and sacrificial service to, those around us. Such a posture is the fruit of the Spirit who is "Love" and "Gift." (3) A grounded hope, faith not in faith itself but in Another, as the Holy Spirit renders the presence of the triune God. As the true God, he is not merely and disappointingly the product of the age's imagination or wishes. (4) A "ruled" life that embraces freedom through restraint; such a stance rejects antinomianism but eschews legalism as well. The Spirit, who directs and empowers sanctification, prompts this bridled and life-giving freedom. (5) A culture of life versus a culture of death, because the Spirit is the "Giver of life." (6) Unity in diversity, as the Spirit unites Jew and Gentile, men and women, old and young, rich and poor, slave and free, Farsi speakers and Cantonese speakers, and much more in the church.

Spirit-Emphasizing Movements

Since the outset of the twentieth century, Christendom has experienced fresh waves of movements emphasizing the Holy Spirit. Three such movements are Pentecostalism, the Charismatic movement, and third-wave evangelicalism.

Pentecostalism

Pentecostalism began at the turn of the twentieth century through a series of events that reached a crescendo with the Azusa Street revival in 1906. From its small beginnings, Pentecostalism has mushroomed into a global movement numbering, according to current estimates, about 600 million adherents, or 27 percent of 2.2 billion Christians worldwide.

The distinctives of Pentecostalism include:[1]

Theological Distinctives:

- baptism in/with/by the Holy Spirit (with various understandings of the nature of such baptism)[2]

---

[1] Some of these distinctives are developed from Bloesch, *The Holy Spirit*. For a popular treatment of the positive and negative aspects of Pentecostalism/the Charismatic movement, see Packer, *Keep in Step with the Spirit*, 151–58; followed by Schreiner, *Spiritual Gifts*, 13.

[2] Frederick Dale Bruner, *A Theology of the Holy Spirit* (Grand Rapids: Eerdmans, 1970), 56–61, opined that the most distinctive element of Pentecostal theology is its "pneumobaptistocentric" feature (59), or centeredness on Spirit baptism. He also engaged in a lengthy study of baptism of the Holy Spirit in the book of Acts (153–218). As Frank Macchia underscores, Steven Land contests Bruner's opinion of this Pentecostal distinctive. See Frank D. Macchia, "The Kingdom and the Power: Spirit Baptism in Pentecostal and Ecumenical Perspective," in *The Work of the Spirit: Pneumatology and Pentecostalism*, ed. Michael Welker (Grand Rapids: Eerdmans, 2006), 112–13. Macchia's reference is to Steven J. Land, *Pentecostal Spirituality: A Passion for the Kingdom* (Sheffield, UK: Sheffield Academic Press, 1993), 62–63.

- separability: regeneration and baptism with the Spirit as two distinct mighty acts of God in believers
- subsequence: baptism with the Spirit taking place subsequently to regeneration, either logically or temporally[3]
- glossolalia (speaking in tongues)
- continuationism

Experiential Distinctives:

- the powerful experience of the reality and presence of God, including "recognition of the vitality and contemporary meaning of the biblical world"[4]
- development of the ability "to pray, to enjoy praying, and to talk about God in a fresh way with joy and power"[5]

---

[3] The doctrines of separability and subsequence are explained in the "Statement of Fundamental Truths" of the Constitution and By-Laws of the General Council of the Assemblies of God, art. 7, "The Baptism in the Holy Spirit":

All believers are entitled to and should ardently expect and earnestly seek the promise of the Father, the baptism in the Holy Spirit and fire, according to the command of our Lord Jesus Christ. This was the normal experience of all in the early Christian Church. With it comes the enduement of power for life and service, the bestowment of the gifts and their uses in the work of the ministry. (Luke 24:49; Acts 1:4; Acts 1:8; 1 Cor 12:1–31). *This experience is distinct from and subsequent to the experience of the new birth* (Acts 8:12–17; 10:44–46; 11:14–16; 15:7–9). With the baptism in the Holy Spirit come such experiences as: an overflowing fullness of the Spirit (John 7:37–39; Acts 4:8); a deepened reverence for God (Acts 2:43; Hebrews 12:28); an intensified consecration to God and dedication to His work (Acts 2:42); and a more active love for Christ, for His Word and for the lost (Mark 16:20). (See https://ag.org/Beliefs/Statement-of-Fundamental-Truths#7; emphasis added.)

For further discussion on the doctrine of subsequence see Bruner, *A Theology of the Holy Spirit*, 61–76. Gordon Fee, a Pentecostal biblical scholar, critiques the doctrine of subsequence in *Gospel and Spirit: Issues in New Testament Hermeneutics* (Peabody: Hendrickson, 1991). For a brief response to Fee, see William W. Menzies and Robert P. Menzies, *Spirit and Power: Foundations of Pentecostal Experience* (Grand Rapids: Zondervan, 2000), 109–19.

[4] Welker, *God the Spirit*, 11–12.

[5] Welker, 12.

- "the abundance and diversity of the gifts of the Spirit," with the dismantling of the clergy-laity distinction and the rejection of hierarchicalism and professionalism[6]
- a two-stage experience of the Holy Spirit: regeneration through the Spirit and baptism with the Spirit; other Pentecostal groups hold to a three-stage experience: regeneration, sanctification, and baptism with the Spirit as empowerment for service

Ministry/Missional Distinctives:

- urgent missionality
- healing "in the context of a theology that regards sickness as a prime manifestation of sin"[7]
- deliverance ministries "based on the supposition that the ultimate adversary of humanity is Satan or demonic powers," thus fostering the need for exorcisms[8]
- openness to ecumenical dialogue, as confessional boundaries are diminished

Concerns about Pentecostalism include:[9]

- its difficulty in communicating the experiences of the Spirit, often repelling people rather than attracting them
- its creation of new hierarchies and elitism, with those who have experienced baptism with the Spirit, speaking in tongues, and the like as the most highly regarded
- its escapism from the powerful structures of technical-scientific rationality that characterize Western culture and that certainly deserve to be critiqued and confronted—but escapism is neither critique nor confrontation, but withdrawal; indeed, should we not expect that the liberating power of the Holy Spirit, claimed to be

---

[6] Welker, 12.

[7] Bloesch, *The Holy Spirit*, 192.

[8] Bloesch, 192.

[9] Some of these concerns are developed from Bloesch, *The Holy Spirit*; and Welker, *God the Spirit*.

experienced by this movement, should address "the dominant cultures' ruling powers of self-endangerment and self-destruction"?[10]

- its emphasis on the unusual, the sensational, the spectacular action of the Holy Spirit—tongues, prophecy, miraculous healing—more as "a reaction against the enlightened skepticism of the average Western mentality, against the rationality, homogeneity, predictability, and foreseeability of the ways in which that average Western mentality goes through life" than as the actual work of the Spirit[11]

- its promotion of unmediated experiences of the Spirit; but God's presence with his people is always mediated, for example, by revelation (Scripture); by atonement, or Christ as the Mediator; by salvation, or the application of Christ's work by the gospel and the Spirit; by structured relationship (the new covenant); by ministry, or church members' serving together and one another through the mediation of gifts of the Spirit; by community, or the church with its divinely appointed leaders and its liturgy, including ordinances/sacraments that both mediate God's presence and shape members' lives into gospel-dominated rhythms; and more

The Charismatic Movement

The Charismatic movement is the "development within mainline churches and denominations (e.g., Anglican, Catholic), beginning in the 1960s, that embraced certain doctrines and experiences of Pentecostal theology. These commonalities were (1) baptism in the Holy Spirit as a mighty act of God in the lives of Christians sometime after their conversion; (2) speaking in tongues as a sign of such Spirit baptism; and (3) the continuing reception and experience of all the spiritual gifts."[12] It is this third emphasis, on the gifts (Gr. *charism*) that gave the name "*Charism*atic" to this movement. Unlike Pentecostalism, from which arose new churches and denominations

---

[10] Welker, 15.

[11] Welker, 15.

[12] Allison, *The Baker Compact Dictionary of Theological Terms*, s.v. "charismatic movement."

(for example, the Assemblies of God, the Church of God, the Foursquare Church), the charismatic movement was largely Pentecostal theology that penetrated and affected already existing churches and denominations.

The movement began in 1960, when Dennis Bennett, rector of St. Mark's Episcopal Church in Van Nuys, California, experienced baptism with the Spirit and speaking in tongues. In 1967, participants at a retreat near Duquesne University experienced a similar phenomenon. That event launched what would eventually become the Catholic Charismatic Renewal in the United States. This movement first met at the University of Notre Dame in 1967, with seventy people in attendance; participation soon exploded exponentially.[13] Several significant charismatic communities developed, including the Word of God community in Ann Arbor, Michigan, and the People of Praise community in South Bend, Indiana.

Distinctives and concerns of the Charismatic movement mirror those of Pentecostalism, with variations occurring with respect to the denominations and churches that embrace the movement.[14] For example, some Catholic charismatics claim greater devotion to the Eucharist and to Mary after their charismatic experience, a claim that charismatic Methodists and Baptists would not make. One also wonders if, for at least some of these people, their charismatic experience of the Spirit marks the moment of their conversion to Christ rather than a renewal of their Christian life.

---

[13] Attendance figures per year were 150 (1968), 500 (1969), 1,500 (1970), 5,000 (1971), 12,000 (1972), 23,000 (1973), 37,000 (1974). See A. Bittlinger, *Charismatische Erneuerung* (Metzingen, DEU: 1979), 5.

[14] For example, Yves Congar, *I Believe in the Holy Spirit*, 2:165–69, raises two concerns about the Catholic charismatic movement: (1) Immediacy: "In the Renewal, Christians look for and find a response or solution in a quick, immediate and personal relationship that cuts out long and difficult approaches." For Congar, the danger of such immediacy is that it may bypass the use of human means such as prudence and decision-making, it may lead to a fundamentalist approach to interpreting Scripture, and it may ultimately result not in a pneumatic or spiritual experience but merely in a greedy or carnal psychical experience. (2) Lessening of social commitment: Because it leads to an experience of intimacy with God and strongly emphasizes an eschatological hope, the Renewal movement "favours a sense of personal and vertical relationship with God and therefore turns its adherents away from action in the world."

Third-Wave Evangelicalism

Historically, Pentecostal theology and practice has come in several "waves" of activity. As just rehearsed, the first wave began in the early part of the twentieth century, with the rise of Pentecostalism. The second wave arose in the 1960s/1970s, with the Charismatic movement. The third wave began in the 1980s and is known as "third-wave evangelicalism,"

> a contemporary type of evangelicalism featuring both similarities to and differences from Pentecostal theology (first wave) and the charismatic movement (second wave). Originating with John Wimber in the 1980s, third wave proponents include Wayne Grudem, Sam Storms, the early Vineyard churches, and [formerly] the Sovereign Grace network. Similar to Pentecostal and charismatic theology, third wave evangelicalism is continuationist, believing that all the spiritual gifts, including the sign or miraculous gifts, continue in the church today. It differs from Pentecostal and charismatic theology in its position that the baptism with the Holy Spirit occurs at salvation, not subsequent to it.[15]

A recent expression of third-wave evangelicalism is found in Reformed charismatic churches such as Renew Church LA, Vintage Church (Los Angeles), Southlands Church (Brea, CA), Aletheia Church (Boston), and those aligned with the Acts 29 network (The Village Church, Dallas; Bridgeway Church, Oklahoma City). Reformed theology, which emphasizes divine sovereignty and such doctrines as unconditional election and the perseverance of the saints, has traditionally "tended to be cessationist, either denying or avoiding the continued practice of charismatic gifts like healing, tongues, and prophecy, believing they were only for the foundational era of the church."[16] Reformed charismatic churches, then, embrace a hearty focus on the extraordinary work of the Holy Spirit, adopting a continuationist

---

[15] Allison, *The Baker Compact Dictionary of Theological Terms*, s.v. "third wave evangelicalism."

[16] Brett McCracken, "The Rise of Reformed Charismatics," *Christianity Today*, December 21, 2017, https://www.christianitytoday.com/ct/2018/january-february/rise-of-reformed-charismatics.html.

stance and seeking to make room in their weekly worship services for expressions of the gifts of the Spirit.[17]

Reaction to Pentecostalism, the Charismatic movement, and third-wave evangelicalism has been mixed and, in some cases, quite vitriolic. Whatever one's opinion may be, an important issue to consider is how to "account for the Spirit's presence and power in the explosive growth of Pentecostal and charismatic Christianities."[18] A charitable, measured pneumatology urges believers and churches to avoid easy reductionism by which Pentecostal and charismatic phenomena are dismissed as either the highest expression of divine blessing or the derelict result of demonic activity.

The Holy Spirit and a Theology of Religions

For the last few decades, several attempts have been made to address the relationship between pneumatology and a theology of religions.[19] For background, the issue often comes down to the differences between exclusivism and inclusivism. Exclusivism is

> the position that salvation comes only through Christ, not through religions like Islam, Buddhism, and Hinduism. Exclusivism makes two affirmations: (1) The person and work of Christ is the ground of salvation; through his life, death, and resurrection, Christ accomplished redemption. (2) Faith in the person and work of Christ is necessary to appropriate salvation; through trust in Christ, sinful people experience redemption. Accordingly, the church is

---

[17] For a fascinating study of the relationship of Baptists to these Spirit-emphasizing movements, see C. Douglas Weaver, *Baptists and the Holy Spirit: The Contested History with Holiness-Pentecostal-Charismatic Movements* (Waco: Baylor University Press, 2019).

[18] Barbeau and Jones, "Come, Holy Spirit: Reflections on Faith and Practice," 246.

[19] For a brief treatment of the Holy Spirit among religions see Kärkkäinen, *The Holy Spirit in Ecumenical, International, and Contextual Perspective*, 157–82; Kärkkäinen, "'How to Speak of the Spirit among Religions': Trinitarian Prolegomena for a Pneumatological Theology of Religions," in *The Work of the Spirit: Pneumatology and Pentecostalism*, ed. Michael Welker (Grand Rapids: Eerdmans, 2006), 47–70.

missionally engaged in proclaiming the gospel to make known the salvation accomplished by Christ so it may be believed.[20]

In contrast, inclusivism is

> the position that salvation comes through Christ yet extends beyond Christianity to include adherents of religions like Islam, Buddhism, and Hinduism. Like exclusivism, inclusivism affirms that the person and work of Christ is the ground of salvation; through his life, death, and resurrection, Christ accomplished redemption. Unlike exclusivism, inclusivism denies that faith in his person and work is necessary to experience salvation. While people from non-Christian religions can be saved only by the salvation accomplished by Christ, they may experience salvation apart from faith in Christ.[21]

Importantly, the historical position of the church is exclusivism, but the move toward inclusivism is accelerating significantly in some circles.

For example, beginning with Vatican II, Roman Catholic theology has embraced inclusivism.[22] If one imagines a series of concentric circles, the innermost circle would represent the Roman Catholic faithful, with the next outlying circle representing the other two expressions of Christendom, Eastern Orthodoxy and Protestantism. Continuing outward, the next circle would represent the monotheistic religions of Judaism and Islam, with the circle still further removed representing non-Christian religions (e.g., Hinduism, Buddhism, Sikhism). Finally, the furthest-removed circle would

---

[20] Allison, *The Baker Compact Dictionary of Theological Terms*, s.v. "exclusivism." Amos Yong, *Beyond the Impasse: Toward a Pneumatological Theology of Religions* (Grand Rapids: Baker Academic, 2003), 22–23, views exclusivism as "the traditional Christian position of *extra ecclesia nulla salus*" (outside the church there is no salvation) that underscores "salvation as ontologically secured (through the person and work of Christ) and as epistemically accessed (through the preaching of the gospel, among other providential means of God)."

[21] Allison, *The Baker Compact Dictionary of Theological Terms*, s.v. "inclusivism." Yong, *Beyond the Impasse*, 23, views inclusivism as the position that underscores "salvation as ontologically secured (through the person and work of Christ) and as epistemically accessed (through the preaching of the gospel, among other providential means of God)."

[22] For further discussion see Allison, *Roman Catholic Theology and Practice*, 163–66, 174–80.

represent "those who in shadows and images seek the unknown God," others
who "seek God and moved by grace strive by their deeds to do His will as it is
known to them through the dictates of their conscience," and still others who
"have not yet arrived at an explicit knowledge of God and with His grace
strive to live a good life." Roman Catholic inclusivism maintains that, while
the fullness of salvation belongs to those in the innermost circle (that is, the
Catholic faithful), salvation extends outward such that anyone, even those in
the circle furthest removed from the center, may experience salvation.[23]

Roman Catholic theology grounds its inclusivism on various points,
including belief in the universal love of God for all people, the unlimited atonement of Jesus Christ, the divine will that everyone would be saved (1 Tim 2:3–
4; 2 Pet 3:9), some type of universal or prevenient grace that prepares people for
the gospel, and the fact that the Roman Catholic Church is "the universal sacrament of salvation."[24] Important for our discussion is the later development of
Catholic inclusivism that appeals to the wind-like activity of the Holy Spirit: as
"the wind blows where it pleases" (John 3:8), so is the movement of the Spirit
unregulated, even in the midst of non-Christian religions and agnosticism, to
prepare people who have no knowledge of the gospel for salvation.[25]

From a Protestant perspective, Amos Yong appeals to the Holy Spirit in his
argument for inclusivism in his *Beyond the Impasse: Toward a Pneumatological
Theology of Religions*.[26] Some of his presentation reflects the elements already

---

[23] *Lumen Gentium*, 13–17.

[24] *Lumen Gentium*, 48.

[25] According to Sullivan, this emphasis on the unregulated blowing of the
Spirit—in other words, his activity outside of the Roman Catholic Church—
is a major theme in the writings of Pope John Paul II (for example, *Dominum
et Vivificantem*; *Redemptoris Missio*; *Ecclesia in Asia*). See Francis A. Sullivan,
"Vatican II on the Salvation of Other Religions," in *After Vatican II: Trajectories and
Hermeneutics*, ed. James L. Heft (Grand Rapids: Eerdmans, 2012), 82. At the same
time, Congar, *I Believe in the Holy Spirit*, 2.35, insisted that the Holy Spirit "is the
Spirit of *Jesus Christ*. He does no other work but that of *Jesus Christ*. There is no time
of the Paraclete that is not the time of Jesus Christ. . . . The catholicity of the Church
is the catholicity *of Christ*. The soundness of any pneumatology is its reference to
Christ" (emphasis original).

[26] Yong, *Beyond the Impasse*. Daniel Castelo, *Pneumatology: A Guide for the
Perplexed* (London: Bloomsbury T&T Clark, 2015), 122, summarizes the relationship between the Holy Spirit and a theology of religions: "Given that the world is
because God brings it to be and given that all of humanity reflects the image of God

noted.[27] These include the wideness of God's mercy, the universal atonement of Christ, the divine will for universal salvation, and prevenient grace, a type of divine favor that is universally given to all people, restoring their ability to meet the conditions (repentance and faith) of salvation. Important for our purpose is the appeal of Yong (often following Pinnock) to the Holy Spirit. Similar to the Roman Catholic view, Yong reasons from the fact that the Holy Spirit blows where he pleases (John 3:8) to conclude that the Spirit cannot be limited to the "institutional forms of the church." Moreover, if this is true, "Why would the Spirit blow 'outside' the church but not at all in the religions" without denying the particularity of salvation in Christ?[28]

Additionally, Yong draws attention to the biblical framework of creation, re-creation, and final creation, noting the universal presence and activity of the Holy Spirit in each aspect.[29] Moreover, he maintains that "the religions of the world, like everything else that exists, are providentially sustained by the Spirit of God for divine purposes." They are not merely human efforts to reach God, he claims, nor are they demonic; they do not "lie beyond the pale of divine presence and activity." Quoting Pinnock, Yong underscores, "It would seem strange if the Spirit excused himself from the very arena of culture where people search for meaning. If God is reaching out to sinners, it is hard to comprehend why he would not do so in the sphere of religion."[30]

---

and not simply self-professed Christians, touch points necessarily exist between the confession of the Holy Spirit and popular religious expressions of various contexts."

[27] Yong often develops ideas proposed earlier in Clark Pinnock, *A Wideness in God's Mercy: The Finality of Jesus Christ in a World of Religions* (Grand Rapids: Zondervan, 1992).

[28] Yong, *Beyond the Impasse*, 20–22. A major difference between Roman Catholic theology and that of Pinnock (seemingly cited with approval by Yong) regards the double procession of the Holy Spirit from both the Father and the Son. Pinnock rejects the *filioque* clause, so that the Spirit proceeds from the Father only. Thus, the work of the Son is identifiably distinct from the work of the Spirit. See Pinnock, *A Wideness in God's Mercy*, 78; discussed in Yong, *Beyond the Impasse*, 111–12; see also Cole, *He Who Gives Life*, 199–202.

[29] Yong, *Beyond the Impasse*, 40–42. For Yong, the emphasis on the Spirit's being poured out at Pentecost on "all" people and "in the last days" (Acts 2:17)—hence transcending both space and time—"begs to be understood in a universal sense that transcends (at least the institutional boundaries of) the church" (40).

[30] Yong, *Beyond the Impasse*, 46. His citation is from Clark Pinnock, *Flame of Love: A Theology of the Holy Spirit* (Downers Grove: InterVarsity, 1996), 203. Yong

Finally, Yong raises a key question: "But how is the Spirit's presence and activity in the world of religions discerned, and how do we confront and pronounce judgment on that which is not of God?"[31] Yong appeals to Pinnock's response: we discern the Spirit in religions whenever we witness "self-sacrificing love, care about community, longings for justice, wherever people love one another, care for the sick, make peace not war, wherever there is beauty and concord, generosity and forgiveness, the cup of cold water."[32] On this latter element, according to Pinnock and cited approvingly by Yong, Jesus showed that insofar as people in general, and particularly those of other faiths,

> gave a cup of cold water to the thirsty[,] they showed where they stood with respect to the kingdom and that they were positively oriented to Jesus himself, even though they did not know him. The good Samaritan too had a heart for God's kingdom as revealed in his acts of compassion, and the inadequacies of his theology as a Samaritan did not worry Jesus, because evidently for Jesus the issue was the direction of his life toward the kingdom, not theological correctness. I believe that Jesus is the criterion of salvation both ethically and theologically, and that it is possible for those who have not known him to do the works of love which correspond to God's kingdom and participate in salvation at the last judgment.[33]

Accordingly, Yong, borrowing from Pinnock, is an example of recent Protestant attempts to trace the presence and work of the Holy Spirit in a theology of religions.

Our doctrine of the Holy Spirit, affirming the inseparable operations of the triune God and being inextricably connected to Christology, is a missional pneumatology that holds to exclusivism and rejects inclusivism. Scripture undergirds the two affirmations of exclusivism (see definition at the beginning of this section). Accordingly, inclusivism's denial of the

---

dismisses the traditional paradigm that views religions as beset by sin and expressive of idolatry. For that paradigm see Daniel Strange, *Their Rock Is Not Like Our Rock: A Theology of Religions* (Grand Rapids: Zondervan, 2014).

[31] Yong, *Beyond the Impasse*, 120.

[32] Yong, *Beyond the Impasse*, 120. The citation is from Pinnock, *Flame of Love*, 209–10.

[33] Yong, 120–21.

second affirmation is wrong. Such rejection puts inclusivism at odds with Paul's insistence on announcing the gospel in order to ignite faith in Christ: "Everyone who calls on the name of the Lord will be saved. How, then, can they call on him they have not believed in? And how can they believe without hearing about him? And how can they hear without a preacher? And how can they preach unless they are sent? . . . So faith comes from what is heard, and what is heard comes through the message about Christ" (Rom 10:13–15, 17). Inclusivism also contradicts Peter's emphasis on the gospel and regeneration: "You have been born again—not of perishable seed but of imperishable—through the living and enduring word of God. . . . And this word is the gospel that was proclaimed to you" (1 Pet 1:23, 25). On the basis of such clear and constant biblical support, the church has historically embraced exclusivism and rejected inclusivism.[34]

Moreover, proposals like that of Roman Catholic theology and of Yong are flawed on several accounts. One problem is their inadequate view of the fallen human condition. Such sinfulness results in nonbelievers' (1) drawing the wrong conclusions from general revelation and thus being condemned by God for their idolatrous response to that universal disclosure (Rom 1:18–25); (2) failing to obey the dictates of their conscience (Rom 2:13–16); (3) reacting superstitiously to God's providential care (Acts 14:8–18); and (4) engaging in idolatry rather than genuine worship of the one true God (Acts 17:22–31). Second, these inclusivist proposals assume that humanity's search for meaning, love for others, concern for justice, appreciation of beauty, desire for unity and peace, and, generally speaking, giving "a cup of cold water" (see Matt 25:31–46) are evidences of an orientation toward the kingdom of God that somehow places such people in the realm of salvation. Without denying the "goodness" of such works, exclusivism considers them to be the responses of intractably sinful hearts, whether they are done altruistically or religiously for the purpose of achieving merit before God. This negative assessment does not at all deny the fact that human beings are divine image bearers, recipients of common grace, and beneficiaries of the universal work of the Holy Spirit. Such presence

---

[34] For a thorough critique of inclusivism, see Christopher W. Morgan and Robert A. Peterson, ed., *Faith Comes by Hearing: A Response to Inclusivism* (Downers Grove: InterVarsity Press, 2008). For a discussion of the development, largely post-Vatican II, of inclusivism in the Roman Catholic Church, see Allison, *Roman Catholic Theology and Practice*, 174–80.

and assistance, however, is not "in any way salvific, that is, effecting salvation, apart from a response of faith to the gospel of Jesus Christ."[35]

Third, inclusivism encounters difficulty with Jesus's statement about "the Spirit of truth. The world is unable to receive him because it doesn't see him or know him. But you [my disciples] do know him, because he remains with you and will be in you" (John 14:17). Jesus's view of humanity is binary: people are divided into two disparate groups. On the one hand are Jesus's disciples, in whom the Holy Spirit dwells, in virtue of whose presence they experience salvation, eternal life, a relationship with the triune God, and the like. On the other hand is the world, in whose citizens the Holy Spirit does not and cannot dwell. In virtue of the Spirit's absence, nonbelievers do not experience salvation, eternal life, a relationship with the triune God, and more. Indeed, "the whole world is under the sway of the evil one" (1 John 5:19). This division does not mean that any particular person or group of people is necessarily excluded from the work of the Spirit to apply the work of Christ for salvation. Indeed, the Spirit "blows where [he] pleases" (John 3:8), but Jesus's affirmation is closely tied to belief in the Son of Man, who "must be lifted up, so that everyone who believes in him may have eternal life. For God loved the world in this way: He gave his one and only Son, so that everyone who believes in him will not perish but have eternal life" (3:14–16). Certainly, the Spirit is free to do as he pleases: he can save anyone, from Nicodemus, (3:10), to a Samaritan woman (chap. 4), from a disabled man (5:1–14) to one born blind (chap. 9). But the Spirit's work is always attached to the death and resurrection of Jesus (exclusivism's first affirmation) and belief in Jesus (exclusivism's second affirmation).[36]

---

[35] Allison, 178–79.

[36] As Holmes, *The Holy Spirit*, 22–23, underscores concerning "the Holy Spirit as the Spirit *of* Christ": "The 'of' makes all the difference. . . . The Spirit never departs from the Son. The Spirit works tirelessly in the economy of grace to expand the community of those baptized into the Son, the living Lord Jesus. Emphasizing this point makes it far more difficult to think of the Spirit apart from Jesus Christ and his Father, our Father. In keeping the Spirit tethered to the Son, as indeed the biblical testimony encourages, the Spirit does not float free of the Son and his Father. The indissoluble bond that exists between Jesus Christ and the Holy Spirit, between the Father who sends him and the Son who breathes him, is thereby honoured."

25

Conclusion

T his volume on pneumatology has developed, in the first half, a biblical theology of the Holy Spirit and, in the second half, a systematic theology (with some attention to a historical theology) of the Holy Spirit. He who inspired the biblical writers has revealed progressively his person, presence, power, work, and mission. This development is traced canonically through the Pentateuch, the Historical Books, the Wisdom Books, the Prophetic Books, the Gospels and Acts, the Pauline Epistles, the General Epistles, and Revelation. As the divine Third Person in intratrinitarian relations with the Father and the Son, the Holy Spirit reveals his trinitarian mission in relationship to creation and providence, Scripture, angelic beings, human beings, human sin, Christ, salvation, the church, and the future. Among the central themes of this revelation are the Spirit's mediation of the divine presence, his speaking of truth, his impartation of both created life and re-created life, his empowerment and uniting of the people of God, and his fostering of renewal and holiness that leads ultimately to eschatological perfection. Wherever and whenever the Spirit is poured out, those whom he fills experience a revitalization that leads to thanksgiving and mission, to the glory of God and the furtherance of the gospel of Jesus Christ throughout the world.

We bring our work to a conclusion with several matters of personal and pastoral application to life and ministry. Each discussion will begin with questions for reflection (for an individual and for a church) followed by applications derived from our pneumatology.

Worshiping, Honoring, and Praying to the Holy Spirit

Are you reluctant to worship the Holy Spirit? If yes, what may account for this hesitancy? If no, how do you express that worship?

How do you honor the Holy Spirit moment by moment in your life?

Do you pray to the Holy Spirit? If no, for what reason(s) do you not pray to him? If yes, for what matters do you pray to the Spirit?

With the affirmation of the Nicene-Constantinopolitan Creed, the church has historically confessed, "We believe in the Holy Spirit . . . who proceeds from the Father and the Son, who with the Father and the Son together is worshipped and glorified." We acknowledge the divine person-hood of the Holy Spirit and his coequality with the other persons of the Trinity as to nature, power, and will. Moreover, the Spirit's eternal procession from both the Father and the Son, together with his names of "Love" and "Gift," highlight the co-eminence of the Spirit in relation to the other two persons. He is God the Holy Spirit, and this truth compels us to adore and honor him together with the Father and the Son.

Concretely, then, church worship services direct praise and thanksgiving to the triune God in prayer and song and responsive readings, expressing honor to the Spirit for his appropriated works of creation/re-creation/perfection. At particular junctures in the liturgy, the Spirit's presence and power are invoked: to unite us in one mind and heart as we worship; to convict us of sin, and to assure us of the Spirit's application of forgiveness; to illumine Scripture as it is read and preached, and to prompt us to trust and obey; to bring blessing and sanctification as new believers are baptized and we celebrate the Lord's Supper; and to direct and empower us as we enter into our mission field of the world.

Personally, as we engage with the Holy Spirit, we honor him moment by moment with our love, trust, obedience, and dependence. These activities by which we revere the Spirit are not different in essence from those same activities of adoration directed toward the Father and the Son. For example, we do not trust the Father, love the Son, and obey the Holy Spirit differently than we trust, love, or obey the other two persons. Indeed, the Holy Spirit as "Love" is the one through whom "God's love has been poured out in our hearts" (Rom 5:5). We cannot know the divine love apart from the outpoured Holy Spirit. Additionally, the Spirit as "Gift" is the highest of the "good gifts" whom the heavenly Father gives us. In turn, our hearts should overflow with joy and thanksgiving for God's wonderful favor—the Spirit himself!

So we may pray to the Holy Spirit. Because he is God and engages in appropriated works (inseparably with the Father and the Son), we may direct specific prayers for his particular attention. This is not different from prayer involving the other two persons. For example, following the way Jesus taught us to pray, we may address "Our Father," i.e., the First Person. Specifically, we may address our prayers to the Father through the Son "in Jesus's name." Also, we may at times choose to address the Spirit directly in prayer as the Third Person of the triune Godhead: "Spirit, help me speak the gospel clearly to my neighbor"; "Spirit, transform me into the image of Christ." On balance, it would probably be most appropriate to address our prayers primarily to the Father through Jesus while occasionally choosing to pray directly to the Spirit.

Relying on the Illumination of the Holy Spirit to Grasp Divine Revelation

How do you understand the interface of the Spirit of God with the Word of God?

Do you rely on the Holy Spirit as you read, study, and meditate on the Bible? If yes, how do you express that dependence? If no, how may your lack of dependence affect your interpretation and application of Scripture?

The Holy Spirit is the one who is responsible for the inspiration, or God-breathed quality, of Scripture. Written by human authors, it is the Word of God because of the Spirit's speaking in and through those writers. Moreover, because he is the Spirit of truth, the Word that he inspired is wholly true (inerrant) in all that it affirms. We have the privilege of trusting all Scripture because all Scripture is inspired by the Holy Spirit and therefore true. In our day, as it seems a growing number of Christians are drifting away from the truthfulness of the Bible, we who rely on the Spirit of God's interface with the Word of God may possess great confidence in divine revelation.

Such dependence is expressed by giving heed to the Spirit's work of illumination. Not only did he inspire Scripture as it was being written in the past; he also illumines Scripture as it is being read and studied in the present. This work of the Spirit is essential for a proper interpretation of the Bible. Some people (mis)understand this illumination to mean that they just sit down with their Bible in hand, ask the Spirit to help them grasp what it means (to them), and almost magically they get it. This naive approach, while quite common, overlooks the fact that the Spirit prompted Scripture to be written with an overarching focus—Christ is the theme from beginning to end—and in different genres—narrative, poetry, prophecy, law, letter—that demand to be read according to different rules of interpretation. Seeking to understand the Bible without a basic grasp of these interpretive principles, even when relying on the Spirit's illumination, may be a recipe for disaster![1]

Rather, reading the Bible in accordance with good interpretive skills and in line with "the Holy Spirit speaking in the Scripture" (Westminster Confession of Faith, 1.10) brings great blessing. Such a reading of Scripture may begin with a prayer for illumination by the Holy Spirit. Again, Huldrych Zwingli provides an exemplary prayer: "Almighty, eternal and merciful God, whose Word is a lamp unto our feet and a light unto our path, open and illuminate our minds, that we may purely and perfectly understand your Word and that our lives may be conformed to what we have rightly understood, that in nothing we may be displeasing unto your majesty, through Jesus Christ our Lord. Amen."[2] This prayer asks for the Spirit's help both in properly understanding the meaning of Scripture and in enacting its rightly understood meaning, whether that is obedience to a command, trust in a promise, confession of sin, praising God, and the like.

Giving Thanks to the Holy Spirit for the Application of Redemption (Re-Creation)

Do you give thanks to the Holy Spirit for his work in applying the salvation accomplished by Jesus Christ? For what particular acts do you give thanks to him?

---

[1] For help in this area, see Andreas J. Köstenberger and Richard D. Patterson, *Invitation to Biblical Interpretation* (Grand Rapids: Kregel, 2011); abridged as *For the Love of God's Word* (Grand Rapids: Kregel, 2015). See also Richard Alan Fuhr, Jr. and Andreas Köstenberger, *Inductive Bible Study* (Nashville: B&H Academic, 2016).

[2] Locher, *Zwingli's Thought*, 28.

From the beginning to the end of our salvation, the Holy Spirit is at work (inseparably with the Father and the Son). Even before we embraced the gospel, the Spirit convicted us of our sin, (self-)righteousness, and (worldly) judgment. His divine disturbance prompted us toward repentance and faith, evangelical virtues stimulated by the Spirit himself, who also united us with Christ for the reception of all the benefits of salvation. Through that Spirit-prompted faith, we were justified, declared not guilty but righteous instead. The Spirit regenerated us, removing our own nature/identity and imparting a new nature/identity that loves God and others. By means of the Spirit of adoption, we acknowledge God as our heavenly Father as we share sonship with his Son. This covenantal relationship is sealed, being guaranteed by the Spirit who is the down payment and firstfruit, and who bears witness with our spirit that we truly belong to God in Christ forever. Christ himself baptizes us with the Spirit, incorporating us into his body, the community of faith in which we live and flourish, united and gifted by the Spirit. As the perfecter of God's purposes, the Spirit is the ground for, and the initiator of, our sanctification, which includes our human activity in growing in Christian maturity. The final work of personal perfection will be our resurrection, as the Spirit transforms our lowly bodies into glorified bodies. Then, we will live forever in the new heaven and new earth, the final and eternal state of blessedness in the presence of the triune God.

By his re-creating work, the Holy Spirit effects salvation. To him we offer our thanksgiving for a work well done.

Keeping in Step with the Holy Spirit

What does being filled with/walking in Holy Spirit look like concretely in your life? What are the biggest obstacles to your keeping in step with the Holy Spirit? What concrete plan can you develop to overcome these obstacles so as to live more consistently in the Holy Spirit (remember: doing more is not necessarily a good plan)?

It could be advised that the very first action in which we should engage as we tumble out of bed each morning is to cry out "Spirit, direct my steps today!" Such a biblically sound prayer guarantees nothing about the circumstances, personal interactions, trials, temptations, heartaches, and joys that will come our way during the day. But as we utter it, we put ourselves into the proper posture with which to start out our day, a posture of dependence upon the one who indwells, guides, and empowers us. Such yieldedness is the right response to the ongoing command "be filled by [i.e., controlled by] the Spirit" (Eph 5:18), an imperative that demands a moment-by-moment reliance on God the Holy Spirit.

Our biggest obstacle to a consistent walk with the Spirit is our own sinful heart ("the flesh"). "For the flesh desires what is against the Spirit, and the Spirit desires what is against the flesh; these are opposed to each other, so that you don't do what you want" (Gal 5:17). Though not our identity as disciples of Jesus Christ, our old self rears its ugly head as we yield to it and give expression to anger and bitterness, pride and lust, idolatry and greed, self-loathing and lovelessness, and more. "I say then, walk by the Spirit and you will certainly not carry out the desire of the flesh" (Gal 5:16). This "Spirit-filled, Christ-centered, God honoring" identity, which is our true, new self, focuses more and more on what pleases the Lord and resists—puts to death—all that is opposed to his will and way.

In terms of concrete plans to actualize this reality, our thoughts often go to specific activities in which we plan to engage: more Bible reading and memorization, more prayer, more evangelism, more fasting, and the like. All of these ideas are certainly welcome! But for most of us, one of the biggest obstacles to keeping in step with the Spirit isn't a lack of spiritual intake; rather, we suffer from a lack of focus on the simple matter of trusting and obeying the Spirit as he leads. For this we need time and concentration, which may look like withdrawal from the frenetic pace of life, work, family, church, responsibilities, busyness, and more. What if our concrete plan would be to establish regular rhythms of "spiritual breathing": crying "Spirit, direct my steps today" as we tumble out of bed, listening to the voice of the Spirit as we meditate on Scripture, checking for sins to confess, creating margins for divine appointments arranged by the Spirit, voicing simple phrases like "Spirit, I adore you" and "Spirit, thank you," praying for the Spirit's guidance, obeying him when he directs us, and the like? While this may appear to be just another list of things to do, these rhythms are actually expressions of a lifestyle that flows from walking with the Holy Spirit moment by moment. And it is to this Spirit-filled lifestyle that we are called: "If we live by the Spirit, let us also keep in step with the Spirit" (Gal 5:25).

Being Guided by the Holy Spirit

Do you seek to be guided by the Holy Spirit? If no, what may account for this hesitancy? If yes, how do you concretely seek his direction?

Are you aware of, and dependent on, the Holy Spirit as the one to whom our good works are to be ascribed?

If someone comes up to you claiming that the Spirit has given her clear direction to embark on a particular course of action, how would you discern if this guidance is indeed from the Spirit?

As we make much of keeping in step with the Spirit, we need reminding of what the Spirit's guidance consists: he leads in both moral matters involving good works and personal direction.

As to the first, the Holy Spirit operates good works through our life: "the fruit of the Spirit is love, joy, peace, patience, kindness, goodness, faithfulness, gentleness, and self-control" (Gal 5:22–23). While often viewed as personal Christlike characteristics—which they certainly are—these attitudes and actions are expressed in community; thus, they are relational good works: Christians do good to other Christians. Scripture calls us to many other types of good works: evangelistic engagement with nonbelievers, merciful care for widows and orphans, selfless bearing of one another's burdens, Spirit-empowered employment of our spiritual gifts, and much more.

An ancient confession of faith reminds us "to whom good works are to be ascribed, and how they are necessary":

> But since they who are the children of God are led by the Spirit of God, rather than that they act themselves (Rom. 8:14), and "of him, and through him, and to him, are all things" (Rom 11:36), whatsoever things we do well and holily are to be ascribed to none other than to this one only Spirit, the Giver of all virtues. However it be, he does not compel us, but leads us, being willing, working in us both to will and to do (Phil 2:13). Hence Augustine writes wisely that God rewards his own works in us. By this we are so far from rejecting good works that we utterly deny that anyone can be saved unless by Christ's Spirit he be brought thus

far, that there be in him no lack of good works, for which God has created him.[3]

Accordingly, as we are guided by the Holy Spirit, we will engage—and must engage—in good works. This claim about the moral guidance of the Spirit is not controversial.

As for personal guidance, which for some is a controversial matter, our pneumatology maintains that the Spirit sets the course for us by giving specific direction concerning the how, when, where, and whom of vocation, marriage or singleness, family, ministry, and more. We expect and long for such personal guidance as we live in the age of the Spirit. Such divine direction does not have to be dramatic or of a miraculous nature, though it may be. Rather, we expect and depend on the Spirit to guide through the most mundane matters of life.

Of chief concern is how we are to discern whether it is the Spirit who is directing a particular course of action or if such an idea is simply the product of one's imagination—or worse. Importantly, we must be "in the Spirit" to discern the Spirit. Though some might complain that such a posture is helplessly subjective, that's just the way it is: Scripture demands that we be filled with/walk in the Spirit for all matters—and that includes discerning the Spirit's guidance. Additionally, several criteria (put in the form of a question) help us to discern the leading of the Holy Spirit: (1) Is such guidance in accordance with the Word of God? (2) Does such direction exalt Jesus Christ? (3) Does such guidance result in sanctification and engagement in good works? (4) Is such guidance directed at engaging others with the gospel? (5) Does the church confirm this direction of the Spirit?

Being "in the Spirit" and using these criteria appropriately will enable us to discern the personal guidance of the Holy Spirit.

Accordingly, we pray "*Veni, Creator Spiritus*" (attributed to Gregory the Great, 590–604):

---

[3] Tetrapolitan Confession (1530), chap. 5. http://apostles-creed.org/wp-content/uploads/2014/09/tetrapolatan-strasbourg-swabian-confession.pdf.

Creator-Spirit, all-Divine
Come, visit every soul of Thine,
And fill with Thy celestial flame
The hearts which Thou Thyself didst frame.

O gift of God, Thine is the sweet
Consoling name of Paraclete—
And spring of life and fire and love
And unction flowing from above.

The mystic sevenfold gifts are Thine,
Finger of God's right hand divine;
The Father's promise sent to teach
The tongue a rich and heavenly speech.

Kindle with fire brought above
Each sense, and fill our hearts with love;
And grant our flesh, so weak and frail,
The strength of Thine which cannot fail.

Drive far away our deadly foe.
And grant us Thy true peace to know;
So we, led by Thy guidance still,
May safely pass through every ill.

To us, through Thee, the grace be shown
To know the Father and the Son;
And Spirit of Them both, may we
Forever rest our faith in Thee.

To Sire and Son be praises meet,
And to the Holy Paraclete;
And may Christ send us from above
That Holy Spirit's gift of love.

BIBLIOGRAPHY

Adewuya, J. Ayodeji. "The Holy Spirit and Sanctification in Romans 8:1–17." *Journal of Pentecostal Theology* 9 (2001): 71–84.

Allen, David M. "The Forgotten Spirit: A Pentecostal Reading of the Letter to the Hebrews." *Journal of Pentecostal Theology* 18 (2009): 51–66.

Allen, Leonard. *Poured Out: The Spirit of God Empowering the Mission of God.* Abilene: Abilene Christian University Press, 2018.

Allison, Gregg R. *The Baker Compact Dictionary of Theological Terms.* Grand Rapids: Baker, 2016.

———. "Baptism with and Filling of the Holy Spirit." *Southern Baptist Journal of Theology* 16, no. 4 (Winter 2012).

———. "The *Corpus Theologicum* of the Church and Presumptive Authority." In *Revisioning, Renewing, Rediscovering the Triune Center: Essays in Honor of Stanley J. Grenz.* Edited by Derek J. Tidball, Brian S. Harris, and Jason S. Sexton. Eugene: Wipf & Stock, 2014.

———. *50 Core Truths of the Christian Faith: A Guide to Understanding and Teaching Theology.* Grand Rapids: Baker, 2018.

———. *Historical Theology: An Introduction to Christian Doctrine.* Grand Rapids: Zondervan, 2011.

———. "Holy God and Holy People: The Intersection of Pneumatology and Ecclesiology." Pages 235–62 in *Building on the Foundations of Evangelical Theology: Essays in Honor of John S. Feinberg.* Edited by Gregg R. Allison and Stephen J. Wellum. Wheaton: Crossway, 2015.

———. *Roman Catholic Theology and Practice: An Evangelical Assessment.* Wheaton: Crossway, 2014.

———. *Sojourners and Strangers: The Doctrine of the Church.* Foundations of Evangelical Theology. Wheaton: Crossway, 2012.

————. "Theistic Evolution Is Incompatible with Historical Christian Doctrine." Pages 926–52 in *Theistic Evolution: A Scientific, Philosophical, and Theological Critique*. Edited by J. P. Moreland, Stephen C. Meyer, Christopher Shaw, and Wayne Grudem. Wheaton: Crossway, 2017.

————. "The Word of God and the People of God: The Mutual Relationship between Scripture and the Church." In *Scripture and the People of God: Essays in Honor of Wayne Grudem*. Edited by John DelHousaye, John J. Hughes, and Jeff T. Purswell. Wheaton: Crossway, 2018.

Archer, Kenneth J. *A Pentecostal Hermeneutic: Spirit, Scripture, and Community*. Cleveland: CPT Press, 2009.

Augustine. *On the Trinity*. In *The Trinity. The Works of Saint Augustine: A Translation for the 21st Century*. Edited by John E. Rotelle. Translated by Edmond Hill. N.p.: New City Press, 1991.

Badcock, Gary. *Light of Truth and Fire of Love: A Theology of the Holy Spirit*. Grand Rapids: Eerdmans, 1997.

Baker, William R. "Searching for the Holy Spirit in the Epistle to James: Is 'Wisdom' Equivalent?" *TynBul* 59 (2008): 293–315.

Barbeau, Jeffrey W., and Beth Felker Jones. "Come, Holy Spirit: Reflections on Faith and Practice." Pages 242–53 in *Spirit of God: Christian Renewal in the Community of Faith*. Edited by Jeffrey W. Barbeau and Beth Felker Jones. Downers Grove: IVP Academic, 2015.

Barth, Karl. *The Holy Spirit and the Christian Life: The Theological Basis of Ethics*. Louisville: Westminster John Knox, 1993.

Bartholomew, Craig. *Where Mortals Dwell: A Christian View of Place for Today*. Grand Rapids: Baker Academic, 2011.

Basil of Caesarea. *St. Basil of Caesarea against Eunomius*. Translated by Mark Delcogliano and Andrew Radde-Gallwitz. Washington, DC: The Catholic University Press of America, 2011.

Beale, Gregory K. *A New Testament Biblical Theology: The Unfolding of the Old Testament in the New*. Grand Rapids: Baker, 2011, 559–650.

Beck, T. David. *The Holy Spirit and the Renewal of All Things: Pneumatology in Paul and Jürgen Moltmann*. Princeton Theological Monograph Series. Eugene: Pickwick, 2007.

Belleville, Linda. "'Born of Water and Spirit': John 3:5." *TrinJ* 1, no. 2 (Fall 1980): 125–41.

Bennema, Cornelis. *The Power of Saving Wisdom: An Investigation of the Spirit and Wisdom in Relation to the Soteriology of the Fourth Gospel.* Tübingen, DEU: Mohr Siebeck, 2002.

Berding, Kenneth. *What Are Spiritual Gifts?: Rethinking the Conventional View.* Grand Rapids: Kregel, 2006.

———. "Who Searches Hearts and What Does He Know in Romans 8:27?" *Journal of Biblical and Pneumatological Research* 5 (2013): 94–108.

Berkhof, Hendrikus. *The Doctrine of the Holy Spirit.* 2nd ed. Richmond: John Knox, 1967.

Bertone, John A. "The Function of the Spirit in the Dialectic between God's Soteriological Plan Enacted but Not Yet Culminated." *Journal of Pentecostal Theology* 15 (1999): 75–97.

Bieder, Werner. "Pneumatologische Aspekte im Hebräerbrief." Pages 251–60 in *Neues Testament und Geschichte.* Edited by Heinrich Baltensweiler and Bo Reicke. Tübingen, DEU: Mohr Siebeck, 1972.

Billings, J. Todd. *Remembrance, Communion and Hope.* Grand Rapids: Baker, 2018.

Billington, Antony. "The Paraclete and Mission in the Fourth Gospel." Pages 90–115 in *Mission and Meaning: Essays Presented to Peter Cotterell.* Edited by Antony Billington, Tony Lane, and Max Turner. Carlisle, UK: Paternoster, 1995.

Block, Daniel I. "The Prophet of the Spirit: The Use of *Rwḥ* in the Book of Ezekiel." *JETS* 32 (1989): 27–49.

Bloesch, Donald G. *The Holy Spirit: Works and Gifts.* Christian Foundations. Downers Grove: InterVarsity, 2000.

Bock, Darrell L. *A Theology of Luke and Acts: God's Promised Program, Realized for All Nations.* BTNT. Grand Rapids: Zondervan, 2011.

Bovon, François. "Der Heilige Geist, die Kirche, und die menschlichen Beziehungen nach der Apostelgeschichte 20, 36–21, 16." Pages 181–204 in François Bovon. *Lukas in neuer Sicht: Gesammelte Aufsätze.* Neukirchen-Vluyn, DEU: Neukirchener, 1985.

Brand, Chad Owen, ed. *Perspectives on Spirit Baptism: Five Views.* Nashville: B&H, 2004.

Bray, Gerald. *God Has Spoken: A History of Christian Theology.* Wheaton: Crossway, 2014.

———. "The Work of the Spirit (Romans 8:1–17)." *Evangel* 19 (2001): 65–69.

Brueggemann, Walter. *Theology of the Old Testament: Testimony, Dispute, Advocacy.* Minneapolis: Fortress, 1997.

Brug, John. "A Rebirth-Washing and a Renewal-Holy Spirit." *Wisconsin Lutheran Quarterly* 92 (1995): 124–28.

Bruner, Frederick Dale. *A Theology of the Holy Spirit.* Grand Rapids: Eerdmans, 1970.

Bruner, Frederick Dale and William Hordern. *The Holy Spirit: The Shy Member of the Trinity.* Minneapolis: Augsburg, 1984.

Burgess, Stanley M. "Holy Spirit, Doctrine of: The Ancient Fathers;" "Holy Spirit, Doctrine of: The Medieval Church;" and "Holy Spirit, Doctrine of: Reformation Traditions." Pages 730–69 in *The New International Dictionary of Pentecostal and Charismatic Movements.* Rev. and expanded ed. Edited by Stanley M. Burgess and Eduard M. van der Maas. Grand Rapids: Zondervan, 2002.

Burke, Trevor J., and Keith Warrington, eds. *A Biblical Theology of the Holy Spirit.* Eugene: Cascade, 2014.

Calvin, John. *Institutes of the Christian Religion.* Library of Christian Classics. Volumes 20 and 21. Edited by John T. McNeill. Translated by Ford Lewis Battles. Philadelphia: Westminster, 1960.

Cantalamessa, Raniero. *The Mystery of Pentecost.* Translated by Glen S. Davis. Collegeville: Liturgical Press, 2001.

Carson, D. A. *The Gospel according to John.* Leicester, UK: Inter-Varsity, 1991.
———. *Showing the Spirit: A Theological Exposition of 1 Corinthians 12–14.* Grand Rapids: Baker, 1987.

Castelo, Daniel. *Pneumatology: A Guide for the Perplexed.* London: Bloomsbury T&T Clark, 2015.

Casurella, Anthony. *The Johannine Paraclete in the Church Fathers: A Study in the History of Exegesis.* Tübingen, DEU: Mohr Siebeck, 1983.

Childs, Brevard S. *Old Testament Theology in Canonical Context.* London: SCM, 1985.

Coakley, Sarah. *God, Sexuality, and the Self: An Essay 'on the Trinity.'* Cambridge, UK: Cambridge University Press, 2013.

Coetzée, J. C. "The Holy Spirit in 1 John." *Neot* 13 (1979): 43–67.

Cole, Graham A. *He Who Gives Life: The Theology of the Holy Spirit*. Foundations of Evangelical Theology. Wheaton: Crossway, 2007.

Congar, Yves. *I Believe in the Holy Spirit*. 3 volumes. Translated by David Smith. New York: Crossroad/Herder & Herder, 2015.

Coulson, John R. "Jesus and the Spirit in Paul's Theology: The Earthly Jesus." *CBQ* 79 (2017): 77–96.

Crisp, Oliver D. "Uniting Us to God: Toward a Reformed Pneumatology." Pages 92–109 in *Spirit of God: Christian Renewal in the Community of Faith*. Edited by Jeffrey W. Barbeau and Beth Felker Jones. Downers Grove: IVP Academic, 2015.

Dabney, D. Lyle. "Why Should the Last Be First? The Priority of Pneumatology in Recent Theological Discussions." In *Advents of the Spirit: An Introduction to the Current Study of Pneumatology*. Edited by Bradford E. Hinze and D. Lyle Dabney. Milwaukee: Marquette University Press, 2001.

Dautzenberg, Gerhard. "Prophetie bei Paulus." Pages 55–70 in *Prophetie und Charisma*. Edited by Ingo Baldermann, Ernst Dassmann, and Ottmar Fuchs. Neukirchen-Vluyn, DEU: Neukirchener, 1999.

Deere, Jack. *Surprised by the Power of the Spirit*. Eastbourne, UK: Kingsway, 1994.

Dillon, Richard J. "The Spirit as Taskmaster and Troublemaker in Romans 8." *CBQ* 60 (1998): 682–702.

Downs, David J. "'The Offering of the Gentiles' in Romans 15.16." *JSNT* 29 (2006): 173–86.

Duffield, Guy P., and Nathaniel M. Van Cleave. *Foundations of Pentecostal Theology*. Los Angeles: L.I.F.E. Bible College, 1983.

Duguid, Iain M. "What Kind of Prophecy Continues? Defining the Difference between Continuationism and Cessationism." Pages 112–28 in *Redeeming the Life of the Mind: Essays in Honor of Vern Poythress*. Edited by John M. Frame, Wayne Grudem, and John J. Hughes. Wheaton: Crossway, 2017.

Dumbrell, William J. *The Search for Order: Eschatology in Focus*. Eugene: Wipf & Stock, 2001.

Dunn, James D. G. *Baptism in the Holy Spirit: A Re-Examination of the New Testament Teaching on the Gift of the Spirit in Relation to Pentecostalism Today*. 2nd ed. London: SCM, 2010.

————. *Jesus and the Spirit: A Study of the Religious and Charismatic Experience of Jesus and the First Christians as Reflected in the New Testament.* London: SCM, 1975.

————. "Spirit Speech: Reflections on Romans 8:12–27." Pages 82–91 in *Romans and the People of God: Essays in Honor of Gordon D. Fee on the Occasion of His 65th Birthday.* Edited by Sven K. Soderlund and N. T. Wright. Grand Rapids: Eerdmans, 1999.

————. *The Theology of Paul the Apostle.* Grand Rapids: Eerdmans, 1998.

Easley, Kendall H. "The Pauline Use of *Pneumati* as a Reference to the Spirit of God." *JETS* 27 (1984): 299–313.

Emery, Giles. *The Trinitarian Theology of Thomas Aquinas.* Translated by Francesca A. Murphy. Oxford, UK: Oxford University Press, 2007.

Emmrich, Martin. "*Pneuma* in Hebrews: Prophet and Interpreter." *WTJ* 63 (2002): 55–71.

Erickson, Millard J. *Christian Theology.* 3rd ed. Grand Rapids: Baker Academic, 2013.

Erlemann, Kurt. "Der Geist als ἀρραβών (2 Kor 5, 5) im Kontext der paulinischen Eschatologie." *ZNW* 83 (1992): 202–23.

Ewert, David. *The Holy Spirit in the New Testament.* Scottsdale: Herald, 1983.

Fatehi, Mehrdad. *The Spirit's Relation to the Risen Lord in Paul: An Examination of Its Christological Implications.* Tübingen, DEU: Mohr Siebeck, 2000.

Fee, Gordon D. *God's Empowering Presence: The Holy Spirit in the Letters of Paul.* Grand Rapids: Baker, 2009.

————. *Gospel and Spirit: Issues in New Testament Hermeneutics.* Peabody: Hendrickson, 1991.

Feinberg, John S. *Light in a Dark Place: The Doctrine of Scripture.* Foundations of Evangelical Theology. Wheaton: Crossway, 2017.

Ferguson, Everett. *The Church of Christ: A Biblical Ecclesiology for Today.* Grand Rapids: Eerdmans, 1996.

Ferguson, Sinclair B. *The Holy Spirit.* Contours of Christian Theology. Downers Grove: InterVarsity, 1996.

Firth, David G., and Paul D. Wegner, eds. *Presence, Power and Promise. The Role of the Spirit of God in the Old Testament.* Nottingham, UK: Apollos, 2011.

Frey, Jörg, and John R. Levison, eds. *The Holy Spirit, Inspiration, and the Cultures of Antiquity: Multidisciplinary Perspectives*. Berlin: de Gruyter, 2014.

Gaffin, Richard B., Jr. "'Life-Giving Spirit': Probing the Center of Paul's Pneumatology." *JETS* 41 (1998): 573–89.

Gentry, Peter J., and Stephen J. Wellum. *Kingdom through Covenant: A Biblical-Theological Understanding of the Covenants*. 2nd ed. Wheaton: Crossway, 2018.

Graves, Robert W., ed. *Strangers to Fire: When Tradition Trumps Scripture*. N.p.: The Foundation for Pentecostal Scholarship, 2014.

Grayston, Kenneth. "The Meaning of Παράκλητος." *JSNT* 13 (1981): 67–82.

Gregory of Nazianzus. *Fifth Theological Oration: On the Holy Spirit*. NPNF². Vol. 7.

Gregory of Nyssa. *On the Holy Spirit against the Followers of Macedonius*. NPNF². Vol. 5.

———. *On the Holy Trinity, and the Godhead of the Holy Spirit*. NPNF². Vol. 5.

Grudem, Wayne, ed. *Are Miraculous Gifts for Today?: Four Views*. Leicester, UK: IVP, 1988.

———. *The Gift of Prophecy in 1 Corinthians*. Washington, DC: University Press of America, 1982.

———. *Systematic Theology: An Introduction to Biblical Doctrine*. Grand Rapids: Zondervan, 1994, 2006.

Gunkel, Hermann. "Influence of Babylonian Mythology upon the Biblical Creation Story." In *Creation in the Old Testament*. Edited by B. W. Anderson. Philadelphia: Fortress, 1984.

———. *The Influence of the Holy Spirit: The Popular View of the Apostolic Age and the Teaching of the Apostle Paul*. Translated by Roy A. Harrisville and Philip A. Quanbeck II. Philadelphia: Fortress, 1979.

Guthrie, Donald. *New Testament Theology*. Leicester, UK/Downers Grove: InterVarsity, 1981.

Guthrie, Stephen R. *Creator Spirit: The Holy Spirit and the Art of Becoming Human*. Grand Rapids: Baker Academic, 2011.

Habets, Myk. "Prolegomenon: On Starting with the Spirit." Pages 1–19 in *Third Article Theology: A Pneumatological Dogmatics*. Edited by Myk Habets. Minneapolis: Fortress, 2016.

————. *The Progressive Mystery: Tracing the Elusive Spirit in Scripture and Tradition*. Bellinghma, WA: Lexham Press, 2019.

Hafemann, Scott J. *Paul, Moses, and the History of Israel: The Letter/Spirit Contrast and the Argument from Scripture in 2 Corinthians 3*. WUNT 81. Tübingen, DEU: Mohr Siebeck, 1995.

Hahn, Roger L. "Pneumatology in Romans 8: Its Historical and Theological Context." *Wesleyan Theological Journal* 21, nos. 1–2 (1986): 74–90.

Hall, Cletus L., III. "The Grounding of Paul's Pneumatology in his Christology in 1 Corinthians 1:18–2:16." PhD diss., Regent University, 2017.

Hamilton, James M., Jr. *God's Indwelling Presence: The Holy Spirit in the Old & New Testaments*. NAC Studies in Bible & Theology. Nashville: B&H, 2006.

————. "Rushing Wind and Organ Music: Toward Luke's Theology of the Spirit in Acts." *Reformed Theological Review* 65 (2006): 15–33.

Harvey, John D. *Anointed with the Spirit and Power: The Holy Spirit's Empowering Presence*. Explorations in Biblical Theology. Phillipsburg, NJ: P&R, 2008.

Hatina, Thomas R. "John 20, 22 in Its Eschatological Context: Promise or Fulfillment?" *Bib* 74 (1993): 196–219.

Hawthorne, Gerald F. "Holy Spirit." Pages 489–99 in *Dictionary of the Later New Testament and Its Developments*. Edited by R. P. Martin and P. H. Davids. Downers Grove: InterVarsity, 1997.

————. *The Presence & the Power: The Significance of the Holy Spirit in the Life and Ministry of Jesus*. Dallas: Word, 1991.

Haykin, Michael A. G. "A High Pneumatology: Leaning on the Holy Spirit in 2 Timothy." Pages 113–25 in *The Empire of the Holy Spirit*. Mountain Home: BorderStone, 2010.

————. "The Fading Vision? The Spirit and Freedom in the Pastoral Epistles." *EvQ* 57 (1985): 291–305.

Heron, Alasdair I. C. *The Holy Spirit*. Philadelphia: Westminster, 1983.

Hesselink, I. John. "The Charismatic Movement and the Reformed Tradition." Pages 377–85 in *Major Themes in the Reformed Tradition*. Edited by Donald K. McKim. Eugene: Wipf & Stock, 1998.

Hildebrandt, Wilf. *An Old Testament Theology of the Spirit of God*. Peabody: Hendrickson, 1995.

Holmes, Christopher R. J. *The Holy Spirit*. New Studies in Dogmatics. Grand Rapids: Zondervan, 2015.

Holmes, Stephen R. "Trinitarian Action and Inseparable Operations." In *Advancing Trinitarian Theology: Explorations in Constructive Dogmatics*. Edited by Oliver D. Crisp and Fred Sanders. Grand Rapids: Zondervan, 2014.

Horn, Friedrich Wilhelm. *Das Angeld des Geistes: Studien zur paulinischen Pneumatologie*. FRLANT 154. Göttingen, DEU: Vandenhoeck & Ruprecht, 1992.

Horton, Michael. "'Let the Earth Bring Forth . . . 'The Spirit and Human Agency in Sanctification." Pages 127–49 in *Sanctification: Explorations in Theology and Practice*. Edited by Kelly M. Kapic. Downers Grove: InterVarsity, 2014.

———. *People and Place: A Covenant Ecclesiology*. Louisville: Westminster John Knox, 2008.

———. *Rediscovering the Holy Spirit: God's Perfecting Presence in Creation, Redemption, and Everyday Life*. Grand Rapids: Zondervan, 2017.

Issler, Klaus. *Living into the Life of Jesus: The Formation of Christian Character*. Downers Grove: InterVarsity, 2012.

Johnson, Bill. *Hosting the Presence: Unveiling Heaven's Agenda*. Shippensburg: Destiny Image, 2012.

Kaiser, Walter C., Jr. "The Indwelling Presence of the Holy Spirit in the Old Testament." *EvQ* 82 (2010): 308–15.

Kamlah, E., J. D. G. Dunn, and C. Brown. "Spirit." Pages 689–709 in *New International Dictionary of New Testament Theology*. Edited by C. Brown. Grand Rapids: Zondervan, 1978.

Kärkkäinen, Veli-Matti, ed. *The Holy Spirit: A Guide to Christian Theology*. Louisville: Westminster John Knox, 2012.

———. *Holy Spirit and Salvation: The Sources of Christian Theology*. Louisville: Westminster John Knox, 2010.

———. "'How to Speak of the Spirit among Religions': Trinitarian Prolegomena for a Pneumatological Theology of Religions." Pages 47–70 in *The Work of the Spirit: Pneumatology and Pentecostalism*. Edited by Michael Welker. Grand Rapids: Eerdmans, 2006.

———. *Pneumatology: The Holy Spirit in Ecumenical, International, and Contextual Perspective*, 2nd ed. Grand Rapids: Baker Academic, 2018.

Keener, Craig S. *The Mind of the Spirit: Paul's Approach to Transformed Thinking*. Grand Rapids: Baker Academic, 2016.

———. *Spirit Hermeneutics: Reading Scripture in Light of Pentecost*. Grand Rapids: Eerdmans, 2016.

———. *The Spirit in the Gospels and Acts: Divine Purity and Power*. Grand Rapids: Baker, 2010.

Kelly, J. N. D. *Early Christian Doctrines*. Rev. ed. San Francisco: Harper San Francisco, 1978.

Koch, Robert. *Der Geist Gottes im Alten Testament*. Frankfurt am Main: Peter Lang, 1991.

Köstenberger, Andreas J. *A Theology of John's Gospel and Letters*. BTNT. Grand Rapids: Zondervan, 2009.

———. "What Does It Mean to Be Filled with the Spirit?" *JETS* 40 (1997): 229–40.

Köstenberger, Andreas J., and Scott R. Swain. *Father, Son and Spirit: The Trinity and John's Gospel*. NSBT 24. Downers Grove: InterVarsity, 2004.

Kuyper, Abraham. *The Work of the Holy Spirit*. Grand Rapids: Eerdmans, 1946.

Legge, Dominic. *The Trinitarian Christology of St Thomas Aquinas*. Oxford: Oxford University Press, 2017.

Levering, Matthew. *Engaging the Doctrine of the Holy Spirit: Love and Gift in the Trinity and the Church*. Grand Rapids: Baker, 2016.

Levison, Jack. "A Theology of the Spirit in the Letter to the Hebrews." *CBQ* 78 (2016): 90–110.

Levison, John R. *Filled with the Spirit*. Grand Rapids: Eerdmans, 2009.

———. "Spirit, Holy." Pages 1252–55 in *The Eerdmans Dictionary of Early Judaism*. Edited by John J. Collins and Daniel C. Harlow. Grand Rapids: Eerdmans, 2010.

———. *The Spirit in First Century Judaism*. Leiden, NL: Brill, 1997.

Lichtenwalter, Larry L. "The Person and Work of the Holy Spirit in the General Epistles and the Book of Hebrews." *Journal of the Adventist Theological Society* 23, no. 2 (2012): 72–111.

Litfin, Duane. "Revisiting the Unpardonable Sin: Insight from an Unexpected Source." *JETS* 60 (2017): 713–32.

Ma, Wonsuk. *Until the Spirit Comes: The Spirit of God in the Book of Isaiah*. Sheffield, UK: Sheffield Academic Press, 1999.

MacArthur, John. *Charismatic Chaos*. Grand Rapids: Zondervan, 1992.

———. *Strange Fire: The Danger of Offending the Holy Spirit with Counterfeit Worship*. Nashville: Thomas Nelson, 2013.

Macchia, Frank D. "The Kingdom and the Power: Spirit Baptism in Pentecostal and Ecumenical Perspective." In *The Work of the Spirit: Pneumatology and Pentecostalism*. Edited by Michael Welker. Grand Rapids: Eerdmans, 2006.

Malone, Andrew S. "Appreciating the Pneumatology of Acts, Part 1: Retrospect." *RTR* 76 (2017): 23–38.

———. "Appreciating the Pneumatology of Acts, Part 2: Prospect." *RTR* 76 (2017): 121–35.

Marshall, Bruce D. "The Unity of the Triune God: Reviving an Ancient Question." *The Thomist* 74 (2010).

Marshall, I. Howard, Volker Rabens, and Cornelis Bennema, eds. *The Spirit and Christ in the New Testament and Christian Theology: Essays in Honor of Max Turner*. Grand Rapids: Eerdmans, 2012.

Martin, Lee Roy. "'Power to Save!? The Role of the Spirit of the Lord in the Book of Judges." *Journal of Pentecostal Theology* 16 (2008): 21–50.

Matthews, Victor H. "Holy Spirit." Pages 260–80 in *The Anchor Bible Dictionary*. Vol. 3: *H–J*. Edited by David Noel Freedman. New York: Doubleday, 1992.

McCracken, Brett. "The Rise of Reformed Charismatics." *Christianity Today*, December 21, 2017.

McDonnell, Killian P. "The Determinative Doctrine of the Holy Spirit." *Theology Today* 39, no. 2 (July 1, 1982): 142–61.

McDonnell, Kilian, and George T. Montague, eds. *Christian Initiation and Baptism in the Holy Spirit: Evidence from the First Eight Centuries*. Collegeville: Liturgical Press, 1991.

McFarland, Ian A. "Spirit and Incarnation: Toward a Pneumatic Chalcedonianism." *International Journal of Systematic Theology* 16 (2014).

McGee, Gary, ed. *Initial Evidence: Historical and Biblical Perspectives on the Pentecostal Doctrine of Spirit Baptism*. Eugene: Wipf & Stock, 1991.

Menzies, Robert P. *The Development of Early Christian Pneumatology with Special Reference to Luke-Acts*. Sheffield, UK: JSOT, 1991.

Menzies, William W., and Robert P. Menzies. *Spirit and Power: Foundations of Pentecostal Experience*. Grand Rapids: Zondervan, 2000.

Miller, John B. F. "Not Knowing What Will Happen to Me There." In *The Unrelenting God: God's Action in Scripture: Essays in Honor of Beverly Roberts Gaventa*. Edited by David J. Downs and Matthew L. Skinner. Grand Rapids: Eerdmans, 2013.

Mills, Donald W. "The Holy Spirit in 1 John." *Detroit Baptist Seminary Journal* 4 (Fall 1999): 33–50.

Moltmann, Jürgen. *The Source of Life: The Holy Spirit and the Theology of Life*. Translated by Margaret Kohl. Minneapolis: Fortress, 1997.

Morales, Rodrigo J. *The Spirit and the Restoration of Israel: New Exodus and New Creation Motifs in Galatians*. Tübingen, DEU: Mohr Siebeck, 2010.

Mowinckel, Sigmund. "'The Spirit' and the 'Word' in the Pre-Exilic Reforming Prophets." *JBL* 53 (1934): 199–227.

Munzinger, André. *Discerning the Spirits: Theological and Ethical Hermeneutics in Paul*. SNTSMS 140. Cambridge, UK: Cambridge University Press, 2007.

Neve, Lloyd R. *The Spirit of God in the Old Testament*. Cleveland: CPT, 2011.

Oswalt, John N. *The Bible among the Myths*. Grand Rapids: Zondervan, 2009.

Owen, John. *Pneumatologia: A Discourse concerning the Holy Spirit*, in *The Works of John Owen*. Vol. 3. Edited by William H. Goold. Edinburgh: Banner of Truth Trust, 1965.

Pack, Frank. "The Holy Spirit in the Fourth Gospel." *ResQ* 31 (1989): 139–48.

Packer, J. I. *Keep in Step with the Spirit: Finding Fullness in Our Walk with God*. Rev. and enl. ed. Grand Rapids: Baker, 2005.

Pannenberg, Wolfhart. "The Working of the Spirit in the Creation and in the People of God." In *Spirit, Faith, and Church*. Edited by Wolfhart Pannenberg, Avery Dulles, and Carl E. Braaten. Philadelphia: Westminster, 1970.

Peterson, David. *Engaging with God: A Biblical Theology of Worship*. Downers Grove: InterVarsity, 2002.

———. *Possessed by God: A New Testament Theology of Sanctification and Holiness*. New Studies in Biblical Theology. Downers Grove: InterVarsity, 1995.

Peterson, Robert A. *Salvation Applied by the Spirit: Union with Christ*. Wheaton: Crossway, 2014.

Pettegrew, Larry D. *The New Covenant Ministry of the Holy Spirit.* 2nd ed. Woodlands: Kress Biblical Resources, 2013.

Philip, Finny. *The Origins of Pauline Pneumatology.* WUNT 2. Bk. 194. Tübingen, DEU: Mohr Siebeck, 2005.

Pinnock, Clark. *Flame of Love: A Theology of the Holy Spirit.* Downers Grove: InterVarsity, 1996.

———. *A Wideness in God's Mercy: The Finality of Jesus Christ in a World of Religions.* Grand Rapids: Zondervan, 1992

Pitts, Andrew W., and Seth Pollinger. "The Spirit in Second Temple Jewish Monotheism and the Origins of Early Christology." Pages 135–76 in *Christian Origins and Hellenistic Judaism: Social and Literary Contexts for the New Testament.* Edited by Stanley E. Porter and Andrew W. Pitts. Leiden, NL: Brill, 2013.

Powery, Emerson B. "The Spirit, the Scripture(s), and the Gospel of Mark: Pneumatology and Hermeneutics in Narrative Perspective." *Journal of Pentecostal Theology* 11 (2003): 184–98.

Poythress, Vern S. "Modern Spiritual Gifts as Analogous to Apostolic Gifts: Affirming Extraordinary Works of the Spirit within Cessationist Theology." *JETS* 39 (1996): 71–101.

Quan, Keith A. "A Pneumatological Retrieval of Neglected Dimensions of the Doctrine of Scripture." Pages 133–52 in *Third Article Theology: A Pneumatological Dogmatics.* Edited by Myk Habets. Minneapolis: Fortress, 2016.

Quinn, Jerome D. "The Holy Spirit in the Pastoral Epistles." Pages 35–68 in *Sin, Salvation, and the Spirit.* Edited by Daniel Durken. Collegeville: Liturgical Press, 1979.

Robeck, Cecil M., and Amos Yong, eds. *The Cambridge Companion to Pentecostalism.* New York: Cambridge University Press, 2014.

Robson, James E. *Word and Spirit in Ezekiel.* LHBOTS 447. New York: T&T Clark, 2006.

Ruthven, John. *On the Cessation of the Charismata: The Protestant Polemic on Postbiblical Miracles.* Sheffield, UK: SAP, 1993.

Sanders, Fred. *The Deep Things of God: How the Trinity Changes Everything.* 2nd ed. Wheaton: Crossway, 2017.

Schnelle, Udo. *Theology of the New Testament.* Translated by M. Eugene Boring. Grand Rapids: Baker, 2009.

Schreiner, Thomas R. *Spiritual Gifts: What They Are and Why They Matter.* Nashville: B&H, 2018.

Scobie, Charles H. H. *The Ways of Our God: An Approach to Biblical Theology.* Grand Rapids: Eerdmans, 2003, 269–300.

Scurlock, JoAnn, and Richard H. Beal, eds. *Creation and Chaos: A Reconsideration of Hermann Gunkel's* Chaoskampf *Hypothesis.* Winona Lake: Eisenbrauns, 2013.

Seaman, M. X. *Illumination and Interpretation: The Holy Spirit's Role in Hermeneutics.* Eugene: Wipf & Stock, 2013.

Shults, F. LeRon, and Andrea Hollingsworth. *The Holy Spirit.* Guides to Theology. Grand Rapids: Eerdmans, 2008.

Smail, Thomas. *The Giving Gift: The Holy Spirit in Person.* London: Hodder and Stoughton, 1988.

Smalley, Stephen S. "'The Paraclete': Pneumatology in the Johannine Gospel and Apocalypse." Pages 289–300 in *Exploring the Gospel of John: In Honor of D. Moody Smith.* Edited by R. Alan Culpepper and C. Clifton Black. Louisville: Westminster John Knox, 1996.

Spawn, Kevin L., and Archie T. Wright. *Spirit and Scripture: Exploring a Pneumatic Hermeneutic.* London: T&T Clark, 2012.

Stanton, Graham N., Bruce W. Longenecker, and Stephen C. Barton, eds. *The Holy Spirit and Christian Origins: Essays in Honor of James D. G. Dunn.* Grand Rapids: Eerdmans, 2004.

Storms, Sam. *Practicing the Power: Welcoming the Gifts of the Holy Spirit in Your Life.* Grand Rapids: Zondervan, 2017.

Studebaker, John A., Jr. *The Lord is the Spirit: The Authority of the Holy Spirit in Contemporary Theology and Church Practice.* Evangelical Theological Society Monograph Series. Eugene: Pickwick, 2008.

Swete, H. B. *The Holy Spirit in the Ancient Church: A Study of Christian Teaching in the Age of the Fathers.* London: MacMillan and Co., 1912.

———. *The Holy Spirit in the New Testament.* 1909. Repr., Eugene: Wipf & Stock, 1998.

Thiselton, Anthony C. *The Holy Spirit in Biblical Teaching through the Centuries and Today.* Grand Rapids: Eerdmans, 2013.

Tsumura, David. *Creation and Destruction: A Reappraisal of the* Chaoskampf *Theory in the Old Testament.* Winona Lake: Eisenbrauns, 2005.

Turner, Max. "Holy Spirit." Pages 551–58 in *New Dictionary of Biblical Theology*. Edited by T. Desmond Alexander and Brian S. Rosner. Downers Grove: InterVarsity, 2000.

———. *The Holy Spirit and Spiritual Gifts in the New Testament Church and Today*. Rev. ed. Grand Rapids: Baker, 2012.

———. *Power from On High: The Spirit in Israel's Restoration and Witness in Luke-Acts*. Sheffield, UK: Sheffield Academic Press, 1996.

———. "The Spirit of Prophecy and the Power of Authoritative Preaching in Luke-Acts: A Question of Origins." *NTS* 38 (1992): 66–88.

———. "The Work of the Holy Spirit in Luke-Acts." *Word and World* 23, no. 2 (2003): 146–53.

Umstattd, Rustin. *The Spirit and the Lake of Fire: Pneumatology and Judgment*. Eugene: Wipf & Stock, 2017.

Van der Kooi, Cornelis. *This Incredibly Benevolent Force: The Holy Spirit in Reformed Theology and Spirituality*. Grand Rapids: Eerdmans, 2018.

Vanhoozer, Kevin J. "Reforming Pneumatic Hermeneutics." Pages 18–24 in *Holy Spirit: Unfinished Agenda*. Edited by Johnson T. K. Lim. Singapore: Genesis Books and Word N Works, 2015.

Vidu, Adonis. *The Same God Who Works All Things: An Exposition and Defense of the Doctrine of Inseparable Operations*. Grand Rapids: Eerdmans, 2020.

———. "Trinitarian Inseparable Operations and the Incarnation." *Journal of Analytic Theology* 4 (May 2016).

Volf, Miroslav. *After Our Likeness: The Church as the Image of the Trinity*. Grand Rapids: Eerdmans, 1998.

Von Harnack, Adolf. *History of Dogma*, 7 vols. Boston: Roberts Brothers, Little, Brown, 1895–1900.

Wainwright, Arthur. *The Trinity in the New Testament*. London: SPCK, 1962.

Wallace, Daniel B., and M. James Sawyer, eds. *Who's Afraid of the Holy Spirit?* Dallas: Biblical Studies Press, 2005.

Waltke, Bruce K., with Cathi J. Fredricks. *Genesis: A Commentary*. Grand Rapids: Zondervan, 2001.

Walton, John H., and Brent Sandy. *The Lost World of Scripture: Ancient Literary Culture and Biblical Authority*. Downers Grove: IVP Academic, 2013.

Warfield, B. B. *Counterfeit Miracles*. New York: Charles Scribner's Sons, 1918.

Weaver, C. Douglas. *Baptists and the Holy Spirit: The Contested History with Holiness-Pentecostal-Charismatic Movements.* Waco: Baylor University Press, 2019.

Welker, Michael. *God the Spirit.* Translated by John F. Hoffmeyer. Eugene: Wipf & Stock, 1994.

Wellum, Stephen J. *God the Son Incarnate: The Doctrine of Christ.* Foundations of Evangelical Theology. Wheaton: Crossway, 2016.

Wenk, Matthias. *Community-Forming Power: The Socio-Ethical Role of the Spirit in Luke-Acts.* London: T&T Clark, 2004.

———. "Holy Spirit." Pages 387–94 in *Dictionary of Jesus and the Gospels.* 2nd ed. Edited by J. B. Green. Downers Grove: InterVarsity, 2013.

White, R. E. O. *The Biblical Doctrine of Initiation.* Grand Rapids: Eerdmans, 1960.

Wiarda, Timothy. "What God Knows When the Spirit Intercedes." *BBR* 17 (2007): 297–311.

Williams, J. Rodman. *Renewal Theology.* 3 vols. Grand Rapids: Zondervan, 1996.

Witherington, Ben, III, and Laura M. Ice. *The Shadow of the Almighty: Father, Son and Holy Spirit in Biblical Perspective.* Grand Rapids: Eerdmans, 2002.

Wood, Leon J. *The Holy Spirit in the Old Testament.* Grand Rapids: Zondervan, 1976.

Wright, Christopher J. *Knowing the Holy Spirit through the Old Testament.* Downers Grove: InterVarsity, 2006.

Yarnell, Malcolm B., III. *God the Trinity: Biblical Portraits.* Nashville: B&H Academic, 2016.

———. *Who Is the Holy Spirit? Biblical Insights into His Divine Person.* Nashville: B&H Academic, 2019.

Yates, John W. *The Spirit and Creation in Paul.* WUNT 2, no. 251. Tübingen, DEU: Mohr Siebeck, 2008.

Yong, Amos. *Beyond the Impasse: Toward a Pneumatological Theology of Religions.* Grand Rapids: Baker Academic, 2003.

Zuck, Roy B., and Darrell L. Bock, eds. *A Biblical Theology of the New Testament.* Chicago: Moody, 1994.

NAME INDEX

A

Adewuya, J. Ayodeji, 143

Alexander, T. Desmond, 5, 203

Allen, David M., 168–69

Allen, Leonard, 230, 258, 396, 415, 422, 424

Allen, Michael, 228

Allison, Gregg R., 224, 228, 231, 239, 242, 248, 257, 260, 279–80, 285, 295, 300–301, 307, 310–12, 316–17, 325, 327, 335–36, 351, 359, 369, 374–76, 379–80, 382, 389, 391–97, 399–400, 402, 404–8, 416–19, 426, 428, 430–31, 435–38, 440–41, 443–46, 450–51, 453–54, 458, 467, 469, 471, 475–76

Anderson, B. W., 296

Anderson, Paul N., 76

Aquinas, Thomas, 225, 248, 256, 261–62, 264, 267, 275–76, 283–84, 292, 339, 348, 353–54

Archer, Kenneth J., 321

Athanasius, 239, 316

Athenagoras, 314

Atkinson, William P., 128

Augustine, 246, 248–50, 256, 260–61, 265–69, 282, 285, 292, 448, 451–52

Aune, David E., 189

Austin, J. L., 309

Averbeck, Richard E., 9, 11, 17

B

Badcock, Gary, 248

Bailey, Kenneth E., 86

Bailey, Mark L., 160

Baker, William R., 167

Baltensweiler, Heinrich, 168

Bandstra, Andrew J., 179

Banks, Robert, 92, 94

Barbeau, Jeffrey W., 231, 374, 461, 470

Barclay, John M. G., 123

Barrett, C. K., 77

Barth, Karl, 14, 248, 249, 323, 342, 380, 382

Bartholomew, Craig G., 11–12, 27–29

Barton, Stephen C., 61, 65, 67, 74, 92, 116, 123, 128, 142, 144, 160, 167, 176

Basil of Caesarea, 11, 243, 246–49, 259–60, 282, 460

Bauckham, Richard, 56, 76, 167, 189

Bavinck, Herman, 344–45

Beal, Richard H., 296

Beale, G. K., 5, 27, 57–58, 153

SUBJECT INDEX

SCRIPTURE INDEX

519

3:3 *134, 137, 218*
3:6 *129, 134, 137, 197, 203, 209,*
  218
3:7–8 *134*
3:8 *134, 137, 218*
3:12 *135*
3:17 *134, 137, 218, 249*
3:17–18 *135*
3:18 *134, 137, 218, 318, 337, 410*
4:3–6 *318*
4:4 *326, 331, 337, 441*
4:14 *360*
5:1–5 *137*
5:5 *54, 133, 135, 137, 152, 197,*
  204, 208, 218, 291, 395
5:17 *132, 134, 372*
6:1 *136*
6:2 *136*
6:6 *135–37, 218*
6:13 *136*
6:16 *153*
6:16–18 *294*
8–9 *132*
10–13 *132, 134*
12:1 *132*
12:9–10 *132*
12:12 *132, 431*
13:13 *242*
13:14 *133, 136–37, 165, 204, 214,*
  218, 438

Galatians

1:2 *425*
1:6–7 *105*
1:6–10 *104*
1:11–2:21 *104*
2:1–14 *109*
2:10 *412*
2:16 *105*
2:20 *374*
3:1 *105*
3:1–4:11 *105*
3:1–5 *104, 114*
3:1–14 *375*

3:2 *105, 107, 112, 208, 218, 292*
3:2–3 *113*
3:2–5 *114*
3:2–6 *376*
3:3 *104–5, 107, 112, 218*
3:4 *106, 114, 183*
3:5 *105, 107, 112–13, 204, 218,*
  292, 430
3:6 *110*
3:7 *106*
3:9 *106*
3:13–14 *106*
3:14 *104–7, 109, 112–13, 207, 218*
3:26–28 *377, 437*
3:28 *48, 106*
4 *197*
4:1–3 *107*
4:4 *352*
4:4–5 *214*
4:4–6 *241, 280, 291*
4:4–7 *107, 164, 214, 331, 377*
4:6 *104–8, 112–13, 142, 197, 204,*
  208, 218, 259
4:12–6:1 *108*
4:21–31 *108*
4:23 *109–10*
4:28 *109*
4:29 *109, 110, 112–13, 218*
5 *155*
5:4 *106*
5:5 *109, 112–13, 218*
5:6 *109*
5:13 *110*
5:13–6:10 *104*
5:14 *109*
5:16 *105, 110, 112–13, 165, 218,*
  233, 482
5:16–17 *406*
5:16–18 *106*
5:16–19 *400*
5:16–26 *110*
5:17 *105, 110, 112–13, 218, 482*
5:18 *110, 112–13, 165, 218*
5:19–21 *110, 406*